THE RIGHT TO KNOW

Volume 4

Edited by: Zoia Horn, Nancy Gruber, Bill Berkowitz

June 1992

Congress shall make no law respecting an establishment of religion, or prohibiting the exercise thereof; or abridging the freedom of speech, or of the press; or the right of the people peaceably to assemble, and to petition the government for a redress of grievances.

— First Amendment to the Constitution

DataCenter 464 19th Street, Oakland, California 94612-2297 (510) 835-4692

This book is dedicated to DataCenter Business Manager Marie Pastrick.
We send her our love and wish her a full recovery.

ISBN 1-880648-04-0

Preface

The Right to Know, volume IV, continues the series of DataCenter press profiles that identify and analyze the barriers that threaten our access to information and our freedom of expression. This 270-page collection of articles has been assembled from DataCenter files and represents a broad range of both mainstream and alternative press sources.

The DataCenter is a nonprofit, public interest research library and information center focusing on politics and economics. This press profile is part of an ongoing publication program on contemporary public policy issues. For a listing of DataCenter products and services please see the flier at the end of this book.

I want to thank the DataCenter Board and staff for their support of this project over the last 10 years, not only in publishing the Right to Know series but also in backing the project's advocacy, outreach, research and documentation program.

We are most indebted to the three staff members, Zoia Horn, Nancy Gruber, and Bill Berkowitz, who, as editors, guided this reader through the many steps of its development — from its early conceptualization through article selection and consultation with authors, and finally in weaving the parts into a comprehensive statement on the current status of the right to know in the United States.

This reader would not have been possible without the particular efforts of Tom Fenton, Nicole Hayward, Christine Karim, Ruth Sill, and Eddie Yuen, DataCenter staff members who assisted with desktop publishing, layout, document retrieval, and overall management of the project.

We are also greatly indebted to two DataCenter volunteers who gave generously of their time to make this book a reality: Jane Scantlebury, for updating the directory of organizations, and Mort Sobell for electronically scanning articles for reproduction and for help with indexing.

The publication of this reader is particularly memorable as it marks the final task at the DataCenter of Zoia Horn, the founding director of our Right to Know Project. She formally retired with the final delivery of the text to the printer. The publication of this collection also marks Zoia's 50th anniversary as a professional librarian and caps a distinguished career as a champion of intellectual freedom and the citizen's right to know. Those of us who are privileged to know Zoia will recognize the overstated notion of her "retirement" and look forward to her continuing contributions.

And finally we are most grateful to the DataCenter's donors and funders whose financial support made the Right to Know Project and this reader possible.

Fred Goff
Executive Director

July 1992

Acknowledgements

We wish to thank the publishers and/or authors of the articles in this collection for granting the DataCenter reprint rights.

The articles reprinted herein are copyrighted by their respective publishers or authors and are reprinted with their permission. The original publishers or authors retain the copyright to these articles, which may not be reproduced without the permission of the copyright holders.

The following publications have requested that this additional information be provided:

CovertAction Information Bulletin is published at 1500 Massachusetts Ave., NW, Room 732, Washington, DC 20005.

Extra! is published eight times a year by Fairness & Accuracy in Reporting (FAIR). For subscriptions ($30/year for individuals, $40/year for institutions) write to FAIR/Extra!, Subscription Service, P.O. Box 3000, Dept;. FAR, Denville, NJ 07834.

"Unlawful, Unelected and Unchecked," copyright © 1991 by *Harper's Magazine.* All rights reserved. Reproduced from the October issue by special permission.

"Save the Public Library," by David Morris reprinted with permission from The Institute for Local Self-Reliance, 2425 18th Street, NW, Washington, DC 20009.

"Public Information Goes Corporate," reprinted from *Library Journal,* October 1, 1991. Copyright © 1991 by Reed Publishing, USA.

"Journalism of Joy"; "Eye of the Storm" reprinted with permission from *Mother Jones* magazine, © 1991/92, Foundation for National Progress.

"A Conservative Look in Newsprint"; "New Tool of Developers..."; "Chilled by Hoover's Ghost"; "Free Speech Is at Issue..."Copyright © 1990/91 by *The New York Times* Company. Reprinted by permission.

"Deregulatory Creep" reprinted by permission from *The Progressive,* 409 East Main Street, Madison, Wisconsin 53703.

"How Rappers Predicted Rioting," by Teresa Moore and Torri Minton. © *San Francisco Chronicle.* Reprinted by permission.

"The Gag Rule One Year later" first printed in *Sojourner: The Women's Forum* Vol. 17, No. 7 (March 1992). 42 Seaverns Ave., Jamaica Plain, MA 02130.

"The Secret Battle for the NEA"; "Blow by Blow" reprinted by permission of the authors and *The Village Voice.*

"Freedom of Information?"; "Computer Networks..."; "Rights on the Line"© 1991 & 92, The Washington Post. Reprinted with permission.

"The President's Hidden Curriculum" (Oct. 1991); "The 'War on Drugs'" (Nov. 1991); "The Fallacies of 'Political Correctness': I" (Jan. 1992); "Free Market Environmentalism" (Dec. 1991); "Domestic Destabilization" (July/Aug. 1991) reproduced from *Z Magazine,* 150 W. Canton Street, Boston, MA 02118. $25/one year. $35 for libraries & institutions.

Contents

INTRODUCTION

by Zoia Horn

Since the publication of *The Right to Know III* in 1992, several events have occurred in the United States that have significant implications for the concerns of this series; these concerns include the unimpeded flow of information, the renewal of constitutional rights and the correction of historical misperceptions.

These milestones—the dissolution of the Soviet Union and the "end" of the Cold War in 1990, the Bill of Rights' 200th anniversary in 1991, and in 1992, the "celebration" of the Quincentennial of the Columbus "discovery" of the Americas—demand a critical examination. But, for the most part, in the mainstream press and in establishment institutions, a "business as usual" pattern is being fiercely maintained, and important opportunities are being missed. This compilation of articles attempts to provide discussion and analysis of these events and their significance for our right to know.

Cold War

A critical re-evaluation of the cold war, informed by an understanding of the dissolution of the Soviet Union is only beginning—this, despite the fact that the cold war has permeated every aspect of life in the United States since 1946. A World War II ally was consciously transformed into an "evil empire." Ideological warfare in the name of "anti-communism" was translated into real wars and invasions in Korea, Vietnam, Grenada, Panama and into secretly funded covert wars in Chile, Angola, Cuba, Nicaragua, El Salvador and others.

The cold war skewed the U.S. budget toward the military and intelligence, made dissent look like treason, and consequently justified spying on people and organizations that were critical of governmental policies and actions. It channeled science into research most useful to the military and invited industry into the lucrative production of weapons and other military hardware, from which they are loath to be weaned.

With the much-heralded crumbling of the Soviet Union, the focus of the hate disintegrated, but cold war patterns and mind-sets persist irrationally. The expected "peace dividend" has been relegated to the realm of myth. The huge military budget is tentatively being targeted for reduction—sometime in the future. And, there seems to be a search for a new enemy.

The "national security" state, with its excessive classification of government information continues to maintain a wall of secrecy between people and their government. The suppression of information, of "whistle-blowers" and of the press, also continue unabated—witness the control of the press during the Gulf War. (see PRESS AND MEDIA section)

Examining the domestic consequences of the cold war might reveal its hidden costs to health care, education, production jobs, and potential racial harmony. It would certainly uncover some of the misinformation that was disseminated as truth about the now defunct USSR.

Bill of Rights

The 200th anniversary of the Bill of Rights, should have been the occasion for a reaffirmation of democratic principles. Unfortunately, it fizzled into just another public relations campaign profiting Philip Morris, Inc., the sponsor of a widely viewed exhibit.

Many people polled during the Persian Gulf war saw no contradiction between the censorship and manipulation of the media by the Pentagon, and the Bill of Rights. Indeed, previous polls have revealed that people on the street, asked to read the Bill of Rights, thought it was a communist document, and thus rejected parts of it. Ignorance of our basic democratic tenets requires a serious, massive, educational campaign at all age levels, through all mediums of communication.

Columbus

The Quincentennial "celebration" of Columbus' "discovery" of the Americas provides an opportunity to examine what has been written as history and the embarrassing realities of incredible cruelties, torture and enslavement that the histories have hidden. Exposed by Native Americans and scholars, the treatment of the "Indians," as Columbus dubbed them, can be seen as a paradigm for U.S. treatment of other non-Europeans—Africans, Latin Americans, Asians, Arabs.

Racism in its ugly, violent manifestations and cold, institutional prejudice and neglect was challenged by the Civil Rights movement in the 1960s. But, one needs look no further than dateline Los Angeles, May 1992, to recognize that the inequities and injustices that affect those who are Black, Brown, or "other" (including women), are still not ended.

The videotaped beating of Rodney King in 1991 and the acquittal in 1992 of the Los Angeles police who beat this African American man, scandalized people around the world. What was common knowledge about police brutality among the inner-city residents became a shocking revelation to the general public watching the televised videotape. The issue had rarely been reported as news, and the scurry for Federal statistics on police brutality revealed there had been little serious interest in the subject in the past.

But the fires of outrage and despair and the looting of property pushed to the side the central issue of racism, poverty and injustice. The attack on property, viewed on millions of TV screens for several days, became the more important moral threat. The looters, identified from TV coverage, carrying sofas, boxes of Pampers, or beer, will fill court calendars for months and will occupy already crowded jails for years.

In contrast, few perpetrators have been held accountable for the plundering and looting by Savings and Loans institutions. The costs of those piracies will be used to justify the reduction of funds for public housing, education, transportation, child care, and employment in South Central Los Angeles and many other places.

Racism, sexism, classism, and homophobia — those learned prejudices — permeate economic and social behavior. A kind of veiled censorship that blots out consciousness of whole groups of people is often accepted and thus promotes ignorance, fear, and self-delusion. (see OTHER HIDDEN BARRIERS section)

The Right to Know

These themes — an appropriate response to the end of the cold war; an effort to protect the Bill of Rights; and racism's degradation of U.S. society — permeate this new collection of articles. Unfortunately, all the barriers to the people's Right To Know, which gave the initial impetus to this series at the beginning of the Reagan presidency, persist.

At present, government information, paid for with tax money, continues to be curtailed and manipulated, sometimes for political purposes (e.g., 1990 Census undercounting, and suppression of negative reports on social conditions), sometimes to suit business interests (e.g., suppression of a Department of Agriculture's nutrition book). The result has been a phenomenal reduction in the dependability of statistics. The expanding practice of privatizing government documents has increased their prices and made them prohibitively expensive, even for libraries. The government can no longer be held accountable for the accuracy of information that has been transferred into private hands, and public access to it is no longer assured.

Information technology, has become a barrier as it falls more and more into corporate hands. Commercial power also defines what is news, what is literature, and what is art as never before. Under-funded public libraries are being pushed to charge fees, and public schools, to provide captive audiences for child-directed advertisements. The rapid and efficient crunching of names and numbers by computers has developed "target marketing" which identifies our purchases, our subscriptions, and our income, while denying us our privacy. Spying has thus taken on a new dimension. (See CORPORATE POWER and TECHNOLOGY sections)

It is little wonder that concerned people are organizing against the many attacks on the right to know and the democratic society that it is meant to maintain. The American Library Association's 1991-92 president, Pat Schuman, chose "The Right To Know: Librarians Make It Happen" as the theme for her year in office; the organization, Computer Professionals for Social Responsibility, is busy encouraging networking, seminars, and conferences on technology as an empowering tool for all; and the Washington Office of the American Library Association maintains an impressive, if depressing chronology of examples of "Less access to less information by and about government." (See AFFIRMATIONS OF OUR RIGHT TO KNOW and ATTACKS ON THE RIGHT TO KNOW sections)

There is anger, skepticism and impatience in the air. The political campaigns of 1992 are exposing the bankruptcy of ideas to solve the economic and social problems that now plague the country. With an assured right to know, using information as a tool, and public debate to test it, people might decide to provide the ideas and momentum needed to make a more honest and humane society.

I. Attacks on the Right to Know

The Bush administration continued in the footsteps of the Reagan administration in attacking the right to know. As articles in this section reveal, it began to undermine the public education system and suppressed needed information in exchange for political gain. The American Library Association's Washington Office continues its disturbing compendium of *Less Access to Less Information...* that had been gathered for the public good and paid for with public tax money.

"We are not afraid to entrust the American people with unpleasant facts, foreign ideas, alien philosophies, and competitive values. For a nation that is afraid to let its people judge the truth and falsehood in an open market is afraid of its people." — John F. Kennedy

"Liberty cannot be preserved without a general knowledge among the people who have an indisputable, unalienable, indefeasible, divine right to that most dreaded and envied kind of knowledge, I mean of the character and conduct of their rulers." — James Madison

"A popular government, without popular information, or a means of acquiring it, is but a prologue to a farce or a tragedy, or perhaps both." — James Madison

LESS ACCESS TO LESS INFORMATION
BY AND ABOUT THE U.S. GOVERNMENT

prepared by the American Library Association Washington Office

INTRODUCTION

During the past ten years, this ongoing chronology has documented administration efforts to restrict and privatize government information. A combination of specific policy decisions, the administration's interpretations and implementations of the 1980 Paperwork Reduction Act (PL 96-511, as amended by PL 99-500) and agency budget cuts have significantly limited access to public documents and statistics.

The pending reauthorization of the Paperwork Reduction Act should provide an opportunity to limit OMB's role in controlling information collected, created, and disseminated by the federal government. However, the bills that have been introduced in the 102nd Congress would accelerate the current trend to commercialize and privatize government information.

Since 1982, one of every four of the government's 16,000 publications has been eliminated. Since 1985, the Office of Management and Budget has consolidated its government information control powers, particularly through Circular A-130, Management of Federal Information Resources. This circular requires cost-benefit analysis of government information activities, maximum reliance on the private sector for the dissemination of government information, and cost recovery through user charges. OMB has announced plans to revise this controversial circular early in 1992, but a draft revision is not yet available.

Another development, with major implications for public access, is the growing tendency of federal agencies to utilize computer and telecommunications technologies for data collection, storage, retrieval, and dissemination. This trend has resulted in the increased emergence of contractual information collected at taxpayer expense, higher user arrangements with commercial firms to disseminate charges for government information, and the proliferation of government information available in electronic format only. While automation clearly offers promises of savings, will public access to government information be further restricted for people who cannot afford computers or pay for computer time? Now that electronic products and services have begun to be distributed to federal depository libraries, public access to government information will be increased.

During 1990, at a time when the American economy never has been more complex, increasing numbers of news articles showed that federal statisticians are losing the ability to track the changes.

The restrictive and controversial information policy imposed by the administration during the Persian Gulf War was the most prominent government information issue of the first half of 1991. In the second half of 1991, numerous articles again reported that poor statistics and inadequate information have led to major miscalculations in the formulation of federal policy. Examples included problems with federal data about early childhood immunizations, prescription drug use, the consumer price index, the 1990 census, and the hazardous waste cleanup.

ALA reaffirmed its long-standing conviction that open government is vital to a democracy. A January 1984 resolution passed by Council stated that "there should be equal and ready access to data collected, compiled, produced, and published in any format by the government of the United States." In 1986, ALA initiated a Coalition on Government Information. The Coalition's objectives are to focus national attention on all efforts that limit access to government information, and to develop support for improvements in access to government information.

With access to information a major ALA priority, members should be concerned about this series of actions which creates a climate in which government information activities are suspect. Previous chronologies were compiled in an ALA Washington Office publication, *Less Access to Less Information By and About the U.S. Government: A 1981-1987 Chronology*. The following chronology continues semiannual updates published from 1988 to 1991. [RTK Ed. note: The chronology has also been published in *Right to Know*, Vols. 1-3. This Introduction has been slightly edited by RTK.]

Less Access...XV
A 1990 Chronology: June - December

JUNE - For more than four decades, the United States and its allies kept a secret list of computers, machine tools, telecommunications equipment, and other high-technology products that could not be sold to the Soviet Union or its East Bloc satellites. However, high-tech companies in the Western alliance never knew what products were on the list, which was compiled by a 17-nation group that polices technology sales, the Coordinating Committee for Multilateral Export Controls, known as Cocom. With the Cold War winding down, East Bloc turning capitalist and Cocom making more advanced technologies available to Moscow, all that has changed. In May, the State Department bowed to a Freedom of Information Act request and made the Cocom list public. It acted 11 years after Congress said the list should be readily available. ("High-Tech List Comes Out of Cold," *The Washington Post*, June 22)

JUNE - Retired Admiral Elmo R. Zumwalt Jr. accused government and industry scientists of manipulating research data to hide what he called clear evidence that Agent Orange may have caused cancers, birth defects and a wide variety of other ailments in Americans who fought in Southeast Asia and their offspring. The admiral, who recently reviewed studies on the widely used defoliant for the Department of Veterans' Affairs, charged that the distortions continue to "needlessly muddle the debate" over the impact of dioxin-laden chemicals on the American public. Forms of dioxins, a carcinogenic agent in Agent Orange, are present in herbicides widely used in American agriculture.

Appearing before the House Government Operations Subcommittee on Human Resources and Intergovernmental Relations, Zumwalt noted that he had suspected that his son, a former naval officer, died of cancers caused by Agent Orange. But Zumwalt said that until recently he had also believed "that there was insufficient scientific evidence to support a linkage between his illness and Agent Orange exposure. That was, of course, the conventional propaganda. The sad truth which emerges from my work is not only is there credible evidence linking certain cancers and other illnesses with Agent Orange, but that government and industry officials credited with examining such linkage intentionally manipulated or withheld compelling information of the adverse health effects...."("Ex-Admiral Zumwalt Claims Manipulation on Agent Orange," *The Washington Post*, June 27)

JULY - "The federal government has come up with a novel approach for handling bad economic news: it has decided to stop reporting it. The statistic in question is the annual assessment of America's global investment standing, which in the past few years has shown that the United States has gone from being the world's largest creditor nation to being the largest debtor nation. The government says the figure is no longer reliable. Critics say the Bush administration is playing politics by not releasing it."("Bad News Is No News," *Newsday*, July 2)

JULY - A top Air Force general knew that the Stealth fighter plane had missed its targets in its first combat mission, but he did not tell his superiors at the Pentagon, a classified report says. The lapse left Defense Secretary Dick Cheney bragging about the plane's "pinpoint accuracy" in the Panamanian invasion even though one of the bombs missed its target by 160 yards.

The general, Robert D. Russ, chief of the Tactical Air Command, which controls the Air Force fighter planes, knew shortly after the mission about the flaws in their performance and should have kept his superiors fully informed about problems in the raid by the planes, the report said. Asked about the report, General Russ issued a statement saying that the Army commanders who led the invasion were responsible for telling top Pentagon officials about what happened in the attack. Soon after the invasion, Cheney said that each of the fighters had delivered a 2,000-pound bomb with "pinpoint accuracy," based on information provided to him by the military. And for months after, the Pentagon continued to insist that it had been a picture-perfect operation. But in early April, after a *New York Times* reporter showed a senior Air Force official a picture of the bombed site, Cheney learned that the bombs had missed their targets. Soon after, he commissioned the report. ("Report Says General Knew of Stealth Fighter's Failure," *The New York Times*, July 2)

JULY - The Bush administration is seeking a change in the federal computer espionage law that would open the door to prosecution and conviction of whistle-blowers and journalists as well as spies. The Justice Department said the proposal would make the espionage law "more useful." It would eliminate a provision in current law requiring proof of espionage and make it a crime to use—or cause the use of—a computer to obtain classified information without authorization. The penalties would be the same as they are now. Violators would be subject to 10 years in prison for a first offense, or "an attempt to commit such an offense." Second offenders could be imprisoned for 20 years.

The proposal was submitted to Congress in June by the Justice Department as part of a package of changes in the computer fraud and abuse statute of 1986. "It seems they want to make far more people spies than actually are," said Rep. Charles E. Schumer (D-NY), chairman of the House Judiciary Subcommittee on Criminal Justice.

Another part of the Justice Department package that drew criticism was a provision that would define information in a computer, as well as computer processing time, as "property." "The thrust of that is to say that if you take information, that's property and you can be accused of stealing," Schumer said. "I think that's very dangerous. We need a law more finely honed than that."

Morton Halperin, Washington director of the American Civil Liberties Union, said the proposals call to mind the controversial 1985 prosecution of former naval intelligence analyst Samuel Loring Morison, the first person convicted under espionage laws for leaking documents "relating to the national defense" to the news media. Morison's lawyers contended that the sections of espionage law used in the case were meant to apply only in a clandestine setting, to spies and saboteurs, and not to disclosures to the news media. As for the theft charges, they protested that making the law applicable to government "information" would give the executive branch unbridled discretion to control what the public may be told.

Under the Justice Department computer espionage proposal, it could be even more dangerous to take the secrets from a computer than to get them on paper. The bill would make it a crime to pluck from a computer any "classified" information, even items stamped secret, because disclosure would be embarrassing. That is a much broader category than documents "relating to the national defense."

Halperin said, "Given the amount of information that is classified and the degree to which debate in the United States depends on that information, we have consistently opposed criminalizing access to classified information by private citizens, except where it involves transfer to foreign powers." Justice Department officials acknowledged that their proposal would cover whistle-blowers and journalists. "No one considered that in the drafting of it," said Grace Mastalli, special counsel in the Justice Department Office of Policy Development. But she said it was "probably not possible to narrow it without destroying the purpose of the bill." "A Revised Computer Espionage Law?" *The Washington Post*, July 5)

JULY - At a time when the American economy never has been more complex, federal statisticians are losing the ability to track the changes. The official statistics report that the nation is in the midst of a period of unsurpassed prosperity—a peacetime record of 7 1/2 years without a recession. But private economists say many of the statistics spewed by the government each month that purport to trace the economy are seriously flawed. Some are so suspect that analysts ignore them in preparing forecasts rather than face embarrassment when the government totally revises its original report. "History is being rewritten on a monthly basis," said Allen Sinai, chief economist of the Boston Co. "It makes it very hard for private-sector analysts and public policy makers to come to correct conclusions."

Bad data triggers more than bad government policy. A number of economists believe the Federal Reserve has been forced to keep interest rates higher this year because of a mistaken easing in credit last year resulting from a mistake in the monthly report on retail sales. The government first reported retail sales fell by 0.1 percent in May 1989, only to discover belatedly that the survey had overlooked $1.4 billion in sales. This, a small decline, turned into a sizable 0.8 percent increase. The initial erroneous report was picked up in the government's broadest measure of economic activity—the gross national product—which originally showed an anemic 1.7 percent growth rate during the spring. After the error in retail sales was caught, the GNP report was revised to show the economy growing at a much more respectable 2.5 percent. But the correction came too late to stop policy makers at the Federal Reserve from acting to cut interest rates for fear the economy was headed into recession.

In studying government data, everyone from the National Academy of Sciences to the National Association of Business Economists has reached the same conclusion: there are serious problems regarding the accuracy and usefulness of the statistics. "Economists Question Accuracy and Value of U.S. Statistics," *The Washington Post*, July 5)

JULY - Officials of Richard Nixon's presidential library said the library will pick and choose who can do research there and probably will keep out Pulitzer Prize-winning Watergate reporter Bob Woodward. The library also will lack a full set of memos, letters, and other documents from Nixon's White House years when it opens later in July. The originals are in the custody of the government, and Nixon has chosen to copy only those he considers important to the library. The actions have irked some scholars who say they mistrust a library where documents will be screened. The library's director, Hugh Hewitt, says every document of any importance, including many relating to Watergate, will be in the library. But he acknowledged that Woodward probably would not be allowed to study them. "I don't think we'd ever open the doors to Bob Woodward, he's not a responsible journalist," Hewitt said.

The Richard M. Nixon Presidential Library will be able to use its autonomy as a privately run facility to choose the scholars it allows to do research. Of the nation's other presidential libraries, only the Rutherford B. Hayes library is privately operated. Eight are run by the National Archives, which will also control the Ronald Reagan library in California. "Nix on Library to Screen Visiting Researchers," *The Washington Post*, July 9)

[Ed. note: A July 12 editorial in *The Washington Post*, "Access to the Nixon Library," said that after the preceding story appeared, inquiries came quickly from Nixon scholars and others, who pointed out that no reputable research library screens access to researchers on the basis of possible disagreement with their conclusions. Library Director Hewitt then said he had been mistaken and that the library's not-yet-assembled archives would be open to all comers.]

JULY - The Government Accountability Project filed suit against the Agriculture Department to obtain a report on its beef inspection procedures. The suit is the latest flurry in a long-running battle pitting the USDA against consumer groups and dissident federal food inspectors who charge that the USDA Streamlined Inspection System is putting dirtier and more dangerous beef in supermarkets. Partly in response to public criticism, the department last year contracted with the National Academy of Sciences to study the inspection system to ascertain whether it posed unacceptable food risks. The department later gave the academy its own report on the program, but refused to make it public. This prompted GAP to file suit in U.S. District Court to obtain the report under the Freedom of Information Act.

"We have very strong suspicion that the USDA defense of the Streamlined Inspection System is a bureaucratic bluff," said Thomas Devine, the project's legal director. "The reason they won't release it is that the assertions they make couldn't withstand outside scrutiny." Agriculture Department spokesman David Schmidt said, however, that the agency had decided not to release its report until the academy had finished its study. The academy said publication was expected at the end of September. "Releasing the report would compromise and politicize the results of a scientific study," Schmidt said. "We don't feel we need to release it to a group that has no expertise in the subject."("USDA Is Sued: Where's the Beef Report?" *The Washington Post*, July 10)

JULY - In a move that will provide more access to government information, Secretary of Health and Human Services Louis Sullivan proposed a set of uniform definitions that would clarify and standardize the labels on virtually every food product sold in the United States. The 400-page proposal, which will be published in the Federal Register updates and expands the list of what nutrients should and should not be listed on food labeling and defines precisely what is meant by previously confusing terms such as "cholesterol-free" and "reduced cholesterol" that manufacturers have used at their own whim. Officials of the Food and Drug Administration said that in the coming months they will follow with two more-detailed proposals. The first will set precise standards for use of terms such as "high in fiber," "lite," and "fresh," and the second will set out guidelines for how food labels should be designed. Final rules are expected to be in place by this fall and full industry compliance is expected a year later.

"American consumers should have full access to information that will help them make informed choices about the food they eat," said Sullivan. Sullivan said the administration had not yet decided whether the federal rules would preempt states in food labeling. Both the Office of Management and Budget and senior White House officials apparently oppose the idea. ("Uniform Food Labels Proposed," *The Washington Post*, July 13)

JULY - In early July, President Bush signed a classified order that revises National Security Decision Directive 145 and eliminates National Security Agency oversight of federal computers containing sensitive but unclassified information . Duane Andrews, assistant defense secretary for Command, Control, Communications and Intelligence told about the Bush action at a hearing on government compliance with the Computer Security Act held by the House Science, Space, and Technology Subcommittee on Transportation, Aviation, and Materials.

The order revises NSDD 145 to clarify the computer security policy role of NSA and the National Institute of Standards and Technology and brings federal computer security regulations in line with the computer security legislation enacted more than three years ago, the official said. The changes to NSDD 145 may resolve an ongoing turf battle between NSA and NIST, which share responsibility under the Computer Security Act for monitoring government computer security plans. Under the changes, NSA no longer will have responsibility for computer systems handling sensitive but unclassified information. As stated in the act, that responsibility will be solely NIST's. The new directive also removes any reference to federal authority over private-sector computer systems, Andrews said. ("Bush Revises NSDD 145," *Federal Computer Week*, July 16)

JULY - A substantial proportion of people who call the Social Security "800" hotline and are told that a local Social Security office will call them back never receive the follow-up telephone call, the General Accounting Office reported. Critics have claimed that Social Security began the toll-free telephone line in an attempt to save money on personnel and, in effect, has reduced the amount of services available at local offices.

The GAO findings showed that of callers who were instructed to expect a return call at a specific time, 89 percent reported getting the call and being pleased with the help they received. However, about 24 percent of those who expected to be called back to arrange for an application for benefits said they never received a call, the GAO reported. Of those receiving benefits who wanted to be called back to discuss problems, 42 percent said they never received a call. In all cases, the follow up did not occur until at least two to three weeks had passed from the date the person initially called 1-800-234-5772. ("GAO Faults Social Security '800' Hotline," *The Washington Post*, July 18)

AUGUST - A test a decade ago revealed an apparent flaw in the main mirror of the blurry-eyed Hubble Space Telescope, but key officials of the National Aeronautics and Space Administration and outside experts charged with overseeing the project say they were never informed of the problem. Tests on the telescope's main mirror in 1981 uncovered a defect called spherical aberration, according to scientists investigating the problem and an optical expert who worked on the mirrors at Perkin-Elmer Corp., the company that designed, built, and tested the telescope's optical system. The test that detected the aberration was discounted because another testing device believed to be more sophisticated found no such flaw, according to a former Perkin-Elmer employee, who asked not to be identified. NASA officials said they knew of no one at the agency who was aware of the discrepancy in the test results. Former employees of Perkin-Elmer, on the other hand, said that NASA representatives were informed at the time.

By discounting the results of one test, the engineers at Perkin-Elmer were, in essence, relying on a single test to assure the mirror was perfect. Optical experts say now that Perkin-Elmer and NASA should have challenged the mirror with at least two or three independent tests. Perkin-Elmer's bid for the project did not include independent tests, although a losing bid submitted by Eastman Kodak did. According to documents obtained by the Associated Press, Perkin-Elmer was awarded the optics contract for $64 million against a Kodak bid of $100 million. Because of massive cost overruns, Perkin-Elmer was eventually paid $451 million. ("Hubble Flaw Was Found in '81," *The Washington Post*, August 6)

AUGUST - Reporters and photographers who sought to cover the landing of American troops in Saudi Arabia were barred from accompanying military personnel by the Pentagon, which said it was honoring a Saudi request to keep the media at bay. Thus, the beginnings of the largest U.S. military operation in the Middle East in three decades went unseen and unheard by the American public.

The last time the Defense Department allowed reporters to accompany the military into combat was during the invasion of Panama in December. Even by the Pentagon's account, the "press pool" arrangement worked badly: journalists who had been given credentials to join front-line combat troops were kept far from the action by U.S. officials. The sequestering of reporters in Panama kept vital pieces of information from the public, such as the military's treatment of Panamanian citizens and the performance of U.S. personnel and weaponry. Recalling that fiasco and the total blackout of the media during the United States' 1983 invasion of Grenada, some journalists suggested that the Bush administration had more to do with keeping the media out of Saudi Arabia than Cheney let on. ("Media Shut Out at the Front Lines," *The Washington Post*, August 9)

[Ed. note: In an August 11 editorial, "Getting Behind 'Desert Shield'," *The New York Times* said that in a wise change of course, the Bush administration has prevailed upon Saudi Arabia to permit firsthand coverage of the U.S. troop deployment by American journalists. A pool of representative reporters will be admitted.]

AUGUST - According to John Markoff in an August 19 New York Times article, "Washington is Relaxing Its Stand on Guarding Computer Security," President Bush has ordered a quiet dismantling of an aggressive Reagan administration effort to restrict sources of computerized information, including databases, collections of commercial satellite photographs, and information compiled by university researchers. The article gives the background of the controversy regarding the creation of a new security classification, "sensitive but classified information," which was aimed at reducing unauthorized uses of computerized information and at restricting authorized uses so that foreign countries could not piece together sensitive information to learn the nation's secrets.

However, the Bush administration move to revise the Reagan administration policy has caused some computer security experts to say that they are concerned that the Bush move goes too far in decentralizing oversight for computer security. A National Security Agency official warned that the United States was now in danger of losing its leadership in computer security to European countries that have been investing heavily in new technologies.

AUGUST - A lack of adequate computer security in the Department of Justice is endangering highly sensitive information, ranging from identities of confidential informants to undercover operators, the General Accounting Office has concluded in a report to be issued soon. Although the department moved its main data center last year to a new "state-of-the-art" facility, GAO said that unauthorized users still could enter and exit the system without being detected. "The threat of intrusion into these systems is serious, and there are criminals who could benefit immensely from such covert encroachments," Rep. Robert E. Wise Jr. (D-WV) said in a letter urging Attorney General Dick Thornburgh to "immediately correct" the security flaws. A department official who requested anonymity said he was dismayed that the GAO assessment failed to cite "a lot of corrective action already taken and more that is under way." "Justice Data Security Faulted in GAO Report," *The Washington Post*, August 23)

6

AUGUST - In a three-page article, "Science, Technology, and Free Speech," in the Summer 1990 *Issues in Science and Technology*, Allen M. Shinn Jr. observed that now that industrialization has spread technological and scientific capabilities around the globe, there is an increased need for American researchers to talk freely with colleagues in other nations. Yet the export laws—in particular, the export Administration Act, the Arms Export Control Act, and the Invention Secrecy Act—may stand in their way. Ironically, what was intended to further national security may now actually hurt it. These laws frequently have been criticized on economic grounds. But there is another, largely unexplored avenue to their reform: as applied to control information, the laws are probably unconstitutional.

Shinn says the export laws violate the First Amendment in three ways: (1) they impose controls through administrative licensing, a form of prior restraint that has been almost uniformly rejected by the courts since the 18th century; (2) the definitions of controlled information are overbroad; and (3) the laws are ineffective in protecting national security. He says that new regulations under the Export Administration Act have both defined and greatly relaxed controls on "fundamental" research. The new regulations, final in 1989, remove constraints on technical data that are "publicly available," that result from fundamental research (essentially, research intended to be published), or that are "educational information."

Shinn believes that these changes establish a policy against using the export control laws against academic research. Although they represent real progress, the new rules still suffer from constitutional defects. He makes a case that when revised, the laws should make clear that the government can require, at most, notification of intent to export, with actual control dependent on its willingness to go into court and seek an injunction. Shinn says, "That is what the First Amendment requires."

SEPTEMBER - Writing in the September 1990 issue of *Natural History*, Michele Stenehjem says that for 40 years scientists knew that radionuclides from reactors along the Columbia River accumulated in body tissue. They decided to keep the information to themselves.

In an eight-page article, "Indecent Exposure," Stenehjem describes how the Hanford Engineer Works in Washington produced the plutonium for the world's first atomic explosion. The secret project was created in early 1943 to produce plutonium for the first American atomic weapons. The enterprise, operated on contract for the federal government, brought spectacular results and for 40 years after the war, the endeavor was praised by those involved or interested in atomic energy.

In 1986, however, with the release of some 19,000 pages of environmental monitoring reports, engineering reports, office memoranda, and letters concerning Hanford's early history, the world learned that there had been a darker side to the vast undertaking. These documents, many previously classified, and the 40,000 pages subsequently released, disclose that in the course of producing plutonium for World War II and the cold war that followed, the Hanford Works released radioactive wastes totaling millions of curies.

The facility released billions of gallons of liquids and billions of cubic meters of gases containing contaminants, including plutonium and other radionuclides, into the Columbia River and into the soil and air of the flat, wide Columbia Basin. Some of the releases were caused by leakage or faulty technology; others were the result of deliberate policies set by scientists convinced of the acceptability of these emissions. In the years of peak discharges, 1944 to 1966, these scientists and policy makers never informed the residents of the region of the emissions or warned them of any potential or real dangers, even when the releases far exceeded the "tolerance levels" or "allowable limits" defined as safe at the time. Instead, on many occasions they told the public that Hanford's operations were controlled and harmless.

SEPTEMBER - The Bush administration opposed a House Democratic leadership proposal to create a federal technology database that would help American companies compete against foreign rivals. The White House said such a program would be costly and unnecessary. The legislation is part of a Democratic package intended to enhance the competitiveness of American companies and signals growing congressional concern over the problems American companies encounter in competing with foreign rivals. The proposed database would include all industrial technology (dealing with physics, chemistry, biology, communications, transportation, medicine, and other sciences) developed with the aid of federal- and state-financed research. The federal government spent $6 billion last year on university-sponsored research. But the administration said that the final project would duplicate existing government databases and that a $25 million pilot project would be too costly.

House Democratic leaders contend, however, that the government's approach has been piecemeal and that access to the current databases depends on knowledge of their existence and protocols—rules governing the communication and transfer of data between machines. They argue that technology transfer through databases provides the biggest return for the investment. Rep. John LaFalce (D-NY), chair of the House Small Business Committee, said that under existing programs a business in need of technical assistance had to know "10 different protocols needed to access 10 different data bases." Joe Shuster of Teltech Inc., a Minneapolis information systems company, said that "smart, world-class competitors are constantly looking for leverage, and nothing today provides more economic leverage than technical knowledge—nothing."("Democrats' Data Plan Is Opposed," *The New York Times,* September 6)

SEPTEMBER - After a century of serving as the public's eyes and ears about the weather, the National Weather Service is changing its mission. The agency has begun to close its phone lines and refer to private weather companies more and more questions it formerly answered. In addition, these private companies have gradually acquired from the government the right to distribute readings from federal observation offices and pictures from its radar systems. Some people who rely on Weather Service data say they worry that the government is abandoning a long-established duty and is forcing the public to pay for information it is used to getting for virtually nothing.

"It's just ridiculous," said Albert Thompson, a cotton grower who was recently told by the Weather Service in Lubbock, Tex., that he would no longer be told the rainfall in West Texas cities. "We pay taxes, and there is no reason we should not get that information from a Government office." Weather Service officials say the changes are designed to get the government out of the business of distributing routine weather information, so it can concentrate on the difficult job of spotting and reporting dangerous weather conditions. Dr. Elbert W. Friday Jr., the director of the Weather Service, said he believes that the change—in effect, making private companies the middlemen between the public and its government—is going to provide greater access to the information and save the Weather Service money.

Dave Powell, president of the National Weather Service Employees Organization said: "The specialized services they are talking about really are things we have been providing since 1890. A lot of the people we serve are on a shoestring, farmers and contractors."

Perhaps the clearest example of the changing Weather Service missions is the signing of 13 contracts with private companies in the South. In each case, the agency closed phone lines providing recorded weather information just as a private company opened its own lines, providing a similar message but preceded with advertisement. The private weather industry has grown to include more than 100 companies that together make $200 million a year.

In Atlanta, for example, the Weather Service is paying the Contel Corporation to electronically distribute national weather information. Contel can charge the public for the information. Contel classified the Associated Press, with thousands of clients, as a reseller and asked for $1.6 million from the news agency for the right to transmit the information. The agency objected to any reseller fee and decided to use a service operated by the government. That service has no reseller fee but gives less information and is slower, said John Reid, vice president and director of communications and technology for the news agency. He said there have been times when severe weather warnings arrived at the news agency after the warnings had expired. ("What's the Weather? Don't Ask the Service," *The New York Times*, September 10)

[Ed. note: In a related story, people in Miami phoning to find out the time and temperature got something else: soft pornography. A voice welcomed them, saying, "She's all alone in the tub. Jump in. It's all wet." Then it gave a 976 telephone number, told listeners that it would cost them $19.95 for a three-minute call, and finally gave the temperature and time. "We have received complaints relative to this ad," said Gary Allington, Southern Bell Telephone & Telegraph Co. By mid-morning the tape was replaced with an ad for a psychic. Southern Bell leases the time number to Ryder Communications of Coral Springs, Fla., which sells ad space on it. ("Soft-Porn Ad on Bell Firm's Tape Pulled," *The Washington Post*, December 13)]

SEPTEMBER - Citing budget constraints and agency policy, only news media, university libraries, heads of university departments, members of Congress, members of the diplomatic corps, and government officials can continue to receive the monthly publication, *World Agriculture Supply and Demand Estimate*, free of charge. The announcement was made in a September 11 letter to "Dear Reader" from Raymond Bridge, information officer for the Department of Agriculture World Agricultural Outlook Board. Others who want the publication were invited to subscribe for $20 a year.

SEPTEMBER - New York City officials challenged preliminary 1990 census figures, charging that the count conducted this spring and summer missed 254,534 housing units in the city and, as a result, hundreds of thousands of New Yorkers. The city said its records showed that the census overlooked at least five housing units on each of 11,957 blocks, or 43 percent of the city's blocks. New York City has been particularly vigorous in challenging census findings, in part because federal funding is tied to population totals. Officials estimate that the city receives about $150 annually for each of its residents. Also, preliminary census figures indicate that the state will lose three congressional seats, in part because of population shifts away from New York City.

The city has participated in a lawsuit to force the Census Bureau to use a statistical adjustment to compensate for residents missed by the census. Other cities also have challenged Census Bureau figures. Los Angeles officials said they found nearly 50,000

units not included on census lists, and Detroit officials said they found errors on almost all of the city's 13,000 blocks. ("New York City Disputes 1990 Census," *The New York Times*, September 20)

SEPTEMBER - The National Library of Medicine announced a new fee schedule effective February 1, 1991, for CD-ROM products containing MEDLARS data in the September-October 1990 NLM Technical Bulletin. Among the categories of annual subscription fees:

1. For a copy of the database on a stand-alone station, the charge to the vendor from NLM will be (and currently is) $100.

2. For the same subscription on a network of two to five stations, the charge is $1000.

3. For the same subscription on a network of five or more stations, librarians have estimated the charge to be between $7,500 and $10,000, since the NLM newsletter gave a formula instead of a specific figure.

These are the charges to the various Medline vendors; the vendors are likely to pass the fee changes on to their users. Concerns have been expressed in the library community that these NLM charges will discourage network access to CD-ROM MEDLINE.

OCTOBER - Wassily Leontief, awarded the Nobel Prize in Economic Science in 1973, decried the "sad state of the Federal statistical system" in an op-ed piece in *The New York Times*. He said that while our system employs very dedicated, highly qualified individuals, the funds appropriated for their task fall far short of what is needed. Moreover, with a rapidly changing economy, the job has become more complex. Leontief said in his own field—the compilation of the input-output tables that describe the flow of goods and services between the different sectors of the U.S. economy in a given year—the situation is as bad as the current difficulties with the U.S. census.

The federal input-output unit has been reduced to 22 people. There is a hiring freeze. "No wonder the input-output tables for 1972 have not yet come out. With the changes in our economy, these figures, when published, will be only of historical interest." By contrast, in Japan the compilation of input-output tables is done by 200 economists and statisticians. A four-volume table for 1975 was published in March 1979. The 1985 table has already been published.

Leontief concluded: "Some proponents of privatization suggest that diminished support for Federal statistical services will eventually be compensated by private corporate data-gathering organizations. This solution seems about as effective as replacing the klieg lights in a baseball stadium with player-held flashlights. As the U.S. struggles to maintain its competitive position in the world, we can ill afford further deterioration in the data base indispensable to the efficient conduct of all public and private business."("Federal Statistics Are in Big Trouble," *The New York Times*, October 1)

OCTOBER - The government's special nutrition program for low-income women, infants, and children (WIC) sharply reduces later Medicaid health outlays for the mother and child, and also results in improved birthweights according to a Agriculture Department study. The long-awaited study has special significance because of a protracted dispute over a study four years ago that came to the same basic conclusion: that WIC enhances the health of the mother and child. Despite its findings, and for reasons never made clear, the Agriculture Department altered the summary statement of the 1986 findings to play down the beneficial health effects. The new study, in contrast, was hailed by the current Secretary of Agriculture, Clayton Yeutter. ("Mothers' Nutrition Program is Effective, U.S. Study Finds," *The Washington Post*, October 19)

Less Access...

OCTOBER - When Congress passed the 1991 military spending bill in October, it imposed little-noticed but significant new restrictions on the President's power to spend billions of dollars on classified programs. Legislators and administration officials struggled over a section of the bill requiring the administration to use money earmarked for secret programs precisely as Congress prescribes. At stake is control over a "black budget" of more than $35 billion hidden in the military spending bill for numerous secret weapons programs and intelligence activities.

In the past, Congress has attached classified reports to military appropriations saying how this secret money should be spent. But the administration has treated the instructions in these classified "annexes" as mere expressions of congressional wishes rather than actual law. When President Bush signed the 1990 military appropriations bill on November 21, 1989, he expressed concern about restrictions that Congress tried to impose through a classified report on the bill. "Congress cannot create legal obligations through report language," he insisted. But now, after a year marked by several disputes over the administration's refusal to comply with secret directives from congressional committees, Congress has given the classified annexes the force of law. ("Congress Changes Spending Rules on Secret Programs for Pentagon," *The New York Times*, October 30)

OCTOBER - The Army fired, handcuffed, and removed from office a veteran engineer for threatening to disclose that many troop-carrying helicopters primed for war in Saudi Arabia lack protection against Iraqi heat-seeking missiles. Calvin Weber, a 16-year Army civilian employee, was fired for seeking information about the vulnerabilities of Army helicopters now in Saudi Arabia and "intimating" he would make it public, the Army said yesterday. "Information regarding equipment vulnerabilities, especially during the pendency [sic] of Operation Desert Shield, is very sensitive, and its disclosure could be highly detrimental to the security of the United States," Col. Thomas Reinkober told Weber in a one-page memo ordering him to leave his office at the Army Aviation Systems Command in St. Louis.

The Army has about 300 Blackhawk helicopters in Saudi Arabia—more than any other type—to ferry troops to the front and to evacuate casualties from the battlefield. Weber estimates about 200 hundred of them lack suppressors which are muffler-like devices installed over the engines. They are designed to cool the exhaust before it leaves the engines and hide the turbine blades from heat-seeking missiles. A 1985 Pentagon study concluded that 90 percent of the aircraft downed in combat in the previous 10 years were destroyed by heat-seeking missiles. Most of the losses were Soviet aircraft downed by Afghan rebels equipped with portable, U.S.-made, Stinger heat-seeking missiles. ("Army Worker Fired Over Copter Data," *The Washington Post*, October 30)

OCTOBER - *The New York Times* editorialized that "Secrecy, which made the Iran-Contra affair possible, is now a huge obstacle to its cleanup. Invoking national security, Attorney General Dick Thornburgh refused to allow classified information for the perjury trial of Joseph Fernandez, a former C.I.A. operative at the Nicaraguan end of the illicit enterprise. That forced Lawrence Walsh, the independent counsel, to drop the case."

After describing details of the case, the editorial went on to say: "There has always been a conflict between the Attorney General's role as investigator and as lawyer for the President. That's why it was necessary to appoint a special counsel in the Iran-Contra cases. But the same conflict exists when Mr. Thornburgh makes a decision about classified information. He left open the suspicion

he's protecting his boss, the President."("Iran-Contra: Secrecy's Victim, "*The New York Times*, October 30)

OCTOBER - The Supreme Court considered the constitutionality of regulations that prohibit federally funded family planning clinics from discussing abortion, with Justice David Souter expressing concern that the rules stop doctors from giving women needed medical advice. Speaking for the Bush administration, Solicitor General Kenneth Staff defended the regulations, which bar physicians and other workers in federally funded clinics from giving women any information about abortion, even on request, or from stating if abortion is medically indicated .

During oral arguments in the case, *Rust v. Sullivan*, Harvard Law School Professor Laurence Tribe told the court: "We depend on our doctors to tell us the whole truth, whoever is paying the medical bill, the patient or the government, whether in a Title X clinic or in the Bethesda Naval Hospital," referring to the facility where the justices receive medical care. He said that under the regulations, "truthful information that may be relevant is being deliberately withheld from people who have every reason to expect it."("Souter Questions Federal Defense of Abortion Counseling Limits," *The Washington Post*, October 31)

NOVEMBER -"*Newsweek* has learned that there were three times more U.S. casualties from 'friendly fire' or accidents during last winter's Panama invasion than the Pentagon has previously admitted. What's more, according to a confidential Pentagon report obtained by *Newsweek*, the Joint Chiefs of Staff kept Defense Secretary Dick Cheney's aides in the dark about the losses.

Last June, *Newsweek* reported as many as 60 percent of U.S. injuries and nine of the 23 deaths may have been due to friendly fire. The Pentagon denied the story. But the report reveals that the Pentagon failed to disclose that 72 of 312 servicemen it counts among the wounded were actually injured in parachute jumps, not by enemy fire. The report also shows the U.S. military death toll was 26 not 23, and at least six may have been the result of friendly fire.

All told, the report concludes that 114 of the 338 U.S. casualties—34 percent—were caused by friendly fire or accidents. Highly placed sources told Newsweek that even this percentage was low. And, the report reveals, the staff of the Joint Chiefs Chairman Colin Powell tried to paint a rosier picture for Cheney. An April 4 memo to Cheney's top aides claimed no U.S. soldiers were killed by friendly fire. The Pentagon's only comment was to confirm the revised figures."("An Accident-Prone Army," *Newsweek*, November 5)

NOVEMBER - The federal appeals ruling during D.C. Mayor Marion Barry's trial that said federal judges may not bar an individual from a courtroom "merely because that individual advocates a particular political, legal or religious" view is about to be swept into legal oblivion. The U.S. Court of Appeals in Washington, D.C., has refused to publish the ruling. It means that this important decision can never be cited by other lawyers in Washington, and many lawyers will never even know about it, unless they trot over to the courthouse and look up the case.

The American Civil Liberties Union, which challenged the original order barring two controversial men from the Barry trial, now is challenging the appeal panel's decision not to publish. "It smacks of a system of secret justice," said the ACLU's Arthur Spitzer. Spitzer argues that the appeals ruling—by a panel composed of Clarence Thomas, Douglas Ginsburg, and Laurence Silberman—could be crucial to individuals barred from future trials. He also argues that the court is flouting its own rules, which weigh in favor of publication. Spitzer is seeking a rehearing on the issue and calling for one before the full court." ("You Could Look It Up, but...," *The Washington Post*, November 5)

NOVEMBER - "The government's end-of-the-year fiscal crunch gave an Education Department employee a novel idea for promoting a new report. The cover letter sent to reporters announced that 'A College Course Map,' which compiles statistics of what courses are taken by college students, has been published, but 'nobody has it. There are 5,500 copies of the book sitting in a warehouse,' the letter said. 'But until we have a budget, there is no money to pay the mailing contractor.' This, the letter noted enticingly, means that reporters are being given data temporarily unavailable to the public. The publicity-hungry writer even suggested which pages to read."(*Education Week*, November 7)

NOVEMBER - American University professor Philip Brenner has tried for three years in federal court to get classified documents from the State Department about the Cuban missile crisis. Last month, he even submitted affidavits from the authors of the papers—nine former high-ranking Kennedy administration officials—urging their release.

Unlike many citizens who take on the federal government, Brenner may find that time is on his side. The reason: legislation passed by the Senate in the 101st Congress would require automatic declassification of State Department documents 30 years after the events they chronicle. For researchers dealing with the crisis that brought the United States and the Soviet Union to the brink of nuclear war, the countdown would stop at October 1992. The proposed law would allow State Department documents to be kept secret after 30 years only if they fit one of three strict exemptions: if their publication would compromise "weapons technology important to the national defense," reveal the names of informants still alive who would be harmed, or "demonstrably impede" current diplomatic relations.

Congress adjourned before the House took up the measure, but Senate supporters are confident of passage in the next session. Brenner and fellow researcher Scott Armstrong have filed a Freedom of Information lawsuit to get access to 4,000 documents they say are being withheld by the State Department. ("Lifting the Cuban Missile Crisis Veil," *The Washington Post*, November 9)

NOVEMBER - Treatment with steroid hormones can halve the death rate from the pneumonia that is the leading killer of people with AIDS, a panel of experts has concluded. But it was five months before the government agency that had convened the experts notified AIDS doctors of the finding—in part because the experts were concerned that early notification might jeopardize the publication of their conclusions in a prestigious medical journal. Even now, six months after the finding, many doctors who treat AIDS patients say they have not been informed of it.

The expert panel was convened by the National Institute of Allergy and Infectious Diseases last spring to determine whether steroids would be effective in treating the AIDS-related pneumonia. The panel reached its conclusion May 15 after reviewing five studies of the treatment, some of whose authors were among the panel's members. But it delayed announcing its conclusion, said Dr. Paul Meier, the panel's vice-chairman, because the members could not agree on how to work their statement. And part of the reason they could not agree, he said, was that their papers had not yet been accepted at the prestigious medical journal, and they feared that an announcement of the finding would jeopardize publication. Many medical journals have a policy against publishing studies that have been previously described in the general-circulation press.

The institute did not alert doctors to the findings until October 10, when it mailed a letter to 2,500 practitioners on a list obtained from a pharmaceuticals company which makes a drug used to prevent the pneumonia. The delay has infuriated some advocates for people with AIDS. Dr. Jerome Goopman, an AIDS researcher at the New England Deaconess Hospital in Boston, said the episode showed that it was time that researchers, administrators, and editors of medical journals together set ground rules for the dissemination of information that could save patients' lives. ("News of AIDS Therapy Gain Delayed 5 Months by Agency," *The New York Times*, November 14)

[Ed. note: Responding to criticism that it had delayed announcing a lifesaving treatment for people with AIDS, the federal government issued a defense in the form of an elaborate chronology of the events that occurred over a five-month period before letters were sent to doctors informing them of the treatment. ("U.S. Denies Any Delay in Announcing Treatment for AIDS Patients," *The New York Times*, November 16)

NOVEMBER - Former Secretary of Defense Caspar Weinberger and former Secretary of State George Shultz made special arrangements to get thousands of pages of classified information to help them with their memoirs. The General Accounting Office says it found irregularities in the handling of the papers for both Reagan Cabinet officers. In a report to Sen. David Pryor (D-AR), the GAO auditors were especially critical of the arrangement for the Weinberger papers, which were deposited at the Library of Congress as though he owned them. "There appears to be an inverse relationship between the level one attains in the executive branch and one's obligation to comply with the law governing access to, and control of, classified information," Pryor charged in releasing the report. ("Special Privileges for Ex-Cabinet Members," *The Washington Post*, November 14)

NOVEMBER - A federal judge has ordered the Food and Drug Administration to release more safety data on silicon breast implants, a move the Public Citizen Health Research Group said will allow patients more access to information about the safety and effectiveness of drugs and medical devices. The Federal District Court judge, Stanley Sporkin, ruled that the FDA has to release information voluntarily submitted by manufacturers. The ruling provides a long-sought goal of freeing up health data sought under the Freedom of Information Act.

"It's a major, major victory," Dr. Sidney Wolfe, director of the Washington-based group, said. "We've been attempting since 1972 to get the courts to say that data on safety and effectiveness of drugs and medical devices should be public. If upheld on appeal..., we will use this precedent to get a lot of data that will help us oversee what the F.D.A. is doing." The Dow Corning Corporation, the country's major maker of silicon breast implants, said it would appeal to prevent disclosure of what it considers information that could be used by its competitors. The FDA has denied some information act requests, saying certain data submitted voluntarily includes trade secrets or material that is company property. ("F.D.A. Is Ordered to Release Data on the Safety of Breast Implants," *The New York Times*, November 29)

NOVEMBER - In memoirs scheduled for publication in February 1991, former senator John Tower says President Reagan and his top aides tried to mislead the Tower commission and cover up White House involvement in a key aspect of the Iran-Contra affair. Tower said he was shocked when Reagan denied that the White House gave advance approval for an August 1985 shipment of missiles to Iran, in Contradiction of an earlier statement by the former president. Portions of Tower's book, *Consequences: A Personal and*

Political Memoir, were published in the November 29 *Dallas Times Herald*. Tower wrote that Reagan's about-face seemed part of a "deliberate effort" to cover up then-White House Chief of Staff Donald Regan's involvement in the affair. The Tower commission report had noted Reagan's shifting stories about the missile sale. But the book marks the first time a principal figure has suggested the changes were part of a cover up. ("Tower Book Accuses Reagan of Coverup," *The Washington Post*, November 30)

DECEMBER - Rep. Jack Brooks (D-TX), Chair of the House Judiciary Committee has accused the Justice Department of withholding documents to frustrate his panel's probe of alleged improprieties in the department's dealings with Inslaw, Inc., a Washington-based computer software company. The committee is considering whether to subpoena the documents or to attempt in some other way to force the department to produce the documents.

The case involves Inslaw, which wrote a computer program that allows the Justice Department to keep track of a large number of court cases. Inslaw and its top executive, William A. Hamilton, have accused the department of conspiring to drive Inslaw out of business so that friends of high-ranking Reagan administration officials could get control of the program and market it profitably. Hamilton's testimony reasserted those claims. A federal bankruptcy judge concluded that the Justice Department "stole" Inslaw's proprietary software and did, in fact, try to drive the firm out of business. Those findings were upheld on appeal by a U.S. district judge, but the legal battle continues. ("Justice Department Accused of Keeping Inslaw Evidence," *The Washington Post*, December 6)

DECEMBER - Acting on behalf of the nation's mayors, New York Mayor David Dinkins made a final plea to the Bush administration to adjust 1990 census totals to compensate for people missed in the census. In a meeting with Commerce Secretary Robert Mosbacher, Dinkins reiterated his concern that the census had missed millions of Americans, many of them low-income minorities living in big cities. In his city alone, census work conducted over the past months has missed around 800,000 residents, Dinkins said. Dinkins said that without an adjustment, which would add or subtract population based on a statistical model, "it could cost us a billion dollars over the next 10 years." Commerce officials, who oversee the Census Bureau, said they remain open to an adjustment, but a decision will not be made until next summer. ("Adjust Census, Mayors Urge Administration," *The Washington Post*, December 13)

DECEMBER - Four United States Senators have written President Mikhail Gorbachev requesting on humanitarian grounds that he help clear up remaining mysteries about the Korean airliner shot down in 1983. Several days after the crash, Moscow acknowledged that the jumbo jet had been downed by a Soviet fighter. But it is not known in the Western world whether the Soviet authorities ever found the main wreckage or remains of the victims. Sen. Bill Bradley (D-NJ) wrote the Soviet President in August urging that the official findings of his country's inquiries be made public. In November, a letter was sent to Gorbachev by Sens. Sam Nunn (D-GA), Carl Levin (D-MI), and Edward Kennedy (D-MA), asking whether the Soviet Union had located the plane's wreckage or the passengers' remains. No answer to either letter has been received.

The recent letters came after months of efforts by the senators and several colleagues to try to get American authorities to help fill in the gaps in the story of Korean Air Lines Flight 007. Strong criticism has been directed at the Federal Aviation Administration and the State Department for taking months to reply to senatorial requests for information. An aide to Sen. Kennedy said that replies by the FAA to specific questions about communications with an air traffic control unit in Alaska the night of the incident were "nonresponsive and evasive."("Senators Seek Soviet Answers on Flight 007," *The New York Times*, December 16)

DECEMBER - Physicians and patients told a congressional panel of an array of health problems associated with silicone breast implants, and urged that Congress require safety testing and risk disclosure. The Food and Drug Administration has received 2,017 reports of adverse reactions from silicone implants, according to Walter Gundaker, acting director of the FDA Center for Devices and Radiological Health. "We were misled, ill-informed and even sometimes misinformed by people we should have been able to trust," said Sybil Niden of Beverly Hills, Calif., who suffered severe complications from breast implants after a mastectomy. "What we needed, what is still needed, is more information," she told the House Government Operations Subcommittee on Human Resources.

Silicone breast implants have been used since the early 1960s. When 1976 amendments to the Food, Drug, and Cosmetic Act required regulations of medical devices, breast implants were "grandfathered" into the market, meaning they did not fall under the new regulation. In 1982, the FDA proposed that silicone implants be classified as high-risk devices. FDA officials said they expect a rule would be in force by March requiring manufacturers to submit safety data or remove their products from the market. ("Hill Told of Silicone Breast Implant Problems," *The Washington Post*, December 19)

Less Access...XVI
A 1991 Chronology: January - June

JANUARY - Workers at a training complex in West Milton, N.Y., have accused the Navy's nuclear reactor program of serious safety lapses and say they were disciplined for raising safety concerns. Their allegations, denied by program officials, have contributed to pressure for wider scrutiny of the training and research centers, which make up the only branch of the government's nuclear defense program with its secrecy mostly intact.

Federal officials and executives of General Electric, which runs several facilities for the Navy, said the program had an enviable safety record and no serious operating problems. But they acknowledge that this was impossible for an outsider to verify, because the records are classified. The classified records include virtually all the information on whether the program has suffered accidents, as four long-time workers assert.

Sen. John Glenn (D-OH), the chief legislative force behind revealing shortcomings of the nuclear weapons program, said: "If there's one thing we have found in the rest of the nuclear weapons facilities, it's that secrecy bred corner-cutting that got us into deep trouble, and has bred contempt for safety and for waste concerns."

Navy officials contend: "A self-regulating organization, such as Naval Reactors, which demands technical excellence and high standards, and employs strict discipline and encourages self-criticisms, can do its job well." But critics—most prominently, long-time employees no longer at the plant—say that self-regulation has meant no regulation.

The struggle over information has at times taken bizarre twists. Aided by the Government Accountability Project, workers sued General Electric over a "security newsletter" that threatened life-time imprisonment for disclosing information without prior approval. After the suit was filed, the lab issued a second newsletter diluting the first. In May 1990, it issued a third newsletter incorporating some of the same language as the first, and in June a fourth notice retracted the third, saying it had been distributed in error.

Illustrating the degree to which security considerations pervade discussions of safety, a G.E. official said that the reactor facility had been the subject of dozens of articles in *The Schenectady Gazette* in the last two years and that an adversary, by accumulating facts that were individually unrevealing, could piece together classified information. Asked if any classified information had been thus revealed, he replied that the answer to that question was classified. ("Questions Raised About the Safety of Navy Reactors," *The New York Times*, January 1)

JANUARY - The Pentagon was eager to announce how many tanks, troops, and airplanes it had arrayed against Iraq. The Pentagon spoke in less-specific, less-grand terms about how many U.S. soldiers could die if war broke out in the Persian Gulf. But what the Pentagon would not say was how many body bags and coffins it had stockpiled in Saudi Arabia to handle those casualties. That information was "classified."("Pentagon Classifies Talk of Body Bags," *The Washington Post*, January 2)

JANUARY - The Pentagon's release of guidelines for media coverage in the Persian Gulf, including a controversial requirement that journalists submit their war coverage to military review, signaled the beginning of what became the biggest government information-related story thus far in 1991.

Gone from the rules as proposed the previous week was a provision that prohibited reporters from approaching military officials unannounced for spontaneous interviews. Also dropped was an outright ban on publication of photographs or video showing troops in agony or "severe shock." Instead, the Pentagon requested that such photographs or video not be released before next of kin have been notified.

The security review would force journalists who cover the war from Pentagon combat press pools to submit their work for review by military public affairs officers. The new language for this controversial process indicated that any material that did not pass review would be the subject of discussions between Pentagon spokesman Pete Williams and news executives. Williams stressed that such a procedure meant the review could not and would not become censorship. ("Rules Set for Media," *The Washington Post*, January 4)

JANUARY - The U.S. Department of Agriculture has 7,000 federal inspectors who inspect meat and poultry products. But the program has become increasingly expensive and threats of inspector furloughs continually hang in the air. So do charges from consumer groups and others that the system is inadequate—inspectors cannot detect by sight or feel chemical residues or bacteria on meat and poultry that can make people sick. In the meantime, health authorities have become more vocal in their concern about the growing number of food poisoning outbreaks—and meat and poultry get a large share of the blame.

Officials at the Food Safety and Inspection Service, the USDA agency responsible for meat and poultry inspection, are currently trying to modernize 80-year-old systems amid a barrage of criticisms about how they are going about it. The latest plan to upgrade inspection is being heavily promoted by the agency, although many charge that FSIS is more interested in reducing its own costs and keeping the industry happy than in protecting public health.

"USDA's approach to modernization is for fewer inspectors to spend less time looking at more food whizzing by at drastically faster line speeds. That's a recipe for food poisoning," said Thomas Devine of the Government Accountability Project.

FSIS has been conducting research in a poultry slaughtering plant in Puerto Rico for the past several years to find out where in the slaughtering process birds might be spreading harmful bacteria, but has so far refused to divulge the results. A former agency microbiologist, Gerald Kuester, publicly accused FSIS last year of hiding the damaging news that nearly 80 percent of the birds that left the plant were salmonella-contaminated. "You never release scientific data until it's been peer reviewed, and it will be," said Lester Crawford, administrator of FSIS. Since the study was begun, however, its focus has shifted to finding ways to prevent the birds from coming into the plants contaminated, since it appears difficult with current slaughtering methods to keep contamination from spreading to other birds. ("Can USDA Inspectors Do More With Less?" *The Washington Post*, January 9)

JANUARY - A six-page article, "Dr. Nogood," in the January 11 *City Paper* discussed the long-awaited National Practitioner Data Bank, a computerized record of medical malpractice payments and disciplinary actions against physicians, dentists, psychotherapists, and other medical professionals. Author Peter Blumberg pointed out:

As a repository of critical information about misdiagnoses, mistreatment, and professional misconduct, the Data Bank is supposed to provide a screening tool for hospitals and other institutions that hire doctors, and to expose bad doctors who shed their reputations by moving from state to state every time they get in trouble. The Data Bank makes finding the skeletons in...[a] closet as simple as dialing a toll-free line and paying a $2 fee.

But there's a catch—the public is explicitly forbidden to tap into the Data Bank. The authorizing legislation, the Health Care Quality Improvement Act of 1986, makes the information available only to "authorized parties." The authorized parties include hospitals, health maintenance organizations, group practices, state licensing boards of medicine, and professional societies, all of which are required to query the Data Bank before granting any staff or membership privileges to a physician. Any member of the general public who extracts information from the Data Bank is subject to a $10,000 civil fine.

Why would Congress create an information clearinghouse to protect the public from bad doctors and then make it off-limits to the very people it seeks to protect? The short answer: Organized medicine pressured legislators to make Data Bank information confidential. The prevailing attitude of the medical community—then and now—is that if the records were open, people would make the wrong judgments about doctors for the wrong reason.

Sidney Wolfe, head of the Public Citizen Health Research Group, says: "This idea that the public is too dumb and will misunderstand the information is just an incredible slap in the face of patients. This 'Don't you trust me?' attitude on the part of doctors is unacceptable in 1990. It should have been unacceptable in 1890, but it reflects several millennia of physicians believing they are above and beyond their patients."

JANUARY - The National Weather Service's $3 billion upgrading is so far behind schedule that the agency is forced to rely on deteriorating equipment, a dependence that meteorologists in and out of government say could jeopardize the service's ability to warn of dangerous storms.

One agency report said a new radar systems that should have been installed beginning last year may not be ready until 1997. Another report, written by an agency consultant, said that management problems have led to costly delays in the program, the most comprehensive retooling in the service's 100-year history. Many weather experts who once viewed the program as the opening to a new age of modern meteorology now say that these problems could leave forecasters without the ability to gather much of the basic information they need to predict the weather.

Most of the report on the new radar describes problems the government perceives with Unisys, the large computer manufacturer. Company executives said that its serious financial problems would not affect its ability to fulfill the contract.

Staffing cuts present still more problems. Three hundred fewer employees are working in Weather Service offices around the country than there were 10 years ago, because the agency began to trim to a level appropriate for the new equipment even though it is not yet installed. Richard J. Hirn, the general counsel for the union of Weather Service employees, said the unfilled jobs hurt the service's ability to issue warnings.

A flood in Shadyside, Ohio, that killed 26 people last summer is cited by the union and the Weather Service as an example of the risks the public faces because of problems at the agency. The Weather Service said the radar outside Akron, Ohio, was too weak to determine the extent of the storm, which could have led to warnings. The union said staffing cuts at the Akron office left meteorologists there unable to gather enough information to adequately warn the public. ("Costly Errors Setting Back Weather Service," *The New York Times*, January 13)

JANUARY - The Defense Department is facing a formidable enemy—multimillion-dollar computer systems that are so complex they threaten to immobilize weapons. Some of the Pentagon's big-ticket items are being held hostage to their computers. According to two congressional investigations, the Army's Apache helicopter, the Air Force's B-1B and "stealth" B-2 bombers, the Navy's Los Angeles-class attack submarines, and the Trident II missile program all have suffered cost overruns and production delays because of the computer system they have in common—called embedded computer systems.

Bugs and design changes in the BUSY 1 and 2 and the ALQ-161 embedded computer systems have left some of the newest weapons of war brainless. Government documents obtained by Jack Anderson's reporter Paul Parkinson show that it takes more than 800 software programmers to input 3.2 million lines of instructions in the BUSY 2 so the Navy's latest super submarine, the Seawolf, can be launched. ("U.S. Weapons at Mercy of Computers," *The Washington Post*, January 16)

JANUARY - A strict information policy was imposed by the Bush administration on the war against Iraq, with few specific details made available to reporters and the public about the first day of the bombing against targets in Baghdad and Kuwait.

In the first hours of the war, reporting pools were deployed to watch as fighter planes took off from Saudi Arabian bases and were allowed to speak with returning pilots. Both print and video reports were screened, and while there did not appear to be significant censorship of the earliest dispatches, reporters said some deletions had been made by military officers.

The reporting regulations are the most restrictive since the Korean War and in some ways even more so, since reporters then were not confined to escorted pools. American reporters generally accepted censorship in both world wars and Korea, but there were few restrictions on reporting in Vietnam: reporters were free to make their way around combat areas and their reports were not screened. There is widespread agreement that the distrust of the press inherent in the Pentagon's rules for coverage of the gulf war is part of the legacy of Vietnam. ("Government's Strict Policy Limit Reports," *The New York Times*, January 18)

JANUARY - Journalists covering the war against Iraq were not the only ones complaining about censorship by the Defense Department. Some of the troops complained too. American soldiers interviewed in remote camps in the Saudi desert said that the amount of news programming on Armed Forces Radio broadcast in Saudi Arabia had been sharply reduced since the war began the previous week. "It's the lack of news that gets people anxious," said Capt. Roger Wandell of Orlando, Fla. "You start to wonder what they are keeping from us."("Soldiers Fault Lack of News Since War Began," *The New York Times*, January 22)

JANUARY - An appeals board will not give 115 fired Chicago air traffic controllers another chance at their old jobs, despite evidence that their agency falsified some of their employment records. The Merit Systems Protection Board said it did *"not* [emphasis in original] condone the undisclosed alteration of agency records submitted for inclusion in the official record." But controllers failed to persuade the board that those records were changed purposely to give the false appearance that the controllers had gone out on the illegal 1981 strike. President Reagan fired all striking controllers.

The controllers asked the board to take another look at their cases after a congressional oversight subcommittee reported the Federal Aviation Administration doctored records to justify the firing of the controllers. The appeals court upheld the decision of the MSPB: "Because of their reliance on a broadside attack against the [FAA's] case," the court wrote, the controllers "failed to address or counter in any way the crucial findings...on the accuracy and the reliability of the documents."("Despite Falsified Records, Fired Controllers Still Off the Job," *Federal Times*, January 31)

FEBRUARY - In a three-page essay in *Time*, Lance Morrow asks, "Where was the truth?" as he describes the allies' struggle to control the flood of news as Saddam forced battered prisoners of war to tell lies on Iraqi television. Quoting Senator Hiram Johnson's 1917 statement: "The first casualty when war comes is truth." Morrow then goes on to say:

"But that is too simple a metaphor for what is happening in the first war of the age of global information. Truth and elaborate lies, hard fact and hallucination, have become central motifs in the gulf. A war of words and images has taken up a life of its own, parallel to the one in the sand....

"The Pentagon and the Bush Administration have come close to achieving their goal of forcing journalists—and the public—to rely solely on the information supplied by briefers or gathered in pool interviews in the field. Doing away with independent reporting has been the Pentagon's goal ever since Vietnam. The military has set up a system of media pools to cover the initial stages of the operation, controlling reporters' movements and their access to sources. The system works brilliantly from the Pentagon's point of view, but it has subverted the coverage of the war and given it a dismal, canned quality.

"In the midst of all the spectacle, items of honest truth have died of manipulation and censorship. The drama in the gulf commands eerie and unprecedented high-tech global attention, and yet the volume of real information about the conduct of the war is small. The public does not know how effective the allied strikes against Iraq have been, for example, or how heavy the civilian casualties may have been. Clausewitz's 'fog of war'—a phrase endlessly repeated these days—has become a bright electrical cloud of unknowing." ("The Fog of War," *Time*, February 4)

FEBRUARY - A book by a former Iran-Contra prosecutor accused the Central Intelligence Agency of bribing officials in Costa Rica to allow the construction of an airstrip to resupply the Nicaraguan rebels. The book, by Jeffrey R. Toobin, also said the CIA hampered the subsequent criminal investigation into the payments to Costa Rican officials. The CIA operation in Costa Rica, which would have violated federal law against aiding the rebels in Nicaragua, is one of several previously undisclosed incidents described in the book, *Opening Arguments*. The affair centered on efforts to provide military aid to rebels in part using profits of secret arms sales to Iran from 1984 to late 1986. The book provides the strongest evidence yet that the United States used its money and influence in Central America to persuade governments there to assist the Contras. President Bush has denied that any such *quid pro quo* agreements existed. Interviews by the prosecutors with CIA officials provided little help. "Our friends at the agency did not remember anything," Toobin wrote. "With a few courageous exceptions, most of our CIA witnesses suffered stunning memory lapses." The book has been at the center of a long prepublication legal battle. The book was filed under seal in court as part of the case, and in early February, Federal District Judge John Keenan in Manhattan ruled that Penguin USA was free to publish it over the objections of Lawrence Walsh, the Iran-Contra independent prosecutor. ("Book Accuses the C.I.A. in a Contra Aid Scheme," *The New York Times,* February 5)

FEBRUARY - Jack Anderson reported: "The Environmental Protection Agency's habit of keeping dirty secrets to itself could prove deadly in several communities across the nation." Government investigative reports he has obtained show widespread lapses in the EPA's handling of the banned herbicide Dinoseb. Huge stockpiles of the chemical are stored around the country waiting for EPA disposal. And some of those stockpiles are leaking, unbeknownst to the emergency planners in the cities and states where the chemical is stored.

In Goldsboro, N.C., nearly 32,000 gallons of Dinoseb were temporarily stored at a warehouse near the river that is the source of drinking water for 70,000 people. In 1989, the EPA inspector general checked the site and found some containers were rusted and leaking, taking the risk of poisoning groundwater. City officials did not know it was there. Laboratory animals exposed to Dinoseb had offspring with serious birth defects. Researchers found increased incidence of sterility among farm workers using it. There is no evidence that the water in Goldsboro has been tainted by Dinoseb, but it appears that the EPA is not interested in assuring that it will not be tainted in the future.

The EPA inspector general team says it found leaking containers there, and put that in writing last year. But an EPA spokeswoman in Washington says there were no leaks, only rust. And a regional EPA official said: "Our records don't indicate there was a leak, so there is not a reason for us to test that area." The inspector general also said local authorities were not notified about the Dinoseb as they should have been. However, EPA headquarters said it's not their job to tell the local authorities, nor is the EPA responsible for making sure the storage site is safe until the EPA officially takes over the site to handle disposal. But firefighters in Goldsboro, whose jurisdiction covers the storage site, did not know the Dinoseb was there. ("EPA Secrets Seeping Through Cracks," *The Washington Post,* February 8)

FEBRUARY - Frustration grew among journalists who said the Pentagon was choking off coverage of the war by refusing to dispatch more than a handful of military-escorted pools with ground forces, and by barring those who ventured into the desert on their own. At stake, in the view of these critical journalists, is

whether reporters will serve essentially as conveyor belts for the scanty information dispensed at official briefings and gleaned from the limited access afforded the pools.

Defense officials offered three basic reasons for insisting that coverage be provided by small pools of journalists—representing newspapers, television, radio, magazines, and wire services—who must give their colleagues left behind written reports of what they see and hear. First, they say the pools are necessary for the reporters' physical safety. Second, military officers must review the pool reports to prevent the release of information that could jeopardize U.S. forces. Finally, officials say, it would be impractical to allow the more than 800 reporters now in Saudi Arabia to roam the desert battlefield at will.

Questions about the pool system are "like asking whether a smoothly functioning dictatorship is working well," said Stanley Cloud, *Time* magazine's Washington bureau chief. "Yeah, it's working well, but we shouldn't have to put up with it. We're getting only the information the Pentagon wants us to get. This is an intolerable effort by the government to manage and control the press," he said. "We have ourselves to blame every bit as much as the Pentagon. We never should have agreed to this system in the first place." The pool system was established by the Pentagon in 1984 in response to complaints that journalists had been excluded from the U.S. invasion of Grenada. ("Journalists Say 'Pools' Don't Work," *The Washington Post,* February 11)

FEBRUARY - In his briefing on the Department of Energy fiscal 1992 budget, Secretary James Watkins disclosed the cost of cleaning up the nuclear and toxic wastes and restoring the environment at the department's 12-state nuclear weapons manufacturing complex. The costs of the cleanup vary according to which Energy Department activities are included, but by current calculations the price tag has risen from $2.3 billion in 1990 to $3.5 billion in the current year to a projected $4.2 billion next year. The costs will approach $5 billion a year by 1996. The Energy Department has said the task will take 30 years and cost many tens of billions of dollars.

In a report released on February 11, the congressional Office of Technology Assessment said bluntly that the Energy Department may not be the right agency to manage this huge task, partly because of its shortcomings and partly because the public does not trust it. The department's "stated goal—to clear up all weapons sites within 30 years—is unfounded because it is not based on meaningful estimates of the work to be done or the level of cleanup to be accomplished at the end of that time," the report said. It said the department lacks scientific evidence to support its contention that the factories present no imminent public health danger, adding that "the technical and institutional resources and processes to make and implement sound, publicly acceptable decisions" are not in place. ("Energy's 'Mountain Building Up'," *The Washington Post,* February 12)

FEBRUARY - U.S. officials partially relaxed their "blackout" on news of the ground invasion of Kuwait less than 12 hours after it was imposed, as some officials conceded the restrictions had gone too far and initial reports showed allied forces faring well. Although Defense Secretary Richard Cheney announced that briefings on the war would be suspended for an undetermined period of time, the administration moved quickly on February 24 to ensure that positive news filtered throughout the blackout.

Howell Raines, Washington bureau chief of the *New York Times,* said Defense Department officials were using legitimate security concerns "as a means of imposing the blanket management of information of a sort we've never seen in this country. If they've loosened it today, it was because they had good news to report and it was in their interest to report it. What they've put in place is a mechanism to block out bad news and to keep good news in the forefront." But Army Col. Miguel Monteverde, the Pentagon's director of defense information, said officials simply realized that some of the restrictions were impractical.

The U.S. blackout stood in sharp Contrast to the 1944 D-Day invasion of Normandy, when 27 U.S. journalists accompanied allied forces and filed stories that day. Military historians say blackouts were not used during the Korean War and were briefly imposed only twice during the Vietnam War. ("U.S. Lets Some News Filter Through 'Blackout'," *The Washington Post,* February 25)

MARCH - The Spring issue of *Drug Abuse Update* cited the following example as "the grossest misrepresentation that we have seen," of how "some for-profit organizations are marketing tax-produced publications outside the spirit of the law":

A publisher in New York, Business Research Publications, Inc., markets a monthly drug-abuse newsletter it publishes for an annual subscription of $189. Subscribers will receive a free report published by the U.S. Department of Labor entitled *What Works: Workplaces Without Drugs*, that Business Research Publications has republished. The marketing piece fails to say that the report is free to ALL citizens, regardless of their decision to pay the hefty $189 annual subscription rate. Without a subscription request, the report is still available from this company for $71. You read it right—a free booklet developed and published by the United States Department of Labor is hawked for $71 by this New York firm. Another publication advertised by the same firm is *Model for a Comprehensive Drug-Free Workplace Program* for $85. This report comes from the National Institute on Drug Abuse.

Material published by government agencies is in the public domain. It is reproducible for no charge. The government, in fact, encourages reproduction to increase circulation. Any organization or individual who reproduces a government publication can in turn charge for the expense incurred in the reproduction. The question is, do $71 and $85 fees constitute a fair-market value for a retyped, government-agency booklet bound by a plastic spiral?

We need truth in advertising, but more important, profiteers need to hear this message: Prevention dollars are too scarce for any of us to pay twice for drug education publications. Human resource managers in the workplace need to hear this message: *What Works: Workplaces Without Drugs* and *Model Plan for a Comprehensive Drug-Free Workplace Program* may be ordered free of charge from the National Clearinghouse for Alcohol and Drug Information, 1-800-729-6686. You can learn about other free materials by ordering a catalog of resources from the Clearinghouse at the same number. ("Public-Domain Prevention Materials Sold for Big Bucks," *Drug Abuse Update,* Spring 1991)

MARCH - Federal courts charge high prices for providing copies of judicial documents to discourage requests. This practice is the subject of a General Accounting Office report requested by Rep. Bob Wise (D-WV), chair of the House Subcommittee on Government Information, Justice, and Agriculture. GAO found that the administrative office of the U.S. Courts does not have a policy on how courts should handle requests for documents. As a result, federal district courts use widely differing procedures. Many federal courts charge 50 cents per page, a fee originally set in 1959. The high price was set to cut down on the workload of the courts.

In releasing the report, Rep. Wise said: "GAO found considerable variability in practice and procedure. Some courts are charging 50 cents a page for copies when some commercial, profit-

making companies were only charging 3.5 cents a page. There is no reason why any federal office should use high prices for public information as a way of discouraging requests. Under the federal Freedom of Information Act, copying charges may not exceed direct costs. The courts should be following the same policy."

Copies of the GAO report, *Information Requests: Courts Can Provide Documents in a More Cost-Effective Manner* [report number GGD-91-30 (February 13, 1991)] can be requested from GAO at 202-275-6241. ("U.S. Courts Charge High Prices for Copies of Judicial Documents," News Release, House Committee on Government Operations, March 11)

MARCH - A General Accounting Office official, Howard Rhile, testified before the House Subcommittee on Government Information, Justice, and Agriculture that the Justice Department may have compromised sensitive investigations and jeopardized the safety of some undercover agents, informants, and witnesses by inadvertently releasing computerized information. GAO said it uncovered "appalling details" of the department's failure to protect its secret computer files. "Our investigation leads to the unmistakable conclusion that at present, one simply cannot trust that sensitive data will be safely secured at the Department of Justice."

The GAO's investigation followed press disclosures in September 1990 that the department had mistakenly traded away a federal prosecutor's highly sensitive computer files for $45. While auctioning off surplus equipment, the department sold computers from a U.S. attorney's office without first erasing electronic copies of sealed indictments and information about confidential informants and federally protected witnesses, according to court records. The department has sued the buyer, a Kentucky businessman, in an effort to retrieve its files. ("GAO Faults Release of Secret Data," *The Washington Post,* March 26)

MARCH - Because of bureaucratic foot-dragging, complex directives from Congress and in some cases ideological hostility, the federal government has failed to carry out major parts of health, environmental, and housing laws passed with much fanfare in recent years. The delays have left Congress stymied, consumer groups frustrated, and businesses sometimes paralyzed in the absence of prescribed regulations. Bush administration officials acknowledge that they have missed many of the deadlines set by Congress for the new laws. But they say Congress is partly to blame because it writes laws of impenetrable complexity with countless mandates and gives federal agencies insufficient time to write needed regulations.

For example, two decades after Congress ordered the Environmental Protection Agency to identify and regulate "hazardous air pollutants," the agency has issued emission standards for only seven chemicals. Even when an agency is eager to carry out a new law, it must negotiate with the Office of Management and Budget, which often demands changes in proposed rules to reduce the cost or to minimize the burden on private industry. Congress itself may not provide the money needed to carry out or enforce a new law.

Michael Horowitz, counsel to the director of the Office of Management and Budget from 1981 to 1985, said Reagan administration officials often viewed "nonenforcement of the law" as an easy way to deal with statutes and regulations they disliked. ("U.S. Laws Delayed by Complex Rules and Partisanship," *The New York Times,* March 31)

APRIL - The operators of nearly half of the nation's underground coal mines have been systematically tampering with the dust samples they send to federal safety inspectors who determine the risk of black lung to miners, according to Bush administration sources. Labor Secretary Lynn Martin announced that the government will seek major civil penalties against the operators of more than 800 of the nation's approximately 2,000 underground coal mines for tampering with dust samples.

In recent months, federal mine safety officials said they have discovered more than 5,000 incidents of sampling fraud. In many cases, mine operators simply blew away or vacuumed some of the dust from government-approved sampling equipment before submitting it for inspection, officials said. ("Coal Mine Operators Altered Dust Samples," *The Washington Post*, April 4)

APRIL - Jack Pfeiffer, a retired CIA historian, sued the Central Intelligence Agency over regulations he said have blocked him from publishing a declassified version of the organization's role in the ill-fated 1961 Bay of Pigs invasion in Cuba. The agency, citing its strict disclosure rules, has refused to declassify his work and a federal court has upheld its decision.

On April 9, in a second lawsuit filed in U.S. District Court, Pfeiffer sought to overturn the CIA's declassification and review procedures, contending they are "overbroad" and violate his free speech rights. In addition, he argued, as he did in a previous lawsuit filed under the Freedom of Information Act, the agency does not want his papers made public because his findings might embarrass senior agency officials. Public Citizen, an advocacy group, filed the lawsuit on Pfeiffer's behalf, accusing the CIA of balking at giving the historian complete copies of its disclosure regulations. ("CIA Ex-Historian Presses for a 30-Year-Old Tale, *The Washington Post*, April 10)

APRIL - The Census Bureau held up release of detailed population data it gathered in the 1990 census while it negotiated with advocacy groups over the agency's count of the homeless. The advocates for the homeless, arguing that the bureau missed substantial segments of the homeless population in its 1990 count, have threatened legal action unless the bureau issues a disclaimer noting the inaccuracy of the numbers. "The danger is this will become the number of homeless people and will be used" to make policy, said Maria Foscarinis, director of the National Law Center on Homelessness and Poverty. ("Holding Up the Homeless Tally," *The Washington Post*, April 11)

APRIL - U.S. soldiers were poorly trained and equipped to confront a chemical weapons attack in the months preceding the U.S. military buildup in the Persian Gulf region, GAO concluded in a report that was withheld from public release during the confrontation with Iraq. The GAO report, completed in January, documents unrealistic Army training exercises, serious equipment shortages, weak planning, inadequate leadership and poor innovation in preparing a defense against possible poison gas attack.

While commanders associated with Operation Desert Storm had declined to estimate how many soldiers would die in expected Iraqi chemical attacks, the GAO report stated that 71 Army chemical specialists interviewed for the report had predicted that more than half of the exposed troops would be killed in a future gas attack due to inadequate training.

Army officials said they had ordered increased training and provided adequate protective gear for the troops. Congressional sources said the Army nonetheless considered the report's conclusions so sensitive that it ordered the document be kept secret during the war. The Army also ordered the deletion of two tables in the report documenting wide-spread shortages of chemical decontamination and protective gear among U.S. forces routinely stationed in Europe, evidently including some deployed to the Middle East for the war. ("Report Withheld from Public Says GIs Were Poorly Equipped for Gas Attack," *The Washington Post*, April 13)

APRIL - Sen. Patrick Leahy (D-VT) secured an amendment to the bill reauthorizing the Commodity Futures Trading Commission (S. 207) to require publication of any dissenting, concurring, or separate opinion by any Commissioner. He explained that his amendment was prompted by an incident last year when the CFTC issued an important and controversial interpretation on the regulatory treatment of certain oil contracts. One CFTC Commissioner dissented and prepared a detailed statement of his reasons. But when the CFTC submitted its interpretation of the oil contract to the *Federal Register* for official publication, the dissent was omitted.

Sen. Leahy said: "In this case, the results was [sic] especially unfair. High-priced lawyers with access to the Commission or to expensive private reporting services had no trouble getting their hands on the dissent. But members of the public who rely on official outlets like the Federal Register had no access to the document."(*Congressional Record*, April 17, p. S4601)

APRIL - The National Practitioner Data Bank has another problem: missing data. The 1986 law creating the data bank requires hospitals and other medical licensing authorities to report adverse disciplinary actions against doctors. The law also requires any malpractice judgment or settlement on behalf of a physician to be reported. Hospital and medical licensing and disciplinary authorities in turn must check the data bank before giving doctors' working credentials.

In practice the data bank is being undermined by what amounts to a giant loophole: Doctors can avoid being reported to the bank if their lawyers can get them removed from a suit before it is settled. Here's how these deals work: A hospital or some other entity—such as the doctor's professional corporation—agrees to pay the plaintiff if the physician is dropped from the suit.

Then, regardless of whether the rest of the suit is settled or goes to court, no doctor's name is left in the action to be entered into the data bank. Even doctors who are the central figures in suits can avoid the data bank this way. Plaintiffs and defense lawyers alike acknowledge that the time-honored litigation technique of getting a client dismissed from suits subverts the policy rationale behind the National Practitioner Data Bank.

Nobody is sure just how many doctors have avoided the data bank in this manner, but it is not hard to find settled suits around the nation that have been structured to bypass the reporting requirements. Officials at the Department of Health and Human Services which has a $15.8 million contract with the Unisys Corp. to run the data bank—say that as of March 22, they had received more than 13,000 reports of malpractice settlements or judgments. More than 425,000 queries for information came in from hospitals and other medical institutions.

Federal authorities have no way, however, of keeping track of malpractice settlements that are not reported because doctors were dismissed from the suits. Many settlement deals struck between plaintiffs and defense lawyers are secret. According to some medical and legal experts, the public-interest intent in creating a full record of physicians' malpractice-claims experience is not being served. Dr. Sidney Wolfe, of Public Citizen's Health Research Group, says the bank's backers never imagined that doctors would be able to avoid the system simply by getting their names dropped from suits before final settlement. "It flies in the face of the law for clever lawyers to make these end runs," Wolfe declared. ("Data Bank Has a Deficit," *Legal Times*, Week of April 22)

APRIL - The Environmental Protection Agency halted distribution of one of its popular consumer handbooks after industry complained that it recommended home measures, such as vinegar and water to clean windows, that had not been assessed for their effect on the environment. *The Environmental Consumer's Handbook*, published in October 1990, was pulled from distribution in February after industry criticism that it was imbalanced, partly because of its suggestion that homemade cleaning solutions might be more environmentally benign than store-bought products.

Industry critics also faulted the pamphlet's assertions that disposable products contribute to litter. "How do these items contribute to litter when it is the users who litter, not the items?" noted a critique by the Foodservice and Packaging Institute, a Washington-based trade association.

The pamphlet was prepared by the EPA's Office of Solid Waste to encourage consumers to reduce, reuse and recycle items that might otherwise add to the burden of the nation's landfills. It quickly became one of the office's most requested documents, with more than 15,000 of 30,000 copies distributed.

In late February, Don Clay, EPA assistant administrator, promised to move ahead quickly on a revised version, saying it would be subject to a "more comprehensive review process" that would include "a cross section of interested parties." The revised version is expected to be available in 30 to 60 days. According to documents provided to Environmental Action Inc. under the Freedom of Information Act, publication of the original pamphlet was followed by a series of memos and letters from industry critical of the document. "Clearly, EPA's action was in response not to the public, but in response to the large consumer product manufacturers," said Joanne Wirks, a solid waste expert for Environmental Action. "We didn't just do it because industry said you should change this," said Henry L. Longest II, acting deputy assistant administrator under Clay, "but because the opponents made good points." ("EPA Pulls Consumer Handbook," *The Washington Post*, April 23)

APRIL - "Secrecy is expensive and the Pentagon has decided that it cannot afford as much of it as it used to buy. Sunday's scheduled flight of a space shuttle, a mission devoted to experiments for the Strategic Defense Initiative, which in the past would have been classified, has been declassified.

According to a Defense Department spokesman, who spoke on condition of anonymity, declassifying military shuttle flights probably will save taxpayers at least $80 million a year." ("Pentagon Pinching Pennies on Secrecy," *The Washington Post*, April 26)

APRIL - Yielding to pressure from the meat and dairy industries, the Agriculture Department has abandoned its plans to turn the symbol of good nutrition from the "food wheel" showing the "Basic Food Groups" to an "Eating Right" pyramid that sought to de-emphasize the place of meat and dairy products in a healthful diet.

The proposed change, hailed by many nutritionists as a long overdue improvement in the way the government encourages good eating habits, represented the basic groups as layers of a pyramid. By putting vegetables, fruits, and grains at the broad base and meat and dairy products in a narrow band at the top, government health experts had hoped to create a more effective visual image of the proper proportions each food group should have in a healthful diet.

But in meetings with Agriculture officials earlier in April, representatives of the dairy and meat industries complained that the pyramid was misleading and "stigmatized" their products. The industry groups said they were unhappy not just with the suggestion that portions of meat and dairy products should be relatively small,

but that their place in the pyramid was next to that of fats and sweets, the least healthful foods.

"We told them we thought they were setting up good foods versus bad foods," said Alisa Harrison, director of information for the National Cattlemen's Association. Harrison said the group felt consumers would interpret the pyramid to mean they should "drastically cut down on their meat consumption." According to Marion Nestle, chairman of the nutrition department at New York University and the author of a history of dietary guidelines, on several occasions over the past 15 years the department has altered or canceled nutritional advice brochures in response to industry complaints. ("U.S. Drops New Food Chart," *The Washington Post*, April 27)

MAY - In a three-page article, Holley Knaus describes "sharp restrictions on citizen access to government information" as a result of an ideological assault on government activity, coupled with the rise of an "increasingly strong information industry lobby." As a result of "privatization," citizens or organizations seeking information from government agencies as varied as the Census Bureau and the Federal Maritime Commission must increasingly rely on data companies such as Knight-Ridder, Mead Data, McGraw Hill, and Martin Marietta Data Systems.

She writes that information disseminated through the private sector is much more remote from the public, primarily because it is often prohibitively expensive. Private information vendors, under no obligation to provide the public with low-cost access to government data, "charge exorbitant prices for their services and products."

One example she cites concerns the Department of Commerce National Trade Data Bank. According to the Taxpayer Assets Project, Commerce offers the NTDB, a database of more than 100,000 documents containing political, economic, and technical information relating to foreign trade from 16 federal agencies, on a CD-ROM disk for $35.

However, Congress has prohibited Commerce from offering online access to the database. To receive the more timely online information, users are forced to turn to commercial vendors. These commercial vendors receive the data on magnetic tape or CD-ROMs at low rates, and then program it so that it is available online to those with computers—"at extravagant rates." McGraw Hill's Data Resources, Inc. charges its users up to $80 per hour and $0.54 per number to receive this information. ("Facts for Sale," *Multinational Monitor*, May 1991)

MAY - The Justice Department has determined a strict set of conditions governing the access it has granted House Judiciary Committee investigators exploring the alleged government conspiracy against Washington, D.C., legal software developer Inslaw Inc. The committee has spent close to a year tracking the Inslaw case and its possible connection to Justice's award of a $212 million office automation contract to another company. Investigators have sought 200 department documents related to litigation on the Inslaw case, as well as documents about other companies or procurements. Justice has consistently denied the request, saying the papers would reveal the litigation strategy involving its appeal against Inslaw and so were being shielded from Congress.

Access to the documents will be tightly controlled. For example, Justice officials will be present while committee investigators review the papers. The investigators will be permitted only to take notes of the documents. Based on those notes, investigators will have to formally request copies. If additional hearings on the Inslaw case were conducted, the committee would need to give the department "the opportunity prior to the hearing or proceedings to present any reasons why the material or any portion thereof should not be publicly revealed." If no agreement could be reached, the matter would be referred to an executive session of the committee. ("Justice Screens Inslaw Document Release," *Federal Computer Week*, May 6)

MAY - "Most people who work at the White House treat an order from the President as holy writ. So everyone expected quick action when George Bush, embarrassed by news stories on the freeloading travels of chief of staff John Sununu, directed him to 'get it all out' and make 'full disclosure' of his expensive trips aboard Air Force executive jets to ski resorts in Colorado and to his home in New Hampshire.

Instead, Sununu stonewalled. At Bush's insistence, he issued a list of his White House travels, but it has proved to be incomplete, inaccurate, and misleading. It conceals crucial information that *Time* has obtained concerning at least four family skiing vacations and a fifth trip to his New Hampshire home that were financed by corporate interests—in violation of federal ethics laws. Sununu declined requests for interviews about his travels, smugly assuring associates that if he simply hunkered down and said nothing more, 'this whole thing will blow over'."("Fly Free or Die," *Time*, May 13)

MAY - The Iraqi missile that slammed into an American military barracks in Saudi Arabia during the Persian Gulf war, killing 28 people, penetrated air defenses because a computer failure shut down the American missile system designed to counter it, two Army investigations have concluded.

The Iraqi Scud missile hit the barracks on February 25, causing the war's single worst casualty toll for Americans. The allied Central Command said the next day that no Patriot missile had been fired to intercept the Scud, adding that the Scud had broken into pieces as it descended and was not identified as a threat by the Patriot radar system. But further investigations determined that the Scud was intact when it hit the barracks, and was not detected because the Patriot's radar system was rendered inoperable by the computer failure.

Army experts said in interviews that they knew within days that the Scud was intact when it hit, and that a technical flaw in the radar system was probably to blame. The Army investigations raise questions why the Pentagon and Central Command perpetuated the explanation that the Scud broke up. Central Command officials denied that they were aware of the Army's initial findings of computer malfunction. "It was not something we had at all," said Lieut. Col. Michael Gallagher, who was a Central Command spokesman in Riyadh.

Family members of some of the victims of the attack have tried to get more information from the Army but say the Pentagon has refused to release any details. Rita Bongiorni of Hickory, Pa., whose 20-year-old son, Joseph, was killed in the attack, said she had written the Secretary of the Army, Michael P.W. Stone, for an explanation, but had received only a form letter saying a comrade was at her son's side when he died. When Mrs. Bongiorni requested a detailed autopsy report, she said the cause of death was listed simply as "Scud attack." "I just want to know the truth, and I'm not sure we'll ever know," Mrs. Bongiorni said. "I don't feel the Army's been up front with us."("Army Blames Patriot's Computer for Failure to Stop Dhahran Scud," *The New York Times*, May 20)

MAY - The head of a Pentagon intelligence unit assigned to account for United States servicemen missing in Vietnam has resigned, accusing Bush administration officials of seeking to discredit and perhaps even cover up reports of sightings of Americans in the

country. The Army officer, Col. Millard A. Peck, left his job on March 28, stapling an unusual memorandum and farewell note to his office door that charged that his department was being used as a "'toxic waste dump' to buy the whole 'mess' out of sight and mind in a facility with limited access to public scrutiny."("Bush Is Said to Ignore the Vietnam War's Missing," *The New York Times*, May 22)

MAY - The Supreme Court ruled on May 23 that federally funded family planning clinics may be prohibited from giving any information about abortion. The court, splitting 5 to 4, upheld federal regulations that forbid some 4,000 such clinics that receive federal money from counseling women about the availability of abortion, even if the women ask for the information or if their doctors believe abortion is medically necessary. The decision in the case turned mostly on whether the regulation infringed on free speech.

Opponents of the regulations, promulgated by the Reagan administration in 1988, vowed to press for congressional repeal. A similar effort last year drew administration threats of a veto and died in the Senate.

The decision in *Rust v. Sullivan* turned on the question of free speech and whether the regulations interfered with the doctor-patient relationship, or kept women from making informed medical decisions about abortion. Justice William H. Rehnquist said they did not. He said the government is entitled to decide what it wants to spend its money on, and that its decision to pay for family planning services but not for information about abortion did not violate freedom of speech or any other constitutional right.

All four dissenters said the court should have struck down the regulations on statutory grounds. Blackmun, Marshall, and Stevens, going on to the constitutional questions, said the ruling represented the first time the court had "upheld viewpoint-based suppression of speech simply because that suppression was a condition on the acceptance of public funds." In addition, they said, "Until today, the court has allowed to stand only those restrictions upon reproductive freedom that, while limiting the availability of abortion, have left intact a woman's ability to decide without coercion whether she will continue her pregnancy to term....Today's decision abandons that principle, and with disastrous results."

"This is worse than we could have imagined," said Rachael Pine of the American Civil Liberties Union, which challenged the regulations on behalf of various clinics and doctors. "This opinion is close to giving the government the blank check it sought" in imposing conditions on federally funded programs, she said. "It's close to sanctioning really any kind of government manipulation of information so long as it's paid for by the government."("Abortion-Advice Ban Upheld for Federally Funded Clinics," *The Washington Post*, May 24)

MAY - On May 28 the Supreme Court let stand a ruling that threatens the conviction of Oliver North in the Iran-Contra affair. It refused to review a 1990 ruling by a federal appeals court that requires prosecutors to re-examine the witnesses against him to determine if any of them had prejudiced the trial's outcome by hearing his earlier testimony before Congress. The Justices, who acted without comment, raised the possibility that much of the evidence used to convict North could be invalidated.

The Supreme Court's action was a serious setback for Lawrence Walsh, the Iran-Contra prosecutor, because it means he must now meet the difficult standards set by the appeals court in its July 20, 1990, decision. North was convicted on May 4, 1989, of aiding and abetting in the obstruction of Congress, accepting an illegal gratuity in the form of a $13,800 home security system, and destroying government documents. The charge of destroying documents was voided outright by the appeals court. Walsh vowed to go back to the lower court and try to preserve the two remaining guilty verdicts. ("North Conviction in Doubt as Court Lets Ruling Stand," *The New York Times,* May 29)

JUNE - The anti-crime bill that President Bush has sent to Congress would permit the government to hold special tribunals in which foreigners accused of terrorism would not be allowed to rebut or even see some or all of the evidence against them. Justice Department officials say the tribunals, which would require the approval of a federal judge, would give the government a needed mechanism to deport alien terrorists without being forced to disclose evidence that would reveal the identity of confidential sources, make public the nature of investigative methods, or damage relationships with foreign countries.

But some civil liberties experts say the proposal would violate fundamental principles of American law: that the government's evidence against a person must be public, and that the accused has a right to be informed of that evidence and rebut it. The provision has been largely overlooked until now in the public debate over the anticrime bill but is drawing increasing fire from civil libertarians as the larger measure nears Senate consideration in June. The Supreme Court has long held that aliens living in the United States who face deportation are entitled to constitutional protections, including a public hearing in which the government is not entitled to keep evidence against them a secret. ("Crime Bill Would Establish Alien Deportation Tribunal," *The New York Times,* June 1)

JUNE - The Defense Department has estimated that 100,000 Iraqi soldiers were killed and 300,000 wounded during the Persian Gulf war, the first official attempt to fix the Iraqi death toll in which military officials said was a "tentative" exercise based on "limited information." Responding to a Freedom of Information Act request from the Natural Resources Defense Council, an environmental group, the Defense Intelligence Agency issued a heavily qualified estimate, which was immediately challenged.

"Upon review, it has been determined that little information is available which would enable this agency to make an accurate assessment of Iraqi military casualties," said Robert Hardzog, chief of the Freedom of Information and Privacy Act staff of the intelligence agency, in a letter dated May 22. "An analysis of very limited information leads D.I.A. to tentatively state the following" and then Hardzog noted parenthetically that the estimates carried an "error factor of 50 percent or higher."("Iraq's War Toll Estimated by U.S.," *The New York Times,* June 5)

JUNE - While the U.S. military has labored successfully in recent years—under the mandate of federal law—to overcome long-standing service rivalries and improve both wartime and peacetime coordination among the Army, Air Force, Navy and Marine Corps, the Persian Gulf War exposed continued shortcomings from war planning to intelligence-gathering. Senior military commanders say cooperation among the services has improved. They say the services are now using the experiences of the gulf war to focus on deficiencies that slowed operations and could have resulted in serious problems against a more aggressive enemy force. Among the deficiencies:

- The Air Force could not transmit bombing target lists to Navy pilots aboard ships in the Red Sea and Persian Gulf because of incompatible communications links. As a result, Navy officials had to hand-carry from Riyadh to ships at sea computer disks containing each day's list of targets.

- U.S. intelligence-gathering operations were so cumbersome and compartmentalized among agencies that com-

manders in the field frequently could not obtain timely intelligence to prepare for war operations.... ("War Exposed Rivalries, Weaknesses in Military," *The Washington Post,* June 10)

JUNE - A one and one-half page story in the *Village Voice* by James Ridgeway described issues and problems with the privatization of government information. "The result has been to slowly cripple the functions of government that we take for granted." Ridgeway pointed out that changes in the amount and type of statistical information collected may seem insignificant, and do not show up in a decline in actual statistical output for several years, but ultimately, they will help cloud not only the true effect of administration policies, but even future planning for economic growth.

For example, probably the best single source of information on the U.S. economy is Japan. The Japanese have statistics on their own economy, and make their own informed estimates on how the U.S. operates. For data on cross-border trade with Canada, U.S. business now relies on Canadian statistics. Even the ability of elected representatives to understand what is going on is affected. The Joint Economic Committee of Congress, which is supposed to keep up on economic trends, recently made a study of interest rates. Since the data was unavailable via computer from the Treasury, the committee ended up buying it from a private company.

The author says, "This vast subsidy to the information industry was made by...OMB rules, which basically say that if private industry can make money distributing info, then the government shouldn't be doing it."

Ridgeway gives examples, including high costs, of the government's reliance on private sources for knowledge it needs to govern, using examples from the State Department, the Department of Agriculture, and the National Weather Service. Additionally, he points out:

"The privatization of information affects the most prosaic governmental services. Let's say you are a journalist or scholar or small businessman anxious to find out about the different civil rights bills now pending before Congress....Congress maintains a bill-tracking service that lists all these pending bills and their sponsors by computer, but to get that information most people would end up using Legislate, a service provided by *The Washington Post.* A professor in Brooklyn inquired about the cost of that Service recently: $9500 a year for an academic, and $14,500 for businesses."

Ridgeway also mentions efforts in Congress to change the government's privatization of information that are supported by ALA, Public Citizen, and other groups that are pushing to create an inexpensive government system that would allow people to access online government databases through the Government Printing Office. ("Stormy Weather," *Village Voice,* June 11)

JUNE - U.S. Central Command chief Gen. H. Norman Schwarzkopf charged that battlefield damage assessments from national intelligence agencies during the Persian Gulf War were so hedged with qualifying remarks that they created serious confusion for commanders attempting to make wartime decisions. Schwarzkopf told the Senate Armed Services Committee on June 12 that battlefield damage assessment "was one of the major areas of confusion."

He also echoed the complaint of many field commanders during the war that intelligence was not relayed to senior officers on the ground in a timely, useful form. He recommended that "the intelligence community should be asked to come up with a system that will, in fact, be capable of delivering a real-time product to a theater commander when he requests that." Such problems were compounded by the inability of U.S. military services, especially the Navy and Air Force, to share intelligence information because of incompatible computer systems, Schwarzkopf said. ("Schwarzkopf: War Intelligence Flawed," *The Washington Post,* June 13)

JUNE - In an opinion piece in *The New York Times,* Charles Stith, president of the National Community Reinvestment Network, urged defeat of two amendments in President Bush's banking reform bill. Stith maintained that amendments added by Rep. Paul Kanjorski (D-PA) would gut the Community Reinvestment Act. The "amendments would exempt 80 percent of the nation's banks from following the law's requirements. The amendments would restrict community groups' rights to challenge banks for noncompliance with the act, as well as reduce the number of banks required to report the home mortgage data that would help identify discriminatory lending patterns." Stith said that the Community Reinvestment Act "has been the only leverage poor communities and nonwhite communities possess to win a fair shake from banks....Enforcement of the law is possible because banks are required to keep public records of their business."("Killer Amendments In the Banking Bill," *The New York Times,* June 17)

JUNE - Ron Pollack, of the Families USA Foundation, charged that more than half of the elderly Americans living in poverty are paying for Medicare benefits they are entitled to receive without charge. According to Pollack, eligible individuals must apply to state agencies to get benefits to help pay for medical services and millions have failed to do so because the state and federal governments fail to notify them adequately.

Rep. Henry Waxman (D-CA), principal author of the 1988 and 1990 provisions that entitled the poor to have Medicaid pay their Medicare bills, said, "It's clear that the Social Security Administration, Health Care Financing Administration and states are not doing their job to get this information out to the elderly who are entitled to this help. We're going to try to push the Social Security Administration to send out notices with the checks and figure out some way to get these people enrolled."("Many Elderly Missing Out on Medicaid Benefits," *The Washington Post,* June 18)

JUNE - The June 17 blast that killed six workers and injured 23 at a chemical plant in Charleston, S.C., was the latest in a series of fires, explosions and poison-gas leaks at refineries and chemical plants around the country. "Since October 1987, when a leak of hydrogen fluoride gas at a Marathon Oil refinery forced the evacuation of thousands in Texas City, Tex., the American petrochemical industry has endured one of the deadliest periods in its history, one that has baffled Government experts and alarmed company executives. The 12 worst explosions have killed 79 people, injured 933 and caused roughly $2 billion in damage."

Although some aspects of the explosion were reminiscent of previous accidents, there is no way to know if factors similar to the previous accidents could have contributed to the recent blast. "And there is not a Federal agency that compiles statistics and investigates every accident the way the National Transportation Safety Board does, for example, with air crashes. Although amendments to the Clean Air Act signed into law in 1990 established a Chemical Safety and Hazard Investigation Board, the White House has yet to appoint any members or provide funds."("Petrochemical Disasters Raise Alarm in Industry," *The New York Times,* June 19)

Less Access...XVII
A 1991 Chronology: June - December

JUNE - The Northrop Corporation has agreed to pay $8 million to settle a lawsuit by two of its former employees who said the com-

pany falsified tests on parts for cruise missiles built for the Air Force. The settlement comes 16 months after Northrop pleaded guilty to federal criminal charges in the case filed in 1987 by Leo Barajas and Patricia Meyer, both employees at Northrop's plant in Pomona, Calif. They charged that Northrop and some of its executives had improperly tested guidance devices called flight data transmitters and had deliberately reported false results to the Air Force. ("Northrop Settles Workers' Suit on False Missile Tests for $8 Million," *The New York Times,* June 25, 1991)

JUNE - The nation's next generation of badly needed weather satellites, designed by the National Aeronautics and Space Administration and built by aerospace contractors, are so riddled with defects that they may never be launched. According to federal weather officials, loss of coverage by these satellites could precipitate a national emergency, depriving forecasters of crucial coverage for tracking hurricanes, floods, and tornadoes. Only one U.S. weather satellite, the GOES-7, is positioned in geostationary orbit directly above the country, and its five-year lifespan normally would end early next year. NASA planned to launch new weather satellites in 1989. Known as GOES-NEXT, the $1.1 billion program is $500 million over budget and more than two years behind schedule. Two of five planned GOES-NEXT satellites have been completed.

GOES-NEXT is so flawed that it may not be launched in time to replace the aging GOES-7, National Weather Service officials said. John Knauss, head of the National Oceanic and Atmospheric Administration, which includes the National Weather Service, said he is so concerned he has ordered contingency plans to investigate building a simple satellite quickly or buying one from Japanese or European makers. Instead of GOES-NEXT, he said, the weather service is facing a "NO-GOES" scenario. Moreover, Knauss said, he is prepared to ask the Europeans to move one of their orbiting satellites closer to the eastern United States, which still would leave half of the country without continuous coverage. ("Crucial Weather Satellites May Be Too Flawed to Use," *The Washington Post,* June 28, 1991)

JUNE - Recently librarians in federal depository libraries have complained that the Office of Management and Budget is not making OMB circulars available through the Depository Library Program. OMB maintains that the circulars—which are key documents if the public is to understand federal regulations and requirements for public and private organizations—are for administrative purposes only, not subject to depository requirements. Now the public and libraries can get access to the circulars through an expensive electronic product available from the National Technical Information Service.

NTIS and Government Counselling Ltd., through a joint venture, have produced a CD-ROM containing OMB circulars, the Federal Acquisition Regulations, Defense Federal Acquisition Regulations, General Accounting Office decision synopses, and full-text of the General Services Administration Board of Contract Appeals decisions. The disk also contains public laws, federal information processing standards publications summaries, procurement and acquisition checklists, quarterly news bulletins, and a variety of commentaries to accompany the regulations.

The CD-ROM is available from NTIS as either a quarterly subscription or as a single disk containing the most recent quarter only. The subscription costs $1,495. The most recent quarter only costs $995. In the future, Government Counselling, Ltd. will incorporate agency-specific information acquired by NTIS with its proprietary product to create a series of custom CD-ROMs. ("New

CD-ROM Makes Government-Wide Procurement Regs Easy to Find," *NTIS NewsLine,* Summer 1991)

JULY - Publishers and executives of 17 news organizations, still concerned about press restrictions during the Persian Gulf War, told Defense Secretary Richard Cheney that independent reporting should be "the principal means of coverage" for all future U.S. military operations. In a late June letter, the news organizations said that combat pools—groups of reporters who are escorted by the military and share their dispatches with colleagues—should be used only for the first 24 to 36 hours of any deployment. In Saudi Arabia, military officials frequently detained reporters who attempted to operate outside such pools.

The media executives also sent Cheney a report providing fresh details of how military officials suppressed news, controlled interviews, limited press access, and delayed transmission of stories. Such restrictions "made it impossible for reporters and photographers to tell the public the full story of the war in a timely fashion," the letter said. "Moreover, we believe it is imperative that the gulf war not serve as a model for future coverage."

"We welcome these proposals," said Pentagon spokesman Pete Williams. He said Cheney "is eager to sit down and talk with members of this group....Nobody should get the impression that because we did it one way during the Persian Gulf War that it's going to be that way forever and ever." Williams said there were good reasons for the press restrictions in the gulf, but that "some things worked well and some didn't."

Among the items in the report were: 1) the Pentagon attempted "to use the press to disseminate disinformation," such as releasing plans for an amphibious assault against Iraq that was a ruse to mislead the Iraqis; 2) a *Newsweek* contributor, retired Army Col. David Hackworth, said that on one occasion "U.S. troops fixed bayonets and charged us;" and 3) two reporters were barred from a Marine unit after their escorts complained that they had asked questions forbidden by military guidelines. ("News Media Ask Freer Hand in Future Conflicts," *The Washington Post,* July 1)

JULY - Columnists Jack Anderson and Dale Van Atta reported that congressional investigators are conducting an enormous probe into allegations that the pro-Iraqi tilt of the Reagan and Bush administrations allowed Iraq to buy technology that it later used in weapons turned against U.S. troops. In one case they examined, the reporters said it appears "the Bush administration not only winked at the export of sensitive technology to Iraq but may have stopped legitimate law enforcement efforts to interdict the trade."

Central to the case is Bob Bickel, an engineering consultant and petroleum expert, who worked for about 20 years as an undercover informant for the U.S. Customs Service. In the course of Bickel's engineering work, he would keep Customs informed about what he thought were suspicious orders filled for foreign buyers. Bickel said he was hired in 1989 by a Houston firm to give advice to a foreign buyer on oil-related technology. The buyer turned out to be an Iraqi, and the technology Bickel was asked to buy included a phased-ray antenna system that could potentially be used in a missile tracking and guidance system. Bickel alerted the Customs contact with whom he had always worked.

A Customs investigation did not get very far. The Customs team sent inquiries to Washington, and Bickel let the Houston broker who had hired him know an investigation was underway into the Iraqi client. The broker's response was unexpected; he allegedly told Bickel and the Customs investigators that he was connected to the U.S. intelligence community.

It was not long before Bickel heard that Customs canceled the investigation. Bickel's contact in Customs called Washington and was told the State and Commerce departments were behind the decision. Some very important people did not want anyone nosing around the technology deal.

Anderson says congressional investigators believe the Iraqi buyer was working for Ishan Barbouti, an Iraqi arms dealer. Barbouti is suspected by U.S. intelligence agencies of having been a major player in the construction of a chemical weapons plant in Libya. He bankrolled at least four businesses in the United States that were producing materials that may have been sent secretly to Iraq for weapons use. Barbouti died mysteriously in London last July. ("How the U.S. Winked at Exports to Iraq," *The Washington Post,* July 8)

JULY - Census Bureau Director Barbara Everitt Bryant disagreed with Commerce Secretary Robert Mosbacher on virtually every element of his decision not to adjust the 1990 census to compensate for an undercount. In a document citing strong evidence that the population of the United States is 5.3 million more than the 248 million counted in the census, Bryant wrote: "In my opinion, not adjusting would be denying that these 5 million persons exist. That denial would be a greater inaccuracy than any inaccuracies that adjustment may introduce."

On average, the accuracy of the census would be improved by a statistical adjustment, Bryant wrote in her advisory opinion, which was released by the Commerce Department along with other expert recommendations that went to Mosbacher in the weeks before his decision. Mosbacher announced he would rely on the results of the initial headcount, rather than figures drawn from a sample survey of more than 170,000 housing units, as the basis for redrawing political boundaries and distributing billions of federal dollars.

Mosbacher was criticized for his decision by Del. Eleanor Holmes Norton (D-DC), who said, "The decision is particularly harsh, even cruel, because it comes after more than 10 years of huge declines in federal support to cities." District officials have estimated that the city will lose millions of dollars in aid over the decade. They and others concede, however, that it is impossible to calculate accurately the fiscal impact of the decision, because many federal programs are capped and rely to different degrees on population data. ("Census Bureau Chief Disagreed With Mosbacher on Adjustments," *The Washington Post,* July 17)

[Ed. note: *The Washington Post* editorialized that Secretary of Commerce Mosbacher "was right to decide to stick to the actual number of people counted last year." The editorial said this intricate quarrel will now move back into the courtroom, where a judge will listen to the statisticians debate their differences. "If the country wants a more accurate census in the year 2000, the way to get it is not to embark on statistical massaging of disputed figures but to spend more money to collect better data in the first place."("Census Accuracy," *The Washington Post,* July 17)

JULY - The former head of the CIA's Central American task force admitted in court he and other senior CIA officials were aware of the secret diversion of funds to the Contra rebels in Nicaragua for months before the scandal broke in the fall of 1986. Alan Fiers acknowledged the agency's complicity in attempts to cover up the affair as he pleaded guilty in U.S. District Court in Washington to two misdemeanor counts of unlawfully withholding information from Congress. His pleas came as part of an agreement to cooperate fully with independent counsel Lawrence Walsh, who has been investigating the Iran-Contra scandal for 4 1/2 years.

Fiers said he willfully withheld information from Congress in the fall of 1986 both about the diversion of funds and about the secret Contra resupply operation that was being run out of the Reagan White House. As a result of those admissions and the prospect he will say more, other officials being investigated by Walsh for possible perjury charges may come under increasing pressure to disclose more than they have to date.

At the same time, investigators probing the unfolding investigation of the Bank of Credit and Commerce International told *Time* that the Iran-Contra affair is linked to the burgeoning bank scandal. Former government officials and other sources confirm that the CIA stashed money in a number of B.C.C.I. accounts that were used to finance covert operations; some of these funds went to the Contras. Investigators also say an intelligence unit of the U.S. defense establishment has used the bank to maintain a secret slush fund, possibly for financing unauthorized covert operations. ("The Cover-Up Begins to Crack," *Time*, July 22)

JULY - House Judiciary Committee Chairman Jack Brooks (D-TX) moved to subpoena Justice Department records to investigate allegations that the agency stole computer software from a private company, Inslaw Inc. The announcement came nearly a week after Attorney General Dick Thornburgh refused to testify before the Judiciary Committee. After Brooks' announcement, a Justice official said the department would provide the documents the committee sought for its investigation of the computer software allegations.

A bankruptcy judge in proceedings involving Inslaw Inc. found there was a conspiracy among Justice Department officials during the Reagan administration to steal the software from Inslaw, which went into bankruptcy protection after the agency withheld payments on its government contract. The software was a case-management system used by federal prosecutors.

The Judiciary Committee announcement also said Brooks planned to seek authority to subpoena a 1989 Justice legal opinion that gives the Federal Bureau of Investigation authority to seize fugitives overseas without permission of foreign governments. ("Brooks to Seek Justice Data," *The Washington Post*, July 25)

[Ed. note: See August 14 entry on same subject.]

AUGUST - The General Accounting Office evaluated the quality of Environmental Protection Agency data that will be used to determine the need for mandatory hazardous waste minimization requirements. All the data quality problems GAO identified in its February 1990 report (PEMD-90-3) as likely to occur did occur. These problems included the system's inability to integrate data, uncertain data validity based on inappropriate measurement, and uncertain data reliability based on inadequate data collection methods. Some of these problems were so severe that EPA had to abandon all of the central analyses of waste minimization progress that the agency had originally planned to give to Congress.

Problems such as the extent of missing data were of special importance in negatively affecting the assessment of progress on hazardous waste minimization. These findings suggest that the information EPA presents to Congress will not be helpful in understanding the extent and determinants of waste minimization or in determining whether mandatory or other requirements may need to be included in the reauthorization of the Resource Conservation and Recovery Act. ("Waste Minimization: EPA Data Are Severely Flawed," *GAO/PEMD-91-21*, August 5, 9 pp.)

AUGUST - An article by Spencer Rich stated that one of the most confusing incidents in the debate over the Medicare catastrophic benefits act of 1988, subsequently repealed, was the dispute over the cost of prescription drug benefits. The Congressional Budget

Office originally projected the drug benefit would cost the government $6 billion from 1990 to 1994 and require the elderly to pay $8 billion in insurance. But revised estimates later put the figures at $12 billion for the government and $9 billion for the elderly.

A new study from a National Research Council panel headed by Eric Hanushek of the University of Rochester explains the reason for the huge jumps in both figures: The only available estimates on prescription drug use at the time the bill was passed were ten years old. The CBO initially had to rely on drug-use figures from 1977-80. A subsequent 1987 survey showed that prescription drug use had grown much faster than the earlier figures had suggested.

This example is one of a number cited in the study, which concluded that bad statistics and inadequate information have led to major miscalculations in the formulation of federal policy. The study notes that the government has been cutting funds for developing the statistics that would enable Congress and the White House to understand better what impact new legislation is likely to have on spending and tax policy.

The article cites other examples of poor data about Individual Retirement Accounts, the Consumer Price Index, and the Current Population Survey. For example, during the late 1970s and 1980s, the report says "the consumer price index overstated the rise in the cost of living by some 1-2 percent a year, with serious consequences for wage escalation and overadjustment of Social Security and other federal entitlements." At least 80 million people were affected, and every one percent error cost the government at least $4.6 billion a year in extra payments or lost tax revenue. ("Bad Statistics Cited in Policy Miscalculations," *The Washington Post*, August 6)

AUGUST - After Rep. Frank Wolf (R-VA) met with two officials of the Central Intelligence Agency, the CIA said it will include a consultant's reasons against moving as many as 3,000 employees to West Virginia in a report that previously had been censored. The agency agreed to return some of the information to a version of the report prepared for public release. Wolf is one of several Washington, D.C., area legislators trying to thwart an attempt by Sen. Robert Byrd (D-WV) to transfer thousands of CIA employees from offices in Northern Virginia to Jefferson County, W.Va.

Wolf complained that the CIA was not making public the reasons against moving to West Virginia. The reasons were contained in a report released to the House Intelligence Committee, but were edited from the version made available to the public. How much information the agency will put back in is unclear. "It is our view that to release the study in its entirety would jeopardize the government in its negotiations," said CIA spokesman Mark Mansfield. Mansfield said the information withheld from the report combined analyses of the advantages and disadvantages of each parcel at four sites that the agency is considering. The edited information also contains estimates of the land costs to the government and financial analyses of the cost to develop the sites.

Wolf said parts of the report stated that West Virginia should be eliminated as a site because a lack of highways in the area, because commutes would be too long for workers now living in the Washington, D.C., area, and because the move would cause some key employees to resign. Wolf questioned the need for secrecy, noting "This is not a covert operation. They are not talking about mining the harbors of Nicaragua. They are talking about purchasing land for a building."("CIA Will Disclose More on W.Va. Site," *The Washington Post*, August 14)

AUGUST - After the confrontation between House Judiciary Committee Chairman Jack Brooks (D-TX) and the Justice Department about a controversial 1989 Justice Department opinion about U.S. authority to act overseas, Justice officials sought to negotiate a compromise that would include permitting some members of the Judiciary Committee to review the opinion without publicly releasing a copy. However, a copy of the opinion was obtained by *The Washington Post*.

The opinion concluded that "serious threats" to U.S. domestic security from "international terrorist groups and narcotics traffickers" would justify the President to violate international law by ordering abduction of fugitives overseas. It asserts that the President and Attorney General have "inherent constitutional power" to order a wide range of law enforcement actions in foreign countries without the consent of foreign governments, even if they violate international treaties. It also argues that "as a matter of domestic law, the executive has the power to authorize actions inconsistent" with United Nations charter provisions barring use of force against member nations. Such decisions "are fundamentally political questions," the opinion states, and therefore do not constrain the chief executive in fulfilling his law enforcement responsibilities.

The opinion from the Office of Legal Counsel, written by then-Assistant and now Attorney General William P. Barr, has been at the center of controversy for nearly two years. Along with a later opinion concluding that the U. S. military could make arrests overseas, it was relied on by Bush administration officials in launching the December 1989 invasion of Panama. But critics have charged that it amounts to a dangerous expansion of Justice Department authority overseas in violation of international law.

Justice Department officials have consistently refused to release the June 21, 1989, opinion, contending that its public dissemination would inhibit department lawyers writing internal opinions. They said it also had the potential to harm the government's position in pending cases, including the trial of ex-Panamanian dictator Gen. Manuel Antonio Noriega, by giving defense lawyers ideas about possible weaknesses in the government's arguments. ("U.S. 'Power' on Abductions Detailed," *The Washington Post*, August 14)

AUGUST - Two examples of less government information being made available to the American people were contained in a letter to the editor of *The New York Times*. Ernest B. Dane of Great Falls, Va., cited the annual report to Congress of the Secretary of Defense, which for many years served as a virtual public encyclopedia of data about the defense establishment, and its equipment and cost to the taxpayer. However, for the last two years the report has been revised to exclude most details needed for real understanding of national security issues.

Dane cited a second example of the Office of Management and Budget midsession review of the budget, issued annually on July 15. "This year, the review omitted data showing interest on the public debt. The amount of that interest, now estimated at more than $327 billion for 1993, might seem embarrassing, but it should nevertheless be published."("Using Cost-Cutting to Limit Public Data," *The New York Times*, August 14)

AUGUST - President Bush signed a bill on covert operations intended to close a loophole blamed for the Iran-Contra scandal. But he made it clear that he would use his own discretion on whether to follow the law's tighter requirements on notifying Congress about secret intelligence operations abroad. Bush protested the inclusion of the first legal definition of "covert action," which he said was unnecessary and infringed on the constitutional powers of the Presidency. The legislation requires the President to provide written approval of covert activities conducted by any federal agency and bans retroactive approval of such operations by the President.

During the Iran-Contra affair, former President Ronald Reagan skirted the Intelligence Oversight Act of 1980, which requires the President to give "prior notice" of all covert activities to the two congressional intelligence committees or to give notice "in a timely fashion" if emergency actions are necessary. He also signed an order that retroactively authorized arms sales to Iran, and he did not inform Congress of the two actions for a year. ("Covert-Disclosure Bill Is Signed by President," *The New York Times*, August 16)

AUGUST - The General Accounting Office looked into the removal of government documents during the Reagan administration by the last two agency heads at the Departments of Defense, Justice, State, and Treasury. It discovered that records of departing agency heads were not controlled by the National Archives and Records Administration, as is done for departing presidents. All eight of the former agency heads removed documents when they left office, and two of the four agencies did not know if records had been removed. Agencies were unaware of classified material in two removed collections and failed to ensure that required security restrictions were followed for a significant amount of classified material in a third collection removed to a private business.

Additionally, at least half of the collections contained original documents agencies did not know had been removed. As a result, GAO believes official records possibly also were removed. Once documents are moved, the government's access to them is not ensured—as evidenced by GAO's being denied access to three of the eight collections. GAO concluded that current internal controls do not adequately ensure that government records and information are properly protected because no independent review of documents is made before they are removed. GAO believes the National Archives and Records Administration should oversee plans by agency heads to remove documents and determine whether their relinquishment and removal are consistent with federal laws and regulations. ("Federal Records: Document Removal by Agency Heads Needs Independent Oversight," *GAO/GGD-91-117*, August 30, 35 pp.)

[Ed. note: *The Washington Post* included a story about this GAO report in a September 24 article, "Leaving Town With the Records." The article mentions that the three who would not allow GAO investigators access to records they had taken were former Secretary of Defense Caspar Weinberger, former Secretary of State Alexander Haig, and former Secretary of the Treasury Donald Regan.]

SEPTEMBER - Government studies of the health risks from hazardous wastes at nearly 1,000 Superfund cleanup sites were "seriously deficient," the General Accounting Office reported. The health assessments, which the Agency for Toxic Substances and Disease Registry was required by law to perform under a tight deadline, "generally have not been useful" to the Environmental Protection Agency and others supervising the cleanups, the GAO said in a report to Congress. "Because ATSDR health assessments have not fully evaluated the health risks of many Superfund sites, communities have not been adequately informed about possible health effects," the GAO said.

The Superfund program was established to identify the nation's worst hazardous waste problems and make sure they were cleaned up. Superfund amendments in 1986 gave ATSDR responsibility for looking into the dangers to human health at each site on the national priority list. The agency, which reports to the Department of Health and Human Services, was so rushed that for 165

Superfund sites, it simply found documents already prepared for other reasons and called them health assessments.

For example, the agency took a 1984 review by the Centers for Disease Control of a Massachusetts Health Department cancer mortality study and called it a health assessment of a site at New Bedford, Mass., even though the site was not mentioned. For more recent assessments, the agency has improved its work by visiting all the sites and contacting state or local health officials, the GAO report said. ("'Superfund' Studies Called Deficient," *The Washington Post*, September 4)

SEPTEMBER - According to Jack Anderson, the Nuclear Regulatory Commission has proposed regulations that would permit radioactive wastes to be recycled into consumer goods such as toys, belt buckles, cosmetics, shotgun shells, fishing lures and frying pans. Anderson said: "Consumers will not find a surgeon general's warning on these products. That's because the NRC has no plans to mandate labeling."

The policy was put on hold after creating a firestorm, but if ultimately implemented, the United States would allow levels of radiation that are ten times those suggested by international standards. An NRC spokesperson said: "We do not take actions that do not protect public health and safety." But an internal briefing paper from the Environmental Protection Agency painted a different picture: "We believe this is…not protective of the public health."

The nuclear power industry clamored for this change and, by some estimates, stands to save up to $100 million each year from this cheaper form of waste disposal. The Nuclear Information and Resource Service, a public interest group, estimates the savings would be $1 per year per utility customer.

The NRC adopted the controversial policy in June 1990 when it raised the level of certain less dangerous forms of radiation to which humans could be subjected, abdicating any regulatory oversight for lower levels. Under the policy, about 30 percent of the nation's low-level radioactive waste could be disposed of in a variety of common outlets, including sewer systems, incinerators, and ordinary landfills where it could seep into drinking water sources. Radioactive waste also, for the first time, would be allowed as recycled material in consumer products. ("No Child's Play in Recycled Waste," *The Washington Post*, September 9)

SEPTEMBER - The U.S. Geological Survey's Water Resources Scientific Information Center announced that monthly issues of *Selected Water Resources Abstracts* (SWRA) will cease with the December 1991 issue. The 1991 annual indexes will not be printed at all. The Geological Survey cited budget exigencies and the wide range of commercial sources which provide access to SWRA as reasons for discontinuing the printed publication. Magnetic tapes can be leased from the National Technical Information Service. The SWRA database of 235,000 abstracts is available online via DIALOG and the European Space Agency Information Retrieval Services.

A CD-ROM version of the SWRA is available from several vendors: the National Information Services Corporation charges $595 a year; the OCLC version costs $750 a year to nonmembers, $700 for members. Since no government agency is producing the CD-ROM version of the SWRA, it will no longer be available to federal depository libraries where the public would have no-fee access to it. ("Selected Water Resources Abstracts Will Cease Publication," *Administrative Notes*, U.S. Government Printing Office, September 15)

SEPTEMBER - An article by Barry Meier highlighted criticism of the Consumer Product Safety Commission in its role as watchdog

of the safety of all consumer products other than cars, boats, drugs, and food. One of the agency's most contentious issues concerns how it discloses information involving hazards. Under its rules, the agency must give a manufacturer a chance to review and dispute any data about a product. The Consumer Product Safety Commission is the only safety agency that operates under such restrictions. Congress, in 1981, also prohibited the agency from releasing any data about product hazards that manufacturers are obliged to report to the commission. As a result, preliminary determinations about product hazards are no longer placed in a public reading room at the agency, said Alan Schoem, a commission lawyer.

Thus, it may be years before the public hears of suspect products. In November 1989, the Consumer Product Safety Commission determined that a popular portable heater might pose a fire risk. But it did not alert the public until August 1991, after the manufacturer agreed to fix 3.6 million units. In those 21 months, while the agency and company investigated and negotiated, eight people died in two fires that may have been started by faulty wiring in the heaters, said David Fonvielle, a lawyer in Tallahassee, Fla., for plaintiffs in some of the cases. The manufacturer said the units caused no fires.

Several other issues, including proposals that disposable lighters should be made childproof and ride-on lawn mowers made less liable to tip, have been unresolved for six years or more. Some CPSC problems appear traceable to its limited resources and slow processes. The FY 1991 agency budget was $37 million, down from $43.9 million in 1979. The agency's success in reducing product-related injuries has slowed. The rate of injuries per 100,000 Americans declined by 24 percent from 1978 to 1982, but between 1982 and 1988 that decline was only nine percent, commission data show. ("Product Safety Commission Is Criticized as Too Slow to Act," *The New York Times*, September 21)

SEPTEMBER - At the insistence of former President Ronald Reagan, 6.3 million pages of White House documents will be made public shortly after the opening of his presidential library on November 4. Stung by earlier press reports about a planned three-year restriction on release of all documents, Reagan urged his staff to do everything possible to make some documents available at the library opening, his aides said.

In a letter to National Archivist Donald Wilson, Reagan waived a 12-year delay on the release of 1.5 million pages of selected presidential records covering routine position papers and offering factual information on issues ranging from agriculture to highways and bridges. Reagan also asked that the archives open up an estimated 4.8 million pages of get-well cards, birthday greetings, and other unsolicited letters.

The remainder of the library's storehouse of 55 million pages of presidential documents—including all Iran-Contra documents—will remain shielded from public view for a decade or more by a variety of restrictions to protect national security, foreign policy, and confidentiality. ("Reagan Library Set to Release Private Papers," *The Washington Post*, September 25)

SEPTEMBER - A lobbying disclosure law is so riddled with exemptions that six big military contractors which spent $5.7 million lobbying the executive branch and Congress last year only reported $3,547, according to investigators for the Senate subcommittee on oversight of government management. Sen. Carl Levin (D-MI) chairs the subcommittee which held a hearing on September 25 to discuss the weaknesses of the lobbying disclosure laws, such as the 1989 Byrd Amendment that requires disclosure by contractors.

In a statement, Sen. Levin said: "Disclosure under the Byrd Amendment is almost non-existent, and it's not because there's so little lobbying. Instead, there's a real problem with the way this law has been interpreted, applied and also studiously avoided." A Pentagon inspector general's survey found that lobbying by 100-plus consultants was not disclosed because of the way contractors interpreted the Byrd Amendment. Their reading of the law was backed by the Defense Department and the Office of Management and Budget. ("Senate Panel Looks at Military Lobbying Law," *The New York Times,* September 26)

SEPTEMBER - Proposals by the Food and Drug Administration to improve nutrition labeling on food and drink have been overruled and weakened by the Office of Management and Budget, a consumer-advocacy group alleged. The Center for Science in the Public Interest released documents it obtained showing that some FDA proposals to implement the Nutrition Labeling and Education Act of 1990 were "substantially changed" by OMB. In the opinion of CSPI, the changes favor the interests of manufacturers and retailers.

However, an FDA spokesman said the changes were not significant and that the consumer group had exaggerated the issue. An OMB spokesman said nothing was forced on the FDA, which had agreed to the changes. According to CSPI, the changes would reduce by about 7,000 the number of grocery stores required to post nutrition information for fresh produce and seafood. "The net effect is that the consumer is less likely to see nutritional information than they would under FDA proposals," said Bruce Silverglade, CSPI director of legal affairs.

The FDA had also proposed that the manufacturers of diluted "fruit drinks" use a standard procedure to determine the percentage of real juice in their product—a figure given on the label. This test will be used by the FDA in any enforcement actions, but the OMB would allow manufacturers to use any test they want. "This leaves juice manufacturers free to use whatever test gives them the highest number for juice content," Silverglade said. In addition, the consumer group claims, citing FDA sources, that OMB is delaying approval of a study to test new nutrition labeling formats intended to help consumers better understand what is in their food.

In a separate move, Rep. John Conyers (D-MI), chairman of the House Government Operations Committee, wrote to the director of OMB demanding information on the OMB review of the FDA proposals. Conyers said OMB's revision "appears to subvert congressional intent as expressed in laws to protect public health and safety." Conyers said the OMB has, in the past, "forced the FDA" to weaken regulations governing health claims on some food. ("OMB Accused of Weakening Food-Labeling Proposals," *The Washington Post,* September 26)

[Ed. note: See November 6 entry for follow-up article.]

SEPTEMBER - Judge Harold Greene ruled that a confidentiality clause in federal health research contracts, which bars private researchers from publishing their preliminary findings violates the First Amendment. The ruling comes in the same controversial area of the law that the Supreme Court addressed last May when it upheld a ban on federal funding for public clinics that give abortion counseling. At issue in that case, *Rust v. Sullivan,* and in the current case involving Stanford University was the same question: How much can government limit speech it is paying for?

Greene distinguished his ruling from *Rust,* saying the earlier case involved the government's right to see that public money is spent the way Congress intended. But in the case involving Stanford University, he ruled that the government was directly limiting the rights of scientists to talk about their work. "Few large-scale endeavors are today not supported, directly or indirectly, by government funds," Green wrote. "If [*Rust v. Sullivan*] were to be given the scope and breadth defendants advocate in this case, the result would be an invitation to government censorship wherever public funds flow."

At issue was a dispute between Stanford and the National Institutes for Health over a $1.5 million contract to do research on an artificial heart device known as the left ventricular assist device. The NIH contract included a clause in the contract barring Stanford scientists from discussing "preliminary" research results or data that had "the possibility of adverse effects on the public." Stanford objected, saying the clause violated its First Amendment rights, as well as the tradition of academic freedom among scientists to discuss their work. Such confidentiality clauses have become common in NIH contracts in the past 15 years and usually are invoked in research involving clinical trials going on simultaneously at different universities. ("Federal Judge Rules NIH Research Confidentiality Clause Invalid," *The Washington Post,* September 27)

OCTOBER - A former top Central Intelligence Agency official testified in Senate confirmation hearings that in the 1980s, the CIA was a politicized cauldron in which estimates were slanted and false information was presented to the White House to match the policy objectives of the agency's director, William Casey. The testimony was presented by Melvin Goodman, a professor at the National War College who worked as a Soviet affairs specialist at the CIA for 24 years, to the Senate Select Committee on Intelligence, which was considering the nomination of Gates to direct the CIA. According to Goodman, Gates was Casey's chief agent inside the CIA intimidating analysts into producing slanted reports—especially on Iran, Nicaragua and Afghanistan. However, another former top CIA official, Graham Fuller, told the senators that Goodman had presented "serious distortions."

The Senate committee made public the testimony by another CIA veteran, Harold Ford, who said Gates failed to take seriously the decline of communism and had offered memory lapses to the Senate committee that were "clever." Ford cited a key analysis he said overstated the depth of Soviet influence in Iran at a time when U.S. arms sales were being justified as a counterbalance to Moscow's influence with Tehran. ("Ex-Aide Calls CIA Under Casey and Gates Corrupt and Slanted," *International Herald Tribune,* October 2)

[Ed. note: See following entry.]

OCTOBER - Robert Gates vigorously denied he had exerted pressure on agency analysts to distort Central Intelligence Agency reports. He acknowledged that in a "rough and tumble" CIA atmosphere during the 1980s, embittered and inflexible analysts perceived such political pressure. "I never distorted intelligence to support policy or please a policy-maker," Gates said in testimony to the Senate Intelligence Committee, which was considering his nomination to direct the CIA. Gates drew on freshly declassified CIA memos to present a counterattack against damaging charges by current and former CIA officials that he slanted CIA analyses to suit White House policy objectives and those of William Casey, then the agency's director. ("Gates Tells Panel He Didn't Order Data to Be Slanted," *International Herald Tribune,* October 4)

OCTOBER - During the debate on the conference report on HR 1415, the Foreign Relations Authorization Act, Fiscal Years 1992 and 1993, Sen. Jesse Helms (R-NC), ranking minority member of the Senate Foreign Relations Committee, discussed classification of government information. He observed:

"One of the handiest tools used by executive branch agencies to keep Congress in the dark..., is needless classification of documents. Proper classification of matter relating to vital national security concerns of the United States have my full support. But classification that covers up information that might merely provide to be an embarrassment is inexcusable." (October 4 *Congressional Record*, p. S14439)

OCTOBER - The owner and publisher of the Santa Fe *New Mexican*, Robert McKinney, fired its managing editor and criticized a series of articles detailing safety and environmental hazards at Los Alamos National Laboratory, the largest employer in the Santa Fe area. The series contained 32 articles published during six days in February 1991. The series, based in part on documents obtained under the Freedom of Information Act, stated that cleaning up 1,800 sites of possible contamination near Los Alamos would cost $2 billion over a 20-year period. The articles further stated that the lab releases large amounts of chemical and radioactive contamination into the environment daily, although the risk to public health is slight to nonexistent.

Lab officials did not cite inaccuracies in the series or ask for corrections. But the *New Mexican* published critical opinion pieces by Siegfried Hecker, director of Los Alamos, and former director Harold Agnew. "Any activity creates wastes," Agnew wrote. "Making a dinner salad, baking a pie....Nuclear wastes are no more dangerous than many other wastes." In late August, Los Alamos released a 308-page internal evaluation highly critical of its failure to comply with safety and environmental regulations, essentially confirming much of what had been in the paper's February series. ("After Nuclear Series, Paper Melts Down," *The Washington Post*, October 5)

OCTOBER - In 1985, at the midway point of the worldwide campaign to raise childhood immunization rates fourfold to 80 percent, public health officials in the United States stopped counting. As a result, the United States is the only country in the world that has no official figures on immunization rates of 1- or 2-year-olds. The official explanation was that data collection was costly and the methodology was suspect, but critics contended that the Reagan administration was embarrassed by the contrast between improving immunization rates throughout the Third World and five consecutive years of decline in the United States.

Even without comprehensive data, problems are evident. Nearly 28,000 cases of measles were reported in 1990—more than 18 times the number reported in 1983, when the disease reached an all-time low, and more than 50 times the goal of 500 cases per year that the U.S. surgeon general had set for 1990. Nearly half the measles patients were under age five. In the wake of the measles outbreak, the government has begun to collect immunization data again.

The measles epidemic, along with outbreaks of rubella and whooping cough, has sparked a debate about whether supply or demand is the problem. The supply-siders hold that federal and state funding has not kept pace with a thirteenfold rise in the cost of the vaccines during the past decade. According to a survey last year by the Children's Defense Fund and the National Association of Community Health Clinics, 72 percent of public health clinics experienced spot shortages of vaccines. The demand-side holds that, while there are access problems, the real barrier is a mix of complacency and poverty. To combat the problem, the administration has called for a $40 million increase in immunization funding for this year; Congress is considering a $60 million to $80 million increase. ("U.S. Immunization Rates Uncertain," *The Washington Post*, October 9)

OCTOBER - The fight to gain release of the adjusted 1990 census figures has expanded to include states and the House of Representatives, with Rep. Thomas Sawyer (D-OH) saying he will seek a subpoena of the count from the Commerce Department if necessary. At least five state legislatures have filed Freedom of Information Act requests, arguing that they need to see the adjusted count to determine which set of figures—the official census number of those adjusted to compensate for an undercount—should be used to redraw political boundaries. Sawyer maintains that pubic access to the data is a matter of fairness: "The American people ought to be able to see and evaluate those numbers. They belong to the American taxpayer, who paid about $35 million to generate those numbers."

Commerce Secretary Robert Mosbacher has refused all requests to make public the adjusted figures, saying the numbers were flawed and their release could disrupt the redistricting process going on across the country. Sawyer said Mosbacher's refusal to adjust the census or even make public the adjusted counts "has left state legislatures all over the country struggling with large and demonstrably disproportionate undercounts of minorities."("Adjusted Census Figures Subject of Wider Fight," *The Washington Post*, October 17)

OCTOBER - The White House Council on Competitiveness, a regulatory review panel chaired by Vice President Dan Quayle, has refused to turn over documents to several congressional committees seeking to determine the council's role in federal rulemaking. Critics of the Vice President's council assert that it has become a "super-regulatory" agency beholden to business interests, revising regulations after they are written by the designated agencies. The White House maintains that the council is simply an arm of the President's executive office and as such has all the power to review and suggest regulations that the President gives it. The council has claimed executive privilege to fend off requests for information on its deliberations.

Sen. John Glenn (D-OH), chair of the Senate Governmental Affairs Committee, commented that presidential regulatory review is "process cloaked by mystery and secrecy and encourages the representation of interests that may unfairly influence agency rule making."("Questions on Role of Quayle Council," *The New York Times*, October 19)

OCTOBER - The National Research Council reported that the nation's mammoth program to clear up toxic waste was hampered by the inability to tell the difference between dumps posing a real threat to human health and those that do not. The research council, an arm of The National Academy of Sciences, said that because not enough money was spent on developing a sound scientific system for setting priorities, the nation faced the prospect of wasting billions of dollars on dumps that posed little or no risk and ignoring dumps that were a true threat to the environment and public health.

In addition to criticizing weaknesses in the management of the Superfund program, the report's recommendations are equally applicable to even more expensive cleanup programs managed and paid for by the Department of Energy and the Department of Defense. The two departments are spending more than $6 billion this fiscal year on cleaning up toxic chemical and radioactive waste sites. "We shouldn't be making decisions on spending billions of dollars out of ignorance," said Dr. Thomas Chalmers of the Department of Veterans Affairs in Boston, Mass., a member of the committee that prepared the report. "We need much more data to determine which sites ought to be pursued and we need to set up a

Less Access. . .

better system of evaluating risks."("U.S. Said to Lack Data on Threat Posed by Hazardous Waste Sites," *The New York Times*, October 22)

NOVEMBER - House Democrats accused Interior Secretary Manuel Lujan Jr. of manipulating the conclusions of a report to Congress that favored development of a geothermal energy plant near Yellowstone National Park, by failing to tell them that the National Park Service had dissented vigorously. Yellowstone's geysers are powered by a vast reservoir of underground heat, a resource developers would like to tap.

The report, compiled primarily by the U.S. Geological Survey, concluded that small-scale geothermal development, such as that planned just outside Yellowstone's border by the Church Universal and Triumphant, would pose little risk to the geysers and hot springs that have made Yellowstone a worldwide attraction. However, Lujan did not give Congress a companion report by the Park Service which argued that any such development could threaten the park. ("Manipulation Charged on Yellowstone Report," *The Washington Post*, November 1)

NOVEMBER - Janet Norwood, commissioner of the Bureau of Labor Statistics, testified before the Joint Economic Committee that the Bush administration is studying new jobs data some economists said could mean the government has underestimated the depth of the recession and prospects for recovery. Norwood's comments appeared to provide the first official federal backing for concerns expressed recently by economists from some state governments that the BLS estimates earlier this year of employment and payroll figures were far too optimistic.

Norwood told the committee that the BLS is studying the states' data, and the result could be a lowering of first quarter 1991 employment figures and payroll estimates. Payroll data collected by state governments show a far weaker job market than the BLS estimate, and, if the states' counts hold up, they could lower the BLS estimates of employed people by at least 650,000, she said. The BLS numbers are given to the Department of Commerce, where they are plugged into the government's national economic accounts. While a decline in the payroll numbers does not necessarily mean a decline in the gross national product, it means that "the GNP has been a whole lot weaker than anyone thought," according to a senior congressional economist. ("Federal Jobs Data Called Too Optimistic," *The Washington Post*, November 2)

NOVEMBER - There was a pattern of delay or denial affecting nearly every family that lost a serviceman to "friendly fire" in the Persian Gulf War, according to an investigation by the Washington Post. The Army, in particular, broke its own rules by concealing basic facts for months from the next of kin, and its efforts to postpone disclosure often led it to stretch the truth. Some families never suspected. Others found out through news reports or enlisted friends of the dead men. Some heard only rumors and begged for details. Still others, including all the Marine families, learned informally that a "friendly fire" investigation was underway. All had to wait months for the final word.

Senior officers, in interviews, denied that any family had been deceived. They said the delay in informing families was for the families' own good, in order to verify all the facts and synchronize public release of the findings. The families, almost unanimously, replied they were entitled to the truth—as much as the services knew, as soon as they knew it.

Military documents obtained through the Freedom of Information Act, together with interviews with Defense Department officials and the families of 21 "friendly fire" casualties, indicated that local commanders had clear evidence of "friendly fire" in 33 of the 35 cases by the end of March, but an interservice agreement withheld that information from the families until August. Of 148 U.S. battle deaths in the war, 35 were inflicted inadvertently by U.S. troops. The article contains many specifics about the experience of several families. ("'Friendly Fire' Reports: A Pattern of Delay, Denial," *The Washington Post*, November 5)

[Ed. note: In a November 5 hearing before the Senate Select Committee on POW-MIA Affairs, Secretary of Defense Richard Cheney defended the delays in information about "friendly fire" deaths as "just a normal, natural part of the process."("Casualty Report Delay Called 'Normal'," *The Washington Post*, November 6)]

NOVEMBER - In a move likely to provide more access to information, the Food and Drug Administration and the Agriculture Department proposed the most sweeping set of new food labeling regulations in U.S. history. The proposed guidelines will extend nutrition labeling to all processed foods, force a far more complete listing of ingredients, and standardize what previously had been a byzantine set of regulations on health claims by food manufacturers. The rules, which are open to comment and will be finalized at the end of 1992, are intended to make it easier for consumers to cut through what Health and Human Services Secretary Louis Sullivan has called the "Tower of Babel" in supermarkets and identify the most healthful foods. ("Food Label Reforms to Be Unveiled," *The Washington Post*, November 6)

NOVEMBER - Former Assistant Secretary of State Elliott Abrams pleaded guilty in federal court to two charges of illegally withholding information from Congress about covert U.S. support for the Contra rebels in Nicaragua. The only State Department official to face criminal charges thus far for covering up key aspects of the Iran-Contra affair, Abrams admitted testifying untruthfully before two congressional committees in October 1986, within a fortnight of the crash of a Contra resupply plane in Nicaragua.

Among the details he held back, Abrams said, was that he had solicited a $10 million contribution from the Sultan of Brunei and had been informed by State Department cable that the money was on its way to a Swiss bank account. In entering the misdemeanor pleas, Abrams averted the threat of felony charges and agreed to cooperate with independent counsel Lawrence Walsh in the final stages of Walsh's investigation of the Iran-Contra scandal. ("Abrams Pleads Guilty in Iran-Contra Affair," *The Washington Post*, November 8)

NOVEMBER - In late October, James McConnell, Securities and Exchange Commission executive director, stopped distribution of the September/October edition of *SEC Employee News*, which had already been printed. McConnell believed an article critical about "tension around race and gender" within the agency was based on insufficient research and thus was unfair, according to Jessica Kole, special counsel to the executive director. Sexual harassment issues emerged as a major problem for the agency three years ago.

McConnell's decision disturbed some SEC employees, sources said, because recent events indicated to them that serious problems at the agency persist. The agency has been under court order to stop sexual harassment and discrimination since 1988, when it lost a sexual harassment case involving employees in its now-defunct Washington, D.C., regional office. The newsletter article, by SEC equal employment opportunity specialist Janis Belk, said there were numerous concerns in the SEC's regional offices about the handling of racial and gender issues. ("SEC Blocks Newsletter Containing Article on Gender, Racial Issues," *The Washington Post*, November 8)

NOVEMBER - An advisory panel told the Food and Drug Administration that silicone-gel breast implants should continue to be available for all women, despite an "appalling" lack of information on the safety of the devices and their effects on long-term health. The panel voted against approving silicone implants made by four manufacturers, but agreed the devices should stay on the market under the same status they have always had while the manufacturers conduct additional research on women who have the devices. The panel also said the FDA should see that women contemplating implant surgery are given more detailed information about the risks and benefits.

Panel members prodded the FDA to demand that the manufacturers quickly produce more detailed studies of the rate of rupture, the amount of silicone—a synthetic polymer—that leaks from the devices, and the long-term effects of chronic seepage, which some have suggested could cause cancer or other illnesses. Breast implants have been on the market for more than 30 years, and more than two million women have them. But because the devices came on the market before the FDA gained authority to regulate medical devices, the agency has never evaluated their safety or effectiveness.

FDA Commissioner David Kessler said the "FDA will make sure the data is collected, and collected expeditiously." Several panel members, however, said they had been disappointed in the past, when FDA failed in 1982 and 1988 to push the manufacturers to produce more detailed studies. The companies that sought approval for their implants were Dow Corning Wright, Mentor Corp., McGhan Medical Corp., and Bioplasty Inc. Several other manufacturers had been asked to submit safety data to the panel; but rather than comply, they dropped out of the business. "Companies can't say these devices are perfectly safe any more because we now see there isn't enough evidence to establish that," said Sidney Wolfe, director of Public Citizen's Health Research Group. ("Breast Implants Allowed," *The Washington Post,* November 15)

NOVEMBER - Acting outside the Constitution in the early 1980s, a secret federal agency established a line of succession to the Presidency to assure continued government in the event of a devastating nuclear attack, current and former United States officials said. The officials refused to discuss details of the plan, the existence of which was disclosed in a television program on the Cable News Network. The CNN report said that if all 17 legal successors to the President were incapacitated, nonelected officials would assume office in extreme emergencies.

The secret agency, the National Program Office, was created by former President Ronald Reagan in 1982 to expand the list of successors and a network of bunkers, aircraft, and mobile command centers to ensure that the government continued to function in a nuclear war and afterward. Oliver North, then a Marine lieutenant colonel and an aide on the National Security Council, was a central figure in establishing the secret program, CNN said.

The CNN report also said the United States had spent more than $8 billion on the National Program Office since 1982, much of the money on advanced communications equipment designed to survive a nuclear blast. The communications systems were technically flawed, however, and prevented the State Department, Defense Department, Central Intelligence Agency, and Federal Emergency Management Agency from being able to "talk to each other," according to CNN.

Administration officials refused to discuss the secret succession plan or the National Program Office. A leading constitutional scholar who appeared on the CNN broadcast, Prof. William Van Alstyne of Duke University, said the very secrecy surrounding the plan could undermine its credibility if it ever had to be put into effect. Who, he asked, would believe an obscure figure claiming to be President under a top-secret plan no one had ever heard of? ("Presidents' Plan to Name Successors Skirted Law," *The New York Times,* November 18)

DECEMBER - In June 1989, the FBI raided the Energy Department Rocky Flats plutonium plant to check reports that workers were burning hazardous waste in an illegal incinerator and violating other environmental laws. Prosecutors, the FBI, and Rocky Flats managers have said little about the progress of the investigation, and no one has been indicted. Most of what is known about the case is coming from Karen Pitts and Jacqueline Brever, who have charged in a lawsuit that Rocky Flats officials and supervisors often disregarded safety rules and harassed the two women for talking to federal investigators.

Pitts and Brever left Rocky Flats in April 1991. Officially they resigned, but they charge in their lawsuit that 19 individuals mistreated and harassed them. Also named as defendants are EG&G Inc., the Energy Department's principal Rocky Flats contractor, and its predecessor, Rockwell International Corp. The Energy Department is not a defendant.

The two women, key witnesses in the 2 1/2-year investigation into alleged illegal activities at Rocky Flats, are telling their stories at public meetings and on radio talk shows, in newspaper and network interviews. They tell of routine safety violations, management indifference to potential disasters, and intimidation of workers who raised questions, and they have become the focus of public debate about the long-running investigation at the troubled plant. ("2 Women at Rocky Flats Plant Tell of Intimidation, Safety Violations," *The Washington Post,* December 28)

DECEMBER - In a switch on the problem of less access to government information, a Tampa firm is claiming "instant access" to a wide range of "confidential" computer data, including government data. For fees ranging from $5 to $175, Nationwide Electronic Tracking, or NET, promised it could provide customers with data on virtually anyone in the country—private credit reports, business histories, driver's license records, even personal Social Security records and criminal history background.

NET may seem like a boon to companies trying to check out job applicants or even homeowners suspicious of their new neighbor. But some federal officials say it also was evidence of a growing computer-age menace—the fledgling "information broker" industry that some experts fear may pose one of the most serious threats to individual privacy in decades.

Law enforcement officials say that as the demand for personal data grows, information brokers are increasingly turning to illegal methods. In mid-December, NET was identified by the FBI as one player in a nationwide network of brokers and private investigators who allegedly were pilfering confidential personal data from U.S. government computers and then selling them for a fee to lawyers, insurance companies, private employers, and other customers.

The information-broker investigation involved what officials say was the largest case ever involving the theft of federal computer data and was all the more striking because it was essentially a series of inside jobs. Among the 16 people arrested by the FBI in ten states were three current or former Social Security Administration employees (in Illinois, New York and Arizona) charged with selling personal records contained in SSA computers. In effect, law enforcement officials said, information brokers such as NET were bribing the government employees to run computer checks on individuals for as little as $50 each. Computer checks were being run "on thousands of people," said Jim Cottos, regional inspector general in Atlanta for the Department of Health and Human Services, whose office launched the investigation. ("Theft of U.S. Data Seen as Growing Threat to Privacy," *The Washington Post,* December 28)

DECEMBER - In an editorial titled, "Say Merry Christmas, America," *Government Technology* editor Al Simmons urged readers to ask their legislators to support two pending House bills that would increase public access to government information. The bills are: HR 2772 introduced by Rep. Charlie Rose (D-NC) and HR 3459 introduced by Rep. Major Owens (D-NY). Simmons called the two legislators "a couple of fearless gents from the old school of representative government who are ready to take on the bureaucracy and the private sector lobby as well."

HR 2772 proposes a WINDO (Wide Information Network for Data Online) to be managed by the Government Printing Office which would act either as a gateway to dozens of federal databases or to provide a GPO online system for direct access to tax-payer supported databases. Simmons wrote, "Further, Rose not only thinks WINDO should be affordable to citizen users, he wants WINDO access without charge to the nation's 1,400 federal depository libraries as a computer extension of the depository library system established more than 130 years ago...."

The Improvement of Information Access Act, HR 3459, would require federal agencies to store and disseminate information products and services through computer networks, and set the price of information products and services at the incremental cost of dissemination.

Simmons took issue with government agencies such as the Bureau of the Census that charge as much as $250 for a CD-ROM, even though the actual cost is about two dollars. He also pointed out there are "the private sector data vendors who spend a lot of money trying to discourage the idea that government information should be accessible by citizens directly from the government."("Say Merry Christmas, America," *Government Technology,* December)

Earlier chronologies of this publication were combined into an indexed version covering the period April 1982-December 1987. Updates are prepared at six-month intervals. Less Access... updates (from the January-June 1988 issue to the present publication) are available for $1.00; the indexed version is $7.00; the complete set is $15.00. A new compilation, 1988-1991, is now available. Orders must be prepaid and include a self-addressed mailing label. All orders must be obtained from the American Library Association Washington Office, 110 Maryland Ave., NE, Washington, DC 20002-5675; tel. no. 202-547-4440, fax no. 202-547-7363.

Better to stay ignorant?

Peter

Aleshire

How can we convince kids to quit having kids? Never mind. George Bush doesn't care. How do we keep AIDS from becoming entrenched on college and high school campuses? Never mind. George Bush doesn't care.

At least, the Bush administration has resolutely refused to gather the information that would help us curb AIDS, teen pregnancy, and reckless sexuality.

Mind you, this isn't a case of indifference. Indeed, staying ignorant required a deliberate, purely political action imposed in the face of the best scientific advice.

Allow me to explain.

We know very little about why, how, and when teenagers have sex — except that they are almost certainly having a lot of it.

The questions are crucial. When do most kids start having sex? Are they mostly responding to peer pressure? Are they strongly influenced by the images generated by the mass media? Why aren't they using birth control? How many experiment with homosexual sex? What do they know about AIDS? Where do they get their information? What sources of information do they trust? What would it take to convince them to talk about these things with their parents? How many start sex early because they've been sexually molested? How many actually want to get pregnant?

We don't really know the answers to any of these questions — which may be why all of our efforts to convince our kids to avoid reckless sex have been so unsuccessful.

So the National Institutes of Health (NIH) decided to undertake a comprehensive study to examine sexuality among the young. University of North Carolina sociologists Ronald Rindfuss and Richard Udry drew up a long servey that they intended to administer to 24,000 children in grades 7 through 11, using an $18 million federal grant. All participants were to have had parental consent.

The project spent a lot of time toiling through the bureaucratic approval process, its backers well aware that teenage sexuality remains intensely controversial. All of the questions were exhaustively reviewed by panels of other scientists, by layers of administrators at the NIH, by NIH Director Bernadine Healy, and by James Mason, assistant secretary of health. Mason's approval seemed a particular triumph, since he had led the administration's battle against the research use of tissue from aborted fetuses.

The intricate process satisfied, NIH cut the first check and Rindfuss and Udry began working on their project.

Then Louis Sullivan, the guy who runs the agency that runs NIH, went on a TV talk show and a caller complained about the sex survey. Sullivan said he would look into it.

Next, Rep. William Dannemeyer of Orange County obtained copies of some of the survey questions. You probably remember Dannemeyer from previous exploits. Suffice it to say he's a craggy, bitterly homophobic, Genghis Khan conservative full of folksy venom — one of the little band of right-wingers that has pushed the administration on issues like abortion, fetal tissue research, and cutting off family planning aid to any countries that allow abortion. He planned to introduce a bill that would have cut funding for the sex survey and all future such surveys.

Why?

He said he was afraid that if a lot of kids said they'd had homosexual experiences then all the other kids would conclude that homosexuality was OK. This is an interesting notion, considering that conservatives have repeatedly insisted that the present, small-scale surveys have substantially over-estimated the amount of homosexual activity in the population. If they believe that, wouldn't they welcome a solid, accurate survey?

In fact, that fear probably underlies most of the opposition to the survey. We would rather remain willfully ignorant, than confront accurate information about what our children are doing and thinking.

Anyway, Sullivan saved Dannemeyer the trouble. For the first time in NIH history, the HHS director canceled an already funded project approved through the peer review process.

Still not satisfied, Dannemeyer introduced a bill that would bar any funding for any future sex surveys. Fortunately, Rep. Henry Waxman, D-Los Angeles, amended that bill to require many layers of ethical and peer review if any such project is undertaken in the future. That amendment passed on a vote of 283 to 137.

Once again, Sullivan and the administration caved into the pressure of a small group of extremists. Once again, the minority rules. The Bush administration has sold another little piece of itself.

It's a shabby bit of business. But at least it means America remains No. 1. No. 1 when it comes to teenaged pregnancy. No. 1 when it comes to teenagers dying of AIDS. And No. 1 in willful ignorance.

Peter Aleshire's column appears on Tuesdays and Saturdays.

THE PRESIDENT'S HIDDEN CURRICULUM

BY STAN KARP

CURRICULUM is a term some educators use to describe the powerful but indirect messages schools send to students not only by what they teach, but by how they do it, and even by what they leave out.

For instance, if a teacher stands in front of a classroom and drones on while 30 kids sink slowly into their seats, one unspoken part of the lesson is that authority is the source of knowledge and learning is a passive activity, something done to individuals, not by them. If a young girl is patted on the head for getting a B on a math test, and a boy with the same grade is challenged to find his mistakes and get an A next time, expectations built into the hidden curriculum can become self-fulfilling prophecies. If one school has metal detectors and chains at every door, paint peeling from the ceilings, and converted closets for classrooms, while another school has a landscaped, open campus, potted plants in the air-conditioned lounge, and nicely upholstered furniture gathered in small clusters so groups can talk or study, we learn a lot about the institutions and their attitudes towards the people in them before the bells ever ring.

George Bush, the education president wannabe, has a hidden curriculum too, one that became a little more visible last spring when he and his new Education Secretary Lamar Alexander gave a campaign-style launch to "America 2000," the Administration's plan for the nation's schools. Now winding its way through congressional committees, the plan indicates where federal education policy may be headed. It also shows how buzzwords like "testing," "choice," and "model schools" fit into the overall conservative push for supply-side schooling, a sort of "voodoo education" that would redefine and, in some cases, reverse decades of federal education policy while promoting a privatized market system. If Bush succeeds, he may be remembered as the "education president" who pushed public schools in the

worst possible direction at the very time they were struggling for survival and renewal.

The Wrong Stuff

OF COURSE, America 2000 is partly public relations pap designed to give Bush a domestic "vision thing" for next year's campaign. It's not easy passing yourself off as the education president when the policies you've been associated with for over ten years have been disastrous for schools and kids. Bush's campaign rhetoric promised "a strategy of investing in our children," but since he took office as Reagan's vice president in 1980, real federal funding for elementary and secondary education dropped about 30 percent. Half a million school kids lost federal compensatory education assistance. The Justice Department virtually abandoned the legal struggle for integration, going so far as to seek an end to Court jurisdiction over historically segregated school systems. Conferences of governors and commission reports were substituted for hot lunches and new textbooks.

The real question is how a leading political figure in administrations with these kinds of policies could present himself as "the education president" without provoking scorn and derision. Burying this record under a flood of campaign hype is a major aim of the America 2000 package.

But the plan also contains some real substance, almost all of it bad. On nearly every school issue, Bush is using the bully pulpit of the presidency to promote the wrong stuff. For example:

- *Testing*: At a time when a broad coalition has formed around the proposition that the 200 million standardized, multiple-choice tests U.S. schools give each year are deforming the curriculum, turning

teachers into full-time test coaches, and discriminating against female and minority students, Bush is calling for yet another system of national tests. While reformers press for developing "alternative assessment" and "performance portfolios," Bush wants to sink millions into the kind of sorting and tracking mechanisms that promote educational stratification and justify inequality on the basis of "merit."

- *Curriculum*: With multicultural education and creative curriculum reform high on the list of innovative ideas, Bush is proposing the creation of "new world standards" in five basic areas that, would, in effect, promote standardization of a narrow, national curriculum and encourage still more teaching to the test.

- *Choice*: Under the banner of "freedom of choice" Bush seeks to channel public funds to private and religious schools and justify federal disinvestment in public education. "Choice" is also being invoked in defense of a plan that would cripple the largest remaining federal education program, the $6 billion Chapter 1 programs targeted to the poor and minorities, by using those funds as a lever to create market competition between schools.

- *Money*: The most crucial battle in education today is probably the struggle between rich and poor school districts over inequitable funding systems, which are currently being challenged in more than 20 state courts. Fiscal inequity and growing social polarization have helped create a dual school system nearly as separate and unequal as the one declared illegal by the Supreme Court in 1954. But Bush proposes investing less new money in his "educational renaissance" than he spent in half a day of the Gulf war. "Dollar bills don't educate students," he intoned lamely. He calls his America 2000 plan "a national strategy, not a federal program," or in the more rabid phrase of Secretary Alexander, "It isn't really a program, it's a crusade." This is Bushspeak for no funds. As radical educator Deborah Meier responded, "I don't think there's any field other than education in which the president could announce a bold new plan for solving an age-old problem—and put no money behind it. 'We're going to do away with heart disease by the year 2000 and this is our plan: we're going to ask doctors to work harder and more imaginatively!'"

Model Schools: The fate of the current reform wave will be largely determined by the success or failure of efforts to restructure and revive existing public schools. But Bush is proposing a new agency, the New American Schools Development Corporation, to create an elite network of model schools shaped by corporate planners. Along with existing private institutions, the new models could create a base for further privatization schemes. The model schools initiative will claim the bulk of America 2000's funds and draw monies away from existing equity programs and more progressive experiments (like innovative public schools that do work). The "new generation of American schools" initiative is structured to provide $1 million in start-up grants (and potential campaign bargaining chips) for models in each congressional district. Executives from IBM, AT&T, Boeing, and other corporate giants will head the agency, design and award contracts, and put business figures firmly in control over educational research and development. "We do not intend to be involved in that except to watch it," Alexander said.

Corporate Curriculum

AMERICA 2000 FRAMES education issues in terms that reflect the need corporate planners see for better elite technical training and for a moderate overall increase in the number of high school graduates prepared for middle- and entry-level jobs. Typically the most pressing problems these analysts identify in the nation's education system are that student scores on math tests compare unfavorably with those in South Korea or Japan (where more authoritarian school systems rigidly track students through the sort of national testing programs Bush wants to see here.) Business interests want an education policy directed to correcting such "competitive deficits," unhampered by commitments to equal opportunity, racial justice, or democratic local control of public institutions. They seek to channel widespread concern over school failure and administrative bureaucracy into support for a more efficient, modernized, more privatized system that can more effectively meet the limited manpower needs of a highly stratified economy.

But that same economy has no real need for universally effective schooling for all. There's no economic need in a profit-driven system for equity claims on educational resources, or for open admission to college, or for reversing the shrinking number of minority teachers, or for empowering teachers and parents in local school governance councils or the many other progressive reform options available. National education policy could be used as a lever for democratic renewal, for increasing the power of ordinary citizens, for expanding the importance of locally-based community institutions, and uniting a diverse population in a more active, participatory civic life. But such plans are not on the education president's list of things to do. Instead America 2000 echoes the basic trends of the Reagan/Bush era: increasing inequality and class polarization, slavish devotion to making government policy serve corporate aims, and retreat from long-standing federal efforts to mitigate, however inadequately, racial and social injustice in favor of privatizing social services.

In some ways Bush is an even more effective proponent of these ends than Reagan was. Reagan tried to back-track in education by cutting funds and invoking "local control." His first Secretary of Education, Terrel Bell, complained, "I couldn't get the Reagan

administration to support any kind of initiative. They said, 'It's not our role.'" Reagan also tried ham-handed measures, like abolishing outright the Department of Education, that never got anywhere.

By contrast, Bush—in what union leader Albert Shanker called a "a turning point in American education"—is pointedly asserting a federal role and redefining it from one of promoting equity, helping the poor and aiding the handicapped, to promoting privatization and stumping for conservative reform. He's moving to put his Administration at the forefront of a sprawling school reform movement that is still moving in many different directions.

Bush's new "education team" clearly reflects an aggressive public relations intent, along with a strong corporate bias. Millionaire Lamar Alexander (whose confirmation as Education Secretary was delayed partly by questions over his ties to Chris Whittle, the pioneer of Channel One and other privatizing school experiments) was formerly the "education governor" of Tennessee. There he made a reputation by courting business involvement and imposing reforms from the top down with little input from teachers and parents. Alexander's assistant secretary is David Kearns, former CEO of Xerox. Kearns made education reform a hobby of sorts a few years back by co-writing a best seller called *Winning the Brain Race*. In it Kearns complained that "business and education have largely failed in their efforts to improve the schools, because education set the agenda. To be successful, the new agenda for school reform must be driven by competition and market discipline, unfamiliar ground for educators. Business will have to set the new agenda...." Another new appointee, Diane Ravitch, for years has been an academic warrior against multicultural education. (As "spin doctors" for Bush's school plans, this high-powered staff has plenty of room for improvement. An analysis of the tenure of Bush's first education secretary, Lauro Cavazos, found that the national media, perhaps in a rare display of good news judgment, gave less coverage to Cavazos' performance than it did to the ups and downs of the President's dog, Millie.)

DataCenter   464 19th Street, Oakland, California 94612 (415) 835-4692

Choosing Bureaucracy

ONE OF THE President's major goals is to use national policy to push the states in the "right" direction. Federal disinvestment in education during the Reagan/Bush years has greatly expanded the role of the states in education issues. As federal dollars declined, the state share of local education budgets rose from less than 40 percent to more than half. A little-noticed consequence of this trend has been a sizable increase in intrusive state education bureaucracies. In the last ten years, over 1,000 state-level school reform measures have been introduced mandating testing programs, curriculum standardization, increased monitoring, and more paperwork for local districts. While Bush still uses the rhetoric of "local control" to explain why the federal government shouldn't come up with money for schools, Washington's abandonment of responsibility for education has actually reduced local options and promoted state bureaucracy on a previously unseen scale.

The shift to the states also tends to underscore the gross inequities in school finance systems. School districts now rely on regressive state and local tax systems for over 90 percent of their funds. Overall education spending did rise 15 percent during the 1980s due to increased local and state expenditures fueled partly by the speculative real estate boom. But inequalities between school districts also grew. Typically differences of thousands of dollars in per pupil spending exist between rich and poor districts. Poor districts with less property wealth to draw on have much less to spend on their schools than rich districts, even when the tax rates in poor districts are many times higher. This translates into daily injustices for school kids in the form of fewer course offerings, worse facilities, less experienced and more poorly paid teachers, and fewer support services.

After the U.S. Supreme Court ruled in 1973 that education was *not* a Constitutional right, public advocates began to bring funding inequities to the attention of state courts with some measure of success. But success in the courts did not necessarily translate into equality in the schools. State legislatures have found many ways to evade or limit the impact of court orders. As New Jersey's Education Law Center, the legal advocacy group that fought and won both of that state's key educational funding cases, noted, "Law books are filled with wonderful paper victories which have never been implemented."

As part of the hype about drawing the entire nation into his "educational renaissance," Bush said he was going to learn how to use a computer himself. If he really wanted to learn how the dual school system works he could check out schools in Princeton, New Jersey, where there's a computer for every eight kids, and then travel a few miles to Camden, where the ratio is one computer for every 58 students. Or he could go to the poor Texas district where students study computer science by pretending to type on an artificial paper replica of a computer keyboard. Federal policy could work to reduce or eliminate such inequality. America 2000, with its competitive mania and privatization schemes, will increase it. For the one-third to one-half of an increasingly multicultural student population that is getting a second- or third-rate education because of class and racial inequality, the education president offers only bootstrap sermons, as if the growing gap between poor urban systems and more privileged suburban, predominantly white ones stemmed from the collective failure of students of color to do their homework.

Pressed by recession, more than half the states are in the process of reducing education spending with no federal safety net to limit the damage.

In Massachusetts, where public schools in America first appeared, the state's education commissioner recently resigned citing the "continuing disinvestment in public education." Pointing to a seemingly endless cycle of reductions and cuts eliminating both reform experiments and basic programs, Commissioner Harold Reynolds declared, "The institution of the school as the centerpiece of the community is under attack. Some of the bitterness is so bad that teachers are being insulted as they go to school. Seeing the anger and bitterness in communities that are divided, it's as if we had done everything possible to develop a system to destroy them."

In California, education advocates thought they'd won a buffer a few years ago when they successfully passed Proposition 98, which presumably guaranteed that 40 percent of the state budget would go to schools. But under the pressure of a $14 billion state budget deficit, accounting gimmickry was used to redefine the funding formulas and over $1 billion in education cuts is being imposed. More than 35 districts face bankruptcy, 10,000 teachers and thousands of other school workers face layoffs. When the state was forced by court order to bail out the bankrupt Richmond school district last spring, the governor tried to condition any state bailout on a suspension of teachers' bargaining rights and contracted wage increases, raising the prospect that austerity will be coupled with broader attacks on workers rights. (At the same time, California governor Pete Wilson maintained spending for prisons, leading one school board member to note that the governor was picking "gas chambers over preschools" while another teacher observed, "It's a real smart move that Governor Wilson appropriated large amounts of money for the jail system because that's where these kids will end up.")

In New York City, a broad coalition of teachers, parents, students, and other education advocates was able to stave off threatened midyear cuts that would have thrown the system into chaos. But as the new school year approached, thousands of teachers were facing layoffs and a school system that never recovered from the city's fiscal bankruptcy of the mid-1970s seemed about to be blasted again. Moreover, each round of cuts increases the disparities between rich and poor areas as political clout and systemic racial and class bias take their toll. The Community Service Society of New York recently traced the way the city was "promoting poverty" by the "shift of resources away from low-income NYC school districts." It found that "funding to the poorest districts was cut disproportionately during the city's fiscal crisis in order to keep middle-class children in public schools." On a state

level, the complicated system for delivering state education aid in 51 different categories leaves lots of room for maneuvering by conservative and suburban political forces to direct resources away from Latino, African-American, and Asian communities. In 1987 this was accomplished by treating each pupil in New York City, where public enrollment is overwhelmingly nonwhite, as 94 percent of a student. The echo of the U.S. Constitution's original calculus of slavery was appropriately symbolic.

School Tax Evasion

EQUITY ADVOCATES ARE also up against the pro-business, anti-tax climate shaping state and local budget priorities. While the corporate sector has steadily gained influence over education policy and churned out glossy brochures hailing business commitment to local schools, it has also sharply reduced its tax support for education. Between 1957 and 1987, the corporate share of local property taxes, historically the largest single source of school funds, dropped from 45 percent to 16 percent. Tax concessions to business by local governments—which unlike many school budgets do not need voter approval—have skyrocketed. In one recent year, Florida granted businesses half a billion dollars in tax abatements and concessions, dwarfing the $32 million Florida firms "donated" :o public education with much fanfare. Facing a $34 million budget deficit, Cleveland schools recently filed a lawsuit attacking a deal that waives all property taxes on a $400 million Society Center development. Similar examples can be found in virtually every state and city.

Having helped create this fiscal crisis with his policies, Bush now hopes to use it to carve up the "bankrupt public education monopoly," and "choice" schemes are one of the main scalpels. Back in 1985 the authors of *Choosing Equality* foresaw that "the federal divestiture of resources in public education and the retreat from equity standards set up a dangerously self-fulfilling prophecy. If these trends intensify, public schooling will undereducate growing numbers of children and will increasingly lose public con-

fidence. In this case...salvaging special schools for the 'best and the brightest,' segregating disadvantaged segments of the student population, subsidizing private school alternatives, establishing market mechanisms of service delivery—will appear more justified and feasible, especially when clothed in the rhetoric of personal opportunity."

Bush's education team has intentionally tried to dress up choice as a boon to the poor, implying that those with the worst educational services could better their lot in a market system that included private schools. Last year the Education Department crossed a line it had previously skirted when it endorsed an experimental Milwaukee plan that allowed a small number of inner city students to use public funds to attend private schools. The fact that the plan originated with one of Milwaukee's black legislators made it especially useful to an administration with little credibility on civil rights.

Court challenges are still pending against the Milwaukee plan, but since it's already being cited as a national model, the way it operated in its first year is worth noting. Of the 46,000 African American students in the Milwaukee system, 1,000 were eligible for the voucher program. About 750 applied and 390 were accepted at private schools. But during the year, several private schools sent "difficult" students back to the public system and another private school folded, leaving students stranded. Enrollment dropped well below 300. "The reality," says education consultant Michael Alves, "is that the urban public school system will always educate children nobody else wants. That is the real message coming out of the Milwaukee program." Moreover, small-scale experimental programs which provide additional options to a few do not begin to focus the inequalities that would be produced by a combination of private school selectivity, continued public disinvestment in urban education, and the use of market mechanisms on a broad scale. The inequalities created by the markets in housing and health care are much more indicative of what to expect.

Used within the public system, "choice" certainly has potential to increase the input of students, teachers, and parents and to help democratize bureaucratic systems. But for Bush choice is a spur to market competition and privatization, not educational democracy. In fact, heavy reliance on private institutions, elite experimental models, and market mechanisms will work to strengthen the hand of a new strata of professional education managers and further remove schools from local public control.

In assessing school choice plans, it's instructive to remember that efforts to use public funds to pay for private schools first appeared as part of racist resistance to court-ordered school desegregation. In Virginia, Mississippi, and elsewhere, white politicians withdrew support for public education and tried to develop formulas that would channel tax revenues to private, segregated academies, going so far as to repeal compulsory education laws or even attempting to shut down public systems entirely until blocked by the courts.

The federal role in decisions about which schools kids should attend also became controversial in the early 1970s when conservatives used the rhetoric of "neighborhood schools" to oppose busing to promote racial integration. As with today's choice debate, the demagogic manipulation of emotional rhetoric had racist undertones. In addition, it's more than a little disgusting to hear George Bush champion a parent's "right to choose" schools as a "basic democratic value," while denying women the right to choose whether to become parents at all.

The education president is well on his way to becoming one of the worst teachers American classrooms ever had. His plans would leave schools less fair and less effective for the majority of students in the year 2000 than they are now. Currently thousands of activist educators are working to take advantage of the openings reform provides to make schools better and more democratic. The Bush administration has an entirely different set of objectives. Who'll win out? As Bush said in introducing his latest plans "No one will conduct our educational revolution for us. We've got to do it ourselves." Z

DataCenter   464 19th Street, Oakland, California 94612 (415) 835-4692

II. Overt Censorship

Blatant, open censorship attempts in schools, libraries and the media persist. Well-organized, vocal, conservative organizations are intent on defining acceptable reading and viewing materials and have sometimes succeeded in forcing religious and fundamentalist values onto school curricula and textbooks.

But articles in this section show that in the last two years there has been an increase in overt governmental censorship as well. The "gag" rule that forbids mentioning abortion as an option in the course of family planning counseling, is an undeniable example. The granting of NEA funds to artists based on an undefined content acceptability of the work is yet another. Government censorship during war is not a new phenomenon, although in the past, it was less practiced in the U.S. than in countries lacking constitutional guarantees of press freedom. The Persian Gulf War showed that this too has changed.

"If we can't think for ourselves, if we're unwilling to question authority, then we are just putty in the hands of those in power." – Carl Sagan & Ann Druyan

"Make the Real Obscenities the Real Issues: Homelessness, unemployment, war and militarism, racism, sexism, AIDS, homophobia." – Dave Marsh and Friends

"...The persistent pattern continued; the censors who read for sedition, blasphemy or obscenity never felt that they themselves would be corrupted. They were only worried for the souls of others." – Morris L. Ernst

The Gag Rule, One Year Later: Clinics Prepare for Tough Choices

by Lisa Billowitz

Assaults on abortion rights and access are nothing new in the United States. Harassment in abortion clinics, lack of abortion providers in many parts of the country, parental consent laws, and lack of funding have compromised reproductive freedom even under the relative boon of *Roe v. Wade*. Now with the implementation of the gag rule, women may soon face health care clinics that cannot provide information about abortion—clinics with severely reduced staff and services, clinics that could even shut down entirely.

Throughout the country, health care clinics will soon be forced to choose between federal funding and their ability to discuss abortion as a family planning option with their women clients. The Supreme Court decision *Rust v. Sullivan* upheld restrictions on women's access to accurate health care information. Clinics receiving Title X funds are now awaiting the federal government's final word on implementation, at which point they must decide whether to continue to accept the money and comply with the restrictions, or to give up their funding and face possible cutbacks or even financial disaster.

Many activists and providers have pointed out that the gag rule will inevitably harm the quality of health care for the poor regardless of how the clinics respond to the restrictions. Mary Russell, director of Boston Family Planning at the Association for Boston Community Development (ABCD), said, "These regulations were designed to be destructive and invasive." If the clinic complies, it will not be able to provide accurate, responsible information about pregnancy options to women in need. If the clinic chooses to reject the funds, it is likely that staff, clinic hours, and services will be cut or monies will be taken from other important areas of social service to compensate for the lost funds. And if a clinic keeps the funds but attempts to work around the restrictions, the clinic will be limited in ensuring that all women are responsibly informed of their options, and it will be legally risky for the clinic as well.

What *Rust v. Sullivan* mandates

On May 23, 1991, the Supreme Court upheld regulations that prohibit physicians and counselors who receive federal funds under Title X of the Public Health Service Act from providing information and referrals concerning abor-

tion. Nearly 5 million low-income women rely on Title X funds for their reproductive health care nationally, through approximately 4,000 clinics, hospitals, and family planning organizations. Services covered by Title X include general preventive care, Pap smears, pelvic exams, STD care, contraceptives, and pregnancy diagnosis. Women are the vast majority of those using Title X services, and over one-third of all Title X clients are adolescents.

In Boston, 23 clinics receive these funds, administered through ABCD. These clinics all provide abortion counseling and referrals in a comprehensive health care context, in contrast to free-standing family-planning clinics elsewhere in Massachusetts. The percentage of funding for these clinics that is provided by Title X ranges considerably, but even a small government contribution can be critical to a poor clinic's survival. Not unlike other clinics throughout the country, only 5 to 10 percent of services provided by the Boston Title X clinics is related to "options counseling," the services related to abortion; nonetheless the clinics stand to lose all their government-funding, if they continue to provide abortion-related services.

Thus, to deprive these clinics of federal funds is not only to undermine reproductive care services, but mental health, preventive medicine, dental, internal, and prenatal care as well. Rachael

Pine, an attorney for the plaintiff in *Rust v. Sullivan* and senior staff counsel at the ACLU Reproductive Freedom Project, said, "Once the gag rule is implemented, there will be a large network of compromised health care for poor women."

If a woman inquires about abortion, under the new regulations, the clinic staff must respond, "The project does not consider abortion an appropriate method of family planning." Even a woman with a medical condition that would make pregnancy dangerous or life-threatening could not be informed about her abortion options. Because of the gag rule's pernicious restrictions, medical practitioners who comply with the regulations could be sued for malpractice in some states, according to the ACLU.

The gag rule regulations were devised in 1988 by the Reagan administration in an attempt to restrict women's access to abortion. They remain unenforced pending the outcome of the legal battles and the release of the Health and Human Services (HHS) Department's specific interpretation of the restrictions. At this point, the regulations have been ruled constitutional by the highest court, and one Congressional attempt to counter the court's decision was successfully vetoed by President Bush. Two other legislative attempts to overturn the gag rule are currently pending, according to Terri Sol-

lom, a policy analyst at the Alan Guttmacher Institute.

It is not enough for a clinic receiving Title X money to provide abortion information through staff and programs funded from nongovernment sources. *Rust v. Sullivan* upholds a regulation stating that clinics must physically and financially separate their Title X programs from abortion services, counseling, and referrals. Thus, government-funded projects cannot share staff, funds, or facilities with organizations that provide full information about abortion options, unless HSS significantly changes their interpretation of the regulations.

How clinics are responding

The primary plaintiff in the Supreme Court case was Dr. Irving Rust, medical director of the Hub, the Planned Parenthood clinic in the South Bronx. He said of the Supreme Court decision, "This case is about suppressing information between a patient and her doctor. The government has interfered in that relationship." This health clinic announced immediately following the ruling that they would give up their Title X funds so that women could receive accurate and unbiased information about their options. Several other Planned Parenthood affiliates across the country have followed suit, while many others await the final form of the regulations to be issued by Health and

Human Services before making final decisions.

The Massachusetts Family Planning Association, which encompasses all of the area clinics receiving Title X funds, issued a statement promising to reject federal funds if the restriction interfered with quality health care. The statement read in part, "[We] will never compromise our commitment to clinics for financial or political reasons." Each family planning institution in the state will assess individually how the restrictions will affect their health care provision and accept or reject the funds accordingly, with ABCD making a collective decision concerning the Boston clinics under its umbrella.

Massachusetts clinics will have somewhat more freedom in their decisions to accept or reject government funds than clinics in many states. Governor William Weld has incorporated a contingency fund of $3.1 million in his 1992 budget that would be used to replace federal funds returned by clinics. This item has yet to be approved by the state legislature, however. Several other states have made similar commitments to thwart the gag rule by replacing Title X funds with state dollars, including California, Texas, New Jersey, New York, and Vermont.

The Impact of *Rust v. Sullivan* on health clinics

The gag rule holds many dangerous ramifications beyond the obvious assault on abortion options. It sets up a blatantly stratified system of health care, with different options and services available to the wealthy and the poor. Even if the federal funds are rejected in an attempt to preserve options for low-income women, few clinics have the economic security to prevent a severe impact on their other services.

Roberta Synal of the national Planned Parenthood office said, "This is a domino effect—there will be further burden on other social services."

Many clinics that have refused the federal funds are cutting back services, including their staff, range of services, and business hours. In Flint, Michigan, the regional Planned Parenthood announced that they could no longer provide free services since refusing Title X money; Synal said that many affiliates have made similar cutbacks. Tom Kring of the California Regional Family Planning Council said, "The cutbacks may force women seeking first-trimester abortions into waiting longer and longer." Thus, health care for low-income women will be compromised by the loss of funds, even if the gag rule restrictions are nullified by the clinics refusing to work within them.

Other reproductive health workers fear that the ruling will undermine the very heart of the preventive care that Title X encompasses, as clients decrease their use of clinics because they believe they will not receive adequate counseling and referrals. One client at Dr. Rust's South Bronx clinic, Brenda Alston, pointed out in *Newsweek*: "No need in coming if you can't talk about the things you want to." Russell said that some clients of Title X clinics in Boston believed the ruling meant that abortion was illegal, or that they were not allowed to mention abortion to the counselors they had trusted for years. "Patients are upset; they feel attacked and confused," she said.

In addition, clinics fear losing practitioners who choose to resign rather than provide substandard care or leave because of concern about malpractice. Joan Henneberry, director of family planning for the Colorado Department of Health, asked, "Why in the world would they continue work-

© Meryl Levin/Impact Visuals 1991

Clients wait to have their blood taken at the Community Family Planning Council's Mobile Unit in East New York.

ing in our clinics with these constraints? . . . Why would they put themselves in such a horrible position from a medical liability point of view?"

Furthermore, clinics providing family planning must cope with the taint of controversy engendered by the mere mention of abortion. In Massachusetts, advocates have fought a long battle to convince the legislature that family planning should be funded by the state; every year, clinics face uncertainty as to whether they will continue to receive funds, according to Russell. She stated that while ABCD "is totally behind abortion . . . we have been trying to protect the services from the cauldron of abortion controversy. We're worried that next time [in the legislature] it will be perceived as abortion counseling, not family planning counseling, and that it will impact on the funding vote. We're trying to keep a balance; it's a continuum of care."

Although the gag rule regulations have not yet been put into effect, clinics are already suffering from the strain of anticipating and planning for the inevitable upheaval. "It's destructive to

operate with a cloud over your head," said Pine of the ACLU. Health care workers and activists speak of the toll on time and resources. "This has taken an enormous amount of energy away from the hard work involved in providing good services," said Russell. Helen Crowell, coordinator of clinical services for family planning programs at ABCD, pointed out that the gag rule has not produced the immediate devastating impact that many prochoicers anticipated: "It's a very subtle drain, all the time we're spending dealing with this is sucking away resources."

Can clinics outsmart the regulations?

Since the Supreme Court ruling in May, there has been much discussion among prochoice advocates of the possibilities for thwarting the gag rule through indirect means of informing clients, if Title X funds are continued. Health care workers have posited forming systems of referral through non-government-funded agencies and manipulating positions within the organization in order to inform women covertly about their abortion options.

Russell hopes that "we might be able to use our other money to pay for the staff who do options counseling," though this is dubious under the new regulations.

Synal of Planned Parenthood pointed out that the success of such measures depends on the environment of the clinic. "If there are a couple of places that clinics could get around [the gag rule] with referrals, that will only work in big cities." Pine said that not everyone has the resources and support to follow a complicated trail of referrals to different organizations: "You can't give a thirteen-year-old a runaround set of referrals and expect she'll get there. No matter how referral [systems] work, there will be some intrusion into medical care."

As the restrictions on legal abortion multiply, the relevance of the landmark *Roe v. Wade* decision diminishes. If access to abortion is restricted for minors, for poor women, for women in rural locations, and now possibly for women whose husbands do not agree with their decisions to abort, the technical legality of the procedure becomes superfluous. "It's one more thing of many undermining our reproductive freedom," said Susan Yanow of the Reproductive Rights Network.

The gag rule demonstrates not only the continuing assault on poor women's access to abortion, but also how the abortion issue can be used as a weapon against health care. Crowell of ABCD said, "The gag rule muddies the waters—they're using the abortion issue to get at other things, like family planning. They're using scare tactics to cut away at preventive health care."

Lisa Billowitz writes occasionally for Sojourner and other publications.

THE SECRET BATTLE
FOR THE NEA
BY BILL LICHTENSTEIN

WASHINGTON, D.C.—Two weeks ago, on February 21, National Endowment for the Arts chair John Frohnmayer, a personal friend and appointee of President George Bush, was forced to resign his position after Republican candidate Pat Buchanan attacked the president in New Hampshire for supporting the "filthy, blasphemous art" funded by the agency.

Frohnmayer's resignation hardly mollified Buchanan, however. Last week, as polls showed the challenger closing with the president in the Georgia primary, Buchanan aired a TV commercial that included clips from a film partially funded by the NEA showing ostensibly gay men in leather harnesses; the ad accused Bush of "investing" federal funds in art that is sexually explicit and "pervert[s] the image of Jesus Christ." To drive the point home, a photo of Bush was strategically placed to protect the viewers' modesty.

But the Buchanan ads, which pilloried Bush as an advocate of free expression in much the same way that Bush himself had ridiculed Michael Dukakis as a "card-carrying member of the ACLU," don't tell the complete story. An investigation by *The Village Voice* has revealed that Frohnmayer's resignation was in fact the culmination of a two-year, internecine assault led by the office of Vice-President Dan Quayle and former White House chief of staff John Sununu aimed at imposing content-based criteria for the funding of arts projects. A series of confidential memos between the NEA and the Justice Department and interviews with more than a dozen current and former top-level NEA officials and Capitol Hill staffers document that the Bush administration sought repeatedly to stretch the Supreme Court's controversial *Rust* v. *Sullivan* ruling to cover arts funding. *Rust*, the so-called abortion "gag" ruling, was the 1991 decision that held the government could forbid discussions of abortion between a federally financed doctor and a patient.

Had it succeeded at the NEA, the Justice Department would have established a second beachhead for *Rust*, reinforcing its position that the government would not fund intellectual pursuits whose political or social messages were unacceptable to the administration. The documents obtained by the *Voice* also reveal that, contrary to Frohnmayer's image among art advocates as an enemy of aesthetic license, the NEA

chair actually fought hard and effectively to stave off the use of *Rust* to censor freedom of expression.

Frohnmayer also stood fast in the face of direct White House intervention in the administration of the agency, firing one White House appointee for allegedly leaking confidential NEA matters to right-wingers in the press and Congress, and vigorously resisting the assignment to his personal staff of a "mole" who had been directed to appear at all of Frohnmayer's meetings on Capitol Hill and report back to the administration.

Perhaps equally misunderstood was the role of John Frohnmayer's old friend, George Bush. A handwritten memo, dashed off by the president to his embattled friend in early 1990, when fundamentalist attacks had reached a fever pitch, clearly indicates that Bush, at least initially, sided with Frohnmayer and the First Amendment.

John Frohnmayer, a Republican loyalist whose brother had served as a GOP attorney general of the state of Oregon, arrived in Washington just as an NEA-funded exhibition of Robert Mapplethorpe photographs was being rejected by the Corcoran Gallery in Washington as offensive, and shortly after the fundamentalist uproar over the NEA funding for an Andres Serrano photograph entitled *Piss Christ*, which depicted a crucifix suspended in urine.

The assumption was that Frohnmayer, as the appointee of an avowedly right-wing administration, would toe the conservative line regarding the arts. And in his first major decision as chair, in November 1989, he certainly seemed to do just that. The NEA had given the New York City Artists Space $10,000 for an exhibition organized by Nan Goldin entitled "Witnesses: Against Our Vanishing." According to former Artists Space executive director Susan Wyatt, the application for the grant was clear in its intent: "Nan was interested in reclaiming sexuality, which had been deadened by the AIDS crisis, and she wanted a celebration of gay sexuality."

Just days before the exhibition opened, Artists Space was asked by the NEA to put up a disclaimer stating that "the opinions, findings and recommendations expressed herein do not reflect the view of the National Endowment for the Arts." According to Wyatt, she was asked to simultaneously take NEA's name off the exhibition *and* keep the disclaimer. Then Frohnmayer asked for the $10,000 back, citing the antic-

ipated display of images involving homosexual acts and sadomasochism. When the story hit the papers and Leonard Bernstein refused to go to the White House to receive a National Medal of Arts, embarrassing the president, Artists Space was told it could keep the money.

Frohnmayer's tactical retreat apparently did not sit well at the White House. According to former NEA public affairs director Jack Lichtenstein and other NEA staffers, six of Frohnmayer's choices for the second spot in the agency were vetoed by the administration in the weeks after the Artists Space incident. Instead, he was instructed by Jeannette Naylor, now special assistant to the president and associate director of presidential personnel, to hire Alvin Felzenberg, the former chief cultural policy adviser to New Jersey Republican governor Thomas Kean and a visiting lecturer at Princeton. Felzenberg made it clear immediately after coming aboard on February 1, 1990, that his agenda at the NEA was to keep the White House apprised of any potential trouble spots at the agency.

Soon after this hesitant start, Frohnmayer accepted an invitation to speak before the National Press Club on March 29. His speech received a standing ovation—and set off alarm bells at the White House. "He told the reporters there that when it came to the Helms Amendment [to the NEA funding bill, which would have limited funds for "indecent" art], there was no middle ground," recalls a former top NEA official. "He said you had to come down on the side of the artists, and the reporters cheered."

Frohnmayer then joked, in a way that would later appear prophetic, "I just hope I can get out of this town alive."

Indeed, one time he did try. In the early spring of 1990, Frohnmayer is said to have attended a meeting at the White House between the president and agency heads. During this meeting, Frohnmayer is reported to have expressed his views on arts funding. Soon after, at a skiing vacation in Wintergreen, Virginia, the White House tracked him down and President Bush personally told Frohnmayer over the telephone that he would like the administration's concerns over the funding of controversial art addressed.

"The feeling was that Bush didn't know what John was talking about," said a former NEA official privy to the contents of the president's phone call. According to several sources close to the controversy, Frohnmayer sent the president a handwritten note on plain paper, dated March 9, explaining his opposition to content-based criteria for arts funding.

"Mr. President: In essence, this is the issue I have been dealing with since I've been here," the NEA chair wrote. "The original legislation states that the government must not impose a single aesthetic standard or attempt to direct artistic content.... This is wise.... The main role of the agency is to provide a climate where great American artists can express themselves.... With my greatest respect, John." Felzenberg wrote the memo, removed his name, and had it circulated.

In response, Frohnmayer and NEA counsel Davis pulled NEA telephone logs in an attempt to identify the source of the press leaks. They found records of calls between Felzenberg's office and columnists Rowland Evans and Robert Novack, including one that lasted "over an hour" and preceded a critical article about Karen Finley's grant proposal. Felzenberg was fired by Frohnmayer on Monday, June 4, only to be given immediate shelter at the White House as head of a government commission exploring delays in the appointment of federal officials. Today Felzenberg, Evans, and Novack all admit there had been telephone contact, but insist that Felzenberg was simply returning a call from the reporters.

In early June, after Felzenberg was ousted, Frohnmayer was summoned to the White House, along with Rose DiNapoli, his director of congressional liaison, to answer what were described as President Bush's concerns over the firing of the chairman's top deputy. There Frohnmayer met alone with John Sununu, not an unusual occurrence; but this time, the Voice has confirmed, the meeting included a particularly heated exchange. According to sources close to Frohnmayer, Sununu told the NEA head that when he was governor of New Hampshire, if there was something he didn't want funded, it didn't get funded—so he didn't understand why Frohnmayer was having a problem putting restraints on the sort of art that the White House found offensive.

Frohnmayer challenged Sununu, defending the artistic process and telling the then-chief of staff that he, Sununu, didn't know anything about it. "You have to understand that with art, you can't always tell how something will turn out one, two, or three years after you fund it," Frohnmayer reportedly told Sununu. The former governor proposed to Frohnmayer that the NEA single out "problem cases" and not fund them, which Frohnmayer took as an official suggestion that he begin "blacklisting" artists. Again, Frohnmayer objected vehemently.

"Sununu's idea was to blacklist—if they have done something offensive before, they

shouldn't be funded," recalls Jack Lichtenstein. "It was his feeling that offensive work was being done by a small group of people, funded by the endowment, and was reflecting badly on the administration."

On June 12, as was not uncommon with those who stood up to Sununu, Frohnmayer, along with his director of congressional liaison Rose DiNapoli, were summoned to a meeting in the office of Andrew Card, deputy chief of staff, to discuss major agency policies. Besides Card, the other administration representatives at the meeting were NEA personnel head Jeannette Naylor and Frances Norris. According to sources knowledgeable about the agenda, the message was to tone down the whole "free-expression thing"—they wanted to tell Frohnmayer that he should use his best judgment and not put the First Amendment first.

A little more than two weeks later, the watershed event of the Frohnmayer NEA administration—the chairman's vetoing of the grants to the so-called NEA 4 (Karen Finley, John Fleck, Holly Hughes, and Tim Miller)—was announced. After Frohnmayer overturned the agency's lower-level approval for funding of their sexually controversial performance art, they sued the agency for reinstatement.

The suit shifted the grounds of debate almost overnight. Now, both NEA officials and White House staffers were forced into a common defensive posture. The issue no longer was what art to fund but what legal strategy to pursue, a question that turned out to be every bit as controversial. According to former top NEA officials and confidential documents obtained by the Voice, this new conflict began in the first week of December 1990, when a meeting was called to bring together the legal teams. Present were NEA general counsel Davis, one lawyer from Boyden Gray's office, and four

Bush replied almost immediately with a note of his own, expressing his support and admiration for Frohnmayer's handling of the difficult situation at the NEA in an intelligent manner. One former NEA official who was shown the note recalled: "Wow, it's neat that the president can be so open on an issue like this given the attitude in Washington." As the official remembered, "[Bush] was, in effect, saying he had never looked at the question of arts funding in that way before."

But of course, George Bush was not in charge of U.S. domestic policy in 1990; John Sununu was. And on March 13, just days after Frohnmayer had received Bush's supportive note, Sununu summoned the NEA chief to his White House office for a talk. According to current and former NEA officials, Sununu told Frohnmayer that the chairman's vision of the agency's mission conflicted with the administration's determination not to fund homoerotic and politically objectionable art. "It will never work this way," Sununu reportedly told Frohnmayer. He also told the NEA head to "stay away from Capitol Hill" and the controversy over the Jesse Helms amendment to the NEA's appropriations bill.

The agency's reauthorization bill, which was pending in Congress, ensured that outside criticism of the NEA's policies continued unabated. The Reverend Donald Wildmon's American Family Association took out full-page ads—beginning February 13 in The Washington Times, and later, on March 23, in USA Today—critical of the NEA's decision to fund particular artists, mentioning David Wojnarowicz, Annie Sprinkle, Serrano, and Mapplethorpe by name. On April 12, the AFA mailed each member of congress and 178,000 Christian pastors a letter protesting NEA policies and reproducing details of David Wojnarowicz paintings (provoking a suit by the artist). The AFA's actions caused what one former official called a "crackling" between the agency and the White House.

To reassure Bush, Frohnmayer sent him another note, assuring that despite the public furor everything was under control at the agency. Within two days, on April 26, 1990, NEA General Counsel Julianne Davis testified before Representative Sid Yates's house appropriations committee on the 1991 NEA budget about the reauthorization bill, and came out strongly against content restrictions in the arts.

The very next day Brett Hatch, the son of Utah Republican senator Orrin Hatch and an assistant to White House counsel C. Boyden Gray, called Davis on the carpet. Hatch said that her stance regarding free expression was "not the position that the administration wants to take." In regard to Frohnmayer's exchange of handwritten notes with the president, Hatch said, "We don't want John communicating with the president about this anymore. Tell him to handle things the way Sununu suggests."

Leaks about controversial NEA grant proposals began to appear frequently in the press; in particular, the details of a May 13, 1990, panel meeting in which it was decided not to fund grant proposals submitted by performance artist Karen Finley and three others. Frohnmayer and his top aides immediately began to suspect his White House-imposed #2, Alvin Felzenberg, of being the leaker.

In fact, according to top-ranking current and former NEA officials, Felzenberg was in frequent touch with William Kristol—Vice-President Quayle's chief of staff and son of neoconservative columnist and former NEA Council member Irving Kristol—behind Frohnmayer's back.

Felzenberg also wrote an unsigned memo around the time of the May 13 Council meeting that ridiculed a number of progressive filmmakers who were requesting money, and in particular Deep Dish Television,

several sources close to the controversy, Frohnmayer sent the president a handwritten note on plain paper, dated March 9, explaining his opposition to content-based criteria for arts funding.

"Mr. President: In essence, this is the issue I have been dealing with since I've been here," the NEA chair wrote. "The original legislation states that the government must not impose a single aesthetic standard or attempt to direct artistic content. . . . This is wise. . . . The main role of the agency is to provide a climate where great American artists can express themselves. . . . With my greatest respect, John."

Bush replied almost immediately with a note of his own, expressing his support and admiration for Frohnmayer's handling of the difficult situation at the NEA in an intelligent manner. One former NEA official who was shown the note recalled: "Wow, it's neat that the president can be so open on an issue like this given the attitude in Washington." As the official remembered, "[Bush] was, in effect, saying he had never looked at the question of arts funding in that way before."

But of course, George Bush was not in charge of U.S. domestic policy in 1990; John Sununu was. And on March 13, just days after Frohnmayer had received Bush's supportive note, Sununu summoned the NEA chief to his White House office for a talk. According to current and former NEA officials, Sununu told Frohnmayer that the chairman's vision of the agency's mission conflicted with the administration's determination not to fund homoerotic and politically objectionable art. "It will never work this way," Sununu reportedly told Frohnmayer. He also told the NEA head to "stay away from Capitol Hill" and the controversy over the Jesse Helms amendment to the NEA's appropriations bill.

The agency's reauthorization bill, which was pending in Congress, ensured that outside criticism of the NEA's policies continued unabated. The Reverend Donald Wildmon's American Family Association took out full-page ads—beginning February 13 in *The Washington Times*, and later, on March 23, in *USA Today*—critical of the NEA's decision to fund particular artists, mentioning David Wojnarowicz, Annie Sprinkle, Serrano, and Mapplethorpe by name. On April 12, the AFA mailed each member of congress and 178,000 Christian pastors a letter protesting NEA policies and reproducing details of David Wojnarowicz paintings (provoking a suit by the artist). The AFA's actions caused what one former official called a "crackling" between the agency and the White House.

To reassure Bush, Frohnmayer sent him another note, assuring that despite the public furor everything was under control at the agency. Within two days, on April 26, 1990, NEA General Counsel Julianne Davis testified before Representative Sid Yates's house appropriations committee on the 1991 NEA budget about the reauthorization bill, and came out strongly against content restrictions in the arts.

The very next day Brett Hatch, the son of Utah Republican senator Orrin Hatch and an assistant to White House counsel C. Boyden Gray, called Davis on the carpet. Hatch said that her stance regarding free expression was "not the position that the administration wants to take." In regard to Frohnmayer's exchange of handwritten notes with the president, Hatch said, "We don't want John communicating with the president about this anymore. Tell him to handle things the way Sununu suggests."

Leaks about controversial NEA grant proposals began to appear frequently in the press; in particular, the details of a May 13, 1990, panel meeting in which it was decided not to fund grant proposals submitted by performance artist Karen Finley and three others. Frohnmayer and his top aides immediately began to suspect his White House-imposed #2, Alvin Felzenberg, of being the leaker.

In fact, according to top-ranking current and former NEA officials, Felzenberg was in frequent touch with William Kristol—Vice-President Quayle's chief of staff and son of neoconservative columnist and former NEA Council member Irving Kristol—behind Frohnmayer's back.

Felzenberg also wrote an unsigned memo around the time of the May 13 Council meeting that ridiculed a number of progressive filmmakers who were requesting money, and in particular Deep Dish Television, a New York–based documentary producer and distributor. Deep Dish had requested a grant of $35,000 to examine Columbus's voyages in a culturally diverse context. The memo accused the company of being "Fidel Castro's propaganda arm in the U.S." It has now been confirmed, through sources at the highest levels of the NEA, that Alvin Felzenberg wrote the memo, removed his name, and had it circulated.

In response, Frohnmayer and NEA counsel Davis pulled NEA telephone logs in an attempt to identify the source of the press leaks. They found records of calls between Felzenberg's office and columnists Rowland Evans and Robert Novack, including one that lasted "over an hour" and preceded a critical article about Karen Finley's grant proposal. Felzenberg was fired by Frohnmayer on Monday, June 4, only to be given immediate shelter at the White House as head of a government commission exploring delays in the appointment of federal officials. Today Felzenberg, Evans, and Novack all admit there had been telephone contact, but insist that Felzenberg was simply returning a call from the reporters.

In early June, after Felzenberg was ousted, Frohnmayer was summoned to the White House, along with Rose DiNapoli, his director of congressional liaison, to answer what were described as President Bush's concerns over the firing of the chairman's top deputy. There Frohnmayer met alone with John Sununu, not an unusual occurrence; but this time, the *Voice* has confirmed, the meeting included a particularly heated exchange. According to sources close to Frohnmayer, Sununu told the NEA head that when he was governor of New Hampshire, if there was something he didn't want funded, it didn't get funded—so he didn't understand why Frohnmayer was having a problem putting restraints on the sort of art that the White House found offensive.

Frohnmayer challenged Sununu, defending the artistic process and telling the then-chief of staff that he, Sununu, didn't know anything about it. "You have to understand that with art, you can't always tell how something will turn out one, two, or three years after you fund it," Frohnmayer reportedly told Sununu. The former governor proposed to Frohnmayer that the NEA single out "problem cases" and not fund them, which Frohnmayer took as an official suggestion that he begin "blacklisting" artists. Again, Frohnmayer objected vehemently.

"Sununu's idea was to blacklist—if they have done something offensive before, they shouldn't be funded," recalls Jack Lichtenstein. "It was his feeling that offensive work was being done by a small group of people, funded by the endowment, and was reflecting badly on the administration."

On June 12, as was not uncommon with those who stood up to Sununu, Frohnmayer, along with his director of congressional liaison Rose DiNapoli, were summoned to a meeting in the office of Andrew Card, deputy chief of staff, to discuss major agency policies. Besides Card, the other administration representatives at the meeting were NEA personnel head Jeannette Naylor and Frances Norris. According to sources knowledgeable about the agenda, the message was to tone down the whole "free-expression thing"—they wanted to tell Frohnmayer that he should use his best judgment and not put the First Amendment first.

A little more than two weeks later, the watershed event of the Frohnmayer NEA administration—the chairman's vetoing of the grants to the so-called NEA 4 (Karen Finley, John Fleck, Holly Hughes, and Tim Miller)—was announced. After Frohnmayer overturned the agency's lower-level approval for funding of their sexually controversial performance art, they sued the agency for reinstatement.

The suit shifted the grounds of debate almost overnight. Now, both NEA officials and White House staffers were forced into a common defensive posture. The issue no longer was what art to fund but what legal strategy to pursue, a question that turned out to be every bit as controversial. According to former top NEA officials and confidential documents obtained by the *Voice*, this new conflict began in the first week of December 1990, when a meeting was called to bring together the legal teams. Present were NEA general counsel Davis, one lawyer from Boyden Gray's office, and four from the civil division of the DOJ, including Lloyd Green and Mark Battan. One of the first administration ideas out of the box was the suggestion by the justice department that the NEA remove from its mission statement a clause saying that every citizen of the United States is guaranteed freedom of expression; the administration lawyers suggested that such language was "just inviting lawsuits." The NEA's Davis objected strongly, and the fat was in the fire.

A series of confidential memos followed between Frohnmayer and Assistant Attorney General Stuart M. Gerson, memos that have been obtained by the *Voice*. From early May through early July 1991, the Department of Justice put pressure on Frohnmayer to stand squarely on the principles of the *Rust* decision, claiming that *Rust* gave the agency the right to withhold funding from the four artists based on the offensive content of their work.

"The Bush administration and the Justice Department had just won the [*Rust*] case, and it was like a new toy for them," says a top former agency official. "They couldn't wait to try it out. They wanted to use the NEA to see how much they could limit the speech of those receiving federal money."

Frohnmayer responded in a confidential memo to Gerson dated June 27, 1991. "I am writing you personally to assure that you understand that the litigation strategy proposed by your office is contrary to the best interests of this agency," Frohnmayer declared. While conceding that the *Rust* defense would be expedient, he wrote that such arguments "are contrary to the NEA's mission and history of funding meritorious artistic projects without regard to the political message or ideas contained in them." He continued, "By statute the NEA is committed to supporting excellence and creativity in the arts. . . . In order to do this, the Endowment must foster and support an atmosphere in which artists are free to pursue their creative impulses and focus on the artistic quality of their work." Pointing out that he had repeatedly stated in public that he opposed content-based restrictions on federally funded art, Frohnmayer said he would disavow any use of the *Rust* ruling should the Justice Department's position prevail. "I trust that this will put to rest any further discussion of the merits of filing the First Amendment and statutory arguments [based on *Rust*] in this case," Frohnmayer concluded.

On July 1, 1991, Gerson answered Frohnmayer in another confidential memo,

chiding the chairman for maintaining the position that "content restriction" did not already exist in the NEA's funding process, and objecting to Frohnmayer's preferred defense, that the grants had been rejected solely on "artistic" grounds.

Gerson went on to compare the sexually explicit work of the NEA 4 to heinous acts of violence, using this as a justification for employing *Rust*. "One would hope that the Endowment would never approve any grant that, in the name of free expression and the examination of all ideas, extolled genocide, promoted presidential assassination or celebrated racial lynching, to cite a few horrific examples. As to these matters, I suggest, 'artistic merit' is an irrelevancy. While any idea may be presented artistically or otherwise made the topic of speech . . . the matter of the public's paying the tab represents a different issue, and for the Endowment a difficult charge.

" 'The First Amendment does not prohibit government funding agencies from denying grants based on objections to the ideas or viewpoints expressed,' " the letter states. "[Such argument] is clearly correct as a matter of law, although it is sometimes also politically controversial. The Supreme Court recently restated the validity of the point in *Rust* v. *Sullivan* and, as the Solicitor General argued for the United States, this rule follows a consistent line of decisions of the court."

Frohnmayer answered in a July 8, 1991, memo, reminding Gerson that "each time the Endowment has been reauthorized by Congress content restrictions have been considered, and every single time Congress has voted on the issue it has refused to allow the Endowment to base its funding decisions on the viewpoints or ideas expressed in the applications. . . . I am particularly troubled that you doubt my assertion that the Endowment awards grants without regard to the political message advanced in the work. You question whether it is even possible to assess artistic merit without passing on the message of the work. While this is an interesting question of philosophy, it has no relevance to the real world operations of the Endowment . . . Artistic merit not only *can* be evaluated completely separately from the consideration of viewpoint expressed in the work, it *must* be so judged. If viewpoint is a consideration, then the Endowment has utterly failed in its Congressionally mandated mission. Federal support for the arts will have become federal control."

To prevent the *Rust* argument from becoming part of the agency's defense in the NEA 4 case (it actually went as far as being written into a draft legal brief), Frohnmayer fought his way up to White House counsel Gray. During a meeting in Gray's office in August 1991, also attended by Gerson, Gray finally acquiesced.

Interestingly, despite Frohnmayer's efforts, there is a single minor mention of

Rust in the NEA brief that was filed February in the NEA 4 case. However, Frohnmayer was said to have considered the fact that it was a minor reference, and not the major defense of the case, to be a victory.

With Frohnmayer out and the NEA 4 suit still pending, the battle for the agency continues. According to NEA observers, including highly placed sources on Capitol Hill, the White House long ago positioned Dr. Anne-Imelda Radice, former director of National Museum of Women in the Arts, and former chief of the division of the creative arts in the conservative U.S. Information Agency, as Frohnmayer's senior deputy chair. After being appointed NEA's number two administrator last March, she is now widely assumed to be Frohnmayer's ultimate replacement.

"Radice was supposed to be the last act in the play to bring the NEA under the kind of control that Sununu had wanted from the beginning," says former *Los Angeles Times* reporter Allan Parachini.

Observers fear that Radice or another conservative will willingly remake the agency into a political instrument, much in the way that Chairwoman Lynne Cheney has retooled the National Endowment for the Humanities.

"Radice is seen as a true soldier and good conservative that can make it like the NEH," says Gary Larson, a former NEA program specialist. "What she would probably do is eliminate the Solo Performance in Theatre and Interdisciplinary Arts Categories—that would get rid of performance art, and would cover Holly Hughes and Karen Finley–types—as well as the Interarts Program. Finally, they could have panels like the NEH recommending the funding for a range of proposals, but let the agency staff actually pick the ones to be funded. That would do it."

No matter who assumes control of the NEA in the wake of Frohnmayer's departure, the agency itself remains in trouble. Frohnmayer himself has expressed concern that the NEA may be disbanded after he leaves, and he feels strongly about the necessity for generating unified support in the art world for the agency's goals.

Interestingly, despite his treatment by the Bush administration, Frohnmayer continues to refuse to speak publicly about his tenure as head of the NEA. Frohnmayer's convictions about the First Amendment are probably irrelevant: the Buchanan assault makes clear just how sensitive the issue of funding for sexual, homoerotic, or politically suspect art is. One of the fatal flaws of public funding for free expression is, as John Frohnmayer found, that there can be no middle ground. The week before he was fired, Frohnmayer told a confidant that when he took the job as chair of the NEA he was "a moderate on the First Amendment, but will leave an absolutist." ■

Research assistance by Billy Treger

a New York–based documentary producer and distributor. Deep Dish had requested a grant of $35,000 to examine Columbus's voyages in a culturally diverse context. The memo accused the company of being "Fidel Castro's propaganda arm in the U.S." It has now been confirmed, through sources at the highest levels of the NEA, that Alvin from the civil division of the DOJ, including Lloyd Green and Mark Battan. One of the first administration ideas out of the box was the suggestion by the justice department that the NEA remove from its mission statement a clause saying that every citizen of the United States is guaranteed freedom of expression; the administration lawyers suggested that such language was "just inviting lawsuits." The NEA's Davis objected strongly, and the fat was in the fire.

A series of confidential memos followed between Frohnmayer and Assistant Attorney General Stuart M. Gerson, memos that have been obtained by the *Voice*. From early May through early July 1991, the Department of Justice put pressure on Frohnmayer to stand squarely on the principles of the *Rust* decision, claiming that *Rust* gave the agency the right to withhold funding from the four artists based on the offensive content of their work.

"The Bush administration and the Justice Department had just won the [*Rust*] case, and it was like a new toy for them," says a top former agency official. "They couldn't wait to try it out. They wanted to use the NEA to see how much they could limit the speech of those receiving federal money."

Frohnmayer responded in a confidential memo to Gerson dated June 27, 1991. "I am writing you personally to assure that ~~you understand that the litigation strategy~~ proposed by your office is contrary to the best interests of this agency," Frohnmayer declared. While conceding that the *Rust* defense would be expedient, he wrote that such arguments "are contrary to the NEA's mission and history of funding meritorious artistic projects without regard to the political message or ideas contained in them." He continued, "By statute the NEA is committed to supporting excellence and creativity in the arts.... In order to do this, the Endowment must foster and support an atmosphere in which artists are free to pursue their creative impulses and focus on the artistic quality of their work." Pointing out that he had repeatedly stated in public that he opposed content-based restrictions on federally funded art, Frohnmayer said he would disavow any use of the *Rust* ruling should the Justice Department's position prevail. "I trust that this will put to rest any further discussion of the merits of filing the First Amendment and statutory arguments [based on *Rust*] in this case," Frohnmayer concluded.

On July 1, 1991, Gerson answered Frohnmayer in another confidential memo,

chiding the chairman for maintaining the position that "content restriction" did not already exist in the NEA's funding process, and objecting to Frohnmayer's preferred defense, that the grants had been rejected solely on "artistic" grounds.

Gerson went on to compare the sexually explicit work of the NEA 4 to heinous acts of violence, using this as a justification for employing *Rust*. "One would hope that the Endowment would never approve any grant that, in the name of free expression and the examination of all ideas, extolled genocide, promoted presidential assassination or celebrated racial lynching, to cite a few horrific examples. As to these matters, I suggest, 'artistic merit' is an irrelevancy. While any idea may be presented artistically or otherwise made the topic of speech ... the matter of the public's paying the tab represents a different issue, and for the Endowment a difficult charge.

"'The First Amendment does not prohibit government funding agencies from denying grants based on objections to the ideas or viewpoints expressed,'" the letter states. "[Such argument] is clearly correct as a matter of law, although it is sometimes also politically controversial. The Supreme Court recently restated the validity of the point in *Rust* v. *Sullivan* and, as the Solicitor General argued for the United States, this rule follows a consistent line of decisions of the court."

Frohnmayer answered in a July 8, 1991, memo, reminding Gerson that "each time the Endowment has been reauthorized by Congress content restrictions have been considered, and every single time Congress has voted on the issue it has refused to allow the Endowment to base its funding decisions on the viewpoints or ideas expressed in the applications.... I am particularly troubled that you doubt my assertion that the Endowment awards grants without regard to the political message advanced in the work. You question whether it is even possible to assess artistic merit without passing on the message of the work. While this is an interesting question of philosophy, it has no relevance to the real world operations of the Endowment ... Artistic merit not only *can* be evaluated completely separately from the consideration of viewpoint expressed in the work, it *must* be so judged. If viewpoint is a consideration, then the Endowment has utterly failed in its Congressionally mandated mission. Federal support for the arts will have become federal control."

To prevent the *Rust* argument from becoming part of the agency's defense in the NEA 4 case (it actually went as far as being written into a draft legal brief), Frohnmayer fought his way up to White House counsel Gray. During a meeting in Gray's office in August 1991, also attended by Gerson, Gray finally acquiesced.

Interestingly, despite Frohnmayer's efforts, there is a single minor mention of

Rust in the NEA brief that was filed February in the NEA 4 case. However, Frohnmayer was said to have considered the fact ~~that it was a minor reference, and not the~~ major defense of the case, to be a victory.

With Frohnmayer out and the NEA 4 suit still pending, the battle for the agency continues. According to NEA observers, including highly placed sources on Capitol Hill, the White House long ago positioned Dr. Anne-Imelda Radice, former director of National Museum of Women in the Arts, and former chief of the division of the creative arts in the conservative U.S. Information Agency, as Frohnmayer's senior deputy chair. After being appointed NEA's number two administrator last March, she is now widely assumed to be Frohnmayer's ultimate replacement.

"Radice was supposed to be the last act in the play to bring the NEA under the kind of control that Sununu had wanted from the beginning," says former *Los Angeles Times* reporter Allan Parachini.

Observers fear that Radice or another conservative will willingly remake the agency into a political instrument, much in the way that Chairwoman Lynne Cheney has retooled the National Endowment for the Humanities.

"Radice is seen as a true soldier and good conservative that can make it like the NEH," says Gary Larson, a former NEA program specialist. "What she would probably do is eliminate the Solo Performance in Theatre and Interdisciplinary Arts Categories—that would get rid of performance art, and would cover Holly Hughes and Karen Finley–types—as well as the Interarts Program. Finally, they could have panels like the NEH recommending the funding for a range of proposals, but let the agency staff actually pick the ones to be funded. That would do it."

No matter who assumes control of the NEA in the wake of Frohnmayer's departure, the agency itself remains in trouble. Frohnmayer himself has expressed concern that the NEA may be disbanded after he leaves, and he feels strongly about the necessity for generating unified support in the art world for the agency's goals.

Interestingly, despite his treatment by the Bush administration, Frohnmayer continues to refuse to speak publicly about his tenure as head of the NEA. Frohnmayer's convictions about the First Amendment are probably irrelevant: the Buchanan assault makes clear just how sensitive the issue of funding for sexual, homoerotic, or politically suspect art is. One of the fatal flaws of public funding for free expression is, as John Frohnmayer found, that there can be no middle ground. The week before he was fired, Frohnmayer told a confidant that when he took the job as chair of the NEA he was "a moderate on the First Amendment, but will leave an absolutist." ∎

Research assistance by Billy Treger

A witch hunt for the '90s: new pages in book banning

By Rob Jenkins

WHEN JERRY FALWELL DIS-banded the Moral Majority in 1989, the mainstream media couldn't resist the temptation to interpret the breakup as the signal that the ultra-conservative social agenda formulated at the beginning of the decade had come to nought. The "Reagan Revolution," we were told, had fizzled, leaving in its wake a nascent "green" movement and a president

CENSORSHIP

of a decidedly less ideological strain. But that was before Robert Mapplethorpe's homoerotic photographs were transformed into the scapegoat for the moral downfall of America.

"The wave of censorship we're experiencing in this country is, I think, aptly described as a culture war," argues David Crane of People for the American Way, a constitutional-liberties advocacy organization founded in 1980 by Norman Lear. "And the main battle—in everything from the NEA [National Endowment for the Arts] controversy to people who want to rid the airwaves of 'offensive' TV shows—is between those who view the arts as essential to understanding the problems and potential of humanity and those who are threatened by creativity and new ways of looking at things."

But while Mapplethorpe, Karen Finley and 2 Live Crew grab all the headlines, plain old-fashioned book-banning is making a comeback in a big way. I refer not to the alleged infringement on Bret Easton Ellis' right to have anything he writes, no matter how putrid, put into print by the publisher of his choice. A problem of far greater significance to the future of censorship in America is the widespread practice of agitating for removal of books from public-school libraries and curricula.

The new witch hunt: School is, after all, more than just classwork. As corny as it sounds, it's where children learn about democracy through such time-honored traditions as student-body elections. And if the idea is to mold future citizens, it is worth considering what kind we'll end up with if the importance of intellectual freedom is not instilled at a young age.

A witch hunt is going on in local districts across the country, organized, in large part, by a byzantine network of far-right groups that promote so-called "traditional American family values." Their goal is to derail what they regard as a massive conspiracy by the educational establishment to indoctrinate chilren into the religion of witchcraft, or Wicca.

"Too many of the books and other educational materials in the schools today are full of occult practices and anti-Christian messages," says Alfred Miller of the Christian Educators Association International. CEAI, based in Pasadena, Calif., puts special emphasis on exposing what Miller calls the "satanic underpinnings" of New Age healing and meditative practices. "The reality is that the strength of New Age is the occult," he says. "And it's well known that these kinds of activities are linked with drugs and heavy-metal music. So what we're saying is, 'Let's put a stop to it.'"

This sort of talk could be dismissed as just another spasm of the lunatic fringe if it weren't so effective. Bear-ing the brunt of the accusations is a multilevel reading anthology called *Impressions*. "Nightmarish Textbooks Await Your Kids," screamed the headline on the front page of the Sept. 17, 1990, issue of *Citizen* magazine, a membership and fund-raising organ of another California-based group, called Focus on the Family. Subtitled "Concerned parents say *Impressions*' violent and occultic content torments even happy, well-adjusted children," the article has almost singlehandedly mobilized a full-fledged anti-*Impressions* movement that speaks openly of its plans for bigger and better things. Not one of the people I interviewed failed to mention either the article, the magazine or the group itself.

The fear in the voices of parents opposing *Impressions* is so real that it's hard to believe it was triggered by the primitive scare tactics used in the *Citizen* cover story. The article, for instance, attacks *Under the Sea*, a third-grade reader in the series, for including an allegedly deceptive illustration showing what appear to be harmless floating objects (a piece of pie, a stove, a teddy bear, etc): "Parents looking at the illustration wouldn't know that the teacher's manual directs the teacher to assign the children to compose a spell. 'Write and chant a magic spell' to make things in the room float, the teacher's manual says, and 'write and chant a magic spell' to return the room to normal." Yet if week after week of watching Darin Stevens get turned into a farm animal on *Bewitched* didn't drive Americans crazy for magic powers, it's hard to believe that *Impressions* will do the job.

Try, try again: People for the American Way's Crane cites two cases in the '80s—one in Hawkins County, Tenn., and the other in Mobile, Ala.—in which fundamentalist "pro-family" groups succeeded in convincing the courts "that textbooks in public schools were teaching the religion of secular humanism." The suits were sponsored by Concerned Women for America and Pat Robertson, respectively, and both were eventually overturned at the appellate level.

But back then the religious right had yet to latch onto the anti-Satan, direct-mail juggernaut. This time around they might have more success, because now they can point the accusing finger at witchcraft. "The secular humanism route didn't work, so now they substitute the words 'witchcraft' and 'Wicca,' and they start over again," says Crane. Believe it or not, it seems that the '80s brand of religious conservatism was too subtle for its own good.

Crane says that when he found out the *Impressions* controversy had taken a litigious turn, he wasn't surprised to find the American Family Association pulling the strings. The AFA filed a complaint in Willard, Ohio, only to withdraw it when the school district invited Crane to help them assemble a defense team. "A few days later they went to Woodland, Calif., to mount an identical suit," he says. It's no accident, he thinks, that the AFA's Don Wildmon (most famous for his crusade against the film *The Last Temptation of Christ*) is focusing on areas where the stage has been set for a high-profile case by previous fundamentalist-led book challenges.

"We've seen a sophistication of this movement," says Crane. "In the past there were a few highly visible national leaders who would orchestrate these campaigns. I think that today the far-right organizations— not all of them religious—are much more advanced in their ability to use direct mail, computers, radio (which is a lot cheaper than TV), and literally go into districts and organize against what they feel are hostile forces in the public schools.

"What we face now," he continues, "is a grass-roots movement taking hold that is much more difficult to get the public to focus attention on because the tendency is to think, 'This is one small district in a state a long way away from me.' It's not as visible as Jerry Falwell or Pat Robertson on TV, but we've found it's much more pervasive and difficult to attack. The good news is that these *Impressions* controversies may make it possible to illustrate the network of organizations behind all this."

Mail barrage: Anson Franklin, a vice president at Harcourt Brace Jovanovich, which publishes the series, says sometimes he still can't believe the controversy has gotten so out of hand. "We've seen signs of serious concern or protest in about 10 percent of the 400 or so districts where it's used," Franklin says. And that doesn't include the immense quantities of mail the company has received telling them not to bring *Impressions* to "our area." "Based on the way the letters are worded, it's fairly apparent which ones have been generated by the *Citizen* article. It certainly accounts for the bulk of them."

The last time the Wheaton, Ill., school district had to cope with a book challenge was at least five years ago, according to Denie Young, a district official. It was John Steinbeck's *Of Mice and Men*. As a heated *Impressions* challenge in her district came to a head in mid-March, Young sounded almost nostalgic for the good old days when sex and profanity were the mainstays of book censorship efforts in public schools.

Though careful always to speak of "addressing the concerns of parents," her time in the trenches during Wheaton's recently concluded war on witches has clearly been a trying experience. Echoing Franklin, she expressed acute incredulity: "I never would have guessed something like this could happen."

As a result of several dozen formal complaints, the school board appointed an *Impressions* review committee, with Rev. John Rodgers, who is not a fundamentalist, serving as chairman. When a children's literature specialist who served on the committee said that the stories in *Impressions* are representative of the world of children's literature, parents opposed to the series charged that the committee was a "stacked deck."

And to the extent that people who work in education are disproportionately likely to place a high value on the written word, they are right. But short of packing the committee with people who place no importance on the role of literature in human development, there's little that can be done. Splitting the difference is not always the wise approach.

At a March 20 meeting, the school board voted to continue using the *Impressions* series in the district. "But with a couple of directives," Young says. These include developing a model of collaboration that teachers and individual parents can follow when attempting to find replacements for those *Impressions* selections that a parent doesn't want his or her child exposed to (provided that they amount to fewer than half the total number of reading assignments). And by 1993-94, the administration must conduct a review of available reading anthologies to see if *Impressions* should be replaced at one or more grade levels. In addition, schools must develop training programs for new teachers to "sensitize them to parental concerns in the areas of values, negativism and the occult."

National scope: Time will tell whether these sops to censorious parents quell the unrest. There are signs, however, that some among their ranks are less than satisfied with the outcome. Review Committee Chairman Rodgers, who has tried to remain neutral throughout the process, didn't want to comment on whether national fundamentalist organizations were involved with the Wheaton *Impressions* challenge.

But CEAI's Alfred Miller confirmed his group's involvement: "I was on the phone with somebody out in Wheaton just this morning," he said less than a week before the school board was scheduled to act on the committee's report.

One problem with national groups jumping into the fray is that they overwhelm the mechanisms school systems have developed over the years to prevent "silent" censorship, in which books are quietly removed from reading lists and school libraries to avoid controversy. To safeguard against this, most districts insist that formal procedures be followed in all cases in which educational materials are challenged.

But it doesn't always work. A teacher in a Midwestern state said she hoped a recent decision to retain a challenged book would send a message that the district, which had earlier banned a book in response to a nationally organized campaign, was not easy prey. She wouldn't di-

The witch hunt going on across the U.S. is organized by far-right groups promoting "values of the traditional American family."

vulge the name of the book that had been challenged and retained, because the case hadn't been made public. They had bypassed the carefully constructed channels by bringing the matter to the book-selection committee, even though the book had been selected a long time ago and the committee hadn't the power to "un-select" it.

How, I asked, could their victory

serve as a deterrent to would-be censors if it was hidden from public scrutiny?

"Well, around here sometimes the less that is said, the less that gets going, if you know what I mean," she replied. What, in fact, she meant is that the district administration, well-meaning though it may be, has been effectively intimidated.

Last fall, North Carolina's and Mississippi's state textbook committees voted not to approve *Impressions*, which means that school districts may not use state funds to purchase the series. To some, this may seem only an inconvenience. But the real nightmare scenario, say civil libertarians, is that fundamentalist groups will use their highly successful, if somewhat crude, anti-Wicca/anti-New Age cottage industry as a cash cow to finance their efforts against real literature with political messages that disturb them. Having learned to prey on parents' fears of what they don't know about their children, groups such as the Traditional Values Coalition and Citizens for Excellence in Education, both based in California, have redoubled their efforts against the former bogeyman of choice: sex.

"Fear really is the key," says Jan Chappuis, a junior high school teacher in Seabeck, Wash., who last year fought a losing battle to keep Maya Angelou's *I Know Why the Caged Bird Sings* in her pilot English class for academically talented ninth graders. The initial complaint, filed by parents David and Shanna McVicker, charged that the scene in which eight-year-old Maya is raped by her stepfather would be too shocking to their child. Chappuis believes that the parents are out of touch.

"They don't even know what their own kids are watching on TV," she says. "And, more generally, they don't understand the level of awareness and the prevalence of sexual behavior, either chosen or unchosen, that these kids or their best friends are going through. And they

can't expect the kids to tell them, so the teachers become the bearers of bad news, in the sense that they are the ones who have to design a curriculum that has some bearing on reality. That's when parents get upset. It's a lot easier to claim, as one of the school-board members did, that the teachers' morals are depraved than to think that this type of material is not foreign to a ninth-grader's life."

Cagey citizen-censors: The McVickers also objected to a section of *I Know Why the Caged Bird Sings* that depicts, in the words of their complaint, the author's "struggle with a lesbian identity and the resulting desire and accomplishment of sexual intercourse with the single purpose of disproving the above identity." Needless to say, the story loses a little something in translation. Even the McVickers acknowledge that. Their main complaint is that the book's "sexually value-laden issues have no moral resolution in the text" and that the material "leaves the values of premarital sexual relations, rape and homosexuality in an 'OK' position."

By insinuating that schools hope to teach kids that rape is "OK," the McVickers are able to divert attention from the fact that they want a specific "value"—that homosexuals are unholy—to be imparted to children. Neither the book nor the teacher's lesson plan calls for anything, aside from a failure to condemn, that could remotely be construed as advocating homosexuality. The question is, at what point does a parent's right to have a say in his or her child's education—even if no attempt is made to keep a book from the school-going public at large—conflict with the state's interest in protecting its future citizens from dangerous forms of ignorance? The problem is that, since there is no agency better equipped to determine where parents' rights end and the state's interest in the students' well-being begins, the schools retain this critical power. When teachers, administrators or school boards are compelled to exercise this authority, they are vulnerable to charges of being anti-family.

Assistant Principal P.N. Orcutt wrote a letter in support of *I Know Why the Caged Bird Sings* to the committee in which she raised the very sensible point that the parents' proposed solution—to leave the book in the school library—would solve nothing. Homosexuality and rape, she argues, are things that are difficult for adolescents to approach, even if they are aware of them. "Is it not more sensible, then, to provide an opportunity to read and discuss the issues in a controlled classroom in the presence of a sensitive, intelligent teacher?"

This reasoning apparently swayed the review committee, which overwhelmingly approved *I Know Why the Caged Bird Sings*. But just when it seemed that everything was back to normal, the school board unexpectedly voted to remove the book from the classroom. By all accounts, this unexpected reversal was largely the result of a last-minute campaign by local minister John Haberlin, a member of the district's Religion in Schools Committee. Chappuis said that she recently learned that an *Impressions* challenge had been mounted in her district. Concurrent controversies over sex and satanism in school books will, she thinks, prove a potent brew.

Nowhere do sex and religion converge more explosively than on the subject of abortion. The introduction of *The Handmaid's Tale*, by Canadian novelist Margaret Atwood, into the 12th-grade curriculum at Rancho Cotati High School in Rohnert Park, Calif., ignited a controversy almost immediately. The book details a society run by militant Christian fundamentalists who force fertile women—"handmaids"—to bear children to men whose wives are unable to conceive. Artificial insemination would be against God's will, so

the reader is treated to one particularly heavy-handed scene in which a military commander performs the ritualized rape of his handmaid in accordance with accepted procedure: his wife straddles the handmaid's open legs with her own to simulate participation in the sex act, which the man is forbidden to enjoy.

New Age masquerade: Gene Tidham, whose daughter will be in the class next year, wasted no time in explaining that *The Handmaid's Tale* is part of a larger plot—including *Impressions*—to get anti-Christian values into the public schools. It was all spelled out to him, he said, by a book called *The New Age Masquerade*, which seems have become a standard reference for today's book-banners. Stidham borrowed the book from another parent active in the protest, Jack Behl, whose son was in this year's class that read *The Handmaid's Tale*.

"It lists all the different names that the heads of education in this country have been using for this stuff since the '50s," he says. "Now the new code word is 'impressions,' and they use terms like 'visualization' and 'self-esteem,' but it's really just a cover for channeling and other New Age occult practices."

Stidham's fear is palpable as he talks about the rise of drugs, gangs and suicide in his area. "And now we've got this book," he adds. The school board, however, failed to see the connection and decided to retain the book. Its suggestion that parents who didn't want their children to read *The Handmaid's Tale* could substitute Aldous Huxley's *Brave New World* didn't go over very well, however. Stidham, Behl and their pastor, Chip Worthington of the Rohnert Park Assembly of God, don't plan to give up.

"All we have to do is show about six sections of the book to the average person here, and at least 30 percent of the people will be absolutely outraged," Worthington says. "You

see, only men who agree with the feminist agenda are looked at positively in the book. Its whole premise is that white, middle-class Protestant, religious men are controlling the U.S. and the world. But if anyone knows anything about this culture, they know that the least powerful people are white middle-class ministers. We're at the bottom rung of the power structure."

As is common among fundamentalist leaders, Worthington continually inverts class, gender and race issues to convince the rank and file that they're on the road to martyrdom. His view is that "the educational elite in any given city are generally insensitive to at least 30 to 50 percent of the people in any given city. In our town, it's this educational elite—which is composed of a handful of administrators and mainly the teachers' union—that is controlling this book."

Like all good dissemblers, he's built his analysis around a kernel of truth. It is, after all, hard to deny that as long as teachers have to go to college in order to get a job, there will always be a gap between some parents and educators.

Those who advocate parental involvement as the answer to the problems afflicting America's schools have to come to terms with the fact that class and educational differences have more serious implications than they realized. The sad truth today is that anyone with a computer, a mailing list, a post-office box and a talent for exploiting the pathos of fear stands a pretty good shot of getting books thrown out of one or more public schools.   □

©1991 Rob Jenkins

Rob Jenkins is a writer living in Cambridge, Mass.

THE PROPHETS OF RAGE; THE MESSENGERS OF HOPE

The band's t-shirt proclaims that they are "2 Black (and) 2 Strong," and when they were hauled away to jail after an adults-only performance at a Florida club, some people wondered if the t-shirt message wasn't really the reason that 2 Live Crew drew the heat, instead of their allegedly obscene lyrics. After all, it did seem a little extreme to arrest performers for saying on stage what can be heard in just about any R-rated movie. Perhaps the real problem is that rap music — most of which is produced by young African American men — is becoming too visible, too political, and too popular with young people of all colors for the comfort of the powers that be. As columnist Barbara Roessner noted in the Hartford Courant, *"as long as rap remained hidden on the streets of the inner city, its run-ins with authority were few... Now rap has crept into the mainstream. Only now does the establishment feel compelled to muzzle it."*

I declare it a new age,
Get down for the prophets of rage . . .
You find that we're quotable,
You emulate,
Brothers, sisters, that's beautiful
Follow the path
Of positivity you go
Some sing it or rap it
Or harmonize it . . .
Left or right,
Black or White
They tell lies in the books
That you're readin'
It's knowledge of yourself
That you're needin'
Power of the people say

— Ridenhour/Shocklee/Sadler (Public Enemy),
"Prophets of Rage," © Def Jam Recordings.

Rap (or hip-hop) music has exploded in popularity over the past several years, and this popularity is strongly connected to a cultural revitalization in the African-American community. As a powerful means of communication, rap has contributed to this reawakening of cultural pride, but rappers themselves draw their inspiration from events and movements in their communities. For example, Jesse Jackson's attempt at the presidency was a big factor, and the increasingly successful movement for freedom in South Africa brought Africa back into the public eye in a much more positive way. Nowadays, a leather emblem of Africa emblazoned with the colors of the African National Congress is as common around the necks of African-American youths as ties on bankers. One of the most popular rappers, Kool Moe Dee, titled his second album "African Pride."

African-American leaders like Louis Farrakhan are becoming more and more popular, and not just those alive today. "I hear people talking about Malcom X so much, if I didn't know it I wouldn't think he was dead," Oakland-based rap deejay Dave Cook remarked in an interview with the *Trendsletter*. The lessons contained in the writings and lives of African-Americans is a primary subject of many rap tunes. And Nelson Mandela's triumphant tour of the U.S. earlier this year both reflected and invigorated a

DataCenter   464 19th Street, Oakland, California 94612 (415) 835-4692

fresh outpouring of solidarity with the struggle of the South African people for freedom in their country.

Rappers on Mandela's Tour

It is no coincidence that at nearly every stop on Mandela's tour rap groups (or "crews") were present. At the event in Oakland, California, KRS-One of Boogie Down Productions, one of hip-hop's most politically advanced acts, flew in from New York to warn "Nelson Mandela is not free, he can't even vote in his own country." "Rap is the reason why we see this consciousness coming out," Cook told the *Trendsletter*, pointing out that rappers deal with everything from crime to drugs to the reason why biblical figures are invariably portrayed as white. Rap speaks a language urban youth understand, and it is very aware of its own power in that regard. For most modern rappers, their position implies a responsibility to "get with the program," i.e. put out a positive message that fights self-destructive actions and attitudes and promotes education and self-respect. As columnist Nelson George puts it, "the ability to communicate is a license to advocate."

And these bands do advocate. Not satisfied with simply "talking a cool line" or bragging about their exploits like earlier rap bands, the crews "on the political tip" (rap slang for being politically sophisticated) combine musical innovation with social analysis. Bands such as Public Enemy, Boogie Down Productions and Kool Moe Dee have made it their business to bring their melodic analysis of African-American life and the system that frames it to prisons, high schools and community groups all across the country. As Dave Cook explains in the following excerpt from an article entitled "What is Rap?" "most of the big rap acts have attempted to use their positions in the rap world as a springboard for political activism."

"Leading the pack is Public Enemy. The group constantly supplements its concert appearances with unscheduled and unpublicized stops in prisons and juvenile halls. Two months ago, lead rapper Chuck D was flown to the Bay Area by San Francisco State's Black Student Union to give a lecture. He made two unscheduled stops while here, one at a Black pride rally held on campus, and the other at San Francisco Juvenile Hall. He made these appearances for free. Other artists like Daddy O of the the group Stetasonic, Ice T, and the Jungle Brothers are constantly making stops to speak at local high schools and to address youth groups during their travels.

"In addition to reaching out to the community, rap artists have attempted to undertake the task of establishing their own organizations capable of addressing societal problems head-on. The Stop the Violence Movement (STVM) was found by KRS-One and other big-name rap acts who, in response to a concert killing, came together and recorded 'Self Destruction,' a timely song calling for an end to senseless violence. The proceeds (some $500,000) went to the STVM arm of the Urban League. On the local scene, Oakland's MC Hammer, who has been donating part of his profits to local charitable organizations, will transfer that altruistic spirit to a national level with the proceeds generated by his new release, 'Help the Children.' Hammer will oversee an organization to fund various schools and shelters nationwide.

"The result of this political activism by those big acts has caused others to follow suit. There has been some serious talk amongst the newer and lesser-known rap groups in the Bay Area to start a west coast version of the Stop the Violence Movement. A lot of this has to do with the pervasive gang violence that has afflicted this area. San Jose-based Red Black and Green released an anti-crack and violence song and accompanying video titled 'Serious as Cancer.' The video is currently being considered by the California legislature for use as an educational tool in public schools. Mellow Mar and J Cutt of North Oakland's APG Crew (recently voted Bay Area Group of the Year) are currently participant in a statewide 'Rap for Life Tour' being sponsored by LA-based *Chill Out* magazine. In addition, the group has given free benefits for San Francisco's

Hunter's Point Boys Club and Rock Against Racism Committee. Female rap act Petite and Elite of East Oakland helped found an organization entitled Y O U T H (Young and Old United to Help.) Here they serve as role models and counselors for their high school peers.

"These rappers are all making attempts to put forth positive images and refute the negative stereotypes hurled at them by the media. Many of the these up-and-coming rappers

The Politics of Rap Repression

Rap shows have been banned from a large number of venues all across the country, supposedly "because of the fear the the violence can spill over from the stage to the crowd," according to an article in Newsweek. are first-time activists and hence are still learning. Within their communities they are attempting to fill the roles and responsibilities left vacant by apathetic parents. Many of them are still young: the average age is sixteen to twenty-four. And those who put out vinyl that 'ain't saying nothing' are increasingly ill-received by the rap audience."*

Newsweek, Time and other publications (whose audiences are primarily white and middle class) have gone out of their way to label rap — and the people who make it and listen to it — stupid, racist, brutal, misogynist and repulsive. Even radio stations, when they play rap music at all, seem to play only the cuts that reflect the most negative images possible, while ignoring the acts that put out a more positive message. The FBI has even gotten in on the act, sending letters to radio stations warning them not to play the song "Fuck tha Police" by the rap group Niggers With Attitude (NWA). The same song inspired a nationwide police FAX network to track the group's movements and prevent them from doing live shows. There is even a rumor floating around in hip-hop circles that the FBI is preparing a report on the threat the rap music poses to national security.

So why all the attention on rap? It stretches the imagination to believe that 2 Live Crew's lyrics are more obscene, say, than the rows of stores in Florida selling X-rated videos and magazines. If the spread of violence from the stage to the crowd were a major problem, then movies, television and operas would seem to be prime candidates for being shut down. And while NWA's lyrics in favor of doing away with a few cops might be a little hard to swallow for people who don't have to constantly deal with police harassment, anti-law officer sentiments are common in popular music. For example, the white punk band MDC's initials stand for "Millions of Dead Cops," and Bob Marley admits "I shot the sheriff, but I swear it was in self-defense."

More to the point, the really sexist, nasty or violent rap music is just a small part of the genre, and most of the media coverage has tended to make it seem indicative rather than exceptional. Rap is not coming under attack because it is more graphic, violent or racist than any other music form, although these elements certainly exist. Instead, rap is getting attention from censors and the "law and order" crowd exactly because it has moved well beyond macho posturing and crude sexual descriptions and has become a major motivating force in a new African-American consciousness that is politically active, culturally aware and youth-oriented.

So, at the same time that rap is becoming incredibly popular (NWA sold two million copies of their first album on word of mouth alone), at the same time that it is bringing together young people of all colors and backgrounds and getting much more overtly political and rebellious, at the same time that it is taking the lead in a reawakening of cultural pride and assertiveness and is offering a model of success for young people to follow, it finds itself under attack. A coincidence? Hardly anybody who is part of the hip-hop scene thinks so.

The Messengers Are the Message

The message of rap is not simply the one contained in the lyrics themselves, although this one is becoming increasingly important as hip-hop and its fans become more sophisticated and self-conscious. The other message — one that mainstream commentators have managed to miss entirely if the articles in Newsweek and other mainstream publications are any indication — is that rap artists are heroes to young people. Successful rappers get the trappings of success and they get the respect and adulation of their peers. And because rap is an easily accessible art form, it also offers itself as relevant example of how to succeed. Rap at its best not only inspires the comment "yo, this is fresh" but also "I could do that too."

Although primarily performed by young African-American men, the hip-hop scene has been going through a major transition over the past year or so. It is attracting all kinds of people, and not just in the U.S. On a recent rap show on a local station in San Francisco, the deejays were discussing the "international rappers" who showed up for New York's New Music Symposium. Apparently, there are rap crews in Denmark, Sweden, Africa, Japan and even the USSR. Two acts that particularly impressed the programmers on the show were a Japanese "ragamuffin hip-hop crew" (ragamuffin hip-hop is rap with a reggae beat), and an Italian emcee who was so fast at cutting and mixing "you know the dude spends ten hours a day practicing with his records."

"More and more people are just coming to it," one of the deejays remarked; he was referring not only to the performers but also to the audiences. If the turnout at shows is any indication, at least half the fans of most hip-hop acts are not African-American. In fact, an article in the San Francisco Chronicle pointed out that at the shows on 2 Live Crew's controversial tour that got them arrested "75 percent of the fans were white." Rap comes out of the urban experience and has its roots in African and African-American culture; "rapping" itself is a mode of self-expression that can be traced back to West African traditions of oral history and rhyming games. While anyone can learn to rap, the source of its energy and creativity come from the African-American community. But hip-hop as a medium crosses cultural boundaries fairly easily — at least for young people. There are now Latino rappers, Asian rappers, feminist hip-hop acts, even religious rappers. As the Digital Underground says in one song, "red white black tan yellow or brown, it doesn't matter if we all get down."

Excerpt used with permission from an article entitled "What is Rap?" by Dave Cook in Folio, the program guide for KPFA radio station in Berkeley, California. Dave Cook, as Davey D, hosts a radio rap show called "Bring on the Noise."

"2 Rappers Seized After 'Nasty' Show, San Francisco Chronicle, 6/11/90.

Adler, Jerry et al. "The Rap Attitude," Newsweek, March 19, 1990.

Cook, Dave. "What is Rap?" Folio, February 1990.

Gates, David et al. "Decoding Rap Music," Newsweek, March 19, 1990.

LeMoyne, James. "Behind the Drive to Bring Down a Rap Groups and 'Nasty' Lyrics," San Francisco Chronicle, 6/12/90.

"Making Rap an Issue," Time, March 12, 1990.

McAdams, Janine. "In '89, a New Black Consciousness, Thanks to Rap, Soul Artists," Billboard, 12/23/89.

Roessner, Barbara T. "Censuring Rap is Not a Cool Move," San Francisco Chronicle, 6/22/90.

Simpson, Janice C. "Yo! Rap Gets on the Map," Time, February 5, 1990.

Sinker, Mark. "Enemy of the People," New Statesman and Society, April 20, 1990

—John Anner.

DataCenter   464 19th Street, Oakland, California 94612 (415) 835-4692

Turning the tables on censorship

Suit blocks airing of documentary about lack of artistic freedom in U.S.

By Jeff Kaye
SPECIAL TO THE EXAMINER

LONDON — An Emmy award-winning British television documentary about artistic censorship in the United States is itself facing problems getting shown in America because of a $2 million lawsuit filed against its producers by media boycott organizer the Rev. Donald Wildmon.

"It's using the legal system as a means of influencing what is shown to the public," complains British filmmaker Paul Yule, who directed and produced the documentary, "Damned in the USA." "It's a tactic just like a boycott."

Wildmon, best-known for organizing advertiser boycotts against TV programs he deems unsuitable for public viewing, appears in the film discussing his philosophical views and operational tactics. Although he consented to appear in the documentary, he says its producers violated an agreement not to screen the work in the United States without his permission.

The producers deny such an agreement was ever made.

The film originally was broadcast on Great Britain's Channel 4 network in April as part of a special series of programs that were either about censorship, or had, themselves, been censored.

Among other subjects examined in "Damned" are the controversy surrounding Andres Serrano's photograph "Piss Christ," the Cincinnati obscenity trial resulting from an art gallery exhibition of photographs by Robert Mapplethorpe, the arrest of rappers 2 Live Crew, and the efforts of U.S. politicians to control the awarding of National Endowment for the Arts grants.

Unlike most of the news media coverage of the arts censorship debate, "Damned in the USA" shows viewers the artistic works in question, including the Mapplethorpe photographs with their graphic homosexual and autoerotic themes.

Wildmon was interviewed at the Tupelo, Miss., headquarters of his American Family Association and is seen in the film giving a tour of the town and pointing out the birthplace of Elvis Presley, whom he says he admired.

He filed suit for breach of contract after "Damned" was shown in September at the Margaret Mead Film Festival at the Museum of Natural History in New York, the only public screening of the documentary in the United States to date. The film went on to win an International Emmy Award on Nov. 26 in New York.

Wildmon declined to comment on the suit.

As a result of the pending litigation, says Yule, "others who might show the film in the States are reluctant." The producer said there had been "loads" of interest from potential exhibitors ranging from universities to PBS. So far, no one has agreed to screen it, however.

Says Channel 4 spokesman Chris Griffin-Beale, "We are talking to people about potential sales, but it's under threat. The scale of money for purchasing rights is quite small, but the threat of legal action is considerable."

Yule said it was only with great difficulty that he was able to get Wildmon to agree to be interviewed in the first place. But despite Wildmon's initial reluctance, says Yule, "I think he saw it as a good platform for himself. The fact that I was a foreigner played a role in it. I think he believed he would be represented in a way he wouldn't be by the American media."

Once Yule and his crew arrived in Tupelo, they found that Wildmon would not participate unless they signed an agreement prohibiting them from using his interview in magazines. He was particularly concerned about having his comments wind up in Playboy, Penthouse or Hustler, the producer recalled.

After Yule signed, filming began. But later, after a lunch break, the film crew returned to find their equipment locked away and a second contract waiting for them, says Yule. "Our equipment was in a room where we couldn't get access until the contract was signed."

According to the producer, the second contract seemed to reiterate what had appeared in the first, so he signed it and the filming continued.

Don Christopher, an attorney for Channel 4 in London, said the legal issue appears to center on a clause in the second contract, which says the producers will not provide Wildmon's interview for "other media presentation."

Wildmon says the wording bars Channel 4 and the producers from showing the film outside Britain.

Robert Raskopf, the New York attorney handling the lawsuit in the United States for Channel 4, says he is "arguing primarily that the contract speaks for itself." He successfully petitioned to have the case transferred from the state court in Mississippi, where it was filed, to the U.S. District Court in Tupelo, saying he preferred to have it heard by a federal judge.

Meanwhile, the film faces an uncertain future in the United States. "It's so ironic," says Yule. "The American public is not being allowed to make up its own mind about a film which is about the American public not being allowed to make up its own mind."

Fighting porn, stifling free speech

A little-known anti-porn bill is scheduled for discussion this week in the Senate Judiciary Committee, and if approved there it's likely to pass on the floor with barely a whimper. The Pornography Victims' Compensation Act of 1991 (S.1521), was first introduced back in July by Sen. Mitch McConnell (R-KY), a man fast making a place for himself at the right hand of Sen. Jesse Helms (R-NC).

Salted with references to hard-core porn, child porn and sexual abuse, the bill would allow the victims of sexually related crimes to sue the authors, producers and distributors of any work— from hard-core books to *Playboy* to rap records — deemed to have "caused" an offender's actions.

It bears pointing out that the Judiciary Committee co-sponsors of the bill include Sens. Orrin Hatch (R-UT), Arlen Specter (R-PA) and Strom Thurmond (R-SC), those noted feminists of Clarence Thomas/Anita Hill fame. And that—the views of President Reagan's Meese commission on pornography notwithstanding—there has never been any demonstrated causal link between pornography and sex crimes.

There is, however, a clear link between S.1521 and the broader pro-censorship movement of the past 10 years. Starting with the Parents Music Resource Center (PMRC), which launched its drive against the barbaric hordes of rappers and metal bands nearly a decade ago, the modern censors have understood that the best way to kill expression in the marketplace is to threaten the pocketbooks of people who disseminate it.

The PMRC's organizers are for "parental information" (i.e., warning labels), not censorship. Just ask them. Of course who can help it if certain kinds of artists—principally rap and metal musicians—are singled out for labeling? Or if several major record chains decline to carry labeled records at all? Or if record companies start forming their own in-house Hays Offices to review and revise the content of records prior to release?

Any censorial effort worth its salt starts with the kind of expression even civil libertarians have trouble defending, be it 2 Live Crew or hard-core pornographers. There used to be a vocal contingent of First Amendment absolutists to raise a flag against those tactics, but their numbers have been compromised in recent years by linguistic and feminist reactionaries who equate image and expression with overt acts of violence. The essential position of Catharine McKinnon and Andrea Dworkin, authors of the early-'80s porn ordinance in Minneapolis, is not that pornography incites violence, but that (like heterosexual intercourse, as per Dworkin) it *is* violence—a civil-rights violation, not a free-speech issue.

Would-be progressives embracing ends-over-means distinctions like these are loading a very big gun that can quite easily be taken from them and pointed at them. This applies not only to the First Amendment, but to civil liberties in general. Consider the little-noted 1990 decision, *Michigan vs. Sitz*. The suit, pushed by Mothers Against Drunk Driving, concerned the legality of random drunk-driving checkpoints. The checkpoints were upheld—and, as a result, the Supreme Court ruled for the first time in American history that police don't need probable cause based on your own suspicious behavior to stop you, detain you, search you.

Look at S.1521, and then at the current Supreme Court. A piece of legislation so baldly designed to chill expression of any kind, even hard-core porn, would have been unthinkable a few years ago—if only because the courts would have struck it down before the ink on the resolution dried. But the Rehnquist Court would not only affirm the Pornography Victims' Compensation Act; given the chance, it would extend it.

Is this paranoid reasoning? On the so-called left we have already heard feminist judicial theorists argue that porn is a civil-rights issue with no worthy connection to speech rights. Is it hard to imagine new constructions of "pornography" and "obscenity" that include any expression thought to sully decent civic discourse and unduly excite the emotions? According to Dave Marsh of the censorship watchdog *Rock & Roll Confidential*, there is currently a bill in the Washington state legislature to extend the definition of obscenity to include images of violence. Is "obscene" political speech out of the question?

It's a difference in application, not principle, to extend the spirit of S.1521 from the pornographer to the newspaper that publishes political criticism which might inspire someone to throw a rock or a punch. And it's sheer naiveté to suppose no one in power will think of that. S.1521 is a good start down the road of suppression. **—Steve Perry**

(A version of this story originally appeared in City Pages, *a Minneapolis weekly. It was distributed by Alter-Net.)*

III. Press and Media

Ben Bagdikian quotes from a *New York Times* article, "There is little mystery about what caused the economic problems. The country is suffering a hangover from the mergers, rampant speculation, overbuilding, heavy borrowing and irresponsible government fiscal policy in the 1980s." He then asks simply, "If it's so unmysterious now, where was our news establishment at the time?" Also in this section, Project Censored's annual listing of neglected or suppressed news stories raises questions about the thoroughness and interests of the U.S. mainstream media.

"The press has a preferred position in our constitutional scheme not to enable it to make money, not to set newsmen apart as a favored class, but to bring fulfillment to the public's right to know." — Justice William O. Douglas

"A free press can of course be good or bad, but most certainly without freedom it will never be anything but bad." — Albert Camus

"If the press is not free, if speech is not independent and untrammeled, if the mind is shackled or made impotent through fear, it makes no difference under what form of government you live, you are a subject and not a citizen." — Sen. William E. Borah

"What is not reported may not be lost forever, but it may be lost at a time when it is most needed." — Ben Bagdikian

Journalism of Joy

by Ben H. Bagdikian

In a roundup of the 1991 recession, an intriguing article in the *New York Times* contained this paragraph: "There is little mystery about what caused the economic problems. The country is suffering a hangover from the mergers, rampant speculation, overbuilding, heavy borrowing and irresponsible government fiscal policy in the 1980s."

It's true. There is little mystery about how the 1980s caused our economic (and social) problems. But if you watched television and read the daily papers during that era, you did not receive a picture of the accumulating wreckage produced by Reaganism. You were fed a steady diet of positive news about the "miracle" of the 1980s, the brilliant achievements of the "Reagan Revolution."

If it's all so unmysterious now, where was our news establishment at the time? Did it sell out?

In a word, yes. And it's clear why it did. The great majority of big media owners have always been happier with conservative Republicans, but in the 1980s they had reason to be ecstatic: as they were dispensing their relentlessly positive news about Reaganism, they were being allowed by the government to create giant, monopolistic media empires.

During the 1980s, for example, the three big news networks were taken over by corporations that might have been deemed unqualified under earlier standards set by the Federal Communications Commission. ABC went to Capital Cities, a large newspaper chain whose acquisition increased cross-media domination. NBC was taken over by General Electric, which not only has a major stake in the news as a leading defense contractor and maker of nuclear reactors but has a remarkable history of convictions for fraud and antitrust violations. And a big real-estate operator, Laurence Tisch, took over CBS and decimated what used to be the best news and documentary operation in the United States.

The FCC also relieved broadcasters of traditional requirements for public service, made it almost impossible for citizen groups to challenge renewal of station licenses, and lifted limits on the number of stations that a single corporation can acquire.

The owners of the daily print press got their share of special government treatment too. The daily-news business was already controlled by monopolies in 98 percent of U.S. cities, but in the 1980s the administration further sedated the antitrust laws to permit the biggest newspaper chains to sweep up these local monopolies. In addition, the National Labor Relations Board became stacked with pro-management members, and the media giants went on a ten-year spree of union busting.

Like all of big business, the broadcasters and print publishers benefited from Reagan's shift of corporate taxes onto the middle class and poor, but Americans did not see much coverage of that on television or in the printed news. Ditto with unemployment. To this day, joblessness continues to be reported as though it were a mysterious plague falling unbidden from heaven rather than a natural result of the speculative corporate debt, financial manipulations that rewarded big investors but weakened the products, and fabulous rake-offs by the merger artists of the 1980s.

When, for example, Time, Inc., and Warner Communications were permitted to merge into the world's largest media firm, the descriptions in the news were like those of all big mergers. It was an exciting battle between empire builders; it would produce more efficiency and creative "synergy." As in other cases, when citing "winners" and "losers" in the takeover battles, the news mentioned only the Wall Street adventurers, not the workers and consumers. Only in 1990 did we learn that one of the merger operators who manipulated the Time-Warner deal, Steven Ross, received an annual compensation of seventy-eight million dollars. The next year he laid off six hundred Time, Inc., employees.

It is clear why owners were happy to delude themselves and the public about Reaganism. But what about the 100,000 print and broadcast journalists who did the actual reporting and editing? Did they, too, sell out the American public?

Unlike their bosses, the majority of working journalists certainly did not acquire more money or power during the 1980s. Like the rest of the middle class, they experienced a decline in real purchasing power.

Journalists as a class are hardly exempt from the sins of vanity, sloth, or greed, but this does not explain the misrepresentation of reality that they helped create. For one thing, during the 1980s, local print and broadcast news outlets periodically produced serious stories about the growing economic and social problems in their own communities. The same was true from time to time at the national level. Though major network documentaries practically disappeared, an occasional mini-documentary produced powerful evidence of the social dislocations caused by Washington policies; daily newspapers occasionally reported the underside of the 1980s, as well.

But for every story of that kind there were dozens of the cheerleading variety, which quickly wiped out the impact of the critical stories. Isolated reports seldom frame the citizen's view of the world; rather, news items that are treated briefly and not pursued soon become forgotten bits of flotsam and jetsam in the great tides of information that hourly and daily inundate the public. It is the *pattern* of coverage that creates the dominant impression.

Nevertheless, even the occasional bits of realistic news were enough to bring White House complaints to media owners and executives. Any negative story was in danger of official condemnation. Meanwhile, the president's spin doctors were orchestrating daily photo ops and sound bites, which were meant to brush aside any notion that all was not well at 1600 Pennsylvania Avenue or in the country.

Media owners and managers openly spread the idea in U.S.

newsrooms that the news needed to be upbeat. Allen Neuharth, then chief of Gannett, the country's largest newspaper chain, announced that it was time for reporters to practice what he called the "journalism of hope."

Soon, the normal restraint exercised by most media owners over inserting corporate propaganda into the news crumbled. For twenty years, neoconservative intellectuals had been hammering U.S. journalists as liberal ideologues who tilted the news against business and conservatives, often against the reporters' own bosses. It was an absurd claim, given the similarity of voting patterns between journalists and all professionals with college educations in the liberal arts. Even so, the campaign bore spectacular fruit. There has always been pressure in newsrooms to "prove you are not being unfair to conservatives." In the 1980s, it simply reached new levels of mandated blindness.

Systematically, David Gergen and other White House "communications" operatives complained to news executives that stories exposing gross consequences of Reagan policies—growing hunger, unemployment, poverty—were "unfair" and "unbalanced," invoking the magic words of the twenty-year campaign against independent journalism. These complaints found sympathetic ears among owners and top editors.

If, in the field, a correspondent showed the White House to be lying, as did the *New York Times*' Ray Bonner in El Salvador, that reporter was pulled back in favor of more congenial correspondents. Eventually, this process led to reporters such as Shirley Christian covering the area. Her stories, it would be fair to say, seemed closer to those that people like Elliott Abrams and Oliver North would favor. It is no surprise that the Iran-contra operation was disclosed by an obscure magazine in Beirut and not by any of the three thousand U.S. correspondents in Washington.

When reporters tried to penetrate the propaganda barricade at the White House, their own managements blocked their efforts. One example involved coverage of the president himself. The White House wanted to project an image of the titular leader of the "Reagan Revolution" as a shrewdly insightful, compelling visionary of policy, a natural genius in command of his administration.

The truth was that, left on his own with reporters, Reagan would have revealed himself to be one of the most ignorant men ever elected president, beating out even Calvin Coolidge, whose picture Reagan proudly remounted in the White House. He was subject to alarming fantasies about himself, slept through crucial meetings, and, even when awake, was easily confused by his own three-by-five cue cards.

What Reagan was really good at was B-movie acting—the cocky toss of the head, the gee-whiz smile of the guy next door, and the John Wayne posture on horseback. So the White House media staff came up with the ideal strategy: no words, just pictures, pictures, pictures. As reported by journalist Mark Hertsgaard, the president's media managers ordered Washington news bureaus to stop sending reporters to cover daily events like visits by foreign leaders. Only TV cameras and still photographers would be permitted. The reporters rebelled, but their home offices ordered them to obey. The result was the constant countrywide repetition on TV and front pages of the image of a masterful policy chief.

The owners' abandonment of their reporters gave White House propaganda a free ticket into the nation's news. During his administration, the media regularly referred to Reagan as the most popular president in the history of U.S. public-opinion polling, even though basic Gallup survey data showed he was not. Franklin Roosevelt, Eisenhower, Kennedy, and Johnson had higher peaks; all except Johnson had higher averages. But the White House's spin doctors got away with their own version.

The eagerness of media owners to accept the propaganda is what did the trick. And the false image of the most popular president in history intimidated his opponents. After Reagan left office, Michael Deaver, coordinator of White House image making, admitted that "Reagan enjoyed the most generous treatment by the press of any president in the postwar era."

The mechanism by which owners control the news succeeds because it is invisible to the public. All owners carefully select their top editor or producer with their corporate needs in mind. In turn, this news executive assigns reporters and camerapeople and decides whether the stories and footage that come back will be used or thrown out, whether they will lead the news report emphatically or be relegated to brevity and obscurity, whether they will be pursued as a theme in future stories or dropped at once. No owner hires a top news executive who is expected to spoil the owner's breakfast too often, nor keeps one who does.

Top editors have always been meticulously screened to make sure that they will not be inclined to offend corporate desires. But during the 1980s, a new twist was added: top editors were made part of the business-management team, responsible for keeping up ad linage and often sent to business schools for special training to make them think more like corporate executives.

To intensify corporate control over top editors, most newspapers now grant annual bonuses and stock options for those who remain in the good graces of the business side. One example, though more grandiose than for most newspapers, involves the managing editors of Time, Inc.'s, publications. They receive about $250,000 in annual salary, plus bonuses of from 50 to 75 percent of this figure—all at the discretion of corporate bosses. In addition, many *Time* editors have options letting them buy stock that in the past has sold for as low as $13 a share and in recent years has sold for as high as $182. They, like many newspaper editors, can, if they continue to please the corporation, retire as millionaires. It is not surprising that these editors start thinking more like stockbrokers and less like journalists.

Owners and media companies vary in the latitude they permit editors and news staffs. But even firms with the best journalistic reputations will eject esteemed editors and producers if they do not sufficiently conform to corporate wishes. Gene Roberts is probably the most respected news editor of this generation. More than anyone else, he personally fashioned and operated the strategy that converted the old *Philadelphia Inquirer* from a national joke to one of the most respected (and prosperous) newspapers in the country. The result was a daily that swept the field in its city and region. Then, last year, Roberts unexpectedly "resigned." As with most such disappearances, the victim said little in public to condemn his old paper and bosses, but his closest associates made it plain that the reason for his departure was his refusal to accept new conditions laid down by the parent firm, Knight-Ridder. The same thing happened to Bill Kovach, the editor who reversed the downward slide of the *Atlanta Journal & Constitution* and re-established it as a respectable force in its area. He had reported important news that too often embarrassed powerful friends of the owners.

Editors learn from these emblematic events. The result is deep and widespread self-censorship from the top down in U.S. journalism. The internalized censorship can continue for years or

DataCenter   464 19th Street, Oakland, California 94612 (415) 835-4692

decades after a single, dramatic demonstration by an owner shows that serious punishment will follow if independent news judgments offend that owner's politics or friends.

The same conditioning and self-censorship occur even more readily among reporters. Like their editors, reporters do not need constant reminders of the penalty for defying censorship imposed from the top. In 1982, a time when such stories, if reported nationally, might have prevented the current banking disasters, Earl Golz, a reporter with thirteen years of experience at the *Dallas Morning News*, wrote that federal bank examiners were alarmed about a local bank with unannounced bad loans. After the bank chairman told the paper's owners that Golz's report was a lie, Golz was fired, as was the editor who had approved the story. The bank failed two weeks later, and the examiners forced the dismissal of the chairman who had indignantly denied everything. But neither the reporter nor his editor was rehired. For a long time thereafter, no reporter or editor needed to be told that stories that anger influential bankers may end your career.

Even the most courageous reporter stops wasting time on stories that won't get on the air or into the paper. Self-censorship becomes epidemic. But it is an invisible epidemic, and all the harder to counter because the public never finds out about it.

Most censorship remains invisible for an ironic reason. Journalistic ethics among working reporters have risen enough to make it embarrassing if the censoring hand of the corporation leaves telltale fingerprints on the news. A frank statement by an editor to a reporter that a story was killed for corporate reasons could end up in one of the country's journalism reviews, or even at another news outlet. For example, when Golz and his editor were fired because of the Dallas bank affair, the *Wall Street Journal* carried the whole embarrassing story.

Owners, like their journalists, have egos. And they prefer to avoid negative publicity that could also affect favorability of the medium for advertising. So most owners have learned not to post embarrassing memoranda. Except for at a few crude operations, editors no longer tell reporters, "The boss wants no more stories like this." Instead, reporters are given professionally acceptable reasons. These include decisions that could be legitimate editing judgments, like "No one's interested in that" or "We did that once." When the real reason involves orders from above or corporate anger at the truth, it is never stated.

Lawrence Grossman, former head of NBC News, revealed recently that, following the stock-market crash in 1987, Jack Welch, CEO of NBC's owner, General Electric, called to say that he did not want the network's newscasts to use language that might depress GE stock. Grossman says he did not tell his staff about the call. He has not disclosed whether the private pressure from the top affected his decisions over what to allow on the news.

There is another management practice that may deeply diminish good journalism for a long time. More than ever before, major news corporations are conducting systematic screenings of new reporters to keep out journalists who might not readily comply with corporate wishes or who might join newsroom unions. Some major news companies, including the nation's second-largest newspaper chain, Knight-Ridder, do the screening through mandatory, lengthy psychological questionnaires of all potential new reporters. Others, including some papers in the largest newspaper chain, Gannett, order editors to be deliberately blunt in interviews so that the applicants know the company wants only "team players" who will not rock the boat and are not in favor of unions. Hiring reporters who are not inclined

to question authority is one way to guarantee bad journalism.

While there is widespread cynicism about such procedures, they seem to have had real consequences. Ben Bradlee, former editor of the *Washington Post,* says that, today, "reporters are more conservative than the previous generation." Older correspondents in the gulf war, for instance, were appalled by the number of younger war correspondents who reported transparent military propaganda as if it were fact.

It is not simple to change trends like these. Strictly for profit reasons, the news monopolies tend to hew closely to overwhelming public sentiment. Consequently, it will take a real alteration of the country's political and social atmosphere to force the media to work harder to serve the public more and its owners' favorite political and economic causes less.

But viewers and readers are not powerless. Protests to the media can produce some change. Clear and individually composed letters and phone calls seldom fail to make an internal impact, even if news organizations pretend they do not. Without such audience response, complaints from the organized right-wing and the powerful will dominate pressure on the news. In the end, the media needs the audience to stay in business.

Within journalism, professional news staffs in corporate media should be permitted to elect their own top editor and have a substantial voice in long-range journalistic policies, as is done at some of the most prestigious newspapers in Europe. This would decrease the invisible corporate influence over the news. But such a reform will not come until media owners recognize that the public is losing confidence in an increasingly monopolistic and arrogant industry.

During the degradations of the 1980s, government lying was too willingly supported by the media; high crimes and misdemeanors by the president of the United States became an accepted public boast; looting the public treasury and cheating the citizens were treated by most editors as necessary for liberation of the marketplace. For almost ten years, the media remained silent on the obvious—that Reaganite politics were taking a frightful toll in human suffering and crippling the economy.

The mass media gave the country a dismal demonstration of what George Orwell saw forty years ago: ". . . political chaos is connected with the decay of language. . . . Political language is designed to make lies sound truthful and murder respectable, and to give an appearance of solidity to pure wind."

From that kind of public morality neither the country nor journalism will soon recover.

> ## *When the* market crashed in 1987, the head of GE told NBC News to avoid language that might harm its owner's stock.
>
> ● ● ●

Ben H. Bagdikian is the author of The Media Monopoly *and a former assistant managing editor of the* Washington Post.

THE PRESS PASSES

*The Gulf War and the middle-class recession lead Project Censored's
annual list of what you didn't read enough about in 1991*

By Chris Norris and Peter Tira

AFTER 16 YEARS of policing media self-censorship, Carl Jensen says this year he's finally found a smoking gun. Jensen, a Sonoma State University communications professor, assembles a nationwide panel of media experts each year to identify the 10 most important underreported stories of the previous 12 months.

Never before has Project Censored's list contained such a clear-cut, documented example of media self-censorship as this year's first-place story: the refusal by CBS and NBC to air uncensored footage from Iraq at the height of the allied air attack.

"This was incredible," Jensen said in a phone interview from his home in Cotati. "Here was unique footage of what was happening in Iraq, and the two top news organizations in the country spiked the story."

Ben Bagdikian, a Project Censored judge and professor emeritus at the UC Berkeley Graduate School of Journalism, commented, "Despite all of the misleading information and media manipulation that the Pentagon and the White House practiced on the mainstream media at the outset, the mainstream media still do not seem to have the will to practice independent journalism.

"Once the war started," Bagdikian continued, "with very few exceptions, the mainstream media became hysterical with jingoism that went far beyond the normal concern the public had for the welfare of the American troops."

Following the Gulf War in Project Censored's rankings was the media's piecemeal coverage of America's recession-racked economy. Project Censored's list also includes a hearty dose of political and governmental corruption and white-collar crime — subjects that score perennial high marks.

This year, Jensen and a team of Sonoma State students sifted through a record 700 entries — weighing the importance of the subject, the number of people affected, and the amount of coverage received — before paring the field to 25 finalists and forwarding them to the judges.

In recent years, Project Censored itself has attracted more media attention, with its findings reported regularly in *Editor and Publisher* and, last year, in a PBS documentary by Bill Moyers. Wider publicity helps promote the project's goals, which Jensen describes as encouraging journalists to cover important but neglected issues and encouraging the public to seek alternative sources of news.

1. CBS and NBC's spiking of footage showing Gulf War carnage (San Francisco Bay Guardian; Pacific News Service)

As it was in 1990, Project Censored's most underreported story of the year concerns the Gulf conflict.

At the height of the air war against Iraq, NBC and CBS executives refused to air some of the most compelling footage of the entire Gulf crisis. Videotapes by Emmy award–winning producers Maryanne Deleo and Jon Alpert showed images of Iraq's devastated countryside and anguished families that powerfully contradicted administration claims of minimal damage to civilians. And, according to *NBC Nightly News* Executive Producer Steven Friedman, "It was stuff on the ground that nobody else had."

Yet despite unanimous approval of the piece by NBC news executives, NBC President Michael Gartner killed it. At CBS, the night before the videotape was to air on *CBS Evening News*, Executive Producer Tom Bettag — who had approved the footage for the news segment — was fired, and the piece was spiked by CBS as well.

Dennis Bernstein and Sasha Futran reported this story in articles that appeared in the San Francisco Bay Guardian and were distributed by Pacific News Service.

2. Operation censorship (*Editor & Publisher;* San Francisco Bay Guardian; *The Progressive Review*)

Military restrictions on the news media, coupled with the mainstream press's own jingoism, produced a distorted and incomplete picture of the Persian Gulf War.

Editor & Publisher magazine detailed the military's hostility toward the press in a July 13, 1991, article.

The magazine quoted a *Newsweek* contributing writer, retired Army Col. David Hackworth, saying, "I had more guns pointed at me by Americans or Saudis who were into controlling the press than in all my years of actual combat."

And only a few stories went beyond the mainstream media's patriotic reports.

Bay Guardian contributing writer Jonathan Franklin, for example, had to pose as a mortician inside the Desert Storm mortuary at Dover Air Force Base in Delaware to get some kind of estimate of battlefield casualties. He wrote: "Even in the Dover mortuary, where the carnage is obvious, military morticians labor to promote the illusion of a bloodless war." He also learned that many battlefield casualties were being disguised as "training accidents."

Even after the war and the lifting of press restrictions, important facts and stories — like the 35 "friendly fire" casualties and the inaccuracy of U.S. "smart" bombs — were played down or not reported.

3. Voodoo economics: The complete story (Philadelphia Inquirer, Knight-Ridder Newspapers; USA Today)

DataCenter   464 19th Street, Oakland, California 94612 (415) 835-4692

Individuals earning more than $1 million a year saw salary increases of 2,184 percent in the 1980s. Meanwhile, the total increase in salaries for people earning between $20,000 and $50,000 amounted to 44 percent, or 4 percent a year.

Those startling facts were among those uncovered by the Philadelphia Inquirer's Pulitzer Prize–winning investigative team of Donald Barlett and James Steele. The reporters spent two years crisscrossing the country researching their five-part series, "America: What went wrong?"

Barlett said the series looked at employment, the changing nature of jobs, corporate taxes, and lobbying.

Although many media outlets have reported some current economic facts, Barlett and Steele were among the few to show a comprehensive picture of the politics, tax policies, and corporate decisions that led to the current crisis — and to identify the Reagan and Bush administrations as the source of many of these policies.

They wrote: "Those in Washington who write the complex tangle of rules by which the economy operates have, over the last 20 years, rigged the game — by design and default — to favor the privileged, the powerful and the influential. At the expense of everyone else."

Similarly, the news media have mostly failed to explain the significance of the federal budget deficit. In a notable exception, USA Today recently explained that during 1992 the interest alone on the federal debt will be the nation's single largest expenditure.

4. The $250 billion political cover-up (*Frontline;* the Center for Investigative Reporting)

While most Americans recognize the savings-and-loan scandal as one of the most costly governmental blunders ever, few know how much the administration's attempts to cover it up added to the price tag. Had the problem been honestly addressed before the 1988 presidential elections, Federal Home Loan Bank Board officials estimate, the government could have saved the country $250 billion. Instead, staff members were told to play down the problem so it wouldn't hurt Bush's candidacy.

According to the executive assistant of one bank board member, Federal Deposit Insurance Corporation head William Seidman said Deputy Undersecretary for Finance George Gould had given orders to "lie" about "or misstate" the enormity of the problem. Later, Seidman denied he remembered any such conversation. *Frontline's* televised documentary on the cover-up aired Oct. 22, 1991, three years after George Bush's lips promised to save the taxpayers money.

5. Operation Ill Wind — DOD's quiet scandal (*Common Cause Magazine; St. Louis Journalism Review*)

In his *Common Cause Magazine* article "The Devil and Mr. Jones," John Hanrahan described the scandal-plagued history of the Northrop Corp. under its then-chief executive officer Thomas Jones. At the time of the article, Hanrahan reported that the huge defense-contracting firm was being investigated by up to seven grand juries for allegations of bribery, deliberate overcharging, and falsifying test results.

Philip Dunn, in the *St. Louis Journalism Review,* revealed that Northrop's operation, and the investigations of it, were not unusual.

He reported that, in 1980, the U.S. Department of Justice launched a major investigation of fraud and bribery in the defense-contracting industry and the roles played by former Department of Defense staffers. The public may never learn the results of "Operation Ill Wind," however. Search warrants, affidavits, and transcripts of wiretapped conversations acquired in the course of the DOD investigation have been sealed by court order.

6. No Iraqi threat to Saudi Arabia at start of Gulf War (In These Times [Madison, Wis.]; St. Petersburg [Fla.] Times)

As the president was rallying support for military action by insisting that an Iraqi invasion of Saudi Arabia was imminent, an article in the St. Petersburg Times described satellite photographs that showed otherwise.

The Defense Department was reporting as many as 250,000 Iraqi troops and 1,500 tanks in Kuwait near the Saudi border, but the photos — taken by a Soviet satellite over Kuwait

— showed no signs of a troop buildup. Reporter Jean Heller quoted two satellite-image specialists who said they found it "really hard to believe" they could miss such massive troop deployment, even if the troops were well camouflaged or widely dispersed. This story raised important questions about the need for U.S. military action in the Gulf — but both the Associated Press and the Scripps-Howard news service refused to carry it.

7. 'FOIA' = oxymoron (*Common Cause Magazine*)

"In 1987 the Reagan administration came to Congress with an urgent problem," wrote Peter Montgomery and Peter Overby in the July/August 1991 issue of *Common Cause Magazine.* "Japanese scientists were exploiting the Freedom of Information Act to snare American space shuttle technology worth millions of dollars. Congress could — must — stop them by exempting the National Aeronautics and Space Administration (NASA) from the information-access law."

The truth is that Japan never used the law to get shuttle information, Montgomery and Overby reported. The administration made up the story to keep American reporters and the public from learning the truth about the space shuttle Challenger explosion.

That particular effort was unsuccessful, but Montgomery and Overby cited it as only one example of the Reagan and Bush administrations' hostility to the public's right to know. This hostility, combined with help from the courts, has led to the sharp erosion of the federal Freedom of Information Act during the past 10 years.

The FOIA, enacted in 1966, aims to limit government secrecy by allowing the public to see any official document unless the government can prove the information is covered by one of nine specific exemptions.

8. Corporate America's anti-environment 'crisis management' (*E Magazine; Greenpeace News*)

Although stories of tree-spiking, fishing-net sabotage, and other tactics used by environmental activists have been common enough this year, little media attention has been given to corporations' sabotage of the environmental movement. In 1991, stories in *E Magazine* and *Greenpeace News* outlined some of these efforts, including multimillion-dollar suits against environmentalists, the infiltration of environmentalist groups, and Clorox Corp.'s "Crisis Management Plan" — an anti-environmentalist guide that was leaked to Greenpeace.

Prepared by Ketchum Communications, Clorox's plan calls for labeling Greenpeace as violent "eco-terrorists," suing newspaper columnists who recommend using non-toxic household cleaners and bleaches, and sponsoring "independent" scientists to discredit research findings against Clorox. The plan exemplifies the aggressive public-relations campaigns corporations use against those who challenge their actions.

9. The Inslaw software theft: conspiracy at the Justice Department (In These Times [Madison, Wis.]; Random Lengths [San Pedro, Calif.])

Federal bankruptcy judge George Bason ruled Sept. 28, 1987, that the Justice Department had robbed the Inslaw software company of its computer program, Promis. The software enables a bureaucracy to track cases — and the people involved in them — through the court system.

Bason awarded the Washington, D.C.–based corporation $8 million. Barely one month later, Bason was denied re-appointment to the bench — a highly unusual move. His successor, S. Martin Teel, was one of the attorneys who unsuccessfully represented the Justice Department in the Inslaw case.

Bason's ruling was eventually overturned in the ongoing legal battle between the Inslaw Corp. and its onetime best customer, the Justice Department. The corporation has charged that the department not only stole its software but also conspired to send Inslaw into bankruptcy and then covered up the whole affair.

The Inslaw case was reported in a number of publications, including the Bay Guardian, the Village Voice, and some daily papers. Articles in In These Times and Random Lengths reported new allegations by Inslaw that the Reagan Justice Department turned the stolen software over to businessman, arms dealer, and longtime Reagan friend Earl Brian as a kickback for Brian's help in the "October Surprise" deal.

10. The Bush family and its conflicts of interest (San Francisco Examiner, Santa Rosa Press Democrat, *Spin*, and the Texas Observer [Austin])

While the media crowed over an unauthorized biography of Nancy Reagan, the current president's relatives got considerably less attention — despite their notable business entanglements.

George's brother Prescott, for example, was paid $200,000 for financial advice by Munenobu Shoji, a Japanese real estate president, and another firm run by a former Japanese crime boss. According to Shoji, the crime boss observed that the president's brother "knows many influential people."

George's son Neil, as director of Silverado Savings and Loan, delayed the S&L's closing until after Election Day, eventually costing taxpayers $1 billion. Later, as director of a cable sports network, Neil promised to "absolutely" continue to communicate with the president in his attempts to fight re-regulation of the cable industry.

Jeb Bush, another son of George's, identified a valuable contributor to his family: Miami builder Leonel Martinez, who was also a supporter of both Reagan and the Contras, and who is currently serving 23 years for importing more than 3-1/2 tons of cocaine and 75 tons of marijuana into the United States.

Finally, George Bush Jr., in his capacity as "consultant" to Harken Energy Corp., managed to get the nearly unknown company a lucrative contract with the Saudia Arabian island kingdom of Bahrain. Then, weeks before Iraq invaded Kuwait, George sold more than 200,000 shares of Harken stock and failed to report the "insider" sale until eight months after the federal deadline for such a declaration. ∎

The 15 runners-up

➤ FinCEN: How the Treasury Department's database threatens privacy and property (*Money Laundering Alert*, April 1991; *Washington Report*, September 1991)

➤ Environmental protection denied to racial minorities (*The Workbook*, Fall 1991)

➤ Congress' negligence in oversight duties (*Common Cause*, July/August 1991)

➤ New "intelligence law" makes congressional oversight meaningless (*Congressional Quarterly Weekly Report*, Aug. 3, 1991; Wall Street Journal, Aug. 16, 1991; Los Angeles Times, Aug. 1, 1991)

➤ Judge thwarts compensation for Agent Orange vets (*Multinational Monitor*, July/August, 1991)

➤ Federal seizure laws make winning drug booty a police priority (Texas Observer, Oct. 18, 1991; Los Angeles Times, April 16, 1991)

➤ U.S. ignores Syrian offers to free hostages (San Francisco Examiner, July 21, 1991; *Extra!*, September/October 1991)

➤ The suspicious death of journalist Daniel Casolaro (Village Voice, Oct. 15, 1991; San Francisco Bay Guardian, Aug. 18, 1991; In These Times, Sept. 4-10, 1991)

➤ The canned hunt: Killing captive animals for sport and profit (*Animals' Agenda*, September 1991)

➤ The EPA failure to enforce environmental laws (Los Angeles Times, July 7, 1991)

➤ Toxic PCB contamination above the Arctic Circle (This World, San Francisco Chronicle, Aug. 11, 1991, from the Los Angeles Times.)

➤ *People Magazine*'s censorship of a report from inside Bohemian Grove (*Extra!*, November/December 1991)

➤ The media's inattention to the "October Surprise" story (*Columbia Journalism Review*, September/October 1991)

➤ Dan Quayle's lobbying for big business in Washington (*Amicus Journal*, Summer 1991; *The Nation*, July 29, 1991)

➤ Risks of fluoridation raised by new public health report (*U.S. Department of Health and Human Services*, February 1991)

DataCenter   464 19th Street, Oakland, California 94612 (415) 835-4692

The Media's War

In the wake of protests over press restrictions during the Gulf War, the Pentagon and major media representatives last year began negotiations on guidelines for coverage of future conflicts. A draft agreement, reached in mid-March, is being hailed as a step forward in the relationship between the military and the media. However, it cannot guarantee that the press will be able to provide comprehensive, objective reporting of future wars.

Although the agreement is based on the concept of open and independent coverage, it is vague and provides no way for the media to compel the Pentagon to abide by its provisions. *Newsday* reporter Patrick Sloyan said in an interview that the document is "total bullshit." Sloyan recently won a Pulitzer Prize, primarily for stories he wrote about the Gulf War *after* the conflict, when he had more access to military personnel and information.

The proposed agreement is supported by Washington bureau chiefs, professional associations like the American Society of Newspaper Editors and high-level executives from electronic and print media.

The document is designed to prevent the Pentagon from controlling the media as it did in the gulf, where journalists were confined to "pools" led by Armed Forces personnel and had limited access to the battlefield. Military officers reviewed pool reports before releasing them and sometimes altered or delayed stories for reasons unrelated to security. America's most-decorated living soldier, retired Army Col. David Hackworth, who covered the conflict for *Newsweek*, called the restrictions a form of "thought control" designed to influence public opinion by providing a "sanitized" and "distorted" picture of the war.

The proposed agreement states that pools should be used only in specific circumstances, such as the opening hours of a conflict; that military and public affairs officers should not interfere with the reporting process; and that the Pentagon will allow news organizations to operate their own communications systems in the field, with limited restrictions.

One serious flaw in the agreement is that no consensus was reached about security reviews. Media negotiators said reviews of news stories prior to release were "unnecessary and unwarranted" in light of the media's excellent record of observing military security without prior review during conflicts such as the Vietnam War. Pentagon personnel insisted that security reviews insure that news material does not violate ground rules that protect military secrecy and U.S. troops. Under the proposed agreement, reporters who violate such ground rules could have their combat credentials suspended and could be expelled from the battle zone.

Another flaw is that the Pentagon has a history of violating agreements about media coverage. Following protests about Defense Department restrictions during the invasions of Grenada and Panama—when journalists were prevented from covering much of the fighting—department officials agreed to implement recommendations regarding wartime reporting. These recommendations, contained in reports written at the department's request, were to insure that future restrictions were based only on considerations of operational security and troop safety. But during Operation Desert Storm, former Pentagon officials and military officers—including several who had helped formulate the recommendations after Grenada and Panama—told the Senate Governmental Affairs Committee that the Gulf War restrictions went beyond what was needed to protect military security.

Despite clear evidence that the Pentagon has not operated in good faith in the past, supporters of the proposed agreement say the document will help the press because it establishes specific principles for the coverage of wars and is backed by an unprecedented coalition of top media executives who could apply political pressure to see that the agreement is kept. But the document contains no ground rules—nor any requirement that the Pentagon consult with journalists before writing such rules.

"What the Pentagon is doing is giving itself a club to use over journalists," says Scripps Howard reporter Joan Lowy, who covered the Gulf War. "They're going to write these ground rules, but we don't know what they are yet. And then if you don't go by their interpretation of the ground rule as they interpret it under security review, they'll kick you out. It's a very effective form of censorship."

During the gulf conflict, Lowy said, the Pentagon interpreted ground rules and guidelines "very broadly, to discourage or outright censor anything that was reflecting negatively on U.S. or allied forces." Two negotiators for the media said in recent interviews that they didn't know what the press would do if the Defense Department violated the proposed agreement. Knight-Ridder Washington bureau chief Clark Hoyt suggested that the agreement might provide the basis for a media lawsuit. When told of Hoyt's suggestion, Franklin Siegel of the Center for Constitutional Rights asked, "Where were they when their case was strong and when it would have made a difference?" Siegel represented *The Nation* and other plaintiffs in a federal lawsuit filed against President Bush and Defense Department personnel in January 1991. The suit maintained that some Gulf War press restrictions were unconstitutional and were based on political, not military, considerations. No major daily newspaper or television news organization joined the suit, which was dismissed in April 1991, after the war had ended.

Negotiator Stanley Cloud, *Time* Washington bureau chief, acknowledged that the media will have to rely on the Pentagon's good faith. In the contest "between the military and the press, one side has weapons and the other doesn't," he said. "In the end, we are forced to abide by their rules even if we don't like it."

The Pentagon's success at managing its wartime image gives the military little incentive to adhere to the proposed agreement. Seventy-nine percent of Americans supported the Gulf War press restrictions, according to a poll taken during the conflict by the Times Mirror Center for the People & the Press.

Jane Kirtley, executive director of the Reporters Committee for Freedom of the Press, said the very existence of the proposed agreement is an admission of how weak the media's position is now. She says endorsing the agreement is "writing your own death warrant."   JACQUELINE E. SHARKEY

Jacqueline E. Sharkey is a journalism professor at the University of Arizona and an investigative reporter. Her book, Under Fire: U.S. Military Restrictions on the Media From Grenada to the Persian Gulf, *is available from the Center for Public Integrity, Washington, D.C.*

Arms and the media: business as usual

The head of the censor rules the heart of the giant military-media complex of corporate America

Martin A Lee

As I watched US television coverage of the Gulf War earlier this year, I was reminded of the scene in the Marx Brothers movie in which a woman who is flirting with Groucho beckons to him, saying, 'Come closer, come closer'. To which Groucho responds 'If I got any closer I'd be behind you'.

Groucho's rejoinder aptly describes the relationship between the US press and the US government throughout the Gulf crisis. The most powerful US news media were solidly behind the war as soon as it began, and their support never wavered.

The failure of the US press to mount any serious opposition to censorship by the Pentagon was largely due to the fact that the news media are sponsored, underwritten and, in some cases, directly owned by military contractors. As a result, news reporting in the USA tends to be slanted to favour the interests of corporate advertisers and owners — and corporate America in general — while discriminating against independent policy critics and viewpoints that forcefully challenge the status quo.

The National Broadcasting Corporation (NBC), one of the three leading US commercial television networks, is owned by General Electric (GE), a major military contractor. As it turns out, GE designed, manufactured or supplied parts or maintenance for nearly every important weapons system employed by the USA during the Gulf War, including the much-praised Patriot and Tomahawk Cruise missiles, the Stealth bomber, the B-52 bomber, the AWACS plane, the Apache and Cobra helicopters and the NAVSTAR spy satellite system.

Few TV viewers in the USA were aware of the inherent conflict of interest whenever NBC correspondents and consultants hailed the performance of US weapons. In nearly every instance, they were extolling equipment made by GE, the corporation that pays their salaries.

A code of ethics set forth by the Chicago-based Society for Professional Journalists, which lays down the professional standards reporters in the USA are expected to uphold, states that journalists should conduct themselves 'in a manner which protects them from conflict of interest, real or apparent'.

Martin A Lee, *co-author of* Unreliable Sources: A Guide to Detecting Bias in News Media, *is publisher of* Extra! *the journal of FAIR (Fairness & Accuracy In Reporting), the New York-based media watch group.*

Yet there are many instances of journalists reporting on subjects that have a direct bearing on the profits of their corporate owners without indicating the relevant financial interests at stake.

GE's ownership of NBC goes a long way towards explaining why NBC executives did not vigorously challenge the restrictive rules imposed by the Pentagon during the war. If NBC had mounted a challenge to the Pentagon, the network would essentially have been pitting itself against the economic life-blood of its parent company, which has secured billions of dollars of Pentagon contracts through non-competitive bids in recent years.

GE and other military contractors also sponsor news programmes on Ted Turner's Cable News Network (CNN), and the two other main US commercial TV networks, Columbia Broadcasting System (CBS) and American Broadcasting Corporation (ABC). With television networks dependent on sponsors for nearly 100% of their revenue, journalists are not encouraged to pursue stories that might reflect adversely on their corporate patrons.

Similar institutional constraints exist in the anaemic public broadcasting system, with companies like GE underwriting news and public affairs shows. The principal news programme on public television, the *MacNeil/Lehrer News Hour,* receives hefty financial backing from AT&T, another military contractor. Moreover, the boards of directors of nearly every large US media corporation include representatives from 'defence' companies, forming a powerful military-industrial-media complex which compromises the integrity of US journalism.

The corporate board of the *New York Times,* for example, boasts such luminaries as former Secretary of State Cyrus Vance, who also sits on the board of General Dynamics, one of the biggest military companies in the USA, and an important media sponsor. CBS board members include Harold Brown, a former Defence Secretary, while another former defence chief, Robert McNamara, holds sway on the corporate board of the Washington Post Company.

During the Gulf War, *Newsweek,* owned by the Washington Post Company, featured a Stealth bomber on its cover with the headline: 'The New Science of WAR'. The sub-head read: 'High-Tech Hardware: How Many Lives Can It Save?' That was the spin — US weapons do not destroy lives; they save them. Ironically, this issue of *Newsweek* was on the news-stands the day US jets bombed a

Baghdad shelter, killing 400 civilians, including many women and children.

Throughout the Gulf War, US television aired photos of bull's-eye bomb attacks against Iraqi targets that seemed to atone for years of waste and corruption on the part of military contractors and Pentagon bureaucrats. A chorus of TV experts praised President Reagan's costly 1980s arms build-up. 'It's gratifying to know the money was well spent,' exclaimed *Dallas Times Herald* editorial writer Lee Cullum, during a guest appearance on the *MacNeil/Lehrer News Hour.*

Few US journalists were impolite enough to mention the Reagan and Bush administrations' role in arming, equipping and financing the USA's erstwhile ally, Saddam Hussein. The news media gave short shrift to key stories about cozy US-Iraq relations before the Gulf crisis, including evidence dug up by congressional probers which indicated that companies, with the approval of the US Commerce Department, had sold bacteria to a major Iraqi military research centre working on germ warfare.

Self-censorship by journalists, who are reluctant to offend sponsors and owners, is prevalent throughout US news media. When the NBC *Today Show,* a popular morning news programme, recently aired a segment on consumer boycotts, there was no reference to the continuing boycott of GE products because of that company's profiteering from nuclear weapons. NBC and other TV networks have refused to air commercials for INFACT, the group leading the GE boycott. When Todd Putnam, editor of *National Boycott News,* urged the *Today Show* to cover the GE boycott, an NBC producer confessed privately, 'Yeah, I'll be looking for a new job on Tuesday.'

Publicly, however, top news executives deny pulling punches to please their corporate patrons. NBC *Nightly News* executive producer Steve Friedman, during a July 1990 appearance on the Financial News Network, insisted that GE's ownership of his network had no impact on news content. Friedman went a step further, claiming that NBC is tougher when it comes to reporting on GE than the other commercial networks. As an example, he cited a recent report on NBC *Nightly News* regarding a US$14 million fine levied by the US government against GE because of its role in the Pentagon procurement scandal. This scandal involved numerous Pentagon contractors who had fleeced US taxpayers by charging inflated rates for items such as hammers (US$500

DataCenter   464 19th Street, Oakland, California 94612 (415) 835-4692

each) and toilet seats (US$1200).

Technically speaking, Friedman was correct. NBC *Nightly News* did announce that the government had fined GE — as did the other networks. But, in each case, the report lasted less than 10 seconds and the networks failed to initiate their own investigation of this scandal.

The policy of ignoring the Pentagon procurement scandal and other matters related to military corruption, except when the government gives the signal, is typically passed off as a business decision by a financially-strapped company, rather than as an instance of self-censorship.

The over-reliance on official sources also had an impact on news coverage. This is not always apparent, especially when reporters appear to be breaking torrid stories about government or military malfeasance. In 1988, for example, the news media began to report on serious health and safety hazards at various nuclear weapons plant factories in the USA. The exposure of down-wind and down-river communities to radioactive pollution spewed by the Hanford nuclear arms facility in Washington, Rocky Flats near Denver, Colorado, Savannah River in South Carolina, and other bomb factories, was suddenly big news.

But it was not a new story: data on health hazards from nuclear weapons plants had long been available to reporters. Had they consulted with scientists associated with environmental and peace groups in and around the communities at risk, rather than relying habitually on federal officials with a pro-nuclear agenda, the story would have come out.

New York Times correspondent Fox Butterfield's front-page declaration 18 years after a 1970 study disclosed alarming levels of plutonium near Rocky Flats was typical. 'Although the study attracted some attention at the time,' said Butterfield, 'only in the last two or three years has public concern about Rocky Flats become widespread in this area as a result of a number of problems.' For years Butterfield and the *Times* had ignored a long record of scientific documentation and public concern that culminated in a series of protest demonstrations in which tens of thousands of people denounced the plant's radioactive releases. Non-violent civil disobedience at Rocky Flats frequently resulted in hundreds of arrests. Yet the headline of Butterfield's article, 'Dispute on Wastes Poses Threat to Weapons Plant'. suggested that the country's newspaper of record was more concerned about the future of the weapons factory than the threat it posed to people's health.

Why the current media concern about the nuclear weapons plant scandal in the late 1980s? And why do news reports continue to highlight problems at the nuke factories?

PALOMO

Largely because they are following the lead of the US Department of Energy (DoE), which has chosen to release such information after years of abuse and cover-up. Acting more like court stenographers than critical, aggressive journalists, US reporters have featured the *mea culpas* of DoE officials without probing the reasons behind their abrupt change of heart. Under the guise of seeking funds to 'clean up' the arms factories, DoE officials are preparing to refurbish and modernise these facilities so that they will be able to produce the next generation of nuclear weapons that are not covered by recent US-Soviet arms treaties.

In the USA, the two biggest sources of environmental pollution are the military and big corporations, among them, notably, GE. According to the US Environmental Protection Agency, GE is responsible for more 'superfund' toxic waste sites around the country than any other company. (Superfund sites are so designated because they are considered to be the worst cases of toxic dumping, and hence are awarded federal funds for clean-up.) Needless to say, NBC has not gone on any crusades lately about ecological despoliation caused by its corporate parent or by GE's principal benefactor, the Pentagon.

A former NBC News employee underscored the dilemma: 'The whole notion of freedom of the press becomes a contradiction when the people who own the media are the same people who need to be reported on. There are political limits, and you have to work within those limits, because ultimately it's unacceptable to stray beyond them.' ∎

The Mysterious Death of Danny Casolaro

David MacMichael

Joseph Daniel Casolaro was one of many freelance investigative reporters stirring the witches' brew of scandal simmering in the nation's capitol. He was also an aspiring novelist, newsletter publisher, and freelance writer for publications running the gamut from the now defunct *Washington Star* to the *National Enquirer*. From a well-to-do family (his father, a doctor, had invested well in northern Virginia real estate), he was 44 years old, divorced, and living alone comfortably on a five-acre estate in Fairfax County, Virginia — home to the CIA.

Casolaro was working on a book aimed at exposing what he called "The Octopus," a group of less than a dozen shadowy figures whose machinations figured heavily, he claimed, in the Inslaw case, Iran-Contra, BCCI, and the October Surprise.

Death Scene, With Instant Embalming

In the first week of August, Casolaro told friends and acquaintances that he was going to West Virginia to meet a source who would provide a key piece of evidence he needed to complete his investigation. He drove to Martinsburg, West Virginia, on Thursday, August 8, and checked into room 517 of the Sheraton Hotel. Two days later, at 12:51 p.m., hotel employees found his naked body in a bathtub full of bloody water. Time of death has been estimated at about 9:00 a.m.[1]

Both arms and wrists had been slashed a total of at least 12 times; one of the cuts went so deep that it severed a tendon.[2] Press accounts differ on minor details of the scene, but there was apparently no evidence of struggle. There was a four-sentence suicide note in the bedroom.

Hotel management called the Martinsburg police who brought along the local coroner, Sandra Brining, a registered nurse. Ms. Brining ruled the death a suicide, took small blood and urine samples, and released the body to the Brown Funeral Home. Without authorization from officials or Casolaro's next of kin, the funeral home embalmed the body as a "courtesy to the family," according to Brining's statement at an August 15 press conference in Martinsburg.

Martinsburg police notified the next of kin, Dr. Anthony Casolaro, also of Fairfax, of his brother's death on Monday, August 12. Casolaro says that police explanations for the delay, like the hasty, unauthorized and illegal embalming, seemed either extraordinarily inefficient or highly suspicious. West Virginia state law requires that next of kin be notified before a body can be embalmed.[3]

Casolaro requested a second examination, which was performed by West Virginia state medical examiner Jack Frost, who stated at the same August 15 press conference that the evidence was "not inconsistent" with suicide. At the same time, he declared that he "could not rule out foul play" and admitted that performing a conclusive autopsy on an embalmed body is almost impossible.[4]

Anthony Casolaro publicly stated his disbelief that his gregarious and high-spirited brother could have committed suicide. Danny was so afraid of blood, he said, that he refused to allow samples to be drawn for medical purposes, and would never have chosen, in any case, to slash his veins a dozen times. Other relatives and friends offered the same assessment: Danny Casolaro was not the suicidal type. Moreover, added a former girlfriend, he hated to be seen in the nude.[5]

Brinings' blood samples showed traces of an anti-depressant drug and the non-prescription painkiller Tylenol 3. Casolaro stated that his brother was not depressed and his medical record showed no prescription for anti-depressants. On the other hand, as Ridgeway and Vaughan reported after examination of Casolaro's medical records and conversations with his personal physician (his brother's professional partner), there was clear evidence that the reporter had been in the earlier stages of multiple sclerosis (MS). He had experienced incidents of loss of vision, a couple of severe falls, numbness in one leg, and persistent headaches. His resistance to blood tests could conceivably be attributed to fear that a diagnosis of MS might be confirmed.

Some press reports hinted at an alcohol problem.[6] Most accounts, however, suggest that he enjoyed the company in bars more than the alcohol; according to friends, he would nurse a few beers all afternoon or take four hours to finish a

---

David MacMichael is a former CIA estimates officer. He is the Washington representative of the Association of National Security Alumni, and editor of its bimonthly newsletter, *Unclassified*.

1. "Source May Have Disappointed Casolaro," *Washington Post*, August 25, 1991, p. A20.

2. David Corn refers to "an X-acto blade…not sold locally." ("End of Story: The Dark World of Danny Casolaro," *Nation*, October 28, 1991, p. 511.) James Ridgeway and Doug Vaughan refer to "a single-edge razor blade — the kind used to scrape windows or slice open packages…" ("The Last Days of Danny Casolaro," *Village Voice*, October 15, 1991, p. 32.) Some accounts mention a broken beer bottle, others a broken motel tumbler.

---

3. Ridgeway and Vaughan, *op. cit.*, p. 38.

4. Author's conversation with freelance reporter Steve Badrich, who attended the press conference.

5. Kim Masters, "The Unlikely Suicide," *Washington Post*, August 31, 1991, p. D1.

6. Robert O'Harrow, Jr. and Gary Lee, "Frequent drinking marked writer Casolaro's final days," *Washington Post*, August 25, 1991, p. A19.

DataCenter   464 19th Street, Oakland, California 94612 (415) 835-4692

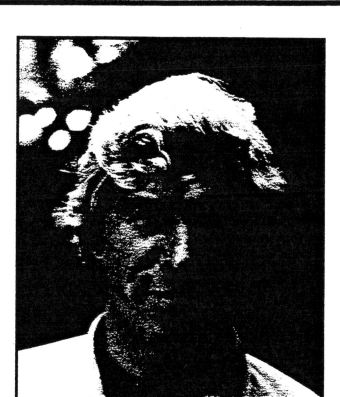

Joseph Daniel Casolaro

business associate, Pat Clawson that he had uncovered a "web of corruption" while investigating the Inslaw case. The "web" involved top-ranking Justice Department officials, New York organized crime figures, and Medellin Cartel drug traffickers, jointly bankrolling "off-the-books" intelligence projects, including Iran-Contra. Their fund-raising schemes, Casolaro said, included: software exports restricted under the Export Control Act, gunrunning, illegal arms sales, bogus mineral and oil investment scams, and drug-smuggling through Canada. Monies generated were so immense, Casolaro said, that government officials regularly skimmed off a hefty percentage. None of this has thus far been documented.

Coincidental Deaths or Parallel Murders?

Casolaro's death was promptly linked to that of other journalists in Guatemala and Chile. On July 29, 1991, Lawrence Ng, a stringer for the London *Financial Times*, was found shot dead in the bathtub of his Guatemala City apartment. Ng had been probing BCCI connections to arms sales in Guatemala.[11] [See Colhoun, p. 45.] Jack Anderson and Dale Van Atta have attempted to link Casolaro's death to that of British military aviation writer Jonathan Moyle — also ruled a suicide when he was found in March 1990 hanging in the closet of his hotel room in Santiago, Chile.[12] Moyle was looking into the activities of Chilean arms dealer Carlos Cardoen, who figures prominently in the Inslaw case.

Anderson and Van Atta take seriously the possibility that both reporters were murdered and that both had been tracking the same "octopus."[13] Both were investigating the activities of Cardoen, a suspected conduit for arms sold to Iraq. According to an affidavit filed in the Inslaw case, Cardoen also played a role in the sale of Inslaw's purloined software to Iraq.[14]

Both Casolaro and Moyle had communicated with Anderson, who believed they were "no further along in the story" than others. "On the surface," Anderson and Van Atta wrote, "neither man had evidence worth killing for."

British journalist David Akerman disagrees, arguing that Moyle had uncovered information on connections between leading British arms makers and Cardoen, who used British licenses to manufacture high-technology weaponry for illegal delivery to Iraq.[15] Because the illegal weapons transfers were generally known among arms dealers, public disclosure would have been sufficiently embarrassing and financially damaging to have placed Moyle's life in jeopardy. There are those who feel just as strongly about the facts surrounding the death of Danny Casolaro.

bottle of wine.[7] Other accounts speculated that his inability to interest publishers in the book he planned to write had made him despondent.[8] He was also alleged to have been worried about his financial situation. He had borrowed heavily to finance his research and publishers' rejections were a blow. In a letter to his agent he referred to his debts: "In September I'll be looking into the face of an oncoming train." Friends, however, dismissed the allegations — debt was Casolaro's usual condition and he was given to overstatement. Said one friend, "Danny would not off himself over money problems."[9] Also, he was negotiating the subdivision of his five acres, a deal that should have netted him several hundred thousand dollars. His employment of a full-time housekeeper suggests that he was not severely strapped.

Casolaro had spoken to family and friends of the danger of his investigations, warning them not to believe it if he died of an "accident." But one of Casolaro's sources claims that despite being cautioned, the reporter was cavalier about taking safety measures.[10]

In April 1991, Casolaro told longtime friend and former

7. Masters, *op. cit.*
8. R. Drummond Ayres, Jr., "As U.S. Battles Computer Company, Writer Takes Vision of Evil to Grave," *New York Times*, September 3, 1991, p. D12.
9. Masters, *op. cit.*
10. Raymond Lavas, one of Casolaro's sources in the California electronics industry; telephone conversation with the author.

11. Rocco Parascandola, "Who killed investigative reporters?" *New York Post*, August 15, 1991, p. 4; Dan Bischoff, "One more dead man," *Village Voice*, August 27, 1991, p. 22.
12. Jack Anderson and Dale Van Atta, "Another casualty in the 'Octopus' case," *Washington Post*, August 28, 1991, p. D16.
13. *Ibid.* Also, ABC-TV, *Nightline*, September 13, 1991.
14. Affidavit of Ari Ben-Menashe, "Inslaw v. United States of America, and the United States Department of Justice, Adversary Proceeding No. 86-0069," United States Bankruptcy Court, Washington, D.C.
15. David Akerman, "The disquieting death of Jonathan Moyle," *Image*, London, July 28, 1991.

The Inslaw Morass

The most politically volatile side of this story is Casolaro's extensive investigation into the Inslaw case. Elliot Richardson is legal counsel to the Washington, D.C.-based computer software company, Inslaw. Widely respected for his ethics and legal expertise, Richardson quit as Nixon's Attorney General in 1973 rather than carry out the order to fire Watergate Special Prosecutor Archibald Cox. In a recent radio interview, Richardson was asked if he believed Casolaro killed himself. He answered:

I don't. I think everything we know makes it much more likely that he was eliminated by a person or persons unknown who feared that he was about to disclose information that would be severely damaging...he told [friends] separately that he had in hand or ready, significant hard evidence pointing to the connections between Inslaw and these other events [Iran-Contra, BCCI, October Surprise]. He said he was going to West Virginia to get additional evidence that would really lock this whole picture into place. Now, that I think is *the* most significant piece of information we have. There's no reason to suppose that he was lying to his friends. Why should he? And there's no reason to suppose that they lied in saying that this is what he told them.[16]

The Inslaw case involves charges that the Justice Department, under Attorney General Edwin Meese, stole the powerful database software PROMIS (Prosecutor's Management Information System) from Inslaw. When a federal bankruptcy court ruled in Inslaw's favor in 1987, presiding Judge George Francis Bason concluded that the Justice Department "took, converted and stole" the software "through trickery, fraud and deceit."[17]

Allegations about the theft of PROMIS have suggested three possible motives: To fund off-the-shelf covert operations; to market a "trojan horse" database to friendly foreign security agencies, which could then be easily monitored by the National Security Agency;[18] and to pay off Reagan Attorney General Edwin Meese's political crony, Dr. Earl Brian. Now president of the floundering United Press International, Earl Brian has longstanding ties to Reagan and served in his cabinet when Reagan was governor of California.

Whatever its motivations, the Justice Department has twice been found guilty of the theft and was ordered to pay Inslaw $6.8 million, plus legal fees. In 1989, the decision was upheld by federal judge William Bryant who said, "the government acted willfully and fraudulently..."[19] Under both Edwin Meese and Richard Thornburgh, the Justice Department stonewalled efforts to investigate, refusing to release documents either to Senator Sam Nunn's Government Affairs Investigations Subcommittee or to Congressman Jack Brooks' House Judiciary Committee.

In June, after eight years of litigation, the Federal Appeals Court of the District of Columbia voided the two previous decisions. October Surprise figure Judge Laurence J. Silberman[20] cast the deciding vote, declaring that the case had been

---

Allegations about the theft of PROMIS have suggested three possible motives: To fund off-the-shelf covert operations; to market a "trojan horse" database to friendly foreign security agencies, and to pay off Reagan Attorney General Edwin Meese's political crony, Dr. Earl Brian.

---

wrongly heard in bankruptcy court in the first place, and must be retried in a federal district court. Inslaw has appealed to the Supreme Court.

The Washington, D.C. bankruptcy court judge who had heard the case and decided in Inslaw's favor was removed from the bench one month after his decision.[21] He was replaced by S. Martin Teel, Jr., one of the Department of Justice lawyers who had unsuccessfully argued the case. According to a writer for *Barron's*, "Even jaded, case-hardened Washington attorneys called the action 'shocking' and 'eerie.'"[22]

October Surprise

October Surprise is the as-yet unproven theory that members of the 1980 Reagan presidential campaign arranged a deal with the government of Iran to continue holding 52 U.S. hostages in Tehran until after the election in order to prevent President Carter from benefiting politically from their release.

The Inslaw case is tied to October Surprise by the sworn affidavit of Michael Riconosciuto, a West Coast computer and weapons technician with self-proclaimed ties to the intelligence community. He testified last March that he had modified the PROMIS software for sale to the Royal Canadian Mounted Police (RCMP) and Canadian Security Intelligence Service (CSIS) at the request of a Justice Department contracting officer named Peter

---

16. Diane Rehm Show, WAMU-FM, Washington, D.C., October 28, 1991.
17. Inslaw v. United States of America, *et al.*, p. 9.
18. Elliot Richardson, "A High-Tech Watergate," *New York Times*, October 21, 1991, p. A17.
19. *Ibid.*

20. Silberman is accused by Abolhassan Bani-Sadr, the first elected president of Iran following the 1979 revolution, and later deposed by Khomeini, of being one of the four Reagan campaign staffers who consummated the October Surprise deal. Christopher Hitchens, "Minority Report," *The Nation*, October 24, 1987, p. 440.
21. Maggie Mahar, "Beneath Contempt; Did the Justice Department Deliberately Bankrupt INSLAW?" *Barron's Business Weekly*, March 21, 1988.
22. *Ibid.*

DataCenter   464 19th Street, Oakland, California 94612 (415) 835-4692

Chilean arms merchant and intelligence asset Carlos Cardoen.
Associated Press

Videnieks and Reagan/Meese crony Earl Brian.[23] In an unsworn statement to Inslaw's president William A. Hamilton, Riconosciuto says he met Brian in 1980 when he helped him deliver $40 million to Tehran to consummate the October Surprise weapons-for-hostages deal.[24]

After Riconosciuto first contacted Inslaw, Casolaro traveled several times to California and Washington in 1990 and 1991 to talk with him. Riconosciuto claims knowledge of many covert activities in the U.S., Latin America, and Australia, and doubtless influenced Casolaro's concept of the Octopus.[25] In his affidavit in the Inslaw case, Riconosciuto declared that Videnieks told him "not to cooperate with an independent investigation...by the Committee on the Judiciary of the U.S. House of Representatives."[26] Riconosciuto also stated that Videnieks threatened him with specific punishments he "could expect to receive from the U.S. Department of Justice..." if he cooperated with that investigation.[27] Within eight days of swearing the affidavit, he was in fact arrested on charges of distributing methamphetamines and has been held without bail in Washington state since March.[28] My appointment to speak with Casolaro upon his return concerned Riconosciuto, in whose wide-ranging, not entirely believable allegations we shared a keen interest.

23. See: Eric Reguly, "Questions grow as 'Big Daddy' watches his empire crumble," *Financial Post* (Toronto), August 19, 1991, pp. 8-11, for background on Brian.

24. Inslaw memorandum to *The Record*, June 28, 1990, "An Assessment of Michael Riconosciuto...," p. 1.

25. Riconosciuto, personal communications with the author.

26. Affidavit of Michael J. Riconosciuto, "Inslaw v. United States of America, and the United States Department of Justice, Adversary Proceeding No. 86-0069," United States Bankruptcy Court, Washington, D.C.

27. *Ibid.*

28. Carlton Smith, "Worldwide conspiracy, or fantasy? Felon's story checks out—in part," *Seattle Times*, August 29, 1991, p. A1.

Videnieks has denied in a sworn affidavit any knowledge of or contact with Riconosciuto. Earl Brian has done the same. Although Videnieks identifies himself as an employee of U.S. Customs in his affidavit, the Customs personnel office has denied any knowledge of him. An independent check with regional Customs officials also produced no evidence of Videnieks. Casolaro, however, told Hamilton that he had contacted Videnieks at Customs shortly before his fatal trip.[29]

Final Rendezvous

What is known about Danny Casolaro's trip to Martinsburg is that he met on Thursday, August 8, at about 5:30 p.m. in the Sheraton bar with a man described by a waitress as possibly Arab or Iranian.[30] This may have been an Egyptian named Hassan Ali Ibrahim Ali. According to documents provided to Casolaro by former Customs informant Bob Bickel, Ali headed an Iraqi front company in the U.S. called Sitico.

According to Ridgeway and Vaughan, Casolaro had shown a photo of Ali to a friend shortly before leaving for Martinsburg. Middle East expert Mary Barrett has asserted that Hassan Ali—known as "Ali Ali"—had close ties to the late Gerald Bull, the American ballistics engineer working on super long-range artillery for Iraq and South Africa.[31] Bull was murdered in Brussels last March, apparently by Israeli agents.[32]

After meeting with Ali, Casolaro waited in the same bar to meet another source, who never arrived. In a conversation with Tom Looney, a fellow hotel guest he met there, Casolaro spoke of the source he was waiting for, explaining that the man had the information needed to solve the Octopus riddle, something which Casolaro described in detail to his skeptical listener. Looney told Ridgeway and Vaughan that he had a hard time believing that just seven or eight men were responsible for 40 years of scandals.

Other Figures from the Shadows

On the following day, Friday, August 9, Casolaro met with a former Hughes Aircraft employee, William Turner, in the Sheraton parking lot at about 2:00 p.m. Turner gave him some papers relating to alleged corruption at Hughes and in the Pentagon.

To further complicate matters, Turner was arrested on September 26 on charges of holding up a rural bank near his home in Winchester, Virginia. In an interview with Ridgeway and Vaughan in mid-August, Turner professed to being "scared shitless" because of the evidence Casolaro had shown him connecting "the Octopus" to Oliver North, BCCI, the

29. William Hamilton, personal communication with the author.

30. Ridgeway and Vaughan, *op. cit.*, p. 39.

31. Barrett, personal conversations with the author.

32. Suspicion of Mossad involvement in Bull's death has been widely reported in the mainstream press. See also: Mary Barrett, "Gerald Bull, the Canadian Ballistics Genius Who Armed Iraq," *Washington Report on Middle East Affairs*, November 1990. Bull's family, according to Barrett, is bitter that the U.S. government is doing nothing to investigate his death.

Keating Five, and Neil Bush and the Silverado Savings and Loan scandal.[33]

Finally, there is the ubiquitous Ari Ben-Menashe, the former Israeli military intelligence officer who claims to have been involved in organizing the October Surprise affair in 1980 and to have been a key element in the subsequent supply of U.S.-provided military equipment to Iran.[34]

On news of Casolaro's death, Ben-Menashe called Inslaw's William Hamilton to say that two FBI agents from Lexington, Kentucky (where the Israeli lived in late 1990 and early 1991), had been en route to Martinsburg to talk to Casolaro about their own investigation of the Inslaw case. Ben-Menashe said the agents were prepared to give him proof that the FBI was illegally using Inslaw's PROMIS software, Hamilton reports.

Ben-Menashe further told Hamilton that one of the agents, E.B. Cartinhour, was angry that the Justice Department was not pursuing Reagan administration officials for their role in the October Surprise. Cartinhour refused to talk to Ridgeway and Vaughan, but a recently retired agent who had worked with Cartinhour told Ridgeway that he knew of Ben-Menashe and "that involves classified information."[35] The ex-agent also claimed knowledge of an investigation about the Hamiltons, computers, the Justice Department, and a coverup. He told Ridgeway that if any FBI agents had been going to talk to Casolaro, it would have been to get information, not to give it.[36]

The Inslaw investigation has extended into Kentucky for very concrete reasons. One of Inslaw's major sources is Charles Hayes, who runs a computer reconditioning business in Kentucky. Hayes, who claims to have been a former CIA asset, has found evidence of the PROMIS software in former Justice Department computers he acquired for his business.[37]

According to Ben-Menashe, Ridgeway and Hamilton had botched what he told them, and had ruined Cartinhour's FBI career by alleging that he was going against Justice Department policy.[38] Ridgeway, for his part, says his reporting is accurate.

Aftershocks

Casolaro's housekeeper reported receiving several telephone calls on Friday, August 9, at Casolaro's house. At 9:00 a.m., a male caller announced, "I will cut his body and throw it to the sharks." An hour or so later another caller said simply, "Drop dead." Between then and 10:00 p.m., when she left for the night, there were three more calls in which there was only silence or the sound of music in the background. The following day, Saturday,

August 10, she got a final call at 8:30 p.m. — approximately twelve hours after Casolaro's death. A man's voice said, "You son of a bitch. You're dead."[39]

On the previous day, around 6:00 p.m., as widely reported in the press, Casolaro called his mother's home in McLean, Virginia, to say he was on the way home but would be too late for a family birthday celebration.

Whether Casolaro was murdered or killed himself, his death has brought the Inslaw case back into the public spotlight. Elliot Richardson, calling the situation "far worse than Watergate," has written to the Justice Department to request appointment of an independent counsel to investigate Casolaro's death.

If Casolaro was murdered because of what he knew, Inslaw is the most probable cause. There is no evidence that his Octopus theory, or his investigations into BCCI and the October Surprise, are likely to have uncovered information worth killing for. Inslaw is a different matter. Here is a real crime, with real people who, if found guilty, would face real jail terms and stand to lose millions. It is possible that Casolaro, who was in close touch with Inslaw owners Bill and Nancy Hamilton, might have been too close to something conclusive which sealed his death warrant.

The possibility of murder remains the subject of serious inquiry,[40] but the suicide theory is gaining rapidly. Ron Rosenbaum, an investigative reporter and longtime acquaintance of Danny's, concluded after a 10-day inquiry that Casolaro elaborately staged his own death. Reviewing Casolaro's history as a journalist, Rosenbaum frames a good case showing that the dead man had neither the investigative track record, nor an adequate understanding of covert operations to make his extraordinary claims credible.[41] He also offers evidence that some of Casolaro's death threats may have been imaginary. Rosenbaum concedes, however, that Casolaro was dealing with dangerous individuals, and that his investigations had uncovered serious new material.

Unanswered questions surrounding Casolaro's death, including the disappearance of his briefcase and a rash of anonymous calls[42] after he died, have generated significant public pressure. Newly-confirmed Attorney General William Barr has ordered a retired federal judge, Nicholas J. Bua, to conduct a 120-day "top to bottom" review of the Inslaw matter.[43] This is a welcome change from the stonewalling of Meese and Thornburgh. It remains to be seen whether Bua will conduct a thorough investigation or simply preside over yet another government whitewash. •

33. Ridgeway and Vaughan, *op. cit.*, p. 40.

34. As with Riconosciuto, some reporters have avoided Ben-Menashe because they consider his information impossible to confirm. One exception is Seymour Hersh. The Pulitzer Prize-winning Hersh relied heavily on Ben-Menashe in his recent book on the Israeli nuclear program, *The Samson Option*.

35. Ridgeway and Vaughan, *op. cit.*, p. 42.

36. *Ibid.*

37. The FBI appears to have had recent contact with Ben-Menashe in Kentucky. In early 1991, FBI officers investigated a dispute between Ben-Menashe and former CIA officer Allan Bruce Hemmings. Ben-Menashe may have the protection of Kentucky Governor Wallace G. Wilkinson. (Hemmings, conversations with the author.)

38. Ben-Menashe, conversations with the author.

39. Ridgeway and Vaughan, *op. cit.*, p. 38.

40. See for example: Liza Featherstone and Peter Rothberg, "Suicide or Murder?" *Lies of Our Times*, November 1991. Featherstone and Rothberg analyze the gaps in mainstream reportage of Casolaro's death.

41. Ron Rosenbaum, "The Strange Death of Danny Casolaro," *Vanity Fair*, December 1991.

42. Following his death, a number of anonymous calls were placed to Casolaro's house, and to at least two journalists, Dan Bischoff, editor of the *Village Voice*, and Pat Clawson of Metrowest Broadcasting in Washington, D.C. Clawson was a friend of Casolaro's for ten years, and a business associate when Casolaro was publishing a computer newsletter.

43. David Johnston, "Bank Inquiry Widened, Justice Dept. Nominee Says," *New York Times*, November 14, 1991, p. B13.

Jo-Ann Mort

HOW THE MEDIA "COVER" LABOR

The Story That's Not Being Told

It is easy to forget that there are still places like Hamlet, North Carolina . . . until something tragic happens to put them on our mind." So the *Washington Post* informed its readers several days after a September 1991 fire in a chicken-processing plant in Hamlet killed twenty-five workers.

It *is* easy to forget . . . especially when no reporters are there to remind you. Consider the facts from Hamlet. The food-processing plant doors were locked to prevent workers from stealing chickens. (These workers were so poor that they had to be buried in donated clothing.) In its eleven years, the factory had never been investigated by the North Carolina Occupational Safety and Health Administration (OSHA). North Carolina, with more manufacturing jobs than any state in the nation, is less than 4.5 percent unionized.

It is this economy that the *New York Times* praised in an article about the Southeast on September 10 for "many of the region's historic business advantages—low labor and living costs, a pro-business, anti-union environment and a good quality of life. . . ." This article was published just seven days after the fire in Hamlet.

Reporting news is, after all, a business. The recession has hit the media hard and things will only get worse. There is pressure for ad revenue and scarce resources for staff. These two factors don't bode well for the labor press beat. When editors look for a beat to cut, labor is the one. The *Los Angeles Times*, which just cut its full-time labor beat, also recently implemented a hiring freeze. Competition for scarce advertising revenue has newspapers framing their coverage for an elite buying public.

The United States doesn't have state-supported media like the British Broadcasting Corporation or the Canadian Broadcasting Corporation, which embody the idea that the media provide a public service.

In the United States, National Public Radio (NPR) is struggling to attain that same status. Yet even NPR, considered a hotbed of radicalism by many of our elites, could do more to cover labor. Union-related issues do make it onto the NPR airwaves, but an economic issues the spin on the story often comes from a management point of view. NPR now has a half-hour show called "Marketplace," a sort of a business page of the air produced with corporate backing and regularly featuring economic commentators from the Conference Board.

Harry Bernstein, veteran *Los Angeles Times* labor reporter, remembers an earlier time when "reporters like Abe Raskin of the *New York Times* began to objectively report the activities of organized labor, which by then had become a major political and economic force in America. . . . Most other major newspapers followed suit and for several years, unions were a legitimate topic for reporting, although seldom mentioned in the electronic media. Within the past five years or so, there's been another shift: organized labor is being ignored on the invalid ground that it is no longer important enough to devote any considerable space or reporter's time to."

Bernstein writes one of the few surviving labor columns in America. Yet, at the time this article is being written, labor coverage is in flux at the *Los Angeles Times*. Bernstein's column, which once appeared on the front page of the business section, has been relegated to the inside of the section. "My own column continues and what I write is not censored in any way," Bernstein reports. "But I just don't know about its future."

Reflecting on the cancellation of his daily labor beat, *Los Angeles Times* reporter Bob Baker says, "This is bigger than one paper or one beat. There's clearly some discomfort at the notion of covering something from the workers' point of view or any individual point of view. This is what's happened to big city journalism; a lot of papers that a generation ago might have been proud to cover society from the bottom up are today much more cautious. . . . The business . . . is run by people who are more comfortable with the top-down, institutional view of the world . . . more distrustful of instinct, more reliant on public opinion polls." When Baker's beat was canceled, he was told to continue covering the Teamsters union—which of course represents the worst face of labor.

Being a labor reporter won't earn you a promotion today. Writing in the *Los Angeles Times Book Review* recently, former *New York Times* labor writer Bill Serrin reflected: "Your colleagues are off covering the White House or the State Department, hyping some trend and getting on Page One. You are camping out in some mountain motel or a bare room with three locks on the door above a sleazy bar writing about coal miners or laid-off steelworkers and hoping your piece isn't held or dumped inside."

After Serrin departed, the *New York Times* changed its labor beat into a national "workplace" beat—which can mean almost anything.

In January 1990, the metro section editors of the *Times* assigned an ambitious reporter, Alan Finder, to cover labor in New York City after several years of a dry spell on the metro desk—but after only ten months, the beat was canceled and Finder reassigned to cover transportation.

The partial reemergence of a metro labor beat at the *New York Times* came only after the paper found itself unable adequately to cover the *Daily News* strike. There was an acknowledgment at the time that labor was important and that the *New York Times* had to do a better job in covering New York City area labor.

Yet, even while the beat was in place, Finder was pulled off to cover stories ranging from racial controversy at City College to the governor's budget. Labor coverage at the *Times* seemed to be a luxury, not a necessity. Now, as the paper launches a larger metro section, with expanded bureaus in the outer boroughs and suburbs, the labor beat has been discontinued, even though there will be an increase of fifteen to twenty reporters in the new section.

"I agree that it's not something that's been done much or well by most papers in the last several years," says Finder, discussing his former beat. "It's a very fertile area with a lot of good, important subjects to write about. I hope the *New York Times* and other papers will begin to address it.

"In many ways the issues don't fit the conventions of daily news, other than strikes or city labor negotiations," Finder adds. "Most kinds of issues worth exploring are not simple hits. You've got to find ways to take individual worker issues and broaden them to a wider theme. Covering labor and workplace issues requires a lot of inventiveness."

One argument used by editors at the *New York Times* for not covering organized labor is the shrinking percentage of the national work force that is unionized. However, the unionized work force in New York City comes to nearly 36 percent, and plays a significant—even pivotal—role in the life of the city.

There are still some exceptions to the disappearance of the labor beat. Frank Swoboda at the *Washington Post* and Phil Dine at the *St. Louis Post-Dispatch* are two reporters who cover labor fairly and knowledgeably.

Swoboda, a senior reporter at the *Post*, combines coverage of legislative issues related to workers with reporting from the field. He also covers, in-depth, the AFL-CIO as an institution. Swoboda is able to leverage the seniority he has at the paper for his beat. And while other newspaper editors are arguing that the AFL-CIO has slipped in importance as an institution, Washington's hometown paper gives adequate coverage to the labor federation.

Phil Dine, younger than most labor reporters, agrees that his generation of reporters knows little about labor today or its historic role and might tend not to think of it as an interesting area to cover. Dine established the labor beat at a time when the *Post-Dispatch* was competing with another paper for readers.

After Dine proved to be successful by reporting his stories with a human-interest angle, his editors approached him to write a weekly column. "They were trying to personalize the paper with more columnists," Dine says. His column combines St. Louis area coverage with national and international coverage. He was recently on assignment in Eastern Europe, where he was able to focus on labor problems in that part of the world.

"There's a lot of interest in the labor movement in St. Louis," Dine states, pointing out that St. Louis has historically been an important union city. The International Brotherhood of Teamsters was founded there and almost one out of every six Teamster members in the country lives in the region covered by Dine's paper. Reflecting on his paper's publisher, he concludes that "the Pulitzer tradition has been for the underdog and the paper's always been sympathetic toward issues like civil rights and improved working conditions."

Newsday, owned by the Los Angeles Times-Mirror Company, has a solid full-time labor reporter, Ken Crowe, who also combines local and national issues, though by default Crowe mostly covers labor stories in the New York City area. The large amount of local stories precludes one reporter from reaching much beyond New York. *Newsday* does have a workplace reporter, too, who assists in covering labor issues, especially health and safety concerns.

But in the great majority of cases, if the labor movement is covered at all, it's from the business page. Although the *Los Angeles Times* has lost its full-time labor reporter, it still has a workplace reporter at the business desk. Whether unions get covered through that beat is an open question. From the business desk, labor issues tend to be seen in terms of the bottom line. A labor settlement, for example, is covered with attention paid to the market share effect it will have on the company, rather than benefits or hardships for the workers.

Interestingly, both the *Wall Street Journal* and *Business Week* buck the trend. Both have full-time labor reporters who cover social policy and workplace issues with great consideration given to the impact of policies on the work force.

Unlike the *Los Angeles Times* and the *New York Times*, most reporters at the *Journal* and *Business Week* make it their business to cover the kinds of people who may not read their publications. Few blue-collar women read the *Wall Street Journal*, yet reporters regularly include a blue-collar perspective. For instance, in a recent piece on the lack of child care, the reporter interviewed women in managerial and top-level white collar positions as well as a woman who was a member of the Oil, Chemical and Atomic Workers. This woman pointed out that most factory workers have two choices: they can either stay home with the child and risk being fired or they can leave a child home without supervision. Her experience was in direct contrast to that of the more relatively affluent women interviewed in the article, who had more flexible options.

When the *Journal* reports on the leveraged buy-out disasters of the 1980s, reporters consistently chronicle the devastating effects on thousands of workers who have lost their jobs

and their pensions. The *Wall Street Journal* regularly opens its op-ed pages to union voices in a special "Counterpoint" feature. Contrast this with the *New York Times*, where it is extremely rare to read a labor point of view.

We can only speculate as to why the *Wall Street Journal* should feel it necessary to cover labor with some thoroughness while the *New York Times* does not: the *Times* is increasingly oriented toward upper middle-class suburbanites and upwardly (or these days, downwardly) mobile yuppies who have neither feeling for nor interest in workers and their organizations. The *Journal* speaks first and foremost to the American business and managerial classes, for whom it is essential to have accurate information about the state of labor. The *Wall Street Journal*'s news staff is independent of the paper's editorial staff, which allows for the *Journal*'s liberal outlook on economic and social policy. The *New York Times*, in contrast, seems to be run these days by editorial and news editors who are liberal on social policy and conservative on economic policy

Business Week has one of the best labor reporters in the country, Aaron Bernstein, whose father is the *Los Angeles Times* labor columnist. Bernstein not only reports on contract disputes and workplace trends, he also writes opinion pieces about subjects ranging from the need for labor-law reform and arguments for increasing the minimum wage. Bernstein is supplemented by a reporter based in Washington who covers social policy and workplace issues with an emphasis on organized labor. The magazine also has pro-labor Robert Kuttner writing a regular column as one of several contributing writers.

Network television on the other hand has never been good at covering labor. In a 1989 study of network news coverage of labor, Fairness and Accuracy in Media (FAIR), a media monitoring group, found that NBC Nightly News devoted a total of forty seconds to workplace safety.

The same study found that striking miners in Siberia had a better chance of receiving coverage than striking miners in Virginia. One example of this was illustrated during the

United Mineworkers' strike against Pittston two years ago. When several thousand miners and their supporters occupied a company facility in Virginia, the occupation was virtually blacked out by the electronic media, even though the incident offered a visually dramatic event.

Last April, CBS reported on the effects on unions of scab workers. After the report aired, a group of right-wing congressmen fighting proposed federal antiscab legislation denounced the story as "outrageously one-sided" and lodged a complaint with CBS president Lawrence Tisch. This complaint, according to FAIR, led to a meeting between the Republican congressmen and CBS Washington, D.C. bureau chief Barbara Cohen.

FAIR quotes from a *Wall Street Journal* article that said Cohen assured the elected officials that "her bureau would produce another piece on the legislation when it reaches the House floor. . . . Ms. Cohen said CBS would work then with Republicans 'to get their recommendations as to the best spokesman for their side.' "

In fact, in the last year, CBS has been particularly good among the networks in pointing out the hardships faced by middle-class and working Americans and union members in today's economy.

It was a CBS news crew that chronicled a portion of the recent organizing campaign at Fieldcrest Cannon Mills, where the Amalgamated Clothing and Textile Workers (ACTWU) tried to organize seven thousand textile workers in North Carolina in the summer of 1991. This was the largest National Labor Relations Board election in North Carolina in six years, when ACTWU last ran an election at the same facility. The union came within two hundred votes of winning, after losing decisively two previous times.

The mill had been sold between election number two and number three to Fieldcrest. The previous owner, California financier David Murdock, held on to the pension fund when he sold the mill. He invested the workers' retirement money in insurance annuities which then defaulted. Workers once expecting about $90 a month for their retirement were to end up with nothing.

CBS News and ABC News both covered Murdock's pension problems, using the Cannon situation as a case study for what is happening elsewhere in America. Both reports were sympathetic to the workers and the union. But the most striking part of the CBS coverage for this viewer was a camera shot from inside one of the mills. Tacked up on the wall was a notice of the union election from the NLRB. Union representatives are not allowed on the premises of a workplace during a union election, a fact probably not known or even considered by most Americans. Yet, a network television crew was allowed access. The only view union staff had of the election notice was on national television!

Shortly after the piece on the Cannon workers' pension problems, the same CBS news show, "CBS Sunday Morning," broadcast a segment on the state of unions. The same producer did both segments. The second segment clearly stated that the presumption of fairness in union elections may be a false presumption. The show portrayed workers being disenfranchised in a union organizing campaign and in a strike.

Unfortunately, one or two sympathetic television producers and reporters aren't enough . . . though they offer drops of water in a drought. The norm in television news coverage is that labor is an afterthought, if considered at all.

In a rare ABC "Nightline" show on workplace danger and negligent OSHA enforcement dealing with the aftermath of the Hamlet disaster—almost six weeks after the accident—ABC reporter Chris Wallace asked his panelists, "Are there other Hamlets out there?"

The answer is yes, many others, with thousands of workers at risk. The real question is, will the investigative work be done to find these disasters *before* more people are killed?

Perhaps "Nightline" and its viewers would be more aware of the dangerous circumstances in today's workplaces if network news shows didn't wait for a disaster in order to investigate workers' conditions. On the eve of the Solidarity Day March on Labor Day 1991, "Nightline" had scheduled a panel to discuss the current state of organized labor with a labor writer, a labor leader, and a business representative. The show was bumped for an interview with Jerry Falwell on homosexuality. The labor panel was arguably timely, tied as it was to a major demonstration in Washington, but the show was rescheduled for a month later and aired on the East Coast much later than normal show time, after "Monday Night Football."

There is no conspiracy in the media not to cover organized labor. Neither the print nor the electronic media are organized systematically enough for a conspiracy. There are two probable reasons organized labor is not getting covered. The first is a class bias on the part of media corporate owners and publishers. The second is the perception that organized labor "doesn't matter" anymore. The latter perception is one that labor must take more seriously.

Editors, publishers, and even some reporters argue that the organized labor movement is too weak today to warrant the kind of press attention it once received. But, even with the decline of union membership, issues remain and may even become more critical.

The media's job is to search out those who desperately need to have their story told. When will our national press corps begin to wonder whether it's really good public policy for this nation to abandon unionism? After how many Hamlets?   □

World Economics Coverage Follows Simple Rules

by Jeff Goodwin and Renee Steinhagen

When mainstream newspapers write about economic affairs around the globe, they follow a few simple rules that are seldom explicit and never questioned, even when they seem to blatantly contradict reality. Indeed, rather than question these rules, the press often simply "fits" reality to them.

Rule 1: Blame economic ills on "socialism." "Socialism" here refers not just to Communist or socialist regimes, but to virtually any form of government intervention in the economy, particularly redistributive measures. (It conspicuously excludes, however, government intervention that benefits business interests, such as tax credits and subsidies, military spending, and S&L bailouts.)

It follows from Rule 1 that all of the economic problems of Communist and socialist regimes are the result of government intervention, especially that dreaded pathology—economic planning. The possibility that such countries might have economic problems due to authoritarianism, historic underdevelopment, trade embargoes etc. is ruled out.

Rule 1 also requires that the economic ills of relatively affluent capitalist societies be attributed to "socialism" or "socialistic" policies. The press invariably blames economic difficulties in countries like Sweden, Germany, Britain and Greece on "socialism" (or "welfare-state socialism"), not on business cycles, financial speculation or the ordinary investment decisions of major banks and corporations.

Moreover, impoverished capitalist countries should be described as "socialist" or following a "socialistic" strategy (to wrack and ruin), whatever the actual reality. India, Algeria and Mexico (at least until recently) are perhaps the prime examples; after former Indian prime minister Rajiv Gandhi's assassination, for example, news stories were filled with tributes to him for understanding "that radical surgery needed to be performed on India's failed socialist polity to spark economic growth." (*Washington Post*, 5/26/91)

However, the fact that most of the poorest countries in the world are capitalist, not socialist, is rather difficult to suppress. This unfortunate fact requires:

Rule 2: Prosperity must be attributed to "unfettered," "freemarket" capitalism; poverty in capitalist societies, by contrast, must be attributed to "interference" with markets. If Third World officials were "committed to allowing market forces to flourish free of government restraints," a *New York Times* article asserted ("Third World Embracing Reforms to Encourage Economic Growth," 7/8/91), "the four billion people who live in the third world could enjoy a better standard of living."

Countries that are conspicuously "free market" in orientation (or simply in rhetoric) are assumed to be prosperous or, at least, on the road to prosperity. Perhaps the most notorious example of this logic is Chile, which the press invariably describes as an economic success story, despite a rather more sordid reality for the vast majority of its people.

Similarly, if a country's economy seems particularly dynamic (at least for the middle and upper classes), then, in the press' view, it must be because of free-market economics. Accordingly, the role of economic planning and "industrial policy" in Japan and the European Economic Community (as well as the role of Europe's strong labor movements) is systematically ignored. Moreover South Korea, Taiwan, Thailand and Indonesia are routinely described as free-market wonders, despite the enormous role of the state in those countries' economic affairs.

Multinational banks and corporations, according to Rule 2, will inevitably bring wealth to all the nations of the world—so long as they are unconstrained by meddling governments. Consequently, the press will look the other way when such institutions withhold capital from particular communities (even in developed countries such as the U.S. and Canada) until "appropriate" concessions have been made regarding wages, working conditions and environmental regulations.

In addition, the press will ignore these institutions' extraction of enormous profits and interest from developing countries—in effect, their decapitalization of the Third World to the tune of $45 billion since 1985. Needless to say, the numerous studies that demonstrate that the free-market nostrums propagated by the U.S. government, the World Bank and the International Monetary Fund (IMF) have done very little good and a great deal of harm in the Third World are rarely mentioned by the U.S. press, and even then quickly forgotten.

The violent repression of popular protests against free-market "reforms"—such as the general strikes and "IMF riots" in Venezuela, the Dominican Republic, Costa Rica, Morocco, Algeria etc.—also receives amazingly little press coverage. In the press' view, however, the repression of popular movements isn't necessarily a bad thing. This brings us to:

Rule 3: Assume that capitalism may be necessary to create democracy, but that authoritarianism may be necessary to create capitalism. "Chileans seem reconciled to the reality that the most brutal dictatorship in their history presided over the creation of the soundest economy in Latin America," the *New York Times Magazine* reported (7/7/91), in a typical application of this thesis.

Since dynamic, free-market capitalism (and hence democracy) is incompatible with active trade unionism, the press has been extraordinarily indulgent towards the various forms of government and private-sector repression of militant (and not-so-militant) unions in Chile, South Korea, El Salvador, Guatemala, Great Britain and, on occasion, in the U.S.

While trade-union opposition to the former Communist regimes was lauded as the legitimate exercise of precious democratic rights, union activity is viewed very differently by the press when unions are operating in a capitalist context. At that point, unions become merely "special interests," and the "national interest" is identified with the needs of business.

While this distinction implicitly recognizes that conflicting interests exist within societies, the press is usually hesitant to analyze economic issues in terms of such conflicts. In fact, the press generally follows:

Rule 4: Discuss the poverty or prosperity of each society as a whole; avoid comparing the economic conditions of social classes, the sexes or other groups within societies. Discussions of "economic miracles" in South Korea, Taiwan, Hong Kong, Chile *et al.* hardly ever mention the rather horrendous conditions of the working or unemployed poor in those societies, particularly the miserable situation of women.

Conversely, discussions of so-called "economic basket cases" such as India, Egypt or the Philippines generally play down the existence of wealthy upper classes in those societies, not to mention their interest in perpetuating the status quo. Such discussions invariably refer to aggregate measures such as Gross National Product and per capita income, but are conspicuously silent about the distribution of income, the concentration of wealth and real wages.

Jeff Goodwin is a sociology professor at New York University. Renee Steinhagen is a labor lawyer.

DataCenter   464 19th Street, Oakland, California 94612 (415) 835-4692

Paul Mavrides

The Plot to Kill JFK

Before Oliver Stone's movie on the Kennedy assassination was filmed, national news media began an effort to destroy *JFK* in the eyes of the public. But moviegoers turned out in droves to see *JFK* and make up their own minds about a film journalists had savaged as irresponsible and paranoid.

FAIR noticed that the news outlets and journalists that attacked *JFK* the most vociferously were the ones with the longest records of error and obstruction in defense of the flawed Warren Commission inquiry, which concluded that Lee Harvey Oswald had acted alone. Indeed, the factual and artistic license taken by Stone in creating his movie often paled in comparison to the gross inaccuracies peddled in national news reports over the last three decades.

DAN RATHER. The **CBS** anchor asked of *JFK* (12/16/91): "Is it an outright rewrite of history?" On the day after the assassination, as the **CBS** reporter covering JFK's trip to Dallas, Rather rewrote the most important piece of evidence in the case: the Zapruder film.

The first journalist to view the 20-second film of the assassination, taken by Abraham Zapruder with his home movie camera, Rather reported to a national audience that the fatal head shot drove Kennedy "violently forward." As viewers of *JFK* know, the Zapruder footage shows just the opposite: Kennedy's head is driven violently backward, suggesting the fatal shot may have been fired from the Grassy Knoll area in front of the motorcade. But the government theory, announced within hours of the killing, had all shots fired

by Oswald from behind Kennedy in the Book Depository.

Dan Rather later explained (in his book, *The Camera Never Blinks*) that he made this mistake because his viewing of the film was so rushed. But this error (in the government's favor) didn't hurt Rather's career; in fact, his rise up the **CBS** ladder was aided by major reporting assignments on documentaries (in 1964, 1967 and 1975) that did evidentiary somersaults in defense of the Warren Commission.

TIME-LIFE, INC. **Time-Life** paid $150,000 to buy all rights to the Zapruder film, and instead of making it available to experts or journalists, spent the next decade trying to prevent the footage from being seen or studied (**Publisher's Weekly**, "Life Sues to Enjoin Book on Assassination of Kennedy," 12/25/67). **Life** publisher C.D. Jackson, who ordered the Zapruder film kept from public view, was a close CIA associate (**New Times**, 10/1/76).

While hoarding the Zapruder film, **Life** magazine repeatedly distorted what the footage showed. One **Life** article (10/2/64) claimed that the fatal shot caused Kennedy's "skull to explode forward." Another argued (12/6/63) that Oswald had shot JFK in the throat from the rear by claiming—falsely—that the film showed the president turning far around to wave to someone in the crowd.

Meanwhile, **Time** magazine assailed Warren Commission critics as "leftists," "Communists," or, in the case of Bertrand Russell, "that sometime philosopher" (6/12/64). Six months before *JFK* opened, with the movie only half-filmed, a **Time** subheadline (6/10/91) referred to Oliver Stone's "strange, widely disputed take on the Kennedy assassination."

NEW YORK TIMES. The "paper of record" has broken all records in heavy lifting for the Warren Commission. From day one in Dallas to opening night for *JFK*, the **New York Times** has specialized in the selective usage of evidence while denouncing people like Oliver Stone for doing the same.

Besides publishing editions of the Warren Report, the **New York Times** compiled a book, *The Witnesses*, which offered highly selective "highlights" of testimony before the commission. The book included a witness' statement that he'd seen a man with a rifle on the sixth floor of the Book Depository, but not his testimony that he'd actually seen two men there, and that an FBI agent told him to "forget it." Deleted from the testimony of Abraham Zapruder and others were their impressions that shots were fired from in front of JFK. Omitted from the testimony of the autopsy surgeon was the bizarre admission that he'd burned the notes and draft of his autopsy.

The day after the Warren Report was released (9/28/64), Anthony Lewis, then the **Times**' Supreme Court reporter, wrote that "the commission analyzed every issue in exhaustive, almost archeological detail." Still supporting the Warren Report 27 years later, Lewis claimed (1/9/92) that TV was fascinated with Stone but "has no time for the man who knows more of the actual facts of the assassination than anyone else: David Belin, who was counsel to the Warren Commission and has seen every document, every CIA file." Belin, who was also executive director of the Rockefeller Commission's 1975 whitewash of the CIA, has been lavished with media attention for decades (most recently, he was on **Nightline**, 1/22/92, and had an anti-Stone op-ed with Gerald

Editor Says Thumbs Down on *JFK* Review

The crossfire aimed at *JFK* has claimed at least one bystander—Pat Dowell, a movie critic for **Washingtonian** magazine, who resigned in protest after editor Jack Limpert spiked her review of the Oliver Stone movie (**Washington City Paper**, 1/24/92). After Limpert killed the capsule review, which said, "If you didn't already doubt the Warren Commission report, you will after seeing Oliver Stone's brilliantly crafted indictment of history as an official story," Dowell wrote in protest: "The editors of **Time**, **Newsweek** and the [**Washington**] **Post**...have all sputtered in protest about *JFK*'s controversial speculations, but those editors felt no need to soften, censor or omit the rave reviews of the movie by their critics."

Dowell demanded that editor Limpert run her review or accept her resignation: "I cannot in good conscience keep my job at the price of tailoring my evaluation of a film's merits to fit someone else's idea of political (or cinematic) correctness."

Limpert accepted her resignation. "My job," he wrote her, "is to protect the magazine's reputation and it seemed to me that Stone's film went to the heart of what kind of city this is."

Dowell told the **New York Post** (1/25/92) that her former editor "identifies with the Washington elite who are policy makers, pundits and government officials, who are accused in the film of possibly taking part in a conspiracy or at least in a cover-up.... I think the heart of Washington is the rest of us poor schmoes."

Ford in the **Washington Post**, 12/17/91). Lewis, who normally supports freedom of information, asks the public to rely, not on the CIA files themselves, but on what a government lawyer says the files say.

After the House Assassinations Committee concluded in 1979 that two gunman had probably fired at JFK, **Times** editors were unswayed (1/7/79): "To the lay public, the word 'conspiracy' is freighted with dark connotations of malevolence perpetrated by enemies. But 'two maniacs instead of one' might be more like it."

Is Oliver Stone's conspiracy theory any more absurd than the **New York Times**' invention of the "two maniacs" theory? Ironically, one of the **Times**' many recent critiques of *JFK* (by Tom Wicker, 12/15/91) was headlined: "Does *JFK* Conspire Against Reason?"

WASHINGTON POST. Throughout the 1960s, the **Washington Post** denounced proponents of a JFK murder conspiracy as irresponsible kooks. But in 1976, the **Post** promoted its own kooky conspiracy theories...as long as the finger pointed at Fidel Castro. One **Post** article speculated that Kennedy was killed by a conspiracy of Castro and the Mafia (who'd been thrown out of Havana by Castro). Seven months

before *JFK* opened, the **Post** returned from kookdom to denunciation mode, accusing Stone of exploiting "the edge of paranoia."

JACK ANDERSON. The columnist has excoriated *JFK* for relying on dubious sources such as Jim Garrison. In the mid-1970s, Anderson penned "Castro killed JFK" columns sourced to Frank Sturgis, the Watergate burglar whose anti-Castro guerrilla activities had been shut down by the Kennedy administration. On the day after the assassination, Sturgis says an FBI agent told him, "Frank, if there's anyone capable of killing the president, you're one guy that can do it." In August 1974, Sturgis told **True** magazine: "The liberals have twisted everything. If I had my chance, I'd kill every one of them." On the subject of who killed JFK, Sturgis was a dubious source indeed.

Oliver Stone made a Hollywood movie, and chose a flawed hero in District Attorney Jim Garrison to drive his drama. Stone acknowledges that his movie is a work of fiction, a "countermyth" to the "lone assassin myth."

Journalists, however, aren't supposed to deal in myth but in facts. In the JFK assassination, they failed. Perhaps that explains the ferocity of their attack on *JFK*. ⌐

Behind Right-Wing Campus Newspapers

By Miles Seligman and Cymbre Simpson

Strongly backed by a well-connected neoconservative institute, right-wing campus newspapers are waging battles over what they see as highly contested territory— the nation's college campuses.

Right-wing newspapers are not a new phenomenon, but over the past 11 years, their influence appears to have grown. The increased clout is owed not so much to the tireless efforts of student editors, however, as to a national network, created in 1980 by the D.C.-based Institute for Educational Affairs—now the Madison Center for Educational Affairs (MCEA). The Collegiate Network, as it came to be known in 1986, now includes 64 papers on 57 campuses across the country, including the **Dartmouth Review**, the **Yale Political Monthly** and the **Princeton Tory**.

The backers of these papers acknowledge that their efforts are extremist: "At a university with 10,000 undergraduates, there are perhaps 30 or 40 right-leaning students who are willing to take a public stand," writes Bob Lukefahr, editor of **Newslink**, the MCEA monthly newsletter sent to the editors of Collegiate Network papers. This translates into .3 to .4 percent of the student body, an extremely small number for a group often able to set the tone of campus debate.

This disproportionate influence is made possible by the hundreds of thousands of dollars in funding and support earmarked each year by MCEA for student journalism. One of the more impressive support services is *Start the Presses*, a detailed guide on how to start and maintain a conservative publication. In addition to its monthly newsletter, MCEA also offers free syndicated columns from such conservative heavyweights as Patrick Buchanan and Walter Williams; regional and national conferences, all expenses paid, allowing young right-wingers to schmooze with their conser-

Miles Seligman and Cymbre Simpson are editorial interns at FAIR.

vative elders; and connections to over 60 right-wing think tanks, magazines and government organizations.

In an effort to "extend the influence of the Collegiate Network into the professional media," MCEA's Editorial Internship Program places students at media outlets such as **Insight** magazine, **NBC News** and the **New Republic**—as well as in the office of Vice President Quayle.

Most importantly, however, the MCEA provides its student publications with operational funding. In 1990, the Center

This homophobic poster published by a right-wing student paper prompted a lawsuit from Bart Simpson creator Matt Groening and Fox TV.

distributed to two-thirds of its papers nearly $140,000 in direct grants. For further fund-raising help, *Start the Presses* promises, "MCEA may know friendly benefactors in your area and can help you make important contacts with your alumni."

The Center itself has been bankrolled by some of the nation's largest corporations, including Mobil Oil, Dow Chemical and Chase Manhattan Bank. The foundations of the conservative movement—Olin, Scaife, Coors and Smith Richardson—also contribute to MCEA.

By funding MCEA, these institutions

seek to shape campus debate beyond the realm of student journalism. MCEA joined the attack on feminist and multicultural scholarship—disguised as a defense against "politically correct" tyranny—by sponsoring Dinesh D'Souza's *Illiberal Education*. The Center is also launching its own college guide: *The Common Sense Guide to American Colleges*. This self-proclaimed "no-holds-barred critical view" will evaluate schools "using old-fashioned standards of academic excellence, social decency, and community spirit."

Another MCEA venture is the "Student Forum," an association of minority students "who do not support the reigning radical agenda." MCEA boasts that the Forum has "grown to more than 80 members on campuses across the country": the founding conference of this tiny group was notable for the attendance of Judge Clarence Thomas.

MCEA has positioned itself as a vanguard in the ideological struggle on campus, which it pictures as "a place where reasoned dissent is punished, standards are lowered or ignored, and 'politically incorrect' students and faculty are silenced."

MCEA literature makes it clear that the right sees this debate as a war. In the May 1991 **Newslink**, Bob Lukefahr writes a "battlefield update" in which he claims that Collegiate Network papers are the "victims of vicious attacks," finding themselves "under attack," "under siege," "invaded" or "sabotaged" by the "disloyal opposition: minority students, homosexuals and liberals in general."

In this "war," as in others, the embattled see themselves as the righteous defenders of virtue, the protectors of free speech and open debate. As Midge Decter, a former IEA board member, told an IEA conference: "You are surrounded by people who, either irresponsibly or intentionally, seek to bring this blessed country down, and you and your future children with it."

But with advice from the right-wing establishment and considerable financial support, MCEA is there to help the conservative press drive back the "P.C." hordes. MCEA has given conservative campus editors an enemy, the means to fight it and the cash to pay for it all.

A Conservative Look in Newsprint

By STEPHEN R. BARNETT

TWO more cities, Little Rock, Ark., and Dallas, recently have lost competing newspapers and joined the near-ubiquitous ranks of one-daily towns. While The Arkansas Gazette and The Dallas Times Herald may have died of natural economic causes, the circumstances were suspect. One wonders if the Justice Department did as much as it should have to keep these papers alive.

In each case, the paper didn't just die but was sold into oblivion for a sizable bounty from its crosstown rival — a payment financed by the monopoly franchise thus bestowed on the rival. In each case, any efforts by the Justice Department to produce a different result were shrouded in secrecy and apparently minimal.

And in each case, the paper that died was politically liberal, while the one permitted to buy it out — Walter E. Hussman Jr.'s Arkansas Democrat, the A. H. Belo Corporation's Dallas Morning News — shares the conservative views of the Bush Administration.

In Little Rock, where the Gannett Company sold the 172-year-old Arkansas Gazette after running it into the ground for five years, Gannett's payoff from Mr. Hussman was a handsome $69 million — more than Gannett had paid for The Gazette in 1986, and plainly including a monopoly premium over what another possible buyer would have paid Gannett.

Antitrust laws barred Gannett from selling to its rival unless no one else would buy The Gazette. The antitrust division of the Justice Department is supposed to enforce this requirement. In the past, it has. In 1984, when Newhouse Newspapers said it planned to close The St. Louis Globe-Democrat, the division intervened to announce that the paper was for sale and to check out prospective buyers (four were found to be qualified) and police the sale.

In Little Rock, the antitrust division did no such thing. According to news reports, Gannett, apparently feeling no responsibility to try to keep The Gazette alive, made its deal with Mr. Hussman before making any effort to look for other buyers.

Stephen R. Barnett is a law professor at the University of California at Berkeley.

Did the Justice Department play dead as two liberal papers were gobbled up?

The antitrust division reportedly required Gannett only to list The Gazette with a newspaper broker. Neither Gannett nor the division announced that The Gazette was for sale. Both stonewalled inquiries from news organizations. And the division apparently did nothing to make sure that Gannett offered the paper at a fair price, without the monopoly premium.

The story in Dallas was similar. The $55 million that The Times Herald's owners got from Belo was a slimmer bounty than in Little Rock, but it surely exceeded what another possible buyer would have paid. The antitrust division again kept silent and apparently did little.

In Little Rock and Dallas it is possible that, whatever Justice might have done, only the monopoly-bent crosstown rival would have bought the paper. But maverick publishers have shown that it's possible to resurrect a "dying" daily — Rupert Murdoch did it with The Boston Herald, McClatchy Newspapers with The Anchorage News and Mr.

Hussman himself with The Arkansas Democrat.

In Little Rock, moreover, the long-dominant Gazette was still about even with The Democrat in circulation when Gannett took the money and ran. In Dallas, The Morning News had a much bigger lead over The Times Herald, but the market was much bigger as well.

Whether either paper could be sold to someone who would keep it alive could not be known without trying. The owners had no incentive to try, and it doesn't appear that they were prodded much. Whether it would have changed the result, a more open and aggressive stance by the Justice Department at least would have offered reassurance, in this sensitive area, that the Government is enforcing the law.

REASSURANCE is particularly needed because, coincidence or not, the defunct Arkansas Gazette and Dallas Times Herald were liberal papers, while The Arkansas Democrat and The Dallas Morning News now have monopoly megaphones for their conservative voices.

An outcome that closes liberal newspapers and entrenches conservative ones may not displease the present Administration. Did political preference keep the Justice Department from making greater efforts to find real buyers for The Arkansas Gazette and The Dallas Times Herald? With the department's role hidden from view, one can only wonder. ∎

Pap Radio

Once again, the Federal Communications Commission has moved to turn the country's radio stations into a homogenized commodity controlled by the largest corporations. The commission has voted to let one corporation own as many as thirty AM and thirty FM stations, up from the present limit of twelve and twelve. (As recently as 1985 the ownership cap was seven AMs and seven FMs.) For the first time in history, the F.C.C. will permit a company to buy additional stations in the same market.

The action is another violation by the present commission of the Communications Law of 1934 and the democratic philosophy behind it, which holds that the public owns the airwaves. An exclusive license to operate on a particular frequency is supposed to be granted to any applicant that demonstrates it will use that frequency "in the public interest, convenience and necessity." And the station operator must prove it is doing so every seven years (formerly three) on the basis of past performance.

The law presupposes that a radio station is a community facility, which should serve the needs of significant groups in that community. That is why every license requires the station to have local studios and transmitters. The owner can operate for profit, but never at the expense of the public interest.

From the infancy of commercial radio in the 1920s, business operators, realizing how much money they could make selling advertisements, have nibbled away at implementation of the law. In the past the commission has denied licenses to corporate applicants that have demonstrated hostility toward unions or other community groups, or because the applicant's other business enterprises had violated standards of fairness. Various F.C.C. members have fluctuated in their support for the law. But in recent years, the commission has abandoned any pretense of following it. The Reagan/Bush appointees have generally acted as if broadcasting is a corporate privilege and none of the public's business.

By steadily relaxing limits on ownership and introducing other new provisions, the F.C.C. has done two things. It has fostered broadcasting that is a nationally homogenized mix of programs, indistinguishable from one market to another, and it has made licensing a game largely reserved for big corporations. More and more, local political, ethnic and social groups, women, minorities and unions are out of the picture.

The new rule permits one corporation to own enough stations to dominate up to 25 percent of the market; in the smaller markets one owner may control half the stations, with no limit on how much of the market it dominates. The commission has raised the extent to which an owner of an AM and an FM station in the same market may broadcast the same programs on both, further reducing diversity and opportunity for outsiders.

The rule is even worse than it looks. The F.C.C. permits joint ventures among competitors, a kind of cartel chiefly benefiting the giants. They can arrange to share programs. The new limit on one owner's market saturation probably cannot be policed: Radio audience measurement is notoriously spongy and unstandardized.

The F.C.C.'s excuse this time is the recession. Last year 153 stations suspended operations. That is ironic. It was F.C.C. deregulation in the 1980s—suspension of public service requirements and enlargement of ownership limits—that sent big operators on a binge of borrowing and empire building. Now, like the banks, they demand more of the same bad medicine. Besides, there are 11,086 radio stations in the United States, so a suspension rate of 1 percent—mostly speculators—does not threaten the industry.

Paradoxically, the F.C.C.'s style of deregulation, by favoring the big operators, almost guarantees the disappointment of some of them. Big operators are in broadcasting for big profits; they aim for mass audiences. They use standard formats in the major markets, each format (rap, rock, etc.) being nearly identical in almost every market.

The answer for the F.C.C. ought to be encouragement of the opposite kind of ownership, directed at the unsaturated, much-needed programming that reflects the reality of the mix of groups in every community. These are not the audiences and stations created and defined by radio's big corporate owners. Such real citizen groupings are increasingly ignored by the F.C.C. It is the smaller operators who operate with far lower costs and expect lower profits or, in subscriber-supported stations, no profits at all.

The new rules do not become final until Congress approves them. There is opposition, led in the House by Edward Markey and John Dingell and in the Senate by Ernest Hollings. They will need a lot of public support against the big lobbies.

As Ralph Nader has said, we the people own the airwaves. The F.C.C. is our broker. But the broker is giving away our airwaves and not permitting us to use our own property. It's time to change brokers—or for Congress to hold that broker responsible for violating its stewardship.   BEN H. BAGDIKIAN

Ben H. Bagdikian is author of The Media Monopoly *and other books on the mass media.*

It's a mad ad world

By Joel Bleifuss

One of the most interesting, and no doubt least reported, studies to come out of Washington, D.C. this year is an examination of how the national news media is being "corrupted in the service of commercialism." The 76-page report, titled *Dictating Content: How advertising pressure can corrupt a free press*, was released last week by the Center for the Study of Commercialism, an organization dedicated to countering the commercial forces that promote consumption over citizenship.

The author of *Dictating Content*, Ronald Collins, sums up the problem of the "new censorship" this way: "The commercialization of the media involves a long-term erosion of principle, with a greater movement away from informing the citizenry and a corresponding movement toward facilitating the advertising/marketing process." An ABC executive is more succinct, saying, "The network is paying affiliates to carry network commercials, not programs. What we are is a distribution system for Procter & Gamble."

The most interesting part of the report is a case-by-case analysis of how corporate interests wield their financial clout to shape editorial policy. Many of the reporters interviewed by Collins feared being fired or blacklisted and therefore requested anonymity. For instance, an East Coast magazine editor "confirmed that he was fired after clashing with his publisher over the issue of advertiser interference, but said he would jeopardize his future in the industry if he talked on the record."

Advertiser influence shapes the presentation of the news in two ways: through direct economic censorship and through journalistic self-censorship—a subtly corrosive malady that all reporters who have worked in the mainstream press are personally familiar with.

Market forces: Particularly hard hit by the "new censorship" are those who cover consumer issues. TV journalist Herb Weisbaum of Seattle spent his time at the 1990 Investigative Reporters and Editors (IRE) convention "trading horror stories with consumer reporters from across the country." As he reported in the fall 1990 *IRE Journal*, "Everyone is feeling the sting of 'economic censorship.' Stories are being killed, stories are being watered down and, saddest of all, stories are not even being attempted because reporters know they'll never make it on the air."

Take the case of the real estate industry, which accounts for 18.5 percent of all newspaper classified advertising. "It is rare for papers to assign tough reporters to the real estate beat," writes Collins, "even though housing is the average family's biggest investment and readers crave consumer-oriented news about the industry." He points out that a *Washington Journalism Review* survey of 42 real estate editors found that almost half claimed that their "publishers and senior editors had prohibited critical coverage of the industry for fear of offending advertisers. More than 80 percent said advertisers had threatened to pull ads because of negative coverage. Over a third knew of advertisers that had done so."

Sometimes the news that is censored involves stories about the media itself. In the section dealing with GE/NBC, this point is made time and again. Take the news about the GE boycott being sponsored by the consumer interest group INFACT. INFACT's former media director, Henry Hughes, says he discussed the boycott in June 1991 with a bureau chief of the American Public Radio financial news program *Marketplace*. Hughes recalls that the *Marketplace* bureau chief, who is *not* employed by GE, was "literally screaming, 'Media censorship—media smensorship—I have a family to support. You're nuts to think we could do anything on it. ... I know for a fact they'd run me out of here.'"

And it is not just stories, but mere phrases that attract the censor's attention. In the November 1991 *Columbia Journalism Review*, Lawrence Grossman, the former president of NBC News, wrote about a phone call he received from GE/NBC Chairman Jack Welsh on Oct. 20, 1987. Welsh had called to complain that NBC was using the term "Black Monday" to describe the previous day's stock market crash. Welsh charged that such negative reporting was hurting the value of GE stock.

The new news order: The media also censors itself, or as Collins puts it, trades "editorial integrity for advertiser approval."

Editors with their eye on the ad dollar rise to the top. Bill Kovach, the former editor of the *Atlanta Journal-Constitution*, told Collins, "The trend for the past decade has been to promote editors who, if they are not business people, then they are business-conscious." The editor of the new order does "nothing controversial," explains an editorial sales representative at the *Houston Chronicle*. "Our only concern is giving editorial support to our ad projects."

The Gannett newspaper chain, for example, sent out a memo to the editors of its papers suggesting that they boost circulation by featuring more coverage of "shopping trends and sales, new products and restaurants" —and less coverage of institutions like local government.

It was in a similar vein, Collins reports, that "last year the Woodbridge, N.J., *News Tribune* took an award-winning investigative reporter off the environmental beat, leaving the beat open, and assigned him to general news. Meanwhile, the paper heralded the renovation of a local mall by creating a regular column called 'Gone Shopping.' One recent column began this way: 'Just because Santa paid a visit yesterday, littering your living room with tinsel, shredded gift wrap and cardboard shirt boxes, don't you dare entertain the silly notion that your Christmas shopping is finished!'"

Coughin' nails: Nowhere is the new censorship more documented than in the role cigarette advertisers play in shaping coverage of health issues. In the mid-'80s tobacco companies spent $400 million exploiting nicotine addiction on the pages of magazines.

In October 1985, *Time* magazine carried a special ad section devoted to health. The American Academy of Family Physicians supplied the informational copy. *Time* magazine provided the editorial expertise that deleted all references to the hazards of smoking—a decision that must have pleased the multinational tobacco corporations who bought seven pages in that same edition.

In February 1988, the editors at *Newsweek* published a cover story titled "What You Should Know About Heart Attacks." The back cover featured an ad for Malibu cigarettes, while on the inside, editors deleted any mention in the story that smoking tobacco contributes to heart attacks.

A *Time* spokesman explained the curious way the major newsweeklies cover health issues this way: "*Time*, as does *Newsweek*, has a lot of cigarette advertising. Do you carry material that's insulting to your advertiser?"

Time and *Newsweek*'s intellectual little brother, *The New Republic*, has been similarly corrupted. In 1985, Martin Peretz, *The New Republic* owner and editor in chief, canned a story about the ill effects of smoking because the article lacked what he termed a "balanced treatment." The article's author, David Owen, went on to publish his story in *The Washington Monthly* and added this postscript: "What was the basis for [*The New Republic*'s] decision [to kill the story]? 'Massive losses of advertising revenue,' said Leon Wieseltier, the editor who had assigned it. Peretz told me that he thought smoking was not as dangerous as doctors had made it out to be and that, therefore, 'this is a costly crusade that I am willing to forgo.'"

Dictating Content's case studies reaffirm the existence of editorial tendencies that have been long suspected. Taking this analysis a step further, one can conclude that the same media that allows its editorial policy to be dictated by corporate advertisers can be similarly influenced by political power brokers who would prefer that nothing be said that will challenge the status quo.

The root of the problem lies not in the fact that advertising is pernicious, but that a corporate-owned media that is dependent on corporate advertising is inherently unable to provide the public with the benefits of a free press. Are there alternatives?

Todd Gitlin in his introduction to the study touches on this question when he writes, "Journalists may properly ask what system of finance would be preferable to the predominance of the big bucks. Instead of thinking the question [is] answered merely by asking it, Americans should pay more attention to systems of public regulation where private media financing is severed from [having any] control—like Britian's Channel 4—or bolstered by state grants —as in Sweden's newspaper subsidy."

And Collins points out, "The First Amendment grants the press special protections that it may assist the people in making informed choices about their political and economic affairs. This is its constitutional business. Yet when the mission of the press becomes otherwise, one of the high purposes of the First Amendment is undermined."

Perhaps there is a constitutionally mandated imperative to re-examine the nature of media ownership. Do businesses have a constitutionally protected right to impose their marketing propaganda on the public? When addressing such underlying questions *Dictating Content* falls short. The study concludes with some worthwhile recommendations for reform. But is it reform we need or restructuring?

For a copy of Dictating Content, *send $10 to the Center for the Study of Commercialism, 1875 Connecticut Ave., Suite 300, Washington, D.C. 20009-5728.*

Sanitizing the Airwaves:
Corporate Media Censorship of Advocacy Ads

You're the head of a national advocacy group. The latest polls show your group's goals are supported by a majority of Americans. Your issue is hot, but you can't seem to get your positions across through the media (somehow they don't get it right). Luckily, your supporters have provided you enough funds for national advertising. You can buy a couple hard-hitting TV spots which will say what you want to say, how you want to say it. Right? Wrong!!

Recently, evidence of corporate media censorship of advocacy advertisements has piled up. In the last months, Planned Parenthood Federation of America and three peace organizations found it almost impossible to get ads on the air. Each of these organizations tried turning to advertising to communicate with the public. And all found out that having money and a message is not nearly enough.

Herb Chao Gunther, the Executive Director of the Public Media Center in San Francisco, explains his frustrations over these recent events: "Commercial air time is the only time we can speak unfiltered and unfettered, exactly the way we want. It's what political free speech is about. Yet there have been no consistent rules about access to the airwaves, particularly paid access. Low-level people whose responsibilities focus on selling ads to car dealers are making decisions about what the public should see or hear. This undermines public debate."

Chao Gunther views these limitations as part of a larger, political trend which began with the Reagan presidency. Chao Gunther claims that "Over the past eleven years our government has embraced the corporate message and technique: we should be consumers and not citizens. They want us to go to sleep and leave it to the experts, which is exactly what they did in the Gulf War. Then they want to wake us up and tell us when the parade is."

Planned Parenthood

Chao Gunther knows about corporate censorship first hand. Public Media Center (PMC), which produces and places ads for Planned Parenthood, has encountered major problems placing Planned Parenthood's TV spots. According to Chao Gunther, both CNN and the Lifetime network refused to air Planned Parenthood ads because of their political content. These ads were a series of five thirty-second spots which dramatized the problems of parental consent laws. For example, one focused on Becky Bell, a young woman who died of hemorrhaging after a "coat hanger" abortion.

CNN felt that two of the five thirty-second spots were too disturbing, and refused to air them. Since Planned Parenthood wanted the five ads shown together, they took their ads elsewhere, and turned to the Lifetime network.

At first, the Lifetime network jumped at the opportunity for a major media buy from Planned Parenthood. Chao Gunther recalled, "A woman from Lifetime, our sales rep, said, 'We're the perfect network for you because Lifetime reaches women. And we're about women and we're about empowerment.

We're 100% behind you on this issue. These spots belong here'".

Lifetime soon changed its tune. "She got back to me with one demand," said Chao Gunther. "She said, 'We would like to run a very brief disclaimer. But we're still willing to run the ads'." Chao Gunther remained open to this possibility as long as the disclaimer was in little "mouse type," consistent with other media disclaimers. The sales rep assured Chao Gunther that this is what her employers meant.

However, Lifetime responded that they wanted a full six to eight second large-type preface to the ad reading, "The following ad does not represent the opinions of the Lifetime Network, Capital Cities, or their employees."

Lifetime's disclaimer angered Chao Gunther and Planned Parenthood, since applying this standard would undercut the message and stigmatize the ads. They decided not to run the ads. Their response proved moot: the Lifetime spokesperson soon called to say the parent company, Capital Cities, was unwilling to run the ads under any circumstances.

Chao Gunther points out that Planned Parenthood's media campaign wasn't "chump-change." The total media buy from CNN and Lifetime would have totalled over $400,000, a significant sale for any network.

Anti-War Advocacy

Just prior to the Gulf War, CNN and three Washington, DC networks refused ad time for the Military Family Support Network (MFSN). The spots showed a photo of the Emir of Kuwait dissolving to flag-draped coffins while a voiceover said "The Emir is waiting for Americans to go to war....Don't send our husbands, wives and children to their deaths for this man and his oil."

These decisions infuriated Alex Molnar, MFSN's founder, whose 21-year-old son was serving in Saudi Arabia. Molnar attacked CNN and the networks in the *Washington Post*, saying, "The government of Kuwait is buying millions of dollars of television and radio time to tell parents their children should die for Kuwait. In the face of this Goliath, a group of family members scrapes together enough money to do a commercial, and we get turned down....It's kind of hard to swallow."

While the DC stations turned down MFSN, the *Washington Post* reported that at least two of the local stations had run spots supporting the Bush Administration's policy towards Iraq.

At the same time, Operation Real Security (ORS) tried a decentralized approach to airing TV advocacy ads on the Gulf War. A video was produced featuring Ron Kovic, the subject of Oliver Stone's film "Born on the Fourth of July." Then ORS sent the video to hundreds of peace groups across the country, urging them to raise money and get the ad on TV and cable. They were successful in many small markets, but according to ORS director, Jim Driscol, they failed in many of the medium to major markets, including all three networks in Chicago, and stations in Atlanta, St. Louis, Phoenix, and San Antonio. (There were not enough funds to try the biggest markets.)

It was a low key spot — Kovic in his wheel chair next to the American flag talking to the audience. But it did mention body bags, and fighting to protect big oil companies, and ended with "stand up and speak out...Didn't we promise ourselves we wouldn't let this happen again?"

A third anti-war commercial produced for Physicians for Social Responsibility (PSR) didn't get on the air either. The spot, produced just prior to the Congressional vote on the Gulf War, panned over body bags and urged the viewers to do something before it's too late — i.e. call Congress. According to producer Bill Zimmerman — who also produced the PSR spot — CNN refused to run it. Upon rejection, they took it to the CNN newsroom which turned the rejection into a news story, running it several times nationally, gaining much more coverage than the ads would have garnered.

Neighbor to Neighbor

In May of last year, the Central American advocacy organization Neighbor to Neighbor developed ads urging viewers to boycott Folger's Coffee. Neighbor to Neighbor asserted that Folger's practice of buying Salvadorean coffee beans linked them to the right-wing death squads in El Salvador.

Television stations in every major media market refused to run the ad until Boston's WHDH ran the ad. In a refreshing but temporary nod to the First Amendment, WHDH's spokesperson stated, "We don't take sides on political issues. We are simply providing a community forum for the airing of different points of view. It [the ad] was factually accurate and met our standards of taste."

Unfortunately, that attitude did not last long. Proctor and Gamble, the producer of Folger's and the nation's largest consumer products company, took exception, and immediately withdrew all of its advertising from WHDH — more than $1 million a year.

After controversy and debate, a new policy emerged at WHDH which required station personnel to verify the accuracy of an ad before it could run. WHDH then convinced Proctor and Gamble to resume advertising in 1991.

In part, Proctor and Gamble returned because of an unpublished report commissioned by WHDH and written by journalist Scott Armstrong. While the *Boston Globe* reported that Armstrong's conclusions revealed, "very substantial links between the Salvadorean coffee industry and violence and human rights abuse," WHDH, however, focused on Armstrong's point that Neighbor to Neighbor unfairly targeted Folger's because nothing "singled Folger's coffee as having any direct....responsibility for the violence."

The Corporate Rationale

In each of these cases of corporate media censorship of advocacy ads, the media corporations have justified their actions through policy statements like those of WHDH. The existence of a standard policy is presented as a measure of fairness: it's the media corporations' assertion that they apply the same rules to each situation. However, both the application of these policies and their content make it clear that protecting the environment for corporate advertising will make it difficult to get on the air. In fact, the corporate policies create wildly subjective rationales which can be used to keep virtually any ideas (as opposed to products) off the air.

In denying the Military Family Support Network advertising time, Stacey Robinson, account executive at CNN, claimed "It is the policy of Turner Broadcasting and CNN not to air controversial commercials at a time when a topic is so top of mind. Considering the crisis in the Middle East is all the public is thinking of and most of what our reporters are carrying, it would not be in the best interest of our networks to run your spot at this time."

In refusing the Military Family Support Network ads, Washington station WJLA wrote that they reject ads "which tend to inflame or incite unreasoned public response rather than reasoned debate, or which make assertions which cannot be documented." DC station WRC claimed a long-standing policy of "not broadcasting controversial issues of social and political importance unless it is done in a format which provides time for fair and balanced exploration of opposing viewpoints [and this] cannot be achieved in a 30- or 60second paid commercial format."

How can stations which use short, 30-second sound bites to cover stories and uniformly air candidate commercials refuse 30- and 60-second ads on the grounds that the issue can't be fully discussed? And when should we debate going to war, if not when our country is preparing to?

When SANE/Freeze's local chapter brought the ORS/Kovic ad to WHDH in Boston, they ran up against the station's changed policy. The ad couldn't run unless the sponsors could demonstrate that the Gulf War was to be fought to protect oil interests, an assertion most people would likely agree with, but one impossible to prove. Now will WHDH apply the same standard to campaign ads or product ads?

Two Views

Herb Chao Gunther and Bill Zimmerman, experienced veterans in advocacy media, share common concerns about advertising access, but they have different approaches to confronting this problem.

Zimmerman suggests that the growing number of rejections of ads may be because more people are trying to get spots on the air. Zimmerman believes, "The ORS experience shows that local advocacy and pressure can get some ads on the air. And when it doesn't, creative organizing can turn it into a local news item for radio, print news and even TV. Usually the local independent stations are more open to advocacy—need the money—while the network affiliates are much more cautious, but unfortunately have the audience numbers. Generally, stations will shy away from material that is very graphic or emotional."

Zimmerman adds a caution, "While we need access to the airwaves to encourage the flow of ideas and protect democracy, I'm afraid of what might happen if the whole system is opened up. The other side has a lot more money than we do, and I'd hate to get into an advertising contest with them. In other words, we might want to depend on creative organizing to get material on the air."

Chao Gunther disagrees with Zimmerman, claiming "It can be defeatist to think that we can't compete with the Right using ads. If our ads are always rejected, then we're left depending on corporate news media to tell our story—effectively marginalizing or trivializing the real issue as just another story of TV ads that were too hot to air."

Chao Gunther continues, "It's not so much the right wing that's the enemy—though they must be fought on many issues—it's the corporate mentality that's breeding the apathy that's destroying us. Ads that are provocative and disturbing need to get on the air to make people think—to wake them up."

Chao Gunther contends, "It's not too far-fetched to think that if we had 3 or 4 million dollars and access to the air waves, we might have prevented the Gulf War. At a crucial juncture the polls showed something like 70% against the war. That was the point to aggressively go on the air and pressure Congress. After the war started and jingoism and easy victory dominated the news, the 70% swung in favor of the war."

Zimmerman counters, "With every action, there's a reaction. The pro-war effort would have countered with much more money and ads. We can't go blindly into these battles without thinking about the long-term consequences."

Overall, corporate censorship seems more a product of commerce than right-wing ideology. The networks, affiliates and cable owners who benefit from the $25 billion a year spent on advertising, concentrate on delivering the audience to the advertiser and treat the advertising environment as sacred. Any controversy is to be avoided for fear of alienating consumers, right-wing advocacy groups or advertisers. They don't want to give viewers a reason to change stations, advocates a reason to threaten a boycott, or advertisers a reason to take their money elsewhere.

Says Chao Gunther, "They don't want their viewers agitated when the Pepsi commercials come on; they don't want to take their minds off buying Lay's Potato Chips. Here's the question we have to ask ourselves: Is Pepsi's right to market its product in a totally pure environment more important than the robust debate we're supposed to have with a First Amendment and a healthy democracy?"

A Call for Equal Access

Censored advertising space is not a new problem, but it's clearly a growing one. Even with the resources to buy $400,000 worth of advertising as Planned Parenthood was prepared to do, corporate media decided to say no thank you. Increasingly, commercial primacy keeps controversial ideas off the airways. Increasingly, television stations are claiming that controversial ideas must be covered by their news reporting, and not in purchased time.

In the past, media corporations used the fairness doctrine to refuse to run ads with sharply defined points of view by saying they would have to make time for the "other side." Now, with the fairness doctrine rendered inoperative by the Reagan appointed FCC, corporate media has no obligation to provide time to answer advocacy ads. Yet they still block the way, saying they will hear disruptive complaints from opposition groups or they argue, "we're a family station and we protect our viewers/listeners from being offended."

Advocacy ads aren't lewd or abusive, but they are dangerous for television because not everyone will agree with them. In one of the little-known contradictions of American "free market" capitalism, if you have the cash for your ad, even if it is factually accurate and not libelous, you can't buy the time. Isn't it ironic that the air waves, belonging to the people and leased for virtually nothing to media corporations, have become essentially unavailable for the exercise of free speech?

DataCenter   464 19th Street, Oakland, California 94612 (415) 835-4692

Right Wing vs. Public TV

*Pressure from the Right: Conservative Media Critics
Want to Reshape Public Television*

by Laurie Ouellette

Because television is so pervasive in our society, and has the power to influence attitudes and beliefs, scores of critics are worried about the commercial nature of TV, and about television's failure to provide the in-depth reporting, diversity, and challenging programming that it could and should offer. Public television, while increasingly influenced by corporate funding, has nonetheless provided what little diversity we do see on free TV today. Yet, even this modest amount of independent-minded programming may disappear if members of a right-wing crusade against public television have their way. Still gloating from the Right's success in attacking individual artists and the NEA, a growing band of conservative media critics has waged an attack against "leftist" bias in public television shows, and the public funding of public television in general.

Grassroots media watch groups—such as Action for Children, which lobbies against rampant commercialism in children's shows, and Fairness and Accuracy in Reporting (FAIR), which criticizes the corporate bias in television news—encourage active television viewing from their constituents and have been influential in making small but important changes on the screen. However, they have not enjoyed anywhere near the clout of their well-funded conservative counterparts with strong connections on Capitol Hill. Conservative media-watch groups operate by bringing controversy and a flood of media attention to the programs they attack. Their increasing influence can be felt across television, and their intimida-tion has had a chilling effect on public television.

Some of the most successful right-wing "media critics" have focused their energies on reshaping the structure of public television. Indicative of what many insiders believe is a shift and expansion of the Right's agenda away from individual arts (exemplified by the contro-versy over NEA grants) and towards the media—public television in particular—conservative critics such as Brent Bozell,

Still gloating from the Right's success in attacking individual artists and the NEA, a growing band of conservative media critics are waging an attack against "leftist" bias in public television...

chairman of the Washington-based Media Research Center, David Horowitz, founder of the Committee for Media Integrity, and Lawrence Jarvik, a scholar funded by the ultra-conservative Heri-tage Foundation to "look into public TV," have waged critical attacks on the public broadcasting system.

So far, the loudest conservative critic to rage about public TV has been former leftist turned right-winger and now self-proclaimed media watcher David Horowitz. Horowitz has launched several well-publicized attacks on public television programs he targets as "biased to the left," including Bill Moyers' "World of Ideas," the documentary series "Eyes on the Prize" and "Making Sense of the Sixties," the "POV" series and "Frontline." A recent addition to his hit list is the Independent Television Service (ITVS), the new funding agency de-signed to provide innovative new sources of programming for public television.

Horowitz's abundant funding, as well as his connections with conservative Republicans in Congress, have ensured him a position of influence far beyond the grassroots level of most media advocacy groups. Considering that his Committee on Media Integrity (COMINT) consists of a post-office box in Hollywood, a short list of advisory board members, a newsletter, and a mailing list of several thousand subscrib-ers in media circles, Horowitz has been remarkably successful in influencing PBS programming and catapulting himself into the public eye.

While his credibility as a media critic is perhaps due to his past association with the Left (as former editor of *Ramparts* magazine) and his subsequent transformation to champion of conserva-tive interests, his ability to draw media attention seems to come from his ability to generate controversy. Take, for instance, his attack on the award-winning program "South Africa Now" last year.

Claiming the program was biased in favor of the African National Congress, Horowitz criticized the show in his newsletter, organized a letter-writing campaign against it, and pressured station managers of PBS affiliate KCET in Los Angeles until he eventually claimed victory for the cancellation of "South Africa Now" on KCET. (The program was reinstated after angry viewers pressured the station to bring it back. It was also temporarily cancelled on another PBS affiliate, WGBH in Boston.)

As a result of the controversy that erupted over his attack on "South Africa Now," Horowitz himself enjoyed considerable media attention, which in turn reinforced his legitimacy as a media critic. In a round of attack and counter-attack published in *Current*, the trade journal for public broadcasting, as well as in *The New York Times* and other newspapers, Horowitz accused public television of "intolerable" and "illegal" bias, directly targeting Bill Moyers and GlobalVision, the independent production company responsible for the award-winning "South Africa Now." Meanwhile, criticisms proffered by his organization COMINT have been cited in *The New York Times*, the *Los Angeles Times* and *The New Republic*.

Those attacked by Horowitz have responded in print by pointing out inaccuracies and irrationalities in Horowitz's reasoning, and the threat that he poses to the free marketplace of ideas. Moyers warns that Horowitz agenda is not "fairness and balance," but unanimity. "They don't want media integrity—they want media subservience to their ideology. To [Horowitz] and his reactionary allies, criticism equals subversion, opposition equals treason, and liberalism is a personal affront."

Jeff Cohen, media-watcher and director of Fairness and Accuracy in Reporting (FAIR), disputes as inaccurate Horowitz's claims of leftist bias in PBS programming. Horowitz and his associates are not worried about the bias seen every week in right-wing and corporate talk programs, such as William F. Buckley's "Firing Line," or "Wall Street Week," nor is he concerned with the "MacNeil Lehrer News Hour," which has been criticized by FAIR for failing to use diverse sources and for repeatedly using "experts" who maintain corporate interests.

Simple math shows the flaws in Horowitz's claims against leftist bias on PBS, says Cohen. Leftist documentaries represent a tiny proportion of public TV's total programming: "Given the near-total exclusion of the Left from public TV's daily and weekly public affairs lineup, a strong argument can be made that the number of such documentaries is too few."

Producer Danny Schechter warns of the consequences of journalists giving equal time to well-funded and ideologically-driven individuals who represent a dubious constituency.

Producer Danny Schechter, a victim of Horowitz's fierce attack against "South Africa Now," believes that organizations such as Horowitz's have a right to exist, and that debate is healthy, he warns of the consequences of journalists giving equal time, in the name of objectivity, to well-funded and ideologically-driven individuals who represent a dubious constituency.

As Schechter wrote in *Current*, Horowitz' well-publicized attacks are reminiscent of the black lists of the 1950s, which were started by one lone grocer in Syracuse, New York, armed with a mimeograph machine and aided and abetted by a well-paid New York publicist. "In essence, one man with a letterhead [Horowitz] used ["South Africa Now"] to catapult himself into the public eye. We inadvertently became his promotional vehicle; the more heated his rhetoric, the more attention he received. This kind of 'balance' forced us into the position of having to continually defend ourselves against charges that have no basis to begin with. Rather than being innocent until proven guilty, we had the onus of proving that we are not 'biased.' "

Horowitz's critics have various theories as to his connections to a larger involvement with a conservative agenda. Schecter believes that Horowitz is a tool of the conservative climate that he helped generate. Self-censorship, in which stations avoid programs deemed controversial by right-wing critics, is a much longer lasting effect of Horowitz's

influence, says Schecter. Another enduring result, he says, will be the inability of certain programs to obtain funding. "Corporations that might be open to sponsoring programming that is more diverse and open to new ideas are less likely to do so when you have organizations that are ideologically driven and appear to have unlimited resources to make such programming a target."

Jeff Chester, director of the Teledemocracy Project—a Ralph Nader supported media watch group—warns that Horowitz must be seen in the context of the right-wing foundations and organizations that Chester believes

---

The real goal of conservative groups is to remove public funding from television and the arts completely, says independent producer Larry Daressa.

---

funded much of Horowitz's work in the 1980s. According to Chester, the attention of these interlocking foundations and advocacy organizations, and their important connections on Capitol Hill, has grown from an attack on the NEA to include a forceful assault on public television.

Larry Daressa is an independent producer who was involved in the grassroots mobilization of independent producers to form ITVS, the new funding agency for innovative public television programming. Daressa believes that attacks by Horowitz and other conservatives against leftist bias on public television mean more than a shift of focus from the arts to public media. Using an attack on alleged leftist bias in public television as a cover, the real goal of conservative groups is to remove public funding from television and the arts, and to get government out of culture completely, says Daressa. He points out that conservatives have been wanting to cut the funding for public television since the Reagan administration first tried, unsuccessfully, to cut the public television budget in 1981.

If the targeting of the public media is recognized as but one dimension of a

DataCenter   464 19th Street, Oakland, California 94612 (415) 835-4692

full-scale right-wing attack on the funding of arts and culture, Daressa says Horowitz can be dismissed as little more than a "serviceable crank." "By pointing out issues framed by his claims of leftist bias, he is able to provide a populist cover for the real economic attack." And, as Daressa points out, even Horowitz can't resist emphasizing economic issues in his COMINT newsletter, which teems with criticism of excessive station manager salaries, expensive trips, and such.

As Daressa points out, it is true that there are some problems with public television as it exists today, including increasing commercialization. Critics from all sides question whether PBS, which was created to serve the public interest with non-commercial, innovative programming not available on network stations, is doing its job as originally intended. Public television gets the major share of its funding from corporate donations or subscriptions, and most programs paid for by such sources end up reflecting corporate interests.

While Horowitz and his conservative cohorts argue that the commercialization of PBS justifies eliminating its public funding, Daressa points out that while most right-wing shows of opinion have corporate sponsors, controversial and unconventional programming is more likely to require government funding. And this, it seems, is the process that conservatives would like to eliminate.

Perhaps that is why the Independent Television Service (ITVS)—which was appropriated $24 million dollars by Congress in 1988 and created in 1989 to provide new sources of PBS programming for three years—has been the latest focus of conservative media critics. The aim of ITVS is to create innovative experimental television that reflects diverse and challenging ideas, along the lines of popular Channel 4 in England. Conservatives, by waging inaccurate and misleading attacks against ITVS, are forcing them into a defensive position even before they can even get started.

Leading this effort is Lawrence Jarvik, who is "looking into ways to improve public TV," including privatization. Jarvick's research is funded by the ultra-conservative Heritage Foundation. He first attacked ITVS in the latest issue of the COMINT newsletter, criticizing ITVS for, as of yet, failing to provide any grants to independent producers or to develop any programming, and calling the organization a "politically correct pork-barrel."

Reminiscent of the publicity enjoyed by Horowitz, Jarvik's attack against ITVS has enjoyed the media spin-effect, and was featured not only in the public broadcasting trade publication *Current*, but cited as a source in a major article about public television in the *Washington*

The new and innovative programming that does air on PBS is important because it is one of the few independent media outlets still available.

Times, a conservative daily owned by the Reverend Sun Myung Moon. Yet ITVS director John Schott, responding to Jarvik in a later commentary piece in the *Washington Times*, points out the flaws in Jarvik's criticisms: "Although Congress

---

The Independent Television Service has been the latest focus of conservative critics, who are forcing them into a defensive position even before they can get started.

---

created the mandate for ITVS in 1989, it was not until June 1991—four months ago—that our contract with the Corporation for Public Broadcasting was finalized. Until that time, we were not authorized, funded, or staffed to make any grants."

Schott further points out that ITVS, whose programming is scheduled to be broadcast sometime in late 1992, will provide an alternative to the shift in commercialized programming that undermines the original purpose of PBS to provide programming otherwise unavailable on network television. "We are by nature "non-commercial," and it is unlikely that we will ever be accused of being "slickly produced."

It is too soon to tell exactly what the

impact of Jarvik's attacks against ITVS will be. Yet one thing is certain: Conservative interest in reshaping public television is not likely to end soon. While Horowitz and other well-funded conservative critics continue to pressure station managers and send memos to their conservative allies in Congress and the White House, other right-wing groups have taken to sending videotapes of offensive programs to each and every member of Congress to sway them to prohibit the Corporation for Public Broadcasting (CPB)—the Congression-

---

"In just a few years, arts funding has been devastated. We don't want the Right to repeat their success with public broadcasting."

---

ally created department that disburses funds and acts as the fiscal agent for public television—from funding "patently offensive" programming. And, as reported in *Current*, Senator Jesse Helms (R-North Carolina) has been rumored to be preparing a bill that would prohibit "patently offensive" programming that employs CPB funds, similar to his bill on the National Endowment for the Arts, which was endorsed by both houses of Congress before being defeated in a conference Committee in October.

As Jeff Chester points out, the new and innovative programming that does air on PBS, such as that planned by ITVS, is important because it is one of the few independent media outlets still available. Chester worries that the leadership of the independent film and arts community have been shocked and are unable to develop an effective strategy to deal with well-funded conservative critics, and points to the need for the progressive community to rally around programming such as ITVS. "In just a few years, arts funding has been devastated. We don't want the Right to repeat their success with public broadcasting, particularly programs that are trying to be innovative and taking risks. These programs are exploring the democratic process at its fullest, by raising questions." ■

IV. Corporate Power Over Information

In a society given to an overarching commercialism, writes Herbert Schiller in this section, "free access to information as a social commitment goes by the wayside. Only data that has commercial value will be collected and retrieved. Democratic participation in government, founded on the right to know and the availability of information will wither." Beside the concentration of the ownership of newspapers, publishing, and media in ever fewer corporate hands, the newly developed information industry is pressing hard to privatize governmental libraries and information resources. News may be filtered through reporters wary of displeasing corporate owners who also own nuclear plants, military hardware factories, and utilities. And the revenue from advertising — not only products but political comments as well — creates more dilemmas for editors and journalists.

"Advertising reduces every problem to a personal problem with the product as a solution. The true solution is political. We need what virtually every industrialized nation in the world has — a national childcare policy and family leave. What we get offered instead is Hamburger Helper and Enjoli perfume..." — Jean Kilbourne, media critic, on Women's magazines

"The unwillingness of the (Supreme) Court to differentiate between billion-dollar corporations and individuals allows power to be exercised brazenly in the national and local arenas of speech, expression of ideas and social policymaking." — Herbert L. Schiller

A society is emerging in which only data with a commercial value will be collected

Public Information Goes Corporate

By Herbert I. Schiller

FEW PEOPLE would link the future of the entire country with the prospects of one profession—especially if that profession was librarianship. Long-term and massively inculcated collective ignorance has made it difficult or impossible for many to see the connection. Nevertheless, what is happening to libraries and the profession of librarianship is one of the most illuminating indicators of what kind of society is emerging in the United States.

Historically, libraries have been the main collectors, organizers, and managers of the nation's information resources. The handling of this function assumes an overarching national goal. What this goal is, or should be, defines the character of American existence.

Central to democratic society

Two dramatically different approaches to the information function can be identified. One is to regard information as a central element in the development and creation of a democratic society. Under this premise, information serves to facilitate democratic decision-making, assists citizen participation in government, and contributes to the search for roughly egalitarian measures in the economy at large.

Comprehensive and well-organized information enables decision-makers to make rational resource allocation decisions; to prioritize social claims; and to maximize social welfare. It allows them to overcome baleful practices that harm the general welfare, like pollution, smoking, and armaments expenditures. Such information resources allow leaders to promote the development of science and invention that are socially beneficial and to

organize the historical experience for meaningful contemporary reflection and use. In brief, comprehensive, well-organized public information enables decision-makers to bring past knowledge and experience to bear on current issues and problems.

Neutrality is no option

A different approach to information collection and management can prevail. Instead of contributing to democratic society it could reflect and facilitate antidemocratic, nonparticipatory institutions and practices, which maintain or extend inequality in the nation.

A variant of this approach is to view information collection, organization, and dissemination as a neutral activity, absent of social direction. It becomes a more or less routine process of stockpiling facts and figures for whatever use they may serve. This is the equivalent of information for information's sake.

In fact, this is not an actual option. Some design has to prefigure what is being done, whether or not that design is made clear. It is there; if it is left obscure, it may be assumed to serve nondemocratic aims.

These opposing approaches to information collection and management cannot be reconciled. To support one is to be in conflict with the other. This may not always be apparent. In America today, this is made less apparent because no responsible voice will admit to seeking a set of informational institutions and practices that are undemocratic and skewed to the benefit of the already privileged.

An undemocratic information system

Now, however, what no "responsible" voice will admit—the development of an undemocratic information system—is precisely what is occurring. As a consequence of fundamental changes in institutional organization, practices, and goals, the antidemocratic approach to information has received an enormous stimulus. At the same time, the democratic vision and practice have been seriously weakened. Several developments have contributed to this alarming condition.

> **D**eregulation has contributed significantly to the erosion of the national information base

Herbert I. Schiller is Professor Emeritus of Communications, University of California–San Diego, La Jolla. This article is an expansion of his remarks at the 1991 American Library Association Conference program on "Preparing Professionals for the Year 2000," sponsored by the ALA Office for Library Personnel Resources

In the last half-century, since the end of World War II, the United States has become a corporate-dominated society. Admittedly, the American economy in prewar years had no lack of big business, exercising considerable weight in political and economic affairs. Since then, however, the transformation of the American economy from strong industrial state to superpower has been the record of corporate growth and expansion.

Corporate wealth and power dominate the political process, the economic activity, and the cultural space of the nation. In the communications sector—press, publishing, radio, television, recording, film, and advertising—the concentration is no less marked. Today, a half-dozen media conglomerates account for a large share of the country's media-informational activity, to say nothing of their share of the international information-al pie (see Greg MacDonald's "The Emergence of Global-Media Conglomerates," *International Labour Office Working Paper No. 70*, 1990).

One immediate consequence of the corporatization of American life is that a great amount of information is withheld from the public because it is regarded and treated as proprietary by its corporate holders. Another consequence is that information in corporate organization flows from the top down, hardly a model for a democratic information condition.

Deregulation of the U.S. economy

A second feature of this era, derivative from the expanded influence of the corporation in national life, has been the deregulatory tide that began in the 1950s in the Eisenhower administration. Slowed somewhat in the intervening years, it was renewed and massively extended in the Reagan-Bush years.

Largely the result of corporate pressure on the political sphere, deregulation has enabled business to do what it wants while its social accountability has been steadily reduced. The effects of deregulation across the entire spectrum of economic and social life have been immense and are yet to be fully chronicled.

In the informational sector, deregulation has contributed significantly to further erosion of the national information base. Business, in one instance after another, has been relieved of making basic data available to the public. Matters as varied as TV station programming logs—records of what is broadcast—and information affecting workers at their jobs have been left unattended or eliminated.

As deregulation is the means for eliminating social oversight, it affects the national information condition directly and severely. Oversight, to be effective, requires information. The elimination of information to support oversight is an accompaniment to the destruction of oversight itself.

In short, deregulation destroys social information. In fact, this is one of the most damaging consequences of the weakening of the regulatory

---

T he conflicting approaches to information can't be reconciled. To support one is to oppose the other

---

agencies (e.g., the Federal Communications Commission [FCC], the Securities and Exchange Commission [SEC], the Federal Trade Commission [FTC]) in the last 20 years. Those agencies were created to protect the public interest.

Pervasive commercialization

A third feature of contemporary American life is the pervasive commercialization of everyday living. This follows inevitably from the growth of corporate wealth and power and the deregulation that that power has successfully demanded.

Commercialization has a powerful, though largely unacknowledged, impact on the national information condition. Not least is its effect on the overall *quality* of information and its progressive debasement, as the bad (or trivial or distorted) drives out the good. One example is the ever-deteriorating condition of the governmental postal services. Overwhelmed with a torrent of third-class commercial mail, rates go ever higher. Publications that are not subsidized by giant firms find it increasingly difficult to survive.

"The business of America is business," said Calvin Coolidge in 1925. He foretold what has come to pass to an extraordinary degree in the current Information Age. Sales messages are omnipresent and nearly all social, athletic, political, and entertainment events and activities serve as backdrops for commercial solicitation. Social information is buried under masses of commercial messages. Worse yet, when it is accompanied by commercial material, the social content is blurred, trivialized, or lost.

Information as a commodity

These developments—expanded corporate wealth and power, deregulation, and the preemption of social space with commercial messages and perspectives—culminate in still another far-reaching change in the economy. What once were social and public spheres of activity have been steadily privatized. Governmental responsibilities in general, and health, educational, and cultural activity in particular, have been parceled out and taken over by private enterprise.

The national informational system especially has borne the brunt of the privatization pressure. The national government has been, and remains, the largest generator, collector, and disseminator of information. The drive to privatization has cut deeply into these functions.

Even so, free access to information, long a cherished principle of American librarianship, was reaffirmed as recently as February 1991 by the American Library Association's Government Documents Round Table (GODORT) in a list of principles, the first of which was: "Access to government information is a public right that must not be restricted by administrative barriers, geography, ability to pay, or format."

This principle is being steadily weakened. Ability to pay increasingly has become the organizing mechanism for acquiring, processing, and disseminating governmental and all other kinds of information. Impoverished state and local budgets that reduce resources for social undertakings and the aggressive drive of profit-seeking enterprise to expand into the information sphere (it prefers to call it the "information market") are changing profoundly American cultural-informational practices and with them no less than the texture and quality of national life.

As the idea of information as a good for sale, a commodity, advances, the idea of information as a social good, the cornerstone of democratic life, recedes. The transformation is already far advanced. ALA has been in the forefront in attempting to alert the public to what is going on. Its bi-annual publication *Less Access to Less Information by and About the U.S. Government* insistently calls attention to these developments. The January–June 1990 chronology carries this preface to its detailed report:

> During the past nine years, this ongoing chronology has documented Administration efforts to restrict and privatize government information.

The destruction and damage to the social information stockpile are detailed in ample and distressing detail.

Social information: an idea in danger

It is not discrete, one-time decisions that are restricting and eliminating the collection of social information. Basic institutional processes are being changed that are leading to a time when the very concept of "social information" will be considered archaic.

The extent to which, for example, the decision to actually collect data is left to private, profit-seeking firms means that whatever the action taken, it is a result not of an assessment of social need but rather a forecast of private gain. Sometimes these coincide, but to rely on such a possibility is to place the entire social agenda at risk. This is precisely what is happening today throughout the entire economy.

The recent decision of the Bush administration to turn over a large chunk of the radio spectrum to the commercial sector is an example. If the decision is implemented, this crucial resource, inherently a public property, will become a private property. Another vital part of the social sphere will be lost, to be disposed of as its new owners see fit (see Peter Passell, "Administration Seeks Profits in Plan To Auction Airwaves," *New York Times*, May 30, 1991, p. 1).

Not only the national government information stockpile is being privatized. Leading research universities, a major producer of what was once regarded as social information, increasingly are contracting with major corporations. In the varied arrangements that result, the laborato-

ries and the research skills and projects of the professoriat are enlisted to produce data from which chemical, molecular biology, pharmaceutical, computer and electronics, and related corporations can make products and money. The research direction of a part of the university is increasingly guided by commercial objectives.

The information that is produced in the labs and studies of the faculty is no longer publicly available. It goes to the sponsoring company. It is no wonder that *Science* magazine finds it necessary to publish articles that inquire, "Data Sharing: A Declining Ethic?" and to comment that, "Com-

> ## As the idea of information as a commodity advances, the idea of information as a social good recedes

mercial pressures and heightened competition [in the universities] are testing the notion that scientific data and materials should be shared" (*Science*, May 1990, p. 952–957).

Derek Bok, in his final "President's Report" to the Harvard University Board of Overseers in the spring of 1991, warned that commercialization may be the greatest threat facing American universities. "It will take strong leadership," Bok said, "to keep the profit motive from eroding the values in which the welfare and reputation of universities ultimately depend" (Liz McMillen, "Quest for Profits May Damage Basic Values of Universities, Harvard's Bok Warns," *Chronicle of Higher Education*, April 24, 1991, p. A31).

Where will we find that leadership Bok describes? For decades it has been recognized that top university administrators spend most of their time seeking funds from the very corporations that constitute the source of the peril.

Can social information be saved?

Can the processes that are leading to the end of social information be halted or, better yet, reversed? This

is the central and transcending social and political issue in the coming years. The outcome will largely decide the kind of society we become.

In this choice, librarianship and librarians, whether they will it or not, are directly involved and certain to be deeply affected. In fact, it is no overstatement to argue that the survival of American librarianship and its principles, as they have been understood historically, are at stake.

Since it would never do to make the passengers uneasy, airline magazines are noted for their enthusiastic articles. Delta Airline's *Sky* magazine (November 1990, p. 78) published an upbeat piece titled "Here Come the 'Infopreneurs,'" and claimed that "In the old days, they were known as librarians. Today, information-brokers wend their way through hundreds of computer databases with the greatest of ease."

Commercial information activities have an important function to fulfill. To imagine that these services are the sum total of a librarian's contribution is to acquiesce to the emergence of a society in which social aims have been discarded.

It would be a society in which commercial goals are achieved efficiently with electronic technology, but in the process, free access to information as a social commitment goes by the wayside. Only data that has commercial value will be collected and retrieved. Democratic participation in government, founded on the right to know and the availability of information, will wither.

What is happening to the American information system, and to a vital segment of its responsible custodianship, are urgent issues of national importance. Some of the most powerful interests in the country support the direction that has been taken in recent decades. Opposition to these forces will not be easy. There is no guarantee of success.

To try to avoid these issues, however, is no less perilous. Information has become increasingly significant in the organization and performance of the national economy. This has forced the effort to defend American librarianship's longstanding democratic goals to be fused with the need to make the overall economy more responsive to the citizenry and less attentive to powerful corporate interests. Right now, at best, the outcome is uncertain.

INDUSTRY COVER-UPS

Hidden Health Hazards of CFCs

R. DENNIS HAYES

Pacific Southwest Airlines (P.S.A.) Flight 350 was high above California en route to San Diego when the pilot, Capt. Richard O'Harren, detected an odorless vapor spewing into his face. A system that normally beaded rain on the windshield had failed, filling the cockpit with what was later described as a "CFC cocktail." Fearing for the plane's safety, O'Harren and his first officer, William Mulcaha, snapped on their oxygen masks and landed at their destination without further incident, but not before P.S.A. officials had assured them by radio that the rain-repellent chemicals were "nontoxic and harmless."

They were hardly that, as was already well known when the incident occurred in late 1984. CFCs, or chlorofluorocarbons, not only accelerate ozone depletion but pose a variety of serious health hazards, from fatal heart arrhythmia to lung disease to memory loss and psychomotor impairment. Indeed, the canister feeding Flight 350's leaky repellent system bore the warning: "Overexposure Can Cause Central Nervous System Depression, Anesthesia and Cardiac Sensitization." The same caution still appears on similar canisters installed on 6,000 to 10,000 other commercial jets, but few pilots notice the admonition since it is hidden from view under their seats or on the rear wall of the cockpit.

The warning's lack of visibility typifies how corporate America has been able to insist for years that CFCs are safe, despite evidence dating back to 1937 that they are significant toxins. After the Environmental Protection Agency banned CFC use in aerosol spray cans in 1978 because the compounds were destroying the ozone layer, companies began scheming with the Reagan E.P.A. to derail further CFC regulation. As a result, during the 1980s chemical and electronics engineers were able to cook up some 200 new manufacturing uses for CFC-113, the particularly versatile product used in the rain repellent and even more widely in Silicon Valley, where electronics firms sprayed or bathed almost everything that goes into a computer in their "solvent of choice."

Were it not for O'Harren, we still might not know the length to which some companies—notably Du Pont and Allied-Signal—went to hide the fact that their CFC products were not exactly benign. Soon after O'Harren was misted with the rain repellent he developed chronic nosebleeds and hypertension. After a required airline physical, a Federal Aviation Administration doctor declared the pilot, then a veteran of eighteen years in the air, medically ineligible to fly, whereupon he lost his license and his job for fourteen months. With San Diego lawyer Lance Schaeffer, O'Harren brought a personal injury and damages claim against Du Pont, Allied-Signal, P.S.A. (now USAir), Boeing and others responsible for manufacturing and employing the repellent. Last Labor Day weekend, in San Diego County Superior Court, a jury awarded O'Harren $454,000 in compensatory damages and the following day assessed USAir $2 million for its negligence. For example, when O'Harren attempted to get the cockpit hazard acknowledged and corrected, P.S.A. refused to warn other pilots. The jury also found against Du Pont for more than $111,000 for failing, in Schaeffer's words, "to warn adequately of CFC's dangers."

Ettienne was shocked by Du Pont and Allied-Signal's brazenness.

The O'Harren trial revealed that Du Pont and Allied-Signal had amassed sufficient evidence that they should have suspected at least nine years ago that their widely used CFC-113 solvent caused rare tumors and fatal lung infections in rats. Yet they failed to warn thousands of unprotected workers nationwide, especially in Silicon Valley. The National Occupational Hazard Survey estimates that, in all, 300,000 workers may have been exposed to CFC-113. Air samples taken and analyzed in 1989 by the Rowland Laboratories at the University of California, Irvine, showed the valley had the highest amount of CFC-113 molecules ever recorded. The two companies also failed to warn the E.P.A. and the United Nations Environmental Program, as well as scientists and consumers. To this day, Silicon Valley electronics industry leaders proclaim CFC-113 safe and nontoxic.

The trial produced evidence that our body cells and tissue can metabolize CFC-113, breaking it down into toxic and carcinogenic compounds. The nearly 3,000 pages of scientific memos and tables of raw data subpoenaed from Du Pont's Haskell Laboratories included the results of toxicity testing of CFC-113 on the rats. Du Pont and Allied-Signal conducted the test over a two-year period beginning in 1980 but published the results only as "highly sanitized" summaries, maintains Dr. Earl Ettienne, a cellular and molecular biologist who testified as an expert witness for O'Harren.

Ettienne, who has held faculty and research positions at Harvard University, the Massachusetts Institute of Technology and Lawrence Berkeley Labs, reviewed virtually every study conducted on CFC-113. He was not surprised by the Haskell Laboratories findings. "The tests as well as subsequent independent reports indicated that CFC-113 was immunosuppressive and biotransformed [by the body] into carcinogenic and nephro[kidney]-toxic compounds," Ettienne said in an interview from his Mill Valley, California, office.

Du Pont designed the two-year experiment to test for nonlethal toxicity and carcinogenicity. In fact, it yielded lethal

---

R. Dennis Hayes lives in San Francisco and is the author of Behind the Silicon Curtain: The Seductions of Work in a Lonely Era *(South End Press).*

results. There was a "massive death of exposed animals possibly resulting from an immunosuppressant action correlated with an ineradicable lung infection," says Ettienne. A tuberculosislike bug known as corynebacterium killed rat after rat despite multiple and prolonged antibiotic treatments known to be effective against this bacterial strain. In the end, 438 rats, more than half the sample, died. Of those, 129 died from the lung infection, the rest of causes Du Pont failed to disclose. The rats were selected for longevity and exposed to "non-lethal" doses of CFC-113, ranging up to 19,000 parts per million. But based on a recent government report, the lab's high kill rates aren't surprising, because the National Institute for Occupational Safety and Health acknowledges that 4,500 parts per million are immediately dangerous to human life. Du Pont failed to attribute any rat deaths to CFC-113 exposure, even though the lung infections occurred first in medium- and high-exposure groups, and even though CFC-113 had an occupational-illness profile as an upper respiratory tract irritant at the time of the experiment.

Ettienne told me he was shocked by Du Pont and Allied-Signal's brazenness. In a scientific summary published six years after their experiments, company chemists wrote that "observations of appearance and behavior, mortality, and clinical laboratory measurements were unremarkable during the 24-month exposure period. . . . Microscopic examination of tissues from rats examined . . . revealed no evidence of compound-related toxicity or carcinogeneity." In fact, the evidence shows that Du Pont simply failed to analyze, clinically and completely, the large number of rats that died in the experiments.

Ettienne adds that Du Pont found but neglected to publicize statistically significant changes in white blood cells, platelets and fluoride and glucose levels in urine (fluoride is represented by the "F" in CFC). Higher fluoride in rats chronically exposed to CFC-113 indicates that the compound has broken down into even more toxic substances, says Ettienne, including two (CFC-122 and CFC-123) that federal agencies describe as carcinogenic. "Du Pont failed to completely report" these results, according to Ettienne, even when the E.P.A. expressed interest in the data in 1983. "The scientific community should be encouraged to review Du Pont's raw data in their entirety," he says.

That is not likely to happen soon. Du Pont has so far succeeded in stalling a court order to release all the scientific data collected in the case. Schaeffer, O'Harren's lawyer, says such protection is extraordinary, and he opposed Du Pont's legal effort to retrieve the data (uncopied) or to have it destroyed. (USAir is playing the secrecy game too, maintaining that O'Harren cannot share his story with the world without its express permission, as stipulated by the airline's contract with the pilots' union. USAir has made it clear to the pilot that if he talks he is out of a job.)

While researching this article, I gained access to the 1,666-page Haskell Laboratories report. I found it in the E.P.A.'s toxic substances database bearing the warning, "Company Sanitized." According to this document, which is not available to the general public, Du Pont revised its summary of the experiment in 1985 before quietly submitting it to the E.P.A.

I asked Cathy Andriadis, of Du Pont's External Affairs department, why it insists on court protection for data that are available to the E.P.A.; why it buried the tumor incidence tables that begin on page 1,634, where they appear suddenly after 288 pages of unrelated tables; why the tumor data are not clearly referenced elsewhere in the document or listed in the table of contents; and why Du Pont chose to understate the tumors linked to CFC-113 exposure. Du Pont provided confusing answers. Two days after the O'Harren verdict, Kathy Forte, another spokesperson for External Affairs, read the following prepared statement: "We continue to believe the case is without merit and we are considering an appeal." As of press time, they had yet to file one.

A mandatory gradual phase-out of the use of CFCs has at last begun, the result of last year's amendments to the Montreal Protocol Treaty and the Clean Air Act. This new regulatory pressure has prompted a few large electronics firms to cut down on CFC use, and others are planning to do so. I.B.M., for example, has returned to the soap-and-water technique it used in the 1970s before investing in CFCs. But most electronics firms continue to use CFC-113 and won't be required to phase CFCs out completely until the year 2000. Meanwhile, a whole new round of experiments is being conducted by Du Pont and Allied-Signal to find new, "safer" solvents, and a consortium of the world's largest chemical corporations is betting billions of dollars on the outcome. The new experiments are to decide the workplace safety of hydrochlorofluorocarbons (HCFCs) and hydrofluorocarbons (HFCs). In short, the companies that pushed CFCs on an unsuspecting public for years are now seeking to do the same with potentially even more hazardous chemicals, and with the cooperation of the E.P.A.

An analysis of the agency's database of CFC-113 toxicity studies indicates that Du Pont alone supplied nearly 70 percent of those used to determine E.P.A. regulatory policy and to prepare E.P.A. technical evaluations. When I asked Reva Rubenstein, of the E.P.A.'s Office of Atmospheric and Indoor Programs, if she was comfortable with this arrangement, she answered, "We have confidence in the industry's data." Du Pont and Allied-Signal are members of the Program for Alternative Fluorocarbon Toxicity Testing (PAFT), an organization controlled by international CFC-producing firms whose chemists are conducting toxicity tests on CFC-related substitutes. In a press release, PAFT claims that "preliminary results of toxicity tests" were sending "a favorable signal to continue research and development" of HCFCs and HFCs, and it maintains that "the [preliminary] results suggest that HCFC-123, HFC-134a and HCFC 141b should show no adverse effects in carcinogen tests to be completed in 1992 or 1993."

Karla Perri, of the E.P.A.'s Office of Air and Radiation, says Du Pont and other industry tests form the basis for the E.P.A.'s technical evaluations of HCFCs and HFCs. Congress uses the E.P.A.'s technical evaluations to make laws such as the recent Clean Air Act amendments; the United Nations Environmental Program and the Montreal Protocol group use E.P.A. evaluations to guide the international process of phasing out ozone-depleting substances and phasing in substitutes. All of these bodies recently adopted guidelines allowing firms to phase in HCFCs during the early twenty-first century despite protest by Greenpeace, Friends of the Earth and other environmental groups. Recent reviews of the scientific literature by Greenpeace suggest that HCFCs could adversely affect climate and deplete ozone. Moreover, even an E.P.A. publication released in January of last year noted that of all the HCFC substitutes under development, "the largest contributors of [ozone-depleting] chlorine would be HCFC-141b and HCFC-22." In fact, the E.P.A. has concluded that "to return chlorine to pre-Antarctic ozone levels, a phaseout of the HCFCs would also be necessary." HCFCs and HFCs are also greenhouse gases that would contribute to global warming.

Du Pont's HCFCs could prove even more toxic than CFC-113. According to O'Harren trial expert Ettienne, the chemical instability that makes HCFCs less harmful to ozone also makes them more dangerous to workers because they are more easily metabolized. In March of last year, the E.P.A. warned that two of the CFC substitutes "may be hazardous to human health." According to an E.P.A. statement based on ten-year-old data, HCFC-133a produced cancer in rats and HCFC-132b damaged liver tissue. The current industry-run HCFC experiments did not yield this awkward news, according to an E.P.A. spokesperson.

The E.P.A. is already concerned about the workplace dangers of HCFCs and HFCs. In a special report issued last November, the E.P.A. wrote that "compared to the CFCs . . . the HCFCs and HFCs exhibit a greater potential for systemic effects." The E.P.A. "urge[s] all companies and workers involved with the production and use of CFC substitutes to take reasonable efforts to ensure that exposures to these chem-icals are controlled while additional data are being developed." The report continued, "The results of these preliminary analyses [from the chemical industry] indicate that HFCs and HCFCs can be used in a manner safe to workers, consumers, and the general population, given appropriate technological changes and exposure control practices in some applications," but the E.P.A. stressed the "interim" nature of its assessment. Nevertheless, it constitutes a go-ahead to the industry.

"Du Pont and Allied-Signal are jumping the gun," says Erik Johnson, of Greenpeace's Atmosphere and Energy Campaign. The world's largest CFC producers, Du Pont and Allied-Signal have already committed in excess of $1.25 billion for this decade in the evolving CFC substitute market that includes HCFCs and HFCs. Last June Du Pont announced it would design four new plants to produce HFCs. After evaluating alternatives to CFC-113 for use by military contractors, an agency for the Pentagon has provisionally approved HCFCs. Yet as Johnson points out, extensive review has turned up "a variety of safe non-CFC alternatives for every major [CFC] application." Among them are solar-powered refrigerators that are cooled by the mineral zeolite, ultrasonic nozzles that eliminate the need for solvents in the manufacture of electronics or, as at I.B.M., just plain soap and water.

The proposition that corporate science is bad science is not new. But the supporting evidence often comes too late. The O'Harren trial showed conclusively that Du Pont engaged in and covered up dubious scientific procedures that may have jeopardized the health of hundreds of thousands of workers. Now Du Pont and its industry kin are seeking to repeat the scenario, to force again a critical chemical choice without benefit of a thorough and public debate. Both the health of our workers and the viability of the planet's radiation shield may depend on what happens next.   □

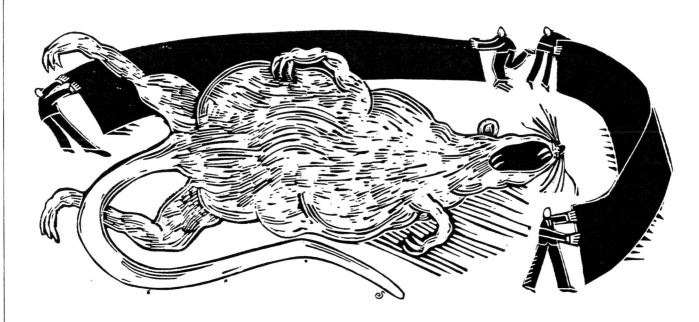

■ THE WHITTLE-ALEXANDER NEXUS

Big Business Goes to School

JOHN S. FRIEDMAN

Channel One, the controversial TV news program for schools, will be televised for the first time in Russia this spring. In the United States, the program is watched every school day in more than 9,000 schools by 6.6 million teenagers—almost a third of all teen students. In fact, more adolescents watch the twelve-minute program than watch the three top network shows combined. In Russia, Channel One will be televised on a test basis in schools in Moscow and St. Petersburg.

But the expansion of Channel One into Russia and its continuing success in America are less significant than another Whittle Communications project, perhaps the most ambitious educational initiative ever undertaken by an American company. In the next few years, Whittle hopes to reshape education by opening a nationwide chain of 200 private schools for profit.

Chris Whittle, chairman and founder of Whittle Communications, represents the new intersection between business and education. Until recently, corporate America, for the most part, has avoided direct involvement in education. But it has now turned to the classroom. The Bush Administration is the point of entry and Chris Whittle is the point man.

Herbert Christopher Whittle is 44 years old. He grew up in Etowah, Tennessee, and earned a B.S. degree in American studies from the University of Tennessee, where he was president of the student body. He began his business career publishing a guide for college freshmen. By 1979 his publishing company was doing well enough to buy and revitalize *Esquire*, which he later turned over to a former partner. Whittle likes to portray himself as a successful businessman and says he hasn't decided if he is a Republican or a Democrat. In fact, his political and financial connections, particularly his many interlocking ties with Education Secretary Lamar Alexander, suggest an agenda far beyond party affiliation.

Whittle Communications is a media company whose properties include specialized magazines, books that contain advertising, a television/magazine service for physicians' offices, wall posters and televised programming. The centerpiece is Channel One.

The Whittle formula is ingenious. His company lends the schools TVs, VCRs and satellite dishes to receive the programming and then wires the system. Besides Channel One, the Whittle Educational Network includes an hour or two a day of noncommercial, educational programming, which is sup-

plied by a regional public TV station, and an occasional professional development program for teachers. In exchange, schools agree to show Channel One to most students on 92 percent of the days in which school is in session.

When Channel One began, the national P.T.A. and a number of other educational organizations opposed it vociferously because of the two minutes of ads on every Channel One program. Critics such as Bill Honig, California state superintendent of public instruction, accused Whittle of "converting the educational purpose of a school to a commercial one."

Buoyed by its $102 million in gross annual revenues from Channel One, Whittle Communications is looking for ways to expand. About nine months ago, Whittle unveiled a plan to "invent," build and open 200 private schools by 1996. His plan resembles the Education Department's original proposal to create some 535 experimental schools by the same year. Referring to his "new American schools," Whittle even echoes some of the rhetoric used by the Bush Administration in its "America 2000" education goals, announced about the same time. Whittle's schools would serve all children from "age 0 to 18," he told *Education Week*. Most likely there would be no admission requirements. If demand exceeded available space, applicants would be selected at random. Tuition for each school would probably be just below the per-pupil cost of public education in its community. Whittle would try to hold the cost of operating his schools to less than that of public schools. One way, he suggests, would be to "harness student power" to reduce support staff. Students might be required to work in the schools, possibly by replacing maintenance or clerical staff or by performing some functions of teachers. (Of course, another way to make such schools profitable would be to reduce the number of teachers by using electronic teaching devices.)

These schools would debut the high-tech school of the future. Students could spend up to three hours a day, Whittle suggests, operating a new electronic learning system that "might include a monitor, printer, computer, CD-ROM, paintboard, fax—even a phone and stereo." He also suggests that pupils might spend up to an additional hour a day watching special television programming.

Whittle estimates that $2.5 billion to $3 billion will be required to put his first 200 schools into operation. By the year 2010, there could be 1,000 campuses, according to Whittle executives, each with day care facilities and elementary, middle and high schools.

For *their* experimental public schools, President Bush and Secretary Alexander want private industry initially to donate $150 million to $200 million for research and development. The federal government would provide start-up grants to model schools, which later would have to rely primarily on local or state funding.

Herbert Kohl, a leading educational theorist and author of numerous books, believes that the Whittle schools and the Administration's new schools all conform to the education agenda of the right wing. "The goal is to set up a limited num-

---

John S. Friedman is a journalist who writes on culture and politics.

ber of exemplary schools," he said, "high-tech schools that pay little attention to teaching moral sensibility and social responsibility. The new schools would represent the privatization of public education. Combined with the voucher system [which lets parents apply tax dollars toward the cost of any school they choose], we would have the corporate plan for education in place—to the ultimate detriment of poor people."

Whittle has said that the $60 million needed for the first, or blueprint, phase of his schools would come from a "variety of sources: our earnings, existing partners, new partners." As he becomes a significant influence in education, Whittle's partners and advisers will be decisive. Who are they? Fifty percent of Whittle Communications is owned by Time Warner. In 1988, before it merged with Warner, Time Inc. acquired the stock for an initial payment of $180 million (Time Warner has an option to buy another 30 percent, and if the option is ever exercised, Whittle can stipulate that the company purchase the remaining 20 percent). By wiring schools to receive Channel One, Whittle accomplished part of a long-unfulfilled goal of Time—the electronic classroom. Time was one of the first corporations to see the business possibilities of merging technology with education. In 1966 Time and General Electric formed the General Learning Corporation (G.L.C.) to integrate "electronic capability with educational materials." But in the mid-1960s schools didn't have any money to spend on computers, which were large and expensive, so the really ambitious computer-related products were never produced by G.L.C., notes Curtis Prendergast in *The World of Time Inc.* G.L.C.'s software became low-tech, such as records and filmstrips, and by 1974 the company was sold. Some fifteen years later Chris Whittle, with his new partner, Time, had the shrewd idea of supplying schools with equipment they otherwise could not afford and charging advertisers for access to classrooms. So eager are Whittle and Time Warner to exploit this market further that Whittle will manage or provide educational computer software and hardware to public and private schools.

The second corporate partner in Whittle Communications is Associated Newspapers Holdings, a diversified British media company, which owns 33 percent of Whittle. The chairman of Associated is Viscount Rothermere (Vere Harmsworth). Lord Rothermere's Associated Newspapers publishes three London tabloids, *The Daily Mail*, *The Mail on Sunday* and *The Evening Standard*. The flagship paper, *The Daily Mail*, was a staunch supporter of Margaret Thatcher when she was prime minister. Editorials on South Africa, for example, matched her opinion that only limited sanctions were required.

While foreign ownership of network television stations is restricted under F.C.C. rules, such rules do not apply to satellite broadcasters like Whittle. Nevertheless, Associated's partial ownership of Channel One raises questions about possible foreign influence over the content of the curriculum.

As for Whittle's relationship with the Bush Administration, it is cozy. Although not a partner in Whittle Communications, Lamar Alexander, Bush's top education official, has, in his own words, been "a good close friend for twenty years" of Chris Whittle. The Alexander-Whittle connection is significant because of Alexander's key position in formulating education policy and programs. Conservative educational theorists and business leaders are important influences on Whittle and Alexander. For example, Chester Finn Jr., the education maven of the right wing who served in the Nixon White House and later was a top policy-maker at the Education Department under Reagan, is also an old friend of Alexander's. "He worked very closely with me on America 2000," Alexander said when interviewed by telephone. Finn, a professor of education and public policy at Tennessee's Vanderbilt University, is advising Whittle on his new schools as well.

David Kearns, longtime C.E.O. of the Xerox Corporation (he relinquished the post in 1990), is Alexander's high-profile Deputy Secretary of Education. From 1978 until he became Deputy Secretary, Kearns was on the board of directors of Time and then Time Warner. Like Time, Xerox recognized the revenue potential of technology in the schools in the mid-1960s. In 1987 Xerox gave $5 million in seed money to the Institute for Research on Learning, a think tank in Palo Alto, California, that specializes in developing new ways to use technology in the classroom. When the New American Schools Development Corporation (N.A.S.D.C.), a private, nonprofit organization, was formed by business and corporate leaders last spring at the President's request to provide research and development funds for the America 2000 schools, Xerox was one of the largest donors.

Reacting to criticism that the board of the N.A.S.D.C. was composed almost exclusively of C.E.O.s, an advisory panel was set up, and Saul Cooperman, a former New Jersey commissioner of education, was named chairman. Cooperman and the other advisory board members—whom he helped select—will evaluate and recommend grants for prototype schools. Cooperman is also founder and president of Edu-

ILLUSTRATIONS BY LISA BLACKSHEAR

cate America, Inc., a public policy organization that advocates national curriculum standards and national testing. Chester Finn is on the board of Educate America. So is Chris Whittle. In 1991 Cooperman became a member of the Whittle Educational Network advisory board. Cooperman denies any conflict of interest and pledged to recuse himself "if Whittle should submit a proposal" to the N.A.S.D.C.

A few years ago, Whittle planned to run for governor of Tennessee; he turned for advice to Tom Ingram, who was Alexander's chief of staff when he served as Governor. Under Ingram's guidance, Whittle took private tutorials at Harvard and Vanderbilt on arms control and welfare. He also had some sessions with Roger Ailes, who had coached Nixon and Bush. Whittle insists he has changed his mind and will not run for office; he believes that Channel One and the new schools are more important.

As Channel One started to absorb Whittle's attention, Ingram steered him through the treacherous shoals of state legislatures and school boards. To make certain that Channel One was accepted, Whittle Communications spent about $3.1 million on lobbying, Ingram said in an interview. Ingram is currently interim director of the new schools for Whittle and also executive vice president for corporate communications. When Alexander was nominated as Secretary of Education, Ingram advised him as well, helping to set up his transition office.

Another of Alexander's former chiefs of staff is Lewis Lavine, head of The Ingram Group, a business and political consulting company that Ingram founded. Whittle Communications is one of its largest clients. Lavine was hired by Alexander as a paid adviser for a number of months, until the Administration's new education proposals were announced last April. Both Ingram and Lavine deny any conflict of interest.

Alexander himself was on the Whittle advisory board that guided Channel One and worked for Whittle after leaving the governorship in 1987. His compensation was $125,000 in consulting fees plus the opportunity to buy four shares of Whittle stock, for which he wrote a $10,000 check, according to *The Wall Street Journal*. When he became president of the University of Tennessee a year later, Alexander transferred the stock to his wife after legal advisers suggested that if Whittle were to do business with the university, there would be a conflict of interest. At the end of 1988, Whittle bought back the stock for $330,000, giving the Alexanders a hefty profit—a matter that came up during Alexander's confirmation hearings.

After his nomination as Secretary of Education, Alexander asked Whittle, Ingram, Lavine, Cooperman and others for their advice. In a series of meetings, three of which Whittle attended, the proposals that became America 2000 were mapped out, along with a voucher system, according to one participant.

After his confirmation, Alexander sold his home in Knoxville, Tennessee, for $977,500. He had paid $570,000 for it about a year before. The buyer was Gerald Hogan, a top executive of Whittle Communications. Hogan received a mortgage of $780,000 from the First Tennessee Bank. Alexander was on the board of the bank's holding company until he be-

came Secretary of Education. Whittle is still on the board.

During his confirmation hearings, Alexander promised to sever his ties with Whittle Communications. The pledge was a "personal recusal from official business that Whittle might have with the department," said Etta Fielek, director of public affairs for the department. Asked in an interview about the sale, Alexander said "the sale of the house doesn't fit in at all" and did not violate his promise. When Whittle was asked about the sale, he said in a telephone interview, "I had nothing to do with it." Questioned about a possible conflict of interest between his connections with Whittle and his position as head of the Education Department, Alexander responded, "Where is the conflict and where is the interest? Whittle has never done any work for the federal government and doesn't plan to." Whittle said that he has no intention of applying for federal funds, although he may apply for state and local funds. As for Alexander, Whittle added, "Ultimately we are trying to do the same things. He is taking the public route. I am taking the private route."

The Whittle-Alexander connection symbolizes the new alliance between business and government to exploit the educational system. Alexander attributes the greater business involvement in public-policy-making to the "different playing field" that developed in the 1980s as competition heated up from Japan, and Japanese firms in the United States demanded better-trained employees. "Corporate America is becoming involved because the public schools are not producing the type of student that business needs," said Arnold Fege, director of government relations for the national P.T.A. "Business wants the curriculum to include a strong business agenda."

Such an agenda, for the most part, could result in a corruption of values, under the guise of being "value free," with a strong emphasis on skills. Kohl, the educational theorist, suggests that questions of labor and worker solidarity would be ignored while the virtues of free enterprise and corporate loyalty would be extolled. "The way to achieve self-validation would be through the corporate structure," he adds. "Desire would be manipulated so that artificial needs could be maintained."

Finally, another reason business is turning to education is that it anticipates profits if the schools are rebuilt and use new learning technologies. Whittle sees nothing wrong in this: "Is there an inherent conflict between profits and education? No way. The biggest contribution business can make to education is to make education a business."

Chris Whittle is an entrepreneur, not an educator. He is not opening new schools to improve children's minds but to make money.

His connections and financial resources give him an inside track to the schools of the future. The Whittle-Alexander-Time Warner corporate nexus will be a dominant force in shaping the schools of tomorrow. Unless parents, teachers and educators provide a strong alternative to the corporate invasion of education, in which Whittle is leading the charge, the nation's schools will be turned into another subsidiary of big business. □

New Tool of Developers and Others Quells Private Opposition to Projects

By KATHERINE BISHOP
Special to The New York Times

SAN FRANCISCO, April 25 — Real estate developers, alleged polluters and even public servants who encounter citizen opposition to their projects have been increasingly using civil lawsuits to discourage such opponents.

These lawsuits, prevalent enough to have acquired a nickname — Strategic Lawsuits Against Public Participation, or "Slapps" — often violate the petition clause of the First Amendment that protects legal attempts to influence governmental action.

And while the citizens who are their targets usually prevail, the time, expense and stress involved keeps many others from speaking out on public issues.

"We are always saying the solution to problems is that people have got to get involved," said Penelope Canan, an associate professor of sociology at the University of Denver who has been conducting research on the subject for five years. "Only 10 percent of the population does so now, and if they are at risk from Slapps, we've got to stop it."

But some argue that developers and others are simply trying to have their day in court.

"So-called citizen activists know they can shut a project down by affecting the developer's ability to get financing" by forcing endless rounds of public hearings and permit appeals, said Richard J. Lyon, a lobbyist for the California Building Industry Association, which represents about 7,000 residential and commercial builders.

"When we try to use the judicial process to shed some sunshine on what we see as an abuse of process," he added, "we're accused of trying to stifle the First Amendment."

States Consider Action

Several states are investigating the issue of Slapps, which researchers define as "lawsuits claiming injury resulting from citizen efforts to influence the government or sway voters on an issue of public significance." California and New York are considering legislation intended to curb such suits by instituting judicial procedures to allow them to be quickly dismissed.

"Our courts are being used by wealthy and special interests to prevent citizens from speaking out on legitimate public controversies," said State Senator Bill Lockyer, a Democrat from Hayward, Calif., who is sponsoring the legislation here.

Dr. Canan and her research colleague, Professor George W. Pring of the University of Denver College of Law, say they began their research to find out why they saw an increasing number of environmental protection advocates being named as defendants in large civil damage cases.

In five years of research, sponsored in part by the National Science Foundation, they looked at 228 such cases involving 1,464 people and 409 groups who had spoken out to a government agency or official, usually challenging a private venture that needed a license or public permit or criticizing police officers, City Council members or other public servants.

They found that the plaintiffs typically charged these individuals or groups with defamation, thereby transforming an issue like zoning or police brutality into one of libel. And while most lawsuits dismissed or winning at trial, it took an average of 36 months to do so.

In one California example cited by Dr. Canan, three homeowner groups and some private citizens were sued

for $40 million by a developer after they successfully campaigned for a ballot measure calling for a moratorium on land development. While the case was dismissed after two years, many citizens withdrew from the groups, and only one defendant chose to countersue, charging violation of his First Amendment rights. He was awarded punitive damages of $260,000.

Counter-Organization Formed

Environmental groups are so frequently the target of such suits that one organization, the Citizens Clearinghouse on Hazardous Wastes, has formed what it calls "Project Slapp Back" to assist local groups threatened with such suits. The 10-year-old not-for-profit organization based in Falls Church, Va., helps 7,500 grassroots organizations around the country address issues of toxic waste and garbage disposal.

Brian Lipsett, a research analyst for the organization, said it has worked with people who have been sued for writing letters to a local newspaper opposing constuction of a medical waste incinerator and for calling a proposed garbage landfill a "dump."

The organization provides information on how best to react to such harassment suits, which he said are "more severe for small, local groups because their budgets are often insignificant." While responding with a countersuit charging interference with First Amendment rights is a possibility, Mr. Lipsett said, local groups can use their time and resources better by taking pre-emptive action to stop such suits before they are filed.

In California, the proposed legislation is intended to screen out harassment suits at an early stage while allowing meritorious claims to proceed. On any suits arising from a person's right to free speech or petition in connection with a public issue, the plaintiff would be required to establish to a judge a "substantial probability" that the claim would prevail before the judge would let the lawsuit proceed. Defendants would be able to recover lawyers' fees it the case was halted by a judge.

The bill is expected to be passed by the State Senate by the end of May and then go the Assembly.

Proposal in New York

In New York, a related bill is pending before the Assembly and is expected to be passed before the session ends in June. Rudy Stegemoeller, associate counsel for the Environment and Energy Committee of the Assembly, said the bill is limited to cases in which the plaintiff in a suit has sought or obtained a permit or zoning change from a local government entity and has been challenged by the defendants.

The bill allows for accelerated proceedings for obtaining a dismissal or summary judgment if the suit is judged to be without substantial basis in fact or law. It also allows for awarding of lawyers' fees and even punitive damages if the suit is shown to have been brought to harass or intimidate the defendants.

Mr. Stegemoeller said work on the bill was done by his unit because "environmentalists are so frequently the targets of Slapps."

The New York Attorney General's office supports the bill and is watching several such suits with the goal of intervening on behalf of defendants in one of them.

"We hope to get New York to develop a good body of law on this issue," said Carol S. Knox, an Assistant Attorney General who works on legislative affairs. "A lot of these cases get dismissed, and that's the good news. But if Slapp plaintiffs win, people get intimidated and go away, and that's bad news."

Defendants Not Entirely Pure

In Florida, the State Attorney General's office is conducting a similar survey of defendants in such lawsuits.

In New Jersey, the Legislature is considering a bill similar to one

passed in Washington State that immunizes from liability citizens who complain to a public entity in good faith and without actual malice. The purpose is to protect individuals exercising their First Amendment right "to petition the government for redress of grievances."

Marina Corodemus, president-elect of the American Trial Lawyers Association, which supports the New Jersey measure, said: "It is a top priority for us. People don't realize how fundamental this is."

But some point out that defendants in such suits are not always entirely pure in their motives. They are sometimes using the system to intimidate or drive away developers, and sometimes using it to practice exclusionary politics that injure the interests of other, less activist citizens.

"Groups bent on stopping development in this state are often trying to stop low-income and high-density projects," said Mr. Lyon of the California Building Industry Association.

"They wrap themselves in the flag of environmentalism when what they really want to do is keep low-income and people of color out of their neighborhoods."

Professor Pring said: "It's definitely true that that happens. These are not cases of black hats against white hats all the time. But that misses the real point. The fact is that in America all points of view deserve to be aired and communicated to our Government representatives."

Correcting the Stereotype

Mr. Lyon also said his group's research shows that, unlike the David vs. Goliath stereotype, most of this type of lawsuits are brought by small developers "whose financial future rides on the success of one or two projects."

Dr. Canan agreed that lawsuits are usually brought by small developers whose economic interests are tied to the community and who, unlike giant corporations, cannot move elsewhere. In some cases "some community groups sandbag them," she said.

But, she said, the remedy is for developers to be sure the city enforces its own codes and regulations rather than to sue citizens who have an opposite point of view.

V. Secrecy and Suppression of Information

Robert L. Park ended his article in *Right to Know III* with these prescient words: "...the 'Iron Curtain' is in tatters. As Soviet society becomes more open, it will be difficult to persuade Americans to move in the other direction. Indeed it may be time for a little western 'glasnost'." Those attempting to use the Freedom of Information Act to obtain data from NASA, CIA and other government agencies may well agree. The articles in this section document the clandestine activities of U.S. intelligence agencies as well as Vice-President Dan Quayle's Council on Competitiveness. And events before and during the Persian Gulf War provided a field day for secret-keepers in the government.

"The very premise of democracy is that 'we the people' are entitled to make our own choices on fundamental policies. But freedom of choice is illusory if policies are kept not only from the public but from its elected representatives." — U.S. Congress. Report of the Congressional Committee Investigating the Iran-Contra Affair. 100th Congress, 1st Session, H. Rept #100-433, Nov. 1987.

"Our government was founded by people...who wrote the First Amendment with the precise idea that things kept secret tend to fester inside the government and are not very good for the country." — Daniel Schorr

"The common folk know
That war is coming.
When the leaders curse war
The mobilization order is already written out."
  — Bertolt Brecht, "When the Leaders Speak of Peace"

ROBERT LAIRD

THE FIGHT TO KNOW

The feds know more than the rest of us.
And they like it that way.

BY PETER MONTGOMERY
AND PETER OVERBY

In 1987 the Reagan administration came to Congress with an urgent problem: Japanese scientists were exploiting the Freedom of Information Act to snare American space shuttle technology worth millions of dollars. Congress could — must — stop them by exempting the National Aeronautics and Space Administration (NASA) from the information access law.

NASA's complaint was powerful, plausible — and false.

In fact, the Japanese never used the law to get shuttle data; a NASA official later admitted that the tale was "apocryphal." The administration concocted the story to keep American reporters, and the public, from learning the truth about the *Challenger* explosion. But NASA's effort to squirm out of the spotlight failed; its corner-cutting and deception lay exposed — thanks largely to the Freedom of Information Act.

The Samurai Shuttle episode, as congressional staffers call it, demonstrates the lengths to which some agencies will go to avoid public scrutiny and skirt the law that guarantees public access to government information.

People seeking government documents "just throw up their hands and go away when they see what some of these agencies make them go through," says David Sobel, a lawyer who specializes in the information access law. "They just decide it's not worth it. And I think the agencies are well aware of that."

The Freedom of Information Act (FOIA, pronounced *FOY-uh*) rests on the premise that government must be accountable to its citizens. It was signed 25 years ago July 4 by a reluctant President Lyndon Johnson, and strengthened over Gerald Ford's veto following the Watergate scandal.

Before FOIA, officials didn't even have to answer requests for government information, much less give it out. FOIA says that anyone can see any official document unless the government can prove that the information is covered by one of nine specific exemptions, including military and law enforcement secrets, sensitive financial

Peter Montgomery is an associate editor. Peter Overby is staff writer.

and business data, information protected by individuals' privacy rights, some internal government documents and some geologic material.

In theory at least, FOIA bucks the bureaucratic impulse for secrecy. In reality, the executive branch and federal courts are stretching the law's exemptions to give that impulse freer rein. Congress last took a shot at FOIA reform in 1986 — a compromise that wound up creating new obstacles for requesters — and since then has paid scant attention to the problems. FOIA's friends can't agree on the next move, if any.

Paul McMasters, a *USA Today* editor who heads a committee on freedom of information for the Society of Professional Journalists (SPJ), sees this bleak future if the law isn't fixed: "more adverse court decisions, more erosion of access rights, more ignoring of FOIA."

OPEN SECRETS

Journalists and authors sometimes think FOIA was written just for them. Indeed, it has helped to uncover significant stories nationally and locally.

A flood of FOIA requests helped demolish NASA's deceptions after the *Challenger* exploded in 1986. Documents and photos revealed that NASA had scrimped on testing critical parts and that the crew cabin, contrary to NASA claims, survived the explosion and probably fell intact to the ocean.

Last year, FOIA helped New Jersey reporter Eric Greenberg expose a coverup — bureaucratic and literal — of munitions abandoned at the site of an Army arsenal where 20,000 people a day now work, attend college or relax in a park. Greenberg obtained an Army consultant's report that mustard gas, potassium cyanide and ammunition remained buried there. The stories prompted a cleanup that has unearthed 20,000 live artillery shells.

Historian David Garrow, author of *Bearing the Cross*, the Pulitzer Prize-winning biography of Martin Luther King Jr., used FOIA to get records of the FBI's surveillance of King. Garrow says he could not have written his book without information he got through FOIA in the 1970s; that material, he says, would have been withheld under restrictions imposed in the 1980s.

Yet writers are actually a minority of FOIA users. Ronald Plesser, a lawyer

specializing in freedom of information, asks rhetorically, "What other three-page or four-page statute has had the kind of impact on government that the Freedom of Information Act has had?"

Because Ralph Nader's Public Citizen sued, many Department of Agriculture meat inspection reports are now public documents. The nonprofit National Security Archive was able to compel release of parts of Oliver North's diaries and the computer message files from the National Security Council during the Iran-Contra affair.

Barbara Crancer, daughter of Teamsters union leader Jimmy Hoffa, filed FOIA requests for Justice Department records on her father's disappearance.

> **Last year the FBI calculated that its average response time to FOIA requests was more than 300 days.**

The government says the 16-year-old case is still active. Crancer is suing.

Far and away, most FOIA requesters don't want to make headlines. The Food and Drug Administration (FDA) processed 40,500 requests last year, with just 6 percent from the media and 1 percent from public interest groups. The others came almost entirely from FDA-regulated companies or their representatives, who use the act to untangle the sometimes Byzantine regulatory process — and to dig up information the government has on their competitors. Despite persistent rumors, business users of FOIA rarely unearth their competitors' proprietary secrets. For example, one manufacturer accused FDA's FOIA staff of releasing a proprietary formula; it had actually been published in the *Physicians' Desk Reference*.

The act has spawned its own industry. An association of government FOIA officers and those who deal with them carries the optimistic acronym ASAP, for American Society of Access Professionals. There are even professional FOIA requesters, whose clients like the convenience of having someone else endure the hassles. Some clients also appreciate the anonymity; logs of FOIA requests, after all, are public documents.

"They all want everything to be released except their own data," Marlene Bobka, marketing executive for FOI Services Inc., says dryly.

CURSES! FOIA'D AGAIN

For someone who railed against Big Government, Ronald Reagan did more than any other recent president to keep government actions secret from the populace. George Bush, the first CIA director to become president, has followed suit.

"In the past 10 years, it has become more difficult and more expensive [to get information under FOIA]. Agencies are less responsive," says military historian Chuck Hansen. "Sometimes I think they have an actuarial table at their side; they try to guess the age and longevity of the requester."

Hansen, a regular FOIA user, asked the Air Force 10 years ago for documents from the late 1940s and early '50s. The Air Force released some, withheld others. He appealed. Then the incoming Bush administration ruled: It wouldn't give Hansen the remaining documents — and he never should have gotten the original batch. Cold War secrets remain locked up.

That kind of response plays well in official Washington these days. Justice Department official Mary Lawton, addressing a FOIA conference sponsored by the American Bar Association (ABA) in May, summed up the Reagan-Bush approach with a snarl: "Some of us who have been plagued by this act for 25 years aren't real enthusiastic about this anniversary."

Conflicts between open government and essential secrets are inevitable. But critics note that "national security" sometimes means "politically embarrassing."

The Reagan administration expansively redefined "national security" to cover virtually all aspects of international activity, including research and development and trade. A 1982 executive order told government officials to classify documents whenever in doubt, and even allowed some material already released under FOIA to be reclassified. The Justice Department also reversed a Carter administration policy to withhold documents only if disclosure would cause "demonstrable harm." The new strategy: Fight every possible case, even if the only defense against disclosure is a technicality.

Blacked out: When this 1941-vintage FBI document was FOIA'd in 1979, just one name was deleted. Requested again in 1985, the Reagan administration released it like this.

puter time, and the Air Force wanted $509 for copying. Two months after the requests were filed, seven agencies of the 21 were still figuring out how to respond.

The exercise made it clear why statistics about FOIA performance are lacking. The amount and usefulness of the information in the logs differs greatly. There's not much help in the congressionally mandated annual reports on FOIA activities filed by all agencies: They are vague, inconsistent and thus worthless for any serious assessment of compliance government-wide.

"Information about the act itself is much more limited than you would expect," says Robert Vaughn, an American University law professor.

Among FOIA frequent filers, anecdotal evaluations vary widely. The Department of Health and Human Services, with little or no classified information, regularly gets high marks. The State Department and Central Intelligence Agency are considered the worst, while the Pentagon's various components get mixed reviews.

David Evans, a military reporter for the *Chicago Tribune*, recently asked the Navy for five years' worth of sensitive reports on emergency crew ejections from combat aircraft. They arrived within two months. But when he asked the Air Force for a study of tactical transport, he was told the 10-year-old document was "internal" and thus exempt. Evans, who as a retired Marine officer sees "a particular poignancy" in FOIA abuses, says that episode "points out how capricious this whole business is" — a complaint echoed by many users who say that success often depends on an official's whim, not the request's merit.

Even critics of agency performance have words of praise and sympathy for some freedom of information officers, whose desire to carry out the law can be frustrated by their bosses.

Quinlan Shea, who worked on freedom of information issues at the Justice Department in the 1970s and at the National Security Archive in the 1980s, blames the Office of Management and Budget (OMB) for ensuring that FOIA offices remain underfunded and understaffed, a universally recognized cause of delay. The Navy's central FOIA office has a staff of two and no fax machine. Emil Moschella, then FOIA director for the FBI, testified

In filling requests, the agencies all seem to be playing by different rules. FOIA is supposed to work this way: You send a letter asking for information. The government has 10 days to fill the request or explain why it won't do so. If the government withholds anything, you can appeal the decision within the agency and in the federal courts. But in many agencies roadblocks are endemic. So are delays, despite the 10-day deadline.

The FDA often takes two years to fill requests, says Bobka; the State Department often takes a year, other requesters say. Last year the FBI calculated that its average response time was more than 300 days. A Navy FOIA officer suggested to one reporter that he'd be better off finding someone to leak the document he wanted. "If you have to file a FOIA request," one media lawyer says, "that means you've failed."

To see how the law is working, *Common Cause Magazine* filed FOIA re-

quests this spring with 21 agencies, asking for recent FOIA logs — lists of requests, when and how they were answered. Four of the 21 — the Federal Aviation Administration, Federal Trade Commission (FTC), Merit Systems Protection Board and Securities and Exchange Commission — met the 10-day deadline.

Several agencies excused themselves by saying their FOIA offices were mere entry points, and once a request was forwarded to the appropriate office no one tracked its progress. Some agencies have computerized logs, others handwritten tracking sheets — one had no logs at all, just a routing slip for each request. The Energy Department at first tried to withhold requesters' names; the Justice Department considers them public information.

Most agencies agreed that *Common Cause Magazine* publishes news and therefore waived fees. The Department of Housing and Urban Development, however, charged $45 for com-

STUPID FOIA TRICKS

NO NAMES I — Greenpeace researcher William Arkin asked for a manual of Navy public affairs officers. The Navy supplied phone numbers and addresses, but blacked out all the names. Arkin calls it "too absurd to appeal."

NO NAMES II — The FBI sent one requester a newspaper clip with all the names blacked out. Another requester got a copy of correspondence with *Look* magazine's public relations director, whose name was blacked out.

WHAT RECORDS? — At the same time the FBI was defending its much maligned "Library Awareness Program," in which agents asked librarians to snoop on patrons' reading habits, its FOIA office was telling requesters it didn't have any records on the program.

OH, THOSE RECORDS — An FDA employee who was notified that he was subject to a random drug test FOIA'd the Department of Health and Human Services for evaluations of the drug testing labs. He was told they didn't exist. When he pointed out that the labs had to be evaluated before they could be certified, he was told that he couldn't have the records.

SO YOU WANT SOME RECORDS? — The National Security Archive asked the CIA for an index of materials the agency had released under FOIA. The CIA finally complied, but set the computer to print the information in a random "dump," producing a 5,000-page mass of unintelligible data.

THE MORAL: MAKE COPIES — Former U.S. Ambassador to Germany Kenneth Rush held secret negotiations with the Soviets in 1971. When Rush retired he gave his notes to the State Department. Now he's writing his memoirs and wants to see his old correspondence. No chance, says the State Department; it's classified.

TIME FOR A CHANGE — When the Federal Aviation Administration got requests for the unclassified bulletins on terrorist threats that are sent to airlines, it stonewalled long enough to write a regulation saying it didn't have to give out the bulletins.

WHO'S ON FIRST? — Writer Bob Trebilcock, researching the Elizabeth Morgan-Eric Foretich child custody battle, filed matching FOIA requests with the Justice Department and the U.S. Attorney for Washington, D.C. Justice said the material he wanted was with the U.S. Attorney. The Attorney's office said it was at Justice.   —*P.M. & P.O.*

al could be assembled, say, for the boss to use in testifying on Capitol Hill.

"It seems to me pretty clear-cut that the motivation behind the act is to get information," he says. "Regardless of the form in which it is stored, information is information."

At least one Reagan appointee regrets the hardball approach to FOIA. Roger Pilon, now at the libertarian Cato Institute, filed requests after he and his wife were wrongly accused of leaking intelligence information to the South African government. "What we'd get back is the standard hiding behind government security," he says. "Having served in State and Justice, I can tell you the amount of material that is classified far exceeds the amount that needs to be classified."

Success with a FOIA request may boil down to a question of cost — and the government decides who must pay and who gets information for free.

The 1986 FOIA amendments were supposed to eliminate search and retrieval costs for reporters and educators and waive copying fees for small requests. The administration turned the reform into an obstacle. Agencies regularly challenge scholars, public interest groups and others to prove that requests are in the public interest. If the government thinks the public knows enough already, it can deny a fee waiver. The FBI, requesters complain, approaches FOIA fees like a car salesman cutting a deal, sometimes offering to waive 10 percent or so.

When a *Common Cause Magazine* writer asked the State Department in January for documents pertaining to President Bush's past travels, and also requested a fee waiver, the department responded with a questionnaire: Had she looked in the public library? What kind of education did she have, especially in foreign affairs? Would she be paid for the article? How much? When the writer protested, an official said the questionnaire had been sent in error.

THE COURTS CHANGE COURSE

FOIA has never been regarded as a precisely drafted law. Over the years, the federal courts have "breathed policy" into it, spelling out by judges' rulings how the government is to comply.

The D.C. Circuit Court of Appeals, which handles most FOIA cases, and the Supreme Court have in the past several years moved aggressively to ex-

last year that his 1991 request for new staff was cut in half by Justice and then "zeroed out" by OMB.

If money is so important, you'd think the administration could tote up the cost of litigating all those FOIA cases. It hasn't. But Justice does track — and has been known to inflate — the cost of complying with the law. The department claimed that compliance with one court-ordered FOIA release would cost $75,000. In 1989 the General Accounting Office found that it actually cost $23,500.

Computers are the newest FOIA battleground. When the act was written in the era of carbon paper and file cabinets, the government had some 3,000 computers. Today it has maybe a million, holding the nation's largest collection of information. But FOIA has never been updated to define the rights of access to that material.

Indeed, the Bush administration seems to regard computers as more worrisome than paper files.

The Justice Department last fall surveyed other agencies about access to electronic records — a process like "polling members of the National Rifle Association on gun control," according to FOIA expert David Morrissey at Indiana University. Among the issues raised: What is an electronic record? Since information can be extracted in virtually any form, can an agency control the form in which it is released? Justice hasn't yet proposed any answers, but the survey's basic premises point toward less FOIA accessibility as more records are put on computer.

"Frankly, I don't understand why there is a problem," Sobel says. If an agency claims material cannot be pulled from a database in the form requested, Sobel would ask if the materi-

pand the government's power to withhold. Journalist McMasters says: "The Supreme Court will let you publish whatever you get your hands on, but won't lift a finger to help you get it."

One problem for FOIA is the changing face of the federal judiciary. Although ideology doesn't necessarily predict votes on FOIA cases, several D.C. Circuit rulings have split between conservatives appointed by Reagan and Bush and liberals appointed earlier. The conservatives hold a majority on the full court.

There's a second, non-ideological problem: FOIA cases eat up too much time. D.C. District Court Judge Louis Oberdorfer says that one of his clerks once spent nearly three months examining thousands of documents the government wanted to withhold. Federal judges don't have the time for such exhaustive analysis anymore — as Oberdorfer said at the ABA conference, their dockets are overwhelmed by drug cases.

The cumulative effect of court rulings since the mid-1980s has been to give the government greater power to deny public access to information and even to discourage cases from being brought.

■ FBI criminal history records — "rap sheets" — have been ruled "categorically" exempt from disclosure. The Justice Department seized on the ruling to encourage agencies to designate other documents as exempt.

■ The Supreme Court held that unless the requested information itself directly reveals government operations or activities, disclosure isn't in the public interest — no matter how it will be used.

■ The Supreme Court vastly broadened the exemption allowing law enforcement agencies to withhold records. Even Supreme Court Justice Antonin Scalia, a staunch conservative, wrote that the decision created a "hole one can drive a truck through."

■ Rulings have broadened the exemption for confidential law-enforcement sources. Anyone who speaks to the FBI now has an essentially "irrebuttable" assurance of confidentiality, even if the bureau never said so.

■ Courts rarely question agency claims that disclosure would compromise "national security." The CIA, in a case involving tests of mind-control drugs on unwitting subjects, won a vir-

tual exemption from court review of its decisions to withhold information. Investigative writer Scott Armstrong, who has used the act extensively, says where national security is claimed, "FOIA for all practical purposes is basically dead."

■ The "balancing" between privacy considerations and the public interest in releasing information is increasingly out of balance. "Privacy wins every single time these days," says Appellate Judge Patricia Wald. In a case now working its way through the courts, news organizations are asking for the audiotape of the *Challenger's* last two minutes. The requesters, citing an inaccurate transcript released earlier by

Since the mid-'80s courts have given government the green light to withhold information.

NASA, say the tape is the only true record of what happened aboard the shuttle. NASA argues that voice inflections make the tape as private as a personnel or medical file. A decision for NASA could radically expand the privacy exemption.

Taken together, these rulings make it harder to get information, especially from such agencies as the FBI and CIA. Says attorney Jim Lesar, whose practice is primarily FOIA litigation: "We may simply have to have a series of disasters before Congress may be impelled to amend the act again."

THANKS BUT NO THANKS
With all FOIA's problems, from interminable delays to hostile court rulings, you'd think users would be beating a path to Capitol Hill for legislative relief. But there's no consensus that getting Congress involved is a good idea.

Hesitant reformers point to 1986, when Sen. Orrin Hatch (R-Utah) added FOIA provisions to an anti-drug bill that was being rammed through before Election Day. In a hastily reached compromise, conservatives got broader law-enforcement exemptions and liberals got the fee-waiver standards. Some FOIA supporters admit they gave away more than they got.

And some advocates fear that tin-

kering with FOIA would give opponents an opening to weaken it. They point to the frequent attempts to write FOIA exemptions into other bills as evidence that beneficial reform is a fragile hope. Says one public interest lawyer, "Are there helpful reforms? Yes. Would I want them at the cost of giving the other side what they want? No."

Any new amendments would be tested in increasingly hostile courts — another reason some advocates say it's smarter to live with the law as it is. For others, the courts' hostility is a major reason to act now. "Given the trend in the courts to read the law narrowly," says Gary Stern of the American Civil Liberties Union, "we believe the statute should be strengthened."

Sen. Patrick Leahy (D-Vt.), chair of the Judiciary Subcommittee on Technology and the Law, may soon ignite the first wide-ranging debate on FOIA in years. For months, his staff has been soliciting comments on draft legislation he hopes to introduce this summer. The bill is expected to clarify the law on electronic records, narrow the recent court rulings on exemptions and impose civil penalties for recalcitrant agencies. It also would require agencies to make information available in public reading rooms and publish indexes of available information.

Some FOIA advocates call it a Pandora's box. But Leahy's staff says FOIA has sustained too much damage to wait any longer. The SPJ's Paul McMasters agrees, saying that if the changes aren't made, "We have a long string of defeats ahead of us."

Meanwhile, everyone pays lip service to open records. Vice President Dan Quayle told a group of newspaper executives in 1989: "An educated and informed public is the foundation of a sound democracy. I have often said that too much government information is classified and that the public would appreciate our national security needs if more data were declassified and released."

It's hard to argue with that. But when *Harper's* magazine asked the vice president's office how many college graduations Quayle had been invited to speak at this spring, his office first said there were too many to count and then withheld the number, claiming security needs.

Harper's is filing a FOIA request. ♦

UNLAWFUL, UNELECTED, AND UNCHECKED

How the CIA subverts the government at home
By Christopher Hitchens

On the first day of August this year, in Room 419 of the Dirksen Senate Office Building, there was a hearing that disclosed little to the eye but a good deal to the skeptical mind. The setup looked unpromising enough. With the exception of vast, choreographed numbers like the Iran-Contra waltz of the summer of '87, congressional hearings are deliberately organized to militate against drama, and this particular hearing was no exception. Experts were on hand to speak in tones pitched to guarantee boredom. Committee members, typically half-prepared and distracted, would ensure monotony and torpor. The Subcommittee on Terrorism, Narcotics and International Operations of the Senate Foreign Relations Committee was taking evidence on the murky workings of an international bank—no big deal in our time.

But the bank in question this day was the Bank of Credit and Commerce International, and the testimony, as it unfolded, had less to do, really, with the financial workings of BCCI than with the intestinal workings of the government of the United States. Ranged in various attitudes of piety and relaxation were Senators Jesse Helms (R., N.C.), James Jeffords (R., Vt.), Claiborne Pell (D., R.I.), Paul Simon (D., Ill.), Alan Cranston (D., Calif., and a nice touch for an investigation of a bank), and John Kerry (D., Mass.), the subcommittee chairman. The two witnesses were Jack Blum, a former investigator for the subcommittee, and William von Rabb, U.S. Customs commissioner under Presidents Reagan

Christopher Hitchens is the Washington editor of Harper's Magazine.

and (until August 1989) Bush, and dull their declarations were not. As Blum and von Rabb got deeper and deeper into their testimony, reporters began to catch one another's eye; in the seats reserved for the public, quiet gave way to murmurs and even a few whistles of astonishment. I was a bit taken aback myself by the Q's and especially the A's:

Did the Federal Reserve possess a list of names of prominent Washingtonians who had taken kickbacks from BCCI? *Yes, it did.*

Had BCCI helped certain "outlaw" states acquire American nuclear technology? *Yes, it had.*

Had payments been made through BCCI to drug runners, gun smugglers, death-squad leaders? *You bet.*

Had the Treasury Department known about BCCI? *Sure.*

What about Justice? (The department, not the concept—we're talking real world here.) *They knew what was up and seemed most concerned that no others would.*

Interesting. But in a way even more interesting (at least to the skeptical mind) than this long scroll of indictments was where the scroll suddenly screeched to a halt. Treasury, Justice...what about the Central Intelligence Agency? I happened to know that the CIA had been politely invited to send someone to appear before the subcommittee. Its members had recently learned from investigators that the agency had stashed money in a number of BCCI accounts to use for covert operations in a number of countries. Senator Kerry's subcommittee—at any rate, Senator Kerry—wanted some answers.

I actually have in my possession a letter from Senator Kerry—whose work on the connection between narcotics and the Nicaraguan Contras was so efficiently interred three years ago—to Judge William H. Webster, director of Central Intelligence. The letter was sent on May 14, 1991, weeks before regulators in several countries shut down BCCI and its worldwide $20 billion criminal operation. In the letter, Webster is asked to furnish a copy of a seven- to ten-page memorandum about BCCI written in 1988 by the deputy director of the CIA, Robert Gates, and to provide as well a "detailed explanation" of the nature and extent of the agency's use of the bank.

Kerry got no reply of any kind from Webster. Kerry *was* told by the agency that no CIA man would appear before his subcommittee unless the hearing was closed. The open hearing did produce an account of how the CIA knew but failed to inform the Federal Reserve that BCCI illegally controlled First American Bankshares Inc., the Washington-based holding company chaired by Clark Clifford; and Jack Blum did place in evidence a deposition from former Contra bagman Adolfo Calero. (Very interesting, the latter—but its contents were not disclosed.) By the end of the day, however, no committee member had formulated a sentence placing in relation the terms BCCI and CIA. This day, as on all too many days since its modest inception in 1947, the CIA was the ghost in the machine. The ostensible processes of open, representative government were not to—and dutifully did not—reveal the agency's role or its reach.

> THIS FALL
> THERE WILL BE MORE
> SORDID ACCOUNTS OF CIA
> OPERATIONS, TO BE SURE,
> BUT I DOUBT THERE WILL BE
> AN ACCOUNTING

There exists a provision in the Constitution requiring of all branches of government "that a regular Statement and Account of the Receipts and Expenditures of all public Money shall be published from time to time." The CIA is exempted from this—hence its easy evasions with regard to BCCI. In truth, the CIA, citing national security, has managed to exempt itself from all manner of scrutiny, be it from the Congress, the press, or ordinary citizens.

The BCCI scandal; the hubristic nomination of Robert Gates to head the agency, despite his umbral connections to the illegal funding of the Contras; the ongoing investigation by special prosecutor Lawrence Walsh into the Iran-Contra affair, now burrowing further and further into the CIA thanks to the attack of conscience and plea-bargains experienced by Alan Fiers, who headed the agency's Central America Task Force from 1984 to 1988; the trial of Manuel Noriega, the CIA's

torture-condoning, coke-dealing "asset"; the mainstream attention given (finally) this past summer to allegations that the Reagan campaign team, led by spookmeister William Casey, sought to delay the release of the hostages held in Iran until after the 1980 election: The CIA, its awful role and lawless reach, is everywhere apparent in Washington just now. Everywhere, and nowhere: This fall there will be more sordid accounts of CIA operations and actions, to be sure, but I doubt there will be an accounting. It would seem to be no one's issue that the laws and institutions of government—that American democracy itself—have been, as they might say inside the agency, "coverted."

"**O**ur real duty is to become the mind of America." Thus Hugh "Harlot" Montague, the pseudo-intellectual spy who is the eponymous center of Norman Mailer's new epic novel about the CIA. Such airs—in life as in fiction—the agency gives itself! The mind of America, yet! But dare we repress the suspicion that there is something all too truthful in this arrogation? Even something that—if we keep in mind how the American political class has delegated numberless dark corners of its "mind" to covert subcontractors—might explain the broadly felt sense of overwhelming political cynicism and disarray? Consider, if only briefly, the postwar role the CIA has played in bending the American mind.

I am going to leave aside the overseas memorials—the graveyards filled by the noisy Americans in and around Saigon; the torture chambers constructed and used in Iran by SAVAK; the jail cell that held Nelson Mandela, whose arrest the CIA played a part in; the statues of dictators propped up by the agency—that mark the CIA's collusion with the most degraded elements in Third World politics. Let us confine the study to America's own internal affairs—including that area of "police, subpoena, or law enforcement powers or internal security functions" that the CIA was, by its founding congressional charter, explicitly forbidden to touch.

Beginning at the beginning, we find the agency secretly finding homes and jobs in the U.S. for several hundred prominent Nazis and Nazi collaborators. Soon after begin the operational pacts with notorious American crime families. Drugs have had a special place in the CIA; it has, over the years, financed experiments with LSD and other hallucinogens and toxins on unwitting civilians, and worked in concert with pilots and middlemen who trafficked not only in information but in heroin and cocaine that wound up on the American market.

As for that other American bogey, spendthrift government: The CIA may be mean but never lean. Its exact funding, naturally, is kept from us, and anyway the "intelligence community" is not only the agency but many agencies, which only means that the generally accepted estimate of the CIA's annual budget—no less than $3.5 billion, in support of 20,000 employees—is on the far side of conservative. In such a case, the smallest vignette may be quite instructive. In 1986, William Casey awarded a $20,000 bonus to Alan Fiers for his "exceptional management" of the CIA's Central America Task Force—Fiers's chief "task," as we now know, being that of circumventing congressional prohibitions on arming Contras and talking trade with hostage takers.

Above and beyond the drugs and the wasting of tax dollars is the matter of American democracy, and the CIA's unrelieved contempt for it. It has bought and suborned senior American journalists and editors, and planted knowing falsehoods in the American press. It has established itself, by means of "deniable" funds and foundations, in the belly of the American academy, although no doubt literature courses influenced by multiculturalism are infinitely more scandalous and threatening to the American way of life. Should I bring up the publishing houses the agency has subsidized to dispense disinformation? How it has further corrupted a political language—think of "asset," "destabilize," "terminate"—already weakened by sordid euphemism? (This is not so much the American mind as the American id: down, dirty, sniggering.) What about the tainted money from overseas—from despots, mostly, as if to sharpen the irony—that, thanks to the agency, has entered the electoral process?

The damage the CIA has done to American democracy is most evident, I think, when we look to Congress. The Senate and House have been routinely deceived by the agency and by foreign governments assisted by the agency—this is the dark heart of Iran-Contra. What is more, the pornography of tough-mindedness, covert action, and preparedness for "peace through strength" has had a predictably hypnotic effect on the legislative branch, turning it from legal watchdog to lapdog. As the agency's most famous counterespionage man, James Jesus Angleton, once peremptorily told an "executive session" of the Senate Committee on Intelligence: "It is inconceivable that a secret intelligence arm of the government has to comply with all the overt orders of the government."

On that occasion—and note, please, the educated contempt with which the word "overt" is employed—the CIA had refused to comply with a congressional call to destroy its supply of Castro-threatening shellfish poison. In recent years senior agency officials have grown somewhat more subtle in their disdain of lawmakers and the law. According to the 1987 report of the House and Senate Iran-Contra committees, Robert Gates testified, in answer to questions that involved the immediate space in front of his nose: "We [the agency] didn't want to know how the Contras were being funded...we actively discouraged people from telling us things. We did not pursue lines of questioning." In his response to a question about how he was advised in October 1986 by an understrapper, Charles Allen, that there might be an Iran-to-Contra "diversion"—bear in mind that this advising from Allen came a full month before the scandal broke—Gates testified that his "first reaction was to tell Mr. Allen that I didn't want to hear any more about it."

Lying? Yes, as it turned out. But in a sense what is more interesting, in an ominous way, is how Gates—how the agency, for it is true of it as well as him—claims the metaphysical power to negate knowledge, even cognition. This is intelligence work of a most peculiar sort. In the hands of the CIA, a well-known, widely reported, public fact—for example, Israel's early and

Illustration by Steve Brodner

crucial role in clandestinely arming Iran with American weapons when there was a congressional ban on such—gets classified a "secret" and is never again mentioned by an elected official. (Israel, comically, went through the Iran-Contra hearings as "Country One.") Similarly, as with Gates and the diversion, a known phenomenon—profits from arms sales to Iran entering the Contras' coffers—becomes "unknown" because a CIA official puts his hands to his ears when knowledge of the phenomenon is about to be uttered in his presence. (The obvious question for Mr. Gates at his confirmation hearings: How did he *know* he didn't want to know any more about it?)

It must be said that over the long haul such conjury does require an audience of almost doltish credulity. This has been furnished time and again by the aptly named intelligence "oversight" committees on the Hill: juries of those not wishing to hear, nodding at witnesses not wishing to tell. In the mid-1970s there did flicker a moment when it was thought that perhaps the CIA should not be a law unto itself—I am thinking of the Church and Pike committees' work—but that moment was quickly extinguished, thanks in no small part to the work of then CIA director George Herbert Walker Bush. An outstanding example of current relations (that is to say, traditional relations) between oversight and the purportedly overseen can be discerned in the matter of the disclosure that Robert Gates, just days before the President nominated him to head the CIA, had been notified that he was a "subject" of Lawrence Walsh's ongoing Iran-Contra investigation. Questioned about this troubling development (troubling even after so much overlooking, one might still think), the White House said it was troubled not at all—that "through an intermediary" it had received "some assurance" from the special prosecutor that Gates was not an actual target of the investigation. And the intermediary? Why, Senator David Boren (D., Okla.), chairman of the Senate Intelligence Committee and the elected lawmaker most clearly responsible for overseeing, not facilitating.

If you had been at CIA headquarters in Langley, Virginia, last March 4—in fact, you would not, by law, have been allowed to have been—you would have witnessed a celebration of such facilitation, as Director Webster invested Republican Congressman Henry Hyde of Illinois and Democratic Congressman

THE "NEW" WHITE-COLLAR CIA HAS BEEN AROUND FOR YEARS, ITS COMPUTER NERDS AND THINK-TANK TYPES TABULATING CONCOCTED NUMBERS

Anthony C. Beilenson of California with CIA Seal Medallions for their "sustained outstanding support to the agency." Both had served long and well (from the agency's standpoint) on the House Intelligence oversight committee, and Webster spoke of the "high privilege" it had been to work with them. Ah, checks and balances. Congressman Beilenson made note at the ceremony of how the CIA had "followed both the letter and the spirit of the law." Congressman Hyde—you might recall his role in making absolutely sure the Iran-Contra hearings self-destructed—contented himself with saying that service to the oversight committee had been "a rare adventure." I dare say.

In its attempt to salvage the Gates nomination this fall and to fend off those, like Senator Moynihan (D., N.Y.), who have begun wondering aloud whether the CIA should not be subject to a full re-evaluation, what with the war it was set up to fight—the Cold War—now over, the agency has gotten the word around town about a "new" CIA: no more plumbers, just computer nerds and specialists of the think-tank variety, white-collar types turning out economic forecasts and drawing up long-range forecasts. The problem with this "new" CIA is that it has been around for years. The tabulation of concocted figures and the drawing from these of fictitious conclusions have long been agency staples. The CIA's annual *Handbook of Economic Statistics* is a perfect example, and its 1989 edition makes for wonderful reading. My favorite number is the one putting the annual rate of growth in the U.S.S.R. during 1981–85 at 1.9 percent, significantly above the rate for those years in Western Europe. The CIA also cooked up the idea that the per capita GNP of East Germany was greater in the 1980s than that of West Germany—the agency's numbers are right there in the 1989 edition of the *Statistical Abstract of the United States*.

To what end, this arithmetical fiction? Well, it wasn't intended to deceive the Russians or East Germans. They never toiled under the illusion that they were outstripping the West. The target here was the American lawmaker and, through him, the American taxpayer. The point was the maintenance of a national mood, one more deeply informed by fear. In such a climate, democracy might be overlooked here and there, and those in power might be given the chance to maintain it and exercise it in the shadows.

When the CIA predicted that the U.S.S.R. would possess *10,000* antiballistic missiles by 1970, it was doing little more than giving an immense boost to the "contractor community," as I once heard it unsmilingly called. The Soviet T-72 tank, recently demonstrated to have extremely combustive properties on the plains of Mesopotamia, was invested with magically sinister capabilities by one CIA report after another. Ditto the Scud. This wasn't the War Brought Home that the anti–Vietnam War demonstrators chanted of. This was the War Bought at Home.

As for the agency's long-range forecasts, they have always been written ultimately with one thing in mind: assuring a continued and prominent foreign-policy–making role for the unelected government at Langley. With the Cold War in the past tense, this will not be easy: New enemies must be found and fast. Drug kingpins? Terrorists? If joining them no longer pays off, one might as well beat them.

It would seem that the agency is also looking to develop *economic* enemies, beginning with Japan. The Rochester Institute of Technology in upstate New York, under the presidency of M. Richard Rose, has evolved into a satellite station of the agency, and last year in Rochester there took place a CIA-sponsored seminar on the Japanese economy. Among the participants were Kent Harrington, director of the CIA's East Asia Department, and former National Security Advisor Robert McFarlane (nice to have *him* back). Col. Andrew Dougherty, a Rochester administrator, worked up a draft report based on the seminar, and I suspect it is something of a template for the "new" CIA.

> THE DARK HISTORY OF THE UNELECTED GOVERNMENT AT LANGLEY MUST BE BROUGHT TO LIGHT IF THIS COUNTRY IS TO REGAIN FAITH IN WASHINGTON

We learn, for example, that the Japanese "are creatures of an ageless, amoral, manipulative, and controlling culture." They are poised to take advantage of Americans, whose natural "optimism" forever "creates a false sense of security and reduces the national will to act." (Sounds here as though Mr. Harrington cribbed a bit from the Fifties forecasts about the U.S.S.R.) In the not too distant future—the report is titled "Japan: 2000"—there will loom the threat of "an economic sneak attack, from which the United States may not recover."

No "new" CIA will be formulated from within the agency itself. Nor will pressure for such come from anywhere in the executive branch. Lest we forget, it was the CIA that molded the plastic figure of George Bush and laid the trail of calamities and cover-ups that helped him along the road to the presidency. Appointed to the directorship by Gerald Ford supposedly as a technocrat—instructive, that, in getting a grasp on nominee Gates—Bush proved staunchly otherwise, beginning right off at his confirmation hearings with one of the more stupendous Freudian syntactical blunders of our time: "I think we should tread very carefully on governments that are constitutionally elected." During his tenure at Langley, the agency set up serious shop in Angola and Jamaica, American journalists continued to be hired on the sly, and General Noriega was even more generously cultivated.

It was also Director Bush who used the agency to tighten the ratchet of Seventies anti-commie paranoia by appointing "Team B" to second-guess the annual intelligence estimates. "Team B," made up of Paul Nitze, Richard Pipes, Lt. Gen. Dan Graham, and others of similar stamp, is perhaps best remembered for its belief in the unfalsifiable superstition that Moscow sought and could obtain strategic superiority. Out of this smoke came the atmospherics of Reaganism.

Bush will do nothing to bring either *glasnost* or *perestroika* to Langley. And he can be counted on to prevent Congress from doing so. Witness his demanding and getting from the Hill in August a new, post–Iran-Contra Intelligence Authorization Act–that, formalities aside, permits the CIA to continue its unchecked, covert ways. Which is not to say that some lonely congressional committee or two still should not make a thorough, concerted inquiry into the CIA a priority. Quite the contrary: There is here, as in the Soviet Union, an entire shadow history that must be brought to light if this country is ever again to regain even a modicum of faith in Washington. One need look back no further than the 1980s—the 1980 presidential election, possibly tainted by William Casey and company; the arms buildup, undertaken on the basis of CIA-confected data; the Contra war, fueled by the CIA against the will of Congress; the cover-up of the latter, smeared with agency fingerprints—to glimpse the breadth and depth of the shadow cast.

Can we take it? The wiseacres inside the Beltway say no, the people could not bear the grim news and do not wish to learn it. Credibility is said to be at stake. Well, yes it is. The full exposure of the shadow government operating out of Langley is a necessary condition for, as people like to say, "putting all this behind us" and "moving the country forward."

No candidate for the highest office in 1992 can be counted as genuine unless he or she announces that the elected government will be the only one.   ∎

David Corn

Freedom of Information?
Not From the CIA

Openness—that's a term that Robert Gates, director of Central Intelligence, has embraced. When his nomination came before a skeptical Senate Intelligence Committee last year, he promised to promote perestroika in Langley. After being confirmed, he convened a Task Force on Openness, which recommended how the CIA could be more forthcoming. (Only under outside pressure did the CIA make public the task force's report, which proposed, among other things, that the agency release material about its successes, admit when it is wrong and "preserve the mystique.") Gates has called for greater declassification of decades-old documents and more background briefings for the press. From a distance, his reforms may seem sincere. But they slip past a key matter.

For several years, I have been working on a book about the CIA. Like many researchers, I turned toward the Freedom of Information Act for assistance and found that when it comes to the CIA, it is almost worthless. The act allows·scholars, reporters and just plain folks to petition various executive branch agencies for documents. There are numerous exceptions to what the government has to release, and amendments to the act in 1984 made it easier for the CIA to withhold some records. Still, the FOIA could be of some small and important value to those seeking to understand what the CIA does, were it not for the way the agency handles FOIA requests—a process that belies the "new" CIA of Gates.

Agency responses to FOIA requests are routinely discouraging, marked by long delays and puzzling answers. Here's one example: I asked for material on the Hmong, an indigenous tribe in Indochina, which the CIA armed and directed in the 1960s and 1970s as part of the so-called "secret war" in Laos. This was one of the biggest agency paramilitary operations in history; its existence is not a secret. The CIA said that it had searched and found not one piece of paper relevant to the request. Operational material detailing the ins and outs of the agency's programs is automatically exempt. But I hoped to find intelligence reports that covered the tribe and its leaders. Surely if the agency supported the Hmong for so long it must have at some time looked at its ally. But there was, the agency said, absolutely nothing.

It is hard to argue with the CIA. Who knows what's in the files? But such responses are hard to accept at face value in light of other Langley decisions. In 1987, the private and nonprofit National Security Archive requested under FOIA an index of all the documents that the CIA had previously released.

After initial denials, the agency sent the archive 12 volumes of about 450 pages each that listed the documents in completely random order. Documents released as part of a single request were scattered throughout the books. This is certainly not how the FOIA office maintains its records, and one can reasonably surmise that it had to program its computer to devise such a random and mean-spirited dump. When I later requested the index information in electronic form—so it could be arranged coherently—the agency told me to get lost. The National Security Archive is still fighting the CIA to obtain the index in computer form.

The only way to use the index is to plow through the volumes. I went through one book and found several documents that looked intriguing. (Almost all the good stuff was released prior to 1981, the year Ronald Reagan assumed office.) I filed a request with the agency for these papers and received the material in three weeks—Olympic speed, by FOIA standards. I then went through the rest of the set and filed subsequent requests. When the CIA realized what I was doing, it seems, it put me in what some researchers believe is the forget-you category. After six months, only one of my other requests has been fulfilled—and that only occurred following the intervention of a lawyer.

The FOIA calls for agencies to respond to requests within 10 days. But that standard has become a farce. Usually it means that the agency acknowledges the receipt of the request within 10 days. Then the request goes to the end of the line, and in some instances years will pass before you hear back. Such delays dilute the power of the FOIA. Few book authors or journalists have the luxury of waiting so long.

If there is any category of request to which the 10-day standard should be applied it is documents already released. The documents I have requested from the index are sitting in a file cabinet in the agency's FOIA office and could be easily retrieved. One request for already-released documents has been held up for more than a year. Not surprisingly, the subject of those records is Edwin Wilson, a rogue CIA employee now in jail.

The agency's FOIA office has acted in a fashion that to outsiders appears capricious and spiteful. Now is the time for Gates to show he is serious about openness. Let him release previously released documents. That's a paltry battle cry, but it shows the sad state of the FOIA in Langley.

David Corn is Washington editor of the Nation magazine and is working on a book on the CIA.

Census fails to quash report on Iraqi deaths

By Jack Colhoun

Washington—The Bush administration has failed in an attempt to muzzle a U.S. Census Bureau demographer who released a report estimating more than 80,000 Iraqi civilians died as a result of the Gulf war.

When the Census Bureau tried to fire Beth Osborne Daponte—charging that she had falsified data and failed to have her study peer-reviewed before making it public—she fought back and won.

"I find it extremely disturbing that the Census Bureau tried to suppress and delay the release of information that is embarrassing to the current administration," Daponte said at an April 13 news conference here, at which she announced that the Bureau had withdrawn the charges against her.

"By trying to do so, the Bureau was effectively keeping the public ignorant of the full impact of U.S. actions in the Gulf area," asserted the 29-year old demographer. "I believe that in the case of the Iraqi information, politics, not a concern to inform the public, governed the Bureau's actions and writings."

'They didn't want any estimate'

Asked if the administration wanted to downplay civilian deaths, Daponte responded, "Not even downplay. Downplay implies they wanted a low estimate. They didn't want any estimate."

Her study estimated 150,000 Iraqis died as a consequence of the Gulf war. The dead included about 40,000 women and 32,000 children, or about 48 percent of the total Iraqi casualties.

Daponte estimated 13,000 civilians were killed immediately by the bombing. But she calculated another 70,000 civilians died in 1991 after the war as the result of the collapse of the Iraqi public health system. U.S. bombing of electric power plants made Iraq's water purification and sewage systems inoperable, creating the conditions for epidemics of water-borne diseases to which children and the elderly are most susceptible (Guardian, April 3, 1991, and June 12, 1991).

According to Daponte's study, 40,000 Iraqi troops were killed in the war. She concluded another 35,000 Iraqis died in the postwar civil uprisings in Iraq by the Kurds in the north and the Shiites in the south, a number which included 5,000 Iraqi soldiers.

11,000 babies, 50,000 old people

Daponte arrived at her figures for civilian deaths resulting from the war by extrapolating from the United Nations' 1987 census of Iraq. She used standard mortality rates and demographic models of excess deaths during public health crises, in which the very old and the very young die at the highest rates.

According to her tables, about 6,000 children age 14 and under died from the bombing, while 11,000 infants under age 1 perished in the postwar period. Only about 400 Iraqis over 65 were killed during the actual war, according to her figures—but almost 50,000 died as a result of the conflict's aftermath.

Her estimate of 40,000 Iraqi military deaths in the war is considerably lower than the 100,000 Iraqi military deaths calculated by the Defense Intelligence Agency in a 1991 document released to National Research Defense Council.

When Frank Hobbs, chief of the Bureau's population studies branch, revised Daponte's study, he reduced the number of civilian deaths from the bombing from 13,000 to 5,000. Hobbs also eliminated her breakdown of civilian casualties according to gender and age.

'Embarrassing to administration'

Daponte said her problems at the Bureau stemmed from her inclusion of Iraqi civilian deaths in her casualty study.

"It's embarrassing to the administration to acknowledge that women and children died in the war," she told the Guardian. "We expect male casualties during war. But the [Gulf] war was portrayed as minimally affecting civilians who weren't involved directly in the war."

Arthur Spitzer of the American Civil Liberties Union, who headed Daponte's legal team, claimed the Bureau's charges against her were trumped up. Daponte produced Bureau documents that proved her study had been peer-reviewed and was approved by her superiors before she made public her findings last January.

Hobbs did not return a phone call from the Guardian.

"The most that might have happened was some miscommunication or misunderstanding between Daponte and one source," Spitzer said, referring to Daponte's

DataCenter   464 19th Street, Oakland, California 94612 (415) 835-4692

contemporaneous notes of a disputed interview with a source that refuted the charge that she falsified data. "We don't even acknowledge there was any misunderstanding or miscommunication."

Neither Daponte nor Spitzer would confirm the disputed interview was with retired Col. Trevor Dupuy, a well-known military historian. But Dupuy informed Bureau officials that he didn't agree with statistical assumptions Daponte made about civilian casualties attributed to him, according to a March 6 story in the Washington Post. Dupuy told the Post, however, that he had "no basis" to conclude Daponte "deliberately distorted what I said."

Daponte doesn't claim her study is the definitive word on Iraqi casualties. She stressed that when she did her research in the fall of 1991, very little information was available. But she noted at her news conference that she intended to do another study later this year on her own time.

Pentagon blanks out Iraqi deaths

Meanwhile, the Pentagon's final report to Congress on the Gulf war puts the administration's familiar spin on the issue of Iraqi civilian casualties. "Conduct of the Persian Gulf War," released April 11, stresses the administration's good intentions and high-tech weapon wizardry.

"From the beginning, Coalition objectives made a clear distinction between the regime and the Iraqi populace—the regime and its military capabilities were the target; the Iraqi people were not," the Pentagon report asserts. "Coalition planners followed stringent procedures to select and attack targets. Attack routes were planned to minimize the results of errant ordnance; the norm was to use precision-guided missiles, rather than less-accurate gravity weapons, in built-up or populated areas."

One lesson the Bush administration learned from the Vietnam War was to downplay civilian casualties. The Pentagon concluded that news stories that depicted the high civilian death toll from U.S. firepower in Vietnam eroded public support for the war. The administration also decided not to make a big deal about the "body count" of "enemy" soldiers killed, as the United States did in the Vietnam War.

"Coalition planners recognized not all weapons would perform in every case as designed and, despite all efforts to prevent collateral damage, some would occur," the 1,300-page report continues. "Although the death or injury of any civilian is regrettable, the apparently low number clearly reflects Coalition efforts to minimize civilian casualties."

The report eliminated a chapter circulating in the Pentagon last winter on the Iraqi death toll. No Iraqi casualty estimates are included in the final report.

Generators bombed

The Pentagon report did reveal, however, that intelligence and communication failures resulted in more bombing runs against Iraq's electric power plants than intended. Pentagon targeters had planned to "target switching systems at electrical power plants because they are easier to repair than other plant facilities," but these goals weren't always passed on to all the air units.

"As a result, many generator halls—which are easier to strike, but harder to repair—were damaged heavily," the report concedes, reopening the issue of U.S. responsibility for the near-complete destruction of Iraqi power plants and the subsequent disruption of the water supply.

In a related development, a Washington Post report on still-classified Pentagon studies undercuts the administration's hype about its wonder weapons' pin-point accuracy. The new analysis, according to an April 10 story in the Post, suggests that the F-117As [Stealth fighter-bombers] placed laser-guided bombs on their primary targets in about 60 percent of the missions flown, in contrast to the 90 percent success rate estimated by top Air Force officers after the war.

The Post added, "The Tomahawks [cruise missiles], 288 of which were fired from surface ships and submarines in the Persian Gulf, Red Sea and eastern Mediterranean Sea, hit their intended targets slightly more than half of the time." The Navy previously announced that Tomahawk cruise missiles hit their targets 85 percent of the time during the war.   ⊙

Deregulatory Creep

Dan Quayle clears the way for industry

BY ARTHUR E. ROWSE

When George Bush announced, during his State of the Union address last January, that he wanted to "weed out unnecessary and burdensome" government regulations that "impede economic growth," he was greeted with one of his loudest cheers. Since then, both Republicans and Democrats have exercised the applause meters with similar promises. Sitting Presidents—and would-be Presidents—have been running successfully against Washington for years.

Yet polls show the general public firmly opposes deregulation of business, especially when the purity of air, water, food, drugs, and other necessities is involved. And seeing what happened to the savings-and-loan and airline industries after deregulation, Americans don't seem to buy Bush's argument that an attack on regulations will do much to combat the recession. According to a survey by Peter Hart last November, people rated "reduced safety and environmental regulations" last among sixteen ways of helping the economy. Professional economists are also skeptical.

But regulation-bashing is almost as popular as football, and it's one game in which Bush is clearly a leader. Since taking office three years ago, he has done more to kick around the rule-making process than any previous occupant of the White House. His chief blocking back is Vice President Dan Quayle, in his capacity as head of a secretive office called the Council on Competitiveness.

Quayle admits to being a "zealot" in fighting "regulatory creep" and has stalled or killed dozens of proposed rules, just as Bush did for eight years in a similar role under Ronald Reagan. Quayle is also the Republicans' outstanding fundraiser, a role that earned him the title of "bag man" for the Bush-Quayle campaign, according to Joan Claybrook, head of Ralph Nader's Public Citizen organization.

Bush got the idea of a regulatory freeze

Arthur E. Rowse is a free-lance writer in the Washington, D.C., area.

from Reagan, whose first Presidential act was to put all in-process regulations on ice for sixty days. But Bush's moratorium is far broader. It includes a complete review of all existing rules. His message to business is clear: Bring us your saddest cases of overregulation and we will cure them—even if it proves fatal to some people.

Five days before the March 10 primaries in Texas, Louisiana, and Oklahoma, the Administration said it would slash fees required of small stripper oil wells on Government land. It also relaxed rules governing the natural-gas industry. Four days before the Illinois and Michigan primaries a week later, Bush broke a seventeen-year impasse by dropping a proposal that automobile manufacturers install fuel filters—at $20 to $30 per car—in cars sold in certain cities. He substituted a proposal for filtering at the gas pump, which would cost service stations $20,000 to $40,000 for new equipment. Independent marketers—who own two-thirds of the nation's stations—claimed the proposal would hurt them competitively against the big oil companies.

Reporters gently suggested that campaign contributions might be motivating some of the changes, but none chose to spice up their stories with available specifics: Congress Watch (another Nader organization) released a report showing that as of December 31, the Bush-Quayle campaign and the Republican National Committee had collected $1,150,360 from petroleum interests and $156,250 from auto interests. But the news was ignored by *The Washington Post*, *The New York Times*,

and the *Los Angeles Times*. The Associated Press transmitted a dispatch, but another ten big-city papers, checked at random, spiked it.

Also before the Illinois and Michigan primaries, Bush blocked a twenty-year effort to limit exposure of six million workers to more than a thousand hazardous products in the maritime, construction, and agriculture industries. Limiting these toxic chemicals might be more dangerous than not limiting them, wrote White House official James B. MacRae Jr. in a bizarre letter to the Occupational Safety and Health Administration. The cost of compliance, he argued, would cause the layoff of workers most prone to serious injury. As acting director of the Office of Information and Regulation in the Office of Management and Budget, MacRae is the White House's chief aide on regulatory matters. Asked to explain, he said, "I'm not on my own. I do what I'm told to do."

This action could doom safety limits affecting additional millions of American workers, according to an OSHA official who chooses to remain anonymous. "Loony" is what Peg Simonario calls it; she is chief of health and safety for the AFL-CIO. *The Times* reported the move after it was leaked from OSHA, but buried the news inside the paper, as did *The Post* the next day. They and other news organizations were more interested in the unpaid lunch bills and check overdrafts of Congress.

Also lost in the excitement on Capitol Hill was any consideration of the timing and motivation of these actions. According to a report available at the time from the Center for Responsive Politics, business had contributed nearly $13 million in "soft money" to Republican committees during 1991, with ten more months to go before the election. Individuals, many of them business executives, donated another $4 million to the GOP. The Republican Party took in a total of $17 million in soft money, compared to $7 million for Democrats.

DAVID SUTER

"Soft money" refers to donations to national party committees. It is supposed to be restricted to state and local "party-building" but often winds up in the states where Federal elections are closest. The soft-money loophole allows wealthy firms and individuals to give large chunks of cash without having to comply with the strict limit of $1,000 per person on regular campaign contributions.

Bush is not the first President to wield his powers of office to advantage in a political campaign. To help with this task, he chose campaign manager Fred Malek, who cut his teeth as director of Richard Nixon's "Responsiveness Campaign" to, in Malek's words, "corral all the goodies available" to ensure the President's re-election. In a memo to Government departments at the time, he advised against putting anything in writing. "In fact," he wrote, "I propose that we stop calling it politicizing the Executive Branch and instead call it something like strengthening the Government's responsiveness."

Bush also is not the first President to give private business a back door to the regulatory process. That custom goes back to the first Nixon Administration. But the current assault on regulations exceeds all earlier ones in several important respects:

¶ *Aggressiveness.* Dan Quayle doesn't just wait for complaints to come in, as Bush usually did as Vice President. Quayle scours the country clubs for them. In a summary of 1991 activities, his office boasts that he made more than 400 political appearances in 200 cities, raising "a new record" of $22 million for Republican campaigns nationwide. He seems to play politics more than golf.

¶ *Skirting the Law.* Quayle appears to come closer than even the Nixon crew to breaking the law against trading Government favors for campaign money. In a profile of Quayle in January, *The Washington Post* reported: "In almost every city he visits as a campaigner, Quayle holds

The Bush-Quayle team makes sure the field tilts in favor of lobbyists who want to score for their clients.

closed-door round tables with business people who have made sizable contributions to the local or national GOP." In speeches, he asks the same business executives to send regulatory problems to him. In response to critics, Quayle's spokesman Jeff Nesbit said that to imply that contributors get special treatment at the Council is "patently false."

¶ *Public Disclosure.* When Bush ran a similar back office under Reagan called the Presidential Task Force for Regulatory Relief, there was some doubt about whether it needed to comply with the Freedom of Information Act, since it was in the White House complex of executive privilege. That doubt was erased last September, when a Federal judge ruled that disclosure was required because of its regulatory activities. The Administrative Procedures Act also requires that the public be informed at all stages of rule-making. But the Quayle Council continues to hide essential details about its operations from Congress, the public, and the press.

¶ *Constitutionality.* Despite unanswered questions about its constitutionality, Quayle's wrecking crew requires agencies to call or drop in before even thinking about issuing a notice of intent to regulate. In 1981, the Congressional Research Service found that the same Reagan Executive Order cited as authority for Quayle's Council violates the separation-of-powers clause of the Constitution, because of its license to kill laws without due process.

¶ *Conflict of Interest.* Unlike Bush, who put his investments into a blind trust to avoid personal conflicts of interest when

he headed the Reagan Task Force, Quayle refused to do so. He apparently continues to work on regulatory issues that can directly affect his family's extensive investments. In January, Allan Hubbard, his principal aide on the Council, quit under fire and joined Quayle's campaign team after being accused by a House subcommittee of similar violations. Other conflicts can arise from the links between top campaign officials and private business. According to Charles Babcock and Ann Devroy of *The Washington Post,* campaign chairman Robert Teeter and campaign manager Fred Malek continue as paid directors or professional advisers to many firms while meeting each morning with top White House officials. When he took office, Bush pledged that ethical conduct in his Administration would be judged not on whether a criminal offense is committed but whether there is "any appearance of impropriety or conflict of interest."

With so many questionable activities under way, one might ask how Bush and Quayle have avoided massive public protests. The answer lies largely in news coverage—or the lack of it. Indiscretions in Congress tend to get much more attention, often beyond all proportion: take the check-bouncing caper, for example. And legislative action on regulatory matters is usually treated like football: as final victories or defeats. But the Bush-Quayle team makes sure the field tilts in favor of lobbyists who may have lost the fight in Congress but who want another chance to score for their clients. Christine Triano of OMB Watch calls the Quayle Council "a convenience store for big-business lobbyists."

Quayle sets the scene as chairman with what he has acknowledged are antiregulation and anticonsumer views. And his Council's permanent members appear to fit the pattern. They include Treasury Secretary Nicholas Brady, Attorney General William Barr, Commerce Secretary Bar-

Selected Government Actions and Contributions to Bush-Quayle and the GOP

INDUSTRY	GOVERNMENT ACTION	CONTRIBUTIONS
Automobile (3 firms)	Proposal for gas-tank canister dropped Stricter auto efficiency opposed	$156,250
Pharmaceuticals (10)	Drug-approval process speeded up "Orphan drug" competition bill vetoed	$185,002
Airlines (9)	Limits on noisy engines reduced	$315,700
Utilities (10)	Rules on boiler pollution relaxed	$385,500
Insurance (2)	Product-liability limits pushed	$450,000*
Air Polluters (11)	Emission standards delayed	$788,270
Oil and Gas (10)	Stripper-well fees reduced Rules on natural gas usage relaxed Limits on hazardous air blocked	$1,150,360
Food (5)	Nutrition guidelines pulled back Nutrition labeling delayed a year	$1,352,000*
Developers (25)	Wetland protection acreage reduced	$2,277,490
Individual "hard" donations to Bush-Quayle in 1991		$9,926,553
Total soft-money contributions to GOP, 1991		$17,134,513
Total contributions to Bush-Quayle and GOP, 1991		$27,061,066
Estimated soft contributions to Bush-Quayle, 1987-1988		$40,000,000

*Soft-money donations to GOP in 1991; other data include soft money for 1987-1991, plus hard money from individuals and political-action committees for 1988 and 1990 elections.

SOURCES: FEDERAL ELECTION COMMISSION, CONGRESS WATCH, OMB WATCH, NATIONAL LIBRARY ON MONEY AND POLITICS, CENTER FOR RESPONSIVE POLITICS

bara Franklin, White House Chief of Staff Sam Skinner, OMB Director Richard Darman, and Council of Economic Advisers Chair Michael Boskin. The staff acts like a vacuum cleaner, sucking up complaints from the business world, then dumping them on the appropriate regulators.

News reports also tend to accept the view of recent Administrations that Government regulations are bad for people as well as for business. The news corps has no deliberate system of tracking issues; it chooses instead to rely mostly on press releases and official notices or leaks. Many journalists also dismiss the other side of the story: the cost in lives, illnesses, and injuries that many rules seek to save.

The three-month delay of pending rules affecting safety in the workplace may have killed as many as 357 people and caused 1,271,503 lost work days, according to figures contained in Bush's own 1993 budget plan. When OMB Watch, a respected public-interest group, pointed out these grim statistics to leading reporters, they yawned.

Some of the lag in implementing laws results from the paper-shuffling that might be expected in an organization as big as the Federal Government. But at least as much comes from the opposition of business interests most affected by the rules and from Government officials unwilling to ruffle those interests. Some long delays affecting human life and health include:

¶ The Clean Water Act of 1972 ordered the Environmental Protection Agency to eliminate all water pollutants by 1985. But twenty years after passage, the agency has

failed to impose controls over effluents from four-fifths of the nation's industrial plants, according to Jessica Landman of the Natural Resources Defense Council. Many states have tried to stem the flow of poisons with their own controls, but Landman says they tend to fall well below even the Federal standards.

¶ The Clean Air Act of 1970 ordered the EPA to attack pollution in many ways. One was to identify "hazardous air pollutants" and to set limits on how much of each could be released by industrial plants. But two decades later, the agency has set emission standards for only seven substances. In 1990, a frustrated Congress passed tough amendments to impose controls on 189 more chemicals. But delays continue to occur.

¶ A 1988 law requires the Government to set standards for clinical laboratories to reduce the number of inaccurate medical tests on patients. But four years later, the Health Care Financing Administration has not yet established standards; it does not even know how many clinical labs operate in the United States.

¶ In 1980, the National Institute of Occupational Safety and Health determined that formaldehyde should be regulated as a potential cancer risk. Ten years later, labor unions and producers of the substance agreed on a compromise limit of exposure below initial recommendations. But final action has been delayed by the Quayle Council and the ninety-day freeze.

¶ A 1987 law ordered the Government to set standards designed to protect nursing-home residents and improve their

care. Yet the Department of Health and Human Services has completed action on only a few standards. Others have been held up at the White House's Office of Management and Budget, where the nursing-home operators want them to remain confined. It didn't hurt the industry to have campaign manager Malek serving as a director of Manor Care, Inc., the second largest chain of nursing homes in the United States.

¶ Beginning in the mid-1980s, the EPA, Food and Drug Administration, and Department of Agriculture tried to develop some controls over the budding biotechnology industry. They worried, as did many scientists, that genetically engineered substances might threaten the environment in dangerous ways. When these efforts failed in 1990, the Quayle Council sailed in, flying the industry's colors of noninterference. The result announced by the Council last year was a set of guidelines designed to ensure that "agencies won't add extra layers of regulations." The payoff: unknown but potentially huge, from an industry Bush has predicted will grow to $50 billion by the end of this decade. (The Association of Biotechnology Companies refused to release a list of members.)

One reason for such delays is the secrecy that enshrouds them much of the time. Secrecy is standard operating procedure for the Quayle brigade. Little of its regulation-bashing would be possible in the glare of publicity. The Council troops are told: "Leave no fingerprints!" All anyone knows about their activities comes from occasional leaks from aggrieved agencies and from efforts of Congressional committees to force the information out by holding hearings and issuing reports.

Leading that effort has been Representative Henry Waxman, Democrat of California, who heads a subcommittee on health and environment. In March 1991, he held the first hearing on the Quayle

DataCenter   464 19th Street, Oakland, California 94612 (415) 835-4692

DAVID SUTER

Council's blockage of 1990 amendments to the Clean Air Act. Waxman wanted to discuss why the Council had blocked a ban on incineration of lead batteries, a major health threat to children, and stalled a rule that would have required 25 per cent of waste to be recycled instead of incinerated.

In this and other hearings, Quayle refused to send a representative or answer written queries. Republicans on the subcommittee also opposed Waxman. When they were not accusing the Democrats of "harassment" and "partisan politics," they didn't show up at all. Waxman's principal foe was Representative William Dannemeyer, Republican of California, who said he feared that the "monster" environmental law would add another level of bureaucracy. As a result of news reports featuring pollution in the Grand Canyon, Quayle eventually agreed to compromise on a 70 per cent reduction in emissions there.

The next day, Quayle issued a sweeping memorandum to all executive agencies and departments claiming the power to review every phase of regulatory activities, including press releases, strategy statements, and advance notices of proposed rule-making. This memo and another on April 6, 1991, stirred Waxman to hold a second hearing on May 1. The April memo included more than a hundred changes made by the Council in EPA's plan for setting up a program of permits to control emissions from chemical plants, oil refineries, and other stationary sources of pollution.

Among changes made by the Council, one would allow polluters to increase emissions if the appropriate state agency did not object within seven days of being notified. Waxman said this was illegal because it rendered the regulatory process "largely meaningless." EPA's own general counsel concluded that the seven-day escape clause was illegal. But the political payoff was substantial. Joshua Goldstein of the Center for Responsive Politics found that eleven big air-polluting firms

Quayle's 'reform' of the legal system would leave insurance companies as the big winners.

donated $788,270 to Bush and Republican committees.

There seems to be no clear behavior pattern by contributors. The nation's top three polluters, Eastman Kodak, General Motors, and Hoechst Celanese were holding their soft money for later in the campaign, as were others, while Atlantic Richfield, which ranks far down the list of polluters, spread it around like butter. By the end of January, the company and its top executives had sent $727,360 to the GOP.

Bush and Quayle also were building up large leads in the race for individual contributors. During 1991, they reported $9.9 million, more than all that raised by the two other Republicans and five Democrats, according to data compiled from Federal Election Commission records by the National Library on Money and Politics. The Bush-Quayle team also led the field in the proportion of givers (63 per cent) with no clues to their occupation or employer, as required by law. That means such data are of limited value.

On July 22, Waxman went at it again with a public hearing on the role of the Council on EPA's proposal to cut pollution from boilers used by utilities. What bothered Waxman here, he said, was how the Department of Energy had "hijacked" EPA's role by drafting major parts of the proposal with the Edison Electric Institute, the industry lobbying group. Waxman released a DOE memo saying, "We do not believe the draft interpretative rule is responsive to the needs of the electric-utility industry." The payoff for Bush-Quayle:

Ten utility firms contributed $385,500 to the GOP by the end of 1991, according to Congress Watch.

In the following months, the Quayle Council stepped up its activity. For example, it forced the EPA to cut in half the number of acres to be protected as "wetlands," despite Bush's 1988 campaign promise of "no net loss." The bottom line here was considerable: $2.3 million from twenty-five members of the National Wetlands Coalition, according to FEC data compiled by Congress Watch.

After receiving a complaint from United Parcel Service through Senator Wendell Ford, a Democrat from Kentucky, home of UPS, the Council managed to get then-Transportation Secretary Samuel Skinner to relax a rule designed to reduce aircraft noise around airports. As a result of some hundred staff meetings, more than a thousand noisy planes will not have to be retired by 1996. The payoff: Nine airlines and air services paid $315,700 in 1991 to Bush and GOP committees. Tiptoeing quietly in the background were Malek, a major investor and former executive of Northwest Airlines, and Teeter, campaign chairman, who doubles as a director of UPS.

Food companies also have received some treats. In March, the U.S. Department of Agriculture announced it would push back the deadline for meat and poultry labels containing nutritional data from May 1993 to May 1994, at industry request. Ellen Haas, director of a food-policy group, called it a "campaign present" to the industry from the Quayle Council. A year earlier, the USDA withdrew nutritional guidelines in the form of an "Eating Right Pyramid" after industry powers objected.

One of the Council's top priorities has been to speed-up the process of approving new medicines, a perennial pain for pharmaceutical makers. As a result, the Food and Drug Administration was ordered by Quayle to cut short its requirements for new drugs destined for patients with such terminal illnesses as AIDS. The crusade continues for other drugs, despite the thalidomide experience of the early 1960s, in which delays by an FDA analyst prevented the deformation of thousands of babies, as happened in Europe.

The drug industry is especially close to Bush's heart. He held stock in and served as a director of Eli Lilly before becoming Vice President. That may explain why he was not interested in a bill passed by Congress designed to lower the cost of some high-priced medicines by increasing industry competition. With the support of the Council on Competitiveness, Bush vetoed the so-called Orphan Drug Bill, an action which benefited Lilly's own orphan drug Humatrope.

News reports on the Waxman hearings gave the public its first glimpse of the mischief caused by the Quayle Council. The wetlands dispute also drew some public attention, largely because of Bush's broken promise. But it wasn't until last December that the Council attained all the elements of a major story. That was when OMB Watch issued a detailed study accusing Hubbard, a multimillionaire, of breaking Federal laws governing conflicts of interest. The copies of his financial disclosure forms indicated that he owned substantial shares of two companies directly affected by EPA proposals he had been vigorously opposing in his role as Council staff chief.

The Washington Post and a few other papers had reported two weeks earlier that Hubbard owned half of a chemical company that could be affected by environmental rules. Here was solid documentation of a serious ethical problem. The Associated Press considered it major news. So did the big three national papers. Only five of eight other big-city papers checked at random carried any mention of it. Television networks ignored the news.

Five days later, the media got another chance, when the subcommittee held a public hearing on charges that Quayle himself had some conflicts of interest in his Council activities. A voluminous staff report offered evidence that Quayle had actively participated in quashing the EPA proposal to mandate recycling of 25 per cent of municipal wastes, while owning $350,000 in stock of Central Newspapers, Inc., a conglomerate controlled by the Quayle family trust.

The report said the company owned seven newspapers, two paper mills, and a new plant dedicated to producing virgin newsprint. The company also was said to belong to industry organizations that actively opposed the EPA recycling proposal, preferring a voluntary system. Media coverage here was better, with seven of eleven large papers running something about the accusations reported by the AP. But only four papers led their stories with Quayle, and TV networks again looked the other way.

Meanwhile, the Council on Competitiveness has been adding its voice to business lobbying efforts in Congress. High on the list is the long-standing battle to limit the right of people to sue for damages when injured by faulty products. Headlines have depicted Quayle as a shining knight for reform of the legal system. But, as Nancy Watzman of Congress Watch suggests, "the real victims of Quayle's plan are not lawyers but people who are injured." The biggest winners will be insurance companies, a potentially large source of campaign contributions.

Quayle has also been riding to the rescue of property owners who may suffer from unjust compensation when they must comply unwillingly with Government regulations. A typical case is a landowner who is prevented from developing his land after it has been designated a protected wetland. The object is not to generate a bonanza for property owners but to plan funerals for regulations that get in their way.

How does the Vice President respond to his critics? Two days before the Congressional hearing accusing him of ethical transgressions, *The Washington Post* published an article of his claiming the Council "is simply protecting America's greatness from overzealous regulators." His own marching orders, he said, come from an editorial written by his hard-right grandfather Eugene Pulliam, entitled WILL THE FEDERAL BUREAUCRACY DESTROY INDIVIDUAL FREEDOM IN AMERICA?

As long as George Bush is President, wrote Quayle, that won't happen. Without touching on the charges that he himself is adding to Government red tape, he declared that the Council seeks to "preserve regulations that truly protect the safety, welfare, and health of American citizens." He added without a written wink, "The Council stands with the worker, the consumer, and the businessman against unelected, selfish, and increasingly powerful special interests."

There are those who say, however, that Quayle's office doesn't come close to addressing the problems of competing with other nations today. Nor is the Council itself without competition in the Federal establishment. The prestigious Competitive Policy Council was created by Congress in 1990 to analyze the nation's economic problems.

In its first annual report this March, it did not cite Government regulations as a major problem. It preferred to discuss the need to improve in such areas as savings and investment, education and technology, and to lower health-care costs. It concluded that the responsibility for improving productivity "lies primarily with American industry and its workers," not Government.

Paging Dan Quayle. ∎

EYE OF THE
STORM

The $200 billion reason we had to go to war in the Middle East.

S VICTORIOUS ALLIED TROOPS WERE CLOSING down their desert outposts in the Persian Gulf last spring, U.S. secretary of defense Richard Cheney flew to Riyadh with a secret agenda for his meeting with his Saudi counterpart, Prince Sultan Abdul Aziz. Afterward, Cheney told reporters that the United States would continue to oppose establishing permanent bases on the Arabian Peninsula, but hinted that something might be going on behind the scenes. "It's still the Middle East," he was quoted as saying, "and therefore a certain amount of discretion is required in terms of what you say publicly. . . ."

In this case, discretion required that Cheney not reveal the truth about his mission, which was to forge the latest in a series of secret oral understandings that have been kept hidden from both Congress and the public for the past ten years. Earlier versions of these agreements had set the stage for U.S. intervention in the Persian Gulf war, probably making it inevitable. The current understandings, which (despite the official line) include a permanent U.S. presence, will shape the futures of Saudi Arabia and the United States well into the next century. Furthermore, these secret agreements obligate the U.S. military to protect the Saudi royal family from all threats, internal as well as external, and therefore make U.S. involvement in future Middle East conflicts unavoidable.

In their discussions, Cheney and Sultan set out to resolve a contentious issue: What kind of access will the United States have to a sophisticated network of superbases and ad-

BY SCOTT ARMSTRONG

vanced weapon systems built almost entirely at Saudi expense, and that now hold the key to military dominance in the region? The combination of state-of-the-art communication and air defense systems, elaborate infrastructure, and advanced weaponry had proved its value in Operation Desert Storm by providing a premixed, dehydrated war machine: Just add American troops and (fresh) water to create the most advanced warfare command system in the world, with conventional military capabilities beyond those available to defend Europe or even the continental United States.

Sultan did not have to be explicit about the reasons for Saudi resistance to a permanent U.S. military presence. Cheney knew from Central Intelligence Agency reports that the royal family was split into two factions. A pro–United States faction, led by King Fahd and his brother Sultan, the defense minister—and pushed by the aggressively pro-American Prince Bandar, Sultan's son and the Saudi ambassador to Washington—was willing to consider deeper involvement with the United States.

Leading the other, anti-western faction was Crown Prince Abdullah, the king's half brother and head of the

Saudi National Guard, the kingdom's internal security force. Abdullah is a traditionalist deeply committed to Islamic and tribal conventions, which include the Koran's admonition that the infidel must never be allowed to tend the two holiest mosques at Mecca and Medina. The legitimacy of the Saudi royal family is based on its unique role as "protector" of the two mosques; for Saudi fundamentalists, as well as devout Muslims elsewhere, reliance on U.S. forces to protect the kingdom implied the royal family's abdication of that status.

General H. Norman Schwarzkopf was not along for the sensitive meeting with Sultan. He had rubbed many members of the royal family the wrong way with his blunt, sometimes undiplomatic handling of his Saudi peers and superiors. But Schwarzkopf well understood the value of the superbase network. In fact, the general had stated that the U.S. military's Central Command (CENTCOM) would not have recommended sending in such a substantial U.S. force in the first place without the mixture of access to advanced military facilities and pre-positioned military equipment that the Saudis made available. Had the network not been there, the Bush administration might never have pushed for the war or, if it had, the war might not have ended in an overwhelming victory for the United States and its allies.

Without the elaborate Saudi infrastructure in place, U.S. planes, missiles, and air defense radar would have operated with "less than one-quarter the efficiency and accuracy" that they achieved during the war, a Cheney adviser says. These systems had been designed with the purpose of allowing CENTCOM forces to swing directly into emergency action against advancing Soviet forces. In the gulf war, according to one of the most experienced Middle East experts on Cheney's staff, the U.S. military was able to draw on "the full potential of every weapon system" to keep its planes in the air longer, to target and route aircraft more efficiently, and to make decisions "in hours which would have taken days, weeks, or even months" in any other theater of war in the Third World. Access to the network of Saudi superbases was the sine qua non for Desert Storm's success.

BEHIND THE STORY

In 1981, while covering the Reagan administration's proposed sale of five AWACS surveillance planes to Saudi Arabia for the *Washington Post,* investigative reporter Scott Armstrong discovered evidence of a new, super-secret plan to establish U.S.-Saudi military dominance in the Persian Gulf. Only $550 million of the $5.5 billion allocated for the AWACS would actually go toward the purchase price of the planes, Armstrong learned. The other 90 percent, he was told by Richard V. Secord, then an obscure air-force general and deputy assistant secretary of defense for the Middle East, was for "spares, training, and some ground equipment." When Armstrong questioned these numbers, Secord and members of an interagency staff he coordinated, including a young marine officer named Oliver North, claimed that it was all part of a "loose arrangement" between the United States and the Saudis.

But from the Saudi side, Armstrong found out that the arrangement was not so loose. Sources within the royal family explained that the sale was part of a package deal that included a U.S. commitment to send the Rapid Deployment Force in the event of a move by the Soviet Union or others against Saudi Arabia. In return, the Saudis were willing to permit the pre-positioning of certain essential material for Rapid Deployment Force use. Through further digging, Armstrong was able to document that what was actually being created by the two countries, almost completely off the books, was an extensive new network of superbases and advanced weapon systems available for use by U.S. forces in the all-too-likely event of war in the Middle East.

When Armstrong's story appeared a few days after the Senate had authorized the sale of the AWACS, it was met with a round of well-coordinated denials by cabinet secretaries and presidential aides, including a denunciation of Armstrong's projected cost for the secret plan, $50 billion. So effective was this reaction – and so tightly held were the details of the secret arrangement – that over the next decade the subject would virtually disappear from public debate.

Several years after the story appeared, one of the officials who had been instrumental in discrediting it apologized to Armstrong, saying that he now realized that the reporter had been right after all. This official, who had seen everything President Reagan saw on the matter, explained that the compartmentalization of information had been so extreme that key figures in the cabinet, members of the National Security Council, and even the president himself could not fully appreciate the scope and sophistication of what was being created.

During the gulf war, the superbase network was central to U.S. success, but because of military secrecy, the public did not know that. For *Mother Jones,* Armstrong reinterviewed his original sources and spoke with new ones from the Carter, Reagan, and Bush administrations, as well as people inside or close to the Saudi royal family. Most insisted on anonymity but otherwise cooperated. Armstrong also reviewed classified and unclassified documents from the Pentagon and the intelligence agencies, and, in the process, discovered that the regionwide cost for the world's most advanced network of superbases had ballooned to nearly $200 billion – four times his original estimate. What that expenditure has bought is military dominance in the Middle East.

While pinning down the story, Armstrong realized that he had discovered one of the unstated reasons the United States went to war last winter – to protect the critical superbase network from Saddam Hussein. He came to two additional conclusions: the United States may well have to go to war again to protect this "asset"; and the idea that this country's military power could be as effective anywhere else in the world is a myth. Nowhere outside Saudi Arabia, where oil wealth paid the bills, does such a useful launchpad for U.S. military firepower exist.

Photograph by Hilary Schwab courtesy of The American University

"Never before in history has the American military had such an enormous battlefield advantage," one of Cheney's chief deputies now says. "And never before has the dominance of that advantage been so dependent on factors beyond our immediate control. Were this [advantage] to fall into hostile hands, we would simply have to reconsider our options. We could not sustain dominant regional force without it."

Two Kings, Three Presidents

WHEN IRANIAN MILITANTS seized U.S. diplomats in Tehran in November 1979, and the Soviets invaded Afghanistan a month later, Jimmy Carter became the first president to face the real prospect of having to send a Rapid Deployment Force to the Persian Gulf. But as Carter and his aides scrambled to consider contingencies, they found the Pentagon's bag of gulf tricks virtually empty. Shortages of port facilities, water rights, access to the gulf, pre-positioned equipment, and the sophisticated electronic and technological support on which the U.S. military had become so dependent made it difficult to plan operations of more than hours' or days' duration. Con-

heney knew from the CIA that the royal family was split into two factions, one pro-U.S., the other Islamic traditionalist.

flicts requiring weeks or months of combat were beyond anyone's imagination. In the phrase of the day, the Rapid Deployment Force was a joke. It was not rapid, deployable, or forceful.

Carter's strategists concluded that the key to projecting U.S. force over the horizon was local basing in the Persian Gulf. The most desirable location, clearly, was Saudi Arabia, but except for a handful of small airfields, it was devoid of usable infrastructure. Change would require a mammoth investment in modern facilities: ports; air bases; air defense equipment; and command, control, and communication facilities.

As discussions with U.S. strategists began, the Saudis' top priority, according to sources inside the royal family, was to maintain a safe distance from western powers. While Saudi purchases of sophisticated arms were considered desirable because they increased the prestige of the regime, any perceived dependence on the United States would be a liability. Furthermore, until the rapid onset of regional turmoil in 1979, no one in the royal family was prepared to discuss offering the United States even temporary use of Saudi bases. But then came a series of events—the fall of the shah, the emergence of

a hostile Shi'a theocracy under Ayatollah Khomeini, unrest in the two Yemens, a coup attempt in neighboring Bahrain, the Soviet invasion of Afghanistan, and the seizure of the Grand Mosque at Mecca by Islamic militants—that necessitated a change in attitude.

The Carter administration worked quietly with the royal family to design a system of gradual weapon purchases, supported by large investments in airfields and ports. But no sooner had Carter announced his resolve to protect the Saudis and their gulf allies—the Carter doctrine—than he had to back away from his staff's recommendations to implement the plan. His 1980 presidential campaign needed Jewish votes and financial backing.

After the election, however, the new Reagan national-security team picked up where Carter had left off and approved the plan to sell the Saudis the linchpin to the superbase network, the Airborne Warning and Air Control System (AWACS). The administration's decision to sell five AWACS planes set off opposition from powerful pro-Israel members of Congress. Anxious to keep the far-greater dimensions of the superbase deal out of congressional debate, the administration and the Saudis launched the plan with a simple oral understanding between Major General Charles L. Donnelly, Jr., chief of the U.S. military group in Saudi Arabia, and Colonel Fahd Abdullah, head of the Saudi air force and an influential member of the royal family. By keeping the agreement oral and at this comparatively low level, both sides had the "understanding" they wanted without formal written agreements, which could leak or be reviewed—and possibly rejected—by the U.S. Congress.

The key to maintaining secrecy lay in minimizing congressional review of Saudi requests to purchase U.S. arms other than the AWACS planes themselves. By breaking additional military purchases into smaller packages that fell below the dollar limits requiring congressional review, the Reagan administration made it difficult for Congress or the media to track the course of the new relationship. In other instances, instead of purchasing military aircraft, which would need congressional approval, the Saudis were urged to acquire commercial versions and upgrade them to military specifications with high-tech gear obtained outside the United States. All of

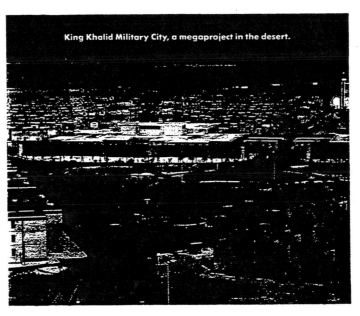

King Khalid Military City, a megaproject in the desert.

this was coordinated by contracting with private U.S. corporate think tanks—including the Boeing Corporation, BDM Corporation, and the Mitre Corporation (a federally funded, but nongovernmental research group)—for advice on how to construct the overall system. In this way, the planners curtailed any official U.S. government paper trail that would have drawn congressional and press attention to the scope of the arrangement.

Meanwhile, inside Saudi Arabia, although the powerful prince Abdullah (soon to become crown prince) still stood in quiet but firm opposition to the growing ties, other senior members of the royal family, most notably King Fahd, decided they were willing to permit a periodic U.S. military presence inside the country, but no permanent U.S. base. In a series of meetings from 1982 to 1986, involving the king, President Ronald Reagan, cabinet officials, and military officers, the two sides came closer to agreement on the nature of the problem: In case of trouble, how could Saudi Arabia's military hold off attackers for a few days while U.S. forces rushed in to defend their ally?

Mitre, in particular, helped the Saudis assess their air defense vulnerabilities. Understanding that the Saudis had deep pockets and the U.S. Air Force deep needs, Mitre representatives recommended that Saudi Arabia integrate its ground-based radar, missile systems, fighter bases, fighters, and command-communication posts into a single network. It was an enormous project. There were only two systems this sophisticated in the entire world: NATO's NADGE system in Europe and the NORAD system in the United States. No other country or group, including the Soviet Union, had anything approaching it.

"This is the most ambitious plan to build a single regional C^{3}I [command, control, communication, and intelligence] system ever undertaken," says Barry M. Horowitz, president of Mitre. As part of its implementation, Saudi Arabia was divided into five sectors, each with its own fully redundant system. These five regional operating centers were linked to a central command headquarters near Riyadh by digital, secure communication and radio networks connected by satellite. The five sectors could operate independently, each capable in an emergency of functioning as the central command to direct an air war stretching anywhere from Egypt to Pakistan, from the southern Soviet Union to the Indian Ocean.

Most significantly—since in times of a major crisis the Saudis would have to operate smoothly with their allies, including the United States—communication and intelligence hardware convertible for U.S. use was installed. Because several scenarios of U.S. gulf doctrine called for using nuclear weapons to stop a Soviet move into the region—to which the

Soviets would likely respond in kind—the six command posts in the Saudi desert were hardened against nuclear attack and linked by shielded communication lines. The facilities to be constructed would provide far-readier preparation for a nuclear war against the Soviets than anything in place in the United States or Europe.

To avoid trouble, the royal family required that its growing military relationship with the United States be kept as covert as possible. One concern of the pro-western members of the family about cozying up to Washington was the possible humiliation of losing a big confrontation with Israel's advocates in Congress. The flip side of this concern was shared by the Reagan administration. Throughout the seventies, every arms sale to an Arab state had been fiercely opposed by influential supporters of Israel. If this significant commitment to an ongoing relationship with the Saudis, which included an elaborate network of superbases tied in with advanced weapons, became public, it would become a lightning rod for the opposition. Thus, development of the bases was kept very, very quiet.

The scale of the Saudi program knew few bounds, but since it remains secret, its costs can only be estimated from various government documents and defense-industry trade publications. In order to create a substantial military presence in the empty territory just south of Iraq and Kuwait, King Khalid Military City was expanded into a six-billion-dollar megaproject with a futuristic design—an instant modern city dropped onto a barren, moonscapelike desert. Elaborate, air-conditioned military command bunkers were installed, below ground, there and at the other superbases. Nearby, one of the region's largest ports was born, almost overnight.

Throughout the early and middle eighties, Congress periodically refused to sell the Saudis certain weapon systems and threatened to block the sales of others. In frustration, the Saudis turned elsewhere for weapons, spending $37 billion with the British and $10 billion with the French. But then, in 1987, Iranian attacks on Kuwaiti oil tankers re-cemented the relationship with the Americans, as U.S. naval forces entered the gulf to work closely with the Saudis.

By the time Iraqi forces crossed into Kuwait in August of 1990, the Saudis had spent about $90 billion for weapons; about $34 billion for military-related construction of new bases and infrastructure; and at least $30 billion for ports, communication facilities, military roads, and emergency fuel storage. A complete picture of the overall investment in military preparation must include the additional $15 billion spent by other Gulf Cooperation Council members at the Saudis' behest on compatible military acquisitions, and $6 billion spent on military-related construction. At the same time, the

Photograph courtesy U.S. Army engineering division

DataCenter   464 19th Street, Oakland, California 94612 (415) 835-4692

United States and Saudi Arabia underwrote billions of dollars in arms sales and military construction for Egypt, which resulted in many of the bases and staging sites used over the past decade by U.S. forces there.

This staggering regional expenditure approaching $200 billion over a decade has created the infrastructure necessary to allow what one Mitre executive called "the kind of smooth integration of our own forces that we dream of but never see. Add to that the integration of other NATO and regional forces and you have the great military achievement which allowed Desert Storm to go off smoothly."

Previously published accounts of the buildup to Operation Desert Storm suggest that the Saudi and U.S. governments stumbled into a closer relationship because of Saddam Hussein's military challenge. This misconception arises from secrecy on both sides about the existence of commitments that have not been officially acknowledged. The continuing reluctance of the Saudi royal family to reveal its agreements with the United States has led to what one former Pentagon official calls the "myth of the virgin intervention," and obscures the

long-term implications of the NATO-sized military network now in place in Saudi Arabia.

The Network Is Tested for the First Time

IN AUGUST 1990, WHEN 100,000 IRAQI TROOPS INVADED Kuwait and deployed as if preparing to move on Saudi Arabia, President Bush called King Fahd to see if he wished to invoke the secret understanding that the United States would aid the Saudis. According to Bush administration officials, Fahd was initially most interested in intelligence reports and a mere assurance that U.S. troops were prepared to assist Saudi Arabia on short notice. The king asked only that the United States announce such an intention, thereby discouraging Saddam Hussein from moving south into Saudi territory for fear of triggering a larger U.S. troop commitment.

To Fahd's apparent surprise, Bush told him he was ready not only to assure the Saudis of U.S. support publicly, but to move in massive numbers of troops and weapons to prevent any Iraqi invasion. Bush was insistent in pursuing an open-ended invitation to utilize the newly constructed

QUESTIONS OF LEGITIMACY

 he current agreement being negotiated with the Saudis by Defense Secretary Richard Cheney is, according to one Capitol Hill staff member familiar with Cheney's private version of the trip to Riyadh, a virtual model for a mutual-defense treaty. "It is a clear demarcation of responsibilities of who will do what under what conditions. It involves committing U.S. forces to defend Saudi soil. It should be a treaty," says the congressional aide.

Under the Constitution, the president may enter into treaties with other governments only with the advice and consent of the Senate. Yet this has not been the case with the U.S.-Saudi agreements on the scope of the advanced systems being put into place in the Persian Gulf.

The tendency of presidents to bypass the Senate has grown over the past decades, as successive administrations have negotiated executive agreements with other countries without Senate involvement. In 1930, 25 treaties and 9 executive agreements were in effect. In 1968, 16 treaties and 266 executive agreements were concluded. Today, treaties number just over a thousand and executive agreements in the tens of thousands.

Moreover, ever since the Carter era, presidential aides have stated that oral "understandings" are not even executive agreements. The claim has been made that each layer of agreement between the United States and Saudi Arabia was not legally binding but simply an "understanding" between the two parties.

This distinction escapes some constitutional scholars. "If the United States and another country both intend to be bound by an agreement – whether written or oral – it is an international agreement and must under the Case Act be reported to Congress," says Michael Glennon, professor of law at the University of California at Davis and an expert

on treaties. "If the agreement contains a mutual-defense pact between the two countries, it is, for all practical purposes, a treaty."

In the past, defense has been precisely the foreign-policy area where the Senate has gotten most involved. In 1969, showing its growing opposition to the Vietnam War, the Senate warned President Nixon that it reserved the right to refuse to implement any executive agreement to which he had agreed. In 1972, the Senate attempted to put its foot down again. Reviewing a presidential agreement with the Persian Gulf state of Bahrain, which provided for use of military facilities, the Senate indicated that the president should submit it as a treaty. The following year, the entire Congress enacted the War Powers Act to assure that the president would not use executive agreements or any other mechanism as justification for military intervention.

As a practical matter, constitutional concerns about this issue have not troubled the Reagan and Bush administrations, which have been successful in co-opting key members of the congressional committees concerned with foreign and defense policy. Furthermore, most of the series of covert U.S.-Saudi relationships involving funds for anti-communist resistance groups in Afghanistan and Africa have been known to Congress' two intelligence oversight committees. Even the Saudis' secret roles in funding the contras and orchestrating an assassination attempt on Lebanese Shi'a leader Sheikh Fadlallah, at the request of former CIA director William Casey, have been passed off by the congressional committees as misguided attempts by the Saudi government to be helpful to the United States.

Because they are fundamentally undemocratic, such secret agreements represent the death knell for the separation of powers that the founding fathers created. Both houses of Congress have refused to respond to the Reagan-Bush incursions into their constitutional prerogatives, as demonstrated in the Iran-contra affair and a variety of other covert operations. What little congressional enthusiasm remained for constraining the unconstitutional operations of the Bush presidency has now been further eroded by the success of the Persian Gulf war.   —S.A.

bases and military infrastructure and equipment pre-positioned for just such a contingency. The president, evidently more at the urging of his NSC staff than Pentagon officials, saw the need both to breathe life into the partially dormant network and to ensure that Saddam would not be able to seize it.

Within hours, according to U.S. intelligence officials, Fahd had consulted others in the royal family, who were, for the most part, unenthusiastic about Americans arriving in large numbers. Crown Prince Abdullah feared contaminating the system of royal patronage and tribal order with U.S. military units of mixed race, sex, and class. Also, according to both Saudi and U.S. sources, the royal family tried to make sure that the Americans understood Saddam's perspective. Beyond his immediate grievances over oil and territorial rights, Saddam believed that Kuwait, the United Arab Emirates, and Saudi Arabia had been flooding the market with cheap oil, over their OPEC-specified quotas, thus pulling down Iraq's price for oil. He further believed that these countries were plotting with the United States against him militarily by conducting joint naval and air exercises in the gulf.

Saddam's paranoia had some basis in reality, the Saudis noted, and the royal family was looking for ways to reassure the Iraqi leader and get him to pull out of Kuwait. But the Bush administration disagreed with any course that would smack of appeasing Saddam; if the United States helped Saudi Arabia, it would not be with a token force that could be overrun by Iraqi troops. Instead, there had to be a commitment by the Saudis to let in 100,000 U.S. troops immediately. Bush instructed Cheney to brief Prince Bandar, the Saudi ambassador in Washington, and to ask that he take that message back to his uncles, the king and crown prince, and to his father, the defense minister.

Bandar gave them the message, but Abdullah and others insisted that a minimum U.S. deployment would be sufficient. Bush then dispatched Cheney to placate Abdullah, a mission that succeeded to the extent that within days, CENTCOM technicians were lashing their top-flight communication and intelligence gear into the waiting Saudi systems. This, along with the elaborate new infrastructure, allowed the largest and fastest deployment of troops to full-battle readiness in military history.

There had only been two major non-oil docks in Saudi Arabia in 1980, each capable of unloading one ship at a time. By 1990, nine major ports could service dozens of

Nowhere else in the world, not even in the U.S., could we fight as successfully as we did in the gulf."

ships simultaneously. The twelve bare-bones airfields of a decade earlier had doubled in number, each now including several long runways, maintenance facilities, and air control systems sufficient to allow a constant influx of U.S. planes filled with troops and equipment. In covering this mass mobilization, American reporters were captivated by the logistics and electronic wizardry—but overlooked the story of the ten years of secret preparation that had made it all possible.

"Nowhere else in the world—not even in the United States—could we fight as successfully as we did in the gulf," says a military planner who has devoted his career to worrying about sending U.S. forces into regions of conflict. "Few of our own people realize this, but we could not have prevailed as completely or as quickly against similar forces from our dedicated bases in the Philippines, [South] Korea, Thailand, or Guam."

Adds a well-placed government consultant: "If tomorrow we had available all of today's technology but no actual offensive and defensive weapons or infrastructure [in the United States], and if we built a system here from scratch with virtually unlimited funds, we would install essentially what the Saudis have put in. The one exception is that we would waste money on tactical and strategic nuclear weapons, which we probably can never use."

The Future

THE EXISTENCE OF SAUDI MILITARY COMmunication systems and the network of superbases, which interlocked so efficiently with U.S. equipment and forces during the gulf war, helps explain why Bush insisted on moving to defend Saudi Arabia so quickly. In fact, the Saudis now have an even more sophisticated system than what was originally intended for them. The software needed to integrate all the electronic information into one state-of-the-art system was so complicated that Boeing had not yet completed it at

DataCenter   464 19th Street, Oakland, California 94612 (415) 835-4692

the time of Iraq's invasion of Kuwait. So when CENTCOM arrived, it brought its own master C^{3}I system and promptly transplanted it into the massive Saudi C^{3}I system connecting the entire country's air defense systems and newly constructed bases.

This final improvement in the Saudi system has made the network more than regionally significant. Furthermore, so advanced are several elements of the system now in place that U.S. strategists have restricted Saudi use of them. That was the backdrop for Defense Secretary Cheney's meeting with Prince Sultan last May. Cheney hoped for Saudi permission for a new, permanent deployment of U.S. troops to protect the system on a continuing basis, leaving these advanced elements in place. If the Saudis insist that nearly all U.S. troops leave, it is unclear whether these aspects of the system will remain or be stripped.

One of the top Pentagon planners accompanying Cheney to his meeting with Sultan believes that the network was a brilliant accomplishment, "the single greatest investment in [military] infrastructure in the history of man." Upgraded by CENTCOM to accommodate the allied command during the war, this accumulation of sophisticated electronic gear and nuclear-hardened facilities was, according to the Pentagon official, Washington's "most important asset in Southwest Asia." From Cheney's perspective, the network is the key to future military security in the Middle East. "That is why we are so determined to protect it," one of Cheney's aides explains.

But this also means that if it ever fell under the control of forces unfriendly to the United States, either through invasion or due to changes within Saudi Arabia, the system could become a terrible liability. What, for instance, would prevent the Saudis from employing this massive military network against Israel, say, or Turkey, or India?

In their meeting, Cheney promised Sultan that Special Forces units would hardly be noticed by residents or, for that matter, by other regional powers such as Iran and Syria. If the increased presence were noticed, it could be explained away as a "routine rotation," he suggested. There would be no admission of a permanent U.S. base; there would be no public treaty. There would be no announcement of any kind. Everything would, as usual, remain secret.

Throughout the first ten years of twists and turns in secret diplomacy, the Saudis had tried to sidestep U.S. requests to base forces in the kingdom permanently. At his meeting with Sultan, Cheney learned that the royal family was balking once again, according to an official on the trip. But Cheney had his own set of realities to lay out. Without a lasting presence, the United States could not guarantee protection to the royal family from external and internal threats.

The two defense chiefs ultimately came to a partial understanding. For its part, the United States again agreed to send military reinforcements from over the horizon, should there be an attack on the Saudis or a request for reinforcements. The United States would leave behind a major portion of its most sophisticated C^{3}I equipment. The royal family, in return, guaranteed Washington continued access to the air base in Dhahran, the naval base in Jubail, and, in case of trouble, the remainder of the Saudi air-base network.

Sources familiar with the meeting and subsequent U.S.-Saudi discussions say that the latest "oral" understanding is not yet complete. According to Saudi sources involved in the negotiations, the Saudis have offered to purchase and pre-position a substantial amount of heavy U.S. armor and supplies and have agreed to tie in their C^{3}I system to a CENTCOM headquarters somewhere in the region, but well-placed Pentagon sources say that the Bush administration has not yet accepted the Saudi offer. In addition, left unresolved are the exact size and composition of the permanent U.S. military contingent. While the Saudis have apparently agreed to permit the United States to station as many as seven thousand military personnel at Saudi bases, including at least some Special Forces advisers, the deployment will be treated publicly, as Cheney suggested, merely as rotating units of technicians on temporary exercises and training assignments.

It is unclear what policy the Bush administration has for dealing with challenges to the Saudi monarchy other than to continue the secret understandings with King Fahd and the royal family. The administration's recent Middle East arms-control initiative has been read by some analysts as a publicly staged attempt to put the U.S.-Saudi relationship at arm's length. But according to Bush administration officials who spoke on background, it is actually something quite different. By calling for restraints on new arms sales in the region, the United States is, in effect, actually locking in the status quo. In any event, the covert, massive Saudi arms-acquisition program will not be affected by anything said in public. The two governments are now so experienced at disguising their massive technology transfers that the entire relationship occurs almost completely "off the books."

Estimated Price Tag for Military Dominance in the Gulf (in billions)

JORDAN
IRAQ KUWAIT $6.0
SAUDI ARABIA
Weapon 90.4
C^{3}I 17.1
IRAN
$2.9
BAHRAIN
QATAR
SUDAN
YEMEN

Total selected Arab States: $223.2 billion
Military: $34 billion; military related: $30 billion
Dollar figures are for the period from 1978 to 1990

Sources: Stockholm International Peace Research Institute yearbooks:
Defense Military sales reports. DISAM Journal: Gulf States Newsletter: and others.

Scott Armstrong is a former reporter for the Washington Post, *investigator for the Senate Watergate Committee, founder of the National Security Archive, and coauthor, with Bob Woodward, of* The Brethren. *He is at work on a book about national-security affairs in the Bush administration. This article was prepared with the research assistance of Kurt Shaw.*

Illustrated by Jim Morton/World Lithographic Services

The NSA goes to school under veil of secrecy

By Andrea Barnett

MISSOULA, MONT.

While searching through the University of Montana's (UM) budget last fall, I was surprised to find that the liberal arts college has a $2,000 teaching and research grant with the Department of Defense.

But I was even more surprised when a UM administrator came right out and told me that the school has a research contract with the National Security Agency (NSA). Not only does the NSA try to keep its contracts secret but it is unusual for a bureaucrat to be so forthcoming.

The UM-NSA contract is projected to last through June 1994 and cost up to $203,620. Like most NSA-sponsored research, the UM contract is with the mathematics department.

The contract includes a non-disclosure clause that prohibits the university from announcing the award or sponsorship of the agreement and forbids the release of any information regarding the government's interest in the project.

Montana state law and a 23-year-old UM Faculty Senate resolution prohibit classified research at the university. The state law probably does not apply because the results of the research will supposedly be published freely.

But the senate resolution, passed in 1969 in response to the Pentagon's "Project Themis," which funded 43 classified military research projects at 35 schools, conflicts with the secrecy of the contract.

"All scholarly activity and research on this campus shall be openly arrived at and the faculty shall be free to publish or not as each individual faculty member sees fit. The only restrictions on the activity of publication and disclosure are those voluntarily imposed by the faculty member in exercising his [sic] professional judgment and discretion."

The purpose of the UM research, according to the contract, is to "expand the use of the greatest deviation correlation coefficient Rg into the multiple linear regression model" and "develop a general framework of regression techniques."

In plain language, this means the project director, UM math Professor Rudy Gideon, is trying to "develop techniques for exploring the relationship of many random quantities," says NSA spokesman Jerry Volker.

"The agency does a lot of work with colleges and universities that aims to improve, if we can, mathematics," he adds. "It's a skill we need very badly."

The War Research Information Service (WRIS) in Cambridge, Mass., runs a non-profit information clearinghouse about military research contracts. WRIS Director Rich Cowan says it is unusual for an NSA contract to be discovered at all. As a result, WRIS has little information about NSA-sponsored research.

Cowan says the information contained in the UM contract is not sufficient to explain the nature of the research, but that it probably has something to do with "voice recognition." Much of the NSA's math research is used for encoding and code-breaking.

The NSA was established in 1952 by a seven-page order of President Harry S. Truman, as a surveillance and intelligence-gathering organization, with its roots in the government's code-breaking brigades of World Wars I and II.

The agency's mission, Volker says, is to collect "foreign intelligence information" and to coordinate "highly specialized technical functions in support of U.S. government activities."

"The agency is essentially the premier technical spy agency we have," says Greg LeRoy, director of Public Search in Houston, Texas, a non-profit organization that keeps track of military and defense research contracts.

Above the law: According to James Bamford, author of *The Puzzle Palace*, there are no laws prohibiting the NSA from engaging in any activity. Unlike the CIA, which was established by Congress and operates under legal restrictions that included prohibitions against operating within the U.S. and assassinating foreign leaders, the NSA has no legal mandate.

In fact, the only laws the NSA must follow are those that restrict the release of information about the agency.

"In addition to being free of legal restrictions, the NSA has technological capabilities for eavesdropping beyond imagination," Bamford writes in *The Puzzle Palace*. "Such capabilities once led former Senate Intelligence Committee member Walter F. Mondale to point to the NSA as possibly the single most important source of intelligence for this nation.'"

In 1962, the NSA began monitoring U.S. citizens on its "watch list," Bamford says. By 1970, then-President Richard Nixon approved the "Domestic Intelligence Gathering Plan: Analysis and Strategy," which, among other things, allowed for NSA electronic surveillance of "individuals and groups in the United States who pose a major threat to internal security," and "surreptitious entry" or breaking and entering into "facilities occupied by subversive elements."

Cowan says the WRIS believes that the NSA uses its massive electronic surveillance capabilities for "eavesdropping on political groups in the U.S. that are opposed to government policy."

Big black budget: According to LeRoy, the NSA is reported to have the largest budget within the U.S. intelligence community—more than the FBI and CIA combined.

LeRoy says the NSA's budget takes up an estimated $12 billion of the country's $350 billion defense and national security budget.

The agency gets its money from the government's "Black Budget," the contents of which are kept hidden even from Congress. According to Tim Weiner's book, *Blank Check*, that budget, which pays for secret defense and intelligence operations, stood at approximately $34 billion in fiscal year 1990.

"The research at UM may not be that insidious," Cowan says, "but the fact that it's connected to a budget that's accountable to no one, and used for a lot of purposes that are not in the public interest, should be of some concern."

Both LeRoy and Volker say that NSA contracts with universities are fairly common.

"You'd be hard-pressed to find a large well-run state university that doesn't have a portion of its science and research funding from defense and intelligence agencies," LeRoy says.

Volker says the number of schools with NSA contracts would comprise a "decent-sized list," including Massachusetts Institute of Technology (MIT), the University of Kansas, Ohio State University and schools in the California university system.

The money for the UM contract came from funds reserved for "historically black colleges and universities," Volker says. "This institution [UM] qualifies because it has a significant number of minority employees."

Only 5.36 percent of UM's faculty, however, are minorities.

LeRoy is critical of military research at universities, saying the enormous amount of money spent for such research perverts the ability of academics to pursue underfunded but non-military studies.

"At MIT, for example, in certain fields, over 90 percent of the research is financed by [military-related] groups," he says. "This overwhelmingly limits who gets access to computers and research materials."

A second drawback to military research, especially contracts with the NSA, is that military interests take precedence over academic inquiry, and professors are often forced to submit their work to the government for censorship if they want to publish it.

Professors and students working on these projects often must pass a security clearance and sign a statement promising to submit anything they might publish to the NSA for review, according to LeRoy.

"This has been especially true in mathematics cases," LeRoy says. "There have been more instances of pre-publication review against mathematicians by the NSA than any other group."

Thus, professors who research for the NSA find that they cannot take credit for their work.

"People who work with the NSA oftentimes find they've

got limited credibility, and they are stuck with the same Black Budget grants over and over again," LeRoy says.

UM math Professor Gideon, who is currently on sabbatical in Seattle, says that, although the NSA is funding his research, he is "doing [his] own thing."

Volker confirmed this, saying Gideon approached the agency with a request for funding. Strangely, Volker claims Gideon has no responsibility to give any data to the NSA, and that the agency will learn of Gideon's results when he publishes them.

But according to the contract, "The government shall receive unrestricted rights to use any ideas, designs, processes or inventions resulting from or used on this contract."

Furthermore, the university must obtain written permission from the NSA to release any information about the contract, even to admit its existence.

LeRoy says this kind of non-disclosure clause "acts to pervert the generally open nature of university policies."

Cowan agrees, saying secret contracts fly in the face of academic freedom and openness.

"It's crazy," he says, "for research to be going on when you can't even find out what it's about." ☐

Andrea Barnett is a journalist living in Taos, N.M.

School of the Americas: A Well-Kept Secret

Mary Swenson

Thousands of Salvadoran soldiers, members of one of the world's most repressive armed forces, have received training at a little-known establishment called the U.S. Army School of the Americas (SOA) at Fort Benning, in Columbus, Georgia.

The following testimony was given by Salvadoran soldiers to the Congressional Task Force, headed by Representative Joe Moakley (Dem.-Mass.), investigating the November 16, 1989, massacre of six Jesuit priests and two Salvadoran women:

> While leaving, Avalos Vargas—nicknamed "Toad" and "Satan" by his comrades—passed in front of the guest room where the two women had been shot and heard them moaning in the darkness. He lit a match and saw the two women on the floor embracing each other. He then ordered a soldier, Jorge Alberto Sierra Ascencio, to "re-kill" them. Sierra Ascencio shot the women about ten times, until they stopped moaning.

What kind of training would lead to such atrocities? According to documentation provided to Rep. Moakley's Task Force by the office of the U.S. Assistant Secretary of Defense, Sgt. Avalos Vargas and four of the other eight soldiers arrested for the Jesuit massacre were graduates of Ft. Benning.

SOA Training

What kind of training does the SOA provide? Colonel William de Palo, Commander of the SOA, and his public relations staff maintain that human rights and "American values" are taught, but refuse to discuss the specific content of their courses. Earlier studies, however, have shown that not only is the human rights and values component of U.S. training insignificant, but that the emphasis on the omnipresence of communism and subversion, and on low intensity conflict, makes the graduates more hostile to popular movements and more ruthless than previously.

The proof of the pudding is in the eating: In Brazil, Guatemala, the Dominican Republic, and elsewhere, torture and death squads followed closely on U.S. intervention and training. In El Salvador, Raymond Bonner pointed repeatedly to the violence of U.S.-trained personnel, giving details on how the "U.S.-trained Atlacatl Battalion" performed at Mozote, with 482 civilian victims, of which "280 were children under fourteen years old" (*Weakness and Deceit* [New York: Times Books, 1984]).

Mary Swenson is a staff member of the Central America Resource Center in St. Paul, Minnesota. For more information on the campaign against the School of the Americas, contact SOA Watch, 2420 Ft. Benning Rd., No. 1, Columbus, GA 31903; (404) 682-5369.

Interesting Reading

The sordid history of the SOA would make for interesting reading if any of the national media were willing to cover it. Established in Panama in 1946 to train Latin American officers and foster anti-communism, its graduates returned to their home countries to overthrow constitutional governments and set up regimes which were characterized by intimidation and, at times, mass murder. Panama demanded the removal of the school as a condition of the Panama Canal Treaty, and the SOA moved to Ft. Benning in 1984. At one point, then Congressman Michael Harrington led an effort to ban the SOA's urban counter-insurgency courses. It was later discovered that the school changed the titles of its counterinsurgency courses, but continued teaching the same material under different names.

The major national commercial media have, overall, chosen not to cover this significant aspect of U.S. involvement in the war in El Salvador. A database search of the major wire services and newspapers revealed only *two* references to the SOA in the last three years: a brief and innocuous Associated Press item on fighting drug traffic (October 22, 1989) and one hard-hitting column by Colman McCarthy in the *Washington Post* (January 28, 1990, p. F2). Not a word in the *New York Times* or any other paper.

Ample Opportunities for Coverage

Not that the press has not been handed ample opportunities for covering the issue. In 1983, a year before the SOA was moved from Panama to Ft. Benning, 525 Salvadoran soldiers were sent to Ft. Benning for training. In protest, three citizens, dressed up as high-ranking military officers, entered Ft. Benning, climbed a tree near the Salvadoran soldiers' barracks and, using a high-powered tape player, broadcast Archbishop Romero's sermon in which he ordered soldiers to stop the killing. The three received 18-month sentences for this.

In the fall of 1990, ten people, including veterans, priests, a teacher, and Salvadoran refugees, staged a 35-day hunger strike in protest of the training of Salvadoran soldiers there. Over the years, the Atlanta Committee on Latin America and other regional organizations have held major demonstrations. On November 16, 1990, the anniversary of the massacre of the Jesuit priests and Salvadoran women, three veterans—including a priest and a former chaplain at Ft. Benning—committed an act of non-violent civil disobedience. They poured human blood on the sign at the headquarters building. They were found guilty and await sentencing. The maximum sentence could be 10 years and a $10,000 fine.

The *New York Times* received numerous press releases on these actions, and during the hunger strike, Atlanta correspondent Peter Applebome was called and encouraged to cover the story. But nothing ever appeared in print.

Meanwhile the SOA continues its questionable and secretive work of training Salvadoran soldiers (400 of whom are currently at the school). Flagrant human rights abuses on the part of the Salvadoran military continue unabated. The number of victims in this U.S.-sponsored war now surpasses 75,000. The evidence is damning. The U.S. Army School of the Americas is implicated in this continuing bloodshed, and the national corporate press collaborates by refusing to cover the story. ●

DataCenter   464 19th Street, Oakland, California 94612 (415) 835-4692

VI. Propaganda, Misinformation and Disinformation

It was Walter Lippman who first used the phrase, "manufacturing consent" to describe propaganda. Edward S. Herman and Noam Chomsky adopted the phrase for the title of their book (see bibliography). The manipulation of public opinion in the commercial sector is done with advertising. (see Corporate Power Over Information section) In the political arena, public relations is used to marshall support for wars, huge military budgets, political candidates; and opposition to communism, "regulation" of business, etc.

Propaganda, Mis- and Disinformation are used to accomplish these tasks. The United States Information Agency, the Public Information Offices of the Defense Department and the other services have thousands of people working behind the scenes to shape public opinion. The FBI, CIA, the National Endowment for Democracy are also active in this field. Contriving a political climate was tried recently by promoting the phrase "politically correct" to ridicule liberal attempts to counter racism, and other biases that undermine justice and equality.

"In countries where the levers of power are in the hands of a state bureaucracy, the monopolistic control over the media, often supplemented by official censorship, makes it clear the media serve the ends of a dominant elite. It is much more difficult to see a propaganda system at work where the media are private and formal censorship is absent. This is especially true where the media actively compete, periodically attack and expose corporate and governmental malfeasance, and aggressively portray themselves as spokesmen for free speech and the general community interest. What is not evident (and remains undiscussed in the media) is the limited nature of such critiques, a well as the huge inequality in command of resources, and its effect both on access to a private media system and on its behavior and performance." — Edward S. Herman and Noam Chomsky, *Manufacturing Consent,"* 1988.

"Paramount among the responsibilities of a free press is the duty to prevent any part of the government from deceiving the people and sending them off to distant lands to die of foreign fevers and foreign shot and shell." — Justice Hugo L. Black

USIA: Propaganda As Public Diplomacy

Robin Andersen

The way the former Director of the United States Information Agency (USIA), Charles Z. Wick, chose to explain his agency's project was: "We are telling the world about the meaning of freedom."[1] And a USIA videotape produced in the early 1980s for the benefit of Congress (to be used for promotion during budget hearings) referred to the agency's mission this way: "President Dwight D. Eisenhower...believed that America's message of freedom and opportunity could win the war of ideas, and help prevent war among nations."[2]

Even though the USIA has been portrayed as a beacon of light "to a world hungry for truth, and anxious for freedom," in fact the agency's *raison d'etre*, from its inception, was much less noble. According to international communications scholar Laurien Alexandre, "the USIA was part of a massive media counterthrust against the 'Red Menace'...from the Russian Revolution through the Cold War to the Reagan Doctrine."[3] In fact, she asserts that the historical anticommunism used to justify international information policy was never intended to bring truth to those locked behind the iron (and later sugarcane) curtain. Rather, it served

to undermine socialist and resistance movements, to alter political perceptions and to create an acquiescent public...International communication and public relations packaging have historically been marshalled in this campaign of ideologically inspired misrepresentations, lies and distortions designed to contain, rollback and defeat the movement of peoples challenging U.S. economic, political and cultural hegemony.[4]

Postwar Propaganda

The USIA was established after World War II in the virulent anticommunist, anti-Soviet atmosphere of the times. It developed as a consequence of President Truman's "Campaign Truth." In order to "combat communist distortions"

and "promote the truth about America," $121 million was appropriated in 1950 to build an aggressive U.S. propaganda apparatus.[5] Various information programs were developed at the Department of State, and in 1953 these programs, together with the existing broadcast service, the Voice of America (VOA — established in 1942) were consolidated under the USIA. The agency, and its flagship service, the VOA, have been the U.S. government's external voice of anticommunism since that time.

The break-up of the domestic Cold War consensus caused by the war in Southeast Asia had repercussions for USIA. Without the clarity of the Cold War mission, USIA suffered budgetary cutbacks, demoralization and general disarray. The agency's identity crisis was felt most dramatically in VOA's news departments. Some editors and reporters felt they were professionals committed to "objectivity," others accepted their new role as pro-detente diplomats, while an older generation still carried on as cold warriors.

During this period the VOA was revamped. Its new charter, signed into law in 1976 by President Ford reads "VOA news will be accurate, objective, and comprehensive," and further that the VOA "will represent America, not any single segment of American society," by presenting "responsible discussion and opinion" on U.S. policies.[6]

The Reagan-Bush Era

Carter's detente policies were quickly rolled back with Reagan's entry into the White House. Under Carter, the USIA had been cut out of Washington policymaking forums and reduced to a "bare-bones operation."[7] But the Reagan White House reasserted the USIA's propaganda function as a key element of foreign policy. Reagan's new director, Charles Z. Wick had access to the highest levels of the U.S. government.

In 1981, the USIA received an enormous injection of funding and support, enjoying one of the largest budget hikes given to any federal agency. Its budget grew 42 percent in the first fiscal year alone. In the previous 15 years, the budget had declined 27 percent, and the staff size was 37 percent below the 1967 level.[8] By 1989, its budget had skyrocketed to its

---

Robin Andersen is a media critic who lives in New York. This article was written with research assistance from John Gowan.

1. Charles Z. Wick, "The Power of Information in the Quest for Peace," *Vital Speeches of the Day*, Vol. 51, No. 17, June 15, 1985, p. 520.

2. Charles Z. Wick, "The War of Ideas: America's Arsenal," *Vital Speeches of the Day*, Vol. 52 No. 1, October 15, 1985, p. 16.

3. Laurien Alexandre, "Anti-Communism and the Voice of America: The Radio's Raison d'Etre," *The Ideology of International Communications*, Laurien Alexandre, ed. (New York: Institute for Media Analysis, Inc., 1991), Monograph Series, No. 4, p. 1.

4. *Ibid.*

5. "Anti-Communism and the Voice of America," *op. cit.*, p. 1.

6. *Ibid.*

7. Carolyn Weaver, "When the Voice of America Ignores its Charter," *Columbia Journalism Review*, November/December 1988, p. 36.

8. "USIA: A Battered But Powerful Propaganda Tool," *US News and World Report*, March 5, 1984, p. 58.

present level of approximately one billion dollars. With this largesse, the agency was expected to accomplish the public relations feat of portraying the U.S. government's anti-Soviet and militaristic foreign policy—which came to be known as the Reagan Doctrine—as ultimately reasonable and democratic.

But in the 1980s, USIA activities were no longer to be restricted to foreign policy. They were also incorporated into the newly developing domestic "public diplomacy" operation. According to Alexandre, "Public diplomacy is the relatively new and rather innocuous sounding term used by Reagan officials to describe the very old practice of propaganda."[10]

Participation in this internal propaganda apparatus included the highest government echelons: the NSC, CIA, Departments of Defense and State, and USAID. Walter Raymond, a veteran CIA overseas propaganda specialist, was brought in to head the domestic strategy sessions which involved the extensive manipulation of the American media for the purposes of creating a climate of opinion favorable to Reagan's foreign policies.[11] Therefore, it is no longer possible to view the activities of the USIA in isolation from its role within the entire policymaking establishment of the executive branch. Propaganda is fashioned along with the domestic and foreign policies it serves to justify.

Charles Wick's Blacklist

One of the great ironies of the USIA in the 1980s was that even in the face of its weighty assignment to put a humane face on the Reagan Doctrine, the agency could not quite manage its own public relations image. The continued bad press generated by director Charles Z. Wick compelled *Newsweek* magazine to call "all publicity agents: You're needed in Washington. After all, someone should create a new image for America's chief image maker."[12] At issue was Wick's compilation of a blacklist, and his secret taping of hundreds of phone conversations. Even though these actions were far closer to those ascribed to disinformation specialists in the KGB than to a department responsible for accuracy and openness abroad, Wick managed to weather the storm and go on to push through TV Marti and other USIA programs.

The scandalous press accounts remained focused on the flamboyant personality quirks of Wick himself and neglected to understand, much less criticize, the workings of the agency he directed. But the secret tapings and the blacklist were not personal idiosyncrasies; they revealed the agency's actual purpose. Even though Wick's numerous public speeches pro-

Associated Press   Associated Press
Coretta Scott King and Walter Cronkite were on the official USIA blacklist of people unfit to represent the U.S. abroad.

claimed public diplomacy under the USIA to be the expression of freedom through democratic ideas and discussions—the international equivalent of the marketplace of ideas at home—the agency's mission was the dissemination of the narrow views of the executive branch.

The blacklist is one of the best illustrations of the divergence between the stated goals of public diplomacy and the real ones. It functioned to exclude scholars and educators whose opinions and analyses fell outside the narrowly defined spectrum of discourse defined by the Reagan White House. Those listed were considered unfit to represent the U.S. abroad.

Under Carter a State Department program, American Specialists, was merged with a USIA program, Volunteer Speakers. The new speakers program was called American Participants, or AmParts, which was then allowed to be administered by the USIA director, instead of a nonpartisan board of scholars. After pressure was brought by certain members of Congress who feared that whatever administration was in power might use the program for their own political propaganda, Carter signed an executive order. "The new Agency's activities," it stated, "...will not be given over to the advancement of the views of any one group, any one party, or any one administration. The agency must not operate in a covert, manipulative, or propagandistic way."[13]

But AmParts was quickly utilized as a platform for the Reagan line abroad. The blacklist was instituted after an incident in the summer of 1981 when it was discovered that four U.S. economists touring Japan courtesy of AmParts "were reported in a USIA cable to have been 'uniform in their criticism of U.S. economic policies and skeptical of the effectiveness of supplyside economics...' "[14] From this incident the blacklist evolved. A host of Americans from Walter Cronkite to Coretta Scott King were deemed too radical to represent

9. *Ibid.*

10. Laurien Alexandre, "In the Service of the State: Public Diplomacy, Government Media and Ronald Reagan," *Media, Culture and Society*, Vol. 9 (1987), p. 30.

11. See: Robin Andersen, "Propaganda and the Media: Reagan's Public Diplomacy," *CAIB*, No. 31 (Winter 1989), pp. 20-24.

Since July 1989, Raymond has been "senior coordinator" of the president's Eastern European Initiative. This "government-wide effort to help Eastern Europe develop democratic institutions" is housed on the seventh floor of USIA headquarters.

12. "Of Blacklists and Charlie Wick," *Newsweek*, March 12, 1984, p. 36.

13. Jonathan Rosenblum, "The Origins of the 'Blacklist:' USIA Today," *The New Republic*, Vol. 191, July 9, 1984, p. 7.

14. *Ibid.*, p. 8.

Medical student "rescued" by U.S. invasionary forces in Grenada kisses the ground back home.

American democracy abroad. Other "liberals" targeted were ABC's David Brinkley, the *Washington Post's* Ben Bradlee and *New York Times* columnist Tom Wicker. (Not surprisingly, former CIA employee Philip Agee was also excluded.) At the same time, in speech after speech, Wick condemned government controlled propaganda, "The message of our product is larger than any society or government. It is, at bottom, the message of freedom itself, and it resides in the soul of every man as an inner measure of his highest and most noble aspirations."[15]

The public statements made by Director Wick in defense of the blacklist and its subsequent cover-up, revealed an attitude toward journalism and truthfulness entirely incompatible with the stated goals of the agency. When accused of lying to reporters by denying that a blacklist existed, his response was telling. "I regard your premise as completely unfair. I did not lie about it...*I do not regard [a reporter]...as a proper forum for me to make an accountable statement...*"(Emphasis added.)[16]

But Wick's personal disdain for the Fourth Estate was only the most public indication of his agency's propensity for ideology over information. A former White House correspondent for Radio Martí learned that the pursuit of professional journalism at that agency was inappropriate behavior.

Reagan's Phantom Interview

Annette Lopez-Muñoz had requested an interview with President Reagan. After months of delay the interview finally took place, but she was not allowed to ask any questions. Instead, on her way to the Cabinet room she was presented with the text of an interview complete with questions and answers already written by the National Security Council. Ernesto Betancourt, then head of Radio Martí, played the role of journalist while Charles Wick directed the episode. President Reagan read only the first paragraph of each response because the answers were to be translated into Spanish. Reagan did not even have to mouth the words. When she

15. Charles Z. Wick, "Glasnost: The Challenge to U.S. Public Diplomacy," *Vital Speeches of the Day,* Vol. 53, No. 14, May 1, 1987, p. 419.

16. "Of Blacklists and Charlie Wick," *op. cit.,* pp. 36-7

complained to a superior about the NSC's control of the interview, the response was, "You have to understand Annette, at this level everything is managed."[17]

In contrast to the agency's true attitude toward the free press are Charles Wick's prepared statements promoting USIA's Worldnet: "These spontaneous, and uncensored, satellite press conferences send a powerful message to the world about freedom of the press and how our country welcomes dissent and open debate."[18]

Censoring Documentary Films

Just how far the USIA goes to welcome public debate is evident from the agency's attempt to block independent U.S. documentary filmmakers. In May of 1988 it took a federal appeals court in San Francisco to halt the USIA from engaging in what the court called a "virtual license to engage in censorship."[19] At issue were USIA regulations used to decide the tax-exempt status of documentary films. The USIA regulations denied certification for duty-free export status to films it

> **The USIA was expected to accomplish the public relations feat of portraying the U.S. government's anti-Soviet and militaristic foreign policy as ultimately reasonable and democratic.**

deemed "propaganda." But the appellate court called the regulations "content based" and thus forbidden under the First Amendment. The regulations limited "expressions and opinions on issues of public controversy."[20] The USIA had approved films which were pro-nuclear power and had denied certification to anti-nuclear films. Other films denied certification depicted U.S. urban drug problems, an award-winning film about the dangers of uranium mining, and "From the Ashes...Nicaragua Today," a film the agency felt left the impression that the United States had been the aggressor in the war against Nicaragua. At the same time the USIA engaged in economic censorship of American documentary films on the basis of content, it was accusing the Soviet Union of exactly the same thing. "Is it 'glasnost' when our music, movies, art and literature destined for Russia, are censored, screened, and excluded on the basis of political content?"[21]

17. Annette Lopez-Munoz, "The Phantom Interview," *The New Republic,* Vol. 196, June 29, 1987, p. 11.

18. Wick, "The Power of Information...," *op. cit,* p. 520.

19. Jane Gross, "Appeals Court Backs Film Makers Over U.S.," *New York Times,* May 18, 1988, p. C14.

20. *Ibid.*

21. Wick, "Glasnost," *op. cit,* p. 420.

Worldnet and the Invasion of Grenada

In Wick's words, "Worldnet was created during the height of the Grenada rescue mission, when it became apparent to me that our motives were misunderstood in Europe. Somehow we needed to do a better job of explaining our point of view—and quickly! We needed the dramatic and visual impact of satellite television."[22]

When U.S. troops hit Grenadian beaches in October 1983 and for three days thereafter, Pentagon press managers excluded the press from the island. Because no independent footage was available, the government was even more free than usual to manufacture and disseminate its own version of events. The controlled coverage served to confirm Reagan's assertion that Grenada was a Soviet-Cuban island stronghold subverting democracy in our hemisphere. Only months and years later did it emerge that all of the U.S. justifications for the invasion were unfounded. The number of Cubans there had been grossly exaggerated and were in no event planning a take-over.[23] The large quantity of guns intended for international terrorism "documented" by Pentagon photographers turned out to be a small quantity of antiquated weapons.[24] And the U.S. medical students who provided a great photo opportunity when they were "rescued," turned out to have been in no danger, except that occasioned by the U.S. invasion itself.

That Worldnet was born as the international information component of a military action, to justify the U.S. military invasion of Grenada, lays bare its true role. In fact promotion of peaceful coexistence is not the goal of this "war of words." On the contrary, the U.S. propaganda apparatus exists to facilitate, support and justify an aggressive, militaristic foreign policy. International propaganda disseminated by USIA in the 1980s became a powerful component of those policies.

Of Propaganda and Credibility

This propaganda success in Grenada marked the first stage of press management which would lead finally to the ability of the military to carry out the invasion of Panama and the Gulf War unencumbered by the media. The power of television images was viewed as key to the creation of favorable public opinion, and so radio, the longtime staple for propaganda dissemination, had to make room for video. Of course propagandists cannot admit the success of their manipulations, especially to the U.S. public, which prides itself on being able to detect the crass maneuvers of propagandists. Indeed most people in the U.S. believe they are protected from propaganda, and U.S. media legitimation rests on its independence. So at the same time that Public Diplomacy created favorable media coverage of Reagan's

---

22. Wick, "The Power of Information," *op. cit.*, p. 520.
23. Anthony Marro, "When the Government Tells Lies," *Columbia Journalism Review*, March/April 1985, p. 39.
24. *Ibid.*, p. 38.

Of Patronage and Public Resources

If the USIA and VOA were primarily journalistic enterprises designed to tell the world about freedom and American democracy, they would be headed by seasoned professionals, men and women of proven integrity and uncompromising standards. That is not the case at the agency. Instead, top appointments directing the largesse of public funding have been used to reward Reagan/Bush loyalists, cronies and fundraisers. A friend of the Reagans since the 1950s, Wick did not, however, enter politics until 1979, as a fundraiser for the Reagan campaign. With his business connections in finance and mortgage companies, Wick is reported to have raised $10 million. With no experience in journalism, directing the USIA was nevertheless his reward.

In 1989, after leaving his position as vice-chair of the Board at Bristol-Myers Company, Bruce Gelb took over from Wick as head of USIA. His principal qualification for the job was also fundraising, to the tune of $3 million as the co-chair of the New York State finance committee for the Bush 1982 campaign. Also like Wick, he has no background in news, but in the late 1950s he was the advertising manager for Clairol hair coloring products. In 1959 his family took control of Bristol-Myers, which in 1976 was served with a lawsuit from the Sisters of the Precious Blood over sales of infant formula in the Third World. Even though Bristol-Myers denied that Gelb was responsible for marketing the product, it is widely felt that he had to have known about the company's actions. The Sisters revealed three outright lies the company told in justifying its sales. In addition, the company disseminated an article in *Fortune* magazine that described church groups protesting the sales as "Marxists marching under the banner of Christ."[1] These issues were public record at the time of his appointment, but nevertheless Congress confirmed the nomination.

After just two years on the job, Gelb was replaced in May by the agency's 12th chief, Henry Catto. President of H&C Communications, a TV film production company, Catto served in a variety of posts for successive administrations: 1969, deputy representative at the Organization of American States; 1971-73, ambassador to El Salvador; 1974-76, White House protocol chief; 1976-77, U.S. ambassador at the United Nations in Geneva; 1981-83, Reagan's first official spokesperson at the Pentagon; and 1989 until 1991, when he took over as head of the USIA, ambassador to the United Kingdom.

---

1. "USIA: A Battered But Powerful Propaganda Tool," *op. cit.*, p. 58, and Wick, "Glasnost: The Challenge...," *op.cit.*, p. 419.

The USIA's Assets

The USIA is a far-flung empire. The VOA broadcasts in 42 languages and claims to reach 130 million listeners. USIA publishes 14 magazines in 20 languages, and operates approximately 150 libraries in over 80 nations. It has its own foreign service corps with more than 200 posts in 127 countries, and a staff of about 8,700 worldwide, 5,100 of them Americans.

In addition, it sponsors people-to-people exchanges, overseas speakers programs, cultural presentations and exhibits, and maintains cultural centers in about 100 countries. It has three foreign press centers in the U.S. serving some 3,000 foreign correspondents. Radio and TV Martí were created in 1985 and 1990 respectively, to broadcast the U.S. government's position to Cuba.[1] Worldnet sends television interviews with top U.S. government officials via satellite to hotels and embassies around the world.

1. *New York Times*, September 26, 1991, pp. A1, 24.

policies in Central America, Wick felt compelled to assert that "If you think you can manipulate the American media—talk to me afterwards—I'd like to sell you the Brooklyn Bridge."[25]

The mendacity of Wick's denials of his own success becomes apparent when compared to his assertion that the Soviets, not the Reagan administration, were in fact able to manipulate the U.S. media. "The Soviets have stepped up their use of Western methods of public diplomacy to take their case to the U.S. people...The *New York Times* has called Mr. Gorbachev 'a PR Commissar's Dream.' "[26] The vast increases in the USIA budget during the 1980s were justified by assertions that the Soviets had indeed been successful at information manipulation, even of the American press.

TV Martí

TV Martí is probably the most inflammatory international broadcast program at USIA. It operates in violation of a United Nations-sponsored treaty signed by both Cuba and the U.S. in 1982 and was "adopted without authorizing legislation or hearings by the appropriate congressional committees."[27]

The situation is potentially explosive. The U.S. says it is defending the rights of Cubans to free information. In fact, Cuba already receives CNN and picks up commercial stations from southern Florida. Cuba views the video invasion as a violation of national sovereignty and has threatened to

retaliate by disrupting U.S. broadcasts "from New York to California." The U.S. in turn has prepared an "active option" of "surgically removing" the offending Cuban transmitters.[28]

TV Martí stands as a dangerous Bush administration boondoggle. Millions of dollars a year are thrown away to please a right-wing anti-Castro constituency. "Its only purpose," observed USIA scholar John Spicer Nichols, "is to pay off George Bush's campaign promises to the rabidly anticommunist Cuban-American community in Florida..."[29]

The public relations firm, Black, Manafort, Stone, and Kelly, lobbied on behalf of TV Martí's advocates during Senate Appropriations Committee hearings. President Bush's then campaign manager, Lee Atwater, was a former Black, Manafort business partner. The PR firm's lobbyist Stuart Sweet also represented Jorge Mas Canosa, a Miami Cuban backing TV Martí.[30] According to Federal Election Commission records, Mas Canosa "gave $6,000 to Mr. Bush and his political action committee."[31] The most absurd fact currently is that the USIA continues to broadcast a signal which is never received; it has been successfully blocked by the Cuban government.

The Limits of Propaganda

In 1983, neither the Soviet Union nor Cuba was the reason the U.S. invaded Grenada, as Worldnet would have the world believe. Melvin A. Goodman, who was chief of the CIA's Soviet-Third World Division under Robert Gates, testified at Gates' confirmation hearings that the "bleak landscape of an expansionist Soviet Union" painted by Gates while CIA Deputy Director in the 1980s was "inconsistent with agency assessments."[32] USIA propaganda does not bring the light of truth and hope to those people whose governments do not believe in the Western renditions of freedom of speech. Rather, it exists to block international criticism of its global military hegemony through the most blatant form of information manipulation. But even an immense international propaganda apparatus cannot sell the U.S. to an increasingly skeptical world on the receiving end of its policies. No amount of propaganda will persuade the Arab people of the justness of the U.S. system in face of the massacre of 200,000 Iraqis. The Soviet Union can in no way be considered a threat to U.S. hegemony, and with the absence of the historical justification for the USIA, reason would predict that the agency is at least being scaled back. But according to John Spicer Nichols, no budget cuts are planned. The billion-plus dollars a year spent on propaganda would be unnecessary if the U.S. were sincerely committed to peace with the world community. ●

25. Wick, "The War of Ideas," *op. cit.*, p. 19.
26. *Ibid.*
27. *Washington Post*, January 25, 1989, p. A19.

28. John Spicer Nichols, "Video Invasion," *The Nation*, April 2, 1990, p. 441.
29. *Ibid.*, p. 442.
30. The authoritarian multimillionaire, Mas Canosa, although disliked and feared by many anti-Castro Cuban exiles, has openly declared himself available for the position of Fidel Castro's successor.
31. Bob Davis, "Television Groups Entangle on Signal to Cuba," *Wall Street Journal*, June 16, 1988.
32. *New York Times*, September 26, 1991, pp. A1, 24.

NED, CIA, and the Orwellian Democracy Project

Holly Sklar and Chip Berlet

The National Endowment for Democracy (NED) was first funded in fiscal 1984, an appropriate year for an Orwellian agency making the world safe for hypocrisy. The quasi-private NED does publicly what the CIA has long done and continues to do secretly. Despite successive scandals, U.S. meddling in the internal affairs of other nations—including their "democratic" elections—has not only thrived, it has become respectable.

U.S. manipulation of foreign elections was standard operating procedure well before the CIA's creation. In 1912, for example, the highly-decorated Marine Corps General Smedley Butler wrote his wife Ethel, "Today, Nicaragua has enjoyed a fine 'free election' with only one candidate being allowed to run...In order that this happy event might be pulled

political process—from manipulating media and public opinion to working to unseat administration critics in Congress. Constitutional checks and balances are voided as Congress exercises its oversight responsibility largely by overlooking wrongdoing, and the courts defer to Congress and the Executive in "national security" matters.

Fronts and More Fronts

The covert side of foreign intervention was officially institutionalized in June 1948, when President Truman signed a National Security Directive (NSD 10/2). "The overt foreign activities of the U.S. Government must be supplemented by covert operations," it read, "[including] any covert activities related to: propaganda, economic warfare, preventative di-

---

We supervised elections in Haiti and wherever we supervised them our candidate always won. —General Smedley Butler, U. S. Marine Corps, 1935

---

off without hitch and to the entire satisfaction of our State Department, we patrolled all the towns to prevent disorders..." In 1935, reporter John Spivak interviewed the then retired Butler, who became a vocal anti-interventionist after being approached to assist a now-forgotten domestic coup attempt against President Franklin D. Roosevelt: "Butler spilled over with anger at the hypocrisy that had marked American interference in the internal affairs of other governments, behind a smokescreen of pious expressions of high-sounding purpose. 'We supervised elections in Haiti,' he said wryly, 'and wherever we supervised them our candidate always won.' "[1] Butler would recognize the old policy of interference behind the new NED smoke screen.

Contemporary covert and overt operatives, working for or with the U.S. presidency, also intervene in the American

rect action, including sabotage, anti-sabotage, demolition and evacuation measures; subversion against hostile states, including assistance to underground resistance movements, guerrillas and refugee liberation groups, and support of indigenous anti-communist elements in threatened countries of the free world."

The Orwellian democracy machine grew quickly in the warm shadow of the Cold War. The CIA provided a home for the "Gehlen network" of former German Nazi spies with experience in the Soviet Union and Eastern Europe. Under the guise of "liberationism," CIA fronts such as the Crusade for Freedom promoted these emigré fascist leaders and collaborators to the U.S. public as democratic freedom fighters in the war against communism.[2] Some became leaders in the Republican Party's Ethnic Heritage Groups Council.[3] Others assisted Radio Free Europe and the various propaganda instruments known collectively as the "mighty Wurlitzer" by its proud conductors. The CIA also influenced U.S. and foreign

Holly Sklar and Chip Berlet are writing a book about NED. Sklar is the author of *Washington's War on Nicaragua* and *Trilateralism: The Trilateral Commission and Elite Planning for World Management.* Berlet is an analyst with Political Research Associates in Cambridge, Mass. His articles have appeared in numerous publications, including the *Boston Globe, Chicago Sun-Times,* the *Des Moines Register,* and *CAIB.*

1. Jules Archer. *The Plot to Seize the White House* (New York: Hawthorn Books, 1973), pp. 57-58 and p. 207, citing John L. Spivak's interview with Butler.

2. See: Christopher Simpson, *Blowback* (New York: Weidenfeld and Nicolson, 1988).

3. Russ Bellant, *Old Nazis, the New Right, and the Republican Party* (Boston: South End Press/Political Research Associates, 1991).

DataCenter   464 19th Street, Oakland, California 94612 (415) 835-4692

labor organizations through such bodies as the International Confederation of Free Trade Unions and AFL-CIO affiliates.

With the help of front groups espousing ant-communism and democracy, the U.S. interfered in elections and destabilized governments in many countries, among them Italy, Greece, Iran, the Philippines, Guatemala, Brazil, Indonesia, Chile, Portugal, Jamaica, and El Salvador. As then National Security Adviser Henry Kissinger said on June 27, 1970, speaking in support of secret efforts to block Salvador Allende's election in Chile, "I don't see why we need to stand by and watch a country go communist due to the irresponsibility of its own people."[4]

In 1967, there was a public outcry when *Ramparts* magazine exposed secret CIA funding of the National Student Association's international activities. Follow-up stories and congressional hearings exposed a network of ostensibly private labor, student, cultural, media and other organizations that were funded by the CIA, using conduit foundations, under its Psychological, Political and Paramilitary Division.

Faced with mounting criticism, President Johnson appointed the three-member Katzenbach Commission which included CIA Director Richard Helms. This commission laid the groundwork for a new funding technique. It recommended that "The government should promptly develop and establish a public-private mechanism to provide public funds

Terry Allen
NED funded a group affiliated with the ARENA party, despite that party's death squad links. Above, ARENA supporter votes in 1989 Salvadoran elections. Note see-through ballot boxes.

I don't see why we need to stand by and watch a country go communist due to the irresponsibility of its own people. — Henry Kissinger

---

openly for overseas activities of organizations which are adjudged deserving, in the national interest, of public support."[5] A bill was introduced in Congress in 1967 to create an "Institute of International Affairs," but it was not approved, and the matter of CIA funding of front groups faded from public scrutiny until Watergate.

The CIA quietly continued covert operations involving front groups and more scandals erupted in the Nixon administration. The congressional Church (Senate) and Pike (House) committees investigated CIA and FBI operations in Watergate's wake and exposed a wide variety of illicit and antidemocratic programs. Domestic operations included CIA propaganda activities and Operation CHAOS, and the FBI's COINTELPRO. Foreign operations ranged from CIA programs to manipulate elections and overthrow governments, to plots to assassinate foreign leaders. Amid calls for placing limitations on the CIA or even abolishing it, George Bush was appointed CIA director, serving from 1976 to 1977.

His mandate was to mollify his former colleagues in Congress while actually limiting CIA reform.

"Project Democracy"

In the 1980s, with former CIA Director Bush in the vice presidency, the Reagan administration legalized through Executive Order many of the covert activities previously condemned as illegal, immoral and antidemocratic.

The Katzenbach recommendation of a "public-private mechanism" finally bore fruit in the National Endowment for Democracy.

NED was the public arm of the Reagan administration's "Project Democracy," an overt-covert intervention and "public diplomacy" operation coordinated by the National Security Council (NSC). In a speech to the British Parliament on June 8, 1982, President Reagan announced that the U.S. would launch Project Democracy to "foster the infrastructure of democracy, the system of free press, unions, political parties, universities, which allows a people to choose their own way."

According to a secret White House memo setting the agenda for a Cabinet-level planning meeting on Project Democracy, officials decided in August, "We need to ex-

---

4. *Newsweek*, September 23, 1974, pp. 51-52; and Seymour Hersh, *The Price of Power* (New York: Summit Books, 1983), p. 265.

5. White House press release, March 29, 1967.

amine how law and Executive Order can be made more liberal to permit covert action on a broader scale, as well as what we can do through substantially increased overt political action."[6]

On January 14, 1983, Reagan signed NSDD 77, a secret National Security Decision Directive instructing the NSC to coordinate interagency efforts for Project Democracy. "Public diplomacy," it stated, "is comprised of those actions of the U.S. Government designed to generate support for our national security objectives."[7]

When legislation was introduced to authorize "Project Democracy" in February 1983, administration officials promised Congress that the CIA would not be involved. A separate bill authorizing funding for NED was introduced in April. The public NED record generally traces its origins to a government-funded feasibility study by the bipartisan American Political Foundation (APF) headed by Allen Weinstein. He served as NED's first acting president until February 1984 and is currently president of the Center for Democracy, an NED grantee.[8]

"A lot of what we do today was done covertly 25 years ago by the CIA," Weinstein told *Washington Post* foreign editor David Ignatius.[9] Calling NED "the sugar daddy of overt operations," Ignatius writes enthusiastically of the "network of overt operatives who during the last ten years have quietly

John Richardson, the current and past (1984-88) chair of the NED board of directors, is an old hand in the CIA's front group network. He was president of the CIA-sponsored Radio Free Europe from 1961 to 1968. From 1963 to 1984, he was variously president and director of Freedom House, a conservative/neoconservative research, publishing, networking, and selective human rights organization. Freedom House is now heavily endowed with NED grants. Richardson later became counselor of the congressionally-funded U.S. Institute of Peace (USIP) which is governed by a presidentially-appointed board of directors dominated by past and present government officials, including Defense and CIA, and members of right-wing organizations such as the Hoover Institution on War, Revolution, and Peace.[10]

Bipartisan Support, Partisan Intervention

The National Endowment for Democracy has already been involved in 77 countries — from Afghanistan to New Zealand, Northern Ireland to South Africa — with most funding going to Eastern Europe and Latin America. NED's major priority for 1991 is the Soviet Union.

As described by a 1991 General Accounting Office (GAO) report, NED

---

*A lot of what we do today was done covertly
25 years ago by the CIA.* —Allen Weinstein, Founding President, NED

---

been changing the rules of international politics...doing in public what the CIA used to do in private."

Actually, CIA footprints are all over Project Democracy, from NED to the Iran-Contra operations. The CIA-NED connection is personified by Walter Raymond Jr. who supervised NED under Reagan. A propaganda expert and senior officer in the CIA Directorate of Operations, Raymond was first detailed by the CIA to the NSC in 1982 as Senior Director of Intelligence Programs. He resigned from the CIA in April 1983 in order to become a special assistant to the President as director of International Communications and Public Diplomacy at the NSC. In mid-1987, he became deputy director of the U.S. Information Agency (USIA), where he now heads the Eastern European Initiatives Office.

plans and administers a worldwide grants program that is generally aimed at fostering a nongovernmental approach to (1) strengthening pluralism through institutions such as trade unions and business associations, (2) developing political parties and electoral processes, and (3) advancing democratic political institutions through civic education and the media.[11]

NED is a bipartisan growth industry for partisan intervention. NED President Carl Gershman was formerly senior counselor to U.N. Ambassador Jeane Kirkpatrick; past resident scholar, Freedom House; executive director of the cold warrior Social Democrats USA (1974-80); former research director for the AFL-CIO and board member of the CIA-linked International Rescue Committee. NED Vice Chair Charles Manatt, of the Washington law firm Manatt, Phelps, and Phillips, is former chair of the Democratic National Committee and on the board of the Center for Democracy.

6. Joel Brinkley, *New York Times*, February 15, 1987, and John Kelly, "National Endowment for Reagan's Democracies," *The National Reporter*, Summer 1986, pp. 23-24.

7. *Ibid.*

8. Diane Weinstein, Allen's spouse, was legal counsel to Vice President Dan Quayle.

9. David Ignatius, "Innocence Abroad: The New World of Spyless Coups," *Washington Post*, September 22, 1991.

10. Sara Diamond and Richard Hatch, "Operation Peace Institute," *Z Magazine*, July-August 1990, pp. 110-12.

11. U.S. General Accounting Office, Report to Congressional Committees, *Promoting Democracy: National Endowment for Democracy's Management of Grants Needs Improvement*, March 1991, p. 8.

DataCenter   464 19th Street, Oakland, California 94612 (415) 835-4692

NED Treasurer Jay Van Andel is a major funder of the Heritage Foundation and the co-founder and chair of the Amway Corporation, which is tied to the evangelical right.

Although registered as a private nonprofit organization, NED is funded by Congress with tax dollars largely channeled through the U.S. Information Agency (USIA) and the Agency for International Development (AID). From 1984 to 1990, NED received about $152 million in congressionally approved funds, including $38.6 million in FY 1990. By law, NED does not carry out grant programs itself, but makes grants to U.S. "private sector" organizations which in turn fund projects by foreign recipients. According to a 1991 GAO report, "The Endowment monitoring procedures have not been effective. Grantee noncompliance with the Endowment's key financial and internal controls has resulted in instances of funds being misused, mismanaged, or not effectively accounted for."[12]

In one controversial NED grant to the University of South Carolina, the university was used essentially as a money laundry. It was allowed to skim ten percent of the NED funds for administrative expenses and simply pass on the remaining money to vaguely described Chilean projects. Some of the funds for these projects were deposited into the personal account of a director of one of three Chilean groups authorized to receive the grant money. Beyond that point there is no documentation of how the funds were spent. According to one newspaper account, some faculty members suspected the process was being used for secret foreign policy initiatives or covert operations.[13]

NED's Core Four

Most NED funds are distributed through four core grantee organizations, profiled below. All but the Free Trade Union Institute (FTUI) were specifically created to serve as NED conduits.

FTUI was established in 1977 by the AFL-CIO's Department of International Affairs. It continued the work of its predecessor—the CIA-connected Free Trade Union Committee—which was founded in 1944 to combat leftwing trade unionism in Europe. The late Irving Brown, who served on FTUI's board and was director of the AFL-CIO International Affairs Department until 1986 and then senior adviser to Lane Kirkland for international affairs, was identified by several former CIA officers as a CIA agent.[14] FTUI executive director Eugenia Kemble is a former assistant to American Federation of Teachers president Albert Shanker. Her brother Penn Kemble, now with Freedom House, was president of PRODEMCA. This "private" bipartisan group supported Reagan's Central America policy and channeled NED grants to the Nicaraguan opposition and the anti-Sandinista newspaper *La Prensa* until 1986.

In addition to providing NED funds to Soviet and European unions and media, FTUI channels NED grants to the AFL-CIO's three established regional organizations. The Latin American program is under the American Institute for Free Labor Development (AIFLD) which was launched in 1962 by Kennedy's Labor Advisory Committee on Foreign Policy. AIFLD's first executive director was Serafino Romualdi, whom former CIA officer Philip Agee called the "principal CIA agent for labor operations in Latin America."[15] William Doherty, Jr., AIFLD executive director since 1965, has also been identified as a CIA agent by Agee and other former CIA officers.

The African-American Labor Center (AALC) was begun in 1964 and first directed by Irving Brown. It supported such "unions" as Holden Roberto's National Front for the Liberation of Angola, which the CIA backed in the 1970s, along with Jonas Savimbi's UNITA. In 1968, Brown transferred to the newly-formed Asian-American Free Labor Institute (AAFLI) which was created to organize Vietnamese labor unions and land reform as part of the multi-faceted U.S. counterinsurgency program.

The Trade Union Congress of the Philippines (TUCP) is a key recipient of FTUI grants, via AAFLI. Following the assassination of opposition leader Benigno Aquino in 1983, funding for the pro-Marcos TUCP jumped. "If people hadn't had assistance then," said Bud Philipps, the AAFLI administrator in the Philippines, "the success of the political left in the [Filipino] trade unions would have been phenomenal. Nationally and internationally it would have been a Waterloo." The money to promote the U.S. policy in the Philippines was spread around CIA-style. "Imagine if you have US $100,000 to give out to families in US $500 chunks," said Philipps. "Your stock goes way up, faster than the stock of any of the militant labour groups."[16]

U.S. support for TUCP continues under Aquino. In September 1991, a scandal erupted in the Philippines over U.S. attempts to buy support for the military bases treaty, implicating among others Senator Ernesto Herrera, the general secretary of the TUCP. On July 19, Herrera, then a critic of the bases treaty, had written President Aquino, saying, "It will be extremely difficult to vote for an agreement which reflects an almost contemptuous disregard of Filipino workers' interest." Herrera reportedly switched his vote in favor of the losing treaty after AAFLI promised $3.7 million in additional TUCP support.[17]

Nor was this the first scandal over FTUI grants. In 1984, FTUI awarded grants to Panamanian union activists promoting the candidacy of Nicolas Barletta, who was backed by the U.S.-supported Panamanian military. That same year, FTUI gave secret grants to two French groups opposed to the policies of President Fran was a student activist group described by a 1982 French Parliamentary Inquiry as a "satellite movement" of the rightwing paramilitary *Service d'Action Civique*. The other grantee was *Force Ouvriere*, a trade union organization which used violence when working with the CIA after World War II to oppose leftwing unions.[18] Through FTUI, NED continues funding regional affiliates of Force Ouvriere in Africa and the Caribbean.

The Center for International Private Enterprise (CIPE), another core NED grantee organization, is the U.S. Chamber of Commerce counterpart to FTUI. Established in June 1983, it supports "free market" policies and business organizations, pro-business media, training of business leaders and mobilization of business in the political process. In Eastern Europe, for example, CIPE has programs to support business organizations, analyze business enterprises and

---

12. *Ibid.*, p. 3.

13. "Government grants stopped at USC on way to Third World," Charles Pope, Dave Moniz, *The State* (Columbia, S.C.), May 12, 1991, p. 1.

14. See: *e.g.*, Jonathan Kwitny, *Endless Enemies* (New York: Penguin Books, 1984), pp. 339-48; Philip Agee, *Inside the Company: CIA Diary* (New York, Bantam Books), 1975, pp. 69, 624.

15. Philip Agee, *op. cit*, p. 64; Kwitny, *op. cit.*, pp. 341-43, 346-54.

16. *International Labour Reports*, No. 33, May/June 1989, p. 11.

17. Peacenet report, October 17, 1991, citing mainstream Manila newspapers.

18. Mark Schapiro and Annette Levi, "NED to the Rescue," *The New Republic*, December 23, 1985; Alfred W. McCoy, *The Politics of Heroin* (New York: Lawrence Hill Books, 1991), p. 58.

Ministries of Truth: Psywar at Home

The Reagan-Bush administrations' "public diplomacy" program involved a network of rightwing donors, organizations, lobbyists and PR specialists working in conjunction with the NSC, CIA and two special offices: the White House Office of Public Liaison and the State Department's Office of Public Diplomacy.[1] In May 1983 the White House Office of Public Liaison, headed by Faith Ryan Whittlesey (former ambassador to Switzerland), established the Outreach Working Group on Central America, a vehicle for packaging PR themes, networking, and mobilizing administration supporters.

On May 20, 1983, NSC official Walter Raymond informed National Security Adviser William Clark that the "Faith Whittlesey effort" was "off to a good start" and discussed the establishment of a "Coalition for a Democratic Central America." In a section headed "Private Funding Effort," Raymond wrote, "I have provided Jeff Davis with a list of funding programs that require private sector support...Roy Godson[2] reported that he met early this week with a group of private donors that [chief of USIA and top fundraiser for the 1980 Reagan campaign] Charlie Wick brought to the sitroom two months ago. The group made their first commitment of $400,000 which includes support to Freedom House, a pro-INF [Intermediate-Range Nuclear Forces] group in Holland, Accuracy in Media, and a European based labor program. These are useful steps forward. More to follow."[3]

Complementing and then superseding the Outreach Group was the State Department's Office of Public Diplomacy on Latin America and the Caribbean (S/LPD), directed by the Cuban-born Otto Reich, a former AID official and instructor at the U.S. Army School of the Americas. Although based at State, the Office of Public Diplomacy was an interagency office, with personnel from State, DOD, AID and USIA, operating under the direction of the NSC's Walter Raymond and Oliver North. "If you look at it as a whole," a senior S/LPD official said, "the Office of Public Diplomacy was carrying out a huge psychological operation of the kind the military conducts to influence a population in denied or enemy territory."[4] Reich's executive officer, Lt. Col. Daniel "Jake" Jacobowitz, had a "background in psychological warfare," according to S/LPD Deputy Director Jonathan Miller. Following a request from Reich to Raymond, five other Army officers were recruited from the 4th Psychological Operations Group at Fort Bragg, North Carolina.[5]

In 1986, Reich became ambassador to Venezuela and was replaced by Robert Kagen. Raymond prepared a secret memorandum for John Poindexter to send to Casey, assuring the DCI that "the departure of Otto Reich has not resulted in any reduction of effort...Although the independent office was folded into Elliott Abrams' bureau, the White House has sent a clear tasker to the community that this limited reorganization in no way reflected a diminution [sic] of activities. On the contrary, the same interagency responsibilities are being exercised, and the group reports directly to the NSC...In reality, the reorganization also means that Elliott Abrams plays a strong public diplomacy role, and in this way we have harnessed one of the best public diplomacy assets that we have in the government."

Raymond noted that he chaired a weekly Central American public diplomacy meeting with participants from the NSC, the CIA's Central American Task Force, State, USIA, AID, Defense and the White House Press and Public Liaison Offices. "This group takes its policy guidance from the Central American RIG and pursues an energetic political and informational agenda."[6] The RIG (Restricted Interagency Group) was made up of officials from State, Defense, the NSC, Joint Chiefs and CIA and was led by the core group of Oliver North, Assistant Secretary of State for Inter-American Affairs Elliott Abrams and CIA Task Force chief for Central America Alan Fiers. In 1991 plea bargains with Independent Counsel Lawrence Walsh, Fiers implicated higher CIA officials in the Iran-Contra coverup and Abrams pleaded guilty to two misdemeanor charges of withholding information from Congress about secret government efforts to support the contras during the Boland ban on military aid.

---

1. See: Holly Sklar, *Washington's War on Nicaragua* (Boston: South End Press, 1988), pp. 240-49, 262-64, 274, 321-23, *passim.*

2. Godson is a Georgetown University professor, 1980 CIA transition team member, and Washington director of the National Strategy Information Center—an intelligence lobby and think tank which Casey was influential in founding, when it provided funding to Arturo Cruz, then a contra political leader. *Report of the Congressional Committees Investigating the Iran-Contra Affair*, Deposition of Roy S. Godson, append b vol 12, pp. 253-305, *passim; Tower Board Report*, p. C-17; *Iran-Contra Report*, pp. 97-98; and James Ridgeway, "The Professor of Conspire," *Village Voice*, August 4, 1987.

3. Memorandum from Raymond to Clark, May 20, 1983, Iran-Contra Hearings, Exhibit OLN-219. Also see: Memorandum from Raymond to Clark, August 9, 1983.

4. Alfonso Chardy, *Miami Herald*, July 19, 1987. See also: Chardy, *Miami Herald*, October 13, 1986, and House Committee on Foreign Affairs, Staff Report, *State Department and Intelligence Community Involvement in Domestic Activities Related to the Iran-Contra Affair*, September 7, 1988.

5. Robert Parry and Peter Kornbluh, "Iran-Contra's Untold Story," *Foreign Policy*, Fall 1988, p. 19.

6. Memorandum for Casey prepared by Walter Raymond, August 1986, Iran-Contra Hearings.

---

provide policy recommendations and assist legislative actions in Hungary, Romania, the Czech and Slovak Federal Republic, and Poland. In Poland it also funds the Krakow Industrial Society's efforts to publish a daily national newspaper "that will cultivate understanding of the role of private enterprise in economic and democratic development."[19]

The National Democratic Institute for International Affairs (NDI), the Democratic Party's vehicle for NED funding, is chaired by former Vice President Walter Mondale. The Institute's president, J. Brian Atwood, assistant secretary for congressional relations in the Carter administration, declared: "Our philosophy is that we should be operating on a non-partisan basis. We do not care who wins an election; all we care about is the democratic system. Our conferences [have been attended] by people across the spectrum, from Social Democrats to conservatives. I think there is a danger we could pervert an election process by getting into a campaign on one side or another."[20]

As shall be seen later, that's just what NDI did in Nicaragua.

The Republican Party also has its own conduit for NED funding—the National Republican Institute for International Affairs (NRI). J. William Middendorf, its secretary-treasurer, was head of the 1980 CIA transition team, former secretary of the Navy, and ambassador to the Organization of American States under Reagan. Until mid-1991, Jorge Mas Canosa, chair of the Cuban American National Foundation and of the Radio Marti advisory board, served on the NRI board of directors. Oliver North's diaries refer to Mas Canosa and the contra support network, for example, in this February 4, 1985 entry: "Felix Rodriguez, still have not gotten dollars from Jorge Mas." The Cuban American National Foundation has

---

19. NED 1990 Annual Report, p. 27.

20. Interview, *Campaigns and Elections*, May/June 1989, p. 34.

DataCenter   464 19th Street, Oakland, California 94612 (415) 835-4692

received NED grants to support the work of the Madrid-based International Coalition for Human Rights in Cuba and to support the U.S. counterpart to the Havana-based Cuban Committee for Human Rights.

Another brief NED mini-scandal erupted in 1989, when NRI was accused of interfering in Costa Rica's elections. NRI supported the successful presidential candidacy of the Social Christian United Party's Rafael Calderon by financing the organization he directed, the conservative Association for the Defense of Costa Rican Liberty and Democracy. NRI grants were used in part for nearly $50,000 in salary paid to Calderon, who in 1986 had lost the presidential race to Oscar Arias of the National Liberation Party (PLN). In its annual reports, Calderon's association said it used some $434,000 in "NED grants beginning in 1986 for seminars and conferences, to fund research for opposition members of the national legislature, to run public opinion polls and to train 200 instructors for a nationwide 'political education program.' " NED grants were also used to fund a magazine, which ran a column by Calderon condemning the Arias peace plan for Central America as "a deformation of masculine values and the defense of our national sovereignty."[21]

"Victory" in Nicaragua

Destabilization campaigns can culminate in invasions such as Grenada in 1983 and Panama in 1989, or military coups such as Guatemala in 1954 and Chile in 1973, or "electoral coups" such as Jamaica in 1980 and Nicaragua, where economic embargo, re-escalating contra war and increased internal opposition to the Sandinistas prevailed in 1990.[22] Angola may be next.

At the March 1990 NED board meeting, President Carl Gershman called the "victory of the democratic opposition in Nicaragua...a tremendous victory for the Endowment as well." The board minutes continued:

Those who head the party and labor institutes, whose tireless efforts helped make these victories possible, are well known to Board members. Still, there are others who made 'a sterling contribution' and Mr. Gershman took the opportunity to pay tribute to them as well: from NDI, Ken Wollack, Donna Huffman, and on-site project manager Mark Feierstein; from NRI, Janine Perfit and project manager Martin Krauze; from AIFLD, Gordon Ellison and Dave Jessup; from the International Foundation for Electoral Systems, Richard Soudriette and Hank Quintero; and from Delphi International, Paul von Ward and Lee Zahnow.[23]

The Washington-based Delphi International Group, which plays a key role for NED in Nicaragua, has offices in San Francisco, Moscow, Beijing, Paris and Dublin. It is headed by Paul von Ward, a former naval officer, NATO adviser, State Department official and U.S. embassy officer. Delphi took over NED's La Prensa grants in 1986 after PRODEMCA too openly supported military aid for the contras. These Delphi grants were first directed by Henry Quintero, former executive director of the Institute for North-South Issues (INSI), which was used by Oliver North to launder money to the contras.[24] Quintero, a former intelligence research specialist for the Department of the Army, State Department and USIA, is now with the International Foundation for Electoral Systems, described below. Delphi also administers NED grants for the right-wing Radio Corporacion and other radio stations, training and "civic education" projects for women and youth, and other assistance to anti-Sandinista groups in Nicaragua.

NDI sent an election survey mission to Managua in September 1988. According to an internal draft report, a purpose of the mission was to see "what program(s) could be developed by NDI to assist the democratic opposition in presenting a unified, effective challenge to Sandinista rule." The NDI group was worried about prospects for defeating the Sandinistas. It described the opposition as "centrifugal in dynamic, fratricidal in outlook" and, in the words of an NDI consultant, "bureaucratic, static, atomized, with low credibility in the population." NDI found that "unification is the single most important ingredient for success by the opposition." NED, the U.S. Embassy, and the CIA successfully forged that campaign unity in the UNO political alliance and its labor and civic affiliates—making UNO the viable choice not just for its political adherents but for disenchanted Sandinista supporters and people worn down by war and economic destabilization.[25]

Although the NED charter prohibits direct funding of political candidacies, it poured $12.5 million into 1989-90 election-related funding. NED supported UNO (insisting this wasn't direct support for UNO candidates) and supposedly nonpartisan UNO front groups such as Via Civica (Civic Way) and the Institute for Electoral Promotion and Training (IPCE). In a meeting attended by one of the authors before the election, U.S. Embassy Charge d' Affaires John Leonard referred to IPCE as an "UNO foundation."

NED support for Via Civica was provided by Henry Quintero and the Washington-based International Foundation for Electoral

---

NED groups often play good cop to the CIA's bad cop.

Systems (IFES), founded in 1989. The chair of the IFES board of directors is F. Clifton White, director of the conservative John M. Ashbrook Center for Public Affairs and member of the boards of the Center for Democracy and NRI. Since he helped win the Republican presidential nomination for Barry Goldwater in 1964, White has been regarded as a leading conservative political strategist. His involvement in the Reagan administration's overt-covert pro-Contra propaganda campaign is evident in a November 10, 1986 memo, written not long before the Iran-contra scandal broke. The memo, from Walter Raymond to then National Security Adviser John Poindexter discusses progress on a bipartisan group to promote U.S. policy in Central America, especially Nicaragua: "Although Pete Dailey [CIA counselor], Bill Casey and Clif White have all been involved in general discussion of what needs to be done, we are going to have to be sure that Pete and Bill are not involved...Hence, Clif is now taking the lead."[26]

In Nicaragua FTUI funds the AIFLD-backed Council of Trade Union Unification (CUS) regarded as pro-Somoza until even the elite turned against the dictatorship in 1978. In 1990, FTUI provided a $73,000 grant to assist CUS "in organizing workers and in strengthening their ability to support workers' rights" and a $493,013 grant to assist CUS "in mobilizing workers and their families to participate in and monitor the electoral process."[27]

21. Doyle McManus, Los Angeles Times, October 14, 1989. See also: Boston Globe and Wall Street Journal, October 13, 1989.

22. Holly Sklar, Washington's War on Nicaragua, p. 390-92.

23. Minutes of March 29, 1990 NED Board of Directors.

24. See for example: Report of the Congressional Committees Investigating the Iran-Contra Affair, November 1987, p. 97.

25. See Holly Sklar, "Washington Wants to Buy Nicaragua's Elections Again," Z Magazine, December 1989 and "Many Nicaraguan Voters Cry Uncle," Z Magazine, April 1990 and William Robinson and David MacMichael, "NED Overt Action: Intervention in the Nicaraguan Election," CAIB, Number 33 (Winter 1990), pp. 33-34.

26. That memo was cited in a September 1988 report of the House Committee on Foreign Affairs (whose subcommittee on International Organizations oversees NED), which condemned the domestic propaganda network. Unfortunately, the report had little impact. House Foreign Affairs Committee Chair Dante Fascell (D-Fla.), a past member of the NED board of directors, personifies continued congressional support for the overt-covert "Project Democracy."

27. NED Annual Report 1990, p. 43. GAO, Aid to Nicaragua, May 1991, Report pp. 30-31.

Good Cop-Bad Cop

NED groups often play good cop to the CIA's bad cop while policymakers pretend that the bad cop CIA is out of the election meddling business. In reality, covert political aid also flows. The CIA reportedly spent $6 million during the election period on the Nicaraguan opposition for "housekeeping costs, election-related contra support, political training for UNO operatives in Costa Rica, radio broadcasts from Costa Rica into Nicaragua, and providing travel funds and stories to European journalists." In addition, President Bush, his son Jeb, Special Assistant to the President for Latin American Affairs William Pryce, White House Chief of Staff John Sununu and other officials worked with the Carmen Group to organize UNO campaign public relations, strategy and "private" fundraising under the guise of the "Committee for Free Elections and Democracy in Nicaragua."[28]

An October 1991 *Newsweek* article titled "The CIA on the Stump" described a secret $600,000 CIA program to pay Miami-based contras to return to Nicaragua and work for UNO in the months before the election. About $100,000 was directed to Alfredo Cesar, a member of IPCE's small governing board and now president of the Nicaraguan national assembly. "[Congress] explicitly banned covert CIA financial support for UNO," the magazine reported, "precisely because it feared the political impact if the payments were discovered. 'Having this election jeopardized by so little money and so few people,' one U.S. intelligence official said of the $600,000 operation, 'it's so stupid.'" The article, illustrating the good cop-bad cop routine, fails to mention the CIA's multimillion dollar election-related support program which *Newsweek* had previously reported but dumped down the memory hole.[29]

Old Nazis and New European Democracies

NED core groups and grantees are heavily involved in shaping the political, social and economic destinies of Eastern Europe and the Soviet Union. NDI, for example, has programs for party building, election-related assistance including seminars in grassroots organizing and civic education, election administration, election monitoring, public opinion polls and electoral law reform. In the Czech and Slovak Federal Republic, it is also convening international experts to help draft a new election law. In Hungary, it is consulting with newly-elected parliamentarians "to enhance their ability to carry out their official duties." And in Poland, NDI is also sponsoring a U.S. training visit for senior staff administrators of the Polish Parliament. Programs are also in place in Bulgaria, Romania, the Soviet Republics, and Yugoslavia.

Some of the U.S.-supported East European parties and groups define democracy as available only to those who have specific racial, ethnic, or religious attributes—an echo of the racial nationalism that underpinned the fascist movements in post-World War I Europe.[30] In fact, some supposed democracy builders are reviving Nazi-collaborationist parties, in some cases with the help of aging pro-Nazi forces forced to emigrate to Canada and the U.S. after World War II.[31]

Margaret Quigley of Political Research Associates documented the problem in the Russian Republic. The Free Congress Foundation not only acts as a conduit for NED funds to Yeltsin's Inter-Regional Deputies Group, but has trained Yeltsin's staff, including his campaign manager Arkady Murashev. According to Quigley, Yeltsin's ties to ultra-nationalist and anti-Semitic groups are much deeper than most people realize.[32]

Yeltsin himself spoke to Pamyat officials at a time when members of the Russian nationalist anti-Jewish organization were distributing copies of the virulently anti-Jewish hoax, *The Protocols of the Learned Elders of Zion*. "It's clear," he said, "that a sense of patriotism motivates you, patriotism about our motherland." Yeltsin's vice president, Alexander Rutskoi, is also the deputy chair of *Otechestvo* (Fatherland) an anti-Semitic, Russian nationalist organization.[33]

That the Free Congress Foundation is a conduit for NED funds should itself be controversial. FCF leader Paul Weyrich is a political reactionary condemned even by some conservative Catholics for his support of the Society for the Protection of Tradition, Family and Property. This renegade neofascist Catholic sect is closer to the ideas of the Spanish Inquisition than current Vatican teaching.

Former Nazi collaborator Laszlo Pasztor[34] is a Hungarian emigre who was founding chair of the Republican Heritage Groups Council into which he recruited individuals of anti-democratic political heritage, such as the Fascist Bulgarian National Front and Romanian Iron Guard and Ukrainian nationalist Nazi collaborators. He works with a project sponsored by Weyrich and housed at the Free Congress Foundation building. Pasztor says that when he visited Hungary, he "unofficially" met with leaders of several new political parties, including the Hungarian Democratic Forum, MDF, a group where anti-Semitism still resonates. MDF has participated in NED-funded projects in Hungary. Pasztor is assisting NED grantees by translating and evaluating proposals by Hungarian and Czechoslovakian groups. In July 1989, Pasztor informed Weyrich of his involvement in obtaining "assistance for the anticommunist democratic opposition behind the Iron Curtain" from NED.[35]

Democracy Doublethink

Imagine the leaders of the Soviet Endowment for Perestroika or even the Swedish Endowment for Social Democracy claiming victory in U.S. elections as NED did in Nicaragua. It's not easy to imagine because public knowledge of such support would likely cause a scandal over violations of our sovereignty. U.S. law rightly prohibits foreign funding of U.S. candidates, and receiving such support, if discovered, would be political suicide.

Imagine more. Imagine a foreign endowment funding the *New York Times*, *Washington Post*, ABC, NPR, etc; funding major think tanks, the Republican and Democratic Parties, the AFL-CIO, the Chamber of Commerce, and an assortment of women's, student and cultural groups.

On May 15, 1991, Rep. Paul Kanjorski (D-Penn.) took to the House floor in an unsuccessful attempt to reduce NED funding. He accused NED of unaccountable and anti-democratic behavior in its foreign programs and heavy-handed tactics against congressional critics. "[I have] an internal [NED] memo," Kanjorski charged, "which indicates that staff members have identified my district, myself, and the makeup of my district. They then attempted to set a portion of my constituency against me because of my opposition to their N.E.D. position in prior congressional hearings." In 1986, for example, the Polish American Congress, an NED grantee, organized opposition to Kanjorski's anti-NED stance in his heavily Polish-American district.[36]

NED cannot be understood in ahistorical isolation. It is an increasingly important player in the longtime overt and covert project to make sure the leaders of other nations conform to U.S. critical standards, and to make democracy safe for the New World Order at home and abroad.   ●

28. Peter Eisner and Knut Royce, *Newsday*, March 1, 1990. On the Carmen Group, see William I. Robinson, "U.S. Overt Intervention: Nicaraguan 'Electoral Coup,'" *CAIB*, Number 34 (Summer 1990), pp. 32-35.

29. *Newsweek*, October 21, 1991; March 12, 1990; September 25 and October 9, 1989.

30. Chip Berlet and Holly Sklar, "The NED's Ex-Nazi Advisor," *The Nation*, April 2, 1990, pp. 450-52.

31. *CAIB*, Number 35, (Fall 1990), pp. 17-32.

32. Margaret Quigley, "Uncritical Coverage," *FAIR Extra*, December 1991, pp. 6-9.

33. *Ibid*.

34. Pasztor has misrepresented his past for years, but leading Holocaust historian Randolph L. Braham fully documented Pasztor's collaboration and conviction in the June/July 1989 issue of *Midstream*, pp. 25-28.

35. Berlet and Sklar, "NED's Ex-Nazi Advisor," *op. cit*.

36. Polish American Congress, Washington office news release, 1986.

DataCenter   464 19th Street, Oakland, California 94612 (415) 835-4692

THE "WAR ON DRUGS"

RICHARD HUTCHINSON

...the United States is faced with one aspect of insurgency in Latin America that offers the greatest threat but one which may yet provide U.S. with a weapon with which to regain the moral high ground we have appeared to have lost. There is an alliance between some drug traffickers and some insurgents... A melding in the American public's mind and in Congress of this connection would lead to the necessary support to counter the guerrilla/narcotics terrorists in this hemisphere. Generating that support would be relatively easy once the connection was proven and an all-out war was declared by the National Command Authority... Those church and academic groups that have slavishly supported insurgency in Latin America would find themselves on the wrong side of the moral issue... Instead of responding defensively to each insurgency on a case-by-case basis, we could act in concert with our allies. Instead of wading through the legislative snarl and financial constraints that characterize our security assistance posture, we could act with alacrity to the threat...we can begin to see the hemisphere as a whole and ultimately develop the vision that has been sorely lacking.

—Col. John Waghelstein, commander of the 7th Special Forces Group (Airborne), Fort Bragg, and commander of the U.S. Military Group in El Salvador in the early 1980s, in Military Review, professional bulletin of the U.S. Army Command and General Staff College, Fort Leavenworth

LTHOUGH U.S. intervention in Latin America carried out under the propaganda cover of the "War On Drugs" (WOD) faded from view during the U.S. buildup and war against Iraq, it never stopped. Now it is reemerging as a major focus. Major U.S. military aid to Peru has just been announced.

The War On Drugs is now the main justification for U.S. military intervention in Latin America. According to the Washington Office on Latin America, "As a result of the administration's Andean Initiative, presented to the nation in September 1989, the Andean region is now the primary recipient of U.S. military aid to Latin America... from a U.S. policy perspective the Andean region is the 'Central America' of the 1990s." The Andean Initiative projects $2.2 billion in military and economic aid for five years for Bolivia, Colombia and Peru.

The "counternarcotics" mission is prominently featured in three recent authoritative government documents: the Report of the Secretary of Defense to the President and Congress (January 1991), the 1991 Joint Military Net Assessment (March 1991) of the Joint Chiefs of Staff, and the National Security Strategy of the United States (the White House, August 1991). And in the sections on drugs, all talk almost exclusively about the Andean Initiative, cocaine and the border, rather than about Asia, the Middle East, or heroin. Counternarcotics, counterterrorism, and counterinsurgency are the three aspects of "peacetime engagement," or "low-intensity conflict" and categories used for the daily targeting of third world populations and movements.

The Pentagon's WOD budget now stands at $1.08 billion. This is only .5 percent of the total, but it represents an increase of 1000 times the 1981 level of $1 million. This budget is *in addition to* the Andean Initiative funding, administered by the State Department. Complementing the low-budget Special Forces operations, this is the high-tech, high-budget component of the drug war. It includes the construction of a region-wide, computer-controlled surveillance and intelligence-gathering system, run out of SouthCom HQ in Panama and linked with files in Washington, and patrols by numerous ships and aircraft. A Counter Narcotics Center has been created at CIA HQ in Langley, Virginia. Satellite surveillance and mapping is underway, AWACS radar aircraft are assigned, and ground radar are under construction in all three countries.

From the December 1989 invasion of Panama to August 2, 1990 the WOD was front and center of Pentagon operations and propaganda. What became known as the Andean Initiative had already been underway for several years however. U.S. AID and DEA counternarcotics programs in Peru and Bolivia were reported in 1984, as they ran into problems. In April 1986, Reagan launched the current drug war by signing one of his many secret national security directives, officially classifying international drug trafficking a threat to U.S. national security. That August, 170 U.S. troops and six helicopters deployed to Bolivia for Operation Blast Furnace, a bungled series of raids on cocaine labs. And the current higher-level Operation Snowcap was launched in 1987. This plan includes U.S.-supported helicopter strikes, training in counterinsurgency tactics, and the construction of permanent bases in the region.

Although it seems as if the same story about U.S. Green Berets operating in the Andes has been recycling for years, actually an important shift has recently taken place. Until the launching of the Andean Initiative, U.S. military aid to Peru, Colombia, and Bolivia took the form of training police forces and sending DEA (Drug Enforcement administration) troops. Green Berets, however, trained the DEA troops (and quietly trained the police). The change now is that the U.S. has established military-to-military relations, and is sending direct military assistance. U.S. Special Forces now train and direct armed forces units in all three countries. By fall 1989 there were 100 U.S. civilians and 50 Green Beret "trainers" working in Peru and Bolivia. The current estimate is that 200 U.S. military advisors are stationed in the Andes. Although the Pentagon must inform Congress of the exact number, Congress agrees not to tell the public.

Following the U.S. invasion of Panama, the Southern Command was planning a massive "hemispheric drug raid," but this was shelved during the war on Iraq. More Panama-style strikes

PLAZA ARMAS. AYACUCHO CITY—JORGE OCHOA. IMPACT VISUALS

remain a distinct possibility, but on a day-to-day basis the war in the Andes is being fought as a classic counterinsurgency war, now classified in Pentagon-speak as "low-intensity conflict."

The Addict Economies

THIS ESCALATING U.S. military intervention is set against a backdrop of extreme economic crisis in the region and IMF (International Monetary Fund) austerity programs in Peru and Bolivia, producing both great misery and popular revolt. The Andean countries are "junkie economies," dependent on the coca trade for their survival. In Peru, exchange controls were abolished as early as the late 1970s to attract coca dollars, and the Central Bank has made Peru as open as Panama for money laundering. The U.S. is not targeting the "narco-regimes," however, but rather poor peasant growers and rebel groups.

In Colombia, just days after Medellin cartel boss Pablo Escobar surrendered (to a luxury jail he had built himself), new propaganda in the U.S. declared that the Cali cartel was now a threat to Western Civilization, justifying

further U.S. military intervention. The Colombian regime does not consider the Cali cartel, whose style is discreet and business-like, to be the same kind of problem as the flamboyant Medellin desperados. Colombian military chiefs have frankly said that U.S. aid is being used to fight guerillas in the northeast, not drugs. It has been reported that U.S. Special Forces were responsible for the interception and killing of Medellin leader Rodriguez Gacha in December 1989. In Bolivia, peasant growers, supported by the national workers' federation, have mobilized against U.S.-led coca eradication. Bolivians are also protesting U.S. airbase construction, which they see as the "Hondurization" of their country, leading to large-scale intervention against increasingly rebel-controlled Peru.

As the War On Drugs intensifies, the coca industry is diversifying and spreading beyond the three core countries, like mercury being hit by a hammer. Coca labs are appearing in the Brazilian Amazon, and Brazil's military is carrying out Operation Calha Norte, or Northern Trench, stationing troops, increasing air and naval patrols, installing radar, and clearing people away from its borders with the Andean

countries. The Pentagon increasingly has a new rationale for military cooperation with all the regimes in South America to replace the old anti-Communist alliance.

Peru: Center Of Andean Counterinsurgency

CENTRAL TO THE aims of the War On Drugs is combating the revolution in Peru. Sendero Luminoso, which calls itself the Communist Party of Peru (PCP), a title which several small legal left groups also claim, now controls or holds dual power in 40 percent of the countryside, including the coca-growing Alta Huallaga Valley. Peru is 60 times larger than El Salvador. U.S. counterinsurgency experts agree that the regime is badly losing the war against the maoist guerrillas, and that Sendero could quite possibly take power. This is the real reason the U.S. has been increasing Green Beret training of Peruvian troops and building Vietnam-style firebases in the jungle. Sendero's own military assessment is that they are now moving from a strategic defensive to a stage of equilibrium, marked by mobile warfare with large units and decisive control of

U.S. SPECIAL FORCES IN COLOMBIA—JOE FISH, IMPACT VISUALS

the trunk of a car and their bullet-riddled bodies were found just hours later in the city morgue in Callao. The Peruvian regime is fighting a brutal counterinsurgency war. Over 20,000 people have been killed since 1980: the rebels' estimate is 35,000. Official tabulations to the contrary, the vast majority of those have been highland Indian peasants massacred by the Armed Forces. Peru has led the world in disappearances for four years in a row, according to the UN Commission on Human Rights. In Huanta, the soccer stadium is known as the Pinochet Stadium, the site of numerous mass executions by the armed forces between 1983 and 1986.

The 1990 U.S. State Department human rights report on Peru notes widespread summary executions, arbitrary detentions, torture and rape by the military, and adds that rape by security forces is so frequent to be considered common practice. Of course there are also widespread claims that Sendero Luminoso commits human rights abuses. These claims are used by the media to obscure the massive violence of the Peruvian regime, especially toward Peru's Indians. No matter to what extent these claims are true, they are no justification for ongoing state terror or U.S. intervention in Peru.

Behind the scenes there has been intense infighting in the U.S. government, in the Peruvian government, and between the U.S. and Peruvian governments over the terms of U.S. military aid. Peru, dependent on coca revenues, wants aid to combat the insurgency, with no strings attached. The U.S., wary of opposition to "another Vietnam" in the Andes, wants the counterinsurgency aid packaged as "counternarcotics" for domestic consumption. The U.S. used aid as a club to enforce its terms on the Peruvian regime. Fujimori has no organized political party and has appointed acting military officers to head the Defense and Interior Ministries, while military-control-

base areas. They are preparing for massive U.S. intervention, which they see as inevitable. Given the prospect of a rebel victory, large-scale U.S. intervention is certainly possible and steady escalation is already underway.

The U.S. is sending "more than 50 advisors, including Green Berets and Navy personnel," to Peru to train two combat battalions, create a river patrol, and upgrade helicopters and jets. The role of these trainers is not strictly academic. According to a Green Beret master sergeant assigned to SouthCom, quoted in *Army Times*, "School is one thing. These jungles are another... It is very difficult to properly train these armies to perform long-range recon patrols for drug targets without supervising them on at least their first few missions." Another article in the same issue, called "Vietnam ghosts haunt soldiers in drug fight," notes that "The long-range reconnaissance patrols that were the staple of Army special forces in Southeast Asia are again at the heart and soul of Green Beret operations in Latin America." U.S. forces, including State Deptartment-contracted pilots, have engaged in at least one large-scale battle with Sendero at the Santa Lucia base in the Alta Huallaga Valley.

After over a year of intense negotiations, the U.S. and Peru signed a new military aid agreement in May, pack-

aged as "counternarcotics." This is not deja vu: exactly the same announcement was made in April 1990, but the aid agreement was held up for a year as the new Fujimori administration took office in Peru. This $94 million package, which is for FY91, includes $34 million in military aid: the rest is economic assistance. Of the economic assistance, about two-thirds is balance of payments support, not development projects. With the terms worked out, an even larger FY92 aid package is likely to be approved soon by the Bush administration. Although this agreement has been a big story throughout Latin America, it was largely censored in the U.S. for months. The *New York Times* never reported on the initial May signing of the accord, and finally reported the story only when the administration rubber-stamped the Peruvian regime's "improving human rights record" and sent the aid to Congress for approval on July 31.

The U.S. must certify the Andean regimes' adherence to human rights and civilian control of the military under the terms of the Andean Initiative. The administration's certification for Peru is a cruel joke, coming as it does at a time when a series of major scandals have rocked the Fujimori regime, including Peru's "Rodney King:" a video camera caught police stuffing three youths into

led Emergency Zones now cover 40 percent of the national territory and 56 percent of the population. All spring and summer, while covering up this major leap in U.S. military intervention in Peru, the U.S. press has been full of stories demonizing the revolutionaries in Peru, thus serving to justify U.S. "assistance" to what is characterized as a beleaguered democratic regime.

The CIA-Drug Connection

FOR YEARS NOW, the Christic Institute has exposed the CIA's drugs-for-guns scam for arming the Nicaraguan contras. The systematic role of the U.S. and CIA in the global drug trade has been documented most recently in two new books, *Cocaine Politics* and *The Politics of Heroin*. This connection was forged in Italy and China during WWII, and has grown and deepened from Southeast Asia during the Vietnam War, to Latin America during the contra war and Southwest Asia during the war in Afghanistan, which is ongoing. So as the CIA now joins the War On Drugs, skepticism is essential.

Contra war veterans are now major players in the U.S. war in the Andes. U.S. ambassadors to Peru and Colombia have extensive covert operations resumes. Anthony Quainton, ambassador to Peru, was counterterrorism coordinator at the State Department in the late 1970s, and was U.S. ambassador to Nicaragua at the time of the CIA mining of the harbors in 1984. Morris Busby, just nominated ambassador to Colombia, headed a State Department office for assistance to the contras in 1987, and moved to counterterrorism coordinator at State in 1989. Air Force Lt. Col. David Rankin, air attache in El Salvador in 1984-85 during the contra resupply operation, had extensive ties with Secord's "Enterprise." Rankin now heads the State Department's Bureau of International Narcotics Matters (INM) air wing, a fleet of 53 copters and planes used in Bolivia, Peru, and Colombia. At least a dozen other contra war veterans are now in Peru, including retired Army Special Forces operatives Richard Meadows and Bruce Hazelwood. Meadows' official position in Peru is director of security at a palm-oil plantation near the Santa Lucia base. There is

also a direct connection to the infamous CIA proprietary in Indochina, Air America, which transported heroin during the Vietnam War. As of June, 1990, the company with the State Department contract for the International Narcotics Matters (INM) air wing was Corporate Jets, operating out of Ope-Locka, Florida under the name National Air Transport. According to the *New York Times*, after Air America was liquidated in the 1970s, "...some of the people who worked for Air America were hired by Corporate Jets and were involved in operations like the firefight in Peru." (The major firefight at Santa Lucia, April 1990.) No wonder the Peruvian people call the U.S. troops in Peru "Los Vietnamitas."

Special Forces And "Private Security"

THE 1980S BROUGHT a sharp increase in funding, troop levels and organization for Pentagon Special Operations Forces (SOF), as well as CIA covert action. The combined intelligence budget (for the CIA, DIA, NSA, NRO, etcetera) has quadrupled since 1980 to $35 billion a year. Despite the above-board escalation, the Reagan administration developed extensive "black" or top-secret networks: "off-the-shelf" capabilities to avoid public and Congressional scrutiny, as exposed by the Iran-contra scandal. One way this was done was to expand operations run through the Pentagon, thus avoiding Congressional oversight of the CIA. This modus operandi is bound to continue, and there is evidence that only the tip of the iceberg is visible when looking at U.S. intervention in Peru.

A factor of growing importance to U.S. low-intensity warfare is the role of private security corporations. From 1988 to 1991 the number of registered security companies operating in Peru jumped from 80 to 350, and 150 more are estimated to skip registering and paying taxes. Many of these firms are what they appear, armored transport and bodyguards for corporations and individuals, but others have further functions. The *Wall Street Journal*, for instance, recently profiled a former U.S. SWAT-team member who runs training sessions not only for businesspeople, but also police special forces.

How many "palm-oil plantation security directors" are former or current U.S. covert action operatives? The Wackenhut Corporation, the world's largest private security firm, operates in many countries, including Peru, and has its own antiterrorism division. This division, as well as Wackenhut's board of directors, is filled with former CIA, DIA, FBI and State Department directors and members. Wackenhut is widely thought to train and cooperate with both official and paramilitary groups throughout Latin America.

As "private" operations expand in scope, without any possible public oversight, there are those who advocate turning counterinsurgency over to the private sector entirely. Col. Rod Paschall, a retired Special Forces commander, has bemoaned two problems in low-intensity warfare: the low priority, and therefore poor personnel, assigned by the military, and the Vietnam Syndrome still infecting the public. Paschall seems to have Wackenhut in mind when he says, "An international corporation composed of former Western officers and soldiers skilled in acceptable counterinsurgency techniques would largely solve both of these Western counterinsurgency problems." William Casey would no doubt be impressed by this bold proposal for the off-the-shelf covert operations pulling the shelf up after them.

Exposing The Threat Factory: Drugs And Terrorism

WAGHELSTEIN'S MILITARY REVIEW article provides a smoking pistol demonstrating that the drugs rationale is nothing but a pretext for U.S. intervention. The flimsy creation, "narcoterrorist," has low credibility even in the armed forces: *Military Review* has printed a sharp rebuttal to this deception. In "The Myth of Narcoterrorism in Latin America" (March 1990), Captain Dan Meyer argues that "...the real danger is that use of the term will lead to an inadequate analysis of the problems posed by traffickers and insurgent groups... [A]ny analysis of an alliance between traffickers and insurgents must be based on the realization that each group has specific benefits in mind when it enters into such an agreement. These alliances are not easily categorized...the long-term

DataCenter   464 19th Street, Oakland, California 94612 (415) 835-4692

goals of the two groups contrast sharply..." So within the military itself, charged with fighting the War On Drugs, there are those who believe the "drug crusade" is based on a lie, and is leading to failure. In fact, through 1988 Secretaries of Defense Weinberger and Carlucci stated that it is not the appropriate function for the military to be involved in fighting drugs, and as recently as 1991 a SouthCom official said that it won't work.

According to a Peruvian supporter of the revolution, "The Communist Party of Peru has stated that the drug trafficking problem is a problem of social-political origin, and that the eradication and elimination of it is an issue that will be addressed after the seizure of power in the entire country, when the New State resolves the problem of corruption, exploitation and genocide of the peasants. Meanwhile, the Party will concentrate their main effort in the coca growing zones, which provide work on which 300,000 peasants depend, on protecting the peasants against the abuse and cruelty of the drug barons and the repressive government forces."

Edward Herman and Gerry O'Sullivan demonstrate that Western state terrorism, in official propaganda, is either defined otherwise or becomes "*anti*-terrorism," while the use of the category "terrorism" is reserved for "anti-Western forces." They document the interlocking government and private sectors of the terrorism industry, (the self-identified "anti-terrorists"). This explains how the U.S.-directed contras, along with the U.S.-backed death squad regimes of El Salvador and Peru, can be described as representing "liberty and democracy."

Why doesn't the press ever discuss addict regimes being "in an alliance with drug traffickers?" Bolivia has been dependent on the coca trade since the Banzer dictatorship began in 1971. In the spring of 1991 it was announced that the UMOPAR drug unit in Bolivia trained by the U.S. for four years was being totally reorganized due to corruption. Corruption is also rampant in Peru, and the Cali cartel is integrated into ruling circles in Colombia. But a major DEA sting operation that would have arrested government officials in Bolivia, Colombia, and Mexico was called off by the CIA.

The real targets of the War On Drugs, despite sporadic efforts aimed at banking regulations or drug cartels, are poor peasants and guerillas in the Andes, and Black and Latino youth of the inner cities in the U.S. Low-intensity warfare, from Lima to Los Angeles, is counter-population war.

The penultimate narcoterrorists never get their hands dirty. According to Jacques Attali, President of the European Bank for Reconstruction and Development (of Eastern Europe), turnover from the world narcotics trade equals that of crude oil sales. It has been estimated as being worth $300 billion a year to the banks. A similiarly revealing *Time* article asserts that: "...drug barons launder as much as $100 billion a year in U.S. proceeds... The world's prosperity depends on a fluid and unfettered financial system, yet the lack of supervision is producing a large shadow economy... In the U.S. a money-laundering center can be spotted by the huge surplus of cash that flows into the local branch of the Federal Reserve System. In 1985 the Miami branch posted a $6 billion excess. But after several years of intense federal probes... [m]uch of the business went to Los Angeles, where the cash surplus ballooned from $166 million in 1985 to $3.8 billion last year."

Jefferson Morley quotes a federal prosecutor, who says "The modern gang doesn't rob banks, it buys banks," and observes that "...the captains of the cocaine economy are no different from the producers of beer, wine, liquor, semiautomatic weapons, cigarettes, phone sex, MTV, fluorocarbons or dirt bikes. They sell pleasurable consumption with varying degrees of alleged antisocial consequences. The cocaine economy is not an aberration in the national consumer economy but a microcosm of it." Morley takes this insight into the drug economy one step further to understand the War On Drugs. "The seizure of drugs—even if it does little to reduce use or availability—can be cited as proof of reinvigorated social and legal authority. It is a reliable law of drug capitalism: Drug profits are the tribute that drug regulators pay to drug entrepreneurs for the right to enforce drug laws..."

It has been pointed out that if the government was really concerned about drugs, they would focus on tobacco and alcohol. Tobacco is responsible for over 300,000 deaths annually in the U.S., and alcohol causes over 100,000, while contributing to another 100,000, including 40 percent of traffic deaths. Meanwhile, the total of deaths attributable to all illegal drugs combined is only 3,000-4,000.

The government-funded RAND Corporation decisively refutes the possibility of shutting down the cocaine trade by "going to the source."

RAND corporation economist Peter Reuter recently testified to Congress that, "Source country programs, whether they be crop eradication, crop substition or refinery destruction, hold negligible prospect for reducing American cocaine consumption in the long-run." Reuter shows that coca farmers receive less than 1 percent of the final retail price of cocaine, and that cocaine exporters and smugglers receive less than 15 percent. The Washington Office On Latin America explains that "[b]ecause over 85 percent of cocaine profits are made outside the source countries, source-country efforts will not drive up the retail price enough to significantly reduce cocaine consumption." According to this analysis, even if interdiction efforts were able to stop 50 percent of cocaine shipments from Colombia, the retail price of cocaine in the United States would rise less than 3 percent. No one has presented data to refute Reuter's analysis.

The Need For Opposition

OPPOSING U.S. intervention in the Andes is no longer optional for anti-intervention activists. This means taking on the propaganda campaign of the "War On Drugs." Although this is difficult, the government has made itself vulnerable. As Waghelstein makes clear, the reason the U.S. has resorted to the Big Lie of the War On Drugs is that they know the public would not support a major counterinsurgency campaign in the Andes if presented honestly. What is needed to stop the momentum, which is now leading to more Green Berets, more firebases, more helicopter gunships, and more massacres, is a public resistance movement that begins to change the terms of debate, and put the Administration on the defensive.   z

Panama: Laundering Casualty Figures

Gary Grass

When the U.S. invaded Panama a year ago, the *New York Times* gave its editorial approval, and its news columns have since provided regular support for a benign view of this venture. The article by Mark Uhlig in the Sunday News of the Week in Review, October 28, 1990 ("In Panama, Counting the Invasion Dead Is a Matter of Dispute," p. E2), rebutting charges of extensive, unreported civilian casualties, is a recent illustration of this pattern.

To avoid the political liability of significant U.S. casualties, the assault was designed for overkill: Panama's 3000 combat-ready troops, without tanks, air, or sea power, against the Stealth fighter bomber, Apache helicopters, Spectre gunships, tanks, artillery, and 24,000 troops. Only 23 GIs were reported killed, and the invasion was widely applauded in the U.S. But although the Pentagon announced early on that only 202 Panamanian civilians were killed, news sources like *60 Minutes* (September 30) presented claims — asserted by opponents of the invasion from the very beginning — that the real total may have been several thousand. (On the other hand, Panamanian *military* deaths were exaggerated; see sidebar, p. 11.)

With mainstream sources airing these claims, the Bush administration faced a threat of scandal. The *New York Times* has now reported twice on this matter, in each case calling into question claims and evidence that would taint the record. Its first story (April 1, p. A12) tilted toward official U.S. body counts, but blamed other, allegedly inflated figures on a lack of information and concluded by citing a human rights leader on the need for an investigation.

Uhlig's recent piece, on the other hand, attacked calls for such an inquiry. He presented the claims of wholesale slaughter as too preposterous for serious treatment. He reported only one side of the debate in detail, claiming acceptance of the official story by many organizations and telling readers 7 times in 15 paragraphs that evidence of unreported deaths was lacking. Uhlig never suggested that the unavailability of much hard evidence was in fact a result of an official coverup.

Rules of Evidence

What counts as evidence? Hundreds of witnesses gave testimony to human rights groups, leading them to believe that thousands of people had been killed.

Panamanians have testified that U.S. troops fired indiscrim-

inately at civilians, rocketed and bombed non-military targets, set fire to homes, bludgeoned injured civilians to death and mutilated their genitals, carried out summary executions, and then covered up their atrocities by confiscating and destroying the physical evidence and intimidating potential witnesses. All this was ignored by Uhlig, irrelevant to his simple body-count issue.

Yet this testimony, along with signs of a coverup, is potentially damning. The press had only sanitized glimpses of the invasion. The Red Cross was denied access to battlefields like El Chorrillo for several days. Ambulances were fired upon despite their markings, and hospitals were occupied and made the site of arrests, so that fearful wounded would not enter. A Panamanian official complained that his team was "not allowed to enter the morgues until ... the corpses were putrefied." Another witness said U.S. troops were "paying a man six dollars for every cadaver" he brought them for burning. A doctor from Santo Tomás Hospital charged that "When the U.S. took control of the hospitals ... lists and registries disappeared." Further admissions went unrecorded. He and colleagues "personally took dozens of children to the [children's] hospital," which subsequently denied receiving them.

These witnesses, and hundreds more, spoke despite fear of military or governmental repression. Nine of the ten doctors on duty at Santo Tomás on December 20 were arrested, fired, or driven into hiding. A pro-government medical ethics organization was revived to assist with a broader purge. Many journalists reported the roundup of anyone fingered as Norieguista. A National Lawyers Guild investigation found that some Panamanians had buried their relatives in secret to avoid repression. Even so, the Red Cross received upwards of 1500 reports of missing relatives.

AP / Wide World Photos

Residents of El Chorrillo picking their way through the rubble caused by the "surgical precision" of the U.S. bombing.

Gary Grass is Executive Director of the Latin America Studies Council of Wisconsin. (The information in this section not otherwise referenced, may be found in: *Report of the Independent Commission of Inquiry on the U.S. Invasion of Panama* [New York, 1990]; *Americas Watch Report: The Laws of War and the Conduct of the Panama Invasion* [New York, May 1990]; and *CODEHUCA Report: Exhumations In Panama: Breaking the Silence* [San José, September 1990].)

While Uhlig dismissed these details as unsubstantiated or failed altogether to report on them, he repeatedly accepted and promoted countering views without evidence. The Southern Command (SouthCom) held all the registries of local hospitals and morgues which might be used in determining how many died. The Commission for the Defense of Human Rights in Central America (CODEHUCA) reported that U.S. Embassy and SouthCom officials refused to provide any information whatsoever. SouthCom also kept what *Newsday*'s Patrick Sloyan called "a secret record" of videotapes and photographs logging the invasion (quoted by Helen Thomas, UPI dispatch, January 31, 1990). This was so restricted that even U.S. Representative Charles Rangel was denied access to invasion footage shot from Apache helicopters. When exhumations were made, the U.S. demanded autopsies *not* be performed. Meanwhile the Panamanian government did not cooperate with exhumations and inquiries. This conduct—telling evidence of inordinate bias—was all of no interest to Uhlig.

Near the end of the article, Uhlig stated that residents of El Chorrillo "accused Noriega forces of starting the fires that destroyed most of the barrio." Although Uhlig was quick to cite Americas Watch for accepting a death toll under a thousand, he failed to note that Americas Watch dismissed this report on the origin of the fires as unsubstantiated.

Hysterical Victims, Sober Authorities

Instead of reviewing the case for each side, Uhlig set up the familiar contest between emotion and reason. On one side was Isabel Corro Rodríguez, the founder of the Association of the Families of the Fallen, the only dissenting voice selected by Uhlig. She was presented as an emotional woman who lost a Norieguist father in the invasion, and was quoted in generalities, basing her estimation of 4,000 dead on "the amount of destruction" and drawing a parallel with the Holocaust. The *Times* credited her with little support except from other victims, even though dozens of church, human rights, and popular organiza-

The Preppy Pirate

Mark Fried

At approximately 4 p.m. on May 1, a crypt containing the remains of Panama's national hero, Gen. Omar Torrijos, was opened, and his ashes were stolen. In an arm's-length account characteristic of Panama's post-invasion "free press," the daily *La Prensa* reported: "It was known that the person who looked after the Torrijos remains made a statement to the effect that the theft could have been committed by two white-skinned persons with a foreign accent…."

Guillermo Endara, the corporate lawyer who began his term as Panama's president at the U.S. Army's Fort Clayton on the eve of last December's invasion, was in Washington at the time and had no immediate comment. Neither did George Bush. But as with so many things, the president may know more than he lets on.

For many if not most poor Panamanians, the figure of Gen. Torrijos is closely identified with the nation itself. Torrijos's 1968 coup d'état brought an end to decades of white minority rule. (Endara personifies the return of that oligarchy on the coattails of the U.S. Army.) He guided Panama out of the thinly veiled colonialism in which it had languished ever since Washington engineered the country's independence from Colombia in 1903. Torrijos was influential in helping the Sandinista Revolution reach victory. Most importantly, he convinced the United States to return the nation's only significant resource: the Canal.

Torrijos died in a mysterious plane crash in 1979, a year after he retired as head of state. Many Panamanians attribute his death to the CIA, and to the Agency's primary contact in Panama, Manuel Antonio Noriega. Torrijos's body was placed in a monument-like mausoleum on Fort Amador, the joint U.S.-Panama military base at the mouth of the Canal. (Torrijos often said he did not want to enter the history books, only the Canal Zone.) And his home in downtown Panama City was turned into a museum with all the characteristics of a patriotic shrine.

During the first hours of the U.S. invasion, the Torrijos Museum was bombed from the air. The precision of the attack left little doubt as to the intended target; the homes and gardens on either side were untouched. Then relatives of the general began receiving phone calls from persons who threatened to desecrate his tomb. On February 17, his family exhumed his body, had it cremated, and deposited the ashes in a crypt in the National Cemetery, from where they were eventually stolen.

Torrijos was not the first enemy of the Empire whose remains were disappeared. Mexican revolutionary Pancho Villa's grave was pillaged a few years after his assassination in 1923, and the head removed from his

body. The head was given up for lost until recently, when a group of retired businessmen in El Paso discovered the unpublished memoirs of a deceased local rancher. As Mark Singer reported in *The New Yorker* last fall, the rancher claimed to have known the man who robbed Villa's grave. The operation, the man told him, was financed by a 150-year-old secret society at Yale University, the Skull and Bones Society.

Skull and Bones is open only to the elite of the elite. Many of the original OSS and CIA operatives were recruited from its ranks. George Bush is a member. The Apache Tribe waged a long and ultimately unsuccessful lawsuit to retrieve the skull of their legendary leader Geronimo from the Society's headquarters on the Yale campus. The El Paso businessmen are convinced Villa's head lies in this trophy room of the old Yankee oligarchy. They hope to convince Bush to return the head as a gesture of good will towards Mexico….

In 1671 British pirate Henry Morgan captured Panama City for 28 days of looting and pillaging. When he tired of the killing, he burned the city to the ground. Our twentieth century Morgan is a kinder, gentler buccaneer. There is something terribly preppie about the theft of Torrijos's remains, somehow appropriate to the president's persona. And it would certainly be in keeping with his cavalier devastation of Panama. But as with all of Bush's adventures, we'll never know for sure.   ●

Editors' Note: The New York Times *mentioned once the fears of members of Omar Torrijos's family that his remains might be disturbed (March 29, 1990, p. A4), but when his ashes were, in fact, stolen, the* Times *failed to report the event.*

UPI / Bettmann Newsphotos

President Carter and General Torrijos, as crowds celebrate the "return" of the canal, Panama City, June 1978.

Mark Fried is the editor of *NACLA Report on the Americas*. This piece is from an article which appeared in the June 1990 *NACLA Report* and is printed with their kind permission.

tions all shared her views. Uhlig dismissed Ramsey Clark, whose commission has steadfastly concurred, as having "*suggested soon after* the invasion that Panamanian deaths *could* reach into the thousands" (emphasis added). In fact, Clark and others made fact-finding trips to Panama, after which they reported that the deaths *did* reach into the thousands.

On the other side, Uhlig accepted SouthCom assurances that "all victims of the two gravesites uncovered by Corro's group had been identified and registered before burial" — a matter not at issue, though SouthCom originally maintained that civilian casualties amounted to 84 and denied the presence of mass graves. In fact, a mass grave at the Jardín de Paz cemetery was opened by the U.S. shortly after the invasion, when it was discovered a GI had been interred there by mistake. The 123 Panamanians also there were tossed randomly back into the pit. Only several months later was the grave reopened and the Panamanian bodies identified and registered. SouthCom's du-

AP / Wide World Photos

Bulldozer covering up the mass grave at Jardin de Paz, December 31, 1989. According to AP caption, "no further information regarding the victims was available."

Elusive Numbers, Handy Facts

Mark Uhlig had a problem with the military casualties, too. His October 28 report cited 314 Panamanian soldiers killed. He called the figure part of the "final official American estimate of casualties for the invasion, released by the United States Southern Command on January 11." However, Uhlig apparently forgot that last March SouthCom abandoned that "final" figure as significantly overstated. A *LOOT* reader, Bill McCallum, sent a letter to the *Times* (unpublished), enclosing a March 27 *Los Angeles Times* article by Douglas Jehl, which reported that the "Southern Command said it now believes that the actual casualty figure for Panamanian forces was about 50...." McCallum noted that the correct figure had been mentioned once in a Tom Wicker column, but nowhere else in the *Times*.

There is also a question to what extent Uhlig has relied on the research of fellow correspondents. *LOOT* reader Julian C. Holmes wrote a letter to the *Washington Post* complaining that it had ignored the September 30 piece on *60 Minutes* that suggested Panamanian casualties may have been in the thousands. The *Post* Ombudsman, Richard Harwood, replied to Holmes October 18 with this brief note: "The *Post* considered the CBS report on civilian deaths in Panama to be erroneous and without substantiating evidence. Our most recent exploration of the subject is contained in the enclosed unpublished report from our Central American correspondent, Lee Hockstader."

The report, which went over the Washington Post Foreign Service wire October 3, contains almost all the material found in Uhlig's October 28 article, some of it in strikingly similar fashion. Hockstader wrote, for example, "Most human rights groups, including Americas Watch and Physicians for Human Rights, say there is no evidence to support the assertions of Corro and others, including former U.S. attorney general Ramsey Clark, that thousands of Panamanian civilians died in the invasion. The groups generally calculate that about 300 to 400 civilians died amid a total of 500 to 700 Panamanian fatalities. ... The Roman Catholic Church here has said it figures 673 Panamanians died in the invasion." Uhlig wrote, "But the general tally of 300 to 700 Panamanian dead has been supported by a vast majority of human rights and religious groups ranging from Americas Watch to Physicians for Human Rights to Panama's Roman Catholic Church. Pointing to the destruction of El Chorrillo, some analysts, including former Attorney General Ramsey Clark, suggested soon after the invasion that Panamanian deaths could reach into the thousands. Yet despite frequent repetition in some news reports, virtually no evidence has been advanced to support such a claim."

Of course, Uhlig changed "most" human rights groups to "a vast majority" of them, and he changed "no evidence" to "virtually no evidence." But, one does have one's pride of authorship.

—William H. Schaap

plicities simply went unreported, and Uhlig improperly credited its view with the support of a "vast majority" of human rights groups.

Uhlig never explained why the body count was important, except in terms of the *60 Minutes* piece generating "what one columnist described as 'a potential scandal of Watergate proportions.'" But to others, the hundreds of acknowledged deaths were scandalous enough. The victims' families are simply pleading for recognition of their losses. The victims' fates are uncertain or unacknowledged, their bodies lost or treated like refuse, their plight ignored by international public opinion, wrapped in what CODEHUCA called a "startling complicit silence." The stubborn insistence that so many did not die is another cruelty. It is as if they had never existed. ●

Another Mass Burial Uncovered

Mark Uhlig dismisses claims of mass murder in Panama for "lack of evidence." But evidence alone is sometimes not enough. In September, 1,500 skeletons were found in a single grave at the Dom Bosco Cemetery in Perus, Brazil, 35 kilometers from São Paulo (*Brazil Post*, September 18, 1990, pp. A1, A3). After more than a decade of suspicions which were not acted upon, and a bureaucratic battle over who would exhume the bodies—officially registered as "beggars"—many were found to have heart pacemakers, gold dentures, and bullet holes in their skulls. These facts strongly suggested that the bodies were not those of beggars, but of political prisoners who disappeared during the military repression of the 1960s and 1970s. Although Brazil's Torture Never Again Movement and the São Paulo Archdiocese Human Rights Commission have called for an investigation, a 1979 amnesty law prevents the relatives of victims from pursuing any charges for political crimes.

The prospects such an example raises for justice in Panama are not encouraging, to say the least. Need we mention that this story has yet to be covered in the *New York Times*?

—Ann Nocenti

DataCenter 464 19th Street, Oakland, California 94612 (415) 835-4692

LEGALITIES

THE FALLACIES OF "POLITICAL CORRECTNESS": I

BY JAMIN RASKIN

W E LIVE in a period much like the end of Reconstruction. The central social and political institutions have lost all interest in, and any energy for, interracial social progress. With social justice and equality fatigue setting in, it becomes both tempting and rewarding to tell people to shut up when they seek to hold the society to higher norms. Because the official motion of society is rightward and primitive emotions have been unleashed, it is easy for conservatives to label progressives nags and censors of people's true feelings. In this environment, affirmative action, the last vestige of the civil rights movement, becomes an eyesore and an irritant, the cause of ceaseless controversy. The main silencing mechanism for this freefall return to the old American baseline of racism and class power is the newly minted charge of "political correctness."

When the leaders of the Great PC-Hunt took their dogs out sniffing at the dawn of the 1990s, their hunger for blood led everyone to think that their prey—political correctness—was really out there. But "political correctness" does not exist, and has never existed, as a body of political ideas. It is not an ideology, like socialism, liberalism, or nationalism, nor is it an organized (or disorganized) social movement. Nor is it a world view, a moral philosophy, a partisan organization, an intellectual trend, or even an academic faction. As a description of political ideas, "political correctness" expresses, literally, nothing. It is an empty vessel of a signifier into which meaning is poured on a purely expedient and ad hominem basis.

To the extent it had any referent prior to its media-made infamy, "politically correct" was a low-level, self-deprecating in-joke among leftists, who sometimes teased one another for confusing radical gestures with radical politics. When I was in college, we used "politically correct" semi-affectionately to describe people at anti-Contra aid rallies who pronounced "Nicaragua" as if they were gargling. (It always struck me as funny to pronounce Central American countries with a Spanish lilt but France and Germany without any trace of an accent at all.)

"Politically correct" thus applied, in a gently reproving way, to people who thought of radical political engagement as the willingness to adopt puritanical language protocols and strike dramatic poses. "PC" people—"progressive" one day, "deconstructionist" the next—were little concerned with the actual consequences of right-wing power in the state; they wore the right buttons but never put their minds

or bodies or lives in the pathway of militarism, repression, and social control. In this sense, "political correctness" described a frozen politics of empty gestures: the "politically correct" were not being faulted for being too radical, but for being too "liberal," that is, having a surplus of preachy self-righteousness but a deficit of analysis and courage. The term's implicit critique was that a person's politics were not ethically serious, and therefore not radical enough.

Outside of that internecine and esoteric context, "politically correct" had no general currency and implied no set table of political positions. The term was thus ripe for the taking by conservative pundits, always searching for the perfect epithet for those who champion freedom and equality. (In the mid-1980s, the witless *National Review* tried to popularize the term "hive" to describe those now tagged "PC," but the word never caught on.) Enforcers of today's brittle status quo now employ "politically correct" to describe any political position which disputes the soundness of our economic life, the validity of the assertion that racism and sexism no longer influence our society, the infallibility of corporate power, the nobility of right-wing culture, the value of militarism, or the wisdom of any given policy of the Reagan-Bush tenure. If your politics are not Republican and you let them out of the closet, you risk the wrath of the anti-PC party.

In its conservative reincarnation, "political correctness" has also come to mean a sweeping, coercive, and official conspiracy to propogandize student bodies and the body politic. This is a most remarkable proposition given the fact that the American Right has been in power for the last 11 years and has worked its ideological will at every level of society (with the possible exception of the church) beyond government. The winds of reaction have blown like a tornado through the business corporation, the workplace, the media, Hollywood, the courts, and indeed the university. Mindful of the fact that social ideology is skewed way to the right, PC-handlers are careful never to examine the real ideological content of American institutions, especially the university.

A number of recent studies, including John Trumpbour's *How Harvard Rules* and Jonathan Feldman's *Universities in the Business of Repression* (both South End Press), document beyond any reasonable doubt the way in which the military-corporate-academic complex shapes American colleges and universities. Next to these empirical studies, the flighty meditations of Allan Bloom or anecdotal exaggerations of Dinesh D'Souza simply vanish into thin air. For example, some college teachers may fetishize the female pronoun in class, but the stark reality is that university faculties are still overwhelmingly dominated by men. Defense and CIA research grants are the lifeblood of many university departments. Right-wing corporate foundation money, such as that which flows from the deep pockets of the Olin Foundation, continues to drive academic thought and research ever rightward. Drop by any college class-room discussion of affirmative action in which young white men are present, and you will quickly find that there is no "politically correct" liberal orthodoxy in place.

It is therefore important for the PC-paladins never to define the meaning of "political correctness." The term works only as a polemical weapon, not a term of serious analysis. It sits there like a bludgeon, ready to be picked up when anyone dares question the status quo or uses the great unmentionables of the Bush period: "racism" and "sexism." Thus, in an impressive turnabout, while "political correc-ness" purports to describe censorious language or policies, it is in fact intended to render unspeakable and unthinkable whole categories of belief about power.

By not specifically defining the content or context of PC, its propagandists are free to base their campaign on pure falsehood and sophistry. The central falsehood is that the rights of conservatives and their allies are being vio-lated by liberals. The sophistry is in the conflation of the fact that conservatives and their allies have rights with the implication that conservatives and their allies are right. The coordination of the falsehood with the sophistry produces the image of an embattled, discriminated-against minority courageously fighting to tell the truth against liberal government censors run amok. This image is an utter fan-tasy which reflects (depending on the commentator) either pure paranoia or the conscious strategy of roping off race, class, gender, sexuality and power as unmentionable topics.

Although "political correctness" is clearly a term of abuse intended to silence, it is important to analyze the falsehood and sophistry which it is built on and which it carries in its train, for many people have fallen for the trick. To begin with, it is perfectly obvious that the complaint about conservatives' rights being violated is, at every turn, fallacious. The following passages, taken from the most coherent PC-diatribes, are grouped so as to illustrate the four basic PC fallacies.

PC Fallacy #1: Where There's Silence, There's Censorship

(A) "*Students censor even the most ordinary of opinions. Nicole Stelle, a Stanford junior, spent this past semester working and studying in Washington, and found it easier to be a liberal in Republican Sen. Robert Dole's office than a conservative in Stanford. 'If I was at lunch [in the dorm] and we started talking about something like civil rights, I'd get up and leave ...I knew they didn't want to hear what I had to say.*" (Newsweek, "*Taking Offense,*" December 24, 1990.]

(B) "*During the panel discussion, [Jeffrey] Shesol said that he'd like to tell new students at Brown to 'speak out on as*

many things as you can,' but 'unfortunately, I'd have to tell you that it all depends on your point of view. There are some things that are simply not discussed here. For in-stance, Shesol added, affirmative action and the man's role in abortion. 'It's a climate,' he said, 'something you pick up as you sit through class.'" [Nat Hentoff, "*Gregorian's Chant,*" April 13, 1991, The Washington Post]

(C) "*In the September issue of the American Bar Asso-ciation's Journal, Geoffrey Stone, dean of the University of Chicago's law school and hardly a conservative, says of the ambiance on certain places of higher learning: "Anyone who disagrees or raises doubts runs the risk of being thought of as racist, sexist or homophobic.*" [Nat Hentoff, The Washington Post, September 21, 1991, "*Whitewashing Political Correctness*"]

THE THREE PASSAGES in Group (1) are typical of the common PC fallacy in which one person's completely voluntary decision not to speak or express herself magically becomes "censorship" by others. These three passages rep-resent, successively, cases in which a student (or professor) decides not to speak because: (A) she supposes others "didn't want to hear," (B) he thinks the overall "climate" is liberal or pro-choice, or (C) it is believed that he or she might "run[] the risk of being thought of as racist, sexist or homphobic." None of these cases has anything to do with censorship of free speech, and if the aggrieved tried to sue on a First Amendment theory, they'd be laughed out of court by judge, jury, and bailiff.

Consider Nicole Stelle's complaint that she "knew" her dorm-friends "didn't want to hear what I had to say" about civil rights. This cri de coeur has absolutely nothing in common with an actionable First Amendment violation or any kind of censorship as we know it. This is for two reasons. In the first place, whatever Stelle feels about them, her luncheon friends at the dorm are not to be confused with the state and their attitudes and reactions are not to be confused with state action.

Secondly, even if Stelle were at a public university and the people with whom she felt uncomfortable expressing her views were state-paid professors and administrators, there would be no free speech problem. A First Amendment violation cannot be established by showing that officers of the state would disagree with a citizen's speech. Otherwise, citizens would have a constitutional right to compel state officials to agree with them, a proposition that is without legal foundation and logically unintelligible.

Perhaps the point is not that Stelle's rights were violated, but that there was a chill in the air. Yet, even taken as an anecdote about the touchy protocols governing conversations between college students about race these days, Stelle's situation can hardly be described as problematic or affecting. Most college students, not afraid to have their own beliefs challenged, will rise to debate fellow students they know to hold contrary political views. Indeed, that moment of conflict embodies, perhaps, the very purpose of education: to engage the views of others and to change and refine one's own ideas. Even (charitably) assuming she is correctly reading the minds of her fellow students, Stelle is just being chicken. Given her experience working in the United States Senate, she should have more faith in the possibilities of dialogue and discussion.

This elementary point is not to minimize the insecurity students with unpopular views often experience in the classroom. But anyone who has been around a campus lately will scoff at the suggestion that the enemies of affirmative action are uncomfortable expressing themselves. From my observation, most conservative students are not members of vulnerable minority groups, but articulate and wealthier young people who have had excellent opportunities, like Senate internships, and will continue to get new ones, like Rhodes Scholarships.

Even if this were not true, the fear of those who remain silent rather than "run the risk of being thought of as racist, sexist or homphobic" is only a weak historical flip-side to the much greater fear of those who remained (and remain) silent rather than run the risk of being thought of as black militant, feminist, gay, lesbian, Communist, radical and so on. Indeed, if one has any respect at all for history, the fear that keeps Rhodes Scholar Jeffrey Shesol from talking about the man's role in abortion cannot be likened (with a straight face anyway) to the fear experienced by, say, African-American children sent to all-white schools in the 1950s, student radicals in the 1960s facing suspension or expulsion for their political views and activities, or gay and lesbian students today who would like to speak up about anti-gay bigotry but tremble at the consequences of coming out. There is no doubt that people often choose silence in reaction to informal social pressures, but the willful historical disorientation of the PC-hunt is dizzying.

For a political tendency which urges women and minority students to have "thicker skins" about racist and sexist language, the anti-PC movement's adoption of Stelle's shrinking violet approach to political discourse is paradoxical, at best. The PC-mongers invite us to believe

that women and African-Americans must endure the vilest of racist and sexist epithets hurled at them in the thick of night but that the rights of conservative students are violated because others might—horror of horrors—disagree with them in the light of day in the classroom. Leading PC-sniffer Charles Krauthammer should only take the hint he imparted to "PC" students: "If some students are offended by what flows from constitutional free speech, too bad. As part of their training for adulthood in an open society, offended students might actually be encouraged to respond and debate, rather than sulk and sue..."

All that Stelle and Shesol and their fellow PC victims have to do to end their horrific isolation and "censorship" is to open their mouths. They might summon up the kind of courage exhibited by Senator Dole a few years ago when he called George Bush a liar. But if these tender young conservatives lack the courage to speak, that is nothing the First Amendment can remedy.

PC Fallacy #2: Disagreement Is Censorship

(A) "When a few students last spring mocked Mt. Holyoke's Lesbian/Bisexual Awareness Week by proclaiming 'Heterosexual Awareness Week,' president Elizabeth Kennan upbraided them for violating the spirit of 'community.'" [Newsweek, "Taking Offense," December 24, 1990.]

(B) "There are professors—Al Gini of Loyola University in Chicago, for instance—who are taping their lectures after having been accused of racism or sexism or homophobia by the Jacobins who the AAUP says do not exist. That way the professors can defend themselves by playing back what they actually said. And professors—as at Princeton and Car-

leton College—have dropped courses after being pressured by the Robespierres and Madame DeFarges in the student body." [Nat Hentoff, The Washington Post, September 21, 1991, "Whitewashing Political Correctness"]

(C) *"Duke is a microcosm of the struggle over PC, which is being fought right down to the shelves in the campus bookstore...[Anti-PC Duke political scientist James David] Barber stalked into the political-science section one day last spring and turned on its spine every volume with "Marx" in its title—about one in seven by his count, a lot more attention than he thought it warrants—and angrily demanded their removal."* [Newsweek]

(D) *"A visiting professor at Harvard University Law School, distinguished in the area of contracts law, is berated by feminists for using the pronoun "he" to refer to judges and "she" to refer to secretaries during a hypothetical. His other crime is to quote a poem by Lord Byron about an indecisive woman at last consenting to the arms of her beloved. Feminists charge the quotation, used to illustrate the give-and-take of contract negotiation, is offensive to women in its suggestion that women consent to rape."* ["The Politically Correct Law School: Where It's Right to Be Left," ABA Journal, September 1991]

PASSAGES IN Group (2) illustrate the ubiquitous PC fallacy of confusing someone else's speech or someone else's negative reaction to your speech with censorship or repression of your own expression. In each case, the party charging "PC" doesn't like the speech they have elicited from others (A,B,D) or doesn't like someone else's ideas (C). None of these cases have to do with censorship.

Again, as a basic threshold matter, the First Amendment has no applicability to these vignettes because there are no state actors involved. Mt. Holyoke, Duke, Princeton, Carleton, and Harvard Law School are all private institutions. It is interesting that the conservatives who have always opposed the legislative extension of citizen rights to the private sector, such as the Civil Rights Act of 1964 (or 1990, for that matter) or the First Amendment rights of workers to call for secondary boycotts, now want to water down the boundary between public and private and create free speech rights in private schools.

That idea, carried out seriously and fully, is fine with me. First Amendment rights should be protected in private universities, which have, over the last 50 years, disciplined or expelled thousands of progressive students and discharged or discriminated against hundreds of leftist professors for reasons of conscience and speech. Furthermore, the First Amendment should be extended to private workplaces, where employers have always had the right to control and censor speech by employees, with minor exceptions for union organizing under the National Labor Relations Act. Free speech should also be extended to private shopping malls, which in most states maintain the right to arrest for trespass anyone who dares to pass out a leaflet or make a speech. The right to own socially useful property, like a university, a shopping mall, or a factory, must yield to the right of the citizenry to speak and interact, which is th great promise of democracy.

Come to think of it, free speech should be extended to the public arena, like the federal arts grants program, which now features Senator Jesse Helms as chief PC arts-censor, and federally-funded family planing clinics, where it is now against the law for doctors to even mention the word "abortion" to their patients. Do the PC-libertarians really agree that the First Amendment should be extended to these public programs, much less the "private" sector where their beloved corporate power rests so heavily on the silence of employees, consumers, and other citizens?

I doubt it. But even if they agreed to drop the "state action" requirement and apply the First Amendment to private universities, the cases classed in Group (2) would present nothing like actionable free speech violations. Case (A) presents a college president who "upbraided" two students for parodying sexual minorities. Censorship? Of course not. President Kennan has as much right to speak as they do. The First Amendment protects moralistic speech by university officials as much as it does feeble, literal-minded attempts at humor by students. Had these young wits been suspended from school—the kind of thing that happens regularly to anti-apartheid protestors who occupy presidents' offices—there might be a First Amendment issue. But here there is none. They can go right on speaking.

Case (B) recounts the agonizing tale of unnamed professors "who are taping their lectures after having been accused of racism or sexism or homophobia by the Jacobins who the AAUP says do not exist. That way the professors can defend themselves by playing back what they actually said."

The mythology buried in this story runs head-first into a national study done last summer which revealed that professors at only 5 percent of all colleges and universities reported any pressure, from left, right, or center, to change the political content of their classes. But let's assume for a moment that Hentoff is describing a true social crisis. If the professors are not in fact saying racist, sexist, or homophobic things, then they have nothing to worry about. If they are saying racist, sexist, or homophobic things, then they still have nothing to worry about because there is no known case of a professor being fired or demoted because of racist, sexist, or homophobic statements or beliefs. (This is in sharp contrast to the well-known history of universities firing radical professors during the 1950s, 1960s, and beyond.) Thus, the complaint here must relate to the fact that students are expressing their own views. But one would have thought that this was not something to be feared but the very purpose of education. There is no guarantee that statements by a professor will be unthinkingly accepted by all students and there is also no guarantee that professors will not be misunderstood. These are professional hazards.

If some professors in fact drop their courses after being "pressured by the Robespierres and Madame DeFarges of the student body," then they are clowns and idiots for doing so. But I doubt that this has ever happened in the real world, as opposed to PC make-believe world. Did it happen? What are the facts? Hentoff, like so many other PC-propagandists, leaves us completely in the dark with these murky charges. Notice also his use of the slippery word "pressured." What does that signify? What actually happened? If any professor were ever to drop a course because some student didn't like it, the fault would be completely the professor's own. If students threaten a professor with violence or harassment, then they should be criminally prosecuted (not appeased). But, otherwise, Hentoff's claims are bombastic and wildly overblown. If there are young "Robespierres and Madame DeFarges" roaming around on campus, they carry no guillotines in their backpacks.

Case (C) demonstrates further the upside-down worldview of PC paranoids. Professor Barber, you will recall, became so frustrated with PC ideology that he "stalked into the political-science section [of the campus bookstore] one day last spring and turned on its spine every volume with "Marx" in its title—about one in seven by his count, a lot more attention than he thought it warrants—and angrily demanded their removal."

Well, now. Finally, at long last, we have an example of would-be censorship, but it comes from one of the avowed enemies of political correctness. The activist Professor Barber wants to impose his politically incorrect anti-Marxism on his students, "angrily" demanding the removal of one-seventh of the books in the campus bookstore—way too many on Marx, he thinks! How many would be the right amount for Professor Barber? What's the right proportion of books on Freud or Rousseau? What about Allan Bloom or Leo Strauss? What if the reason there are so many books on Marx is because no one is buying them any more? What if the book doesn't have "Marx" in the title but has significant chapters on him? Do those count?

The absurdity of this vignette, loyally reported by the PC-watch at *Newsweek*, lies in the fact that it is meant to suggest the lengths to which God-fearing professors will go to combat the horrors of leftist political correctness. In fact, it evokes the sophomoric and utterly reactionary spirit of the PC-bashers, who in other places at other times might be burning books about Marx instead of just "angrily demand(ing) their removal." The real instinct for censorship remains with the Right, as this vivid and irredeemably petty anecdote unconsciously reveals.

Case (D) is boiler-plate PC-noise. Obviously, no censorship can be alleged here. Is there a problem with students paying attention to whether secretaries are always "she" and judges always "he"? I don't think so. Students are aware that if we want a society in which it is possible for men to be secretaries and women to be judges, changes may have to occur in the way we think and speak about men and women. Do students have the right to complain to the professor about the fact that all judges are "he"? Of course they do. Does the professor have to follow the students' requests to make some judges "she"? Of course not. He can go his merry way, and even call up the ever vigilant Nat Hentoff to complain about his feminist students. But there is no more of a guarantee that students will refrain from upsetting professors with anti-sexist speech than there is that professors will refrain from upsetting students with sexist speech.

I have found my own students to be remarkably cool about the gender of pronouns, and most of them even regard outright sexism with much equanimity or humor. In the last two years, I have heard only two complaints about

pronouns, and they were both about a casebook which used the masculine pronoun for judges and lawyers and policemen but the feminine pronoun for nurses, school-teachers, and so on. If this is all much ado about nothing, and language has nothing to do with ideology, then why don't the editors and professors simply reverse the assignment of gender to these roles? At the very least, they should stop their sobbing when they occasionally get called on their stubborn addiction to sexual stereotype.

Merits aside, the real intention of retelling boring stories like (D) is to undermine feminism and delegitimize attempts to expose and politicize the sexism embedded in academic discourse and legal parlance. One may agree or disagree with the premise that hundreds of years of sex-segregated education and male-dominated legal institutions have combined to create a gendered language of legal pedagogy. But why would one want to stifle the discussion? Not having the discussion is one way to decide things in favor of the party in power.

PC Fallacy #3: The Senate Censors When It Doesn't Consent

(A) "If Carol Iannone had been a regular contributor to the Nation *or the* Village Voice, *with a couple of degrees from an obscure and undistinguished school, her present critics would have been silent. But if the real Iannone is sent down because of her views, this Senate action will have told other independent professors down the line to censor themselves if they aspire to official recognition."* [Nat Hentoff, July 8, 1991, Washington Post]

(B) "The issue at stake in the Iannone nomination is whether it will be impermissible in this country to say such a thing ["that several books authored by blacks have been honred with awards not on merit but as a form of literary reparation."] Rejection would mean that the public discussion of racial bias will be regulated by the liberal establishment. The discussion of discrimination against minorities is highly encouraged. The discussion of discrimination in favor of minorities is highly dangerous: It may be deemed such an act of deviance as to render the discussant unfit for public office." [Charles Krauthammer, "Clarence Thomas and the Liberal Orthodoxy," The Washington Post, *July 12, 1991*]

(C) "[Clarence] Thomas is a living threat. His confirmation would repeal the current official recognition of the civil rights establishment as the sole legitimate representative of black people in America...Most important, it would mean that, black or white, rich or poor, even the politically incorrect can aspire to serve on the highest court in the land." [Charles Krauthammer, "Clarence Thomas and the Liberal Orthodoxy," The Washington Post, *July 12, 1991*]

THE QUOTES IN Group (3) form a more dangerous and grown-up variant of the juvenile PC fallacy found in Group (2). Here, the fallacy is that, by exercising its constitutionally designated powers of advice and consent in a way the writer (and the Republican Party) disagree with, the United States Senate engages in censorship of the views of the nominee for high office or the Supreme Court. This fallacy emerges from an operation conducted like a three-card monte. First, the elusive "political correctness" is established, by which the writer means something like progressive liberalism. Second, the nominee becomes the nemesis, indeed the antithesis, of "political correctness." Third, the Senate (or any other democratic body) cannot now question this nominee without imposing a bar of political correctness on him or her and, if it actually votes to reject the nominee, it has moved to censor and regulate public dialogue. Thus, an impressive trick has been pulled off: the Senate can only accept, but not reject, a "politically incorrect" nominee. Thus the meaning of the PC game is finally revealed: the "politically incorrect" becomes the politically mandatory.

Most PC-propagandists understand the basic political motivation of this sleight-of-hand, but Nat Hentoff sadly falls for the trick as he tries to perform it himself at home. His comic obtuseness is in full flower with regard to the nomination of Carol Iannone to the National Council on the Humanities, the right-wing non-tenured adjunct professor at NYU, who had written no books after 20 years of teaching English but had contributed a few vitriolic essays to *Commentary*, where she argued that African-American writers had been getting literary awards as a form of official "reparation." Restraining his tears for Iannone, Hentoff proclaimed that if she "had been a regular contributor to the *Nation* or the *Village Voice*...her present critics would have been silent." True, but had she been a regular contributor to the *Nation* or the *Village Voice*, she never would have been nominated to the post by President Bush in the first place. Would that have been censorship? And if she had, by some miracle, been nominated by President Bush (or a mythical Democrat in the future), all of the people chanting "PC witch-hunt" would be calling her a do-nothing, non-performing part-time academic with nothing to show for her decades hanging around the English Department.

Yet Hentoff charges ahead, claiming that if Iannone were to be rejected (she was, by a 9-8 vote of the Senate Labor and Human Resources Committee), the "Senate action will have told other independent professors down the line to censor themselves if they aspire to official recognition." This is idiotic. If Iannone had been confirmed, would that have told other "independent professors down the line to censor" any progressive views they have on race in order to get appointed to the National Endowment for the Humanities? Does Clarence Thomas's Supreme Court confirmation now tell "other independent professors down the line to censor" their support for affirmative action or abortion rights "if they aspire to official recognition"? If Hentoff and Krauthammer are not trying to create a constitutional right for anti-choice, racial conservatives to pass the Senate confirmation process, then they are simply whining about the Senate fulfilling its duties in a way they don't approve of. But the Constitution does not require the Senate to give its consent whenever Nat Hentoff and Charles Krauthammer think it's the PC or, excuse me, un-PC thing to do. (By the way, what is an "independent professor"? Someone who agrees with Hentoff? And what are the other professors "dependent" on—rational thought?)

Hentoff's self-righteous solemnities about liberal censors withholding "official recognition" of neo-conservatives are doubly appalling after 12 years of air-tight Reagan-Bush control of the federal government. This control has permitted an absolute stuffing of right-wing ideologues into every nook and cranny of the federal government. Take, for example, the National Council on the Humanities itself, the 26-member board which advises National Endowment for the Humanities Secretary Lynn Cheney on the distribution of hundreds of millions of dollars in grant money. Hentoff obviously knows nothing about the composition or activities of the real Board. Christopher Lukasik has shown in *In These Times* that "the council has been quietly packed with Republican cronies and conservative ideologues" over the last two administrations. It now includes: Bruce Benson, "an oil company president and head of the Colorado Republican Party," who with his wife donated more than $80,000 to the Republicans; Philadelphia socialite Margaret Ducker, another big Republican contributor; Helen Crawford, "a New Orleans oil and investment consultant" and yet another generous Republican contributor; Republican donor and "former Texas oil baron William Wright"; Michael Malbin, a former speechwriter for Defense Secretary Dick Cheney, the husband of NEH Secretary Cheney; and Harvey Mansfield, perhaps the most conservative professor in the Harvard Government Department who launched a ceaseless attack on the idea of a Women's Studies major and who was confirmed even as the Senate drew the line at the hapless Iannone. (The rejection of Iannone demonstrates that most liberal Democrats will stand up to the Reaganite steamroller only when they can base their opposition on meritocratic grounds.)

Can Hentoff seriously reconcile the Senate's confirmation of so many Republican Party activists and neanderthal academics to the Council with his suggestion that appointees will now have to genuflect before an altar of liberal political correctness? Can he really believe that the federal government is composed of people who have passed liberal litmus tests? If Hentoff is not completely paranoid, he is employing the language of censorship, official recognition and political correctness to mask his own rapid, though perhaps unconscious, drive to the Right.

Krauthammer also tries to insinuate that there is something improper about the Senate actually considering the qualifications and views of a presidential appointee. He says the "issue at stake" in the Iannone nomination "is whether it will be impermissible in this country to say" stupid and vaguely racist things. He says that if Iannone goes down, "public discussion of racial bias will be regulated by the liberal establishment," and that it "may be deemed such an act of deviance as to render the discussant unfit for public office." These scare words not only falsely imply that an official test for public office has been imposed, but remarkably suggest the very opposite of what power relationships are today. If anything, Iannone's platitudes about advantages and awards being conferred unfairly on blacks is now the norm in both the popular media and academic discourse. If "discussion of racial bias" is "regulated" by any "establishment," it is the conservative establishment which includes not only Mr. Krauthammer, but George Will, Patrick Buchanan, James Kilpatrick, Jeane Kirkpatrick, William F. Buckley, R. Emmett Tyrell, Evans and Novak, etc. ad nauseam: the endless parade of redundant and irritating commentators that dominate every Sunday morning talk show and every op-ed page in America.

On the Clarence Thomas affair, Krauthammer is equally deluded. "His confirmation would repeal the current official recognition of the civil rights establishment as the sole legitimate representative of black people in America," he says, then proceeding from the merely false to the astonishing with his melancholy observation that Thomas's confirmation "would mean that, black or white, rich or poor, even the politically incorrect can aspire to serve on the highest court in the land," as if Thomas would constitute some kind of a minority on the Court in terms of his consistently reactionary views. Excuse me, Mr. Krauthammer, but at this point, every justice on the Supreme Court is "politically incorrect" in your Orwellian terms. Was Thomas's confirmation really necesarry to prove that rightwingers hostile to affirmative action, abortion, and personal freedom could get on the Court? It is an outstanding accomplishment of the PC-provocateurs that they have been able to convince so many people that, in a state and an economy administered by right-wingers, it somehow pays to be progressive and hurts to be conservative.

PC Fallacy #4: Liberalism Is Totalitarianism

(A) *"PC is, strictly speaking, a totalitarian philosophy."* [Newsweek, *"Taking Offense,"* December 24, 1990.]

(B) *"Today...it is college presidents. deans, and faculties—not students—who are the zealots and enforcers of Political Correctness...Students and others just emerging from the grip of political and cultural dictatorship elsewhere in the*

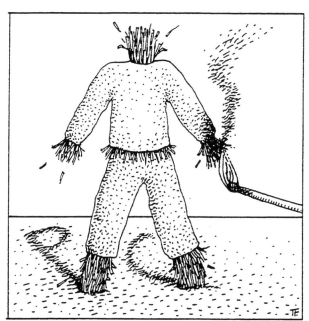

world must look with astonishment at the eagerness with which the people charged with managing American universities have embraced thought control, political re-education and other basics of totalitarianism." [The Wall Street Journal, *November 26, 1990]*

WITH THIS FOURTH fallacy, the anti-PC witchhunt advertises two important dimensions of its work: the desperate search for ever more dramatic claims to describe a mostly non-existent phenomenon and an essential contempt for historical meaning and memory. Whatever else PC may or may not be, it is not totalitarianism. That term was developed to describe Stalinist and Nazi societies, where the state controlled all aspects of social life, turned mass murder into public policy, destroyed dissent and public space, and elevated racism, anti-Semitism, nationalis,m and imperialism to official state dogma. Anyone who now uses "totalitarianism" to describe racial sensitivity workshops or the use of "he or she" exhibits far more hatred for liberalism than respect for the memory of those swallowed up by fascism and Stalinism. Indeed, it is important to say that those who make this connection between "PC" and totalitarianism are spreading a brazen lie.

Of course, to hold the PC-propagandists up to a standard of historical accuracy or moral proportion in their use of "totalitarianism" is to relocate their discourse from political polemic to honest critique. Seen simply as a rhetorical device, the use of "totalitarian" in this context is a classic Orwellian move. How to deal with people who, in a period of profound reaction, continue to raise questions about racism, sexism, anti-Semitism, militarism, and homophobia, the very historical ingredients of totalitarianism? Simple: call them "totalitarian" themselves. But, as we shall see in the next installment, it is the commentators carelessly flinging about "PC" and "totalitarian" who have always sought, and continue to seek, a more closed, repressive society.   z

Next Installment: PC Sophistry and Do Conservatives Really Support Free Speech?

The Tyranny of the Media Correct
The Assault on "The New McCarthyism"

By Laura Fraser

THE LATEST TREND IN INTELLECTUAL (AND NOT-SO-INTELLECTUAL) magazines, lest you have been asleep, is a widespread denunciation of the Tyranny of the Politically Correct. Featured on some half-dozen magazine covers, this new "crisis" on American campuses has taken on as many catchy new labels: "The New McCarthyism," "New Fascists," "New Orthodoxy," "Thought Police," "The Cult of Multiculturalism," and "The Hegemony of the Politically Correct."

The idea is that the academy is under siege by leftists, multiculturalists, deconstructionists and other radicals who are politicizing the university and threatening to undermine the very foundations of the Western intellectual tradition. These radicals, the theory goes, are the left-wing graduate students of the '60s who sneaked into tenured positions in the '90s and are now promoting an agenda of cultural relativism. Armed with affirmative action admissions and hiring, as well as new French literary theories, the politically correct hope to transform the university into a den of multiculturalism— silencing everyone who would dare dissent by calling them "sexist," "racist" or "anti-deconstructionist."

This critique of the politically correct was fathered by writers on the establishment right, notably Allan Bloom (*The Closing of the American Mind*), Roger Kimball *(Tenured Radicals)*, and, most recently, Dartmouth Review editor-turned-Heritage Foundation scholar Dinesh D'Souza *(Illiberal Education)*. It was nurtured by such organizations as Accuracy in Academia (an offshoot of AIM whose President John LeBoutillier and several board members were members of the World Anti-Communist League (an organization that, as Sara Diamond reports in **Z Magazine** (2/91), was "one of the most important coordinating bodies for death squad activities in Central America and elsewhere"). Only recently have mainstream magazines, including **The Atlantic, New York, Time,**

Laura Fraser is a freelance writer whose media criticism appears regularly in the San Francisco Bay Guardian.

DataCenter   464 19th Street, Oakland, California 94612 (415) 835-4692

Newsweek, The New Republic, as well as several newspapers (led by the **New York Times'** Richard Bernstein), followed suit to attack the multicultural movement with haughty condemnations of the "politically correct."

Despite this mad rush of publicity, the term "politically correct" is hardly new. When I was in college 10 years ago, the term "politically correct" was used to gently poke fun at someone who had gone a little overboard in their particular worldview. When another femi-

nist would tell me, for example, that you had to be a lesbian to be a real feminist, I could shrug and say she was being a little "too PC" for my tastes, which ran toward men.

Thus the political communities (whether feminist, anti-racist, gay, ecologist, etc.), with all due respect to each other, kept themselves from taking "PC" too seriously.

There were, however, serious issues that weren't considered "too PC." It wasn't being too PC to suggest to the administration that when a woman was sexually assaulted by a drunken frat guy, it wasn't just a case of boys being boys. Nor was it too PC to raise the consciousness of a white male professor of 20th Century American intellectual history who neglected to put any blacks or women on the syllabus. And it wasn't too PC to wonder if the hierarchical

structure of a text made it inherently male-dominant. It was just interesting.

Ten years later, admittedly, things have heated up on campus. The president's office at my alma mater was recently fire-bombed by a student who, according to the **New York Times,** was concerned with "minority interests." At Harvard Law School, a faculty member who supported a sit-in demanding the hiring of more minority and women professors was recently stabbed to death (though the possible connection

to "majority interests" was not made explicit in newspaper accounts). Clearly, as the academy's predominantly white male history clashes with the increasingly multicultural present, people are going overboard on all sides. A respectful and lively debate is indeed in order, and should eventually result in a more tolerant academy that has incorporated a broader range of human arts and experience.

Unfortunately, as things stand, only one side of this debate has made its way into the national media. From all the talk about the ideological hegemony of the multiculturalists, you might expect it would be the PC side that was getting all the print. But no. All the articles are by none-too-liberal men, usually white, defending the traditional academy. In these articles, the PC point of view is only described in caricature,

without the kind of depth that might count as either "objectivity" (highly valued among the anti-PCs) or honest intellectual inquiry. Most of the arguments follow a very similar line, drawing upon the same body of outrageous cases. The orthodoxy of the anti-PC articles is, in fact, quite remarkable.

It's the new Tyranny of the Media Correct.

The Media Correct (MCs) have painted a diverse group—**New York**'s John Taylor (cover story, 1/21/91) defines them as "multiculturalists, feminists, radical homosexuals, Marxists, New Historicists"—with broad strokes, lumping them together because of their "conviction that Western culture and American society are thoroughly and hopelessly racist, sexist, oppressive," as Taylor puts it. Then they are given a name—in **New York**'s case, "new fundamentalists" —because after naming them, it is possible to write about them monolithically, no matter how diverse their views. "They believe that the doctrine of individual liberties itself is inherently oppressive," says Taylor, as if there were a *they* and that *they* all shared such a belief. He seems to be safe in making those assertions, because he never interviews or otherwise presents an honest view of what any of them really think.

After creating this strange monolith of PCs, the Media Correct describe a broad range of issues which the PCs seem to threaten. Freedom of speech on campus is allegedly being threatened by changes in the literary canon, affirmative action, discussions of date rape, and, most improbably, new literary theories. Included, really, is anything that threatens the status quo; anything, as **Time** put it (1/1/91), that is a "reversal of basic assumptions held by the nation's majority." It's difficult to understand how a group whose sole purported unifying characteristic is diversity could be so orthodox in its beliefs. Nevertheless, as **Newsweek** put it (cover story,

12/24/90), "PC is, strictly speaking, a totalitarian philosophy. No aspect of university life is too obscure to come under its scrutiny." It's also hard to know how a philosophy that supposedly rejects hierarchy can be totalitarian, but leave that to the MCs.

The MCs then display their evidence of this new fascism—bizarre, isolated incidences that in themselves may be troubling, particularly ones limiting free speech on campus, but in total don't add up to a multicultural conspiracy. A lot of these examples are meant to be outrageous, but don't strike one as such. Dinesh D'Souza, in the March **Atlantic** cover story, writes that students at Holyoke College, University of California at Berkeley, Dartmouth College, and Cleveland State University all have ethnic course requirements; this is evidence that the "core curricula...are now under attack."

He seems scandalized that a Duke English class studies gangster books and movies and finds that organized crime is "a metaphor for American business as usual" (**Time** also uses that example; examples of the "new totalitarianism" seem to be scarce). D'Souza, along with **Time** and Richard Bernstein

in the **New York Times**, makes much of a Duke English professor's paper called "Jane Austen and the Masturbating Girl," without ever giving a hint about what the paper's about. (I'd love to read it.) The point of this exercise is to mock anyone who deviates from strict readings of, say, Nathaniel Hawthorne, and mark them with a big scarlet PC.

The idea that new multicultural texts might be included in the canon is also made fun of, by juxtaposing venerable texts with ones with silly titles. This game is played in almost all the MC articles. D'Souza writes of Plato's *Republic* and Machiavelli's *Prince* being replaced by *I, Rigoberta Menchu*, the political odyssey of a Guatemalan peasant woman, and Frantz Fanon's *Wretched of the Earth,* "a passionate argument for violence against colonial oppression." John Taylor in **New York** frets that "instead of models of clarity like E.B. White, essays such as 'is not so gd to be born a girl,' by Ntozake Shange" are assigned. **Time** imagines a literature class that "equates Shakespeare and the novelist Alice Walker, not as artists but as fragments of sociology." And **Newsweek** worries that Rabelais is being dropped for Toni Morrison. None

of the articles quotes any real live professor who would actually make these swaps, or gives any respect to multicultural authors or the idea that our understanding of humanities may be broadened if we include more of humanity.

Many of the articles decry affirmative action in admissions or hiring, describing how blacks with lower SAT scores are getting into school over whites and Asians with high scores, and how black, Latino and women professors are increasingly sought by schools. There's no nod to the idea that SATs might not be the only indicators of ability, or that they are biased toward whites (as has been argued extensively).

The articles also dismiss Afrocentric theories—which claim that much of Western culture was borrowed from African sources—out of hand, and characterize their existence as the "most problematic" aspect of PC, as **Time** put it. Nowhere is there evidence of right or wrong, or a confidence that if wrong, other academics would debunk the theories. Both affirmative action and Afrocentric materials are described in tones that could only be used by someone who feels his culture is inherently, perhaps genetically, superior.

Finally, in decrying semiotics and deconstructionism, the MCs lament that PCs "deny the notion of objective reality," as D'Souza puts it. Richard Bernstein sees this as the worst the PCs have to offer—"some even question the very notion that there is such a thing as disinterested, objective scholarship." But before there were PCs, did academics always agree on the objective meaning of, say, James Joyce's *Ulysses*? Has there always been one way to interpret a book? One truth?

The MCs seem to think so. That truth is the truth of the white male establishment, which, incidentally, still holds the reins of power in the universities, and is scared of giving even a little bit away. MCs must also believe that their articles—which are full of generalizations, one-sided accusations and paranoias (not to mention racism, sexism and anti-deconstructionism)—are also objective, also the truth.

Hegemony? New McCarthyism? New Fascists? Hmmm.❑

The "Myth" of Racism

The movement against the "New McCarthyism" often treats discrimination as a PC myth. "Students and university administrators often behave as if the civil rights and women's movements of the 1960s and '70s never existed," wrote Amanda Foreman in a **New York Times** op-ed. "Every setback, every racist or sexist incident is seen as proof that intolerance is pervasive."

That intolerance is pervasive in our society was documented by a survey released early this year (**Washington Post**, 1/9/91). In the University of Chicago's National Opinion Research Center survey of racial attitudes in the U.S., non-black respondents showed widespread prejudice: 53 percent thought African-Americans were less intelligent than whites; 51 percent thought them less patriotic; 56 percent believed them to be more violence-prone; 62 percent said they were lazier; and 78 percent said they were more likely to "prefer to live off welfare" and less likely to "prefer to be self-supporting." Majorities expressed similar prejudices against Latinos, and sizable numbers held the same views about Asian-Americans.

One might expect such dramatic confirmation of racial prejudice in the U.S. to be the subject of extensive commentary, including an examination of the media's role as the main source of information about minorities for most whites. But the study did not spark a major discussion in the press—commentators as a group seem more interested in denouncing calls for multicultural curricula as the "New Tribalism" than in criticizing discriminatory attitudes as the same old racism.

—FAIR

National Security Education

Title VIII of the 1992 bill contains the "National Security Education Act of 1991." This interesting legislation, pet project of Senate Intelligence Committee Chairman Boren, establishes a $150 million trust fund administered by the Defense Intelligence College under direction of a board of trustees—"The National Security Education Board"—headed by the Secretary of Defense (and of which the Director of Central Intelligence (DCI) is a member). It has the worthy objective of providing scholarships for undergraduates to study abroad, graduate student fellowships for foreign language and area studies, and grants to universities to establish or improve foreign language and area studies programs. For the first year of the program (fiscal 1992), $35 million has been appropriated from the fund. Perhaps a clue to the extent of future intelligence budget cuts is the fact that the $180 million originally proposed for the trust fund in the Senate bill was reduced by $30 million, approximately 15 per cent.

In a statement of November 26, Senator Boren declared: "For four decades, the world came to us and spoke our language. That era is over. Now, to compete economically and to protect our diplomatic and national security interests, we need to think internationally. This means improving our skills in the areas of international and regional studies and developing more foreign language fluency. If we fail to do so, we will be ignoring a critical threat to our national security and to our ability to remain a world leader." (See also, David L. Boren, "Ignorance of World puts America at risk," *Atlanta Constitution*, September 19, 1991).

CIA Prep

An important objective of the Act is to: "produce an increased pool of applicants for work in the departments and agencies of the United States Government with national security responsibilities" (Sec. 801, (c) (3)), and one of the

tasks of the National Security Education Board is to devise means to recruit student beneficiaries of fellowships and programs to work for federal national security agencies. However, the conferees amended the bill to make clear that no US intelligence agency can use students for any purpose while they are in the program. This, the conference report explains, is to make foreign governments and organizations understand that "US citizens...under this program...are engaged in purely academic pursuits." (*Report*, p.32) Whether foreign governments and universities will fully appreciate the distinction between hosting and supporting future US national security officials without a current link to intelligence agencies and those with an existing connection remains to be seen. At any rate, the committees deserve credit for sensitivity and even a certain delicacy.

The Academic Response

As Boren noted in his press release of November 26, the Department of Education (DOE) now provides $18.6 million for foreign study programs and the Department of State budget includes $9.78 million in foreign study grants to colleges and universities for a total of about $28.4 million. Thus, the national security establishment, with its $35 million authorization for this year, becomes the dominant funder in the US government foreign studies support effort. (Note: To be fair, Boren's calculation leaves out the far greater sums spent, principally by the US Information Agency (USIA), on a variety of educational and quasi-educational exchange programs—UNCL).

Throughout the Cold War period, national security (or "national defense," as it used to be called) served as justification for all manner of federal spending. The great interstate highway program, for example, was begun in the Eisenhower administration as the National Defense Highway Act. Reaction to the Soviet Union's launching of Sputnik in

1958 was the National Defense Education Act, intended to redress assumed shortcomings in US scientific education. What is puzzling here is that with the Cold War declared over, a federal effort to deal with the alleged failure of US higher education to devote sufficient resources or attention to the teaching of foreign languages and knowledge of other cultures should be mounted under the banner of national security and responsibility for it given to the Department of Defense (DOD).

It would seem logical that DOE be in charge of responding to educational problems, even though one of the goals of this act, admittedly, is to increase the pool of potential qualified applicants for the foreign services, including the intelligence and military services, of the United States. Indeed, where the particular needs of those services for language-trained individuals are concerned, evidence is abundant that the intensive training provided at military language schools has been more than adequate to meet demand and usually superior to university language training. The CIA also has excellent in-house language training capabilities. One would think that the most appropriate and efficient response for national security institutions in meeting their language and area study needs would be improvement of their own training and educational bases, not expanding on to civil campuses.

In fact, Senator Boren's original plan was to have his initiative funded in DOE's budget. However, this sensible approach was blocked by the federal Office of Management and Budget (OMB). According to sources in the educational community who followed the process closely, OMB ruled that under last year's budget summit agreement which put national security and domestic spending in separate compartments with no transfer of funds from one to the other permitted, a national security education proposal had to be funded from the defense budget. Hence, the apparent anomaly.

If Everything Affects National Security, Then the National Security System Must Control Everything

Another point for concerned analysis, something which does not appear in the report on the 1992 intelligence authorization, is the manner in which the term national security is broadened so far that it becomes virtually meaningless, on the one hand, and on the other provides justification for a greater and more controlling role of the military services and intelligence agencies on the nation's campuses. Many educators, especially from institutions notorious for their traditional ties to the national security establishment, seem willing and eager to provide a rationale, especially since they stand to gain. James Alatis, Dean of Georgetown University's School of Languages and Linguistics exulted: "This is the most important legislation for our profession since the National [Defense] Education Act. It creates a much needed and long overdue dialogue between the education, intelligence and defense communities. NSEA [the National Security Education Act] will produce the expertise necessary, not just to defend our nation militarily, but compete economically and function effectively in the international community." (Press Release, National Council for Languages and International Studies, 26 November 1991).

The Good News — US Lead in Loopy Logic Unchallenged

The Association of Professional Schools of International Affairs (APSIA) was likewise ecstatic. Its statement provided an even more all-encompassing rationale:

"*Without a renewed commitment to international education, our competitive edge will continue to erode in the increasingly interdependent world economy. Few Americans will be competent to understand and work effectively with Japanese business leaders, Arab oil ministers or European Community officials to advance U.S. interests and values. As the Cold War recedes into memory and the world threatens to become increasingly unstable, more—not fewer-qualified individuals will be needed to understand and analyze issues around the globe—from rising nationalism in East Central Europe and the former Soviet Union to the proliferation of weapons of mass destruction worldwide; from the complexities of the Middle East peace talks to the crushing debt burden of our Latin American neighbors; from the steady erosion of the world's natural resources to the insidious spread of international narcotics trafficking.*"

(UNCLASSIFIED cannot help noting that, judging from APSIA's press release, the US international lead in purple prose and loopy logic is not yet threatened).

APSIA's members are the School of International Service at The American University; the Graduate School of International Relations and Pacific Studies, University of California, San Diego; School of International and Public Affairs, Columbia University; Graduate School of International Studies, University of Denver; Edmund A. Walsh School of Foreign Service, Georgetown University; The Elliott School of International Affairs, The George Washington University; John F. Kennedy School of Government, Harvard University; The Paul H. Nitze School of Advanced International Studies, The Johns Hopkins University; Graduate School of Public and International Affairs, University of Pittsburgh; Woodrow Wilson School of Public and International Affairs, Princeton University; School of International Relations, University of Southern California; The Fletcher School of Law and Diplomacy, Tufts University; Yale Center for International and Area Studies, Yale University.

Vision, Leadership and (Ahem) Money

APSIA's acceptance of national security system funding for, and even some measure of control of, its foreign affairs programs by the military is not surprising. Most of the member institutions already have strong links to the security system. At least one (Tufts) has established a major field of "national security studies." However—even allowing for the severe financial stringency under which the US educational system at all levels is laboring and its consequent and understandable reluctance to question the propriety of any source of support—it is a bit odd that the Liaison Group for International Educational Exchange, a coalition of higher education and exchange organizations dedicated to promoting international student exchange linkages between the United States and other nations, accept this without question. Its executive secretary, Dr. Norman Peterson, said on November 25: "We applaud Senator Boren for his vision and leadership in putting this program together, and pledge ourselves to helping make it a success."

In fairness it must be said that both APSIA's executive secretary, Kay King, and the Liaison Group's Peterson, in discussing the Act with UNCLASSIFIED, expressed reservations. King agreed that there would be problems with perceptions by foreign institutions despite the pains Boren had taken to allay their fears. The problems would be addressed in earnest as actual programs are developed, she said.

Can Higher Education Civilize the Intelligence System?

As for the breadth of definition of national security, King believes it is proper to put economic and even environmental concerns in the same program with military security. She argued that,

DataCenter   464 19th Street, Oakland, California 94612 (415) 835-4692

as the Gates hearings, in her opinion, had demonstrated, the intelligence apparatus is undergoing basic change that would allow it to function effectively in an open society. She hoped that the universities would help push it toward that change. When UNCLASSIFIED described the recent events at Rochester Institute of Technology (UNCLASSIFIED, Vol. 3, Nos. 4 and 5)—with which, she said, she was not familiar—as showing the danger that the university was more likely to be changed than the intelligence system, she replied that if there were abuses her organization would have to reconsider its cooperation.

National Security Scholars—Sheep in Wolves' Clothing?

APSIA, according to King, will not have to worry too much about foreign reaction since the large majority of its graduate fellowship programs, as she envisions them, will take place on US campuses. Also, the Act provides that only US citizens can take part. However, Dr. Peterson of the Liaison Group, whose organization will be placing undergraduate National Security Education Act scholars in foreign countries, anticipates difficulties based, he says, in appearances. "We're keeping our fingers crossed," he told UNCLASSIFIED. "We have to convince our friends that this is not a wolf in sheep's clothing, but, instead, a sheep in wolf's clothing."

Peterson, who advised Boren on the Act, says that the Defense Intelligence College has a good reputation among academics and he expects no real problem in working under its administrative control. However, he expressed some

discomfort, indicating he would be happier with more traditional educational sponsorship. He described how Boren tried first to work through DOE, and, when OMB blocked that, sought, with the help of Senator John Kerry (D-MA), to use the Foreign Relations Committee, tacking the proposal on to the US Information Agency budget. However, Foreign Relations would approve only $4 million. He was surprised, he said, that "this president" (meaning "Education President" Bush—UNCL) showed no interest.

UNCLASSIFIED wonders how the educational bureaucrats and careerists now blistering their palms with applause will explain to their foreign counterparts that they want them to collaborate in scholarly exchange programs whose announced purposes are not the traditional promotion of international understanding but the enhancement of US "national security." Moreover, they will be hard pressed to convince them that they should cooperate in the training of future intelligence officers who will use their knowledge of the language, culture and politics of the host country to, perhaps, carry out covert operations in it in the future. Foreign educational institutions may also question the fact that the programs in which they are asked to cooperate are administered by the Defense Intelligence College or by private institutions contracting with the US DOD. Transcripts of these explanations will doubtless make interesting reading.

A Question of Turf — And Integrity

Finally, it is curious that the DOE, whose new secretary, Lamar Alexander of Tennessee, is, arguably, the most politically potent and ambitious individual ever to hold the post, apparently acquiesced in this unprecedented intrusion of the DOD and the intelligence system on to educational turf without a struggle. In fact, neither the DOE's public affairs office or its legislative reference officer

were even aware of the National Security Education Act when contacted by UNCLASSIFIED on January 6.

Increased federal government action to address the lamentable neglect of foreign language and foreign area studies by US colleges and universities, if, in fact, such action is necessary, should be the responsibility of the Department of Education. UNCLASSIFIED and the Association of National Security Alumni believe that close and direct relations between the intelligence system and the university pose unacceptable dangers for the independence and integrity of the latter.

That Alexander does not defend the role of his Department, despite the OMB decision, is puzzling. That university leaders do not express concern about, indeed, seem to welcome, military-intelligence control of international studies programs is distressing.

The Surprising Opposition

So who's opposed? Perhaps surprisingly every Republican member of the House Intelligence Committee announced opposition to Title VIII during conference. Peterson was puzzled since, as he explained to UNCLASSIFIED, they had been lobbied by universities in their districts to support the bill. He speculated that the campus contact persons probably talked to the legislative aides in the congressmen's offices who dealt with education, not national security. Hence, the message didn't get through. It would be nice to believe that such as ranking minority member Bud Shuster (R-PA), himself a Ph.D., were worried about academic integrity. UNCLASSIFIED may yet see Shuster and his colleagues joining a CIA Off Campus demonstration. ∎

OPPOSITION RESEARCH

FREE MARKET ENVIRONMEN- TALISM

BY SARA DIAMOND

NVIRONMENTALISM POSES a unique challenge to the usual guardians of the status quo. Were all things possible, corporate profiteers would just as soon enjoy clean air and water along with the rest of us. But there's one species of green stuff that takes precedence over all others. Environmentalists—especially those committed to a social justice approach—ought to expect opposition on a variety of fronts.

Thus far, corporate and government responses to "radical" environmentalism are taking shape in at least four forms: physical violence against activists and whistleblowers; covert and legal harassment of movement groups; the construction of an ongoing propaganda campaign against "ecoterrorists;" and, most subtly, the corporate-sponsored building of a "free market" answer to growing public concern about the environment.

Full coordination among the various players is not evident. Nor is it necessary to have a destructive effect. Those who write anti-Earth First! newspaper columns can, even inadvertently, create the kind of hostile political climate that gives a green light to physically violent conspirators.

Direct Action

THE MAY 1990 car bomb assassination attempt on Earth First! leaders Judi Bari and Darryl Cherney remains unsolved. The whole set of circumstances surrounding the FBI and local law enforcement's mishandling of the case effectively sends a message that activists are fair game for anti-environmental vigilantes. In March 1991, Greenpeace scientist Pat Costner's rural Arkansas home and office were burned to the ground in what investigators consider a case of arson. The apparent target was Costner's 20-year collection of research material on toxic waste.

Writing in the July/August 1991 issue of *Humanist* magazine, Political Research Associates analyst Chip Berlet chronicled stepped-up police and legal harassment of environmentalists across the country. Activists have been jailed illegally without charges or bail. Local authorities,

private spook agencies, and even the EPA have begun collecting photographs and dossiers, as if to prepare for future covert operations against the movement.

The FBI itself spent $2 million to set up Arizona Earth First!ers for an alleged conspiracy to sabotage nuclear facilities.. Last summer's trial proceedings, in which the prosecution accepted defendants' plea bargain to lesser charges of vandalizing a ski resort, revealed just how far the feds are willing to go to bust up the movement. One of the government's informants within the Arizona group was a heavy LSD user named Ron Frazier who was subjected to FBI hypnosis sessions as part of his "training." The seedier sides of the Arizona case escaped much press scrutiny, in sharp contrast to the barrage of media speculation about whether Judi Bari, a single mother of two young daughters, might have blown herself up as a publicity stunt.

Seeing Red

THE TIMING OF one strident piece of anti-environmentalist disinformation was particularly striking. A week before scheduled Earth Day events in northern California, the San Francisco Sunday *Examiner*, on April 14, 1991, featured "Tale of a plot to rid Earth of humankind." It was a tale, all right. The story, by a Jonathan Tilove of Newhouse News Service, reported as credible the assertions of ex-CIA officer Vincent Cannistraro that a cabal of "radical environmentalists" were cooking up a recipe for a virus that could kill humans but leave other species unharmed. The *Examiner* featured the article on page two, with a photo of Earth First! cofounder David Foreman.

Cannistraro concocted his mad-scientist fantasy while on staff with the National Strategy Information Center, a CIA-linked think tank that publishes books and holds conferences to promote "low intensity conflict" and "terrorism" as cornerstones of U.S. military doctrine. As a sidekick to Oliver North on the National Security Council, Cannistraro helped manage the CIA's funding of contra leader Arturo Cruz. NSIC president Frank Barnett is a veteran of the Cold War-era Institute for American Strategy, itself a spin-off of the private American Security Council. Since 1955 the American Security Council has provided dues-paying cor-

DataCenter   464 19th Street, Oakland, California 94612 (415) 835-4692

porations with intelligence reports on U.S. citizens, including the kind of information the FBI is prohibited from circulating.

Last May, Cannistraro told Zack Stentz, an environmental reporter for the *Anderson Valley Advertiser*, that he's an "environmentalist," too, and that he had no intention of defaming Earth First! "The environment just isn't something we focus on here," Cannistraro told Stentz. But disinformation and psychological warfare are things the NSIC focuses on, and propaganda might be most effective if it

doesn't claim to be factual, but merely leaves readers feeling fear and loathing toward environmentalists.

Psy-war might also work best if its sources are multiple and difficult to track down. Newhouse reporter Jonathan Tilove also relied on an anonymous letter advocating biological warfare against humans, published in a 1984 Earth First! newsletter. Tilove lifted this tidbit from a 1990 report prepared by Cato Institute analyst Doug Bandow on assignment for the Heritage Foundation.

Bandow's paper "Ecoterrorism: the Dangerous Fringe of the Environmental Movement" was released as a Heritage Foundation "Backgrounder" in April 1990, marking the 20th anniversary of the first Earth Day. The purpose of these "Backgrounder" reports is to provide free ammunition to the Heritage Foundation's cultivated list of media hacks, coast to coast. Coinciding with heightened media attention to environmentalism, Bandow's paper rehearsed a litany of activist "crimes" against private property and portrayed "radical" environmentalists as spaced-out nature worshippers and misanthropes.

But Bandow also hinted at some of the essentials of an anti-environmental movement strategy. He reported that "the Washington Contract Loggers Association [has] created a Field Intelligence Report to track the activities of ecoteurs and has established a reward program for information leading to the apprehension of such criminals. Similarly, the Mountain States Legal Foundation, based in Denver, Colorado [has] established an ecotage hotline...In the first two months of hotline operation, Foundation President William Perry Pendley received reports of ecotage from California, Colorado, Idaho, Nevada, Oregon, and Washington. Mountain States [has] also established a clearinghouse to file civil damage actions against saboteurs and to assist the government in prosecuting violators."

Aside from advocating increased intelligence gathering and collaboration between states and corporate-backed law firms, the point of Bandow's paper was to initiate a classic divide-and-conquer strategy, by positing "ecoterrorists" as a threat to "mainstream" environmentalists. "The best defense against ecotage is for mainstream environmentalist community and political leaders and for businessmen [sic] to speak out frequently on the issue," Bandow stressed. He explicitly slammed David Brower, veteran leader of the Sierra Club and Friends of the Earth, for having given office space to Earth First! and for defending its civil disobedience tactics. Bandow advocated that "mainstream" environmentalists purge the movement of radicals in the same way that "in the 1950s the American labor movement purged itself of most communist members and influence....The political organizations closest to the terrorist group's ideological views should separate themselves from its activities and help mold a broad social consensus against its activities."

Shoring Up Bulwarks

SHORTLY AFTER THE Heritage Foundation released Bandow's version of the divide-and-conquer proposal, another Heritage affiliate published an intelligence report on Greenpeace. The Capital Research Center tracks dissidents and provides its big corporate benefactors with early warning of anti-capitalist trends.

Here, too, the backgrounds of the Center's Executive Committee members are telling. Frank Barnett of the spooky National Strategy Information Center is on board. Richard Allen, head of the Heritage Foundation's Asian Studies Center, was Reagan's first National Security adviser, before he had to resign over the embarrassing revelation that he had accepted an expensive wristwatch from the Japanese government. Heritage trustee Midge Decter, who

founded the recently disbanded Committee for the Free World, has taken credit for launching the National Association of Scholars and the whole hullabaloo over "political correctness." Norman Ture was a Reagan administration Treasury Department official and a key architect of tax cuts for the rich.

Capital Research Center's "Organization Trends" report expands the notion of "fringe" to include Greenpeace. The apparent rationale is the discovery that some activists have worked with both Greenpeace and Earth First!, and the fact that Greenpeace helped Earth First! hire a detective to solve the Judi Bari bombing case. Greenpeace is charged with "hostility to free enterprise" because it "condemns pirate whalers, specific toxic polluters and 'commercial greed.'"

But what really irks Capital Research Center is Greenpeace's organizational success: its millions of grassroots supporters and its near independence from corporate donations. Greenpeace has developed good relations with some of the "established" environmental groups, like Friends of the Earth and the Cousteau Society and, according to the Capital Research Center, "is drawing more 'mainstream' groups to the left." The Center recommends that businesses decline to donate to environmental groups. "Corporations might be tempted to shore up the 'moderates' as a bulwark against Greenpeace and organizations like it but the fact is that the entire movement is inherently anti-corporate."

Planting A Cash Crop

SOME FARSIGHTED CORPORATIONS are finding that the best "bulwark" against "anti-corporate" environmentalism is the creation and promotion of an alternative model called "free market environmentalism." Here the idea is not to pit "radical" environmentalism against a crude, devil-may-care capitalist message. The preferred plan is to cultivate a "reasonable" approach based on "balancing" the "individual rights" of big corporations with the rights of society and the planet to survive into the 21st century. "Free market environmentalism" has sprouted into a virtual cottage industry for a slew of libertarian-oriented think tanks, publishers, and conference organizers.

At the vanguard is the Montana-based Political Economy Research Center (PERC), started in 1980 by a group of Montana State University professors. Its advisory board includes an impressive list of academicians. Its board of trustees includes executives from the oil, chemical, and financial industries. With generous funding from corporate foundations, including Carthage, Bradley, Earhart, Scaife, the Liberty Fund, and the M.J. Murdock Charitable Trust, PERC sponsors educational seminars for undergraduate students and for journalists assigned to the environmental beat. PERC's photo-filled newsletter conveys the think tank's laid-back approach to political advocacy. These are the kind of people who wear fuzzy flannel shirts and Levi's and enjoy the great outdoors. But their love of nature is matched by their commitment to corporate sovereignty.

PERC's leading thinker is Montana State economics professor Terry Anderson. With coauthor and PERC associate Donald Leal, Anderson's book *Free Market Environmentalism* was published last spring by Westview

Press, in a joint deal with the Pacific Research Institute in San Francisco. The "property rights paradigm" boils down to the argument that "market incentives" are the key to both protection and clean-up. Expansion of private ownership—including eventual control of what are currently public lands and resources—will increase environmental integrity. That's because "individuals," including corporations with the legal status of individuals, will want to protect the price or value of what belongs to them. Local community input on problems like toxic waste sites, deforestation, or the construction of nuclear power plants is all well and good, but, lacking actual "ownership," the public has little incentive to make sound decisions. Should people living in an environmentally threatened area organize politically and pressure government agencies to restrain corporations on their behalf, this "command-and-control environmentalism" will threaten "democracy" because no one will be able to make an unlimited amount of money. The free marketeers invoke formerly "communist" governments' disastrous mishandling of environmental problems as if to prove that only individual property owners ought to make decisions for everyone concerned.

The elitism of "free market environmentalism" is only one of its many flaws. In a lengthy telephone interview, I queried Professor Anderson about the obvious problems when a company like Exxon can accidentally destroy a huge part of Alaska. His quick answer was that high liabilities ought to be an integral part of what he calls "making incentives matter." In other words, if Exxon knew it would have to pay exorbitant penalties and litigation costs, it wouldn't hire drunken ship captains. But this argument, of course, assumes rationality and forethought on the part of corporate decision makers. It also neglects the fact that the only way to build into the "incentive structure" a liability high enough to restrain short-term greed is through political pressure, i.e. when citizens use "democracy" to force some sort of representative state agency to limit what capitalists can get away with.

Recycling Free Market Advocacy

THE "FREE market environmentalism" concept is fertilizing a number of corporate-backed think tanks. In general, the role of think tanks is to frame the terms of policy debates before they arise and to generate the kind of empirical data activists can use to influence policymakers. Since environmental problems are multifaceted, there's room for numerous organizations to develop expertise in special areas.

Citizens for the Environment, started in 1990 as a spin-off to the Washington, DC-based Citizens for a Sound Economy, has chosen to focus on solid-waste management at the regional and local level. Because CSE has built a claimed membership of 250,000 since 1984 and functions as a lobby against taxes and government regulation of industry, its new advocacy on environmental issues is liable to fall on receptive ears. In a June 1991 conference on "The Politics and Science of Garbage" CFE drew speakers from the Environmental Protection Agency, from the plastics and packaging industries, and from two "respectable" environmental groups, Resources for the Future and the Natural Resources Defense Council. Transcripts of the conference presentations indicate that a major theme was the need to privatize recycling, landfill use, and hazardous waste management systems. In an interview, CFE director Stephen Gold expressed concern that local governments are "dictating to the private sector" because "the public's demanding a solution, like a lynch mob."

In June the libertarian Cato Institute launched its own Environmental Studies program with a two-day conference on "Global Environmental Crises: Science or Politics?" attended by about 200 people. Cato assembled an impressive array of scientific experts, including climatologists and meteorologists, with diverse viewpoints on the hot topic of "global warming." Cato's Environmental Director Robert J. Smith acknowledges that there's serious scientific debate on the extent of this crisis. But in a memo following the conference, Smith alluded to the Institute's political concern that "many government leaders continue to rush toward the June 1992 United Nations 'Earth Summit' in Brazil determined to bring central planning to all the world's nations on the basis of presuppositions about the world's climate." Environmental hazards caused disproportionately by First World polluters are not to be solved through multilateral diplomacy.

Both Citizens for the Environment and the Cato Institute receive major backing from Charles G. Koch, whose $15-billion-a-year oil and gas corporation is one of the largest privately held firms in the world. Koch Industries specializes in oil pipeline production but also has subsidiaries dealing with crude oil transport and coal mining. Koch has been the mainstay of the libertarian movement—which just happens to be the political tendency most actively pushing "free market environmentalism."

Acting Locally

IN THE NEXT few years, much of the environmental debate is likely to occur on the state and local level. It's, therefore, no coincidence that in the past decade, the Right's biggest growth industry has been the formation of small public policy institutes, already numbering 55 in 29 states. A recent study by the National Committee for Responsive Philanthropy, a liberal group that monitors trends in the foundation world, reported on the Madison Group, which is coordinating activities among the new state institutes and some of the more established national advocacy groups. (The Madison Group is a project of the American Legislative Exchange Council, created in 1973 to organize right-wing state legislators.) Member think tanks in the Madison Group include the Political Economy Research Center in Bozeman, Montana, and the Pacific Research Institute in San Francisco.

The Colorado-based Independence Institute, with a $200,000 budget and a donor list dominated by oil and coal companies, has begun issuing position papers on environmental questions most relevant to the southwest. Here, obviously, water is the central issue and the Independence Institute is applying "free market environmentalism" to advocate "water marketing." Proposals include conversion of state and federal water projects—already beholden to business interests—into totally private ownership. For starters, the Institute has recommended that Colorado "auction water rights to the highest bidders who meet reasonable standards," including the Audubon Society and the Nature Conservancy. But once water rights enter private hands, they're fair game for less conservation-conscious marketeers.

In the northwest, where clear-cutting and preservation of public lands top environmentalists' agenda, the counter-movement's catch phrases "wise use" and "multiple use" imply that forests can be exploited and preserved at the same time. Leading the charge for "wise use" is the Bellevue, Washington-based Center for the Defense of Free Enterprise. The group's vice president, Ron Arnold, has been an active ally of Unification Church front groups, including the American Freedom Coalition, which has promoted "wise use" in its monthly newspaper. Arnold makes frequent speeches for logging and oil industry associations. In 1990 Arnold told executives with the American Petroleum Institute that "they face complete destruction unless a serious public support movement is built at the grassroots nonprofit level." Arnold's Center has also been raising funds for an apple growers' lawsuit against the Natural Resources Defense Council and CBS News over the defendants' claims that people were getting sick from eating apples sprayed with the chemical alar.

What Shade Of Green?

FREE MARKET ENVIRONMENTALISM threatens the genuine article, not just because its proposals may give policymakers room to foot drag or pursue half-way measures, at the expense of the environment. The target audience for the free marketeers also seems to be the liberal and "moderate" activists who would just as soon not take on the root causes of environmental degradation. Though they can't be counted on to link true economic democracy with sane environmental policies, liberals do believe in citizen input on policy matters, and they have the kind of advocacy track records that make them the voices policymakers will listen to. Also, liberals sometimes condemn crude and violent attacks on dissidents. For these reasons and because they do reflect large constituencies, "mainstream" environmentalists can be tactical allies to social justice greens, on issues of shared concern. But coalition work between "mainstream" groups and those who see the connections of race and class to environmentalism will be threatened to the extent that free marketeers successfully frame policy debates in terms of property rights versus bureaucratic red tape. Given a respectable alternative that will ensure their access to economic and political elites, the liberal conservation-type groups just may jump on the "free market" bandwagon.   z

DataCenter   464 19th Street, Oakland, California 94612 (415) 835-4692

VII. Dissent Control

The First Amendment guarantees our right to assemble and to express our opinions, no matter how unpopular. In light of that, the articles in this section ask some pertinent questions: Why is the FBI probing foundations? Why was a former Black Panther framed? Why has Geronimo Pratt spent nineteen years in prison for a crime "the government knew he had not committed?" "Why do immigrants face punitive U.S. action after speaking out on political issues?" And why is the environmental movement being threatened and infiltrated with agents provocateurs?

"We must not confuse dissent with disloyalty." — Edward R. Murrow

"In a democracy, citizens are their own governors. As a consequence, government officials are prohibited from suppressing or otherwise restricting any speech that bears on public affairs." — Elizabeth Hull

"[No country] can live in freedom where its people can be made to suffer physically or financially for criticizing their government, its actions or its officials." — Justice Hugo L. Black

"The government is constitutionally precluded from unbridled and inappropriate covert activity which has as its purpose or objective the abridgment of the First Amendment freedoms of those involved." — Judge Roger G. Strand, U.S. District Court, Phoenix, Arizona, Dec. 10, 1990

Chilled By Hoover's Ghost

By John R. MacArthur

Like many Americans, I assumed that the collapse of the cold war would put an end to Government surveillance of individuals and domestic political groups that oppose U.S. foreign policy. But last week my family foundation — which makes a point of defending freedom of speech and the press — was forced to sue the Federal Bureau of Investigation to find out why it is keeping files on the foundation and its president, Lance Lindblom. The agency refuses on "national security" grounds to disclose virtually any of the information it has collected about us.

Unfortunately, we are not alone. At least two other foundations that share some of our interests are pursuing Freedom of Information Act appeals to discover what makes the F.B.I. so curious about their activities. There are almost certainly more foundations in similar straits. But they either lack the money for litigation or fear the political consequences of it being known the F.B.I. is watching them. They tell themselves — foolishly, in my opinion — that what they don't know won't hurt them.

It's conceivable, of course, that the Bureau is conducting legitimate investigations of grant recipients whom it imagines to be engaged in criminal activity or espionage. But somehow I doubt it. The files on our foundation go back at least five years, and in that time we have given money

John R. MacArthur, publisher of Harper's magazine, is a member of the board of the J. Roderick MacArthur Foundation.

only to legal, tax-exempt organizations. And my family, now in its third generation of successful capitalist enterprise, must always have seemed a poor prospect for recruitment by the Soviet Union.

The more likely explanation for our files is that the F.B.I. still views opposition to Government policy as subversive and dangerous, particularly when it involves Latin America and Southeast Asia. Some of our money defends human rights in El Salvador and Guatemala, two countries with egregiously repressive governments that are heavily supported by the U.S. And Mr. Lindblom accompanied opposition leader Kim Dae Jung in his

Why is the F.B.I. probing foundations?

return trip to South Korea in 1985, when U.S. policy still favored the dictatorial President, Chun doo Hwan.

It evidently matters little to the F.B.I. that for years we backed underground publications in Eastern Europe and the Soviet Union, as well as investigations of human rights violations in Albania, Cuba and North Korea. The traditions of J. Edgar Hoover die hard, and enemies have to be created.

The F.B.I. has little incentive to change its ways. In his 1988 campaign, President Bush successfully demonized the American Civil Liberties Union, our lawyers in the case against the F.B.I., and one of our

major grant recipients. The Center for Constitutional Rights, which discovered our F.B.I. files, is one of the Bush Administration's staunchest foes on civil rights policy and war powers. The center is another of our favorite charities.

We think it is outrageous that the F.B.I. won't tell us the truth, and we stand willing to press our case until we get damages and an apology for this blatant violation of our privacy. But even if we win our lawsuit, it won't be sufficient. The greater damage caused by F.B.I. intrusions is the chilling effect it might have on already far too cautious foundation executives. How many will now think twice before giving money to human rights organizations in countries, including our own, where the government has violated the civil liberties of its citizens? Nobody, after all, wants an F.B.I. file.

Three solutions propose themselves. The first is to restore the Carter-era standard — rescinded by the Reagan Administration — making it harder for the Government to classify information in the first place.

Second, Congress, which this year finally repealed the McCarthy-era McCarran Act, ought to complete the process of glasnost in our Government by passing proposed legislation that would prevent the F.B.I. from investigating the First Amendment activities of U.S. citizens and organizations.

Lastly, Congress should hold hearings on the role of the F.B.I. in the post-cold-war world and banish once and for all the ghost of Hoover, its founding director. After more than 40 years as a quasi political police force, the Bureau should devote its full attention to its original purpose: catching criminals. □

The framing of Geronimo Pratt

*How the FBI railroaded
the ex-Black Panther leader
into life imprisonment
for a murder he
didn't commit*

By John Roemer

D
ARKNESS HAD FALLEN along the Santa Monica seafront when Kenneth Olsen and his wife Caroline arrived at Lincoln Park for a game of tennis. The couple had been going through marital difficulties and were living apart. Their plan to play tennis on this mild Southern California evening a week before Christmas in 1968 was the first tentative step toward rebuilding their marriage. But this marriage would not be saved.

Around 8:10 pm, Olsen flicked the switch that turned on the massive floodlights overlooking the tennis court. Within moments, the high school vice-principal and his wife, herself a second-grade teacher in the Los Angeles public schools, found themselves in the most horrific of urban nightmares. Two men with guns appeared and demanded the couple's money. The Olsens offered no resistance, turning over $18 in cash and their car keys. But their assailants then ordered them to lie face down on the court surface and pray to god. Trembling and crying in terror, the couple did so. The two men shot them both and left them to die, fleeing the scene in a red and white convertible.

Caroline Olsen died, although she spent 10 days in the hospital clinging to life. Her husband survived, offering authorities a description of the young black males who had shot them.

The motiveless, cold-blooded killing attracted major media attention. Two years later, in December 1970, prominent L.A. Black Panther Geronimo Pratt was indicted for Caroline Olsen's murder. Kenneth Olsen positively identified Pratt as one of the killers, and another witness testified she saw Pratt and another black man near Lincoln Park just before the shooting. During a 1969 raid of a Los Angeles Panther house, where Pratt and 17 others were arrested and a number of weapons seized, police say they found a .45 caliber handgun that, in later tests, matched shell casings found on the tennis court. Julius Butler, a former Panther who knew Pratt, swore that Pratt had admitted the shootings to him. And if all that were not enough, Geronimo Pratt owned a red and white convertible.

Pratt has served 20 years in state prison — the first eight in solitary confinement — since his conviction in 1972. All the while, this articulate Vietnam war hero and former Panther leader has forcefully protested his innocence. Over the years, the evidence against Pratt has gradually unraveled, and it has become painfully clear that the tennis court shootings in 1968 had three victims. True justice was never meted out for the murder of Caroline Olsen or the shooting of Kenneth Olsen — and Geronimo Pratt has suffered needlessly for a crime he did not commit.

Prior to the murder, Pratt had been a major target of COINTELPRO, the FBI's counterintelligence program aimed at destroying the Black Panther Party by eliminating its leaders. Caroline Olsen's death provided the government with a perfect device to get Pratt off the streets forever.

M. Wesley Swearingen, a former FBI agent who was close to the original Pratt investigation, says bluntly that Pratt was "framed" by the bureau. Other evidence comes from former Panthers who have finally decided to break their silence, as well as from the FBI's own files, which include wiretap logs and correspondence showing that Julius Butler, the prosecution's star witness, was an FBI informant. All the available evidence points to one conclusion: Pratt is innocent of the murder, and is in fact a political prisoner dating from former FBI director J. Edgar Hoover's ruthless campaign to annihilate the Black Panthers at all costs.

I
T MAKES ME want to cry," said Jeanne Hamilton, one of the jurors who convicted Pratt in 1972, as she details the information Pratt's attorneys have shared with her in the last year. Hamilton, a certified public accountant and business teacher at the California Polytechnic Institute in Pomona, says her conscience has bothered her ever since Pratt's lawyers showed her the new evidence.

"I know now that Pratt is a man who is principled and intelligent — and innocent," Hamilton said. "I've destroyed his life, though I feel I was a victim, too. I was 22 years old. The government had a lot of credibility. They betrayed us. We did not have the whole story. It is amazing to me that they won't give this man a hearing now. It's a crime. We would never have convicted him if we knew what we know now."

Bob Bloom is the attorney who shared his findings with Hamilton and who wants the world to know what Hamilton now knows. For the past two years, Bloom has been digging through Pratt's voluminous FBI records in search of evidence of a frame-up. He has found plenty.

In one box of papers, Bloom found a reference to a former Panther named Tyrone Hutchinson who had been questioned in 1970 about the tennis court shootings. Hutchinson's name and his testimony had been concealed from Pratt's defense at the time of his trial. Bloom wondered why.

His curiosity led him last spring to an interview room at Pelican Bay State Prison on California's north coast. Hutchinson, imprisoned there on robbery charges, provided Bloom with crucial information. When he'd been interrogated by Los Angeles police, Hutchinson told Bloom, he had said that he knew who had killed Caroline Olsen. Hutchinson told the police two men who were at the tennis court at the time of the killing gave him the details of what had happened. Hutchinson named the men, whose current whereabouts are unknown.

The L.A. police took extensive notes during his statement, Hutchinson remembers, then warned him not to discuss it with anyone "if I knew what was good for me." Hutchinson understood what they meant. "I took this to be a threat on my life at the time and I still do," he said in a sworn declaration to Bloom. "I take their threats seriously. I am in fear today of what the police, the D.A., the parole board and the Department of Corrections might do to me for disclosing what I overheard. But I know that Geronimo had nothing to do with the tennis court murder."

Bloom had a second, and unexpected, breakthrough last year at a San Francisco party celebrating the parole of Johnny Spain, a longtime San Quentin inmate linked to George Jackson. At the party, Bloom ran into Patricia Richartz, a longtime investigator for Panther attorney Charles Garry.

Richartz had a remarkable story to tell. In 1975, Garry had won a court order that allowed him to examine FBI wiretap logs relating to a pending Huey Newton case. It was a unique chance for the Panthers to penetrate the high security enemy camp. High above Golden Gate Avenue in the San Francisco Federal Building, Richartz and another investigator working for

Garry, David Fechheimer, looked through records containing names of dead and imprisoned members of the Panther movement.

Suddenly Pratt's name all but leapt off the wiretap log Richartz was holding. It was a routine FBI entry, noted in the chilly bureaucratese of federal eavesdroppers, that detailed a phone call from a woman who spoke to Geronimo Pratt on December 18, 1968, at about 5:30 pm, while he was at a Panther house in Oakland. Richartz immediately saw that it was highly improbable Pratt could have committed a murder 400 miles south of Oakland less than three hours later.

"He was here all the time," she said to herself. "It says so right here."

She showed the document to Fechheimer. Their eyes met. Nothing was said until the two left the building, amazed but frustrated that they were not allowed to take the telltale log with them. (Both have signed affidavits affirming what they saw in the log.)

Could Pratt have possibly gotten from Oakland to Santa Monica by eight o'clock that night? Perhaps he could have sped to Oakland Airport, immediately boarded a plane for the hour-long flight to Los Angeles, and raced 20 miles north on the San Diego Freeway to the Lincoln Park tennis courts to rob a couple of $18 — an unlikely, but certainly possible, scenario

But some hypothetical madcap dash to the murder site would contradict the prosecution's contention that the Panther leader had been in Los Angeles all along. The government's case relied heavily upon Julius Butler, who testified that Pratt had been with him during the daylight hours before the shootings. December 18, the day of the killing, is one of the shortest days of the year, a day in which darkness falls in California by 5:30 pm. When Pratt was on the phone in Oakland, it was already dark.

News of Richartz's find got sidetracked in the internal political warfare that tore apart the Panthers in the early 1970s, and stayed that way for 15 years. Until she mentioned the wiretap log to Bloom at Johnny Spain's party, no one on Pratt's defense team knew it existed. Richartz and Fechheimer say they spoke of the matter to various attorneys, but never pressed it.

The wiretap finding made Bloom realize that a number of people must have known that Pratt was in Oakland when the murder occurred. In seeking them out, Bloom was plunged into the murky political infighting within the Panther organization that had kept witnesses for Pratt silent for years.

How AND WHY the Panthers fell apart into contending camps that pitted Huey Newton against his old comrade Eldridge Cleaver was a mystery until the night of March 8, 1971, when unknown persons broke into FBI storage files in Media, Pennsylvania, outside Philadelphia, and removed thousands of pages of classified documents.

Published during the following week by the *Washington Post*, the documents alerted the public to the FBI counterintelligence program,

code-named COINTELPRO, intended to neutralize black groups like the Panthers. Senate hearings in 1975 on the program revealed that Panther leaders like Newton, Cleaver and Pratt were singled out for special attention as "key black extremists."

The documents uncovered an FBI poison-pen campaign used to drive a wedge between Newton in Oakland, and Cleaver, then exiled in Algeria. Pratt was seen as aligned with the Cleaver faction and expelled from the party by Newton. When Pratt was put on trial for murder, the Newton-run party newspaper published explicit instructions that no Panther was to associate with Pratt or testify on his behalf. None did.

· In the internecine battles provoked by COINTELPRO, attorney Garry, who died last year, lined up with the Newton faction. The crucial evidence of the wiretap log was never passed to Pratt's defense, Pratt attorney Stuart Hanlon said this week. "Garry iced it. I found it really disturbing."

A 1969 FBI document makes it clear that the bureau was out to get Pratt and other Panther leaders. It states, in part, that "constant consideration is given to the possibility of the utilization of counterintelligence measures with efforts being directed toward neutralizing PRATT as an effective BPP [Black Panther Party] functionary."

Bloom has now found witnesses willing to come forward on Pratt's behalf. Six former Panthers from the Newton faction, including chief of staff David Hilliard and co-founder Bobby Seale, have signed declarations swearing that Pratt was in Oakland on December 18, 1968. "I have carried feelings of guilt and remorse since my refusal to help Geronimo [at his trial] in 1972," Hilliard wrote. Others have echoed his regrets.

THE MAXIMUM SECURITY prison at Tehachapi sits in a range of dun-colored mountains that rise between Bakersfield and the Mojave desert. The complex looks like a space colony, but time, not space, is the chief preoccupation here.

Inside, thick glass and heavy automatic doors confining several thousand men produce an atmosphere of profound strain that is evident in the taut demeanor of the guards. Geronimo Pratt, by contrast, appears relaxed and at ease.

Twenty years ago, when Pratt entered prison at age 21, the FBI seemed to believe it had put away a dangerous revolutionary who had learned the ways of warfare in Vietnam. Pratt was indeed a war hero, earning the Silver Star, two Purple Hearts and two Bronze Stars, among the highest commendations awarded to soldiers. "I joined up to do something and I was true to it," he said. "I didn't betray the oath I had taken with the 82nd Airborne. To this day, I feel pride when I hear about the 82nd, even though they took Grenada and went into Panama, and I opposed that."

But Pratt's loyal military service was used against him by the FBI. A 1970 FBI profile

quotes with concern a *Los Angeles Times* article about him: "Geronimo is what many feared would be a disastrous by-product of the Vietnam war, a black man trained as a soldier who returned home to turn his skills against the establishment."

A few years later, California Department of Corrections officials used similar rhetoric to justify placing Pratt in a punishment isolation cell known as "the hole" for the first eight years of his sentence. They branded him the new George Jackson, after the celebrated Panther field marshal who was shot to death by San Quentin guards under suspicious circumstances.

"I went to prison in the wake of the George Jackson thing, though I never met him," Pratt said. "It made things triply difficult, not only from the state and the administration but from prisoners who had known George Jackson. They felt slighted that this outsider from Louisiana was being thrust forward as George's successor. That's prisoner mentality. So I was getting it from all sides."

With nothing to see, no one to talk to and nothing to read, Pratt began meditating to maintain his sanity. "I just had a hole in the floor and a bunch of violence all around me," he said. Throughout his incarceration, Pratt has protested his innocence from his prison cell. "The government can't afford to reopen the investigation because it would ultimately end up right in the lap of the FBI," he said.

RETIRED FBI AGENT Swearingen, who now lives near Santa Fe, New Mexico, says he knows that Pratt is innocent from what he learned while working in the Los Angeles office of the FBI in the early 1970s. "I know that Geronimo Pratt didn't do the tennis court murder," Swearingen said. "I knew in 1972 he was innocent and the FBI was going to try to get him out of the way. I didn't believe it was going to work. I didn't think innocent people went to jail. I get angry every time I think about it. In my career I had thought that the FBI was above this kind of behavior."

Swearingen says that FBI agents Brendan O. Cleary, Richard Held and Richard Bloeser all knew Pratt was innocent. Cleary was the agent in charge of Pratt's case during the trial, while Bloeser led the "Extremist Intelligence" squad, in charge of investigating black radicals.

The three agents helped manipulate the evidence to frame Geronimo Pratt, Swearingen claims. "Just before Pratt's trial began, these agents held a conference at which I was present. Bloeser told how Mr. Olsen had personally identified two other black men and how the Los Angeles police had got him to change his testimony [to] say that Mr. Pratt had killed his wife," Swearingen said. "I had been in the FBI about 18 years, and I knew all about how you get eyewitnesses to change their stories."

In a signed affidavit, Swearingen has sworn that during the Pratt investigation he overheard Cleary tell someone over the telephone, "The son of a bitch was in Oakland." Swearingen is sure that Cleary was talking about Pratt. "Based on the context in which I heard Cleary's comment," his affidavit continues, "I took that to mean that Cleary knew that Pratt was in Oakland at the time the crime was committed in Santa Monica."

FBI agent Cleary, now stationed in Boston, would not respond to Swearingen's charges this week. "This thing has been through the courts a thousand times," he said. "I'm not at liberty to comment."

Held, who now is special agent in charge of the FBI's San Francisco office, called Swearingen's allegations "absolute baloney, absolute nonsense." He refused to comment in detail, but said, "Not now, not in the past, not in the future have I had authority to frame anyone and I never have done it."

Bloeser, now retired from the FBI, did not return repeated phone calls.

The prosecution's star witness against Pratt was Julius Butler, a former Los Angeles County sheriff's deputy who had "joined" the Panthers. Since the trial, attorney Bloom has located two retired Los Angeles Police Department officers who confirmed that Butler worked for them as an informant for some time, including the period when he was Pratt's principal accuser.

Los Angeles investigator David Bernstein, who has filled his garage with extensive files on the Pratt case, also discovered that Butler had been an FBI informant. Various FBI documents, with names deleted, had been turned over to Pratt's defense team under a court order some years ago. While poring through them, Bernstein realized that the FBI had neglected to purge numerous references to Butler from documents that revealed him as a "probationary racial informant — ghetto."

Butler had told Pratt's jurors under oath, "I have never been in the world a snitch." Now he stood revealed as an informant whose undercover work for the government may well have led him to falsely accuse Pratt of murder.

Butler currently works as a paralegal at a Los Angeles law office. He refused to take a reporter's calls, but in previous statements he has denied that he ever worked as an informant for any government agency. "Julius feels betrayed by the government," said Bernstein. "They kind of threw him to the wolves when they let [his] papers get to [Pratt's] defense."

Bloom has also been able to explain away other parts of the prosecution's case against Pratt. The sighting of Pratt's red and white car at the scene of the crime has never really been an issue, since seven witnesses, including Butler, testified that Pratt had allowed the vehicle to become a "Panther car," available for use by any party member.

Nor does the gun present a big problem for the defense. The connection of the weapon to Pratt was so tenuous that the trial judge at first refused to admit it into evidence. Butler was the only witness who said the gun was Pratt's.

"The FBI agents talked about how the barrel was missing from the gun they were going to introduce in evidence," said Swearingen, "and how the LAPD ballistic expert would testify falsely that the shell casings matched the gun."

Bloom also believes that eyewitness testimony from both Kenneth Olsen, who died of natural causes in 1979, and others can be challenged. They repeatedly described the men they saw the night of the shootings as clean-shaven. But nine witnesses, including Butler, testified that Pratt always wore a goatee and mustache in those days.

Bloom charges Pratt's 1972 prosecutor, Richard Kalustian, with intentionally suppressing evidence about Butler's status as an informant. At one point in the trial, when a witness mentioned the FBI, Kalustian broke courtroom rules by declaring, "The FBI's never been involved in this case and you know it."

Kalustian, now a Superior Court judge in Los Angeles County, said last week in a telephone interview, "I didn't suppress anything from anybody." Butler, he said, "wasn't working for the FBI, he was providing innocuous information to the FBI. There's a difference. It's a very involved question."

Regarding Bloom's compilation of new evidence, Kalustian said, "It's a rehash of the same old stuff. It's full of conclusions, not evidence. I read it and I threw it away."

That's also about what happened last year when a Los Angeles judicial colleague of Kalustian's received Bloom's 147-page petition and the 300-page sheaf of exhibits that accompany it. Bloom and veteran Pratt attorney Stuart Hanlon tried to have the petition heard in San Francisco, arguing that many of the current judges in Los Angeles are former prosecutors at the D.A.'s office where Kalustian worked.

The change-of-venue effort failed, and the job of hearing the petition went to L.A. Superior Court Judge Gary Klausner. It was Bloom's worst nightmare: Klausner had been an L.A. district attorney when Kalustian was originally prosecuting Pratt. Klausner received the voluminous petition and substantiating accompanying evidence at 11 am on August 14. By ten o'clock the next morning, Klausner had dismissed Bloom's request for a new trial. Klausner's three-line order said there were "insufficient grounds" to re-open the case.

In December 1991, three California appeals court judges turned down the case in one word: "Denied." Bloom is now preparing to file another appeal. In the meantime, he has lined up support for Pratt from organizations such as Amnesty International and the National Black Police Officers Association.

But at the Los Angeles District Attorney's office, the prevailing view of Pratt as a time bomb hasn't changed much. "I think we still have a revolutionary man," said L.A. Deputy District Attorney Diane Visanni at Pratt's 1987 parole hearing. "If he chooses to set up a revolutionary organization upon his release from prison, it would be easy for him to do so."

To this day, politics — his politics, and those of the U.S. government — remains the principal factor that keeps Geronimo Pratt behind bars.

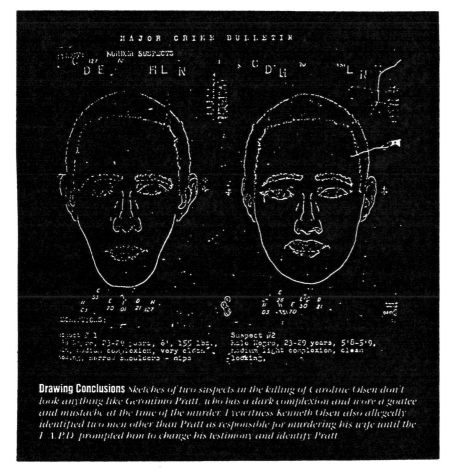

Drawing Conclusions *Sketches of two suspects in the killing of Caroline Olsen don't look anything like Geronimo Pratt, who has a dark complexion and wore a goatee and mustache at the time of the murder. Eyewitness Kenneth Olsen also allegedly identified two men other than Pratt as responsible for murdering his wife until the LAPD prompted him to change his testimony and identify Pratt.*

COINTELPRO:

The 19-Year Ordeal of Dhoruba bin-Wahad

Robert J. Boyle

On March 22, 1990, before a packed New York City courtroom, former Black Panther Party leader Dhoruba bin-Wahad was ordered released on his own recognizance after serving 19 years in the maximum security prisons of New York State for a crime the government knew he had not committed.

One week earlier, Justice Peter McQuillan had vacated Dhoruba's conviction for the 1971 attempted murder of two police officers on the ground that the prosecution had failed to disclose the existence of pre-trial statements by its chief witness which exonerate him. Dhoruba's freedom came only after a 15-year struggle to expose a politically motivated frame-up designed to neutralize an effective Black spokesperson.

More than 300,000 government documents obtained during this legal fight vividly illustrate how the U.S. government uses its criminal justice system as part of a counterinsurgency campaign against domestic liberation movements.

The Black Panther Party and COINTELPRO

In the 1960s, people throughout the world were successfully challenging the imperialist policies of the U.S. government. The Vietnamese people were defeating the most sophisticated war machine on Earth. In Africa and Latin America, national liberation movements began to expose and fight against western colonialism.

Inside the United States, Black people were organizing a mass movement to overturn 400 years of domestic colonialism driven by a racist culture and society. Thousands of Black people took to the streets to demand jobs, food, adequate medical care, housing, education, and an end to racist police brutality and murder. In short, Black people were demanding control over their own lives. Many organizations emerged from this struggle for Black power. One such organization marked a significant development in the struggle of Black people — the Black Panther Party.

The Black Panther Party for Self-Defense (BPP) was organized in Oakland, California, in 1967. Its 10-point program demanded, among other things, community control of the police and education, the right of Black people to defend themselves from racist attack, and an end to the draft of Black men into the military. The BPP instituted and maintained free breakfast-for-children programs, community health clinics, and classes in political education. It captured the imagination of the Black youths who swelled its ranks. By 1969, the BPP had 27 chapters throughout the United States.

The BPP program, particularly its vocal advocacy of armed self-defense, was viewed with racist paranoia by federal and local law enforcement agencies. They responded with armed confrontations around the country which resulted in the deaths of numerous BPP members.[1] On the national level, the FBI embarked on a disinformation campaign, publicly labeling the BPP the "greatest single threat" to the internal security of the United States. Covertly, the FBI instituted a counterintelligence program, known by its acronym, COINTELPRO, designed to "disrupt" and "neutralize" target groups and individuals. According to the final report of the Church Committee:

> Many of the techniques used would be intolerable in a free society even if all the targets had been involved in violent activity but COINTELPRO went far beyond that. The unexpressed major premise of the programs was that a law enforcement agency has the duty to do *whatever is necessary* to combat perceived threats to the existing social and political order.[2]

Labeling groups working for civil and human rights as "Black Nationalist-Hate Groups," FBI Director J. Edgar Hoover sent a letter to all field offices in March 1968 describing COINTELPRO's goals as follows: (1) to prevent the "coalition of militant black nationalist groups which might be the first step toward a real Mau Mau in America"; (2) to prevent the rise of a "messiah" who could "unify and electrify" the movement, naming Martin Luther King, Jr., Stokely Carmichael, and Elijah Muhammad as its leaders; (3) to prevent violence on the part of black nationalist groups by pinpointing "potential troublemakers" and neutralizing them "before they exercise their potential for violence"; (4) to prevent groups and leaders from gaining "respectability" by discrediting them to the "responsible Negro community" and to the white community; and 5) to prevent the long-range growth of these organizations, especially among youth, by developing specific tactics to "prevent these groups from recruiting young people."[3]

Other FBI documents of the operation speak even more frankly about COINTELPRO's racist nature and goals:

> In seeking effective counterintelligence, it should perhaps be borne in mind that the two things foremost in the militant Negro's mind are sex and money. The first is often promis-

---

Robert J. Boyle is a criminal defense and civil rights lawyer in New York who, together with Elizabeth Fink and Robert Bloom, represented Dhoruba bin-Wahad.

1. A report issued by BPP attorney Charles Garry in 1970 estimated that between 1966 and 1970 more than thirty members of the Black Panther Party had been killed by police gunfire. This includes the December 4, 1969, murder of Chicago BPP members Fred Hampton and Mark Clark who were killed during a pre-dawn raid by Chicago police while they lay sleeping in their beds.
2. U.S. Senate Select Committee to Study Government Operations, 94th Cong., 2d Session, Report No. 94-755, Book III, p. 3, emphasis added.
3. FBI Memorandum dated March 4, 1968, from Director to all field offices captioned "Counterintelligence Program, Black Nationalist-Hate Groups."

---

cuous and frequently freely shared. White moral standards do not apply among this type of Negro. You don't embarrass many Negroes by advertising their sexual activity or loose morals....

The Negro youth and moderates must be made to understand that if they succumb to revolutionary teaching, they will be dead revolutionaries.[4]

The BPP became the primary target of the FBI's COINTELPRO operations. According to the Church Committee, almost 90 percent of all counterintelligence activities aimed at the Black Liberation Movement targeted the BPP. In a letter dated November 25, 1968, Hoover ordered all field offices to submit "imaginative and hard-hitting counterintelligence measures aimed at crippling the Black Panther Party."[5] Proposals were to be submitted every two weeks and field offices were ordered to inform Hoover immediately of any "tangible results" achieved by each operation.[6]

Local police agencies worked closely with the FBI to "neutralize" the BPP. While the FBI worked covertly with its disinformation campaign, electronic surveillance, and informants, local police agencies were conducting their own campaigns against the BPP. They physically attacked and arrested Panthers while sharing all intelligence information with the FBI. The New York City Police Department (NYPD) for example, was assigned three undercover officers to work full-time as BPP members. One of these officers, Ralph White, was a founding member of the BPP chapter formed in the Bronx.[7] A March 1969 FBI "Inspectors' Review" (a quarterly report of FBI intelligence activities) noted that the NYPD had

a "program" of arresting BPP members on spurious charges.[8] Such activities severely hampered the BPP because Party members spent much of their time raising bail money and defending against false criminal charges at the expense of the community programs.

Maximum Surveillance and Disruption

Dhoruba bin-Wahad, then known as Richard Dhoruba

Mahmood Nadia/Impact Visuals

April 27, 1990. Dhoruba bin-Wahad one month after his release. Before him are part of the more than 300,000 government documents obtained in his case — documents which vividly illustrate the U.S. counterinsurgency campaign against domestic liberation movements.

Moore, joined the Black Panther Party in the summer of 1968 and worked out of the Harlem and Brooklyn, New York offices. An articulate speaker and organizer, he quickly rose to the rank of Field Secretary, becoming responsible for organizing BPP chapters throughout the Northeast. Law enforcement responded with alarm to these First Amendment-protected activities. On September 5, 1968, the day Dhoruba attended his first BPP meeting, the NYPD commenced a "criminal" investigation of him.[9] By January 1969, the FBI had commenced its own "investigation" of Dhoruba, placing him on the "Security Index" — a list of American citizens subject to internment in the event of a "national emergency."[10] In April 1969, the FBI labeled Dhoruba a "key leader" of the New York BPP and a main target for their counterintelligence activities.[11]

On April 2, 1969, Dhoruba bin-Wahad and 20 other New

4. FBI Memorandum dated April 3, 1968, from San Francisco to Director, captioned "Counterintelligence Program, Black Nationalist-Hate Groups, Racial Intelligence," emphasis added.

5. FBI Memorandum dated November 25, 1968 from Director to all field offices captioned "Counterintelligence Program, Racial matters, Black Panther Party."

6. Among the numerous counterintelligence activities directed against the BPP in late 1968 and early 1969 were several efforts to divide the BPP internally. In one operation, the FBI sent former BPP leader Eldridge Cleaver a spurious note warning him that New York Panthers were going to murder him. At the same time, the FBI anonymously informed the New York Chapter that Mr. Cleaver had misappropriated funds from a speaking tour. (See FBI memoranda dated October 22, 1968, and October 30, 1968, captioned "Counterintelligence Program, Black Nationalist-Hate Groups.") Distribution of the BPP newspaper, the major source of the organization's funds, was also disrupted. As stated in a December 2, 1968, memorandum to Hoover, the FBI's New York Office was making "[e]very effort to misdirect the operations of the BPP on a daily basis."

7. Ralph White's role was disclosed during the 1969-71 conspiracy trial of the "Panther 21" discussed below.

8. FBI Inspectors' Review of the New York Office, January 1969, through April 1969, p. 20.

9. In bin-Wahad's civil rights lawsuit against the NYPD and FBI, the former agency disclosed that they commenced a criminal investigation of him merely because he attended a meeting of the Black Panther Party.

10. FBI Memorandum from Director to New York dated June 5, 1969, captioned "Richard Moore."

11. FBI Inspectors' Review, *op. cit.*, n. 7, p. 17.

DataCenter   464 19th Street, Oakland, California 94612 (415) 835-4692

York Panthers were indicted and arrested on a New York State indictment charging them with conspiracy to commit murder and arson, the "Panther 21" case. The indictment only charged conspiracy—no act of murder or arson was actually alleged—and was based entirely upon the testimony of the three undercover NYPD officers. The entire New York leadership of the BPP, including Dhoruba, was incarcerated in lieu of exorbitant bail.

By March 1970, fund-raising efforts were successful enough that bail money could be posted for a few Panther 21 defendants.[12] Party members chose Dhoruba for release to act as

> ...prevent the coalition...which might be the first step toward a real Mau Mau in America...prevent the rise of a messiah who could unify and electrify the movement...pinpoint potential troublemakers and neutralize them...prevent...leaders from gaining respectability by discrediting them to the responsible Negro community...

spokesperson for the Panther 21 and build support for BPP programs. Notified of his release, the FBI ordered immediate and continuous surveillance.[13] In succeeding months, Dhoruba's whereabouts were recorded, his speeches taped, and information concerning him disseminated to state and local police agencies. In June 1970, Dhoruba was placed on the FBI's "Agitator Index" solely because of his "extensive public appearances on behalf of the BPP."[14] This index, established in 1967, was "a convenient list of primary targets for COINTELPRO activity."[15]

Dhoruba bin-Wahad then became a target of a sophisticated plan carried out by the FBI during 1970 and early 1971 to divide the Panthers internally. In executing this plot, the FBI manipulated differences in political perspective and exacerbated personality conflicts to create two violently opposed factions within the Party, one on the West Coast loyal to BPP leader Huey P. Newton, who was released from prison in August 1970, and the

other on the East Coast loyal to Eldridge Cleaver, then in exile in Algeria. As one of the few Panther 21 defendants on bail, Dhoruba became a pawn in this plan.[16]

A myriad of counterintelligence operations were directed at Huey P. Newton, causing him to fear many loyal BPP members. In one such operation, in October 1970, the FBI anonymously warned Newton that Cleaver intended to "set up" Newton through New York BPP members.[17] Through the efforts of high-level informants, provocateurs, fictitious letters, and manipulation of the media, an unprecedented level of fear and suspicion existed within the BPP by late 1970. Numerous loyal members were expelled by Newton and others demoted. This internal strife was noted by J. Edgar Hoover in a memorandum to several field offices on January 28, 1971. Observing that counterintelligence operations have caused Newton to react violently to criticisms, the Director ordered that:

> The present chaotic situation within the BPP must be exploited and recipients must maintain the present high level of counterintelligence activity.... Immediately furnish Bureau recommendation for further counterintelligence activity designed to further aggravate the dissension within BPP leadership.[18]

The field offices responded with enthusiasm. On February 1, 1971, the New York Office proposed a letter be sent to Eldridge Cleaver, purportedly written by the Panther 21, criticizing Newton.[19] In early February 1971, Newton began a speaking tour of the East Coast. The FBI used this opportunity to further heighten existing tensions. An anonymous letter was sent to Newton's brother, Melvin, warning him that Huey would be killed by East Coast leadership while on the tour.[20] As an outspoken member of the New York Chapter and a Panther 21 member, Dhoruba bin-Wahad was suspected of making this alleged threat. Dhoruba found out, and he, along with three other BPP members fled New York for their safety in mid-February 1971, jumping bail in the Panther 21 case.

---

12. The brutal overt repression of the BPP did arouse some support for them in the liberal white community. For example, in January 1970, noted composer and conductor Leonard Bernstein hosted a fund-raising party for incarcerated Panthers. The FBI responded by mailing copies of articles from the BPP newspaper which expressed support for the goals of the Palestine Liberation Organization to Jewish guests at the event. Through this mailing, the FBI hoped to expose the alleged "anti-Semitic posture" of the BPP. The New York FBI office was instructed to sign the letter "with an anonymous name with additional phraseology such as 'Concerned and Loyal Jew,' or other similar terminology." Memorandum from Director to New York dated February 25, 1970 captioned "Counterintelligence Program." Alienation of Jewish support for the BPP was a frequent goal of FBI counterintelligence operations.

13. Teletype dated March 26, 1970, captioned "Black Panther Party-Travel of Leadership."

14. FBI Memorandum from Director to New York dated June 1, 1970, captioned "Richard Moore."

15. *Op. cit.*, n. 2, p. 511.

16. This tactic had been successful earlier in bringing about the expulsion of the entire BPP International Staff. Commenting upon this operation, the FBI noted as follows:

"To create friction between Black Panther Party leader Eldridge Cleaver in Algeria and BPP Headquarters, a spurious letter was sent to Cleaver, who accepted it as genuine. As a result, the International Staff of the BPP was neutralized when Cleaver fired most of its members. Bureau personnel received incentive awards from the Director for this operation."

See FBI Memorandum from G.C. Moore to William Sullivan dated May 14, 1970, captioned "Counterintelligence Program, Black Nationalist-Hate Groups."

17. FBI Memorandum from New York to Director dated October 7, 1970, captioned "Counterintelligence Program, Black Nationalist-Hate Groups." The New York Office notes further:

"The NYO believes the proposed may bear fruit because it would appear that Huey P. Newton is apparently unstable and suffering from a sort of complex."

18. FBI Memorandum from Director to Boston dated January 28, 1971, captioned "Counterintelligence Program, Black Extremists, Racial Matters."

19. FBI Memorandum from New York to Director dated February 2, 1971, captioned "Counterintelligence Program, Black Nationalist-Hate Groups."

20. FBI Memorandum from San Francisco to Director dated February 2, 1971, captioned "Counterintelligence Program, Black Nationalist-Hate Groups."

Dhoruba's fears of FBI-inspired factional violence were not unfounded. In March 1971, COINTELPRO was successful and the BPP erupted into bloody factionalism.[21]

The Arrest and Frame-Up of Dhoruba bin-Wahad

The split in the BPP did not bolster the weak case against the Panther 21. On May 13, 1971, all defendants, including Dhoruba *in absentia*, were acquitted of all charges. Alarmed by the acquittal, J. Edgar Hoover ordered an immediate intensification of FBI operations against all acquitted Panther 21 defendants.[22]

On May 19, 1971, two New York City Police officers who were guarding the home of Manhattan District Attorney Frank Hogan (the prosecutor in the Panther 21 case) were shot and seriously wounded. Two days later, two other officers were shot and killed in Harlem. In communiques issued a few days after each shooting, the Black Liberation Army, an armed clandestine organization, took credit for both actions.

These shootings, claimed by a previously unknown organization, prompted a coordinated federal, state, and local campaign to capture anyone the government thought could have been involved. This investigation, given the name "Newkill," was launched at a White House meeting on May 28, 1971, attended by President Richard M. Nixon, Attorney General John Mitchell, assistant Attorney General for internal security Robert Mardian, J. Edgar Hoover, and representatives of local police agencies.[23] Nixon ordered a "no-punches-pulled" campaign to imprison Black political fugitives. The minutes of this meeting have allegedly been lost by Nixon.[24]

The "Newkill" investigation marked the formalization of the FBI and local police strategy to prosecute Black political activists under the guise of "criminal" investigations. "Newkill," and the later "Chesrob" investigation[25] served as the basis for the hunting down, murder, torture, and prosecution of Black revolutionaries forced into hiding by the successful COINTELPRO operations of the FBI.[26]

At the time of the May 19, 1971 shooting, Dhoruba was still a fugitive in the Panther 21 case as the result of the BPP split. Federal and local law enforcement agencies believed he was in Algeria. On June 5, 1971, Dhoruba and three others were ar-

rested in the Bronx at the Triple O Social Club, an after-hours narcotics hangout, while committing an armed robbery of that club.[27] A machine gun of the caliber used to shoot the officers on May 19 was recovered at the scene. The police and FBI now had all they wanted: They had a machine gun; they had in custody one of the most vocal BPP leaders; and they had a way out of the deep embarrassment caused by the recent acquittal of the Panther 21.

But other than the alleged weapon, the government had no evidence. Of the seven eyewitnesses to the shooting, none could

---

Not satisfied with incarcerating an innocent man for 19 years, the Manhattan District Attorney's Office is currently appealing the decision releasing Dhoruba. Moreover, they have stated that if they fail on appeal, they will seek to try Dhoruba for a fourth time.

---

identify Dhoruba after viewing a lineup. Indeed, two witnesses chose another participant in the lineup as closely resembling one of the perpetrators. Then, on June 12, 1971, the NYPD received an "anonymous" telephone call from a woman who stated as follows:

> The four men you are holding are not suspects. They may know who did it. They did not do it, either the [May 19] or [May 21] shooting. They were at my girlfriend's house, 757 Beck Street, Bronx. Her last name is Joseph.... They did nothing until the Social Club incident. I will call again.

The anonymous caller turned out to be Pauline Joseph herself. Scores of police descended upon 757 Beck Street, arrested Ms. Joseph, and had her committed as a material witness. For nearly two years Ms. Joseph remained in the exclusive custody of the New York County District Attorney, mostly living at the old Commodore Hotel in Manhattan with various NYPD officials. This tragic woman who had a history of mental disorders and was recently diagnosed as a paranoid schizophrenic, was literally brainwashed by the FBI, NYPD and District Attorney to become the chief witness against Dhoruba. Through the 20 months she was in custody, her story changed from exonerating Dhoruba to being present during certain comings and goings at the time of the shooting.

In order to achieve Dhoruba's false conviction, prosecutors then proceeded to stack the case. First, all prior, recorded statements of Pauline Joseph, including the text of her "anonymous" telephone call, were withheld from the defense, precluding defense counsel's most effective weapon in cross-examination. Second, Pauline Joseph was fed details, allegedly "corroborated" by uncontroverted physical evidence, so that her testimony might seem plausible. Third, exculpatory

---

21. In March 1971, Robert Webb, a BPP member loyal to Cleaver was shot and killed in New York, allegedly by Newton supporters. In April 1971, Sam Napier was killed, allegedly by Cleaver supporters. In an April 5, 1971, memorandum, the FBI congratulated itself for the Webb murder noting that the high state of confusion in the BPP was a direct result of their counterintelligence efforts.

22. In a May 24, 1971, letter, Hoover frantically ordered the New York field office to:
"Intensify investigations of [the Panther 21]. Target sources at determining their black extremist activities. Develop additional sources and informants close to these individuals in order that the Bureau can be advised on a timely basis as to their day-to-day activities and associates of a black extremist nature."

23. FBI Memorandum from E.S. Miller to A. Rosen, dated November 23, 1971, captioned "Newkill."

24. "Break-In Memos Allegedly Missing," *New York Times,* June 22, 1978, p. 16.

25. "Chesrob" is the FBI acronym given to its search for Assata Shakur (Joanne Chesimard) and other suspected BLA members.

26. For example, BPP members Twyman Meyers, Frank Fields, Zayd Malik Shakur, Harold Russel, Anthony Kimu White, and Woody Green were all shot and killed by police and or FBI agents who claimed they were merely trying to apprehend suspects in BLA-related cases. Yet none of these individuals had criminal charges pending against them.

27. Stating that this action was an attempt to rid the Black community of drugs, Dhoruba subsequently pled guilty to this robbery.

DataCenter   464 19th Street, Oakland, California 94612 (415) 835-4692

ballistics and fingerprint examinations performed by the FBI and NYPD were withheld and/or destroyed. Finally, although the FBI was intimately involved in every aspect of the prosecution, its activities were kept secret, as was all information concerning the counterintelligence program.

In response to defense motions at trial for exculpatory information, the prosecuting District Attorney (now U.S. District Judge) John F. Keenan swore in October 1971 (four months after Pauline Joseph's telephone call) that no exculpatory information existed and that all evidence "ineluctably" pointed to Dhoruba's involvement.[28] The District Attorney's office repeatedly represented that, except for a one-paragraph statement taken on the night of her commitment, there were no recorded statements from Pauline Joseph, a woman kept under 24-hour police guard for nearly two years.

Dhoruba's first trial commenced in the fall of 1972 and ended with a hung jury, with a majority voting for acquittal. The second trial, begun in January 1973, ended in a mistrial after the judge, Joseph Martinis, became ill with a "cold" during jury selection and after several Black jurors had been sworn.[29] Jury selection for the third trial began one week later. To the defense's astonishment, Black people accounted for only five percent of the jury panel.[30] Confronted with a stacked jury pool, fabricated evidence, prosecutorial misconduct, and ignorant of the fact that he was a target of COINTELPRO, Dhoruba was convicted and sentenced to life imprisonment.

All direct appeals from the conviction were denied. In 1975, after Church Committee disclosures concerning COINTELPRO, Dhoruba began a civil rights lawsuit in federal court in New York charging that he was the victim of an FBI/NYPD frame-up. The litigation stagnated until 1980. The NYPD maintained that they possessed no documents relevant to Dhoruba's claims. The FBI produced documents from Dhoruba's "name" file but maintained that additional papers did not exist. In May 1980, confronted with documents obtained from a related litigation showing that the NYPD and FBI were committing perjury, U.S. District Judge Mary Johnson Lowe finally ordered the FBI to produce its massive files on the BPP and Dhoruba.

From 1980 to 1984, the FBI produced approximately 300,000 pages on Dhoruba, COINTELPRO, the BPP, and related investigations. However, the contents of these documents were nearly two-thirds excised on "executive privilege" and other grounds. Thus, over the next several years, Dhoruba's lawyers were forced to conduct a document-by-document review to submit legal challenges to these deletions. Finally, in 1987, the FBI produced an almost uncensored copy of its "Newkill" file, including documents generated during the investigation of the May 19, 1971 police shooting. Among these 5,000 pages were over 30 prior interviews with Pauline Joseph, contradicting every aspect of her

FBI documents obtained years after conviction also show that evidence was fabricated and exculpatory evidence suppressed for political reasons...

trial testimony. Also included were exculpatory scientific tests and documentation showing that the District Attorney, with the cooperation of the NYPD and FBI, intentionally misrepresented the existence of this exculpatory material.

A motion for a new trial was filed in April 1988. Nearly one year later, New York State Supreme Court Justice Peter McQuillan issued a five-page decision finding that the DA had wrongfully withheld the prior statements and, had they been disclosed, Pauline Joseph would have been "successfully impeached." However, the court denied the request for a new trial on technical grounds and refused to rule on the documented allegations of misconduct.

On February 8, 1990, Justice McQuillan was reversed by the appellate court and essentially ordered by that court to vacate Dhoruba's conviction. A bail hearing held on March 22, 1990, finally resulted in Dhoruba's release.

Not satisfied with incarcerating an innocent man for 19 years, the Manhattan District Attorney's Office is currently appealing the decision releasing Dhoruba. Moreover, the Office has stated that if it fails on appeal, it will seek to try Dhoruba for a fourth time. The decision only underscores the political nature of this case.

The District Attorney surely knows that the racist, politically motivated prosecution of Dhoruba bin-Wahad was not an aberration. His prosecution was part of a counterintelligence strategy designed to neutralize the Black Panther Party and thereby weaken the movement of Black people in the United States for self-determination and human rights. Other members of the BPP who were direct and/or indirect targets of COINTELPRO were prosecuted in the early 1970s and remain in prison today; others were murdered. The juries which convicted those targeted by the FBI were also unaware of COINTELPRO. In these cases, FBI documents obtained years after conviction also show that evidence was fabricated and exculpatory evidence suppressed for political reasons.[31] Thus, it is expected that federal and state law enforcement agencies will use all their efforts to re-incarcerate Dhoruba not only to prevent him from continuing the political work he began 20 years ago, but to prevent a precedent which might ease the release of the remaining Black political prisoners in jails throughout the country.

The existence of Black political prisoners in the U.S. is a consequence of the vicious racist repression of illegal COINTELPRO activities under the pretext and guise of the criminal law. Their existence exposes the U.S. government as one of the most hypocritical violators of human rights in the world. The freedom of U.S. political prisoners is therefore something that must be supported by all freedom-loving peoples.   •

28. Affidavit of John Keenan submitted in *People v. Richard Moore*, Ind. 3885/71, New York County.

29. In accordance with established procedure at the time, Joseph Martinis was chosen by the District Attorney to preside over Dhoruba's trials.

30. The usual percentage of Black people was about 25 percent.

31. For example, in the case of the "New York Three" (former BPP members Albert Nuh Washington, Herman Bell, and Anthony Jalil Bottom), convicted for the 1971 murder of two police officers, the prosecution withheld the results of an exculpatory FBI ballistics comparison. In another well-known case, documents obtained through the Freedom of Information Act show that former BPP leader Geronimo ji Jaga (Pratt), a documented COINTELPRO target, was in fact under FBI surveillance in Oakland, California, at the same time that the state maintained he was committing a murder 400 miles away.

Free Speech Is at Issue as a Palestinian in U.S. Fights Deportation

By SETH MYDANS
Special to The New York Times

LOS ANGELES, Nov. 29 — Khader Hamide is the kind of immigrant the United States says it does not want. Although he arrived here legally and holds a regular job as an airline ticket salesman, Mr. Hamide, a Palestinian, holds politically unwelcome views and expresses them loudly.

In a deportation case the Government has pursued against him since 1987, Mr. Hamide and seven other immigrants who entered the country legally are accused of being members of the Popular Front for the Liberation of Palestine, a self-described Marxist group that was involved in several airline hijackings in the 1970's in its quest for a Palestinian state. The Federal authorities say the eight were distributing literature of the popular front, advocates subversive activities.

Mr. Hamide and seven others have denied being members of the group, though Mr. Hamide says he supports the Palestine Liberation Organization, of which the popular front is a radical faction. The deportation case against the eight, which is now expected to be heard by an immigration judge next spring, raises questions about the free-speech rights of non-citizens and about the Government's right to exclude foreigners who may voice unwelcome views or who may advocate terrorism. The case also demonstrates the Government's continuing effort to bar foreigners for their political views, although last year Congress repealed a provision of the 1952 McCarran-Walter Immigration Act that provided for such restrictions.

New Charges Are Added

That repeal allowed for the completion of pending prosecutions under the act and also provided a new standard for exclusion of aliens, the advocacy of terrorism. Now Mr. Hamide and one of his seven colleagues face deportation charges under both the old and the new statutes.

The Government said that if it was forced to choose between the statutes, it would elect to proceed on the old ideologically based charges rather than the new charges of advocacy of terrorism.

The Government's lawyer in the case, Michael P. Lindemann, who is in the Justice Department's office of immigration litigation, said he could not discuss the case because "there are an awful lot of aspects that are in litigation."

The continuing vigor of the Government's effort to exclude the eight takes on a new perspective in light of the opening of peace talks in the Middle East, which include the P.L.O.

"You would hope the Administration would be more tolerant of the Palestinian viewpoint, given that the P.L.O. and the Palestinian people have made a genuine step towards peace," said Mr. Hamide, 37 years old, whose wife, Julie Nuangugi Mungai, is expecting a child. Ms. Mungai, a native of Kenya, is the only non-Palestinian among the group.

Deeper U.S. Motive Is Seen

Mr. Hamide said he believed that the tenacity of the prosecutors reflected a desire to win a case that would allow for the deportation of all foreigners who espouse views hostile to those of the United States Government.

Prosecutors acknowledge using a double standard for non-citizens in terms of the First Amendment's guarantee of free speech. "It goes without saying that if they were United States citizens, nothing would be applicable to them," said Mr. Lindemann, referring to prosecution on the basis of their expressed views.

It is this double standard, in part, that has delayed the proceedings for so long. In December 1988, a Federal district judge blocked the deportation order, a ruling that was overturned for technical reasons on appeal.

"In this case the Government is trying to stifle certain ideas from entering our society from certain aliens through its immigration power," said Judge Stephen V. Wilson in issuing the ruling. "Our society, however, was built on the premise that only through the free flow of ideas can our nation grow and prosper.

"Logically, to say that resident aliens have First Amendment rights in the domestic context but not in the deportation context is to deny them First Amendment rights at all."

The repeal of the ideological sections of the McCarran-Walter Act made clear that foreigners are entitled to the same rights of free speech as citizens.

The act, a product of the Communist scares of the McCarthy era, was promoted as protecting citizens from subversive ideas. Over the years, the Government used it to keep out thousands of foreigners, including the leader of the P.L.O., Yasir Arafat.

The act set up 33 categories for barring foreign visitors and those seeking to become residents, including espionage, drug trafficking, polygamy and deviant sexual behavior. It also included ideological provisions barring advocates of Communism or totalitarian dictatorship.

'I Have Strong Views'

Despite the Congressional repeal of these ideological provisions, Mr. Hamide said the case itself has served to curtail the range of his public speech as he stays away from statements that could offer fuel to his prosecutors. But he is far from silenced, and accepts invitations to speak out in public about his own case as well as about Middle East issues.

"I have strong views about the right of the Palestinian people to an independent Palestinian state," he said. "I believe the Israeli occupation is wrong and illegal. I support the P.L.O. as the sole legitimate representative of the Palestinian people. And I will continue to express these viewpoints."

When Mr. Hamide and his colleagues were arrested early in 1987 by the Federal authorities, they were charged with subversion and held for almost three weeks. An immigration court judge ordered them released, some on bond and others on their own recognizance, saying the Government had failed to show evidence of specific illegal actions. The Government later acknowledged that the eight had not committed any criminal act.

"The initial statement by the Immigration and Naturalization Service was that they were arresting a group of terrorists in Los Angeles," said Marc Van Der Hout of the National Lawyers Guild, the lead counsel for the defendants. "Then it came out that they were charging them with distributing literature, publications, and they were deporting them because they didn't like the content of the publications," he said.

"This has been a relentless attack on Palestinians doing lawful, legitimate, First Amendment-protected activities."

As the case moved slowly through the courts, the charges of subversion were dropped against all eight, and the ideologically related charges under the McCarran-Walter Act were dropped against all except Mr. Hamide Michael Shehadeh. These charges against the two were augmented by charges of advocating terrorism. The other six are now only charged with technical violations of the immigration laws.

Mr. Hamide, who was born on the West Bank now occupied by Israel, came to the United States as a student in 1971 and later received both a bachelor of arts degree in psychology and a master's degree in business administration from the University of Oregon.

As his case has dragged on he said, he has accommodated to the situation. "My wife and I delayed having a child but now we gave up delaying because it looks like this case has taken on a life of its own," he said.

Targeting the Environmental Movement:

Bombs, Lies and Body Wires

Johan Carlisle

- An FBI agent provocateur infiltrates an activist group and instigates members to sabotage a power line. Those involved—except the agent—are arrested and charged with terrorism. Other members are arrested for conspiracy.
- Two activists are repeatedly threatened on the phone and in person. A poster with their portraits, with the crosshairs of a rifle scope superimposed, is put on their office door. Soon after, they are seriously injured in a car bombing. The police arrest them in the hospital as prime suspects.
- A right-wing group publishes bomb-making diagrams, falsely attributes them to an activist group, and is caught planting a fake bomb at an activist's office.
- A major news service distributes an unconfirmed story based on an "ex"-CIA counter-terrorism expert's theory that activists and mad scientists are secretly plotting to unleash a virus to wipe out humanity.

In the 1960s the FBI unleashed COINTELPRO, a campaign designed to divide and destroy Black liberation and anti-Vietnam War, feminist, and other social movements of that turbulent period. At the time, the FBI program seemed like a series of unconnected incidents and anyone who had suggested a coordinated government campaign would have been dismissed as a paranoid conspiracy theorist.

Eventually, tenacious investigation uncovered hard evidence that the U.S. government used propaganda, promotion of internal splits within organizations, physical intimidation, disinformation in the media, conspiracy trials and murder to eliminate movements it considered undesirable.

The incidents above could have been taken from the files of COINTELPRO. In fact, they all happened within the last few years and were directed against the environmental movement. Increasingly, these radical (*i.e.*, effective) organizations have been harassed, infiltrated, smeared in the media, and even threatened by assassination attempts. Increasingly, serious researchers and activists are concerned—given the similarity to the techniques employed in COINTELPRO—that there could be tolerance or coordination from above.[1]

The two environmental groups under the heaviest fire are Earth First! and Greenpeace. Both are outspokenly nonviolent yet considered radical because they practice direct action, carry out high-profile media events and civil disobedience, and because they are affecting corporate profits with their numerous successful campaigns to halt or slow environmental destruction.

Johan Carlisle is a San Francisco-based freelance journalist and managing editor of *Propaganda Review*. Research assistance by Sheila O'Donnell.

1. See: Ward Churchill and Jim Vander Wall, *Agents of Repression: the FBI's Secret War Against the Black Panther Party and the American Indian Movement* (Boston: South End Press, 1988).

Earth First!

On the morning of May 24, 1990, Earth First! organizers Judi Bari and Darryl Cherney were driving from Oakland to Santa Cruz, California. They planned to address a rally promoting the upcoming Redwood Summer protests against the destruction of the last remaining old growth forests in northern California. Suddenly, a pipe bomb with nails taped to it exploded directly under Bari's seat. She was severely injured and at first doctors thought she might not survive. A year later, she is still in pain, has trouble walking and cannot stand or drive for long periods of time. Doctors say she will be permanently maimed. Cherney was nearly blinded in one eye.

The attack on Bari and Cherney was the culmination of a steady build-up of death threats and confrontations in northern California. A year later Bari said:

The bombing represented the end of innocence for our movement. Sure, we had seen violence before, but this was different. The logger who broke Mem Hill's nose, the log truck driver who ran me off the road—themselves victims of the timber industry—in the heat of the moment took out their anger on us. But whoever put that bomb in my car was a cold and premeditating killer.

The FBI's attempt to frame me and Darryl...made us realize what we are up against. Not only are they willing to use lethal force to protect their 'right' to level whole ecosystems for private profit; they are also backed by the full power of the government's secret police."[2]

---

2. Bari is a unique threat to the timber industries. She is also a Wobblie (Industrial Workers of the World) union organizer, and the first to bring timber workers and Earth First!ers together.

Although neither activist had a record of violent activities and both were ardent proponents of nonviolence, the Oakland police and the FBI immediately targeted them as the prime and to this day only suspects. Cherney was treated and released from the hospital the night of the bombing and then taken to jail. Bari was placed under arrest in her hospital bed.

A letter containing detailed information was sent to the Santa Rosa *Press Democrat* four days after the bombing. "The Lord's Avenger," writing in flowery, biblical prose took credit for the attack. The FBI's immediate reaction, despite lack of evidence, was to ascribe the letter to Bari (written from her hospital bed) or her accomplice. It failed to consider other suspects or follow up other explanations.

Day after day, local media dutifully reported "evidence" which the Oakland police – citing the FBI – offered as proof that the Earth First!ers had been transporting an anti-personnel bomb which allegedly detonated prematurely. Police claimed the bomb was on the floor in the back of the car when it went off and that therefore Bari and Cherney must have known about it.

Now, 16 months later, no charges have been filed. Bari and Cherney remain prime suspects despite the fact that their attorneys and investigators have developed and fed the police a number of leads which the police and FBI have apparently failed to investigate including: an alleged agent provocateur, who persuaded Bari to pose with an automatic rifle (the picture of which was later sent to the local police and was published in a local newspaper); a series of memos[3] from the director of public relations for Pacific Lumber Company to the company president which showed a clear pattern of approval for violence against Earth First! activists; and dozens of death threats prior to the bombing.

In May 1991, Judi Bari and Darryl Cherney filed a federal lawsuit against the FBI and several law enforcement agencies seeking damages for covering up the identity of the real bomber by obstructing the investigation.[4]

"I don't know if the FBI had anything to do with putting that bomb in my car," said Bari in a speech at a May 5th rally, "but I know for certain that they tried to frame me for it and made sure the real bomber wasn't found. They removed my [car's] whole floorboard with a blowtorch and sent it to their crime lab in Washington, D.C., thereby destroying the evidence that would prove they were lying about the location of the bomb."

Associated Press
Richard W. Held's involvement in operations targeting social change movements spans decades.

The Missing Link?

The FBI agent in charge of the Bari/Cherney bombing investigation is Richard W. Held, a name familiar to activists from the Black Hills of South Dakota to Puerto Rico to Los Angeles.[5] Held was the director of the Los Angeles COINTELPRO operations in the late 1960s, when the Bureau conducted a massive disinformation, harassment and alleged assassination program against the Black Panthers and numerous other activist groups and individuals.[6]

Held was instrumental in the Los Angeles-based part of the FBI campaign which used cartoons and forged letters to create divisions in the Black Power movement.[7] Eventually, this national effort decimated the movement and led to the shooting death of two Panthers who believed the forgeries.

Later, from 1969-72, down Highway One in San Diego, a secretive FBI-funded right-wing paramilitary group called the Secret Army Organization (SAO) waged a vicious campaign against the underground press, Black and anti-war activists. Held was involved there as well.[8]

In a July 1976 press conference, Held acknowledged that he had also worked in Minneapolis where he was responsible for COINTELPRO activities during the 1960s and 1970s.

Held went on from there to the Pine Ridge, South Dakota campaign conducted by the FBI and Pentagon which resulted in the death of at least 70 American Indian Movement activists, the 1975 military assault on the reservation, and the framing and jailing of Leonard Peltier.[9]

---

5. Richard W. Held should not be confused with former deputy to J. Edgar Hoover, Richard G. Held, his father, who retired in 1987.

6. See *CAIB*, Number 24, pp. 26-7 and Number 25, p. 54.

7. In December 1969, "four days after a similar raid on a Panther apartment in Chicago (a raid which left Mark Clark and Fred Hampton dead), 40 men of the Special Weapons and Tactics (SWAT) squad, with more than a hundred regular police as backup, raided the Los Angeles Panther headquarters at 5:30 in the morning...The Panthers chose to defend themselves and for four hours they fought off police, refusing to surrender until press and the public were on the scene. Six of them were wounded. Thirteen were arrested. Miraculously, none of them were killed." (Churchill, *op. cit.*, p. 82.) *See also for reproduction of the cartoons: CAIB*, Number 36, pp. 34-35.

8. *San Diego Union*, January 11, 1976; *New York Times*, January 11, 1976; "Nanda Zoccino, "Ex-FBI Informer Describes Terrorist Role," *Los Angeles Times*, January 26, 1976.

9. This was one of the first-known joint military/FBI/SWAT operations in "Operation Garden Plot," the Pentagon national master plan for civil disturbance control which is still in effect. It was the product of paranoid government leaders who were convinced that widespread armed revolution was inevitable. Peltier is still in prison, sentenced to two consecutive life terms, and is considered a political prisoner by Amnesty International.

---

3. The memos were obtained from Pacific Lumber by Cherney's lawyers.

4. *San Francisco Chronicle*, May 22, 1991, p. A7.

In 1978 Richard Held was transferred to Puerto Rico where as Special Agent in Charge (SAC) he oversaw a massive surveillance and counter-insurgency operation against a growing independence movement. The state police intelligence agency admitted in court that files were kept on at least 74,000 people. Over a 15 year period preceding and during Held's tenure, hundreds were attacked, bombed, and shot. Pro-independence newspapers were bombed repeatedly and activists' houses were burned to the ground. "Although rightwing organizations claimed credit for nearly 70 of these attacks, not one person has ever been arrested or brought to trial."[10]

According to Ward Churchill, "During the 1980s, the FALN [Fuerzas Armadas de Liberación Nacional Puertorriqueña] and other pro-independence organizations have been the target of some of [the FBI's] most intense covert operations. FBI activities on the island culminated on August 30, 1985 with a massive paramilitary operation bearing a striking resemblance to the operations on the Pine Ridge and Rosebud Reservations a decade earlier. More than 300 heavily armed FBI agents and U.S. marshals participated in raids throughout Puerto Rico, kicking in doors, conducting warrantless searches, wrecking the contents of homes, impounding personal property and arresting scores of activists on 'John Doe' warrants."[11]

Richard W. Held was rewarded once again and became Special Agent in Charge in San Francisco where he is currently leading the investigation into the Earth First! bombing.

Associated Press
Judi Bari, recovering from carbomb.

The Monkeywrench Gang

Meanwhile, in Prescott, Arizona, the U.S. government is prosecuting five Earth First!ers for an alleged conspiracy to sabotage power lines, nuclear power plants, and a ski resort. Two First!ers were arrested May 1989 in the desert. A heavily-armed FBI SWAT team caught them cutting a power transmission tower. The next day, a third activist, Peg Millett, who had escaped the previous evening's bust, was arrested at work. Earth First! co-founder, David Foreman was rousted out of bed in Tucson by heavily-armed FBI agents and taken to jail in Phoenix. The fourth member of the tower cutting crew was not arrested—and the Earth First!ers quickly real-

ized that their trusted comrade, Michael Fain aka Mike Tait, was an FBI agent provocateur and that he, and paid informant Ron Frazier, had set them up with the FBI.[12] "[Fain] was a fellow monkeywrencher," said Earth First! spokesperson Karen Pickett, "who had not only encouraged the plan but had facilitated its implementation by renting the acetylene tanks, filling his truck with gasoline and driving the crew out to the desert where SWAT lay in wait." Fain had slowly worked his way into the activists' confidence, trying to get to Foreman, the ultimate target. Pickett said, "He was a dinner guest in their homes, he took Peg out dancing and was dating one of her closest friends. He played on their sympathies and compassion. Then he brought out the big screw."[13]

The FBI's real plan, behind the estimated $2 million intelligence operation, was revealed when defense attorneys read in their opening remarks the now-famous line mistakenly recorded by Fain's body wire as he chatted with a fellow agent, unaware that he had neglected to turn off his recorder: Fain was frustrated at his inability to get Foreman to incriminate himself. "Foreman isn't the guy we need to pop. I mean, in terms of an actual perpetrator. [Foreman] is the guy we need to pop to send a message. And that's all we're really doing..." The message is the same one sent by COINTELPRO: the more effective a movement for social change, the more tenaciously it will be targeted.

The Sahara Club

In Spring 1990, as Earth First! prepared for Redwood Summer, a small group of off-road bikers launched a new organization. The Sahara Club, said founder Rick Sieman, would provide an alternative to groups like Sierra Club and Earth First! which are full of "eco-pigs" bent on "spreading panic and hysteria" about environmental threats. "We want people to be able to get under one umbrella organization to fight the eco-freaks and the Nature Nazis," he continued. "Everything we do—including the name Sahara Club is designed for maximum irritation."[14]

---

10. Churchill, *op. cit.*, p. 368; quoting from Alfred Lopez, *Dona Licha's Island* (Boston: South End Press, 1987), p. 146.

11. Churchill, *op. cit.*, p. 386.

12. Karen Pickett, "FBI Targets Earth First!" *Anderson Valley Advertiser* (Booneville, California), July 3, 1991, p. 8.

13. Pickett, *ibid.*

14. "Sahara Club Targets 'Eco-Freaks'," *San Francisco Chronicle*, Associated Press, December 12, 1990, p. B4.

Not much is known about this small group of burly bikers which claims 4,000 members. Their political debut was a direct action campaign launched against Sen. Alan Cranston (D-Cal.) for his Desert Protection bill which would prevent them from riding their motorcycles in the environmentally sensitive desert outside Los Angeles. They now appear intent on destroying Earth First!.

"They crashed [Earth First!er] Mark Davis's talk in California at a religious college," Bari told *CAIB*, "There were about 30 of them wearing normal clothes who suddenly stood up, removed their shirts to reveal matching black T-shirts with a picture of someone strangling an Earth First!er. They not only shouted Mark down but they pushed their way up onto the stage and took away his microphone."

The group's newsletter has grown more vicious as well as more sophisticated over time. Issue #2 contains a highly detailed schematic drawing of a semi-buried booby trap explosive described as "one example of a death trap from Earth First!...This deadly device is planted in the ground over a trail that bikes or ATVs use, and when the wheel makes contact, the shell is fired, shooting the charge up into the face of the rider." The newsletter contends that the illustration "is taken directly from an Earth First book on how to set traps to kill or maim dirt bikers. This is not a joke folks."

Indeed, no one is laughing. Earth First!, unable to get a copy of the manual at the Grenada Hills, California address listed in the newsletter, doubts that the publication exists. If it does, charges Bari, "it was obviously made up by them, not by us...that this diagram came out one month before I was bombed may be significant."

The Sahara Club newsletter supports Bari's contention that the Club promoted harassment. During Redwood Summer, the Club newsletter boasted that the group held dirty tricks workshops for local anti-environmentalists. "Whether they did or not," noted Bari, "dirty tricks started to happen to us shortly after these guys arrived on the scene." On August 30, 1990, for example, alleged Sahara Clubber Timothy Harold Haynes delivered a bundle of his organization's newsletters to an Earth First! office in Arcata, California. He or someone had wrapped the package in duct tape so that it appeared to be a bomb. He was later arrested and convicted of a misdemeanor count for "placing a facsimile bomb."

Oakland Tribune
An endangered old growth redwood.

Greenpeace

In an act of state-sponsored terrorism, in July 1985, French intelligence agents in New Zealand bombed the Greenpeace ship, *Rainbow Warrior*, killing photographer Fernando Pereira. Since then, Greenpeace has grown stronger and is now involved in nonviolent environmental actions around the globe. Its opposition has responded with violence and harassment.

In March 1991, Pat Costner, a research scientist working with Greenpeace, returned home to find her office and rural home burned to the ground. More than 20 years research on toxic waste and, ironically, incineration, was destroyed in the fire which local officials classified as an accident. Greenpeace, however, hired investigators who found evidence of arson and plans to offer a reward for the arrest and conviction of the arsonist.

Harassment campaigns against the organization are becoming increasingly sophisticated as Greenpeace's effectiveness and influence threaten vested interests. Using the same techniques which resulted in media portrayal of Earth First! as "Eco-Terrorists," major corporations are devising secret strategies to marginalize and smear environmentalists.

A confidential plan developed by the Pittsburgh-based Ketchum Public Relations firm for Clorox Corporation and leaked to Greenpeace reveals the siege mentality which has been observed at other corporations, private security conferences, and government agencies.[15] "Crisis Management Plan," a 60-page memo, advised how to counter "worst-case scenarios" for environmental issues "which hold potential for presenting a public relations crisis" for Clorox.

Ketchum prepared a strategy to greenwash its image, neutralize "green journalists" and counter Greenpeace's campaign against the toxic effects of chlorine.[16]

---

15. *Pensacola News Journal*, "PR Firm's Damage Control Plan for Bleach Company is Leaked," May 13, 1991, p. 2A.

Chip Berlet, an investigative journalist for Political Research Associates in Cambridge, Massachusetts, reports that in conversations with participants at the American Society for Industrial Security (ASIS) conference in 1988, he detected a "troubling trend among a few hard-line outfits. Over breakfast a Navy security staffer said he had attended a naval intelligence briefing where Greenpeace was described as a 'terrorist' group with ties to 'international communist groups.' See also: Chip Berlet, " Taking Off the Gloves," *Greenpeace Magazine*, September/October 1990, p. 17.

16. *Greenpeace Magazine*, July/August 1991, p. 6.

- The Issue: Greenpeace has announced a worldwide effort to rid the world of chlorine by 1993 — Chlorine Free by '93, they call it. Greenpeace is well known, both for its dramatic campaigns, often associated with violent tactics, and with spurious research, generated more for its shock value and fund-raising appeal than its scientific utility.
- Industry Association (Chlorine Institute?) advertising campaign: "Stop Environmental Terrorism."
- Conduct research to determine if and how a slander lawsuit against the columnist and/or Greenpeace could be effective.
- [Use] third party scientific spokespeople [who] are prepared to cast doubts on the methodology and finding of the reports [damaging to Clorox and still unwritten].
- Enlisting the support of the union and the national union leadership since jobs are at stake.

Excerpts: Ketchum Public Relations "Crisis Management Plan."

In an attempt to spin this embarrassing leak, Clorox told the press that it was "not involved in [the plan's] preparation, and [is] not acting on its recommendations. The consulting firm's language and overly descriptive analysis detracts from its central theme."

The corporation apparently had no problem with the central theme itself — how to discredit environmentalists in the press and local communities where controversial environmental issues are being debated. Bill Walker, a Greenpeace public relations and media spokesperson, recently attended a convention of the Public Relations Society of America (PRSA). The title of the conference was "Our World in Transition" but Walker observed that after looking through the program it looked more like "How to Make Your Corporation Look Like a Friend to the Planet While Reaping Billions in the International Waste Trade."[17]

One workshop at the conference, "Building Public Support by Resolving Disputes Through Consensus," focused on how corporations should learn to neutralize activists and build relations with the locals. According to a participant:

When you're dealing with a group of outside agitators — Greenpeace or somebody like that," remarked a participant, "they usually have a different agenda than the people in the community where you're trying to place

your facility. If you let them rant and rave and foam at the mouth, the community will sometimes get turned off and...then you can arrange a private meeting behind [the activists'] backs."

The War on Eco-Terrorism: Who Drafted the Press?

Sometimes charges concocted against targeted groups are so wacky that it is hard to imagine anyone will take them seriously. "Ex"-CIA agent, Vincent Cannistraro[18] recently revealed to the press that he has "evidence" that a few "highly educated scientists" are secretly developing a virus that will kill all humans but leave all other species intact. He offered no proof of these "small organized clandestine cells" but assured the press that they constituted "potentially the most lethal of all terrorist movements."[19]

Newhouse News Service assigned a young reporter to research Cannistraro's theory. Jonathan Tilove spent three weeks talking to all kinds of environmentalists and was still unable to come up with any proof.[20] Tilove explained to CAIB that his article was written in an obviously ironic, tongue-in-cheek style which no one would take seriously.

Entitled "Mad Scientists Plot End of Mankind," the article went out on the New York Times syndicate to hundreds of papers around world. It was published on Sunday, April 14, 1991, weeks before the first anniversary of the Bari/Cherney bombing, by the San Francisco Examiner. Its Sunday edition is read by hundreds of thousands of people in northern California, an area where Earth First! is very active and where it is treated by many with suspicion, fear and violence.

Although Cannistraro's statements to the press did not name any environmental groups, Tilove's Newhouse News Service article printed in the Examiner mentioned Earth First! eight times.[21] The Examiner published the story as a serious news feature on page two along with a picture of Earth First! co-founder David Foreman.

---

17. Bill Walker, "Green Like Me," Greenpeace Magazine, May/June 1991, p. 9.

18. Cannistraro was giving a paper on the many terrorist threats around the world at the inaugural meeting of the Counterterrorism Study Group. This body was convened by and is run out of the Washington office of the National Strategy Information Center, a right-wing think tank co-founded by William Casey in 1962.

Cannistraro is no ordinary spook. For one thing, he calls himself an environmentalist. He was also a career CIA operations officer who, until the Iran-contra scandal in 1986, was CIA Director William Casey's "man" at the National Security Council where he was detailed as Oliver North's assistant in charge of monitoring covert operations. He slipped through his testimony unscathed at the Iran-Contra hearings and moved back to CIA headquarters, where he was the head of counterterrorism until his early "retirement" in 1989.

19. Jonathan Tilove, "Tale of a plot to rid earth of humankind," Newhouse News Service, April 14, 1991 by San Francisco Examiner, p. A-2.

20. Zack Stentz, freelance writer from Santa Cruz, noted that: "La-Rouche followers have been especially active in the campaign against environmentalists through their group 'Stop Eco-Fascism,' who last year distributed a videotape that juxtaposed shots of Earth First! demonstrations with Nazi rallies." Anderson Valley Advertiser, June 19, 1991, p. 12.

21. It should be noted that the Examiner, the Hearst flagship paper, has become decidedly more liberal since Will Hearst III took over a few years ago. Its excellent environmental reporter, Jane Kay, told CAIB that she had no involvement in the decision to run the "mad scientist" article.

In light of the violence directed against Earth First! in northern California, the publication of this article shocked a number of media analysts and environmentalists. An *ad hoc* group organized a protest outside the *Examiner's* office and forced a meeting. On April 23, Steven Cook, the senior editor who ran the "mad scientist" article, listened to representatives from Earth First!, Greenpeace, *Earth Island Journal*, and *Propaganda Review*. He admitted that he hadn't given much thought to the article. It was, he thought, "an interesting look at the subject of population control."

Eventually, he apologized and promised to give more thought to future articles about environmental groups. Judi Bari, outraged by the "mad scientist" article, wrote an op-ed which the *Examiner* printed the following Sunday challenging Tilove's lack of documentation. The best the author of the article can come up with, Bari charged, "is an anonymous letter-to-the-editor from a 1984 *Earth First! Journal*, carefully excerpted for maximum shock value."[22]

Bari was skeptical that a reporter in Washington, D.C. would have waded through 10 years of *Earth First! Journals'* letters to the editor[23] just to find this one letter. As it turned out, Tilove saved himself the legwork and got the letter from a paper on "eco-terrorism," written for the Heritage Foundation by Doug Bandow, an analyst for the Cato Institute.[24]

"We want...one umbrella organization to fight the eco-freaks and the Nature Nazis."

Rick Sieman, Sahara Club Founder

Looking Back, Moving Forward

The environmental future of our planet is looking worse each day. Given the obvious fact that all other social movements will be meaningless if the earth is uninhabitable, the radical environmental groups may well be at the forefront of political and social change. "The effectiveness of the environmental movement," said Greenpeace activist Josh Karliner, "can be measured not only by the documented attacks, but also the fact that the movement is growing every day."[25]

Associated Press

The Greenpeace Rainbow Warrior was sunk by French intelligence agents in New Zealand in 1985, killing one person.

In the 1960s, activists had no idea how extensively the FBI, the CIA and the military were infiltrating and harassing their organizations. The daring investigative work of progressive journalists, researchers and activists in the 1970s revealed the scope and horror of those massive espionage operations aimed at wiping out the challenges to authority that characterized a broad spectrum of U.S. society in the 1960s.

In the 1990s, said Earth First!er Chris Manes, "The government is treating [environmentalists] like terrorists although no person has ever been hurt by an Earth First! action."[26]

Given the potential economic and political impact of an effective movement, it is only reasonable to anticipate a strong, organized and even violent reaction from those interests which profit from the status quo. "The reason why corporations are 'greenwashing' their images, the reason why we have an 'environmental president,' and the reason why Judi Bari and Darryl Cherney got blown up," said Karliner, "is the increasing threat posed by the environmental movement."

While it is true that many radical environmentalists advocate profound changes in our polluting, wasteful, consumer society, they are not terrorists and there is no evidence that anyone is plotting such absurdity as wiping out humanity. When the press repeats this type of bizarre and undocumented disinformation it feeds the myth that groups like Earth First! and Greenpeace have a secret agenda of terrorism and total destruction of the American way of life.

Evidence of government reaction is mounting. "We need to deal with the repression of our movement," Carliner warned, "but we should not dwell on it."   •

---

22. Judi Bari, " 'Tabloid Attack' on Earth First!," *San Francisco Examiner*, April 21, 1991, p. A19.

23. The letters to the editor feature of the Earth First! Journal is discreetly titled "Dear Shit fer Brains."

24. According to Zack Stentz, "Bandow himself was not above spreading disinformation in the past. In a 1990 *Wall Street Journal* op-ed, Bandow included among the crimes of 'eco-terrorism' the bombing of sawmills and the stringing of piano wire to decapitate motorists. 'The sawmill bomb he's talking about was planted by the same person who tried to kill me,' said Bari, 'and the only people who claim to have seen this piano wire are Sahara Clubbers.' " See: Zack Stentz, "Disinformation Epidemic," *Anderson Valley Advertiser*, June 19, 1991, p. 1.

25. Interview with author, August 8, 1991.

26. Stentz, *op. cit.*, p. 12.

VIII. Technology : First Amendment & Privacy Rights

The ability to gather, sort, arrange, and select desired information electronically has proved to be a great boon and a great danger. Through interrelated electronic databases, businesses identify potential customers, credit companies amass personal information, and government agencies gather private information on citizens who are innocent of any crimes. The authors in this section alert us to such inconveniences as "target" marketing, and the dangers to First Amendment rights inherent in network "spying".

"Modern technology is essential to the modern world. The danger is that the instantaneity of its techniques defines its aims. Instant greed. Instant prestige. The instant future. This is why a sense of history has become a condition for our survival." — John Berger

"This Constitution's protections for the freedoms of speech, press, petition, and assembly, and its protection against unreasonable searches and seizures and the deprivation of life, liberty, or property without due process of law, should be construed as fully applicable without regard to the technological method or medium through which information content is generated, stored, altered, transmitted, or controlled." — Laurence H. Tribe, Proposed 27th Amendment

Does new technology threaten consumer privacy?

Target Marketing: Turning Birds of a Feather into Sitting Ducks

by ROBERT ELLIS SMITH

SOME CALL it "target marketing," others call it "database marketing," or "targeting by taste." Whatever it's called, there is a startling change taking place in the way wholesalers and retailers try to get their products into the hands of consumers.

No longer are they content to advertise in the mass media — spending millions of dollars for messages that may fall on deaf ears — and hope that customers will find their way to stores where items are displayed. Manufacturers and many retail outlets now want to target customers directly and lock them into consistent buying patterns.

Robert Ellis Smith, an attorney and journalist, publishes *Privacy Journal,* a monthly newsletter based in Providence, Rhode Island.

The way to do this, of course, is to use precise lists for mail or telephone solicitation or to identify customers loyal to your brand and somehow manipulate them into buying your products over and over. The only way to accomplish this successfully is to know everything possible about your customers — their age, income, ethnicity, family size, credit cards, and buying habits.

Some target marketers, like Quaker Oats Co., want to know their customers' political and social views. In its current massive direct marketing campaign, Quaker Oats asks customers, including many children, their views on drug testing, school prayer, and gun control, on the theory that their responses indicate whether they are traditionalists or open to new ideas.

Kids and adults who ordered the Cap'n Crunch Dick Tracy wrist watch radio through a Quaker Oats offer in cereal boxes last summer were sent an intrusive questionnaire that asked about these three political issues, as well as street address, income,

---

"The stores have other uses in mind for the information you provide."

---

what credit cards the family uses, the names, ages, and preferences of smokers in the household, and who has what diseases in the family. It also asks the wrist watch radio users to agree or disagree strongly or moderately with the statement: "My dog is like my baby." (Quaker Oats makes Ken-L Ration and Gaines dog food.) The company plans to use the data to market other products directly to the family, based on its preferences. It will then track the purchases so that it can reinforce patterns by marketing the identical products and allied products in the future. Customers will receive different levels of discounts depending on their family characteristics. Quaker Oats will "overlay" television, radio, and newspaper advertising and monitor the varying responses, thus completing the manipulation of the buyer.

ORWELLIAN INNOVATIONS

When women reach the cash register at Casual Corner or August Max clothing stores, the clerks ask them for their telephone number, which is then entered into the cash register. We are conditioned to provide information like this innocently, because we have been led to believe that it will help the merchant track us down if a check bounces or a credit card transaction is erroneous or invalid.

But the stores have other uses in mind for the information. They are gathering phone numbers from cash customers as well. The stores are using new computer software called REACT, which links the phone number with the customer's identity and address, age and income brackets, dwelling type, and previous purchases in the store. All of this information — on 55 million persons — has been stored in the retailers' in-house computer system.

Combining this information with a description of the current purchases permits the stores to court customers by mail, by telephone, or in the store for purchases for which the customer is known to be vulnerable. REACT is a "computerized tracking system" that "allows retailers to turn every single customer into a loyal customer," according to Direct Marketing Technology in Schaumburg, Illinois, and Retail Consumer Technology in Connecticut, which developed it for $15 million. One of REACT's officers used the term "targeting by taste."

The REACT people stress that information is kept confidential by the stores and that providing the telephone number is purely voluntary. A customer is told, they say, that the phone number is requested for marketing purposes. No privacy threat.

But is that the end of the debate?

There are no prohibitions against Casual Corner or August Max peddling that personal information to other "target marketers." Nor is it correct to imply that customers know the consequences of providing a phone number when they do so innocently at the point of purchase.

It is a myopic view of privacy to say that as long as information is protected, the individual's privacy is protected. Privacy, in the 1990s, includes not only the right to control personal information about oneself and how it is used, but also the right to be free of manipulation, whether in the marketplace or by the government. Privacy includes the right to exercise autonomy in one's life and personal affairs.

Too often, when the trade press describes these retailing innovations, it includes the obligatory line, "Privacy advocates are concerned about the implications of the new technique." And that is the end of the analysis.

By the same token, in testifying before Congress in May 1990 on innovative target marketing by Citicorp Point-of-Sale Information Services, its president, Jerry Saltzgaber, said: "The answer to privacy concerns is not to prohibit or restrict the collection, access, or use of personal information by marketers. Instead, consumers should be given, as we have already done, adequate disclosure of the uses of such information and be provided with the capability to 'opt-out' by denying the use of personal information for unauthorized purposes."

"The database would be available to anyone who uses an Apple computer."

Saltzgaber also proclaimed, "The time when manufacturers could market one product to all of us using mass market media is gone. The future of marketing is based on actual household purchases.

With advancing technology, retailers and marketers can learn the preferences of their customer households and then have the ability to give each household the product it wants."

Saltzgaber's use of the verb "give" was curious, and his declaration of victory over mass marketing was premature. It came just six months before Citicorp POS was forced to shut down a large part of its operation and let go 174 of its 450 employees. It abandoned a test called "Reward America," in which customers of the Ukrops supermarket chain in Richmond, Virginia, received discounts (in the form of "electronic coupons" credited at the point of sale) in exchange for permitting Citicorp to monitor each of their purchases and sell back the data in aggregate to merchants.

The Citicorp subsidiary will continue its other target programs, including those that track supermarket purchases with magazine readership, identify "lapsed shoppers," and segment customers into groups of coupon-sensitive buyers, new-product triers, price-sensitive shoppers, health-conscious shoppers, and longtime brand loyalists.

The Uniform Product Code, placed on groceries to activate cash registers and to track inventory, is the key to many of these Orwellian innovations. Remember that the UPC appears on drugs, books and periodicals, personal hygiene products, beverages, condoms, diapers, and any number of other products that provide telltale traces of our lifestyle choices. Our traditional assumption that we may purchase these products anonymously is being lost.

CREDIT WHERE CREDIT IS DUE

Two separate ventures with the unfortunate names ScanAmerica (part of Time, Inc. and Arbitron) and Behaviorscan (a Chicago operation) track the purchases of volunteer families through the UPC. Behaviorscan goes one step further, altering the television commercials that each family receives over cable and then tracking the responses as soon as the family goes shopping.

The tracking technology goes much further than anything we had anticipated and so do the privacy concerns. While the technological marvels receive the attention when the products are unveiled, the privacy concerns get no more than a fleeting glance.

The very real threats to privacy can be seen best when highlighted against a new unholy alliance of Equifax, Inc., the largest credit bureau/consumer reporting company in the United States, and Lotus

---

Neither Rain, Nor Sleet, Nor Privacy

The U.S. Postal Service is quietly working on the first nationwide list of American addresses — a cost saving measure that is making the direct-mail industry happy and privacy advocates worried.

The post office plans to license the electronic list to private database companies that sell personal information to mailers, investigators, and debt-collectors. Though the list's use would be heavily restricted and it wouldn't have names attached to the addresses, critics still worry that the post office is making privacy a lower priority than pleasing junk mailers.

The post office has never before had a single national list, even for inernal purposes. Officials say the address directory will be ready next year, with about 85 million of the nation's roughly 100 million addresses.

— *The Wall Street Journal*
December 13, 1990

Development Co., maker of advanced software. Equifax and Lotus this year had planned to launch "Lotus MarketPlace: Households," a computer compact disk, read-only-memory (CD-ROM) with demographic data on 80 million households. The disk would have been available to anyone who uses an Apple personal computer. The database was to include name, address, age range, sex, marital status, income bracket, dwelling type, shopping habits, and "products or lifestyle category."

Users could have browsed through the database, selecting demographic and consumer characteristics that fit their specialized needs, and then rent the names and addresses that fit their targets. Lotus called this "desktop control."

What is shocking about this disk is that the source of the information was to be Equifax's millions of credit reports. Equifax is not extracting information about creditworthiness or specific purchases from the credit bureau database, as it is quick to point out. But the basic list of names was generated by credit files, as well as approximate data on credit card usage, buying frequency, and types of purchase choices. Census information (not individually identifiable, but refined to "census blocs" of 200 or so persons) adds to the demographic portraits.

Using techniques available elsewhere to identify its current clientele, a small business could have prowled through "MarketPlace: Households" to find more customers who are similarly situated. (As one target marketer told his open-mouthed colleagues, "We take 'birds of a feather' and make them 'sitting ducks.'")

In January Equifax and Lotus suddenly cancelled plans for the new product, after pressure from privacy advocates and computer professionals. "Lotus cannot afford a prolonged battle over consumer privacy," said Jim Manzi, president of Lotus. He called the opposition "an emotional firestorm about consumer privacy."

"We should know that unwanted mail is not the only harm that can result."

Equifax said that it was not using individual credit information. But in its advertising to the trade Equifax said, at one point, "Lists include data from credit files as well," and at another point, "[Our lists are] based on financial, credit, and public record information."

Its major competitor in this massive transfer of credit/bureau information to the marketing business, TRW Information Services, claims in its trade advertising that its lists will describe a random consumer: "Bill Hayes is 32 years old, makes over $40,000 a year, uses his credit cards, and just moved to Florida because he loves to scuba dive. The result is an in-depth profile of your customers' buying habits, product needs, financial lifestyle, and history."

Credit files are a notoriously inaccurate source for any kind of information. The companies themselves report that fully one-third of the people who examine their own records, as permitted by federal law, find errors.

The intent of the Fair Credit Reporting Act (FCRA) when it was enacted in 1971 was to confine the use of information in credit reports to determining eligibility for credit, insurance, or employment. The Federal Trade Commission, which enforces the FCRA, has said that extracting any information from a credit file, even if only a name and address, is the same as disclosing a full-dress credit report and triggers all of the consumer protections of the act. Equifax and TRW ignore this.

The Fair Credit Reporting Act reflects principles of "Fair Information Practices" carefully devised in the 1970s by a task force of the Department of Health,

Education, and Welfare, by a respected IBM study, by the drafters of the 1974 federal Privacy Act, and by study commissions in Europe. The most important provision in the code of Fair Information Practices is: "Personal information gathered for one purpose (in this case credit) ought not to be used for another purpose (marketing), without the express consent of the individual."

This is fundamental fairness but there is a practical reason for the principle. Incidental information gathered originally is rarely checked for accuracy but may take on monumental significance when used in a totally different context much later. If the individual has a chance to provide or withhold consent, he or she becomes the best check for accuracy. For example, most people don't care whether their age is accurate on a credit application, but if that information is used to determine insurance premiums it takes on new importance.

TRW and Equifax have repeatedly said they abide by this code. But both Equifax and TRW omit this key principle from the Fair Information Practices principles they distribute with their new lists.

Beyond that, the CD-ROM offering violates a principle of the right to privacy that has been recognized in American law since 1902. It has been called "the right of publicity." University of San Francisco trademarks expert J. Thomas McCarthy has written, quite simply: "The Right of Publicity is the right of a person to control the commercial use of his or her identity."

APPROPRIATE APPROPRIATION

The preeminent authority on the law of torts, William L. Prosser, in 1960 labeled this personal tort "appropriation" and applied it to the commercial use of one's likeness, name, or facts about his or her persona, for someone else's profit. It creates, "in effect, for every individual, a common-law trade name, his own, and a common-law trademark in his likeness . . . much more extensive than those which any corporation . . . can expect."

Most privacy scholars have said that the rationale for protecting this right is to prevent "ripoffs," the unjust enrichment of a corporation for misappropriating the property of another, his or her name, or face. But one, Edward G. Bloustein, the late president of Rutgers University, had argued that what is being protected by this principle of law is "a wrongful exercise of dominion over another. The wrong involved is the objective diminution of personal freedom rather than the infliction of personal suffering or the misappropriation of property." At any rate, most states have come to recognize this right in the years since New York first enacted explicit protection in 1903.

To date, courts have turned to the "right to publicity" mainly in cases involving the use of a name or likeness, without consent, in advertising, especially when an endorsement is implied. No court has been willing to apply the rule to the use of a name in a commercial mailing list. The invasion of privacy has been regarded as slight; "the walk from the mail slot to the trash can is a short one," wrote one judge.

"Quaker Oats wants to know its customers' political and social views."

But that should change in the 1990s. Target marketing is a whole new dimension of misappropriation. What is being disclosed here is not merely one's name, but also revealing information about how one spends his money and, consequently, how one conducts his life. This entitles the individual to compensation. Rather than exposing a person to a onetime use of the name and address (for which the damages are no more than a dime or a quarter in the current market), ventures like MarketPlace exploit the person's name for an unlimited number of uses, by an unlimited number of personal computer users, many of whom have no moral compunctions about using their cyper-imaginations to play dirty tricks.

IS IT SAFE?

It is this vulnerability that elevated the Equifax-Lotus product to an extreme privacy threat: Individual data is now in the hands not merely of businesses subject to federal, state, and local regulatory schemes and to public scrutiny but also to any computer user who can put together an Apple computer and the $695 retail price of the software.

We should know from experience that unwanted mail is not the only harm that can result. There have been several cases of men consulting a database, the public listings of registered drivers in each state's motor vehicle department, to stalk young women. The man who was obsessed with television actress Rebecca Schaeffer in 1989 learned of her home address through California's motor vehicle records.

Six weeks later the man shot Rebecca Schaeffer to death outside her Los Angeles apartment. The people at Lotus call this example "unnecessarily inflammatory."

Is it safe to make millions of home addresses — and indirectly millions of listed and unlisted home telephone numbers — available to anonymous individuals tapping on their keyboards in their bedroom?

The Federal Trade Commission and if necessary the Congress must make sure that the limits of the Fair Credit Reporting Act are obeyed. Information gathered for credit purposes ought to be used only for that purpose, unless the individual consents otherwise.

The target marketing companies, including the marketing divisions of the major credit bureaus, must refrain from offering over-the-counter packages of personal information, unless they compensate the persons who are listed.

TRIVIAL PURSUIT

Customers must insist upon shopping in the old-fashioned way: leaving absolutely no "paper trail" if paying by cash. If they use credit cards, they should provide no information beyond a signature. Upon getting authorization, the merchant is assured of payment and needs no telephone number, address, or Social Security numbers. If they pay by check, conversely, consumers should present valid identification, but refuse to provide credit cards and especially refuse to permit merchants to put Social Security numbers or credit card numbers on the back of checks. Consumers should fill out credit applications judiciously. This will deny merchants and marketers much of the grist for their manipulative mills.

In the end, the segmentation of America belittles us all. It is not the best use of our talents and resources, including our computer technology, to package people in little boxes so that we may sell them more products they don't need. Why is it that computers are used for the most trivial of our pursuits?

Just as gossip journalism demeans and cheapens public figures and drags the rest of us down to a level of peeping Toms, target marketing lessens all of us by peddling our personal information without our permission and by manipulating our personal choices in the marketplace. That, more than any breach of confidentiality, is the invasion of our privacy.   ❏

Dangerous Games

Why did the Secret Service raid an Austin game company?

BY R.U. STEINBERG

O N THE MORNING OF March 1, 1990, U.S. Secret Service agents raided Steve Jackson Games of Austin. The officers were investigating evidence against Jackson and his staff that they believed involved possible breaches in computer security, some of which could have had serious national consequences. Computer equipment and the private computer files were seized, including an unpublished fictional game rule book that was found in one of Jackson's computers. The Secret Service judged that the rule book was not fictional in nature, as claimed, but rather a manual on computer hacking and committing computer crimes.

Far from shutting down an "illegal" computer network, however, the raid led to a lawsuit that may have far-reaching effects on the rights of computer users guaranteed by the First and Fourth Amendments of the U.S. Constitution. Last May, Jackson filed suit against the government, contending that the Secret Service violated the Privacy Protection Act of 1980, the Electronic Communications Privacy Act and his constitutional rights of free speech, freedom of press, and freedom of association. Even though Jackson and his staff were never formally charged with any crimes, they have yet to have all of the equipment returned.

New Frontier

In the gaming business since 1976, Jackson formed his own company in 1980. A law-school dropout, he had enjoyed writing throughout college and even served as editor of the Rice University student newspaper. "Of course, back then I was concerned about the First Amendment," he said. "But I never really dreamed that freedom of speech was ever going to impinge on a game publisher."

Jackson's games are similar to the game Dungeons and Dragons, in which participants act out the parts of heroes or villains. His biggest product is the Generic Universal Role Playing System or GURPS. "We release source books on dozens of genres including outer space, fantasy, Arthurian England, the Old West, and China. Eventually cyberpunk came along, but it's purely fiction — the idea that anyone would even find it objectionable never occurred to us," he said. Depicting a future that mixes economic and social struggle with cowboy-like computer hackers, cyberpunk (computer-spy) activities were the basis of the game rule book, called *GURPS Cyberpunk*, that was seized in the Jackson raid.

The Secret Service was especially interested in Jackson's activities on his computer bulletin board. Every day, thousands of computer users log in on bulletin boards (BBSs) via telephone connections. Farmers and ranchers get up-to-date commodity information about agriculture and livestock. Business people get Wall Street quotations or access wire news services right in their offices. Others use BBSs as a means of exchanging information. To many, getting on a BBS is a form of camraderie.

Steve Jackson said he uses his BBS to communicate with customers of all ages throughout the world to get an early evaluation of his new games and to survey his potential market before he makes heavy investments. The name he uses for his BBS, the Illuminati, comes from his award-winning game based on mysticism.

The government's investigation of Jackson's business began in

R.U. Steinberg is an Austin freelance writer.

The book that was seized by the U.S. Secret Service! (See p. 4)

The book that caused all the trouble.

December 1988, after BellSouth of Atlanta, Ga., discovered that their computer system had been infiltrated by someone via telephone hookup. The electronic intruder stole a computer file describing the operation of the emergency 911 system and details about 911's automatic location and number information systems. Their parent company, BellCore, relayed the information to the Secret Service's Computer Fraud and Abuse Task Force in Chicago, which shares investigations of computer fraud cases with the Federal Bureau of Investigation.

A nationwide investigation of various individuals and computer bulletin-board systems (BBSs) followed. Agents and BellCore employees discovered that the file had been made accessible to a few BBSs throughout the country, including the Phoenix BBS, which was privately operated by one of Jackson's employees, Loyd Blankenship.

Looking for more evidence, agents also logged into Jackson's BBS, where they read the draft of a game rule book written by Blankenship that they thought looked suspicious. When agents hooked up to the bulletin boards, they found themselves in the company of known computer hackers, particularly members of an alliance called "The Legion of Doom," which they suspected was involved in distributing the illegally obtained 911 document.

Before dawn on March 1, 1990, several agents, with guns drawn, entered the Blankenships' apartment, found him and his wife in their underwear, interrogated him for hours, and seized his computer equipment. Later that morning, the agents took Blankenship to Steve Jackson Games, where they continued their investigation, which in-

cluded the questioning of Jackson and his staff and a search of the premises.

When it was all over, the agents had seized a total of four computers and two laser printers from Blankenship's residence and Steve Jackson Games, as well as various software, manuals, printouts and computer equipment. The Secret Service's inventory of seized equipment totaled about $8,000, but because various accounting and product files were also taken in the raid, Jackson estimates that the loss might eventually reach seven figures.

"They looked at everything that could be opened, and a lot of things that couldn't be opened, they opened anyway," said Jackson. "At first, I felt a lot of stark unbelief. Then, I started to feel like it must have been my fault in some way. Finally, there was hot indignation and cold anger."

Blankenship, who had been up late working on the game rule book, was equally angered. "They asked me a bunch of questions, including how long my wife had worked for Lawrence Livermore Labs, a defense research company in California," he said. "Since she had never worked for Lawrence Livermore Labs and was teaching history at Southwest Texas State University, that sort of threw me for a loop."

During his interrogation, Blankenship revealed that he first obtained the 911 file from Craig Neidorf, the editor of Phrack, an electronic newsletter. Neidorf had experienced a similar raid in February 1990, and was taken to trial by the government the following July. During the trial, a BellSouth employee revealed that the file wasn't actually top secret, and was available to the general public for less than $30. The government dropped its case against Neidorf in exchange for a promise from Neidorf "to stay out of trouble" for a year.

"Fear the government that fears your computer"

On July 19, 1991, Jackson convened a meeting at his South Austin headquarters to discuss the possible formation of a chapter of the Boston-based Electronic Frontier Foundation (EFF). Formed in May 1990 by Mitch Kapor, one of the main creators of Lotus 1-2-3; Steve Wozniak, founder of Apple Computers; and several others, EFF is an advocacy organization devoted to protecting the rights of computer users. About 75 people showed up, including computer users, game players, lawyers and grassroots politicians.

"People are here tonight because they are interested in civil liberties of the high-tech age," said Jackson. "There are a lot of things going on now that were never contemplated when the Constitution was written. But the Constitution still applies to things like computers and BBSs. We're still talking about freedom of speech, freedom of the press and freedom of association."

One of those present at the meeting was Bruce Sterling, an Austin science-fiction writer who has published six novels and many short stories in the last 17 years, and who founded the cyberpunk science-fiction movement with writer William Gibson in the mid-1980s.

"My immediate reaction [to the raid] was that Jackson was guilty," said Sterling. "I doubted that he was any major league computer criminal, but I figured that he had done something bad enough to have attracted the Secret Service's attention. A couple of months went by, and then it began to dawn on me that he hadn't done anything wrong." As Sterling recently wrote about the Jackson case in EFF's newsletter, "The cyber police have leaped where angels fear to tread." He also has an idea for a new button: "Fear the government that fears your computer." Jackson has already taken to wearing a button that reads: "I love my country. It's the government I fear."

Responding to these concerns in their defense motion to Jackson's suit, the government states that their warrant affidavit "did not contain intentionally or recklessly false statements, did establish probable cause, was sufficiently specific, and was carried out in good faith," and that Jackson's rights had not been violated. Secret Service spokesperson Allan Carter and Assistant U.S. Attorney Mollie Crosby both declined to comment on the pending case.

In spite of the trepidation some Texas computer users are experiencing in the wake of the Secret Service's seizure of Jackson's equipment, Chris McCubbin, who is now the operator of the Illuminati BBS, said that he doesn't feel threatened by what has already transpired. "I feel completely safe and think that our BBS is pretty secure from harassment right now. That doesn't mean we're not careful. A lot of young kids who are into hacking have asked if we have technical information about breaking into systems," he said. "We tell them in no uncertain terms that we don't, and try to scare them off by telling them that the Secret Service is intercepting their messages."

While Jackson and his lawyers wait for U.S. District Judge Walter Smith of Waco to rule on preliminary motions, things at the game company are proceeding apace. "We're in the process of putting out a relatively silly board game called Hacker," said Jackson. "Players will represent evil hackers, where they can crash systems, or they can be good hackers. You have to have a good sense of humor about all of this."

The federal court will soon decide whether there are sufficient legal grounds by Steve Jackson Games for a trial to proceed. Sooner or later, however, the courts will be confronted with a complex challenge, namely, to decide what rights of computer users shall prevail. On one hand, computer users want to protect their elusive and never-clearly-defined rights of privacy from invasion, either by accident or by design. On the other hand, computer users don't want to commingle in an electronic culture that is so stifling that it would not permit or encourage personal freedoms or the exploration of new horizons. The question is: where does the one leave off and the other begin? ❏

FREEDOM AND PRIVACY
IN ELECTRONIC LIBRARIES

Steve Cisler
Apple Computer Library
Cuppertino, California

When you ask people what they like about the libraries they use, the range of answers will include praise for the staff, the various resources, and the attractiveness of the physical facilities. Almost everyone has a sense of place about a particular library or libraries in general. For some, the library is a place to retreat and relax; for others it is an important institution that binds their community together; and for some it is an efficient center for the dissemination of information and knowledge that meets the deadlines of busy users.

Whether you ask a librarian or library user, most of these concepts are tied to a physical place. However, many people are spending an increasing amount of time working, studying, and relaxing in the realm of electronic communications. When you begin exploring this area (and many librarians are doing just that), it is hard to see the edges of this virtual terrain. It includes our telephones, televisions, radios, the networks that connect our computers, pagers, and facsimile machines, and ATM and credit card machines. This realm has been called Cyberspace, The Electronic Frontier, and The Homeland of the Information Age.

The library is a part of this emerging landscape. What are the qualities of our present libraries that will be valued in the time when many more people will connect electronically to our services rather than walk in to talk with a reference librarian and browse through the books and magazines and CD's? What will set the library apart from other institutions that successfully take root in the electronic arena? One of the most important distinguishing characteristics may prove to be a perception by electronic library users that the staff is really trying to help guide them through the intricacies of the information age. If we can project the sense of service we now have, support for the electronic librarian will grow. While delivery of the requested information might continue to be our primary indication that we have succeeded, we might do well to remember that many people do not associate human beings with satisfactory electronic transactions. How many of us think warmly of the staff that fills the ATM machines with money every day, or of the systems person that tweaks the program that keeps your account straight? Librarians will remain intermediaries, but how prominent will we be to the average user? Another quality of what I'll call the library experience is the trust that people place in the staff and the institution. The importance of

privacy issues and society's increasing awareness of them will make this a very important factor to consider in operating the electronic library.

In March 1991, I attended the First Conference on Computers, Freedom, and Privacy in Burlingame, California. Drawn together was a strange assembly of computer hackers, libertarians, librarians, law enforcement officials, network administrators, computer consultants, writers, lawyers, public policy analysts, and employees of the National Security Agency, the Central Intelligence Agency, the FBI, and the Secret Service. It was a time to meet, to discuss crucial issues, and to begin face-to-face discussion in confronting a variety of problems. Some of the discussion at the CFP Conference and in other fora have explored social implications of technology that are likely to reach new levels of relevance for libraries, too, as they become tied into increasingly complex multi-purpose communications networks. Some of the more important of these include:

1. First amendment rights;
2. The practice of gathering, using, and selling personal information;
3. Monitoring of employees in the electronic workplace;
4. Monitoring of citizens in Cyberspace;
5. Security of personal information on networks.

FIRST AMENDMENT RIGHTS

In Freedom, Technology, and the First Amendment, Jonathan Emord traces the history of the government's stricter curtailment of First Amendment protection for radio, television, and cable broadcasters when compared with the more sacrosanct print media. From early in the 20th Century, when the U.S. Navy sought to put the entire wireless telegraphy industry under complete government supervision, to Supreme Court decisions in 1940 that justified federal controls over the broadcast media on the basis of spectrum scarcity, these industries have not been afforded the same degree of freedom as have print publishers.

The early regulations of the Federal Radio Commission and the more powerful Federal Communications Commission came about partly from broadcasters asking the government to limit the number of licenses, and partly from legislators and government officials trying to legislate what constituted "public interest". As Emord describes it:

The restrictions tempered the willingness of licensees to engage in controversy, coerced them into offering certain kinds of bureaucratically "preferred" programming, and caused them to become tools for the use of incumbent politicians and special interest groups who desired to influence the nature of public debate.

Even though libraries continually face one kind of censorship battle or another, the restrictions placed on traditional print media — and hence on traditional library services — have not been as tight as they have been with respect to the radio, television, and cable industries. For libraries, what are the implications of these disparities in the treatment of different media? Libraries will be hooked into a national network of electronic information sources which eventually may even include entertainment on demand provided by radio and television broadcasting companies.

As various kinds of media are publicly accessible through a single end-user source, it may become more difficult for libraries to continue to enjoy as much freedom as they historically have as handlers of print media. The libraries without walls will open up their collections, and what we provide access to generally, to scrutiny by even more interest groups than we have known in the past. We must be prepared to confront the challenges of being part of a media-rich information delivery network on which there may be more content restrictions than we have been accustomed to. What librarians do, and what advocacy roles we assume, may help to define the extent to which our users continue to view us as upholders of First Amendment rights.

GATHERING, USING AND SELLING PERSONAL INFORMATION

Recently, I served on a panel at a conference at Stanford University hosted by the First Amendment Congress. Most of the people in attendance were from Stanford or from the radio, television, and newspaper industries. I was discussing the privacy of library circulation records, and many in the audience had not even considered the potential threats involved in not protecting that information. However, in light of the case involving the disclosure of Judge Bork's videotape rental records, most everyone there realized that personal reading and viewing habits are tenuously protected in the age of the computer. It was gratifying to be able to claim that librarians were already on top of this issue and had been for some time.

At the CFP conference John Baker of Equifax, the company that supplied Lotus with data for its direct mail product, Lotus Marketplace, discussed attitudes toward privacy by the American people of whom 25% can be called Privacy Fundamentalists, 58% Privacy Pragmatists, and 17% of whom don't care about the issues. The Privacy Fundamentalists are the ones with unlisted numbers; they use personal name variations to track the re-use of magazine subscription information; they don't give out their Social Security number to anyone but the IRS and their banks. It is this group that

will probably help shape the way businesses, government agencies, and even non-profits treat personal information gathered on individuals.

The Bureau of the Census encounters a great deal of resistance from libertarians, minority groups, and other segments of America who distrust parts (or all) of the federal government. Various three-letter government agencies (IRS, FBI, CIA, NSA, DOD) have mission statements that allow them to spend huge sums on automated systems to store, link, and search for patterns in vast files of personal information about Americans and people living in America. But government agencies are not the only ones collecting large amounts of personal information. In fact, we should probably be even more concerned about the private sector, and especially credit firms such as TRW and Equifax. It is commerce that will always want more information about its customers or potential customers. And it is also in the free market where the existence of such information becomes a prized economic commodity in itself. A lot of the unexpected, often unwanted, mail and telemarketing calls you receive originate in a computerized mailing list bought from someone you sometime did business with.

Most niche market direct mail promoters will tell you that the recipients want to get that catalog of biodegradable hiking boots, or the announcements about the latest concerts, or that credit card where part of the fee goes to some worthy cause. Using the profiles of estimated income and lifestyles, merged with the subscription lists of hi-tone periodicals, a direct mailer can target a group with the assurance that the return rate on responses will be much better than the average mailing list. Book and grocery chains are offering membership cards to regular customers. In return for a few benefits, the stores learn about buying patterns of the customers and for the geographical area in which the store is located.

Some people, I'm sure, advocate the use of marketing techniques for libraries like those described above, and I'm sure there have been a number of mailing list experts who have worked with friends, groups or movements to support the passage of some library bond measure. In the quest for more funds and more support, there may be a strong temptation to use some of these tools and perhaps even to change the rules on how circulation records are used, in order to seek supporters in the library community. Before taking advantage of such marketing techniques, however, librarians will no doubt need to reflect on the practical implications and on some very basic philosophical issues about using these types of personal data for purposes other than that for which they were originally recorded.

Librarians should also be aware of information gathered in the library that could even potentially be collocated with other databases through standard personal identification numbers. Many universities, for example, use the Social Security number (SSN) as a common number for all student activities. Unless it is a conscious decision by the library management, the SSN should not be used for access to the online library system or for checking out books. As a nation we have resisted the call for a national ID card, unlike many countries in Europe. But the use and abuse of the SSN makes it a piece of information that can be used to link disparate databases in commerce and in government. In a CFP conference panel, Evan Hendricks of *Privacy Times* recounted some abuses by government and industry involving secretive matching of personal information across multiple databases through matching on SSNs by TRW and the Social Security Administration. Investigators found that in two databases of names (150,000 names in one list and one million in the other) about 20% of the SSNs were inaccurate! Depending on one's perspective, this is either extremely frightening or in some perverse way a ray of hope that, despite the apparent simplicity of national scale surveillance, it has not yet reached very efficient proportions. Certainly we can do better than having to settle for either of these.

In many automated library systems, there are ways to generate unique ID numbers. Even though it may seem that none of the data collected by libraries about their users will ever become a source for cross-database matching, the use of non-SSN identifiers does provide an extra safeguard.

There is a growing controversy over the secondary use of gathered information. Some progressive organizations have a box on registration and membership forms allowing the individual to opt in and allow the personal information to be re-used by the organization or to be re-sold to worthy causes, or to anyone at all. Alan Westin, a privacy expert and consultant for Equifax, predicts that by the year 2000 marketing databases will be consensual and that the participants will be compensated for the use of their information. One positive step that the library world could make is to ask the American Library Association to add an "opt in" box on conference registration forms; this would make it easy to prevent them from re-selling your name to dozens of vendors and exhibitors, whose communications you may not want in your mailbox. At the time of this writing I had to scribble a proviso on my application not to re-sell the information they collected from me. Whether it works, I will know by the time you have this essay.

(Note from author: The American Library Association did not take my name from the conference mailing list as I requested. Consequently, I received over 50 pieces of unsolicited mail.-Steve Cisler)

MONITORING OF EMPLOYEES IN THE ELECTRONIC WORKPLACE

If you have called 411, booked an airline ticket, ordered a computer program via mail order, had a catalog keyed in by an off-shore data conversion firm, or read a newspaper, you have come into contact with someone who has been or is being electronically monitored by their supervisors. The devices available to eavesdrop, to monitor, and to blatantly mold electronic workers' performance is well developed. Operators are timed to see how fast they get you a requested phone number or book a flight. Data entry people have their keystrokes counted, and some reporters

have told horror stories of seeing a warning screen pop up with the words "our colleague in the next cube is working faster than you."

Librarians can envision how, in their places of work, electronic surveillance could be used to monitor the productivity and accuracy of staff performance. At present, there seems to be fairly little discussion of potential abuses of electronic monitoring of employees in the library world, unless perhaps it is at a clerical workers' union gathering.

MONITORING OF CITIZENS IN CYBERSPACE

There exists a large, anarchic computer conferencing/bulletin board system that is known as Usenet. On an average day more than 110,000 articles, totaling over 200 Mbytes, are submitted from 11,000 different Usenet sites. Within 24 hours all the computers on the network have received these messages. Usenet is accessed mostly by Unix-based computers and workstations that reside in an enormous variety of environments, including hobbyists' basements, computer science departments, corporate MIS rooms, and government agencies.

Many of the administrators who keep this network running voluntarily have a deep distrust of the intentions of the government, especially of the agencies charged with surveillance of Americans and foreign nationals here and abroad. Some of the more paranoid believe that powerful text processing engines are combing these messages 24 hours a day, flagging those where certain terms are used. Consequently, a number of users like to throw electronic monkey wrenches in this alleged monitoring by including at the bottom of each message sensitive terms like nuclear, terrorist, Bush, Communist, Tri-Lateral Commission, CIA, etc., in an effort to slow down the surveillance mechanism they suspect exists. My own hunch is that it could exist but does not.

At present there is an ongoing debate about the extent to which the FBI monitors electronic bulletin board systems. There is evidence that the boards run by or for "phone phreaks" and "computer crackers" receive very close attention from the law enforcement crowd. But incidence of surveillance of more middle of the road boards is more difficult to document. The Computer Professionals for Social Responsibility (CPSR) have filed Freedom of Information Act requests that the FBI has ignored. The CPSR may have to go to court to get relevant records released, much as the library community did with the Library Awareness Program.

The integrated online systems in libraries have the potential to monitor the circulation records of users. Through transaction analysis, if combined with user-specific authorization numbers to log on, libraries could even gather personal data about searches in online catalogs. Libraries have a good record in terms of rejecting monitoring of library users. Just as with some of the other concepts discussed here, the future may require more vigilance than ever before as

Freedom and Privacy...

libraries begin to plug into multi-purpose information networks.

SECURITY OF PERSONAL INFORMATION ON THE NETWORKS

One of the more interesting but arcane debates that is spreading around Cyberspace is the need for encrypted information. The general consensus among those who talk about it (and the government generally does not) is that while encryption schemes are necessary, the government has set limits on how powerful an encryption scheme networks can employ. Some in government want to maintain their edge by controlling the use of encryption programs by the public.

Librarians should be aware of these developments because with the greater connectivity among future networks will come a greater need for security. Libraries are generally relatively open places, in an intellectual sense. It will take some creative tactics in the virtual library of the future to both maintain that atmosphere, and at the same time to protect personal information from other users, from law enforcement investigators, and from virus outbreaks or the introduction of hostile worm programs. Even the use of computer agents—software surrogates that travel around the network performing various functions such as searching for material on a subject or sorting electronic mail—will demand a whole new code of ethics by librarians and network administrators. How much will one agent be able to communicate to another agent, if both are looking for information about a patent or a sensitive research issue? How will the confidentiality of the questioner be preserved? And will this processing overhead slow the network down to unacceptable speeds?

CONCLUSION

This has been a rapid survey of several issues that I have been following at conferences and through online sources. Some of this discussion will be found in technical journals, the popular press, and even television. The library community will have to figure where it fits into these complex puzzles. Probably libraries will fit many places, sometimes in opposition to some government agencies, to some businesses, and even to some scholars. I am sure this LITA President's Program will provide a good forum for discussing some of the issues.

An organization that is at the forefront of advocacy of privacy rights in the electronic networking environment is the Electronic Frontier Foundation, 155 Second Street, Cambridge, MA 02141, (617) 864-0665. The EFF has given support to another active group, the Computer Professionals for Social Responsibility, Box 717, Palo Alto, California 94302. Members of these groups participate in Usenet newsgroups such as comp.risks (risks of computers, automation, and reliance on the technology); alt.privacy (an open forum to discuss privacy issues); eff.org.talk (discussion group for the Electronic Frontier Foundation); comp.admin.policy (new group to discuss e-mail privacy, user access to networks, security).

You may also contact the author electronically on The WELL: ac@well.uucp or on the Internet ac@apple.com. The WELL offers access to a number of electronic discussion groups on censorship, information policy, the Electronic Frontier Foundation, and library issues. Phone 415-332-4335 for more information.

Computer Networks and the 1st Amendment

Advanced Technology Raises New Questions and Concerns About an Age-Old Issue

By Sandra Sugawara
Washington Post Staff Writer

Would you want someone monitoring your phone calls to make sure you weren't saying anything that struck them as morally offensive or sexually lewd? Probably not.

Would you want your child to open up a newspaper and read graphic descriptions of sexual activities or comments that mocked your religious beliefs or were racist? Probably not.

For telephone companies, which have been around for decades, and newspapers, which have been around for centuries, the rules of the game are fairly well-established. But computer and communications technologies have created a new animal—personal computer networks that allow personal computer users to write notes and send them over telephone lines to other users.

Like the telephone, these personal computer networks are a communication tool. But as with newspapers, there can be a wide audience for these notes, making it an easy way to disseminate rumors, falsehoods and offensive material.

"These companies are really in a genuine ethical bind in terms of what to do here," said Chris Elwell, analyst with Simba Information Inc, a Wilton,

Conn., company that publishes newsletters on the information industry.

Much of the problem is that new technology has rendered old notions obsolete, according to Harvard University constitutional lawyer Laurence Tribe. "As with other aspects of the computerized communications revolution, the legal framework was built on a model that didn't anticipate anything like this," said Tribe. "I don't think these issues are adequately addressed by our legal system."

Although many users object to censorship, all major commercial

> ## "These companies are really in a genuine ethical bind in terms of what to do here."
>
> —analyst Chris Elwell

computer networks reserve the right to block messages that don't conform to policies the users agree to when they subscribe to the networks. They don't all do it the same way, though.

Prodigy, which is owned by International Business Machines Corp. and Sears, Roebuck & Co. and is the largest or second-largest online network (depending on whether you look at subscribers or households), has taken the most aggressive role in trying to police its network. It is the only major online network that pre-screens public messages, about 100,000 weekly, before letting them run on the system.

There are two ways that users can send notes on online systems. One was is for a user to send a message addressed specifically to another user. That note, known as electronic mail, is not screened by Prodigy.

The other way is by public messages that are posted on electronic "bulletin boards," or places in the system that all subscribers can read. Those messages are first scanned by a Prodigy computer that is programmed to catch several dozen potentially obscene or offensive words or phrases.

Notes that are flagged by the computer are reviewed by Prodigy employees, according to Mark Krefting, who oversees the group monitoring the bulletin boards.

"I'm trying to do a balancing act with freedom of expression that is consistent with standards of a family service," said Krefting, who was a news writer at CBS for six years. "It's not unlike my previous job at CBS, where we would often say: Is this appropriate to put on the air? Is this too graphic? And I face those decisions here daily."

Genie, the third-largest consumer-oriented online service, which is owned by GE Information Services in Rockville, also has come under criticism for censorship.

It does not pre-screen messages, but instead has 120 people under contract who work from their homes monitoring specific bulletin boards. They are the arbiters of what is obscene, indecent, offensive, defamatory, abusive, harassing or inconsistent with decorum and good taste—all banned on Genie.

H&R Block Inc.'s CompuServe, which vies with Prodigy as the largest network, also has managers who monitor bulletin boards. But analysts

said CompuServe has been able to avoid major censorship controversies by establishing different bulletin boards for different user interests. For example, graphically sexual messages might not be allowed in many areas of the system, but they are allowed on its human sexuality bulletin boards.

"Our philosophy is a little different," said Stephen Case, president of Vienna-based America Online, the fourth-largest consumer online service.

Case said America Online views itself as a "town square," where people can stand on their soap box and make their opinions known." He said that America Online rarely deletes messages—about once a year.

ADL officials say they have not gotten complaints about such free-wheeling networks, probably because "when you're dealing with a system that says anything goes . . . subscribers know what they are buying," said Jeffrey P. Sinensky, director of ADL's civil rights division.

But when a service such as Prodigy is advertised as one that will adopt family standards appropriate for children, then expectations change, he said.

ADL is still upset over the decision of Prodigy to allow discussions about whether the Holocaust was a hoax, a claim historians dismiss. Prodigy and ADL officials plan to meet on Monday to try to work out this controversy. But civil libertarians and many users will be waiting to protest any further infringement of what they view as their right to free speech.

Said Henry Heilbrunn, Prodigy senior vice president, "We are pioneers, whenever pioneers go forth, they are going to get a few arrows in the back."

Computers

Rights on the Line

Defining the Limits on the Networks

By Don Oldenburg
Washington Post Staff Writer

At the University of Massachusetts, Douglas Abbott struggles to weigh the free-speech rights of students who use an academic computer network to distribute prurient stories against arguments that the network shouldn't be used for transmitting pornography. "We've been trying to come up with some guidelines that might be enforceable," says Abbott, the university's associate vice chancellor in charge of computing and information systems. "But, generally, the way it's defined is the old conundrum: I know it when I see it."

Some 3,000 miles across the nation, nearly an instantaneous computer transmission away in Sausalito, Calif., managers of a network called The Well say they draw the line in their wide-open forums at two troublesome kinds of communication—libel and illegally obtained information. Otherwise, its 5,000-plus subscribers create their own standards over the modem lines. "What we are selling is access to other people and what they have to say," says The Well's managing director, Cliff Figallo. "So we have always maintained that you should be able to say whatever you want to say on our system."

Though used by a small population compared to telephone callers, computer networks such as these are the up-and-coming exchange of electronic conversation. Their high-tech interaction creates an electronic commons in which computer users chat casually, get on their soapboxes, share ideas, exchange graphic images—in other words, where they do practically everything they could do meeting face to face, absent of the physical senses. It is a "virtual reality," a wall-less and dimensionless place novelist William Gibson labeled "cyberspace."

For all its futuristic implications, cyberspace is mostly filled with the same kind of talk that decades ago took place over back-yard fences, the subjects at any given hour of the day or night ranging from politics and sex to recipes and sports. Even religion. Most network regulars would contend that good computer networks make good neighbors.

But what happens when the neighbors aren't so good? When slander or harassing remarks appear on a network? When disruptive messages are transmitted? When illegal material is sent? Or when obscenities find their way onto screens?

Questions such as these make the chatty networks something of a First Amendment frontier. At issue is how far the Bill of Rights extends into cyberspace?

Trouble struck one such cyberspace neighborhood recently when a massive on-line network called Prodigy showed a dozen of its subscribers to the exit button after they tried to foment an electronic uprising. Like most networks, Prodigy, a joint venture of Sears, Roebuck & Co. and International Business Machines Corp., hosts topical "conferences" on its electronic bulletin board where users can "post" their comments. It provides an electronic mail service (generically called E-mail) where users can send private messages to specific users. Beyond that, Prodigy offers educational programs, computer games, electronic shopping, and other consumer services, all accompa-

BY STEVE MAGNUSON FOR THE WASHINGTON POST

nied by commercial advertising, for a single monthly fee.

But Prodigy's lines heated up last November when the giant network abruptly changed its policy and hiked the fee for high-volume E-mail users. A handful of Prodigy rebels considered the change to be contrary to their subscription agreement and sent hundreds of angry messages through the system to some of the network's 900,000 subscribers. Most of those messages never got past Prodigy's operators, who quickly put the protesters' memberships on hold.

There had been other objections to Prodigy's policy of monitoring and occasionally not publishing messages transmitted to its bulletin boards. Suddenly, in computer circles, the word censorship had surfaced. Three weeks later, Prodigy's director of market programs and communications, Geoffrey Moore, defended the action on the New York Times's Op-Ed page. Prodigy, he argued, had no constitutional mandate to publish messages that seek information on the least painful methods of suicide, charge someone with embezzlement, request pornographic contacts, or provide instructions for illegally hot-wiring an HBO cable connection—all examples of actual transmissions that never made it past Prodigy's managers.

"Some authors have made the bizarre suggestion that Prodigy is required to publish whatever is submitted and that failure to do so is censorship," wrote Moore. "The Constitution bestows no rights on readers to have their views published in someone else's private medium . . . "

In fact, every network draws the line somewhere. "Most of them are quite restrictive, but it varies from system to system as to what they're restrictive about," says Jack Rickard, editor and publisher of Boardwatch, a magazine about on-line services published from Littleton, Colo. "There are 50,000 bulletin boards out there . . . some will tell you no profanity and others will tell you explicitly this is a place where we talk dirty."

Rickard says ongoing friction between users and bulletin board operators isn't unusual, nor is it usually a constitutional dispute. In a conference where the announced topic is cooking, for instance, the moderator will quickly cut short a user trying to change the subject. "The alternative is chaos," says Rickard, adding there are other conferences that specialize in chaos for those so inclined.

Among the conferences offered on the Arlington-based Meta Network is Salon, which is promoted as "the information equivalent to a free-trade zone," where topics and opinions are wide-ranging and all content is free to be copied or distributed without the writer's permission. But when it comes to restricting content, Meta Net's Frank Burns says community standards tend to prevail in his and many smaller networks.

"If you're running a public system that anybody can join, it is somewhat analogous to running a resort hotel that anybody can stay at," he says. "One doesn't presume that if you run a resort hotel you can tell people what they can say or not say at the dinner table, as long as they're not creating a disturbance. In our system, we put all of the responsibility on our community of users to do whatever policing they want."

At The Well (Whole Earth 'Lectronic Link), managers call that kind of self-policing "the white corpuscle effect," because users "rush to the scene of the infection" and eliminate the problem themselves. "The greatest application we've had is when people make remarks that are highly offensive to other users—and meant to be highly offensive," says Cliff Figallo. "But we think being tolerant even toward offensive kind of behavior is something we should stand behind."

In some systems, "flaming" (ad hominem attacks on other users) is a way of life, explains Figallo. "You say the wrong thing or make a politically incorrect remark and you might be called anything. We try to run The

Well in a way that it feels more like a small town where you don't want to create a lot of personal enmity. There is a definite community standard."

Included in The Well's community standard is one conference called Eros, which Figallo describes as "pretty wide open to any of the most erotic ideas and writing you want to come up with." In Eros, the ground rules are less prohibitive than they are cautionary: Those who enter are forewarned. "People can choose whether they want to attend," says Figallo, "and it's a lot easier to quit than getting out of a strip joint you've wandered into."

Douglas Abbott drew the same line two years ago at the University of Massachusetts, in Amherst, when a dispute arose over a sex-oriented conference called Cyberlust on Nearnet (the New England Academic and Research Network). "There are people who have great objections to having that material on the network, even though it is well-identified and you have to log into it to read it," says Abbott, who reviewed the files, held hearings and let the controversy blow over. "We wanted to err on the side of leaving it alone."

Still, network operators wonder how the First Amendment will eventually apply to their form of expression. "I'm just afraid that they might decide that the lowest common denominator of what is acceptable is going to become the rule," says Figallo, "that the main concern is that nobody be offended. . . . Does the fact that people type these words into a machine give them some different status than if they were just speaking out on the street corner?"

DataCenter   464 19th Street, Oakland, California 94612 (415) 835-4692

Who Are You Talking To?
And Who's Listening?

by Jim Warren

What if you recorded every word you said in most phone conversations, and they were automatically typed into a computer? Then searches could easily be automated for any topic or word or phrase you may have mentioned.

What if they were saved for years? What if most of your private, confidential, informal, candid, off-the-cuff business conversations, job gossip, and even your highly personal discussions with close friends were permanently identified as your comments and stored in this easy-to-search form, instead of evaporating when your voice stopped reverberating?

Getting nervous yet?

What if the computer where years of your comments were stored wasn't under your control? It might be a company computer where your computer-aided boss could review your confidential conversations. And—lest surveillance-minded bosses view this too favorably—note that they, also, have overseers—shareholders, tax auditors, unending government agencies, etc. Further: What if the computer wasn't even under company control? And curious eavesdroppers could monitor and search from the comfort of their home or office—perhaps internationally.

What If contingency-based litigation attorneys could automatically search through every one of your conversations—and those of your staff—to discover any ill-considered comment that you or anyone else may have ever made—and then use it to extort money from you or your company?

Could you survive such surveillance? Could your job? Could your company?

Major National Security Threat

Short of nuclear attack, this may be the greatest danger that high technology poses to a free people—a clear danger, present now.

The preceding scenario is exactly the situation with almost all electronic mail—and use of email is escalating at a rate far exceeding the explosion of personal computing that began in the mid-'70s.

If email passes through a file server or host computer, more than likely a copy is permanently retained—at the least, on the backup tapes that are essential for any reliable system operation. This is especially true for any commercial system that purports to be reliable—such as Prodigy, MCI Mall, CompuServe, etc. Even decades ago, when tape storage was far less dense and far more expensive, commercial time-sharing systems usually copied all files onto nightly backup tapes, and week's-end or month's-end tapes were often retained for years, at least.

Easy retrieval of an individual's deleted files has long been an additional valuable benefit of such backup systems, especially useful to fleet-fingered users who too quickly stroked the delete key.

But retrieval of your files for someone else's review—and possible use against you—is just as easy.

Email to or from you may pass through a proprietary network—or Fidonet, the Internet, or other networks that have numerous independent-but-cooperating host computers. In both proprietary and public networks, system administrators all along the transmission path can usually access your email as it passes through their system. Among other things, sysops need essentially unlimited ability to access files—including email files—so they can maintain their systems, trace and fix problems, and occasionally assist delete-prone users.

Most of us who use email think of it as confidential, use it like a telephone, and "speak" with the candor typical of lunchroom—or bedroom—gossip. That's how it should be if we are to gain the massive benefits possible through computer-based communications—benefits that far exceed those of the telephone or the Pony Express.

But most current email systems also involve orders of magnitude greater danger for the users than if they were telephones "merely" having permanent wiretaps and tape recorders. Email permits anyone who can gain access to the files to conduct automated surveillance and searches by topic or "speaker"—even through years of "recordings." And access can be obtained by operator permission, court order, or illegal electronic entry.

Contingency-fee attorneys are rapidly expanding their use of email "discovery" in shareholder litigation, wrongful termination suits, harassment allegations, etc. It's big-bucks business and your every keystroke is fair game for these hunters. Improper or ill-phrased comments that would be momentary and often forgotten if spoken on the phone can be damning when permanently stored in email and provocatively exposed to a naive jury.

Defend It Or Lose It

The greatly enhanced utility and power of email must be counterbalanced by a greatly enhanced prohibition against its access and abuse by others—limited perhaps only to the most serious of criminal investigations. (Remember that Iran-Contra investigators obtained major evidence against North and Poindexter by reviewing backup tapes that retained copies of their "deleted" email.)

Laws can protect us against lawyers. But the best protection that individuals and companies can provide for themselves and their private communications is to encrypt all communications. That requires agreeing on a crypto-system, and public-key cryptography is recognized as the safest and most useful system currently available. To avoid the possibility of a hidden back door, we need a public-key implementation with program code and complete algorithm design available for public review. The government's current and proposed crypto standards fail this essential test—among others.

DataCenter   464 19th Street, Oakland, California 94612 (415) 835-4692

IX. Other Hidden Barriers

Bias and discrimination against the poor, racial and ethnic minorities, the gay and lesbian community and women remain endemic in U.S. society. Through the growing incidence of "hate speech" and "hate crimes", the rights of these groups have been drastically curtailed. Through stereotyping and underrepresentation in the arts and the media, we all suffer the deprivation of our right to know each other. As authors in this section show, the "celebration" of the Columbus Quincentenary and the Los Angeles uprising in May 1992, are driving the ugly face of racism into the public consciousness; whether public corrective action will be taken remains to be seen.

"The flames that rose in Los Angeles have died, but dust from the city's ashes remains on each of us." — Mayor David Dinkins, New York City

"Ignorance is the mother of prejudice." — Ramsey Clark

"The true test of one's commitment to constitutional principles is the extent to which recognition is given to the rights of those in our midst who are the least affluent, least powerful and least welcome." — Judge Leonard Sand

"Racism, sexism, homophobia and class oppression have silenced far more people than the withdrawal of National Endowment for the Arts grants since the summer of 1989." — Barbara Smith

"When language fails, violence becomes the language." — Elie Wiesel

"The quincentennial (Columbus)...is a year not for T-shirts but for introspection. It offers a chance for a fresh effort at harmony among races, if only in atonement for past crimes." — Hans Koning

"Freedom from want is the most fundamental freedom because in poverty we lose the capacity to be what we are. The freedom to know is the second most important freedom." — Ramsey Clark

■ OTHER RODNEY KINGS?

Let's Make It a Federal Case

PAUL CHEVIGNY

On March 3 last year, the Los Angeles police unmercifully beat a black man, Rodney King, who had been stopped for speeding, and shot him with darts from a nonlethal gun called a taser, which is supposed to be used to catch fleeing suspects. Fortuitously videotaped by a bystander, the beating was memorably broadcast on television all over this country and abroad. The resulting furor, including a condemnation of the beating by President Bush, focused unprecedented attention on violence by local police forces. Ten days after the attack, then–Attorney General Dick Thornburgh asked his staff to review past complaints about police brutality "to discern whether any pattern of misconduct is apparent."

A year later, the federal government still has no clear idea of the answer to that question. Although a blue-ribbon commission in Los Angeles later found a pattern of such abuses in the L.A.P.D., the question has sunk out of sight as a national issue. Was such a police beating common or rare? Are such incidents declining in the nation? Is the L.A.P.D. particularly brutal compared with other local police forces? Are there some accepted measures that could be taken to reduce such police violence?

Questions like these are perennial; they nag at us every time an incident like the L.A. beating occurs, and then they are gone with the headlines. We never make much progress in finding the answers, and I finally understand why. The federal government, in all its functions—judicial, legislative, executive and administrative—has been organized, with occasional exceptions, to know little and do nothing systematic about local police abuses. I suppose I always knew this in the way that we Americans all know that police problems are supposed to be peculiarly "local." But I did not grasp how complete is the learned—no, studied—incapacity of the federal government until I was asked by Human Rights Watch during the L.A.P.D. scandal to look at federal oversight of local police as a problem in international human rights. I had to step back from our system and look at it as one might examine relations between the national government and local police in another federal system, for example in Mexico or Argentina.

International standards for law enforcement, developed at the United Nations over the past fifteen years, are straightforward. As embodied in the U.N.'s "Basic Principles on the Use of Force and Firearms by Law Enforcement Officials," they provide that police may use force "only when strictly necessary and to the extent required for the performance of their duty," and that the use of nonlethal, as well as lethal, weapons "should be carefully controlled." They call for a superior officer to be held responsible when he knows or should know about abuses by officers under his command, and they man-

---

Paul Chevigny is a professor at N.Y.U. Law School. His latest book is Gigs: Jazz and the Cabaret Laws in New York City *(Routledge).*

date effective reporting and review procedures for incidents of injury or death. Although the Constitution also sets some general limits on officials' use of force, the federal government does not monitor local compliance even with constitutional, not to speak of international, standards; there are, for example, no federal "reporting and review" procedures for local police violence. The federal government is largely ignorant about compliance with police standards at the local level; it knows little about how local police use force, what they do to control the use of weapons or whether commanding officers are held responsible.

During the L.A.P.D. flap, the Justice Department's Assistant for Civil Rights, John Dunne, sought to soothe a momentarily agitated Congress:

> We are not the "front-line" troops in combatting instances of police abuse. That role properly lies with the internal affairs bureaus of law enforcement agencies and with state and local prosecutors. The federal enforcement program is more a "back-stop" to these other resources.

That is still a fair statement of the existing situation, but it only emphasizes how the federal government has never had the stomach to recognize and use its powers to stop local police brutality. Yet the use of excessive force can be a violation of constitutional rights—a denial of due process of law, for example—and the deliberate violation of constitutional rights by a local official is a federal crime. The Justice Department's work on crime, however, has made very little difference in our knowledge about the incidence of police brutality. The department has received about the same number of criminal civil rights complaints, including some for police abuses, every year for the past decade. Prosecutions have been few because Justice has a longstanding policy of not pressing a federal case when the local district attorney is already acting under state law and because the federal prosecutor is obliged to prove, in each case, that the accused official acted with the "specific intent" to violate constitutional rights.

The jurisdiction on the civil side is even more stunted; there is no statute authorizing the government to bring a case, for example, to enjoin a pattern of police abuse. During the notorious regime of Mayor Frank Rizzo in Philadelphia, Jimmy Carter's Justice Department sued the city to stop the "widespread [police] practice of violating the rights of persons they encounter in the streets and elsewhere in the city." The U.S. Court of Appeals for the Third Circuit dismissed the case, claiming that to recognize an implied power in the government to bring such a suit would create a remedy of "incredible breadth and scope." The Philadelphia case was the Waterloo of federal intervention against local police; no wonder Dunne preferred to claim a modest role for the national government.

That limitation on civil lawsuits undoubtedly ought to be changed; Congress should give the Justice Department the power to intervene against systematic local abuses of constitutional rights, as the A.C.L.U. and the N.A.A.C.P. were urging during the scandal a year ago. But that change—which would be politically difficult to bring about—would probably do little to affect national consciousness about police problems. The narrowness of existing federal jurisdiction reflects how much local officials fear criticism, and how eager federal officials are to accommodate them, all in the name of some vague localism. If national powers to intervene were expanded, it is very unlikely that an Attorney General in a Reagan-Bush sort of administration would want to exercise such a power, and in any case it would not give us systematic information about local police.

If our aim is to increase public consciousness and gradually improve local practices, then direct federal-state confrontation may not be the most useful approach. There are, however, some federal tools available that would be easier to use and perhaps more successful. There are a number of programs in which the wall of localism has already been broken down, primarily because federal officials wanted it breached and local officials wanted federal help. Those programs could be reshaped at minimal cost and with little legislative change to give us nationwide information about police, and even to affect local practices.

The Office of Justice Programs within the Justice Department administers a group of agencies dedicated to "Justice System Improvement," including the Bureau of Justice Statistics, which collects data on aspects of the justice system, and the Bureau of Justice Assistance, which gives advice and grants for special programs to local law-enforcement agencies. In 1990 the Office of Justice Programs spent $762 million.

The Bureau of Justice Statistics collects an extraordinary variety of data, mostly from local sources. It has published a report, for example, on the racial composition of prisoners throughout the United States (which has changed from 78 percent white sixty years ago to 44 percent black in 1986) and others on the social characteristics of criminals and victims. Its *Sourcebook of Criminal Justice Statistics* is a 700-plus-page compendium of figures on crime, police, courts and prisons; if you want to know how many wiretap orders were issued in 1989, the number is 763 and it is on page 472. Since the Los Angeles scandal, the *Sourcebook* has reprinted some data from a Gallup poll on public attitudes toward police brutality, but as far as I can tell, the Bureau of Justice Statistics publishes nothing else about police misconduct.

Nevertheless, the bureau clearly has the power to collect data that would throw light on the problems of police violence. The *Sourcebook* publishes the number of police officers killed in the line of duty (sixty-six in 1989), for example, but not the number of civilians shot by police. The federal government seems to collect no figures on the police use of deadly force, although it would not be extraordinarily difficult to do and might be very useful. James Fyfe, once a policeman and now a noted criminologist, was able to show more than a decade ago, by an analysis of police shooting statistics in New York City, that restrictions on police use of weapons could reduce the number of citizens shot without reducing arrests or increasing crime or injuries to police. If figures on shootings by police were correlated with figures on crime, arrests and injuries, we could compare cities throughout the country; the results would be extremely illuminating.

The federal government has the power to collect information on the number and type of citizen complaints against the police; on officers disciplined by departments and the nature of their offenses; on the number of officers prosecuted for local crimes; and on systems of review, command-control and accountability within local departments. If the government used that power, it might give us an idea how widespread police violence is, in what cities it is prevalent and what can be done to decrease it. Because we have no systematic knowledge on the national level—either of the prevalence of police violence or what can be done about it—we simply don't recognize it as a persistent problem. The systematic ignorance of the federal government works very well to keep police violence off the national agenda.

If the government did have such information it could more actively promote reform by withholding federal assistance to local police forces. Although existing aid programs explicitly forbid "direction, supervision or control" by any federal official over local police, the National Institute of Justice is authorized to conduct research on and make suggestions for the improvement of the criminal justice system. The Bureau of Justice Assistance provides funds to local police for equipment and to assist specific programs, such as drug enforcement. If the federal government possessed adequate information about police violence, it could establish guidelines on the use of nonlethal weapons, on adequate command responsibility and on fair review of complaints of police brutality. These could legitimately be disseminated to local departments, just as the Justice Department now gives advice and funds for law enforcement against drug trafficking and money laundering.

The next step would be to make federal assistance to local law-enforcement agencies conditional on their compliance with basic principles of due process and respect for human rights. It is common for federal grants to be made conditional on compliance with federal law, and in fact that device is already used, in a limited way, in the Justice Department programs. Federal law-enforcement assistance can be suspended if it is found that the local police have engaged in discrimination in employment. Regarding police brutality, I would make the following proposals:

1) When the Justice Department is satisfied that there is a widespread and continuous pattern of the use of excessive force or other violation of basic rights, federal funding to the local police authority should be terminated. There should be a hearing procedure to determine the facts, as there is under the present system when a department is accused of discrimination.

2) When resources supplied under a federal program have themselves been used in connection with acts of police brutality, an equivalent sum should be returned to the government. Think, for a moment, about that taser gun used on Rodney King. In many cases police have obtained sophisticated hardware through federal programs; when that hardware is used to abuse citizens, local departments should pay for it in full.

These proposals are the minimum Washington ought to ask in return for the millions of dollars it spends on law-enforcement assistance. The fact that they are not on the agenda is partly a result of ignorance, cultivated over generations, about local violations of citizens' rights. If the government collected such information, it might begin to seem natural for it to do something about those violations. And not incidentally, it might enable America to comply with international standards for law enforcement.   □

DataCenter 464 19th Street, Oakland, California 94612 (415) 835-4692

How Rappers Predicted Rioting

*By Teresa Moore
and Torri Minton*
Chronicle Staff Writers

Los Angeles

As the smoke of hundreds of fires darkened the skies above Los Angeles, young blacks drove up and down Crenshaw Boulevard in the heart of the riots, blasting rap from their car stereos and raising their fists in the sign of black power.

The hard-core raps were more than mere soundtracks to the looting and burning that followed the verdicts in the Rodney King case: They had presaged the social upheaval and gave voice to the experiences and emotions of the disenfranchised.

Beat Master V., drummer for the rap group Body Count, stood watching a liquor store burn in his old South Central neighborhood. "I've seen all kinds of crazy things since the verdict came down," he said, staring at a dark column of smoke. ". . . It may not be right, but it's only logical."

For years, rappers have chronicled urban decay, police brutality, racism and economic disparity. Within hours of the verdict, their direst predictions came to life.

You were put here to protect us but who protects us from you . . ./

If I hit you, I'll be killed/

If you hit me I can sue/

Looking through my history

book I watch you as you grew/

Killing blacks and calling it the law/

*— "Who Protects Us From You,"
by Boogie Down Productions,
featuring KRS-One.*

"Every rapper's been talking about this," said South Central Los Angeles rapper WC, 23, of WC and the Maad Circle. "But nobody listens until their house catches on fire. It's nothing but a modern-day slavery, changed from whips to billy clubs."

Speaking the gut truth of urban survival, rage and despair, rappers are the heralds of inner-city reality — even more so, some say, than the leaders, politicians and media who are expected to play that role.

Rap is the CNN of black America, says Chuck D, leader of Public Enemy, the most influential hard core rap group.

"Bush came on the news and said don't loot, but the savings and loans have been looting us for years," said Michael Franti, 26, of the Berkeley-based Disposable Heroes of Hiphoprisy. "He said stay in your homes, but a lot of our people are homeless. He said be fair, but what kind of fairness do we see in the courts?"

Desperate Straits

In their raps, the Disposable Heroes take to task a government that has cut education financing and social programs while tolerating high unemployment and ignoring the desperate straits of poor people of color. Franti said the destruction that greeted the Los Angeles police verdict was "not a reaction, but a revolt."

James Bernard, 26, senior editor of The Source, a rap magazine, said, "If anybody had paid attention to the music at all, they would have known" about the impending explosion.

"The rappers are expressing a lot of anger, especially among people of our generation," he said. "That anger is tinged with a lack of faith in the traditional civil rights structure."

On the "Death Certificate" album, rapper Ice Cube criticizes Jesse Jackson, as well as George Bush. The controversial album has gone platinum, selling more than a million copies since October.

Distrust for Politics

Frustration with establishment politics is a running theme in rap. At a recent Berkeley concert, rapper KRS-One, who preaches black awareness and education, exhorted his young audience not to vote.

The kids "pay absolutely no attention to the politicians. They do not trust them at all and have no reason to," says Simba Kenyatta, 39, a professor of African American history at the University of California at Santa Cruz.

In jail cause I can't pay the mother/

Held back in life because I'm a color/

Now this is just a little summary/

Of us/

But y'all think it's dumb of me/

To hold a mirror to your face but trust/

Nobody gives a f - - - about —/

— "Us," by Ice Cube.

Rap is a growing force, with centers in California and in New York, and a hold on urban youth since the late '70s.

Black music in the Recording Industry Association of America's "Urban Contemporary" category, including rap, has shot up from 11.6 percent of the $5.5 billion dollars spent on recordings in 1987 to 18.3 percent of the $7.5 billion spent in 1990.

While many people are put off by the swearing and violence in hard core rap, fans and rap artists say they should pay more attention to the form's deeper political messages.

Cecil Hale, a former vice president of Capitol Records who teaches popular music and communications at Stanford University, points to NWA, hard-core rappers who have drawn a lot of heat.

"They were so rough in the things they said that (one of their) records never got any air play," Hale said. What you hear in their lyrics is "outright frustration, then rage, then a definition of a lifestyle ... which is downright criminal but they also say in their music that there is no other way."

Shut Off From Mainstream

Hale said that the music captures and broadcasts the experience of generation that feels shut out from mainstream culture and trapped in an environment that forces them to seek other routes to success.

"It's a reality that mainstream America simply does not want to deal with." Hale said.

Close your eyes it can't happen here/

Big brother in a squad car's coming near/

*— "California Uber Alles,"
by Disposable Heroes of Hiphoprisy*

Some rappers deplore violence as counterproductive. Others say the violence that seared the country after the verdicts brought people together.

"The looting and everything I thought was unnecessary," said El Cerrito rapper M.C. Spice, 25. "It shows that we as a race don't know how to come together properly.

"I think some rappers can help stop the violence," she said, "just by getting a positive message out about what is going on."

While it hurts to see people beaten, said WC, on the whole the violent outrage "felt good. Because I've never seen so much unity in my life (among people of color). Rival gangs, young folks, old folks, the working class ..."

For once, he said, those being beaten weren't black.

"I just wish we could have burned more homes in Beverly Hills," said WC, "so they can get up every day and they can look at the frustration, look at the anger. They could be the ones out there a week later with the brooms sweeping up."

Martyr Rap

Franti turned his rage over the verdict into a five-page rap, "The Day They Made Rodney King a Martyr," delivered in a San Francisco club on the third night of rioting. "I feel that any way that you can bring about the energy of a mass of people is positive," he said.

Rappers certainly have not been the only musicians with a message of outrage at societal inequities. The anger has been there for years in other forms of black music, like reggae, but that theme has gone largely unnoticed by mainstream America.

"African music in America in general has expressed a message for quite some time that African American people hold in their hearts but are afraid to put out for fear of retribution from the larger white society," said historian Kenyatta.

It is a point of view that white America generally doesn't acknowledge, said Davey D, 27, a Bay Area rap writer and radio disc jockey.

Rap's influence could rise significantly if it acquires more mainstream popularity. Rap's audience among young whites is large and growing.

But for most white fans, said Davey D, the focus has been more on the art than the message.

"Chuck D is not seen as this insightful well-read black man. ... He is seen as an angry black man," Davey D said, speaking of the leader of Public Enemy. "People see this rage and they look at it with amusement and they don't take it seriously and then when things blow up they say, 'Wow, I guess they were serious.'"

DataCenter   464 19th Street, Oakland, California 94612 (415) 835-4692

BLOW BY BLOW

BY LISA KENNEDY

What becomes of a technology deferred?

For those unfamiliar with the receiving end, the events in L.A. offered the chance to know what racism feels like. Art tries to make another's point of view our own (and succeeds from time to time), but nothing in recent history has done this as dramatically as the Rodney King tape and the Simi Valley 12's audacious denial of its reality. His reality, our reality.

As an outraged François Mitterrand said, We've all seen it. We know what we saw (and some of us who watch Court TV know what the jury saw as well). With those acquittals, for one shocking moment we all knew what it meant to feel something, to know it like the back of your hand, the bruise on your jaw, and then to have it denied. No, what you saw, experienced, suffered was really something other than what you saw, experienced, etc. This is one of the great tactics of racism (sexism, homophobia, classism). After a while, it's enough to make you crazy. It's enough to make you angry.

Here's a newly minted joke. The Rodney King jurors have reconsidered the Zapruder film and concluded that JFK's wounds were self-inflicted. In *JFK*, the surprise witness was another movie, a jumpy 8mm piece of history. In the Koon, Powell, Wind, Briseno trial the star witness was 81 seconds of videotape. What happened? Here was the witness who'd come forward immediately, whose 81 seconds of testimony seemingly could not be worn down by attorneys; this witness wouldn't crack under pressure; this witness was objective. But when the 81 seconds became hundreds upon hundreds of seconds, backward, forward, frame by frame, the witness, according to the jurors, began to tell a different story. Slowed down enough, a reflexive jerk of the leg, a movement set in motion by a "stomp" or a swat of Powell's baton, became Rodney King kicking at the cops.

Face it, if Kevin Costner had been the D.A. and the final argument had been scripted by Oliver Stone, those four good ole boys in blue would be in the clink. Instead, while Costner's frame-by-frame deconstruction of the snap and slump of Kennedy's head breathed life into one conspiracy theory, the defense team's manipulation of the Rodney King beating video attempted to put another to death: the one that suggests a thing called racism exists, that it is systemic.

What would be the jurors' conclusion? That JFK's wounds were self-inflicted. Or at least Rodney King's were. And in some twisted way, of course, that is what the jury found. Fleeing at high speed, ignoring traffic signals, resisting arrest—in the light of these (and a record), force became not a legal definition but a "state of mind," as defense attorney Howard Weitzman called it. Ladies and gentlemen of the jury, you are now entering the land of projection, racial anxiety, racism: Welcome.

Of course, that land was as close as the Simi Valley 12's backyards. And during the "insurrection," as congresswoman Maxine Waters so correctly called it, other obscene images flickered across our screens. (For some the world is as an eye for an eye, a video for a video.) There was the footage of people being robbed of their proper names, their dreams, their sense of individuality as they were dragged from a car or a truck and stupidly, gleefully beaten. Unhh! Take that. Unhh. This is for Rodney King. But what was especially sickening was the naïveté with which the media initially met the challenge. Not since the Thomas/Hill hearing has it been so starkly clear that not only are the nation's decision makers overwhelmingly white, and mostly male, but so are its storytellers, its reporters.

All that gee whiz, how come, omigod, omigod reporting of the first 24 hours was revolting. Maybe Peter Bart, editor not of the New York or L.A. *Times* or the Wash *Post*, but of *Variety*, the entertainment mag, was right: those reporters were intoxicated with the Big Screen of it all. The helicopters cutting and swooping through the smoke in the night, like *Boyz N the Hood*. No, strike that, that's a view of the copters from the ground, from that very hotspot, South Central L.A. This was like *T2*, or something not as fun, like the gulf war.

Never has the gulf between black and white been so clear as when it became obvious that part of the reason we weren't getting fed images from the ground was that the image feeders were afraid of the frenzy. Don't blame 'em on one level but do on a host of others. There was the patronizing Greg Lamotte on CNN doing his damndest to win a Peter Arnett Award. There was the painfully hysterical voiceover—*"Jesus, that's attempted murder!!!"*—as Reginald Denny was yanked from his truck and pummeled by several manboys. A new word must be coined for the response that goes beyond ordinary empathy, a term for one's own racial terror presented as objective reportage. Maybe that term exists already: bias.

One wonders, didn't any of these reporters and anchors take in the best movies of the last few years: *Do the Right Thing* and *Boyz N the Hood*? Or did they view them as just so much ethnography? Why did Mookie throw that garbage can through Sal's window? was a zeitgeist koan if ever there was one. Figure that out, or at least don't fear it, and maybe your lead-off question won't be, "Congresswoman Waters, Reverend Jackson, Representative Conyers... Why are *they* so angry?" From the get-go it was clear that many of us were not considered part of the privileged viewing audience; for us, the answer to that question is as apparent as a city block. Then there were phrases like "When the violence started" or "When the violence stops," thrown around as if their truth value were uncontested. In South Central the violence didn't begin with the acquittals and it doesn't end with the withdrawal of federal troops. Of the 58 dead, most were black and Hispanic men from the nabe.

If the S&L scandal were televisual, the physical evidence as persuasive as watching citizens take freely from a supermarket, what would it look like? All of New York City burnt to the ground—block after block looted then destroyed. Perhaps the entire state singed and smoky. White men running in suits, oh why not, walking casually with sacks of dough. Fuck the color TVs guys, we'll bumrush the networks and studios. And gosh, though we the TV audience seldom got to see it in human terms, those gulf war videos of bombs hitting their targets proved that even if white men can't jump they can kill with the best of them. If those Brooks Brothers hoods had to, they could do the deed.

There is no denying that video has a way of grabbing us. We're in second grade and it's our nation's show-and-tell. Still, as a country we shared an extraordinary moment: the polls showed that pretty much all of us agreed that the cops were guilty of using excessive force. Less than half of whites polled, however, agreed with the following statement: The justice system is biased against African Americans, while nearly 90 per cent of blacks did. A video can show us only so much, and then we must rely on history, reporters, politicians, teachers, our own minds to tell us what is going down. Maybe TV is only as good as its viewers? In response to one juror's explanation that they had to take into account not only the 81 seconds of the Rodney King beating, but the many minutes leading up to that teeny, diminished 81 seconds, a friend said, Yeah, and the rest of us had only taken into account the last 100 years. ∎

DOMESTIC DESTABILIZATION

ON DRED SCOTT AND
AFRICAN-AMERICAN ELECTED LEADERS

BY LORETTA J. WILLIAMS

COLIN POWELL IS the darling of the media these days. Neo-conservatives gloat: we entrusted our very national security to a black American general—that's a sure sign integration's working. A white conspiracy against blacks? No. That's just the rhetoric of the left.

Saner voices, however, speak to reality. In November 1989, the National Council of Churches of Christ, USA, (NCCC) passed a resolution condemning racially-motivated "acts of aggression" against African Americans in government. It speaks plainly: "The issue is not the possible innocence or guilt of each of the many elected officials who have come under attack. The issue is the fact that this pattern of attacks by agencies of the government in itself con-stitutes criminal activity on the part of the government because it subverts and undermines the democratic process itself."

The destabilization of black leaders and of the emerging exercise of black political power is a particularly blatant example of political repression. Some call this the attempted decapitation of the African-American community.

Nationwide, the 2 percent of elected officials who are black face formidable stumbling blocks: innuendo, media slander, leaks from grand juries, a variety of tactics which drain public trust and funding. Of the known federal sting operations 14 percent target these 2 percent of elected officials. On the state level: in 1989, for example, one-third of the 1,166 African-American elected officials in Alabama were under investigation or indictment.

Elected officials who do not mirror the traditional white male elite power structure of this country continue to be the targets of covert "low intensity" warfare. Witness the media lynching of Cleveland's current mayor, Michael R. White. Was it mere coincidence that he was subpoenaed by a grand jury while hosting a gathering of the nation's black mayors? Witness Congressperson Floyd Flake, the senior minister of one of Brooklyn's largest African-American congregations, after months of media speculation, is "cleared" in April of "abusing" his ministerial discretionary funds.

Dred Scott Phenomenon

THE WORK OF persons serving in public office can be compromised by more than their own actions. What we have here is Dred Scott revamped.

The question before the Supreme Court in the 1850s was: "Can a Negro, whose ancestors were imported into this country, and sold as slaves, become a member of the political community formed and brought into existence by the Constitution of the United States?"

No, said the Court. The Constitution protects the owner of the slave, not Dred Scott who is the owner's property. Chief Justice Taney ruled: "In the opinion of the court, the legislation and histories of the times, and the language used in the Declaration of Independence, neither the class of persons who had been imported as slaves, nor their descendants, whether they had become free or not, were then acknowledged as a part of the people, nor intended to be included."

African Americans were deemed beings of an inferior order, unfit to associate with the white race either in social or political relations.

Fast forward to a recent affidavit from Hirsch Friedman, a practicing lawyer and an undercover agent for the FBI in Atlanta: "Shortly after I began working with the FBI in 1979, I was made aware of an 'unofficial' policy of the FBI which was generally referred to as *Fruhmenschen* [German for primitive man] the routine investigation without probable cause of prominent elected and appointed black officials in major metropolitan areas throughout the United States. I learned from my conversations with special agents of the FBI that the basis for this policy was the assumption by the FBI that black officials were intellectually and socially incapable of governing major governmental organizations and institutions."

Friedman provided testimony on attempts to entrap and discredit Maynard Jackson, Reginald Eaves, and other elected and appointed Atlanta officials. He recalled the special agent in charge telling him "that they would pursue an investigation because Eaves was a Fruhmenschen and would thus have to break the law." Innate criminality is assumed.

DataCenter 464 19th Street, Oakland, California 94612 (415) 835-4692

This harassment has parallels in the Reconstruction era, when southern elites moved to disfranchise southern blacks from participation in the political life of the region. What began in Mississippi in 1890 spread across the South in domino fashion. By 1910 every southern state had written white supremacy into its state constitution. Technically these statutes have been deleted. But selective persecution and prosecution can achieve the same effect.

It is difficult to document these activities. Yet there is fertile context for them. Black and Latino agents within the FBI have challenged internal discrimination. The Donald Rochon case, for example, documented acts of overt racial hostility within the Bureau. It is not surprising, therefore, that agents feel free to act out their racial hostilities in the so-called line of duty. Racial ascription as non-white is suspicion in itself. The harassment of African-American leaders represents the exercise of political power by white male elites. The goal is not formal prosecution, but dissuasion from any encroachment on white power.

Historical Antipathy To Black Leaders

EACH JANUARY, corporate and civic praise is heaped upon sanitized memories of Dr. Martin Luther King Jr. Forgotten is how the IRS Criminal Division harassed him. Forgotten, too, is his indictment for tax evasion. King is but one in a steady progression of African Americans harassed by government agents: Marcus Garvey, a non-elected organizer with a clear constituency in the Universal Negro Improvement Association; Paul Robeson, artist and internationalist; Representative Adam Clayton Powell, the first and most powerful African-American member of Congress; Rep. Charles Diggs, targeted as he rose to seniority in the House; 50 percent of today's congressional Black Caucus members such as Mervyn Dymally and Floyd Flake; Colorado's former Lt. Gov. George Brown (he and Dymally were particularly vulnerable as the first two African-American lieutenant governors); 21-year-old Black Panther Fred Hampton shot in his bed; mayors past and present such as Carl Stokes, Richard Hatcher, Eddie Carthan, Richard Arrington, Michael White; sheriffs, judges, state representatives, city councilors—the litany could be much longer.

Some call this a "new middle passage." Others speak of it as a slow holocaust. Dhoruba ben Wahid, recently freed from two decades of imprisonment for being a Black Panther, reminds us: "You let them destroy, kill and incarcerate young Black males who were about the business of community empowerment. They came for us, they will come for you too."

The TV docudrama "Separate But Equal" made it painful to recall the euphoria after the Brown decision by the Supreme Court in 1954. The rallying slogan and buttons reading "Free by '63" seem incongruous now. Integration as a singular operating goal was a trap. It unfortunately superceded the longer-standing organizing goal of expanding democracy to include social, economic, political, and racial parity. Recognition of the fundamentally rooted nature of white supremacy has been stymied by advocacy of racial integration. Racial democracy has proven even more illusory than participatory democracy.

The Hoover Legacy

THE FBI IS a factor here. Some background: J. Edgar Hoover had no desire to be involved in racial justice issues. Two years after the FBI was founded, Hoover was asked to investigate a series of lynchings of blacks. His response: We have "no authority to protect citizens of African descent." Hoover thought segregation was okay, and long resisted getting involved, citing states rights and community standards.

In 1934 a mob lynched Claude Neal, who was suspected of murdering a white woman. Newspapers advertised when it would occur. Thousands watched it. The Justice Department refused to send the FBI to investigate. Kidnapping for purposes of monetary gain? Yes, the FBI will investigate. Kidnapping for purposes of murder? Not in the FBI mandate.

A case from the 1940s: Atlanta police used a hot branding iron to get a confession from a 16-year-old black male suspected of burglary. The FBI, asked to investigate whether this was routine practice, said no, without an investigation. A big public relations hassle over the controversy resulted and the FBI had to say it would investigate—but only if the victim filed charges, and if the victim turned out to have a good reputation. The case was dropped.

Hoover saw everything through a filter of anti-communism. Loyalty was the issue. The FBI monitored the black press and anyone protesting the frequent lynchings. Advocacy of racial justice was subversive, and civil rights activism was un-American. Surveillance was approved and encouraged by president after president, even President Kennedy. While John F. Kennedy came to be uncomfortable with Hoover's leadership, Robert Kennedy prevailed, respecting the power base that Hoover had built.

The FBI did not act in a vacuum. While the NAACP spoke of "Free by '63," a manifesto was written and published in 1956 by 100 members of Congress pledging themselves to resist desegregation by every legal means.

The right-wing ideological bent of J. Edgar Hoover still shapes the FBI and the structured ways Bureau personnel attempt to render African-American leaders politically impotent by questioning the authority and exercise of the power of the position they have attained; by dishonoring, discrediting, demoralizing, and disrespecting black political power and earned leadership, says Dr. Joann Watson, Detroit NAACP executive. There are few checks and balances upon the intelligence community. Agents collect information and build cases any way they feel like it.

The Media's Constant Drumbeat

FRUHMENSCHEN PRACTICES ABOUND, too, in the media as their spotlights shine brightly on alleged wrongdoings of African-American elected officials. The Marion Barry deathwatch sold newspapers long before the videotaped sting rendezvous. But the media scrutiny, and lynchings 1990s style can better be seen in the *Washington Post* allegations about William Gray, chair of the House Budget Committee, when he was running for the majority whip position. The *Washington Post* trumpeted unsubstantiated leaks from the Justice Department. By going on the offensive publicly, Gray and his competent staff fought back at the unsubstantiated claim of "ghost" employees. He won the majority whip position.

The media convey a "constant drumbeat" of rumors and out-and-out lies leveled against strong Black leaders. For this reason, the congressional Black Caucus commissioned a study of media coverage of members in 1987. Among the findings: the press "often (unwittingly or consciously) served as a 'handmaiden' for Justice Department leaks to be widely spread although most of the allegations were never substantiated."

The rumor-mongering takes its toll: financial toll, energy toll, toll on day-by-day functioning. Friends become nervous, colleagues distance themselves, the public is suspicious. As Congressperson Mervyn Dymally (D-CA) notes: "Once the words 'under investigation' are hung on you, no one returns your calls. You lose contracts and clients. The banks call in notes. Your credit stops."

Contemporary Cases

SOCIAL PSYCHOLOGISTS USE the concept of moral exclusion to explain how a group is placed outside the boundary in which moral values, rules, and conditions of fairness need apply. African-American elected and appointed officials are victimized by such practices of moral exclusion.

I do not contend that African Americans are the sole targets of such activity. Even the U.S. General Accounting-Office acknowledged FBI surveillance of the Arab community in the U.S. similar to that of the Japanese community during the ten years before their internment. And the FBI is said now to be investigating the rap group NWA.

I contend that a disproportionate number of those targeted for repressive destabilization are people of color, particularly blacks. no more cattle prods, now it's specious charges, derogation, disparagement of those assumed to be inferior.

The National Interreligious Commission on Civil Rights held hearings recently in Milwaukee, Indianapolis, Detroit, Louisville, Montgomery, Kansas City, and New York on the status of civil rights. A diverse array of African-American public officials and tales of repeated and selective harassment have come forth. Some excerpts:

RICHARD ARRINGTON, BIRMINGHAM MAYOR: The first Black mayor in Alabama was the target of a sting operation. A developer, to gain leniency on the sentence for his own wrongdoings, tried unsuccessfully to entrap Richard Arrington on a zoning matter. Arrington had advanced the economic interests of those not previously privy to city contracts. This opening of economic doors was perceived by the old elites as a threat. He went public with the details and ordered a full-scale investigation by the city. The resulting report damning the federal operation has received little press attention.

PATRICIA DAVIS. BIRMINGHAM. AL: Patricia Davis, seven-year member of the state legislature, a junior college teacher, and wife of a minister, chaired the Public Utilities and Transportation Committee. As the only black chairper-

son in the Alabama House, she was indicted on conspiracy and bribery charges. This was preceded by rumors, leaks to the press, the bugging (learned later) of office and home phones, talk of drug use. Through her trial she came to know that an agent listening in on her tapped phone heard Davis say to her young son: "Baby, go back please and get me some Coke." Davis testified: "I don't drink, never have. I am not, and have never been, involved in any kind of drug. The strongest drink? a Coke—Coca-Cola." She immediately took every form of drug test known and gave the results to the press. But the seed had been planted.

JUDGE ALCEE HASTINGS, FL: Found innocent by a jury in 1981, Judge Alcee Hastings, federal judge in Florida, was retried by the U.S. Senate on what was subsequently agreed was the same charge, despite restrictions on double jeopardy. He was found guilty and impeached.

STATE SENATOR ANDREW JENKINS, NY: Accused of operating a mythical bank, Andrew Jenkins has been audited by the Internal Revenue Service, the Attorney General's office, and the FBI. A battering arsenal of investigatory techniques has been arrayed one right after the other. The IRS is the willing servant of political intelligence, ready to do whatever it is told. The positive media coverage Jenkins had been receiving prior to this abruptly changed to rumor mongering about campaign irregularities. Jenkins was followed everywhere by government agents. His phones were tapped. Eventually a political show trial led to an indictment and a career was derailed.

EARL JONES, GREENSBORO, NC: A Greensboro City Council member, three times unopposed in reelection campaigns, was approached by what turned out to be a bogus corporation of FBI agents. A black public relations firm set up a meeting with Jones to talk about relocating a Peach State manufacturing plant. Jobs would be created. The company wanted to be a good corporate citizen, they said, and thus wanted 'to contribute to your favorite charity, Mr. Councilor.' After giving a mini-lecture on ethics, and referrals to the Chamber of Commerce and United Way, Jones left the room. He says he thought them "kind of shaky" at the time, but never imagined that they might be FBI undercover agents. One man followed Jones down to his car and asked him to do a favor. The so-called president of the company pulled out a pouch, saying that he owed the public relations firm owner some money and did not have time to take it over to him before leaving town. Earl Jones was asked to carry this money over. He declined saying he didn't want to be involved in a business relationship. He left and, troubled by the sequence of events, called his lawyer. He, and the Christic Institute South, held a press conference to make public what had happened. This key response, making public the events as they occurred indicating that he had nothing to hide, has protected Jones thus far.

STATE SENATOR CLARENCE MITCHELL III. MD: Investigated and cleared 19 times during his 24 years of service in the Maryland State Legislature, Mitchell was indicted finally for an alleged Wedtech impropriety. Initially there were no criminal charges. When the lawyer moved to set aside the

DataCenter 464 19th Street, Oakland, California 94612 (415) 835-4692

indictment on this basis, the judge, according to Mitchell, said "No, I'm not going to entertain the motion. The prosecutors will find something to charge you with." When Mitchell appealed that decision, a 1910 statute was dusted off. "The grand jury system is a farce," says Mitchell. "They do whatever the prosecutors ask them to do. You and your lawyer have no opportunity to inject any information." After serving 15 months in prison, Mitchell began a nation-wide campaign to assist other elected and appointed officials in stopping prosecutorial abuse and the other elements of harassment. The Clarence Mitchell Jr. Memorial Fund, named in honor of the stalwart NAACP Washington strategist, is a result.

CONGRESSIONAL CANDIDATE FAYE WILLIAMS, LA: Leading in the polls as the 1986 Democratic contender for a Louisiana congressional seat, attorney Faye Williams was flying to a last campaign speech on the eve of the election. Her chartered helicopter was ordered to land immediately. It did, on Air Force property. "We were met by a full show of military readiness including armored personnel carrier, fire trucks and 30 or 40 men with guns drawn on us," said Williams. "We were surrounded and ordered out of the helicopter with our hands up." The next morning the papers featured Air Force charges that candidate Williams had been "rude, abusive, and threatening to the military" in her treatment of the gun-toting airmen. She lost the election by less than 1 percentage point. She still has not received an official explanation for the order to land. She, and others, contend that the incident was contrived to block her becoming the first African American elected in Louisiana since Reconstruction.

The Tales Continue

THERE ARE NUMEROUS other cases of attempts to block the expansion of African-American leadership. Some persons are arrested on one charge and tried for another. Sheriff Richard Lankford of Fulton County, Georgia, after much harassment, faced charges for underreporting his income. Congressperson Floyd Flake (D-CA) says, "If they can't get you on anything else, they'll try tax fraud or tax evasion. Something to do with your lifestyle," he notes. Mayor Unita Blackwell, Mayersville, Mississippi, current president of the National Conference of Black Mayors, speaks of this pattern of harassment as "a new way to keep us in check."

What comes out from the individual stories is a pattern of unequal treatment, of harassment using the same modus operandi. It is not surprising that individual public servants feel overwhelmed by the necessary struggle to survive. The chilling effect takes its toll as young black men and women say "No way am I going to run for public office and have my private life dragged through the media."

Russell Owens, of the Joint Center on Political and Economic Studies, believes that the American public, black and white, has grown increasingly intolerant of malfeasance in office by all elected officials. With few exceptions, he says, allegations of illegal and/or improper conduct by elected officials have proven to be the kiss of death. "Black voters, in particular, did not change the political landscape

only to expect more of the same from their public officials. However, they expect their public officials to receive the kind of careful and constitutional protections guaranteed to all citizens of the country, and therefore, would be particularly repelled by the alleged patterns of discrimination," he says.

Official Denials And Public Complicity

FBI DIRECTOR William Sessions denies the existence of a Fruhmenschen policy and, using convoluted verbiage, cites the excellent in-house guidelines which put limits on such things. The policy on paper has not been found. However, the practice of harassment remains. Just as the government denies that there are political prisoners in the U.S., so the government denies the attack on African-American elected and appointed officials.

The public is complicit in this denial to African Americans of earned tangible political gains. The public has ceded authority to bureaucrats who have wide permission to protect so-called national security. Liberal fears about the Cold War over the years legitimated the emergence of a quasi-independent intelligence community that has no bounds.

Overreaction to McCarthyism insulated bureaucrats from external accountability. The general public looked to "professional administrators" to rid the country of the dreaded Communists. The bureaucrats—they'll act in the public interest, some said. And the national security apparatus grew and grew with broad and ill-defined investigatory and intelligence powers. Political scientist William Keller says that in the early 1950s members of the liberal political community envisioned "an FBI based on a model of domestic intelligence. But because they are not prepared to impose ministerial controls over the FBI, the bureau soon began to resemble more the model of the secret police. The liberal theory of international security therefore spawned a host of unintended consequences with serious implications for the rights of citizens and democratic government more generally."

Deep in our national fabric, our public culture, is permission and determination not to see what is plainly visible. Adamant naivete, intentional innocence, and aggressive ignorance operate to the collective diminishment of communities of color. We must come to better understand the culture of middle class quiescence, its groundedness in individualism and in a false idol of white control.

What To Do

STRUCTURED RACIAL ANIMOSITY must be factored into our conversations and strategies about covert government actions. We must:

- Inform others.

- Advocate a full congressional investigation publicly examining the misuse of the criminal and civil justice system that harasses and drains the resources of African American elected and appointed officials. Justice Department leaders held a "summit meeting" in February to speak with (read "cool out") those calling for such an investigation. Public pressure is particularly needed now.

- Donate funds to the Clarence Mitchell Jr. Memorial Fund. Tax exempt contribution can be sent to the National Council of Churches, earmarked for the Clarence Mitchell Jr. Memorial Fund at NCCC, Prophetic Justice Unit, 475 Riverside Drive, New York, NY 10115.

- Respond in quicker fashion when delegitimation attempts are underway. Help define the issue as an attack on popularly elected leadership.

- Become more active anti-racists. Passive anti-racism is a mirage; the reality is complicity with the status quo. Tap into what activist Anne Braden speaks of as the "reservoir of decency" in each of our networks and communities that can be mobilized.

- Remember that not all government officials are the enemy. Young people—African Americans, Latinas, Americans of Asian descent—are they to be discouraged from moving into the public arena? Our strategizing must become more mature. Change requires both those chipping away from the outside to bring the walls down, as well as those inside making sure that the wall coming down does not crush those in the streets.

- Support people when they are going through this public nakedness. The Marion Barry case can not continue to be used as a rationale for non-involvement. It is unfortunate that the media spotlight on the downfall of Mayor Barry has clouded focus upon unsavory actions by government agents. Perpetually under scrutiny, Barry had countered a media assault for more than five years. Few people now recall the economic advancement for black entrepreneurs that occurred during the early years Barry served the nation's capitol community. Without apologizing for Barry's personal proclivities, one can see

the toll of the spotlight scrutiny and its resulting erosion of constituency support for Barry. Destabilization works.

Conclusion

THE EPIDEMIC HARASSMENT of African-American elected officials is not an aberration. It is part and parcel of a systematic denial of shared power to persons who do not have the correct property right: white skin. In our lifetime, or, at least in our children's lifetimes, we said we would dismantle segregation's structures and practices. We would transform America, so many of us said. Yet white supremacy remains a key regulatory force in the Americas and in the world. We forget this at our peril.

Supreme Court Justice Thurgood Marshall, addressing the Second Circuit Judicial Conference, September 8, 1989, said: "History teaches that when the Supreme Court has been willing to shortchange the equality rights of minority groups, other basic personal civil liberties like the rights to free speech and to personal security against unreasonable searches and seizures are also threatened. We forget at our peril that less than a generation after the Supreme Court held separate to be equal in Plessy v. Ferguson, it held in the Schenk and Debs decisions that the First Amendment allowed the United States to convict under the Espionage Act persons who distributed antiwar pamphlets and delivered antiwar speeches... On the other side of the ledger, it is no coincidence that during the three decades beginning with Brown v. Board of Education, the Court was taking its most expansive view not only of the equal protection clause, but also of the liberties safeguarded by the Bill of Rights."

America has never been one nation indivisible. As 1992 approaches with its glitzy federal and local celebrations of the 500th anniversary of Columbus "discovering" America, we know that we are not moving towards a "more perfect union." It is time for progressives to "run to those who are attacked," says Clarence Mitchell III, "not away from them. We must rally around and stand together." Let us directly confront Dred Scott destabilization. Unless we do this consciously, the color line, distributive even in covert actions, remains rooted.   Z

Loretta J. Williams, sociologist and activist, chairs the National Interreligious Commission on Civil Rights, which works in conjunction with the National Council of Churches and the Clarence Mitchell Jr. Memorial Fund to counter this "low-intensity warfare."

THE BLACKS ARE COMING! — THE BLACKS ARE COMING!!

GEORGE BUSH'S CIVIL RIGHTS RIDE.

DataCenter   464 19th Street, Oakland, California 94612 (415) 835-4692

Killer coverage: Black stereotypes in the media

By Salim Muwakkil

THE PERSISTENT PROBLEM OF RACIAL stereotyping by the mass media has once again emerged as a major grievance among African-American leaders and organizers. Black groups spanning the ideological spectrum are raising objections to what they contend is a growing tendency by the major media to portray African-Americans as either criminals or parasites.

This is a venerable complaint. Enslaved Africans and their progeny have always struggled to assert their humanity in a culture that had such a stake in dehumanizing them. The Christianity professed by this nation's slave-holding Founding Fathers mandated human brotherhood, so black slaves had to be portrayed as less than human. Indeed, the U.S. Constitution itself regarded African descendants as two-thirds human. Negative stereotyping of African-Americans thus is as old as the country itself.

While the problem of racist stereotyping has never vanished, most analysts would agree that in the last two decades—in the wake of the civil-rights revolution—it has become less blatant. Today, media portrayals of African-Americans span a much wider range than in the days when blacks were presented exclusively in demeaning contexts. But a chorus of concern is rising from organizers in black communities across the country who argue that racist media stereotyping has reached a new high and may be just as dangerous as the inflammatory coverage that once provoked murderous nightrides by white supremacist vigilante groups.

Stereotypes in effect: The recent spurt of concern about the issue was provoked by several widely publicized incidents that were fueled by stereotypical assumptions. For example, the Los Angeles police whose savage assault on black motorist Rodney King was surreptitiously recorded on videotape had probably categorized him as a useless drug abuser and probable criminal before mercilessly bludgeoning him. The widely broadcast videotape of the incident horrified viewers and added credibility to black youths' chronic complaints of brutal treatment by police.

But many whites, terrified by stereotype-fed images of crack-crazed black street gangs storming the barricades of civilization, rallied behind L.A.'s tough police chief Daryl Gates when outraged organizers demanded his ouster. Many blacks expressed dismay that the controversial Gates retained such a large degree of white support and said it demonstrated the power exerted by anti-black stereotypes.

African-Americans have expressed concern that anti-black stereotyping has had a powerful influence in other racially charged incidents across the country.

● The "wilding" black youths charged in the 1990 Central Park jogger rape and beating case were thoroughly demonized and convicted, while three of four white St. John's University students accused of gang-sodomizing a black female student—charges corroborated by eye-witness accounts—were exonerated.

● A white police officer in Teaneck, N.J., was acquitted by an all-white jury of charges he killed a black teenager in April 1990, despite scientific evidence indicating that the youth was shot while his hands were raised in a gesture of surrender.

● A white police commander in Chicago accused of systematically torturing dozens of black suspects for more than a decade, caused Amnesty International to place the city on a unique torture watch. In response to the charge, members of the city's police department held a huge rally in support of the alleged torturer.

● A female Korean merchant in Los Angeles who was videotaped last March shooting a black teenage girl to death after an altercation about shoplifting, was tried and sentenced by a sympathetic judge to five years probation and community service.

Black men and the 5 D's: These are incidents that have caught the attention of African-American analysts who discern the influence of negative stereotyping in them all. Some of these analysts contend that the steady diet of anti-black stereotypes is part of a renewed assault on the humanity and potential of African-Americans. "The mass media have exhibited an appalling degree of distortion, bias and insensitivity in promoting negative stereotypes and misconceptions about young black males and in failing to present a more balanced picture of poverty, crime, drug use and social dysfunction in America," writes Jewell Taylor Gibbs in the December 1991 issue of *Focus*, the house organ for the Joint Center for Political and Economic Studies (JCPES) in Washington, D.C.

Gibbs, a professor in the School of Social Welfare at the University of California at Berkeley and a visiting fellow at JCPES, argued that young black men are consistently described by what she called "the five D's": deviant, disturbed, delinquent, disadvantaged and dumb. "These images reinforce the long-held view of many that young black males are somehow less than human," Gibbs wrote, "providing educators, politicians and business executives with a justification to ignore their problems, dismiss their needs and blame them for a host of ills afflicting American society."

Gibbs warned that such stereotyping undermines the strength of this country by aggravating deep-seated racial antagonisms that must be eased if the U.S. is to compete succcessfully with the industrialized nations of Europe and Asia, and be spared the social disruptions resulting from increased crime, welfare dependency and civic distress. Gibbs' argument is couched in the language of social utilitarianism, but other critics are much less circumspect in their condemnation. ·

The media and "modern racism": Boycotts of offending media are growing in popularity in several cities. In New York City, for example, both the *Daily News* and the *New York Post* have come under intense criticism and boycott pressure for what many black organizers charge is consistently negative coverage of the African-American community. "The *News* and *Post* are racist publications, pure and simple," said Elombe Brath, a New York-based black organizer and media analyst. "You can't convince dedicated racists to change simply by the power of argument. In this case, it's the power of the pocketbook that is the most effective method of persuasion."

Major publications in Detroit, Houston, Chicago, Washington, Indianapolis, Miami, New Orleans and Birmingham also have been boycotted by African-American watchdog groups in recent years. While much of this protest activity is being sparked by groups with reputations for radicalism, it is gaining increased support among more moderate constituencies. The campaign against anti-black media stereotyping is one struggle that unifies African-Americans across the political spectrum.

Broadcast media have also come under fire for perpetuating negative images of African-Americans. A recent study of Chicago's local television news shows, for example, concluded that these shows feed racial anxiety and antagonism by according dramatically different treatment to black and white criminal suspects. The study, "The Images of Blacks on Chicago's Local TV News Programs," was conducted by Northwestern University Associate Professor Robert Entman and found extensive racial bias in local television. Entman, who specializes in communication and political science, charged that Chicago's television stations encourage "modern racism"—the continued, though muted, antagonism between races that centers largely on issues of crime.

"The strong resurgence of anti-black stereotypes, particularly of blacks as criminals, is part of a general conservative trend in this country," says Vernon Jarrett, a columnist and editorial board member of the *Chicago Sun-Times*. Jarrett blames much of the problem on the national leadership of Presidents Ronald Reagan and George Bush for popularizing the notion that white Americans bore no further responsibility for racial inequality. "Naturally," Jarrett says, "if whites weren't responsible then blacks' condition must be their own fault. Increasingly, whites, even those with good intentions, began blaming the victims for their victimization, and the media simply picked up the theme."

In the 1990 book *The Mugging of Black America*, author Earl Ofari Hutchinson detailed an informal survey of several national publications that revealed how often African-Americans were linked to drug use and crime: he found that black suspects—in handcuffs, in prison, detained at gunpoint, awaiting trial in a courtroom, selling drugs on the street or as murder victims—were routinely used to illustrate the crime stories. Hutchinson compiled a list of negative terms the publications used to describe accounts of crime in the ghetto. "The warning is clear," he wrote. "Crime, violence and death lurk behind every doorway and under every archway in African-American neighborhoods. For their own health and safety, suburbanites best stay away. Crime gives the media another excuse to continue its centuries-old practice of manipulating images that promote a negative view of African-American life," Hutchinson added.

The black press defense: Representatives of the black press are attempting to increase readership of their publications by capitalizing on the African-American community's widespread discontent with the mainstream media. Despite some small successes, it's been a hard sell. "Today's black newspaper is not the same paper it was 30 years ago at the height of the civil-rights period," says Steve Davis, executive director of the National Newspaper Publishers Association (NNPA), a national organization that represents most black publications. "We've lost our cutting edge and our urgency in getting the black side of the story to African-Americans."

As the NNPA and other organizations mark the 165th anniversary of the black press—the initial issue of *Freedom's Journal*, the first black-owned newspaper, was published March 16, 1827—it's instructive to recall that the landmark publication was created explicitly to counter the blatantly anti-black stereotypes that dominated the media of that period. Riding that rationale, black-owned newspapers developed into vibrant and enormously influential forces for change within the African-American community. These days, however, most of those publications are short of both resources and passion. "The black community's anger and frustration with a mainstream media that consistently misrepresents them offers us a golden opportunity to make a strong case for the continuing need of the black press," Davis said. "Let's just hope they're listening." □

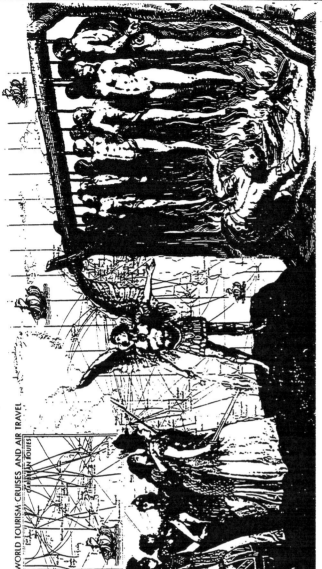

WORLD TOURISM CRUISES AND AIR TRAVEL

GUARDIANGRAPHIC BY MASSATO OTSUKA

Manning Marable

ALONG THE COLOR LINE

Columbus myth at the heart of racism

For the next 12 months across the United States, cultural and public events will be held celebrating the 500th anniversary of Christopher Columbus' "discovery" of America. For much of white America, the mythology surrounding Columbus is a central part of their racial identity. But to accept a mountain of lies as historical fact undermines the humanity of people of color and destroys any possibility of genuine multicultural dialogue.

For generations, white history books have related the tale about the supposedly humble son of a Genoese weaver. The Italian sea captain was convinced that the world was round and persuaded Queen Isabella of Spain to finance an expedition to the west. After a difficult and dangerous journey, the brave navigator and his intrepid crew landed on the island of San Salvador on October 12, 1492. Because he believed that he was only miles from the Asian mainland, Columbus called the gentle people who met him along the shore "Indians." Thus, we are told, white Western civilization finally arrived to what would become America.

The historical reality is that neither Columbus nor any other white European was the first to contact the indigenous people of America. Scholar Ivan Van Sertima, in "They Came Before Columbus," documents that Africans had accomplished this voyage by 700 B.C., traveling to the southern coast of Mexico. Influences of Africa can be seen in agricultural technologies, mound-building and even in the structure of some Native American languages.

The myth of Columbus' "discovery" is also based on the erroneous idea that 15th-century Europeans believed that the world was flat. But the historical fact is that nearly all learned Europeans of the 1400s knew that the world was indeed round, and that uncharted lands were located in the west. Columbus' chief pilot and business partner, Martin Olonzo Pinzon, had found documents in the library of Pope Innocent VIII that confirmed territories west of the Atlantic Ocean.

What motivated Columbus and the Spanish conquista-

dors was the lure of gold and the possibility of exploiting the people and resources of these new lands. Within several decades, the Spanish initiated a series of repressive laws that in effect enslaved millions of Native Americans in a system of forced labor. "Civilization" meant the destruction of indigenous cultures and societies. When the Indians resisted, the Europeans showed no mercy. In the Mayan revolt in the Yucatan in the 1520s, Indian chiefs were burned alive, the arms and legs of captured warriors were cut off and Indian women by the thousands were raped and lynched. In one century, Mexico's total population of 25 million declined to 1 million.

The exploitation of the Americas required a large labor force, so Europe turned to Africa. As early as the 1460s, about 1,000 Africans were imported annually into the Iberian peninsula as slaves. The Catholic Church was prepared to sanction the expansion of the slave trade to the Americas. In 1488, Pope Innocent VIII accepted 100 Moors as his own personal slaves as a gift from the Spanish King Ferdinand. In 1517, Bishop Bartholomé de Las Casas urged the importation of 12 African slaves for every white Spanish settler. Over the next three centuries, between 10 to 15 million Africans were involuntarily shipped to the New World. This figure does not include the millions who perished in the transatlantic crossing, the notorious "Middle Passage," in which their bodies were hurled overboard. Nor does it account for the millions of families that were divided, the children torn away from their parents, the daughters sexually molested before their mothers and fathers.

Slavery required the development of an ideology of domination. It was inevitable that Africans ceased to be described by their languages or cultures, and only by the most superficial distinction that separated them from most Europeans—their skin color. "Blacks" were defined by the boundaries of their skin. Conversely, the Europeans began to call themselves "whites," a racist term, rooted in power, privilege and violence.

By recognizing the genocide and slavery that was the real legacy of Columbus, we might begin to appreciate the dignity of Native American cultures and the history of African people. And by learning from the truths of the past, we might begin to forge the basis for honest interaction and dialogue across racial lines today.

Manning Marable is a professor of political science and history at the University of Colorado, Boulder. "Along the Color Line" is his internationally syndicated column. ○

The media's Asian Invasion complex

By J.K. Yamamoto

"EVERY ONCE in a while, you open up the paper and you really get pissed off at what you see," said Jon Funabiki, director of the Center for Integration and Improvement of Journalism (CIIJ) at San Francisco State University. He was addressing an audience of Asian American journalists, and everyone seemed to know exactly what he was talking about.

Slurs, stereotypes, and otherwise unbalanced coverage of Asian Americans by the news media, even when inadvertent, convey an unsettling message: Asian Americans are still regarded as outsiders. Sometimes, their very existence is not acknowledged.

During the national convention of the Asian American Journalists Association (AAJA) last month in Seattle, Funabiki presented "The Good, the Bad and the Ugly," a joint report by AAJA and CIIJ, which gave "special recognition" to examples of ignorance or insensitivity toward Asian Americans on the part of the mainstream media. It was an idea whose time had come; nominations were limited to items that had been broadcast or published between Jan. 1, 1990, and March 31, 1991. But the 10-year-old AAJA could easily have presented the "awards" annually throughout the 1980s. For example:

▶ *The New Republic* ran an editorial in 1985 titled "How to Gyp the Japs." In response to protests, the editors condescendingly wrote: " 'Japs' is not an ethnic slur, like 'niggers' or 'kikes.'... It is a national nickname." In other words, Japanese Americans had no right to be offended.

▶ That same year, the Long Beach Independent Press Telegram ran a photo of the winning entry in a sand-sculpture contest, described in the caption as a "buck-toothed Chinaman." To add insult to injury, the contest was co-sponsored by the newspaper.

▶ In a story (complete with pie-charts) about the composition of Congress in 1987, The New York Times stated that the Senate was 100 percent white. The paper's staff somehow overlooked Sens. Daniel Inouye and Spark Matsunaga from Hawaii. They missed the Asian and Pacific Islander members of the House as well.

As "THE GOOD, the Bad and the Ugly" shows, the media's old "yellow peril" syndrome continues to turn up even in the 1990s.

▶ The Daily Breeze, published in Torrance (Los Angeles County), carried the banner headline "Asian Invasion"

across Page One of its March 24, 1991, Sunday edition. The article charted the growth of the area's Asian American communities. Commonly used in print news accounts, *invasion* suggests that Asians are a threatening outside force rather than fellow American residents and citizens.

▶ "Honorable mention" in the inflammatory headline category went to a New York paper, Downtown Express. It used the headline "There Goes the Neighborhood" for a package that included a story about the expansion of Chinatown into the Lower East Side.

▶ Radio talk show host Cliff Kincaid of WNTR in Silver Springs, Md., twice referred to CBS News' Connie Chung as "Connie Chink" when he criticized her alleged liberal bias. He later told the Washington Post that "it's a play on words on her last name."

▶ Newsday columnist Jimmy Breslin made headlines when he called a Korean American co-worker, Mary Yuh, a "yellow cur" (among other things) when she had the nerve to criticize one of his columns. He then appeared on Howard Stern's WXRK radio talk show in New York City to discuss his nephew's engagement to a Korean woman, allowing Stern to have fun with the topic: "Are you sitting in the lotus position ... to show that you love the Orientals?... You can absolutely go to the wedding, but you must eat with chopsticks and wear a kimono."

▶ Just as Asian ethnic groups are often mixed up (a kimono is hardly a Korean costume), Americans of Asian descent are sometimes confused with Asian nationals. The San Francisco Chronicle's Herb Caen, in a September 1990 column, mentioned the purchase of the Hellman mansion by "a Japanese couple" as another example of the buying up of America by foreigners. A month later, he ran a correction — the buyers were American-born.

▶ The New York Times was cited for its lopsided coverage of the *Miss Saigon* controversy. The paper sided with producer Cameron Mackintosh, who canceled the Broadway musical when Actors Equity refused to allow Caucasian actor Jonathan Pryce to play the Eurasian lead character. Under pressure, Actors Equity reversed its decision. The Times seemed preoccupied with Mackintosh's artistic freedom. In-depth pieces on the Asian American actors' perspective — the scarcity of opportunities on Broadway, even when Asian roles are being cast — did not appear until after Equity reversed itself, whereas opinion pieces by Dick Cavett, Frank Rich, and Anna Quindlen supporting Mackintosh and/or ridiculing the opposition ran while the issue was still pending.

The timing was suspect. In

contrast, the New York Daily News, San Francisco Examiner, Oakland Tribune, and Los Angeles Times carried pieces on the Asian American perspective prior to Equity's reversal.

The New York Times' first editorial on the subject dismissed as "nonsense" the idea that Asian Americans would be offended by a white actor in "yellowface" — without quoting any of a number of offended community members, playwright David Henry Hwang among them. Only in a subsequent editorial did the newspaper say that Equity had a "legitimate complaint."

A MORE AMBIGUOUS case was the much talked-about article in the Examiner's Dec. 2 *Image* magazine, "Asian Women, Caucasian Men: The New Demographics of Love." Some AAJA members who reviewed the story defended the writer, Joan Walsh, Larry Shinagawa, a Sonoma State University professor, said that Walsh's findings "really hold water." On the other hand, television producer Deborah Gee called the story an "egregious example of shoddy reporting."

One criticism involved the stereotype of Asian women as submissive and exotic, an image held by some of the white males quoted in the article. Walsh has pointed out that some critics confuse her viewpoints with those of the people she interviewed. Others recognize the difference but maintain that she failed to debunk the stereotypes.

Many AAJA members felt there was no basis for treating interracial dating as a hot new trend. TV personalities Connie Chung, Wendy Tokuda, and Jan Yanehiro, all of whom married Caucasians, are cited (but not quoted) as examples of the trend. Yanehiro, who has been married for more than a decade, later said it was news to her that she was doing something trendy.

The story did leave one clear impression: No women find Asian men desirable. One Asian woman's reason for dating Asian men was that she was wary of white male fantasies (Asian men thus win her by default). Tracking down a woman who actually finds Asian men attractive appears to have required more work than Walsh was willing to invest.

It should be noted that no one is accusing Walsh of being a racist; she's no Jimmy Breslin.

The number of nominations (nearly 50) for inclusion in "The Good, the Bad and the Ugly" indicates that the problem won't go away anytime soon. But the report is more than just a gripe session for Asian American journalists; as stated in its conclusion, it will serve as an educational tool to help the media "set aside old conventions and view subjects from new perspectives." ■

J.K. Yamamoto is the English-section editor at Hokubei Mainichi, an English-Japanese bilingual newspaper serving Northern California. Copies of the report are available for $2 from the Asian American Journalists Association, 1765 Sutter, Room 1000, SF 94115. 415-346-2051.

Busting Dow

P.J. Corso

Print coverage of the ban on silicone gel breast implants can indeed be described as topheavy. Try these measurements on for size. In a random survey of 17 *New York Times* articles published in January and February, 66 of the 77 sources quoted were from the top—the Food and Drug Administration, Dow Corning Corporation, plastic surgeons, lawyers, and crisis-management experts. Eleven were either women who had silicone gel breast implants or representatives of organizations concerned with women's health and consumer issues and more than half of these sources appeared in one article, "As Silicone Issues Grow, Women Take Agony and Anger to Court" (January 19, 1992, p. 1). Thirteen of the 17 articles—more than 75 percent—did not cite a single consumer source to comment on the nearly 30 years of FDA oversight and Dow negligence.

Because the *Times* used so few female sources, it failed to explore nuances that distinguish the approaches of women who put safety first, those who defend their freedom of choice despite safety concerns, and those who insist women are entitled to both safety and choice.

Pervasive Sex Bias

Perhaps the sex bias in the news coverage is a mirror image of what occurs in the medical field. A January 29 *Times* article quoted crisis management experts as saying Dow's "mistakes" included extending "too little sympathy and support for women who say they were harmed, and failure to get the worst news out quickly" ("Dow Corning's Failure In Public Opinion Test," p. D1). Yet the same criticisms could be applied to members of the print media. Take the headline published the day after a panel recommended restrictions for silicone gel breast implants: "Breast-Implant Plan Upsets Surgeons" (*New York Times*, February 22, p. 6). *Newsweek* magazine also emphasized that the moratorium could "kill" the industry in "Calling a Halt to the Big Business of Silicone Implants" (January 20, p. 56). This article went on to relay Dow Corning chair Robert Rylee's petulant threat: "If we're going to have to continue to work under a very hostile environment from the FDA, we may well decide to exit." The women whose health is threatened by the implants was apparently a less immediate concern.

The *Wall Street Journal* maintained its allegiance to the manufacturers. As the story broke, the paper reprinted excerpts of the Dow Corning press conference defending silicone breast implants under the heading, "Breast Implants Are Safe and

The Real Terrorists

According to a former federal prosecutor and CIA officer named Ignacio Rivera Cordero, the so-called Defenders—really a covert unit of high-ranking police officials trained by the FBI and armed by a U.S. marshall—became terrorists under the banner of counterterrorism, killing members of the independence movement and other political enemies.

One member of the unit, Julio César Andrades, became an FBI informant after the Defenders disbanded, and provided the Bureau with detailed information of their previous activities and their links to the Cerro Maravilla killings. The FBI refused to follow up until 1990, when an embarrassed Director William Sessions delivered a letter of apology to the Puerto Rican Senate for not having conducted a formal investigation of the case. But it was too little too late.

Senator Marco Antonio Rigau, chair of the Puerto Rican Senate Judiciary Committee, told the *Philadelphia Inquirer* that through the 1970s, police officers planted "scores" of bombs all over Puerto Rico in order to exaggerate the threat of terrorism. And according to Rigau, the police acted with the knowledge of the FBI. "Terrorism had to be created before it could be eliminated," Rigau told Weiner.

Contrary to the *Times* account, which carried Romero Barcelo's uncontested claim that not a "shred of evidence" existed to link him to the Cerro Maravilla affair and others like it, the *Inquirer* reported that in May of 1978, the then-governor signed a secret "internal defense plan" which called for the "elimination or neutralization of insurgent leadership and infrastructure." During 1977 and 1978, the FBI trained the Puerto Rican police in counterinsurgency techniques, giving them manuals which read, in part, "Nothing less than the death of a terrorist will keep him from repeating his act."

Weiner's story stressed that Cerro Maravilla was, in reality, part of a much larger pattern of surveillance and neutralization against Puerto Rico's independence movement, repressive practices encouraged by the FBI and CIA. The *Times*, on the other hand, emphasized the almost singular nature of the Cerro Maravilla affair, conceding only that the FBI (no mention here of the CIA) had "infiltrated legal pro-independence groups to influence their actions."

Again, soft-pedaling the Bureau's illegal activities, the *Times* quoted Senator Fernando Martín, a member of the Judiciary Committee, as saying that Cerro Maravilla had been an "example" of the "harassment" suffered by *independentistas*.

In fact, the strongest terms used to describe the repression of pro-independence forces are attributed to Marco Antonio Rigau, who was quoted briefly and only at the close of Navarro's piece: "This is a process of purification.... We have to get the truth out—how people have been persecuted for political reasons and how the pro-independence ideology was criminalized—so that something like this is never repeated." Like they did with Dash,

the *Times* leaves Rigau, one of the most outspoken members of the Judiciary Committee, sounding relatively moderate.

Other Maravillas

As Tim Weiner's account for the *Inquirer* suggested, there have been other Maravillas. Unmentioned in either the *Times* or *Inquirer* stories, though, is the case of a murdered union leader judgment implied in the press's repeated references to others as "simply" desiring to "exaggerate their natural contours," as *Newsweek* so delicately put it ("Calling a Halt to the Big Business of Silicone Implants").

First of all, many women did not "simply" want to enlarge their breasts. This pejorative adverb discounts the pressure women face to buy into the culture that the cosmetic-industrial complex promulgates. As Katha Pollitt pointed out in *The Nation*, plastic surgeons have even invented a name for the "disease" of small breasts—micromastia. ("Implants: Truth and Consequences," March 16, 1992, p. 1). Big breasts, women are told, can help them find a husband, advance their career, or make them more of a woman if they are "boyish" or "deformed." Women's own attitudes about their bodies, including the size of their breasts, cannot be separated from society's obsession with big breasts. One instance where the *Times* made the connection was in noting that the reason Japanese doctors experimented with silicone breast injections in the first place was to please American soldiers' preference for women with larger breasts than those of most Japanese prostitutes ("Strange History of Silicone Held Many Warning Signs," January 18, p. 8).

Secondly, the procedure does not "simply" result in making the breasts larger, as numerous examples of silicone leakage and subsequent scleroderma, arthritis, and lupus have shown us. It is disingenuous to object to restrictions on women's right to "choose" implants if they are not informed of the possible health consequences. Choice, as Pollitt points out, "implies awareness of possible consequences, precisely what implantees were denied."

What Is Not Covered

What the media chose *not* to address in its silicone breast implant coverage is evidence itself of the broader issue involved—the bias against women in health research. The FDA could not even decide initially whether the implants themselves were subject to agency regulation, or were a cosmetic device. Permitting the manufacture of the silicone gel breast implants without requiring adequate safety studies is one more example of how women's bodies apparently are not worth the care and respect given to men's bodies. A recent political cartoon by M.G. Lord aptly suggested that the only way to get silicone implants banned for good is to link them to cancer in men (*New York Newsday*, February 24).

•

X. Affirmations of Our Right To Know

Re-examination of first principles and how they have been applied is always in order, especially when the ground is shifting and the fires are nearing. It is also the time for strong affirmations and creative action to preserve and expand our right to know.

The following collection of articles covers a wide field. An article by an outstanding historian assesses how the First Amendment has fared over the years; Pat Schuman, president of the American Library Association (1991-92), pleads eloquently for maximum public awareness and support of that endangered institution – the public library; a non-librarian reminds us that "The American public library is the envy of the world;" and some benefits of the computer revolution are explored by an activist who proposes "Worldwide networking for social change."

"The nation's libraries...are not in danger of dying, but they are being diminished. As they decline, they take America down with them." – Haynes Johnson, columnist, *Washington Post*

"Not since backroom printing presses of the revolutionary 1700s has technology offered such powerful tools enabling citizen -based freedom and democracy. This time, the power is via networked personal computers. And, not since Hitler's Third Reich and Stalin's Russia has technology so threatened personal freedom, equitable democracy, and personal privacy. Which will dominate depends greatly on guaranteeing that 18th century civil liberties – speech, press, assembly, limits on search and seizure, etc. – are protected against technological encroachment in the 20th (and 21st) century." – Jim Warren, *Microtimes*, May 11, 1992

Second Thoughts on the First Amendment

*The Bill of Rights guarantees free speech and freedom of the press—
except when the government decides that it doesn't*

HOWARD ZINN

Growing up in the United States, we are taught that this is a country blessed with freedom of speech. We learn that this is so because our Constitution contains a Bill of Rights, which starts off with the First Amendment and its powerful words:

> Congress shall make no law respecting an establishment of religion, or prohibiting the free exercise thereof; or abridging the freedom of speech, or of the press, or the right of the people peaceably to assemble, and to petition the government for a redress of grievances.

The belief that the First Amendment guarantees our freedom of expression is part of the ideology of our society. Indeed, the faith in pledges written on paper and the blindness to political and economic realities seem strongly entrenched in that set of beliefs propagated by the makers of opinion in this country.

As I am about to argue, however, to depend on the simple existence of the First Amendment to guarantee our freedom of expression is a serious mistake—one that can cost us not only our liberties but, under certain circumstances, our lives.

"No Prior Restraint"

The language of the First Amendment looks absolute. "Congress shall make no law . . . abridging the freedom of speech." Yet in 1798, seven years after the First Amendment was adopted, Congress did exactly that; it passed laws abridging the freedom of speech—the Alien and Sedition Acts.

The Alien Act gave the president the power to deport "all such aliens as he shall judge dangerous to the peace and safety of the United States." The Sedition Act provided that, "if any person shall write, print, utter, or publish . . . any false, scandalous and malicious writing or writings against the government of the United States, or either house of the Congress of the U.S. or the President of the U.S., with intent to defame . . . or to bring either of them into contempt or disrepute," such persons could be fined $2,000 or jailed for two years.

The French Revolution had taken place nine years earlier, and the new American nation, now with its second president, the conservative John Adams, was not as friendly to revolutionary ideas as it had been in 1776. French immigrants to the United States were suspected of being sympathizers with their revolution back home and of spreading revolutionary ideas here. The fear of them (although most of these French immigrants had fled the revolution) became hysterical. The newspaper *Gazette of the United States* insisted that French tutors were corrupting American children "to make them imbibe, with their very milk, as it were, the poison of atheism and disaffection." The newspaper *Porcupine's Gazette* said the country was swarming with "French apostles of Sedition . . . enough to burn all our cities and cut the throats of all the inhabitants."

In Ireland, revolutionaries were carrying on their long struggle against the English, and they had supporters in the United States. One might have thought that the Americans, so recently liberated from English rule themselves, would have been sympathetic to the Irish rebels. But instead, the Adams administration looked on the Irish as troublemakers, both in

Europe and in the United States.

Politician Harrison Gray Otis said he "did not wish to invite hordes of wild Irishmen, nor the turbulent and disorderly of all parts of the world, to come here with a view to disturb our tranquility, after having succeeded in the overthrow of their own governments." He worried that new immigrants with political ideas "are hardly landed in the United States, before they begin to cavil against the Government, and to pant after a more perfect state of society."

The Federalist Party of John Adams was opposed by the Republican Party of Thomas Jefferson. It was the beginning of the two-party system in the new nation. Their disagreements went back to the Constitution and the Bill of Rights. Jefferson, a former ambassador to France, was friendly to the French Revolution, while Adams was hostile to it. President Adams, in the developing war between England and France, was clearly on the side of the English; historian James Morton Smith has called the Sedition Act "an internal security measure adopted during America's Half War with France."

Republican newspapers were delivering harsh criticism of the Adams administration. The newspaper *Aurora* in Philadelphia (edited by Benjamin Bache, the grandson of Benjamin Franklin) accused the president of appointing his relatives to office, of squandering public money, of wanting to create a monarchy, and of moving toward war. Even before the Sedition Act became law, Bache was arrested and charged on the basis of common law with libeling the president, exciting sedition, and provoking opposition to the laws.

The passage of the Sedition Act was accompanied by denunciations of the government's critics. One congressman told his colleagues, "Philosophers are the pioneers of revolution. They . . . prepare the way, by preaching infidelity, and weakening the respect of the people for ancient institutions. They talk of the perfectability of man, of the dignity of his nature, and entirely forgetting what he is, declaim perpetually about what he should be."

The atmosphere in the House of Representatives in those days might be said to lack some dignity. A congressman from Vermont—Irishman Matthew Lyon—got into a fight with Congressman Griswold of Connecticut. Lyon spat in Griswold's face, Griswold attacked him with a cane, Lyon fought back with fire tongs, and the two grappled on the floor while the other members of the House first watched, then separated them. A Bostonian wrote angrily about Lyon: "I feel grieved that the saliva of an Irishman should be left upon the face of an American."

Lyon had written an article saying that, under Adams, "every consideration of the public welfare was swallowed up in a continual grasp for power, in an unbounded thirst for ridiculous pomp, foolish adulation, and selfish avarice." Tried for violation of the Sedition Act, Lyon was found guilty and imprisoned for four months.

The number of people jailed under the Sedition Act was not large—10—but it is in the nature of oppressive laws that it takes just a handful of prosecutions to create an atmosphere that makes potential critics of government fearful of speaking their full minds.

It would seem to an ordinarily intelligent person, reading the simple, straightforward words of the First Amendment—"Congress shall make no law . . . abridging the freedom of speech, or of the press"—that the Sedition Act was a direct violation of the Constitution. But here we get our first clue to the inadequacy of words on paper in ensuring the rights of citizens. Those words, however powerful they seem, are interpreted by lawyers and judges in a world of politics and power, where dissenters and rebels are not wanted. Exactly that happened early in our history, as the Sedition Act collided with the First Amendment, and the First Amendment turned out to be poor protection.

The members of the Supreme Court, sitting as individual circuit judges (the new government didn't have the money to set up a lower level of appeals courts, as we have today), consistently found the defendants in the sedition cases guilty. They did it on the basis of English common law. Supreme Court Chief Justice Oliver Ellsworth, in a 1799 opinion, said, "The common law of this country remains the same as it was before the Revolution."

That fact is enough to make us pause. English common law? Hadn't we fought and won a revolution against England? Were we still bound by English common law? The answer is yes. It seems there are limits to revolutions. They retain more of the past than is expected by their fervent followers. English common law on freedom of speech was set down in Blackstone's *Commentaries*, a four-volume compendium of English common law. As Blackstone put it:

> The liberty of the press is indeed essential to the nature of a free state, but this consists in laying no *previous* restraint upon publications, and not in freedom from censure for criminal matter when published. Every freeman has an undoubted right to lay what sentiments he pleases before the public; to forbid this is to destroy

> ## The number of people jailed under the Sedition Act was not large, but it takes just a handful of prosecutions to create an atmosphere that makes potential critics of government fearful of speaking their full minds.

the freedom of the press; but if he publishes what is improper, mischievous, or illegal, he must take the consequences of his own temerity.

This is the ingenious doctrine of "no prior restraint." You can say or print whatever you want, and the government cannot stop you in advance. But once you speak or write it, if the government decides to define certain statements as "illegal" or "mischievous" or even just "improper," you can be put in prison. An ordinary person, unsophisticated in the law, might respond, "You *say* you won't stop me from speaking my mind—no prior restraint. But if I know it will get me in trouble, and so remain silent, that *is* prior restraint." There's no point responding to common law with common-sense.

That early interpretation of the First Amendment, limiting its scope to "no prior restraint," has lasted to the present day. It was affirmed in 1971 when the Nixon administration tried to get the Supreme Court to stop the publication in the *New York Times* of the Pentagon Papers, the secret official history of the U.S. war in Vietnam. The Court refused to prevent publication. But one of the justices held up a warning finger: he pointed out that the Court was making its decision on the basis of "no prior restraint"; if the *Times* went ahead and actually printed the documents, there was still a chance of prosecution by the government.

So, with the doctrine of "no prior restraint," the protection of the First Amendment was limited from the start. The founding fathers, whether liberal or conservative, Federalist or Republican— from Washington and Hamilton to Jefferson and Madison— believed that seditious libel could not be tolerated, that all we can ask of freedom of speech is that it does not allow prior restraint.

"Well, at least we have that," a hopeful believer in the First Amendment might say. "They can't stop free expression in advance." It turns out, however, that such optimism is not justified. Take the case of a book, *The CIA and the Cult of Intelligence*, written by Victor Marchetti, a former CIA agent, and John Marks, a journalist. The book exposed a number of operations by the CIA that did not seem to be in the best interests of democracy and that used methods an American might not be proud of. The CIA went to court asking that the publication of the book be stopped or, at least, that some 225 passages affecting "national security" (or, as Marchetti and Marks argued, embarrassing to the CIA) be omitted from the book.

Did the judge then invoke "no prior restraint" and say,

> This is the ingenious doctrine of "no prior restraint." You can say or print whatever you want, and the government cannot stop you in advance—but you can be put in prison afterward.

"We can't censor this book in advance; take action later if you like"? No, the judge said, "I won't order 225 deletions from the book; instead I'll only order 168 deletions."

Free Speech and National Security

The Sedition Act of 1798 expired, but in 1917, when the United States entered World War I, Congress passed another law in direct contradiction of the First Amendment's command that "Congress shall make no law . . . abridging the freedom of speech, or of the press." This was the Espionage Act of 1917.

Titles of laws can be misleading. While the act did have sections on espionage, it also said that persons could be sent to prison for up to 20 years if, while the country was at war, they "shall wilfully cause or attempt to cause insubordination, disloyalty, mutiny, or refusal of duty in the military or naval forces of the United States, or shall wilfully obstruct the recruiting or enlistment of the U.S."

This was quickly interpreted by the government as a basis for prosecuting anyone who criticized, in speech or writing, the entrance of the nation into the European war or who criticized the recently enacted conscription law. Two months after the Espionage Act was passed, a socialist named Charles Schenck was arrested in Philadelphia for distributing 15,000 leaflets denouncing the draft and the war. Conscription, the leaflets said, was "a monstrous deed against humanity in the interests of the financiers of Wall Street. . . . Do not submit to intimidation."

Schenck was found guilty of violating the Espionage Act and sentenced to six months in prison. He appealed, citing the First Amendment: "Congress shall make no law. . . ." The Supreme Court's unanimous decision, written by Oliver Wendell Holmes, whose reputation was that of an intellectual and a liberal, said that the First Amendment did not protect Schenck:

> The most stringent protection of free speech would not protect a man in falsely shouting fire in a theatre and causing a panic. . . . The question in every case is whether the words used are used in such circumstances and are of such a nature as to create a clear and present danger that they will bring about the substantive evils that Congress has a right to prevent.

It was a clever analogy. Who would think that the right of

free speech extended to someone causing panic in a theater? Any reasonable person must concede that free speech is not the only important value. If one has to make a choice between someone's right to speak and another person's right to *live*, that choice is certainly clear. No, there was no right to falsely shout "Fire!" in a theater and endanger human life.

A clever analogy, but a dishonest one. Is shouting "Fire!" in a crowded theater equivalent to distributing a leaflet criticizing a government policy? Is an anti-war leaflet a danger to life, or an attempt to save lives? Was Schenck shouting "Fire!" to cause a panic or to alert his fellow citizens that an enormous conflagration was taking place across the ocean? And that they or their sons were in danger of being thrown into the funeral pyre that was raging there? To put it another way, who was creating a "clear and present danger" to the lives of Americans: Schenck, by protesting the war, or Wilson, by bringing the nation into it?

Also prosecuted under the Espionage Act was socialist leader Eugene Debs, who had run against Wilson for the presidency in 1912 and 1916. Debs made a speech in Indiana in which he denounced capitalism, praised socialism, and criticized the war: "Wars throughout history have been waged for conquest and plunder. . . . And that is war in a nutshell. The master class has always declared the wars; the subject class has always fought the battles."

Debs' indictment said that he "attempted to cause and incite insubordination, disloyalty, mutiny, and refusal of duty in the military forces of the U.S. and with intent so to do delivered to an assembly of people a public speech." Debs spoke to the jury:

> I have been accused of obstructing the war. I admit it. Gentlemen, I abhor war. I would oppose war if I stood alone. . . . I have sympathy with the suffering, struggling people everywhere. It does not make any difference under what flag they were born, or where they live.

He was convicted and sentenced to 10 years in prison, the judge denouncing those "who would strike the sword from the hand of this nation while she is engaged in defending herself against a foreign and brutal power."

When the case came to the Supreme Court on appeal, again Oliver Wendell Holmes spoke for a unanimous Court, affirming that the First Amendment did not apply to Eugene Debs and his speech. Holmes said Debs made "the usual contrasts between capitalists and laboring men . . . with the im-

plication running through it all that the working men are not concerned in the war." So, Holmes said, the "natural and intended effect" of Debs' speech would be to obstruct recruiting.

Altogether, about 2,000 people were prosecuted and about 900 sent to prison under the Espionage Act—not for espionage but for speaking and writing against the war. Such was the value of the First Amendment in time of war.

The Espionage Act remains on the books, to apply in wartime and in "national emergencies." In 1963, the Kennedy administration proposed extending its provisions to statements made by Americans overseas. Secretary of State Dean Rusk cabled Ambassador Henry Cabot Lodge in Vietnam, saying the government was concerned about American journalists writing "critical articles . . . on Diem and his government" that were "likely to impede the war effort."

Free speech is fine, but not in a time of crisis—so argue heads of state, whether the state is a dictatorship or a democracy. Has that not proved again and again to be an excuse for stifling opposition to government policy, clearing the way for brutal and unnecessary wars? Indeed, is not a time of war exactly when free speech is most needed, when the public is most in danger of being propagandized into sending their sons to slaughter? How ironic that freedom of speech should be allowed for small matters but not for matters of life and death, war and peace.

On the eve of World War II, Congress passed still another law limiting freedom of expression. This was the Smith Act of 1940, which extended the provisions of the Espionage Act to peacetime and made it a crime to distribute written matter or to speak in such a way as to cause "insubordination or refusal of duty in the armed forces." The act also made it a crime to "teach or advocate" or to "conspire to teach or advocate" the overthrow of the government by force and violence.

Thus, in the summer of 1941, before the United States was at war, the headquarters of the Socialist Workers Party was raided and 18 members arrested on charges of "conspiracy to advocate overthrow of the government of the United States by force and to advocate insubordination in the armed forces of the U.S." The evidence produced in court against them did not detail their use of violence or even their alleged plans to use violence—instead, it was simply their Marxist literature, seized by the police. Their crime, apparently, was that they were all members of the Socialist Workers Party, whose Declaration of Principles, said the judge who sentenced them to prison, advocated "an application of Marxist theories

> **Free speech is fine, but not in a time of crisis—so argue heads of state, whether in a dictatorship or a democracy. How ironic that free speech should be allowed for small matters but not for matters of life and death.**

and doctrines to . . . social problems in America." The judge noted that, in the raid of their headquarters, a "large number of communistic books were seized." The appeal of the party to the federal courts lost, and the Supreme Court refused to take the case.

The Communist Party, a bitter rival of the Socialist Workers Party and a supporter of World War II, did not criticize its prosecution. After the war, it was itself prosecuted under the Smith Act and its leaders sent to prison. Here, again, the evidence was a pile of seized literature—the works of Marx, Engels, Lenin, and Stalin.

The First Amendment, said the Supreme Court, did not apply in this case. The "clear and present danger" doctrine laid down by Holmes was still a principle of constitutional law, and now Chief Justice Fred M. Vinson gave it a bizarre twist. He said that, while the danger of violent overthrow was not "clear and present," the conspiracy to advocate a violent overthrow in the future was a *present* conspiracy and so the conviction of the Communist Party leaders must stand.

The First Amendment was being subjected to what constitutional experts call "a balancing test," where the right of free expression was continually being weighed against the government's claims of national security. Most of the time, the government's claims prevailed. And why should we be surprised? Does the executive branch not appoint the federal judges and prosecutors? Does it not control the whole judicial process?

It seems to me that the security of the American people—indeed, of the world—cannot be trusted to the governments of the world, including our own. In crisis situations, the right of citizens to freely criticize foreign policy is absolutely essential—indeed, a matter of life and death. National security is safer in the hands of a debating, challenging citizenry than with a secretive, untrustworthy government. Still, the courts have continued to limit free debate on foreign policy issues, claiming that national security overrides the First Amendment.

Police Powers and the First Amendment

As we have seen, the national government can restrict freedom of speech in relation to foreign policy through judicial reinterpretations of the First Amendment. But what about *state* laws restricting freedom of speech or the press? For over a century, the First Amendment simply did not apply to the states because it says, "*Congress* shall make no law"; the

states could make whatever laws they wanted.

And they did. In the years before the Civil War, as abolitionists began to print anti-slavery literature, the states of Georgia and Louisiana passed laws declaring the death penalty for anyone distributing literature "exciting to insurrection" or with "a tendency to produce discontent among the free population . . . or insubordination among the slaves."

When in 1833 the Supreme Court had to decide if the Bill of Rights applied to the states, Chief Justice John Marshall said that the intent of the founding fathers was that it should not. Indeed, James Madison had proposed an amendment forbidding the states from interfering with various rights—including freedom of speech—and the Senate defeated it.

Madison's intent seemed finally to become part of the Constitution with the passage of the Fourteenth Amendment in 1868, which said that no state "shall deprive any person of life, liberty, or property, without due process of law." But in 1894, someone wanting to make a speech on the Boston Common was arrested because he had not gotten a permit from the mayor as required by city law. When he claimed that the Fourteenth Amendment now prevented any state from depriving persons of liberty, including freedom of speech, the Supreme Court ruled unanimously that the mayor could "absolutely or conditionally forbid public speaking in a highway or public park," that the Fourteenth Amendment did not affect the "police powers" of the state.

This was a localized version of the national-security argument for limiting freedom of speech, and it prevailed until 1925. In that year, 137 years after the ratification of the Constitution, the Supreme Court finally said that the states could not abridge freedom of speech, because of the Fourteenth Amendment. However, this still left freedom of speech as something to be balanced against the "police powers" of the states. In the years that followed, the balance would sometimes go one way, sometimes another, leaving citizens bewildered about how much they could depend on the courts to uphold their rights of free expression.

For instance, in 1949, after Chicago police arrested Father Terminiello, an anti-Semitic preacher who had attracted an angry crowd around his meeting hall, the Supreme Court ruled that Terminiello had a First Amendment right to speak his mind, and the fact that this excited opposition could not be used as an excuse to stop his speech. It said that one "function of free speech under our system of government is to invite dispute."

> **Before the Civil War, the states of Georgia and Louisiana declared the death penalty for anyone distributing literature "exciting . . . discontent among the free population . . . or insubordination among the slaves."**

Shortly after that, however, Irving Feiner, a college student in Syracuse, New York, was making a street-corner speech from a small platform, denouncing the mayor, the police, the American Legion, and President Truman, when one of his listeners said to a policeman standing by, "You get that son-of-a-bitch off there before I do." The policeman arrested Feiner, and the Supreme Court upheld the arrest, saying this was not free speech but "incitement to riot," although the tumult and excitement around Terminiello's speech had been far greater than in Feiner's case.

For a long time, the public has been led to believe in the magic word *precedent*. The idea is that the courts follow precedents—that if a decision has been made in a case, it will not be overturned in similar cases. Lawyers and judges understand, however, what laypeople often do not: that, in the rough-and-tumble reality of the courts, precedent has as much solidity as a ping-pong ball. All a court has to do is find *some* difference between two cases and it has grounds for giving a different opinion. In other words, judges can always find a way of making the decision they want to make, for reasons that have little to do with constitutional law and much to do with the ideological leanings of the judges.

The point in all this is that citizens cannot *depend* on the First Amendment, as interpreted by the courts, to protect freedom of expression. One year the Court will declare, with inspiring words, the right of persons to speak or write as they wish. The next year, they will take away that right. Nor is there any guarantee, should you decide to exercise your right of free expression by speaking in public or distributing literature and you get arrested, that the Supreme Court will even *hear* your case on appeal. It does not *have* to take appeals in free speech cases, and your chance of getting a hearing in the Supreme Court is about one out of 80.

An even more serious problem with the First Amendment is that most situations involving freedom of expression never make it into the courts. How many people are willing or able to hire a lawyer, spend thousands of dollars, and wait several years to get a possible favorable decision in court? That means that the right of free speech is left largely in the hands of local police. What are the police likely to be most respectful of—the Constitution or their own "police powers"?

I was forced to think about this one day in 1961 when I was teaching at Spelman College and several black students showed up at my house to talk to me about their plan to go into downtown Atlanta to distribute leaflets protesting racial segregation in the city. I was teaching a course in constitu-

tional law, and they wanted to know if they had a legal right to distribute leaflets downtown.

The law was plain: a series of Supreme Court decisions made the right to distribute leaflets on a public street absolute. It would be hard to find something in the Bill of Rights that was more clear cut than this, and I told my students so. But I knew immediately that I must tell them something else: the law didn't much matter. If they began handing out leaflets on Peachtree Street and a white policeman (all police were white in Atlanta at that time) came along and said, "Move!" what could they do? Cite the relevant Supreme Court cases to the policeman? "In *Lovell* v. *Griffin*, sir, as well as in *Hague* v. *C.I.O.* and *Largent* v. *Texas*. . . ."

What was more likely at such a moment: that the policeman would fall prostrate before this recitation of Supreme Court decisions? Or that he would finger his club and repeat, "Move on!" At that moment, the great hoax in the teaching of constitutional law—the enormous emphasis on the importance of Supreme Court decisions—would be revealed. What would decide the right of free expression of these black students in Atlanta in 1961, what would be more powerful—the words in the Constitution or the policeman's club?

It wasn't until I began to teach constitutional law in the South, in the midst of the struggle against racial segregation, that I began to understand something so obvious that it takes just a bit of thought to see it. It is something so important that every young person growing up in America should be taught it: our right to free expression is not determined by the words of the Constitution or the decisions of the Supreme Court but by who has the *power* in the immediate situation in which we want to exercise our rights.

> The CIA operates in a clandestine world where the Constitution can be ignored. When there was talk of the CIA's activities violating the First Amendment, CIA official Ray Cline told Congress, "It's only an amendment."

Secret Police in a Democracy

In our country, so proud of its democratic institutions, a national secret police has operated for a long time, in a clandestine world where the Constitution can be ignored. I am referring to the Federal Bureau of Investigation and the Central Intelligence Agency. It was CIA official Ray Cline who, when there was talk of the CIA's activities violating the First Amendment, told Congress, "It's only an amendment."

We might comfort ourselves with the thought that the FBI and the CIA are not as fearsome as the KGB of the Soviet Union or the death squads that have operated in right-wing

DataCenter 464 19th Street, Oakland, California 94612 (415) 835-4692

dictatorships supported by the United States—El Salvador, for instance. The *scale* of terror is not comparable. A radical critic of American foreign policy is not likely to be picked up in the middle of the night, immediately imprisoned, or taken out and shot. (Although it is sobering to recall that the FBI conspired with Chicago police in 1969 to murder Black Panther leader Fred Hampton in his bed.) The actual apprehension of dissidents is on a much smaller scale in our country compared to others. But the mere existence of organizations secretly collecting information on citizens must have a chilling effect on the free speech of everyone. According to a Senate report of 1976, the FBI has files on 500,000 Americans.

However, the FBI goes far beyond the collection of information. We learned this from a mysterious raid in 1971 on FBI offices in the town of Media, Pennsylvania (its perpetrators have not yet been found). The FBI files were ransacked and the documents leaked to a small radical magazine that published them. Many of the documents were headed with the word *CO-INTELPRO*, and only later was it discovered what that stood for: "Counter-Intelligence Program." The Senate committee investigating the FBI in the mid-1970s wrote in its report:

> COINTELPRO is the FBI acronym for a series of covert action programs directed against domestic groups. In these programs, the Bureau went beyond the collection of intelligence to secret action designed to "disrupt" and "neutralize" [the FBI's words] target groups and individuals. The techniques . . . ranged from the trivial (mailing reprints of *Readers Digest* articles to college administrators) to the degrading (sending anonymous poison-pen letters intended to break up marriages) and the dangerous (encouraging gang warfare and falsely labeling members of a violent group as police informers).

The program began in 1956, according to the Senate committee, ending in 1971 because of the threat of public exposure. (The raid on the Media office took place on March 8, 1971; the FBI decided to terminate COINTELPRO on April 27, 1971.) The Senate report said:

> In the intervening 15 years the Bureau conducted a sophisticated vigilante operation aimed squarely at preventing the exercise of First Amendment rights of speech and association, on the theory that preventing

the growth of dangerous groups and the propagation of dangerous ideas would protect the national security and deter violence.

Again, the excuse of national security. James Madison, back in 1798, had warned about this in a letter to Thomas Jefferson: "Perhaps it is a universal truth that the loss of liberty at home is to be charged to provisions against danger real or pretended from abroad."

In a totalitarian state, we assume that the head of state is aware of the operations of his secret police. In a country like the United States, however, the higher officials may claim that they don't know what is going on. Former Attorney General Nicholas de B. Katzenbach said he didn't know about COINTELPRO—but couldn't have stopped it anyway. Officially, the attorney general is higher in rank than the director of the FBI, but the FBI has a power that attorneys general—and even presidents—have been afraid to challenge.

> James Madison, back in 1798, had warned in a letter to Thomas Jefferson: "Perhaps it is a universal truth that the loss of liberty at home is to be charged to provisions against danger real or pretended from abroad."

Even so, it should not be thought that the president or the attorney general strongly disapproved of these activities, illegal as many of them were. J. Edgar Hoover's successor, FBI director Clarence Kelley, told the Senate committee, "The FBI employees . . . did what they felt was expected of them by the President, the Attorney General, the Congress, and the people of the United States." How the FBI knew what "the people" wanted is not clear, but the bureau did have a fairly good idea of what the president wanted and what would get support in Congress.

There is a long record—at least from 1953 to 1973—of illegal opening of citizens' mail by the FBI. There is also a long record of illegal break-ins—"black bag jobs," sometimes called "surreptitious entry." The report of the Senate committee concluded:

> We cannot dismiss what we have found as isolated acts which were limited in time and confined to a few willful men. The failures to obey the law and, in the words of the oath of office [of the president], to "preserve, protect and defend" the Constitution have occurred repeatedly throughout administrations of both political parties going back four decades.

What happens to members of the secret police who engage in illegal acts? Hardly anything. If there is a particularly flagrant set of actions that are exposed to the public, there may be a token prosecution of one or two minor figures. But they certainly will not be sent to prison, as would ordinary people who intercepted mail or broke into people's homes.

One notorious example occurred in 1973, when Tom Huston, a staff assistant in the Nixon White House, drew up a plan (approved by the president) that included wiretapping, mail coverage, and "surreptitious entry." He said, "Use of this technique is clearly illegal. It amounts to burglary. It is also highly risky and could result in great embarrassment if exposed. However, it is also the most fruitful tool and can produce the kind of intelligence which cannot be obtained in any other fashion."

One wonders about the FBI files on those 500,000 people. (Or is it one million or two million? How can we tell?—the FBI operates in secret.) We know from the records of the loyalty investigations of the 1950s that the FBI filed reports on government employees who had been seen entertaining black people, or who had been seen attending a Paul Robeson concert, and so on.

The FBI also maintained files on a number of famous American writers. (This was disclosed when journalist Herbert Mitgang managed to get the documents under the Freedom of Information Act.) There was a file on Ernest Hemingway, whom the FBI labeled a drunk and a communist. Novelists John Steinbeck and Pearl Buck were in the FBI records as people who promoted the civil rights of blacks. John Dos Passos, William Faulkner, and Tennessee Williams were all on the list. About Sinclair Lewis, on whom there was a dossier of 150 pages, the FBI said his novel *Kingsblood Royal* was "propaganda for the white man's acceptance of the Negro as a social equal."

> ## The FBI maintained files on members of radical groups, whose names were put on a "Security Index," which at one time listed 15,000 people who were to be picked up and detained in case of a "national emergency."

There were more serious FBI files than these—the ones kept on members of radical groups, whose names were put on a "Security Index," which at one time listed 15,000 people who were to be picked up and detained without trial in case of a "national emergency." In 1950, Congress passed an Emergency Detention Act, which provided for a set of detention centers (perhaps more accurately, concentration camps) for those people on the Security Index. Although the Act was repealed in 1971, the FBI continued its index.

When the former head of the FBI's Racial Intelligence Section was asked if, during the 15 years of COINTELPRO, anyone in the FBI questioned the legality of what was being done, he replied, "No, we never gave it a thought."

It is hard to tell how many people lost their lives as a result of COINTELPRO, but documents from FBI files, obtained under the Freedom of Information Act, indicated that in the late 1960s and early 1970s, when the FBI was trying

to break up the Black Panther organization, 19 Black Panthers across the nation were killed by law-enforcement officials or by one another in internal feuds, some of which were provoked by the FBI.

One of those deaths was of Fred Hampton, the Chicago Black Panther leader. It turned out that his personal bodyguard, William O'Neal, was an FBI infiltrator, who gave his FBI contact, Roy Mitchell, a detailed floor plan of the apartment occupied by Fred Hampton and others. In a predawn raid, Chicago police fired hundreds of bullets into the apartment, and Hampton, asleep in his bed, was killed. There was an FBI memorandum from the Chicago field office on December 8, 1969 (a few days after the raid):

> Prior to the raid, a detailed inventory of the weapons and also a detailed floor plan of the apartment were furnished to local authorities. . . . The raid was based on the information furnished by the informant.

Although COINTELPRO was declared suspended in 1971, the FBI continued to keep tabs on organizations that were carrying on nonviolent political activities in opposition to official government policy. In 1988 it was revealed (in documents given to the Center for Constitutional Rights under the Freedom of Information Act) that the FBI had infiltrated and kept records on hundreds of organizations in the United States that were opposed to President Reagan's policies in Central America. There were 3,500 pages of files. The FBI's official excuse was that it was concerned about terrorism, but the records showed a concern for what these organizations were *saying*, in speech and in writing. A dispatch from the FBI field office in New Orleans in 1983 said:

> It is imperative at this time to formulate some plan of action against CISPES [Committee in Support of the People of El Salvador] and specifically against in-

Howard Zinn is a professor of history and political science emeritus at Boston University and the author of A People's History of the United States. *This article is adapted from his most recent book,* Declarations of Independence: Cross-Examining American Ideology.

dividuals who defiantly display their contempt for the U.S. government by making speeches and propagandizing their cause.

The most striking evidence that the FBI was not acting against terrorism or to protect national security but was in fact interfering with the First Amendment rights of government critics was its harassment of Martin Luther King, Jr. The 1976 Senate committee report on the FBI stated:

> From December 1963 until his death in 1968, Martin Luther King, Jr., was the target of an intensive campaign by the Federal Bureau of Investigation to "neutralize" him as an effective civil rights leader.

William Sullivan, the FBI man in charge of this operation, told the committee:

> No holds were barred. We have used similar techniques against Soviet agents. . . . We did not differentiate. This is a rough, tough business.

Of course, King was not a Soviet agent but an American citizen exercising his constitutional right to speak, write, and organize. The FBI tried its best to stop him from doing this effectively by discrediting King in various ways; it tried to get universities to withhold honorary degrees from him, to prevent the publication of articles favorable to him, to find "friendly" journalists to print unfavorable articles. It put microphones in his hotel rooms and offered to play the recordings to reporters. In May 1962 the FBI included King on its "Reserve Index" as a person to be rounded up and detained in the event of a national emergency.

What all of this indicates is that, despite the Constitution, despite the First Amendment and its guarantees of free speech, American citizens must fear to speak their minds, knowing that their speech, their writings, their attendance of meetings, their signing of petitions, and their support of even the most nonviolent of organizations may result in their being listed in the files of the FBI, with consequences no one can surely know. It was Mark Twain who said, "In our country, we have those three unspeakably precious things: freedom of speech, freedom of conscience, and the prudence never to practice either." ▣

Your Right to Know: Librarians Make It Happen

Inaugural Address of Patricia Glass Schuman

President, American Library Association
July 3, 1991
Atlanta, Georgia

Librarianship represents much more than just a job to me—it is a way of life. But it is one I happened upon almost by accident. I would not now be president of the American Library Association had I not answered a blind ad in the *New York Times* which read: "College Graduates: Study for Master's degree while training." As a new college graduate, an English major with no typing skills, I had grown used to reading the want ads. I used to tell my parents that I was going to "open an English store."

One week after I answered the ad, someone from the Brooklyn Public Library called to suggest an interview. I hesitated. I truly had no idea what a librarian's work involved. I needed a job, so I went. But first, I took off my engagement ring, pinned back my hair, put on my plainest dress, and washed off my makeup. Yes, I was almost a victim of a stereotype. To my astonishment, ten minutes into the interview, thanks to the skills and tolerance of the librarian interviewing me, I realized that librarianship offered me a chance to be part of a challenging, intellectually fascinating, and socially rewarding profession.

Yet I never dreamed, when I stood up to speak for the first time at the Atlantic City ALA Conference, that I would be president of ALA some 22 years later. In 1969 I was young and hopeful. Now I am older but still full of hope.

I have met and worked with so many wonderful people since then—people who constantly renew my faith in the power of librarians to make a difference, people who make me proud to be a librarian. Because of the trust ALA members have placed on me, I now have what one of my favorite sages, Pogo, would call an "insurmountable opportunity": an opportunity to work with you to make a difference for our profession and for our society.

I am well aware that my presidency will be only a fleeting moment in the life of ALA. A year is a very short time to make a difference. But, together we can—and we must. We are at an important crossroads, not just for our profession but for our society. By speaking out now, we can protect not just the future of libraries and librarians—but the future of the American people's right to know.

Tonight I want to enlist you in ALA's Right to Know campaign, a campaign to capture public attention so that people are informed about the value of librarians. It is a campaign that will influence policy makers to fully support our profession, and our services; a campaign to insist that the public has a right to know—and that librarians make this right to know happen.

Our profession is intrinsically bound to the ideals of democracy. Our very existence stands in defense of the First Amendment—and in defense of equality. When we are at risk, when library services are threatened and librarians are not valued, then the very basis of our democracy is endangered. And we are at risk. These are frightening times for librarians, for all who care about our right to know. We've talked a lot this week about the tremendous obstacles we face:

- the shocking rate of illiteracy in both children and adults;
- the dangers and the potential of new technology;
- the privatization of public information;
- the closing of library schools and the difficulties of recruiting and educating library professionals;
- the rapid deterioration of materials of all kinds in our nation's libraries;
- the widening gap between the information rich and the information poor;
- the physical, financial, linguistic, psychological, and intellectual barriers that continue to widen that gap;
- declining public funds for public services;
- attempts to restrict the freedom to speak, view, and listen.

The list could go on. The litany of problems is all too familiar. It is almost overwhelming. But we cannot afford to be overwhelmed. The challenges we face remind me of a story about Yogi Berra ordering an extra-large pizza with the works. When the waitress asked Yogi if he wanted the pizza cut into six or eight slices, Yogi replied: "Six. I don't think even I can eat eight slices."

Of course, we can slice our pie many ways. But we should not forget that these slices are all part of one whole, one central issue: libraries and librarians are essential. Without them, without open and equitable access to information, America's right to know is at risk: America's right to know—and remember—our past; America's right to know—and understand—our present; and America's right to know—and evaluate—information that can determine our future.

Benjamin Franklin's novel idea, the free public library, was a radical concept: the distribution of books to everyone, regardless of age, sex, class, or income. Our library system is a national treasure, unique in the world. Librarians who work in the more than 115,000 school, public, academic and special libraries throughout the nation have enabled millions of Americans to learn, to achieve, to flourish, and to prosper.

Pieces of this national treasure are eroding rapidly. Protecting this system involves no less than preserving the public's right to know. We can no longer sit back and assume that, because our cause is just, the value of libraries and librarians will be recognized. The reality is that even though we know all that librarians can do, must do, and *do* do—the American public often does not. Neither, unfortunately, does the pool of talent from which we hope to recruit future librarians. Too often, we have assumed that the virtue of our cause is self-evident. The result is what Sydney Levy calls "the impotence of virtue."

In ALA's 1986 Communications Audit, our longtime public relations consultant, the late Betty Stearns, warned us that we must "move out of the field huddle and into action." She said: "Passivity is not a virtue. It is a luxury ALA can no longer afford." Perhaps we've sat on the sidelines because of our own image of ourselves as the "organizers" and "keepers" of the world's knowledge. This is a self-limiting view. Our information society requires an active professional stance. We can't continue to assume the attitude of Oscar Wilde after the unsuccessful opening of one of his plays: "Oscar—how did your play go tonight?" asked a friend. "Oh," said Oscar loftily, "the play was a great success, but the audience was a failure."

Even when we are active—even when we effectively promote library buildings, collections, and services—we often forget to tell people about our most powerful resource. The most valuable asset of any library goes home every night—the staff. It's one thing to tell people to come to a place; it's quite another to invite them to come in and consult a highly trained professional.

Librarians are disseminators of information, not merely its guardians. We are often considered society's gatekeepers, but librarians are actually the gateways. Librarianship is the one profession dedicated to ensuring the right to know. We must never lose sight of this mission, despite the seductive siren song of our information-age mythology. Simplistically, this mythology holds that information, our most crucial capital resource, will flourish only in an unfettered economic environment. The *hero* of this free market is competition. Aided by the *deus ex machina* of the marketplace's "invisible hand," competition's quest is for the greatest good—profit. Competition boasts that information is a precious commodity. Only competition can nurture it!

Only competition can make sure it will flourish! Only competition can guarantee prosperity, diversity, and choice!

Information is not simply a product, a commodity to be bought and sold to the highest bidder. The cost of information is often independent of the scale of its use. A given piece of information is often independent of the scale of its use. A given piece of information—a stock price or a scientific discovery—costs the same to acquire whether the decision to be based on it is large or small. Research leading to the treatment of AIDS will cost the same whether it is used to help 100 or 100,000 patients. But the value and the influence of that information is vastly different.

Lobbyists for more privatization of government information say that competition will encourage companies to produce better, cheaper products. Despite the hyperbole, what they are really asking our government to do is to turn over public assets to private interests—to a handful of multinational media conglomerates. To date, privatization has resulted in less access and higher costs for the American public. If we accept the commoditization of information, if we tolerate our government turning over public information functions to private companies, if we institute fees for services, we will diminish the public's right to know: the right to know information about our environment critical to our health and the future of our planet; the right to know business and economic information we need to survive in today's global marketplace; and the right to know how to participate effectively in our democracy.

Information itself is not power. Let's not confuse the transmission of data—or facts—with the uses people make of them. Information is simply raw material—a powerful tool. It is valuable only when processed by the human mind. Information is a catalyst—a means to create knowledge or wisdom. Salespeople sell information products. Librarians on the other hand, help people use information to solve problems. Information is like trust, or love. It becomes infinitely more valuable when shared. Here is where library services have their greatest potential, their force, their vital impact. Here is where information is a critical resource, a public good essential for a humane and just society.

People cannot exercise their right to know unless information is organized and available. None of us can exercise our right to know unless we are intellectually able—and psychologically motivated—to access and use information. The right to know is much more than free speech. To truly have the right to free expression, people need more than Constitutional guarantees; they need societal commitments as well. If you have no job, no education, no money—your voice will not carry very far. You may have the right to know, but if you don't know how to use it—if you're not aware of it—it will do you no good. Books, magazines, and databases are of little value to people who cannot read. Illiteracy costs this country more than $225 billion annually in lost productivity, welfare payments, crime, accidents, and lost taxes.

We will not live in a true information society unless—and until—we ensure that people have access not only to information, but to cultural content. We will not live in a true information society unless—and until—people have the skills and the resources to use this content. We will not live in a true information society unless—and until—public policy makers recognize that an informed citizenry is a public good that benefits us all. We will not live in a true information society, we will not achieve equal opportunity and justice, unless—and until—all people have the library services they need to learn, live, work, participate, and enjoy our democracy.

If we truly believe that information can be used for powerful purposes, we must persuade people that librarians dispense tools for empowerment. We must convince them that the services librarians offer are an essential part of the solution to problems such as illiteracy, drugs, poverty, crime, pollution, illness, and unemployment. We must remind them that librarians continue to open doors for millions of immigrants and native-born Americans.

Despite our problems, libraries have never been more alive: with programs for new immigrants; with programs for low literate adults and their families; with new technological services for students and business people; with AIDS information services; with programs for latchkey children and the homeless. Across the country, librarians are designing innovative services: services to help people use and share information resources to their fullest potential; services to help people exercise their right to know.

Librarians like Galen Avery at the Toledo-Lucas County Public Library in Ohio who established a government procurement center to help local businesses exercise their right to know how to participate in the complicated federal purchasing process and their right to know as much as their larger competitors.

Librarians like Robin Gaebler at the Spokane (Wash.) Public Library whose afterschool program, Discover Reading, is helping children discover the joys of reading and learning—and helping parents exercise their right to know that their children can succeed in this information age.

Librarians like Carla Montori at the University of Michigan whose preservation program is saving thousands of books that were in danger of total deterioration, helping not just the people of Michigan, but all of us exercise our right to know that what is known now will be preserved for future generations.

Librarians like Carol Cribbet-Bell at the Carrillo Magnet School in Tucson, Arizona, who created the Carrillo Heritage Center to ensure that Hispanic and Native American students can exercise their right to know their history and culture.

Librarians like Charles Townley, at the University of New Mexico at Las Cruces, who initiated a citywide literacy program to ensure that people can exercise their right to know how to decode information.

Librarians like Dorothy Puryear of the Nassau County Library System who initiated the Long Island Business and Education Partnership. The partnership includes businesses, schools, libraries, colleges, and government and voluntary organizations, and helps to ensure that job seekers can exercise their right to know the skills they need for productive careers.

Librarians like Jim Welbourne and Bob Croneberger, who through the Carnegie Library of Pittsburgh's Neighborline Project, offer free access to economic and community information databases to ensure that small business and nonprofit groups can exercise the right to know information that will contribute to their community's economic health and development.

These librarians are just a few examples of how we librarians help people put the "know" in knowledge. Librarians help children to explore, business people to succeed, and adults to discover. Librarians like these demonstrate that the business of librarians is not information. The mission of librarians is understanding through knowledge. Librarians are knowledge navigators, professionals ethically committed to the organization and dissemination of information, the dissemination of knowledge, and the tools for empowerment.

If we truly believe the words carved above the portals of many libraries—that "Knowledge is power"—we must accept responsibility for the exercise of that power. We hold information in trust. Libraries are both the first source and the ultimate repository. Librarians keep information affordable, accessible, and available. We deliver that materials and services that undergird the public's right to know.

We have more outlets than McDonald's. Our impact will be massive if we speak out; if we inform people about the crucial role librarians have in making their right to know happen; if we articulate our message to the media in ways that will influence opinion leaders and decision-makers; if we insist on being heard.

To capture the public imagination we need not be concerned with how pretty people think we are—or even how smart. Our challenge is to show them how useful, necessary, and important we are to their everyday lives and work. ALA has dubbed the nineties "the decade of the librarian." Now we must prove that librarians are members of a dynamic profession fighting for the right to know.

Dick Dougherty and I have worked with ALA staff to develop a long-range communications plan. The June 29th rally in front of the Georgia World Congress Center, the caravan to the White House conference, and the rally at the Washington, D.C., Martin Luther King Library, kick off a year-long mobilization to capture the attention of the nation's decision-makers. Our strategy will build on ALA's existing strengths and our successful, visible campaigns: National Library Week, Freedom of Information Day, the Library Card Campaign, Banned Books Week, etc. The J. Morris Jones/World Book/ALA Goal Award will fund media training for ALA chapter and division presidents-elect. This training, along with fact sheets, briefing books, and other materials, will launch an ALA speakers network. Our objective is to speak out clearly and articulately, with a unified voice.

I have appointed two special presidential committees that will be pivotal to the Right to Know campaign. The Committee for the Right to Know, chaired by Margo Crist, will work to ensure that we have the power tools—fact sheets, briefing papers, and contacts—to tell our compelling story effectively. The Committee on Cultural Diversity, co-chaired by Gloria Leonard and Yolanda Cuesta, will develop strategies to foster and promote programs and services that make the right to know a reality for people of all cultures.

These steps are a beginning. Every member of ALA can contribute. Our collective power within ALA is formidable. Remember, no one person can whistle Beethoven's Fifth; it takes a whole orchestra to play a symphony. What I am asking for is commitment: commitment to spend less time talking to each other about the inner workings of our institutions and our associations; commitment to not splinter ourselves within our profession. To lay people we are all librarians. Our cause is virtuous and powerful. Our task is to work together to tell the full library story to leaders in government, business, education, and the general public.

We must speak with a unified voice. We must support one another. Each of us must reach out and be visible as librarians. Consider every communication an opportunity. You are the key to delivering the right to know message to your users. Use our fact sheets and briefing papers. Localize them. Be alert for issues you can relate to the right to know and library services in your community—the environment, health, education, careers, safety, recreation, housing, law, diversity, and myriad other topics. Write letters to the editor. Write articles. Participate in community, parent, or faculty groups. Make them aware of library resources. Sponsor forums. Give speeches.

Please keep in touch to share your successes and your failures. Let us know what you are doing. The Right to Know campaign depends on facts, cases, and examples from the front lines that specifically show how librarians and libraries help—and how the lack of them hurts. My monthly "President's Column" in *American Libraries* will report on Right to Know activities.

By working together we can seize the initiative to use the Right to Know campaign to convince the public at large, and public policy-makers, that the demographic, social, economic, and cultural realities of the late twentieth century require effective library services—library services easily available to all individuals where they live, where they study, and where they work. We must articulate our concerns, those of our users, and, perhaps more importantly, the concerns of those who do not use libraries but need our services. Our objective is to capture the public imagination—to excite people about what librarians do, where we do it, and, most important—why.

We will use the collective power of ALA to inform public opinion, to tell people that they have a right to know and that librarians make it happen. Capitalizing on our strengths we will influence the press and public policy makers, and convince them that libraries and librarians are fundamental to our democracy. We will put the "I" in information. We will marshall our forces to insist that libraries and librarians are essential for a literate and informed citizenry; that libraries and librarians are as critical to our lives as hospitals, police, and schools.

Far from being overwhelmed by the challenges, we will take charge of our destiny. Together we will fight to strengthen libraries and librarianship. Our cause is crucial to the creation of an ethical, enlightened, equitable information age.

Together we will speak out. We will speak loudly. We will speak proudly. Together you and I can—and we must—make a difference.

Save the Public Library

by David Morris

The public library seems to be an institution out of time. In an age of greed and selfishness, the public library stands as an enduring monument to the values of cooperation and sharing. In an age where global corporations stride the earth, the public library remains firmly rooted in the local community. It wouldn't be hard to view the public library as an anachronism, an idea whose time has passed. Except for one thing. It works, marvelously well.

The American Public Library Is the Envy of the World

The public library is the one government institution no one jokes about. And for very good reason. Since that chilly day in April 1833, when the citizens of Peterborough, New Hampshire, established the world's first tax-supported free lending library, the American public library has been the envy of all other nations.

Across the nation, on average, there is a public library for every 18,000 people. At least once a year, more than six out of every ten Americans, more than 120 million in all, visit one of 9,000 central libraries or 6,500 branch libraries. Four out of ten of us use the library every month. Library use varies by class and race, by age and educational level. But the majority of blacks as well as whites, old as well as young, poor as well as rich, high school dropouts as well as university graduates, make use of the public library.

The public library is the best deal in town. Last year the Windsor, Connecticut, Public Library brought that point home by hosting an Open House bluntly named "I Got My Money's Worth at the Windsor Public Library." For less than 2 percent of the city budget, equivalent to $26.61 per person per year, Windsor residents can borrow more than $7 million worth of resources, including books, records, tapes, compact discs and videos. And if someone can't get to the library, Windsor's librarians, like those everywhere in the country, will graciously and expeditiously answer their questions by phone. Last year, across the nation, this service alone had 250 million satisfied customers.

When we think of libraries, we think of books, and rightly so, for public libraries are our largest bookstores. In 1989, while we bought about 2 billion books, we borrowed almost as many, about 1.5 billion, from the public library.

But libraries are much more than bookstores. About 30 percent of the people who visit libraries do not borrow books. For a greater number of people than we might care to believe, the library serves as a warm and dry sanctuary, a place they can sit without fear of being bothered. For others it is a refuge from loneliness, a place full of hustle and bustle where they can attend a concert, or hear a lecture or read a magazine, all free of charge. For the young, the library is a portal to the world, a voyage of discovery. For the student it is a place to do homework. For the unemployed it is a place to begin a job search and to find out how to write a resume. For the homeless the library offers information on the nearest shelter or soup kitchen. For the immigrant it provides an introduction to the culture and the language. For the traveller the library offers maps, a calendar of current events, local newspapers, and local history. For the community activist, the library is a source of information on what other communities are doing, and who might be allies at home.

Libraries Fall on Hard Times

Despite their singular success, and high public ratings, libraries even in the best of times have never been well-funded. Robert Reagan, Public Information Director of the City of Los Angeles library, observes, "Everybody loves libraries, but mostly they are mute about it." In 1988, 68 percent of Rhode Island's voters approved a constitutional amendment that required state government to adequately provide for public libraries. In 1989, armed with this Constitutional mandate, the citizens successfully persuaded the legislature to establish a goal—the state would meet 10 percent of local libraries' operational expenses. At the time the legislature agreed to this, state spending was only 6 percent of total library spending. This year it fell to 2.3 percent. "We could get in on the books," says Joan Reeves, former trustee of the Providence Public Library and founder of the Coalition of Library Advocates, "but we couldn't translate it into bucks."

"(L)ibraries are plagued by the image that we are nice, but not essential," a librarian once complained to the *Washington Post*. People will defend their libraries, but only when the lights are about to go out. In 1985, the biggest library fire in American history destroyed 450,000 books and damaged 600,000 more at the L.A. central library. Fifteen hundred volunteers showed up to help out. Los Angelenos raised $10 million to replace the lost books, and later, approved a $211 million bond to renovate the central library and still later, another $53 million to upgrade their branches. In 1990 Detroit's citizens, faced with the imminent closing of 5 branches, agreed to raise their taxes by $5 million to support their libraries. In 1991 Brooklyn was faced with having to close half its 58 branch libraries, but citizen outrage restored sufficient money to keep the branches open.

In the 1980s the lights stayed on, and for the most part, library budgets increased. But the cost of books and the demand for services increased even faster. Libraries responded by becoming even more efficient. Automation allowed them to serve more customers with the same staff. Regional agreements allowed libraries, through interlibrary loans, to share resources. And otherwise, they simply made do. Regina Minudri, director of Berkeley's public library, describes her 60-year-old central building this way: "plump lady whose dress is too tight. We can't shoehorn in another book."

But despite their best efforts, many libraries fell behind. John Kallenberg, director of the Fresno, California, public library observes, "You're dealing with mass production, no longer individualized attention." It takes longer and longer to reach phone reference. Many libraries are once again closing on Sundays, or are opening later during the week. Fewer hours translates into fewer uses. Vanderbilt economist Malcolm Getz once calculated that, for a big city library, cutting library hours by one hour a day reduces library traffic by more than 15,000 visits a year.

The current recession has transformed a slow decline into an impending collapse. For many libraries, no longer is the problem one of slowly falling behind, but rather, of survival itself. "Libraries have experienced this kind of difficulty before. But usually in the past it's been geographically isolated," says Charles M. Brown, president of the Public Library Association and director of the Arlington County, Virginia, library. "This time around, it seems like almost a financial assault on America's libraries coast-to-coast."

Half of Brooklyn's branch libraries are now open only 2-3 days a week. Seven San Francisco branches have been downgraded to "reading centers," open on average 3 hours a day. Eight of Detroit's 25 branches have had their hours cut in half, to 20 hours a week. In 1991 Worcester, Massachusetts, Public Library closed 6 of its 7 branches, leading head librarian Penelope Johnson to sadly comment, "You have to wonder when what you're offering is a viable library service or not."

Gary Strong, California's State Librarian, surveys his state and concludes, "One half of city libraries are in very serious trouble, and some are damn close to shutting down." James Fish, city librarian of San Jose, agrees. "Right now, we're just trying to stem the bleeding and then later we'll (perform) reconstructive surgery."

"We will survive, but I'm an optimist," says Kallenberg. "What we will look like and what kinds of services we provide is a whole other matter."

The crisis in the public libraries comes hard on the heels of the collapse of school libraries. During the last decade, for example, half of California's school libraries have been closed, putting more pressure on the public library system. With shrinking budgets, public libraries may no longer be able to take up the slack. At the Clinton Hill branch of Brooklyn's public library, the almost century-old tradition of hosting weekly class visits from eight local elementary schools came to an end in 1951. "Many city schools don't have their own libraries any more, so for a lot of kids, that visit was their first introduction to any type of library, and to the whole world of books," says head librarian David Mowery. At the end of their visit each student had received a library card.

A Few Points of Light

This picture of gloom and doom is not uniform or universal. Some communities maintain well-nourished and healthy library systems. Invariably, this is a result of these communities creating dedicated, secure sources of funding. In Berkeley, when Proposition 13 threatened to decimate their library system, 70 percent of the voters approved a unique library-dedicated tax based on the size of buildings. In 1988, 68 percent agreed to double the tax, and allow the City Council to raise the tax to keep pace with inflation. Homes pay 8 cents per square foot, about $100 a year for a typical single family house. Businesses pay 11 cents per square foot.

Berkeley's budget has almost tripled between 1980 and 1991. Its staff increased by more than 25 percent. This city of 100,000 people is spending $6.9 million on its libraries, a remarkable $69 per capita. "Almost anybody would be happy with these figures," Ms. Minudri happily admits.

At the state level, Ohio leads the way. In 1985 the state established a state library fund and dedicated 6.3 percent of its state income tax revenues to it. Last year that came to $250 million. The result? "I feel like we're living in a bubble," says Marilyn Mason, head of the Cleveland Public Library. Ohio is unique not only in its method of funding, but in the way it allocates those funds. Poorer, rural communities receive more than richer, metropolitan areas. This helps to equalize funding levels that, before 1985, had varied by as much as 20 to 1. Alan Hall, incoming President of the Ohio Library Association, can testify to the effects. As director of the Steubenville Public library, located in southeast Ohio on the edge of Appalachia, Hall has seen his county's library budget increase almost three fold since 1985. Its libraries are open seven days a week. Circulation is up 50 percent.

State funding not only makes poorer and richer communities more equal in their ability to access information. It brings them together psychologically. Hall remembers, "Before there was some division between the Clevelands and Columbus's and Cincinnatis and others, but now that financing comes out of the same pot, we have grown together."

Ensuring the Public's Right to Know

Rich or poor, small town or big city, public libraries uncomplainingly continue to pursue their unique mission. "Librarianship is the one profession dedicated to ensuring the right to know," declares Patricia Glass Schuman, president of the American Library Association. In pursuit of that objective, the Worcester public library in 1872 opened its doors on Sunday. Many viewed it as a sacrilege, but head librarian Samuel Green responded that a library intended to serve the public could do so only if it were accessible when the public could use it. Six-day, 60-hour workweeks meant that if the libraries were to serve the majority of the community who earned their living by the sweat of their brows, they must be open on Sundays.

More than 100 years later, Sundays remain the busiest day of the week at public libraries. And Sunday closings are often the first sign of fiscal distress.

In 1894, the right to know led Denver's public library to pioneer the concept of open stacks. For the first time patrons were allowed the heady pleasure of browsing. In the

1930s, the right to know led Kentucky's librarians to ride pack horses and mules with saddlebags filled with books into remote sections of the state to serve the mountain communities. Today the Louisville, Kentucky, Free Public Library continues the tradition by offering disabled citizens at its computer center over 20 adaptive devices that allow users to operate the computer with a clap, a voice, or a light attached to the user's head.

Access doesn't only mean physical access. It also means being able to locate the information one needs. In the 1970s, Sanford Berman, head cataloguer at the Hennepin County, Minnesota, Library, concluded that the card catalog itself constituted a major obstacle to public access, and made it his life's mission to eliminate that obstacle. Berman offers dozens of examples of headings that will frustrate the user. Want information about light bulbs? You have to look under "Electric Lamps, Incandescent." Need to locate a book to help you deal with your child's bed wetting? You must inquire under "Enuresis." Need information on slipped discs? Look under "Intervertebral Disk Displacement." Under Berman's guidance, the Hennepin County Library does its own cataloguing, and libraries around the country have adopted its system.

In the 1990s the public library's dedication to the people's right to know may face its greatest challenge: what does public access mean in an age of electronic information?

Over the last decade, public libraries have crept into the computer age step by step. First, they automated checkout systems. Replete with laser scanners and bar coded books, today's library checkout counters look much like supermarket checkout counters. Next, libraries computerized the card catalogs, and then their reference systems.

The Library in the Age of Electronic Information

Having automated their internal operations, librarians are now entering the next phase of their technological evolution: linking up with those outside the building. Just as Sunday openings and open stacks reflected a previous generation's commitment to public access, facilitating computer connections characterizes this generation's commitment.

Depending on where you live, your public library may be two years into, or two or three years away from, allowing outside access. Just before Christmas, Minneapolis opened its catalogue to outside searching. For several years, the Denver public library has allowed patrons to search not only its holdings, but those of all 44 member libraries of the Colorado Association of Research Libraries (CARL). Berkeley's catalogue is now on-line, but the user cannot interact with it. By next summer, someone outside the library should be able to dial up, locate a book, discover whether it has been checked out, and if so, when it is due back, and electronically reserve it.

Phone reference is also moving into the electronic era. Many librarians now use computer data bases to answer questions. San Bernardino, California's, public library's MicroLink goes a step further. It allows computer owners to dial up 24 hours a day and leave questions in a message box under the caller's name. The librarian answers these electronically.

Since people often ask the same questions, and since electronic questions and answers can be stored and retrieved, some libraries envision data banks of Q and As, searchable by patrons. Tom Grunder, director of Cleveland FreeNet, a community information network operated out of Case Western Reserve University, dubs this a "living encyclopedia," not only because it constantly becomes smarter, but because, by definition, it contains information people want to know.

When standard reference tools, like almanacs, and dictionaries and encyclopedias, become electronically accessible, Marilyn Mason, director of the Cleveland Public Library, believes it could "satisfy 80 percent of the questions that come in," freeing up Cleveland's 6-7 phone reference librarians to serve other customers. Says Michael Walsh, computer scientist at the Enoch Pratt Free Library in Baltimore, "My goal personally is that if you call the Pratt Library you should be able to access all reference materials as if you were walking through the door." "Technologically speaking, nothing stops us from doing it," adds Walsh. "The only thing that stops it is the licensing."

Borrowing Electrons vs. Borrowing Books

And there's the rub. For no one has yet figured out how to charge for information in the information age. In the past, when a publisher sold a book to a library, he or she expressly permitted that book to be accessible to anyone. But books are concrete objects. When someone is using a book, it is unavailable for anyone else.

Electronic information is different. Says Mary Birmingham of MetroNet, a regional serve provider for Twin Cities libraries, "You can use it without taking it from someone else." Very soon, libraries will be able to scan their magazines, and even books, into computers, and thus transform them from physical objects to electronic information. With inexpensive optical storage technologies, I can tap into the library and transfer information into my home computer. And with the advent of cheaper and faster printers, I can even print out a hard copy of the information at my convenience. And all the while, the initial information will remain in the library, available to others.

In this new world, how should a publisher price a book or a magazine? What role should the public library play in establishing the rules for this new order of things? Mary Birmingham advises librarians, "We need to have our values straight, and to be flexible in all other ways." True to their mission, public libraries are insisting on free access. They oppose licensing agreements that charge users by the minute or by the number of documents viewed or retrieved. Just as libraries now pay an annual fee for unlimited searching and use of the compact discs which store not only bibliographic indexes but, increasingly, full text of articles, so they want to be able to pay an annual subscription fee that allows all their citizens free access. But what should the price of that licensing fee be? Says Walsh, "Publishers do not yet know what is a reasonable fee for the entire city of Baltimore."

Complicating the problem for public libraries is that commercial networks already exist that charge users for information. I can subscribe to PRODIGY, for example, and access commercial encyclopedias, or to DIALOG and access bibliographic or full text reference services.

Right now the libraries are still working out the rules. The CARL system, for example, carries the same encyclopedia as do a number of commercial networks. According to Terry Parks, operations manager for CARL, anyone can dial up the system and use its cataloguing or electronic bulletin board portions, but only those with passwords can access the encyclopedia. All member library card holders are given a password.

Low cost scanners offer another option to libraries: self-publishing. The Boulder public library has mounted city council minutes, searchable by those inside and outside the library. Baltimore will soon mount the city charter. Cleveland FreeNet has gone a step further. In the last election, it scanned in issue papers of candidates for a wide range of state offices. After the election FreeNet deleted the losers' policy papers but retained those of the winners. Grunder calls it a "permanent record" which may help hold candidates accountable to their campaign promises (or conversely, encourage them to promise less the next time around).

Will the increased reliance on computerized information undermine the library's function as a community center? Marilyn Mason says no. "You don't have to have a computer in the home or office to take advantage of our electronic marvels," she insists. All of Cleveland's branches, most of which are within walking distance of the vast majority of the city's inhabitants, are equipped with computers and fax machines. "A child can walk into a branch library, and with the librarians' assistance, can search downtown's 30,000 periodicals and 2 million books, and can request the information via computer. At the end of the day the librarians pull off the requests and fill them. The next day, the branch will receive the item." And if there is an urgency? "We will fax the document to the branch," Mason adds.

The Attack on Free Public Information

One might expect that public information would always be free. If you do you've been asleep for the Reagan years. In 1985 the White House Office of Management and Budget demanded that the federal government, the nation's single largest generator of data, should privatize its information. Circular A-130 required "maximum feasible reliance on the private sector for...dissemination of products and services." OMB explicitly prohibited agencies from undercutting private enterprises by duplicating systems already available from the private sector.

The result of OMB's directive has been that data collected at taxpayers' expense and previously available free or at a nominal charge is now being given away free to private companies who then copyright the machine-readable information in their own name and charge high prices for access. The Securities and Exchange Commission, for example, spends tens of millions of dollars to gather and compile the nation's most comprehensive corporate database, one of the key sources of reliable information on companies' assets, debt, stock and long-term plans. But except for three public information rooms the SEC maintains in Washington, Chicago and New York, the system can be accessed only through Mead Data Central, a private vendor. Mead charges users $45 per hour plus $20 for each record accessed. Calling up 10 corporate reports in an hour on Disclosure, one will shell out $245.

The federal policy of privatizing public information outrages the library community. ALA President Schuman declares, "To date, privatization has resulted in less access and higher cost for the American public. If we accept the commoditization of information...we will diminish the public's right to know."

The Best of Times: The Worst of Times

It is both a difficult, and an exhilarating, time for public libraries. Never before have they been under such financial strain. Never before has their voice in support of public access to information been so needed. Never before have the technologies of information storage and retrieval made their abilities so great.

The struggles of public libraries are by their nature local battles, out of sight of most of the majority of us who get our news largely from the national media. That is regrettable because, given their increasing interconnectedness through interlibrary loans and computer networks, libraries are really a national institution, and a national treasure. As John N. Berry III, editor-in-chief of the *Library Journal*, reminds us, "We decided...that the public library was a public good because whenever any citizen used it, every citizen benefitted."

The public library is a uniquely American institution. It is not free, except in terms of access, but it is astonishingly inexpensive, requiring about 1 percent of local government budgets. The return on that small investment is incalculable. The public library serves many roles. But the argument that first persuaded communities to support their libraries is still the most important. The right to vote must be accompanied by the right to know. Access to information makes citizens of us all.

Gary Strong, California's state librarian, sums it up. "If we let the library system fail we have forsaken what democracy is all about."

David Morris, author, lecturer and consultant, is a columnist for the *St. Paul Pioneer Press*. Portions of this article were first published in *MediaCulture Review*, January 1992.

Time to End the Cold War At Home

by Jeanne M. Woods

In March 1946 in Fulton, Missouri, Winston Churchill declared that an "Iron Curtain" had descended on Eastern Europe. A year later the United States adopted the Truman Doctrine and the policy of "containment" of communism through ideological warfare and economic aid. New legislation set up the National Security Council and created the CIA. The "Cold War" had begun.

This militaristic characterization of the post-war political milieu rapidly gained currency among policymakers, in part, at least, because it provided a rationale for the adoption of measures unprecedented in peacetime. Many traditions of wartime, including military censorship, government secrecy, and restrictions on civil liberties, became institutionalized. By statute, executive order, regulation, and simple practice, Americans were deprived of rights based on the assumption that limits on constitutional rights were necessary to fight the Cold War.

In 1990, nearly half a century later, the end of the Cold War abroad is the definitive event of our time. Yet, while many of the most flagrant violations of the rights of Americans associated with the Cold War (e.g., McCarthyism) are long gone from the American scene, other anti-democratic practices persist. The time is now at hand to eradicate these vestiges of an unseemly chapter in our nation's history, and to establish safeguards to ensure that new "threats" do not replace the Cold War as justifications for eroding our constitutionally guaranteed liberties.

Government Secrecy. The Cold War era produced a carefully structured system of government information control. Today, there is vast overclassification of government information in the name of national security. A 1985 House Committee staff report found that roughly 90% of classified information was classified needlessly. The right to classify and to deny the release of information rests on executive orders. Although the Freedom of Information Act was designed to provide some review, very few courts are willing to overrule the executive's determination that information should be kept secret. The budget of the intelligence community continues to be kept secret in violation of the Constitution, and the very existence of at least one intelligence agency -- the National Reconnaissance Office (NRO) -- is still considered a secret.

Security Clearances. As a result of the overclassification of government information, close to four million government and contractor employees are now required to obtain security clearances. The government has recently reinstituted the practice of asking those whose jobs require a clearance whether they have ever been members of the Communist Party, and it continues to examine the political beliefs and activities and sexual orientation of applicants for these and other positions. The right to challenge a denial of a clearance is very narrow and the Bush Administration is considering proposals to further limit it.

Ideological Exclusions. One of the most infamous measures of the Cold War era was the McCarran-Walter Act, a law barring communists from admission to the United States either as visitors or as permanent immigrants. Under this law, many distinguished foreigners invited to speak to American audiences have been denied visas. Despite recent changes in the law, persons seeking to visit the United States are still required to answer questions about their political beliefs and affiliations, and to apply for a waiver if they have ever belonged to a communist organization. Foreigners wishing to become permanent residents are still completely barred on these grounds.

Travel Restrictions. The government has the authority under the economic embargo laws to effectively prevent Americans from traveling to "enemy" countries. This authority is used to ban travel to Cuba for most Americans and to severely restrict travel to Vietnam and Cambodia. The government can also deny passports to those whose travel it asserts will harm the national security.

Government Surveillance. The Cold War intensified the already existing practice of government surveillance of persons and groups in the United States engaged in lawful political activities. In the name of "counterintelligence" and national security, the government has systematically harassed and spied upon disfavored groups. The cost has been significant, resulting in infringements on the First Amendment rights of free speech and political association, and erosion of the Fourth Amendment protection against unreasonable searches and seizures. The government continues to assert that it has inherent power to investigate political opponents, obtain financial and other private records, wiretap telephones, and even break into homes without a warrant under the guise of protecting the nation from foreign powers and their agents.

Erosion of the Adversary System. Another effect of the increase in government secrecy and judicial deference to claims of national security has been an erosion of the fundamental right to an adversary court proceeding. In more and more contexts where a claim of national security is raised, the courts have been willing to examine evidence *ex parte* and *in camera* (in closed chambers, without representation for the defendant) and to base important decisions concerning individual rights on such secret proceedings. The administration goes so far as to assert that individual claims of political harassment and violations of constitutional rights should not even be heard by the courts if the executive asserts a national security "state secrets" privilege, the

"actual basis of which is not even shown to the individual claimant.

Draft Registration. The continuing requirement to register for the draft impacts adversely on those who are conscientious objectors to draft registration and are thereby denied student loans and the opportunity for government employment.

Covert Operations and War Powers. A new doctrine has emerged during the Cold War that the President has inherent power to use force, either overt or covert, at his own discretion without the approval of Congress. The Constitution, on the other hand, makes it clear that only Congress has the power "to declare war." Nonetheless, the executive has engaged in covert paramilitary operations and overt military invasions in direct violation of the Constitution.

The Environment. The impact of the Cold War on American society has extended even to the environment. The nuclear weapons industry, the embodiment of America's response to the Cold War abroad, has itself become a threat to Americans at home. The industry has a shocking record of contamination, unsafe working conditions and nuclear accidents. Much of the information needed to study the health effects and conduct clean-up of hazardous waste, and to make informed decisions about future weapons production, remains classified.

At this moment of fundamental change in the world situation, vigorous debate on the future direction of U.S. policy is crucial. A meaningful debate on the critical issues brought to the forefront by the end of the Cold War is impossible if Congress and the public are denied access to vital information. The Center for National Security Studies is launching a project designed to eliminate the domestic vestiges of the Cold War. CNSS is preparing a public policy report that will analyze the restrictions on civil liberties and their profound impact on American society. Planning has begun for a major national conference on "Ending the Cold War at Home," scheduled for January 1991, which is being cosponsored by a broad array of public interest, professional, religious and peace organizations. The two day conference will begin with an overview of the problem, conduct workshops that will focus attention on specific issues, and close with a discussion of the steps necessary to eradicate these restrictions on our liberty, including the creation of a coalition to work toward this objective. ∎

DataCenter   464 19th Street, Oakland, California 94612 (415) 835-4692

Worldwide Networking for Social Change

by Brock N. Meeks

If you've ever wanted to effect a change, there's a niche with your name on it somewhere within the Institute for Global Communications. IGC Networks, including Peace-Net, cast their virtual "nets" into the ether and cover an astounding array of subjects. Within the electronic borders of IGC there are no "stars"; this is a global network of local heroes and heroines, strung together with the silicon equivalent of duct tape, chewing gum and bailing wire. And it works—for an amazing variety of projects and causes.

*You can participate in the environmental, political and social transformation handbook of the '90s, Macrocosm USA, being developed online in "macrocosm." Chapters include social issues and remedies, directories, bibliographies and other resources concerning today's planetary crises.

*Wondering "What's Left" of the role of the Left Movement in the '90s? See the topic of the same name in "udc.media." Related discussions are taking place in the "whatsnext" conference.

*EcoTerrorism or Nonviolence? What do you think? Redwood Summer and other Earth First! actions are listed and discussed in "ef!.general." Nonviolent forms of disobedience are discussed in the new conference "nonviolent.action." Related items include "Nonviolence and Property Destruction" in "ed.general" and "Navy Nuclear Weapons-Columbia River" in "gp.press."

*Democracy's Political Prisoners—See "Letter from Chile's PP" in the conference "reg.samerica."

The electronic landscape here is vast. Hundreds of conferences wrap into thousands of topics and tens of thousands of messages and responses. Even the "dead" conferences are worthwhile; rummaging through a dormant conference is like wandering through Tiffany's and being allowed to stuff a stray diamond, here and there, in your pockets.

Association for Progressive Communications

At the heart of IGC Networks is APC, the Association for Progressive Communications. "Back in 1987 IGC helped to develop an international cooperative effort that would link like-minded groups via the computer," says IGC director Geoff Sears. "At the time, the only additional member we had was GreenNet based out of London." Short pause. "But we've come a ways since then." He smiles and his eyes light up.

"PeaceNet's been around since '86," Sears says. "IGC was formed shortly thereafter, so in a sense you have the situation where the child spawned the parent."

Since those humble beginnings, APC has added the Web (Canada), EarthNet (Australia), Alternex (Brazil), FredsNaetet (PeaceNet Sweden), and Nicarao (Nicaragua). Each of these networks share conferences and email with each other. "You can converse with people in more than ninety countries," says Sears. Soon Moscow and Germany will be added to APC's ever-widening group of networks.

With the comparatively new technology of computer-based communications, the gathering and processing of news and information is accelerated. Speed obviously goes hand in hand with volume. If you can transmit information more quickly, you can use the same resources to transmit more information.

The "global village" brought about by geo-synchronous satellite TV is still just a one-way street, regardless of speed. But groups like APC create the "global conference," which draws decision makers together across time and space in conversations that pierce the isolation in which policies have traditionally been formed and implemented in the past.

The War and More on PeaceNet

Formally, IGC is a nonprofit organization that acts as an umbrella for a mixture of networks: PeaceNet, EcoNet, HomeoNet and ConflictNet. PeaceNet, as you might imagine, houses the peace-activist-oriented conferences and read-only information resources.

One of the hottest topics on PeaceNet at press time is the Gulf War. The system is virtually blazing with message traffic about the conflict, with no less than six conferences addressing various war-related issues.

The quality of information is nothing less than stellar—reports stream in from bulletin boards and correspondents in Saudi Arabia, Britain and from others monitoring the world press. Information seen on PeaceNet in the morning often turns up in the headlines tomorrow, and sometimes the information beats the print media by days. For example, take this excerpt from the Mideast.Forum conference dated January 3, 1991:

"During the 1980s, Saudi Arabia spent nearly S50 billion on an air defense system built to US and NATO specifications. At the same time, the US spent $14 billion building a network of (uninhabited) military bases across Saudi Arabia. At this time, the US was allied with (and arming) Iraq. What were the bases for? Isn't it a serendipitous coincidence that they just happened to be there to support the most massive bombing campaign in world history? Source: 'From Rapid Deployment to Massive Deployment' by Joe Stork and Martha Wenger in *Middle East Report* #168 (MERIP, DC)."

This snippet of information was widely played on by the Op-Ed pages just a few days later. Other facts, played widely on the nightly news, are given a decidedly "un-CNN" spin.

PeaceNet also boasts Amnesty International and the Christic Institute. The latter uses the network for electronic distribution of their newsletter and to keep people informed of the institute's activities.

Journalists and activists find PeaceNet a valuable tool and resource. When speaking before a Christic Institute conference, Tony Avirgan, a well-known investigative reporter, said that information he pulls from IGC is vital to his work. "[PeaceNet's] information base is a fantastic source of information, up-to-date, hour-by-hour, on peace, social justice and environmental issues."

Other Networks

EcoNet concerns itself with environmental issues. From backyard recycling to rain forests, there are groups on EcoNet fighting the good fight.

Here you'll find groups like Global Action Network (GAN). GAN is based in Idaho and specializes in helping people take an active role in their environment. Extracting from research papers, government documents, and publications written by environmental experts, GAN supplies users with precise information that can be downloaded and acted on the same day.

For example, *The Action Guide : A Guide for Citizen Group Action*, a kind of do-it-yourself eco-version of "how to fight city hall," is online in full text. There's also the address and phone numbers of environmentally oriented US government agencies, as well as key House and Senate committees and subcommittees.

The conference *Greenstore* is moderated by internationally recognized consumer advocate Debera Lynn Dadd, author of *Nontoxic, Natural & Earthwise*. Greenstore puts you in touch with an abundance of information about ecologically sensitive projects.

EcoNet was honored last year by Renew America's "Searching for Success" as the most extensive environmental computer network in the world.

ConflictNet, according to IGC's newsletter, "is dedicated to providing nonviolent and collaborative problem-solving by bringing people in the conflict resolution movement together with peace and environmental activists." Here you'll find the Academy of Family Mediators, who use ConflictNet as a resource for planning and information. Others use it for drafting legislation, breaking research on "assessment tools" for organizational conflict, and issuing calls for papers. Journals and newsletters such as the Conflict Resolution Notes are online.

HomeoNet focuses on the practice of homeopathic medicine. It's a small but growing network. The network links homeopath practitioners in the US with those in the UK, Australia, and, soon, Brazil.

Case Study: Alternex in Brazil

Yes, the rain forests in Brazil are in peril, but there's more to Brazil's problems than rain forests. For example, homeless children are dealt with harshly. vigilante groups simply kill them rather than house them.

Outrage? Sure. Unnoticed? Hardly. A group known as IBASE (the Portuguese acronym for Brazilian Institute of Social and Economic Analysis) focuses on socio-economic analysis and deals with just this sort of problem, and it's one of the first groups to use Alternex. Their success has encouraged other non-governmental organizations (NGOs) to follow suit. "Results breed results," says Sears.

Until IGC hooked up with IBASE, the NGO was struggling to make efficient use of data communications, "but the weight of paying the 'data freight' internationally was killing them," says Sears. Enter Alternex.

The collaboration between IBASE and IGC resulted in Alternex, a multi-host PC-based "store and forward" system linked to IGC's international computer network. In July 1989, only a few months after approval of the project, Alternex was fully operating 24 hours a day. Today, more than 130 individual and group users in Brazil and elsewhere participate in the network, and this number is increasing daily. Users pay a monthly fee, the equivalent of about US$7.50, which includes one hour of online connection. Online connection runs approximately $5 per hour, cheaper than nearly all other electronic mail services.

Some of the results:

*Local environmental organizations tap into IBASE's computerized directory of environmental development donors and the projects they finance when looking for resources.

*Groups active in the Foreign Debt Campaign, which mobilizes support for alternative solutions to Brazil's debt crisis, use electronic mail to coordinate joint activities.

*NGOs use the system to communicate easily with donor agencies throughout the world or as the cheapest and most appropriate channel to distribute their news clippings or press releases.

*Several NGOs are also acting as community email agencies, providing electronic communication services to

DataCenter   464 19th Street, Oakland, California 94612   (415) 835-4692

small local groups and permitting interaction with their counterparts around the world.

So, What's the Catch?

Is all this too good to be true?

Well, there are problems. The entire system is "an experiment" according to Sears. He acknowledges that the technology is out of the reach of most. Computers are still expensive. "Is that really a problem, or just an obstacle to hurdle?" asks Sears. He's maneuvering the conversation. But he's right on target.

"You have to think of IGC as being close to the top of an 'information chain'," explains Sears. "These [networks] aren't accessible to poor people, they are supporting mid-level NGOs, who are empowered by the computers to do their job better: help people. The networks are an augmentation to these groups, not some kind of miracle drug. Bottomline, people still have to do the work, but now they have better information, they get it faster and can share it internationally."

Since IGC is funded by foundations and private individuals, I ask Sears why, if I had $100 grand to donate, I should give it to him and not to the local homeless shelter. "You have to weigh how much of a multiplier the PC is," he says. "Our theory is that linking all these different micros together is going to have an increased effect of allowing these groups to get more information out to more people. The whole operation is elitist, to a certain extent. Computers aren't reaching the peasant farmer on his plot of land."

Does the peasant farmer need a computer? "You tell me," Sears says. "We don't know what the farmer needs; but the local NGO does, and that's who we're helping. We try hard to stay out of the way. There's been enough of the 'We're American, we know what's best for you' mentality."

Peace: The Next Generation

When the last pixel's phosphor fades from green to black, we're going to leave this all to the children, to the next generation of activists. Is IGC reaching the kids? Read this letter from those waiting in the wings:

Dear PeaceNet,

We are a group of 5th and 6th grader gifted students who attend a magnet school in Miami, Fla. We are (through class discussion and projects) learning about how to become peacemakers. In our gifted center we have already learned a lot about becoming peacemakers, such as being aware of what is going on in the world, and being open minded; however, we would like more information. Could you please send us some information on becoming peacemakers. Thank you.

Sincerely,
Future Peacemakers of America

There's a letter in the mail. (IGC, 3228 Sacramento St., San Francisco, CA 94110, 415/923-0900. Fax: 415-923-1665)

Selected Bibliography

Bagdikian, Ben H. *Media Monopoly*. 4th ed. Boston: Beacon Press, 1992.

Berman, Paul, ed. *The Controversy over Political Correctness on College Campuses*. New York: Laurel/Dell, 1992.

The Bush Administration and the News Media. Washington, D.C.: The Reporters Committee for Freedom of the Press, 1992.

Chevigny, Paul. *More Speech: Dialogue Rights and Modern Liberty*. Philadelphia: Temple University Press, 1988.

Childers, Thomas. *The Information-Poor in America*. Metuchen, N.J.: Scarecrow Press, 1975.

Computers, Freedom & Privacy: Pursuing Policies to Safeguard American Freedoms in the Information Age. Video Library Series, Sponsored by Computer Professionals for Social Responsibility. P.O. Box 912, Topango, CA 91290.

Confronting Columbus. Eds. John Yewell, Chris Dodge and Jan DeSirey. Jefferson, NC: McFarland, 1992.

Criley, Richard. *The FBI v. The First Amendment*. Los Angeles, CA: First Amendment Foundation, 1990.

Dictating Consent. Washington, D.C.: Center for the Study of Commercialism, 1992.

Donner, Frank. *Protectors of Privilege*. Berkeley, CA: University of California Press, 1990.

Emord, Jonathan. *Freedom, Technology and the First Amendment*. San Francisco: Pacific Research Institute for Public Policy, 1991.

The First Amendment Handbook. 2nd ed. Washington, D.C.: The Reporters Committee for Freedom of the Press, 1989.

Fitzgerald, Frances. *America Revisited: History Schoolbooks in the Twentieth Century*. New York: Vintage Books, 1979.

Foerstel, Herbert N. *Surveillance in the Stacks: The FBI's Library Awareness Program*. New York: Greenwood Press, 1990.

Free Expression and the American Public. Washington, D.C.: American Society of Newspaper Editors Foundation, 1991.

Gelbspan, Ross. *Break-ins, Death Threats and the FBI: The Covert War Against the Central America Movement*. Boston, MA: South End Press, 1991.

Gentry, Curt. *J. Edgar Hoover: The Man and the Secrets*. New York: Norton & Co., c1991.

Glasser, Ira. *Visions of Liberty: The Bill of Rights for All Americans*. Boston, MA: Arcade Publishers/ Little Brown, 1991.

Grieder, William. *Who Will Tell the People: The Betrayal of American Democracy*. New York: Simon and Schuster, 1992.

Herman, Edward S. and Noam Chomsky. *Manufacturing Consent: The Political Economy of the Mass Media*. New York: Pantheon, 1988.

Hull, Elizabeth. *Taking Liberties: National Barriers to the Free Flow of Ideas*. Westport, CT.: Praeger, 1990.

Information, Freedom and Censorship: World Report 1991. Compiled by Article 19 International Centre on Censorship. Chicago, IL: American Library Association, 1991.

Kozol, Jonathan. *Savage Inequalities: Children in America's Schools*. New York: Crown, 1991.

Leahy, James E. *The First Amendment, 1791-1991: Two Hundred Years of Freedom*. Jefferson, NC: McFarland, 1991.

Lee, Martin A. and Solomon, Norman. *Unreliable Sources: A Guide to Detecting Bias in the News Media*. New York: Carol Publishing Group, 1990.

Less Access to Less Information by and about the U.S. Government: A 1981-1991 Chronology. Washington, D.C.: American Library Association, January 1992. Continued by a semi-annual publication of the same name.

Marsh, Dave and friends. *50 Ways to Fight Censorship and Important Facts to Know about the Censors*. New York: Thunder's Mouth Press, 1991.

Meyer, Howard N. *The Amendment that Refused to Die: Amendment XIV*. Rev. ed. Boston: Beacon Press, 1978.

Mills, Ami Chen. *CIA Off Campus: Building the Movement Against Agency Recruitment and Research*. 2nd ed. Boston: South End Press, 1991.

The Privacy Project: Personal Privacy in the Information Age. Compact discs of 13-part Radio Series. Walnut Creek, CA: Pacific Multimedia, 1991.

Robins, Natalie. *Alien Ink: The F.B.I.'s War on Freedom of Expression*. New York: William Morrow, 1992.

Ryan, Charlotte. *Prime Time Activism: Media Strategies for Organizing*. Boston, MA: South End Press, 1991.

Salinger, Pierre, and Eric Laurent. *Secret Dossier: The Hidden agenda behind the Gulf War*. New York: Penguin Books, 1991.

Schiller, Herbert. *Culture, Inc.: The Corporate Takeover of Public Expression*. New York: Oxford University Press, 1989.

Shiffrin, Steven H. *The First Amendment, Democracy and Romance*. Washington, D.C.: Howard University Press, 1990.

Solomon, Norman. *The Power of Babble: The Politician's Dictionary of Buzzwords and Double-talk for Every Occasion*. New York: Dell, 1992.

Stockwell, John. *The Praetorian Guard: the U.S. Role in the New World Order*. D. Boston, MA: South End Press, 1991.

Thinking and Rethinking U.S. History. New York: Council on Interracial Books for Children, 1988.

Wyatt, Robert O. *Free Expression and the American Public: A Survey Commemorating the 200th Anniversary of the First Amendment*, for the American Society of Newspaper Editors. Murtreesboro, TN, Middle Tennessee State University, 1991.

Zinn, Howard. *Declarations of Independence*. New York: Harper & Row, 1990.

Organizations

The organizations listed below have shown concern for defending the "right to know" and freedom of the press. Some are national in scope. Others are national with local chapters. Still others are local groups given here as examples. (Revised 4/92)

A.F.L./C.I.O.
815 16th St. N.W.
Washington, DC 20006
202/637-5000

Advocacy Institute
1730 Rhode Island Ave. N.W.
Washington, DC 20036
202/659-8475

Alliance for Justice
1601 Connecticut Avenue, N.W.
Washington, DC 20009
202/332-3224

American Assn. for Higher Education
One Dupont Circle, Ste. 600
Washington, DC 20036
202/293-6440

American Assn. for the Advancement of
Science
1333 H St. N.W.
Washington, DC 20005
202/326-6639

American Assn. of University Professors
1012 14th St. N.W., Ste. 500
Washington, DC 20005
202/737-5900

American Assn. of University Women
1111 16th St. N.W.
Washington, DC 20036
202/785-7700

American Booksellers Foundation for
Free Expression
560 White Plains Road
Tarrytown, NY 10591
1/800/637-0037, ext. 267

American Civil Liberties Union
132 W. 43rd St.
New York, NY 10036
212/944-9800

American Civil Liberties
Union/Washington Office
122 Maryland Ave. N.E.
Washington, DC 20002
202/544-1681

American Council for the Arts
1285 Avenue of the Americas, 3d Fl.,
Area M
New York, NY 10019
212/245-4510

American Council of Learned Societies
228 E. 45th St., 16th Fl.
New York, NY 10017
212/697-1505

American Council on Education
One Dupont Circle N.W.
Washington, DC 20036
202/939-9300

American Friends Service Committee
1501 Cherry Street
Philadelphia, PA 19102
215/241-7000

American Historical Assn.
400 A Street S.E.
Washington, DC 20003
202/544-2422

American Library Assn./Intellectual
Freedom Committee
50 E. Huron St.
Chicago, IL 60611
312/944-6780; 800/545-2433

American Library Assn./Washington
Office
110 Maryland Ave. N.E.
Washington, DC 20002
202/547-4440

American Newspaper Publishers Assn.
P.O. Box 17407
Dulles International Airport
Washington, DC 20041
703/648-1000

American Political Science Assn.
1527 New Hampshire Ave. N.W.
Washington, DC 20036
202/483-2512

American Society of Access Professionals
7910 Woodmont Ave.
Bethesda, MD 20814
301/913-0030

American Society of Journalists &
Authors
1501 Broadway, Ste. 1907
New York, NY 10036
212/997-0947

American Society of Newspaper Editors
Freedom of Information Committee
P.O. Box 17004
Washington, DC 20041
703/648-1144

American Writers Congress
Division of Nation Institute
72 Fifth Ave.
New York, NY 10011
212/463-9270

Media Coalition/Americans for
Constitutional Freedom
900 Third Ave., Ste. 1600
New York, NY 10022
212/891-2070

Amnesty International of the USA
322 Eighth Ave.
New York, NY 10001
212/807-8400

Assn. of American Law Schools
1201 Connecticut Ave., N.W
Washington, DC 20036
202/296-8851

Assn. of American Publishers
1718 Connecticut Ave., N.W.
Washington, DC 20009
202/232-3335

Assn of College & Research Libraries
50 E. Huron St.
Chicago, IL 60611
312/280-2516

Assn. of National Security Alumni
2001 S. St., N.W., Ste. 740
Washington, DC 20009
202/483-9325

Assn. of Research Libraries
1527 New Hampshire Ave. N.W.
Washington, DC 20036
202/232-2466

California First Amendment Coalition
2218 Homewood Way
Carmichael, CA 95608
916/485-2912

Center for Constitutional Rights
666 Broadway, 7th Fl.
New York, NY 10012
212/614-6464

Center for Investigative Reporting
530 Howard St., 2nd Fl.
San Francisco, CA 94105-3007
415/543-1200

Center for Law in the Public Interest
11835 W. Olympic Blvd.
Los Angeles, CA 90064
213/470-3000

Center for National Security Studies
122 Maryland Ave. N.E.
Washington, DC 20002
202/544-5380

Center for Science in the Public Interest
1875 Connecticut Ave., N.W.
Washington, DC 20009
202/332-9110

Children's Defense Fund
122 C St. N.W.
Washington, DC 20001
202/628-8787

Christic Institute
1324 N. Capital St. N.W.
Washington, DC 20002
202/797-8106

Coalition on Government Information
c/o American Library Assn./Washington
Office
110 Maryland Ave. N.E.
Washington, DC 20002
202/547-4400

Committee to Protect Journalists
16 East 42nd St., 3rd Fl.
New York, NY 10017
212/983-5355

Computer Professionals for Social
Responsibility
687 High St.
Palo Alto, CA 94301
415/322-3778

Common Cause
2030 M St. N.W.
Washington, DC 20036
202/833-1200

Council for Democratic & Secular
Humanism
Box 5, Central Park Sta.
Buffalo, NY 14215
716/834-2921

Council of Professional Assn. on Federal
Statistics
1429 Duke St.
Alexandria, VA 22314
703/836-0404

Council on Interracial Books for Children
1841 Broadway, Rm. 608
New York, NY 10023
212/757-5339

Council on Library Resources
1785 Massachusetts Ave. N.W.
Washington, DC 20036
202/483-7474

DataCenter
Right to Know Project
464 19th St.
Oakland, CA 94612
510/835-4692

Educators Against Racism and Apartheid
164-04 Goethals Ave.
Jamaica, NY 11432

Educators for Social Responsibility
23 Garden St.
Cambridge, MA 02138
617/492-1764

Electronic Frontier Foundation
666 Pennsylvania Ave. S.E., Ste. 303
Washington, DC 20003
202/544-9237

Fairness & Accuracy in Reporting
(FAIR)
130 West 25th St.
New York, NY 10001
212/633-6700

First Amendment Congress
1250 14th St.
Denver, CO 80202
303/556-4522

First Amendment Foundation
1313 West 8th St., Ste. 313
Los Angeles, CA 90017
213/484-6661

First Amendment Lawyers Assn.
c/o Wayne Giampietro
125 S. Wacker Dr.
Chicago, IL 60606
312/236-0606

Freedom of Expression Foundation
5220 S. Marina Pacifica
Long Beach, CA 90803
213/985-4301

Freedom of Information Center
20 Walker Williams Hall
University of Missouri at Columbia
Columbia, MO 65211
314/882-4856

Freedom of Information Clearinghouse
P.O. Box 19367
Washington, DC 20036
202/785-3704

Freedom to Read Foundation
50 East Huron St.
Chicago, IL 60611
312/280-4226

Friends Committee on National
Legislation
245 Second St. N.E.
Washington, DC 20002
202/547-6000

Fund for Constitutional Government
121 Constitution Ave., N.E.
Washington, DC 20002
202/546-3732

Fund for Free Expression
485 Fifth Ave.
New York, NY 10017
212/972-8400

Government Accountability Project
Ste. 700, 25 E St. N.W.
Washington, DC 20001
202/347-0460

Gray Panthers
1424 16th St., N.W.
Washington, DC 19107
202/387-3111

Index on Censorship
39C Highbury Place
London N5 1QP
England

Institute for Media Analysis
145 W. 4th St.
New York, NY 10012
212/254-1061

Institute for Policy Studies
1601 Connecticut Ave. N.W.
Washington, DC 20009
202/234-9382

Intellectual Freedom Committee
California Library Assn.
717 K St., Ste. 300
Sacramento, CA 95814-3477
916/447-8394

Inter-American Press Assn.
2911 N.W. 39th St.
Miami, FL 33142
305/634-2465

International Centre Against Censorship
90 Borough High St.
London SE1 1LL
United Kingdom
071-403-4822

Investigative Reporters & Editors
100 Neff Hall
University of Missouri
Columbia, MO 65211
314/882-2042

Laubach Literacy Action Inc.
Box 131
1320 Jamesville Ave.
Syracuse, NY 13210
315/422-9121

Leadership Conference on Civil Rights
2027 Massachusetts Ave. N.W.
Washington, DC 20036
202/667-1780

Media Alliance
Bldg. D, Fort Mason
San Francisco, CA 94123
415/441-2557

Media Island International
Box 10041
Olympia, WA 98502
206/352-8526

Meiklejohn Civil Liberties Library
Box 673
Berkeley, CA 94701
510/848-0599

Missouri Coalition Against Censorship
4557 Laclede Ave.
St. Louis, MO 63108
314/361-2111

Movement Support Network
c/o Center for Constitutional Rights
666 Broadway, 7th Fl.
New York, NY 10012
212/614-6464

National Alliance Against Racist &
Political Repression
11 John St., Rm. 702
New York, NY 10038
212/406-3330

National Assn. of Government
Communicators
80 S. Early St.
Alexandria, VA 22304
703/823-4821

National Assn. of Schools of Public
Affairs & Administration
1120 G St. N.W.
Washington, DC 20005
202/628-8965

National Campaign for Freedom of
Expression
P.O. Box 50245, F St. Station
Washington, DC 20004
202/393-2787

National Center for Freedom of
Information Studies
Loyola University of Chicago
820 N. Michigan Ave.
Chicago, IL 60611
312/670-3116

National Center for Science Education
2107 Dwight Way
Berkeley, CA 94704
510/843-3393

National Coalition Against Censorship
2 West 64th St.
New York, NY 10023
212/724-1500

National Committee Against Repressive
Legislation
National Offices
236 Massachusetts Ave. N.E.
Washington, DC 20002
202/543-7659

National Consumers League
815 15th St. N.W.
Washington, DC 20005
202/639-8140

National Coordinating Committee for
the Promotion of History
400 A St. S.E.
Washington, DC 20003
202/544-2422

National Council for Geographic
Education
Indiana University of Pennsylvania
16A Leonard Hall
Indiana, PA 15705
412/357-6290

National Council for the Social Studies
3501 Newark St. N.W.
Washington, DC 20016
202/966-7840

National Council of Teachers of English
1111 Kenyon Rd.
Urbana, IL 61801
217/328-3870

National Education Association
1201 16th St. N.W.
Washington, DC 20036
202/833-4000

National Emergency Civil Liberties
Committee
175 Fifth Ave.
New York, NY 10010
212/673-2040

National Federation of Press Women
1105 Main St.
Box 99
Blue Springs, MO 64013
816/229-1666

National Lawyers Guild
55 Sixth Ave.
New York, NY 10013
212/966-5000

National Newspaper Assn.
1627 K St. N.W.
Washington, DC 20006
202/466-7200

National Public Radio
2025 M St. N.W.
Washington, DC 20036
202/822-2000

National Resources Defense Council
40 W. 20th St.
New York, NY 10011
212/727-4400

National Security Archive
1755 Massachusetts Ave. N.W., 5th Fl.
Washington, DC 20036
202/797-0882

OMB Watch
1731 Connecticut Ave., N.W.
Washington, DC 20009
202/234-8494

Organization of American Historians
112 North Bryan St.
Bloomington, IN 47408
812/855-7311

Parents' Choice
P.O. Box 185
Newton, MA 02168
617/965-5913

PEN American Center/Freedom to
Write Committee/ Freedom to Read
Committee
568 Broadway
New York, NY 10012
212/334-1660

People for the American Way
2000 M St. N.W.
Washington, DC 20036
202/467-4999

Philadelphia Lesbian and Gay Taskforce
1501 Cherry St.
Philadelphia, PA 19102
215/564-0919

Physicians for Social Responsibility
1000 16th St. N.W.
Washington, DC 20036
202/785-3777

Politician Watch
1850 Union St., #1412
San Francisco, CA 94123
415/281-0859

Project Censored
c/o Carl Jensen, PhD
Department of Communication Studies
Sonoma State University
Rohnert Park, CA 94928
707/664-2149 or 664-2500

Public Citizen Open Government Project
2000 P St. N.W.
Washington, DC 20036
202/293-9142

Radio for Peace International
P.O. Box 10869
Eugene, OR 97440
503/741-1749

Radio-Television News Directors Assn.
1717 K St. N.W.
Washington, DC 20006
202/659-6510

Reporters' Committee for Freedom of
the Press
1735 Eye St. N.W.
Washington, DC 20006
202/466-6312

San Francisco Community Television
Corporation
1095 Market
San Francisco, CA 94103
415/621-4224

Scholars & Citizens for Freedom of
Information
c/o John A. Scott
School of Law, Rutgers University
Newark, NJ 07102
201/648-5687

Scientists Institute for Public Information
355 Lexington Ave., 16th Fl.
New York, NY 10017
212/661-9110

Society of Professional Journalists/Sigma
Delta Chi
16 S. Jackson
Greencastle, IN 46135
317/653-3333

Southern Poverty Law Center
P.O. Box 2087
Montgomery, AL 36102
205/264-0286

Special Libraries Assn.
Government Relations Committee
1700 18th St. N.W.
Washington, DC 20009
202/234-4700

Student Press Law Center
1735 Eye St. N.W., Ste. 504
Washington, DC 20006
202/466-5242

Unitarian Universalist Assn.
Washington Office for Social Concern
100 Maryland Ave. N.E., Rm. 106
Washington, DC 20002
202/547-0254

WAMM Media Watch
Women Against Military Madness
3255 Hennepin Ave.
Minneapolis, MN 55408
612/827-5364

Washington Coalition Against
Censorship
5503 17th N.W., #640
Seattle, WA 98107
206/784-6418

Women in Communications
2101 Wilson Blvd.
Arlington, VA 22201
703/528-4200

Women's Institute for Freedom of the
Press
3306 Ross Place, N.W.
Washington, DC 20008
202/966-7783

Cumulative Author Index: *Right to Know*, Volumes I-IV

* *The Right to Know,* volumes I-III, are available from the DataCenter. For ordering information see flier at end of this collection.

of the arts, III: 191-192, 193; IV: 39,-41, 49
of computer networks, IV: 198, 199-200
of films, I: 74-75; II: 50, 72, 115-116; IV: 49
in the media, I: 157-161, 162, 167-172; II: 125, 160-161, 170, 187-191, 206; IV: 26
of recordings, I: 138; II: 157-159; III: 191, 194
of research publications, II: 47, 49, 56
of textbooks, I: 129-130; II: 180-182, 183
Census, Bureau of, I: 46; II: 49, 52, 97
1990 census, II: 68, 69, 71-75, 77, 79, 81, 83, 100; III: 62, 90-91
censorship by, IV: 110-111
Undercounting in 1990 census, IV: 8, 11, 16, 21, 26
Center for Constitutional Rights, II: 117
Center for International Private Enterprise (CIPE), IV: 137
Center for Strategic and International Studies, III: 131-132
Central Intelligence Agency (CIA), II: 54, 55, 199-201; III: 52; IV: 25, 104-108, 134-140, 159-161, 228-231
and Bank of Credit and Commerce International, IV: 104, 105
and censorship, I: 36-37; IV: 22
and Contras, II: 20, 23-24, 136-137, 138
and covert activity in Nicaragua, II: 134, 140, 141, 142; III: 44-45
and disinformation, II: 52-53, 68
and drug smuggling, III: 156-157; IV: 144
and FOIA, I: 25-26, 159, 162; IV: 109
and funding of research, II: 6, 7
and helicopters to North Korea, III: 60
and revelations by former agents, I: 20, 36-37; II: 29, 30, 34-35, 215; IV: 16, 25
and savings and loans scandal, III: 51
and secrecy oaths, II: 69, 76
Chamorro, Edgar, II: 136-137, 141
Channel One [television "current-events program" for schools], III: 145; IV: 93-95
Chemical plants, accidents in, IV: 20
Chemical warfare industry, II: 128
Chernobyl (USSR), II: 55, 62
Chomsky, Noam, II: 123, 201
Chlorofluorocarbons (CFCs), IV: 90-92
Christic Institute, II: 21-22, 25, 190
Cigarettes testing program, II: 63
CISPES see Committee in Support of the People of El Salvador
Civil disturbances, II: 41
Civil rights, II: 86-91, 117-118, 216-217
Reagan administration attack on, I: 158, 162
Classification of information, I: 12, 46, 47-48, 53; II: 13, 20, 61, 70; III: 31, 89-90; IV: 25-26
increase in, I: 3-9, 23; II: ix, 4-5, 46, 47, 78; III: 4-5, 9, 77
in computers, II: 47; IV: 5-6
and secrecy oaths, II: 30, 35, 55, 69, 72, 78
"Classifiable" information, II: 4-5, 68, 69; III: 57, 60
Classism in media coverage, II: 165-166; III: 224, 225; IV: 67-69
Cleaver, Eldridge, IV: 171, 175
Climate-related information, II: 62
Closed government meetings, III: 64, 91
Coal mines, safety in, IV: 16
Coalition for Better Television (CBTV), I: 167-167
Coalition on Government Information (COGI), II: xi
Coast Guard, III: 64
COINTELPRO, I: 70-72; III: 113-119
and Blacks, I: 82-83, 84-85
Cold war, II: 30, 127, 153, 171, 199; III: 113; IV: 240. See also Anticommunism
College newspapers, right-wing, IV: 73
Collegiate Network, IV: 73
Colombia, IV: 141
Columbus quincentenary, III: 212, 215, 219, 222; IV: 217
Commerce, Department of, II: 51, 53, 60, 62, 65

publications, III: 86; IV: 17
Commercial speech, II: 177-178
Commercials in the classroom, III: 145
Commission on Civil Rights, II: 69
Committee in Support of the People of El Salvador (CISPES), II:103-106; III: 107
Commodity Futures Trading Commission (CFTC), IV: 16
Communications Act (1934), II: 207
Community Reinvestment Act, IV: 20
"Compartmentalized" information see "sensitive" information
Computer espionage law, IV: 4
Computer hackers, I: 52; III: 63, 245-246; IV: 192-193
Computer security, III: 63, 64; IV: 5-6, 15, 201 See also Privacy rights
Computerized data, restrictions on access to, I: 65; II: 64, 76; III: 6; IV: 12. See also Databases
Computer software copyright, III: 87, 245
Computers in centralization of power, I: 173-174
Congressional publications, II: 52, 53, 83. See also Government publications
Conservative attacks on public television, IV: 81-83
Conservative bias on television news programs, III: 126-132, 133-135
Constitutional restraints, II: 87-91
Constitution, II: 86
ignorance of, II: 175
Consumer Information Center, I: 49; II: 46
Consumer issues, censorship of, IV: 24, 76
Consumer Product Safety Commission, II: 64; IV: 24
Contras, II: 61, 64, 65
and drug trafficking, II: 21, 23-27, 139, 190
in the media, II: 122, 129-130, 135, 138.
See also Iran-contra affair
Corporate abuse of power, I: 165-166; II: 216-217; III: 123, 175-177, 181; IV: 78-80,
Corporate control of information, IV: 28, 87-89, 187-189
Corporate propaganda & disinformation, II: 177-178, 216-217; IV: 54
Corporate secrecy, II: 35; IV: 90-92
Cost recovery of government information, I: 46, 49
Costa Rica, II: 135, 137
Council of Trade Union Unification (CUS), IV: 139
Council on Environmental Quality, II: 53
Council on Library Resources, II: 95
Counterfeit Access Device and Computer Fraud and Abuse Act of 1984, I: 52
Counterinsurgency training, IV: 126
Courts, Federal, politicization of, III: 10
secret opinions in, III: 72. See also Supreme Court
Covert action by CIA, II: 29, 215; IV: 134-140
in Central America, I: 158-158, 162; II: 19, 21-22, 27
Cranston, Senator Alan, II: 33
Creationism, I: 133, 134-135; II: 184
Cruise missile guidance system, III: 70
Cuba, propaganda to, see TV Marti
Cuban missile crisis, documents on, IV: 10
Cuban periodicals, I: 11
Daponte, Beth Osborne, IV: 110
Databases, government, III: 96
inventories of, II: 65
privatization of, I: 53; II: 46, 58, 67, 71, 84, 94-95; III: 93; IV: 8
restrictions on access to, I: 64, 65; II: 6, 54. See also Fees for government information; Computerized data, restrictions on access to
Davis, Deborah, II: 199-201
Dead Kennedys (musical group), II: 157-159
Debt, Third World, III: 139-140
Decency in Broadcasting, II: 160
Declassification of information, II: 4, 13, 47, 67, 78; III: 71; IV: 17
Defense contractors, III: 82, 90; IV: 57
lobbying by, IV: 24-25

Kampuchea, in U.S. propaganda, II: 128. See also Cambodia
Kennedy, John F., assassination of, IV: 71-72
Kenyatta, Muhammad, I: 84-85
Koop, C. Everett, II: 32-33
Korean Air Lines Flight 007, IV: 11
La Penca (Nicaragua) bombing, II: 21-22; III: 44-45
La Prensa (newspaper), II: 131, 134, 137; III: 219
Labor coverage in the mass media, II: 165; III: 225; IV: 67-69, 70
Labor, Department of, I: 12, 59
Labor Institute for Public Affairs, II: 166
Labor unions image campaigns, II: 165
Labor Statistics, Bureau of, I: 46
Landsat satellite system, II: 58, 61, 73; III: 70
LaRouche, Lyndon H., III: 158
Laxalt, Senator Paul, I: 161
Lead poisoning, II: 66
Leaks, information, I: 9, 15; II: 34, 69. See also Secrecy in government
"Legal Analysis of OMB Circular A-122: Lobbying by Non-Profit Grantees of the Federal Government," I: 47
Less Access to Less Information by and about the U.S. Government, I: 45-53; II: 45-82 ;III: 55-92; IV: 3-29, 89
Libel suits, I: 92-93, 94-95; III: 248-249
Libraries, I: 47, 52; II: 94-95, 113; III: 101, 250; IV: 232-235, 236-239
    censorship in, III: 195-196
    grant programs for, I: 49.
    See also Library Awareness Program
Library Awareness Program, II: 3, 69, 77, 80, 81, 82, 113-114; III: x, 5, 58, 80, 89, 105, 106, 242-243
Library of Congress, II: 52
Library Services and Construction Act, I: 46; II: 46, 52, 60
Libya and chemical weapons, III: 165-168
Lie detector tests see Polygraph testing
Literacy programs, II: 57, 176
Los Alamos National Laboratory, safety and environmental hazards at, IV: 26
Lying, public, III: 178, 180-183
MacNeil/Lehrer News Hour, III: 133
Manufacturing statistics, faulty, III: 63
Mapplethorpe, Robert, III: 192
Mariona prison (El Salvador), II: 191
Martial law contingency plans, II: 41
Martin Marietta Data Systems, II: 48, 49, 58, 84, 96
Marxism, II: 173-174
McCarran-Walter Act, I: 4, 8; II: 214; III: 10, 111, 112
McCarthyism, I: 70-72; II: 127, 214; III: 3
McFarlane, Robert, II: 72, 75
McKinnon, Catherine, IV: 50
Meat and dairy industry, IV: 17
Meat and poultry inspection, IV: 5, 12
Media, attacks on by New Right, I: 86-91, 167-172
Media bias & manipulation, II: 121-123, 125-127, 165-166, 167, 187-191, 198, 202, 207; III: 126-132, 133-135, 139-140, 146-155, 156-158, 178, 181-183
    on Afghanistan, III: 125
    ageist, III: 227-230
    anti-Arab, III: 169-172
    anticommunist, II: 171
    homophobic, II: 170, 206
    in Persian Gulf War
    on attempted assassination of the Pope, II: 143-150
    on China, III: 146-147
    on El Salvador, III: 136-138
    on Nicaragua, I: 119-123, 158, 162; II: 129-142
    on Panama, IV: 146-148
    racist, II: 203-205; III: 216-218; IV: 209, 215-216
    and "war on drugs," III: 159-160.

See also Freedom of the press; News, Government-controlled; Propaganda
Media concentration, I: 163-164, 165-166; II: 187-191, 192-197, 198, 201; III: 5-6, 181; IV: 53-55, 60-61, 74, 75
Media omission, I: 157-161; II: 187-191, 198
Media self-censorship, IV: 55, 56, 60-61
Medicaid, information about, IV: 20
Medicare drug benefits, IV: 22
Medical malpractice reporting, IV: 16
Meese, Edwin III, II: 46, 49
Merit Systems Protection Board, II: 46
Microfiche shortage in depository libraries, III: 68
Misinformation, government, I: 103-115, 116-118
Miskito Indians, II: 142
Morison, Samuel Loring, I: 15-16, 21-22; II: 50, 51; III: 9, 15-25
Moscow Embassy security problems, II: 64; III: 68
Motion pictures see Films
Movement Support Network, II: 118
Mozambique, III: 124
Multiculturalism, IV: 156-160
National Aeronautics and Space Administration (NASA), I: 52; II: 67; III: 88
    and FOIA exemptions, III: 42-43, 71; IV: 57, 99-103
    privatization, III: 79
    restrictions on NASA RECON database, III: 55
National Archives, I: 54-55
National Center for Education Statistics, II: 52
National Commission on Libraries and Information Science (NCLIS), II: 46; III: 251
National Computer Security Center, III: 64. See also Computer security
National Committee Against Repressive Legislation (NCARL), I: 70-72
National Democratic Institute for International Affairs (NDI), IV: 138
National Endowment for Democracy (NED), IV: 134-140
National Endowment for the Arts (NEA), III: 192, 193; IV: 39-41
National Environmental Policy Act, II: 53
National Farmers Union, I: 50
National Institute for Occupational Safety & Health (NIOSH), II: 98
National Library of Medicine database, IV: 8
National Oceanic and Atmospheric Administration, II: 62
National parks, III: 91-92
National Policy on Protection of Sensitive, But Unclassified Information, II: 57, 64
National Practitioner Data Bank, IV: 12, 16
National Program Office, IV: 28
National Republican Institute for International Affairs (NRI), IV: 138
National Right to Life Committee, II: 40
National Security Agency (NSA), I: 25, 29-31, 174; II: 5, 83; IV: 124, 125
National Security Archive, II: 36, 76, 81; III: 88, 241-244
National Security Council, II: 6, 67, 153
    destruction of computer tapes, III: 67
    and Iran-contra affair, II: 61, 68, 72
    and propaganda operations, II: 124, 130; IV: 131
National Security Decision Directives (NSDD), II: 20; III: 32-36, 56, 76
    NSDD 84, I: 14, 24-25, 33-35, 36, 41, 51, 159, 162; II: 6, 34, 39, 68, 74; III: 9, 36
    NSDD 145, IV: 5-6
    NSDD 189, II: 5;
    NSDD 192, II: 70;
    NSDD 196, II: 50
National Security Education Act, IV: 159-161
National security issues, I: 19-22, 48; II: ix, 3-5, 12, 57, 70; III: 4, 92
    and classification, I: 23, 46; II: 47
    and FBI, II: 113
    and federal employees, II: 50, 78
    and FOIA, II: 20, 103
    and martial law, II: 41
National Technical Information Service (NTIS), I: 47, 63; II: 46, 57

DATACENTER PUBLICATIONS & SERVICES
Effective 6/15/92*

* The rates for DataCenter publications and services may change periodically without notice

---

Providing information in the public interest. 464 19th Street, Oakland, California 94612 (510) 835-4692

CUSTOM RESEARCH SERVICES

Search
Service

Professional research services: $90.00/hour for one week service. Rush service available on request. Pro bono services available for qualifying clients.

Clipping
Services

The DataCenter will monitor any or all of the 500 publications we receive monthly for topics that interest you. Rates vary according to number of periodicals being monitored and frequency of delivery. Call or write for more information.

SERIAL PUBLICATIONS

Information Services Latin America (ISLA): Monthly. 350 pages. $580/year (full service); $190/year (each regional section); $370/year (microfilm). Airmail postage extra. Back issues available of printed and microfilm editions. Twice yearly index free to full service subscribers.

Corporate Responsibility Monitor (including "Plant Shutdowns Directory"): Bi-monthly. 150 pages. $450/year (commercial and government users); $340/year (nonprofit organizations). Also available: monthly PLANT SHUTDOWNS ALERT, $450/year.

Third World Resources: A Quarterly Review of Resources from and about the Third World: Quarterly. 24 pages. U.S. & Canada: $35/one year (organizations); $35/two years (individuals). Outside North America $45/one year (organizations); $50/two years (individuals). Back issues available. Annual index free to subscribers.

PUBLICATIONS IN PRINT

The Right to Know: Nancy Gruber and Zoia Horn, eds. Note: Vol. IV contains a cumulative index for Volumes I - IV. For postage and handling for each book ordered include $2.00/(4th class); or $3.50/(1st class).
  Vol. I (1985. ISBN 1-880648-01-6. $10)
  Vol. II (1988. ISBN 1-880648-02-4. $15)
  Vol. III (1990. ISBN 1-880648-03-2. $20)
  Vol. IV (1992. ISBN 1-880648-04-0. $20)
  One complete set of all four volumes (ISBN 1-880648-00-8. $55)

The Persian Gulf War Series: Bill Berkowitz and Marie Pastrick, eds. Classroom and Bulk Order rates available upon request.
  Background & Analysis (1991. 64pp. $6 postpaid)
  Iraq Under Fire (1991. 60pp. $6 postpaid)
  The Media and Our Right to Know (1991. 78pp. $7.50 postpaid)
  One complete set of above three volumes ($16 postpaid)
  Update (1992. 56pp. $5 postpaid)

Third World Resource Directories. Thomas P. Fenton and Mary J. Heffron, eds. Orbis Books, Publisher. Prices include domestic postage. Add $3 each for airmail printed matter postage overseas.

Asia and Pacific (1986. 160pp. $14.95)
Latin America and Caribbean (1986. 160pp. $14.95)
Africa (1987. 160pp. $14.95)
Middle East (1987. 160 pp. $14.95)
Women in the Third World (1987. 160pp. $14.95)
Food, Hunger, Agribusiness (1987. 160pp. $14.95)
Human Rights (1989. 160pp. $14.95)
Transnational Corporations and Labor (1989. 160pp. $14.95)
Third World Struggle for Peace with Justice (1990. 180pp. $14.95)

LIBRARY USE

Users pay a two-tiered day use fee ($6.50 individual or $25 professional) or may take out a membership. In addition to individual memberships, the library also offers organizational rates, special contract use agreements, and pro bono discounts.

Hours: Tuesday and Thursday, 1:00 to 5:00 pm;
Wednesday 5:00 to 9:00 pm. Open 10:00 am to
3:00 pm the first Saturday of every month.

MEMBERSHIP

Library day use fees are waived for members of the DataCenter. Members also receive discounts on photocopying in the library and have access to the DataCenter's archival library collections. Annual fees: $75 (professional); $30 (individual); $20 (student semester rate). Inquire for fees and benefits for organizational membership.

(Return the coupon below with your check made payable to **DataCenter**. California residents add 8.25% sales tax for all publication orders. Our address: DataCenter, 464 - 19th Street, Oakland, CA 94612.)

_____ Please send me more information about:_____

_____ I wish to subscribe to: _____

_____ Please send me a sample of: _____

_____ Please send me the following items: _____

_____ Here is my membership fee of $ _____

_____ Here is a donation of $ _____

                          Total Enclosed: $ _____

Name: _____

Address: _____

City/State/Zip: _____

Telephone: Home (___) ___ - _____ Work (___) ___ - _____